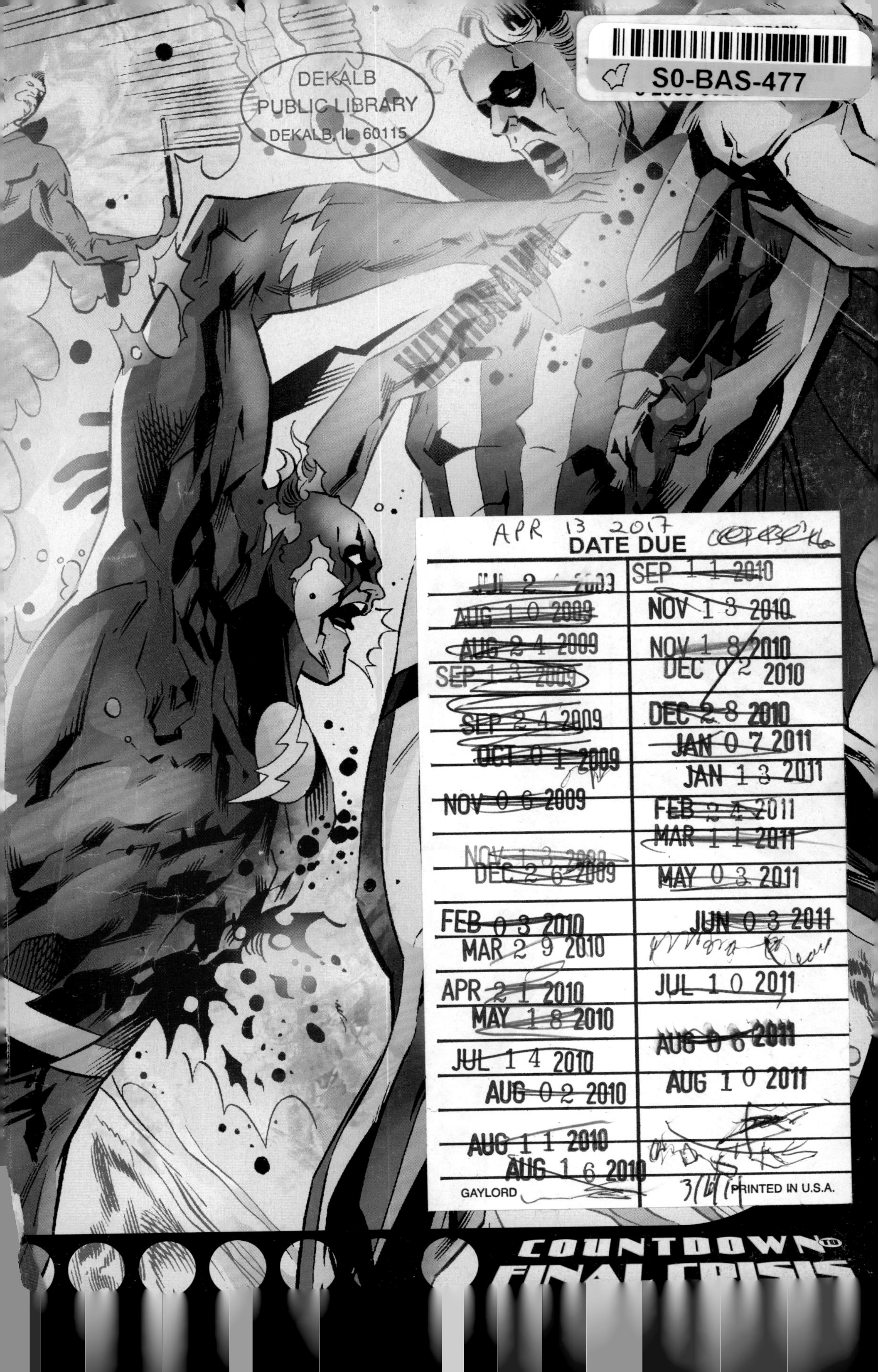
COUNTDOWN TO FINAL CRISIS

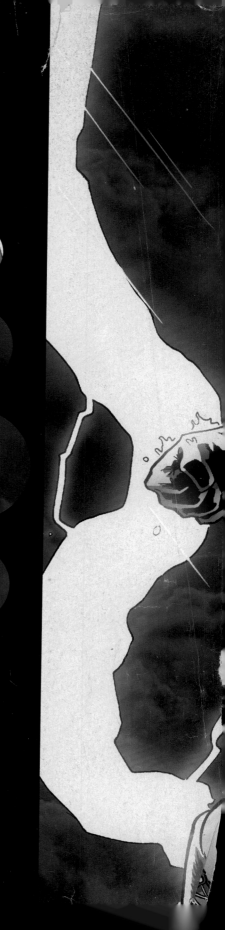

Paul Dini with...
Jimmy Palmiotti &
Justin Gray
Tony Bedard
Adam Beechen
Sean McKeever
Writers

Keith Giffen
Story Consultant

Jesus Saiz
Jim Calafiore
Carlos Magno
David Lopez
Tom Derenick
Manuel Garcia
Dennis Calero
Pencillers

Jimmy Palmiotti
Mark McKenna
Jay Leisten
Don Hillsman
Alvaro Lopez
Andrew Pepoy
Jack Purcell
John Stanisci
Dennis Calero
Inkers

Travis Lanham
Pat Brosseau
Jared K. Fletcher
Rob Leigh
Phil Balsman
Ken Lopez
Letterers

Tom Chu
Rod Reis
Guy Major
Pete Pantazis
Colorists

Dan DiDio Senior VP-Executive Editor **Mike Marts** **Mike Carlin** Editors-original series **Jeanine Schaefer** Associate Editor-original series **Elisabeth Gehrlein** Assistant Editor-original series **Bob Joy** Editor-collected edition **Robbin Brosterman** Senior Art Director **Louis Prandi** Art Director **Paul Levitz** President & Publisher **Georg Brewer** VP-Design & DC Direct Creative **Richard Bruning** Senior VP-Creative Director **Patrick Caldon** Executive VP-Finance & Operations **Chris Caramalis** VP-Finance **John Cunningham** VP-Marketing **Terri Cunningham** VP-Managing Editor **Alison Gill** VP-Manufacturing **David Hyde** VP-Publicity **Hank Kanalz** VP-General Manager, WildStorm **Jim Lee** Editorial Director-WildStorm **Paula Lowitt** Senior VP-Business & Legal Affairs **MaryEllen McLaughlin** VP-Advertising & Custom Publishing **John Nee** Senior VP-Business Development **Gregory Noveck** Senior VP-Creative Affairs **Sue Pohja** VP-Book Trade Sales **Steve Rotterdam** Senior VP-Sales & Marketing **Cheryl Rubin** Senior VP-Brand Management **Jeff Trojan** VP-Business Development DC Direct, **Bob Wayne** VP-Sales

Printed in Canada. First Printing. ISBN: 978-1-4012-1789-1 Cover art by Andy Kubert, Tim Townsend and Dave Stewart.

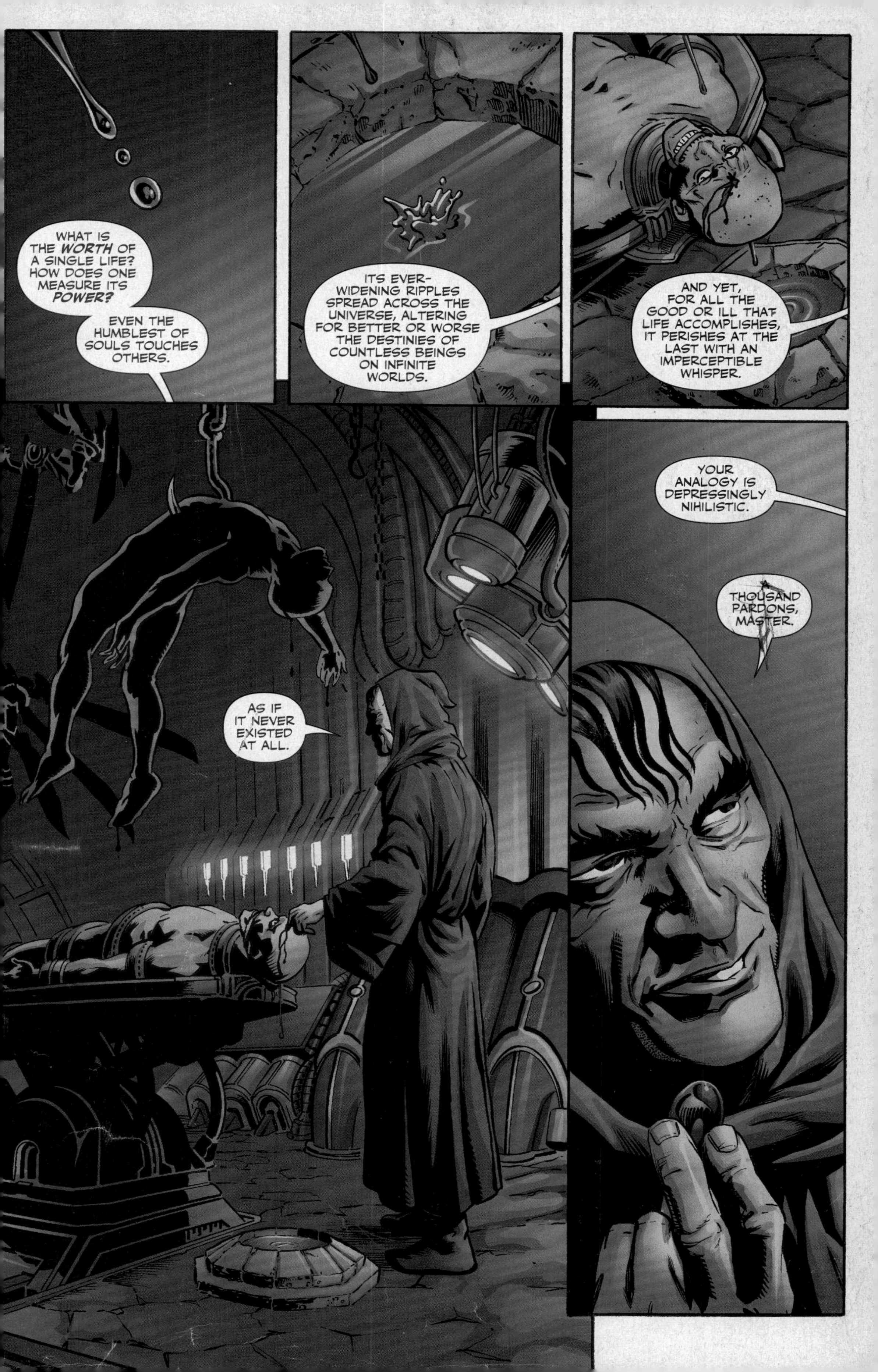
WHAT IS THE WORTH OF A SINGLE LIFE? HOW DOES ONE MEASURE ITS POWER?
EVEN THE HUMBLEST OF SOULS TOUCHES OTHERS.
ITS EVER-WIDENING RIPPLES SPREAD ACROSS THE UNIVERSE, ALTERING FOR BETTER OR WORSE THE DESTINIES OF COUNTLESS BEINGS ON INFINITE WORLDS.
AND YET, FOR ALL THE GOOD OR ILL THAT LIFE ACCOMPLISHES, IT PERISHES AT THE LAST WITH AN IMPERCEPTIBLE WHISPER.
AS IF IT NEVER EXISTED AT ALL.
YOUR ANALOGY IS DEPRESSINGLY NIHILISTIC.
A THOUSAND PARDONS, MASTER.

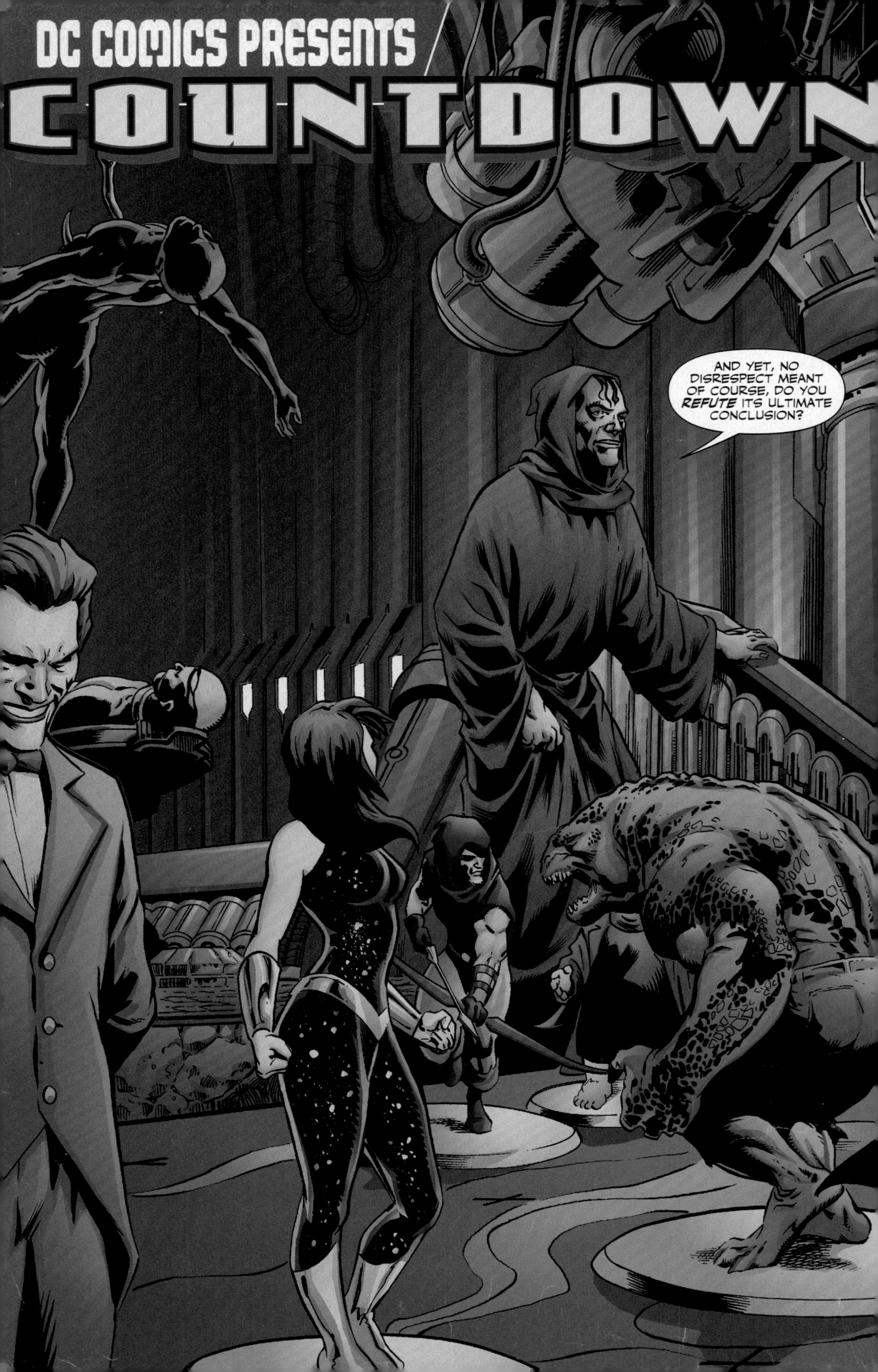
DC COMICS PRESENTS
COUNTDOWN
AND YET, NO DISRESPECT MEANT OF COURSE, DO YOU *REFUTE* ITS ULTIMATE CONCLUSION?

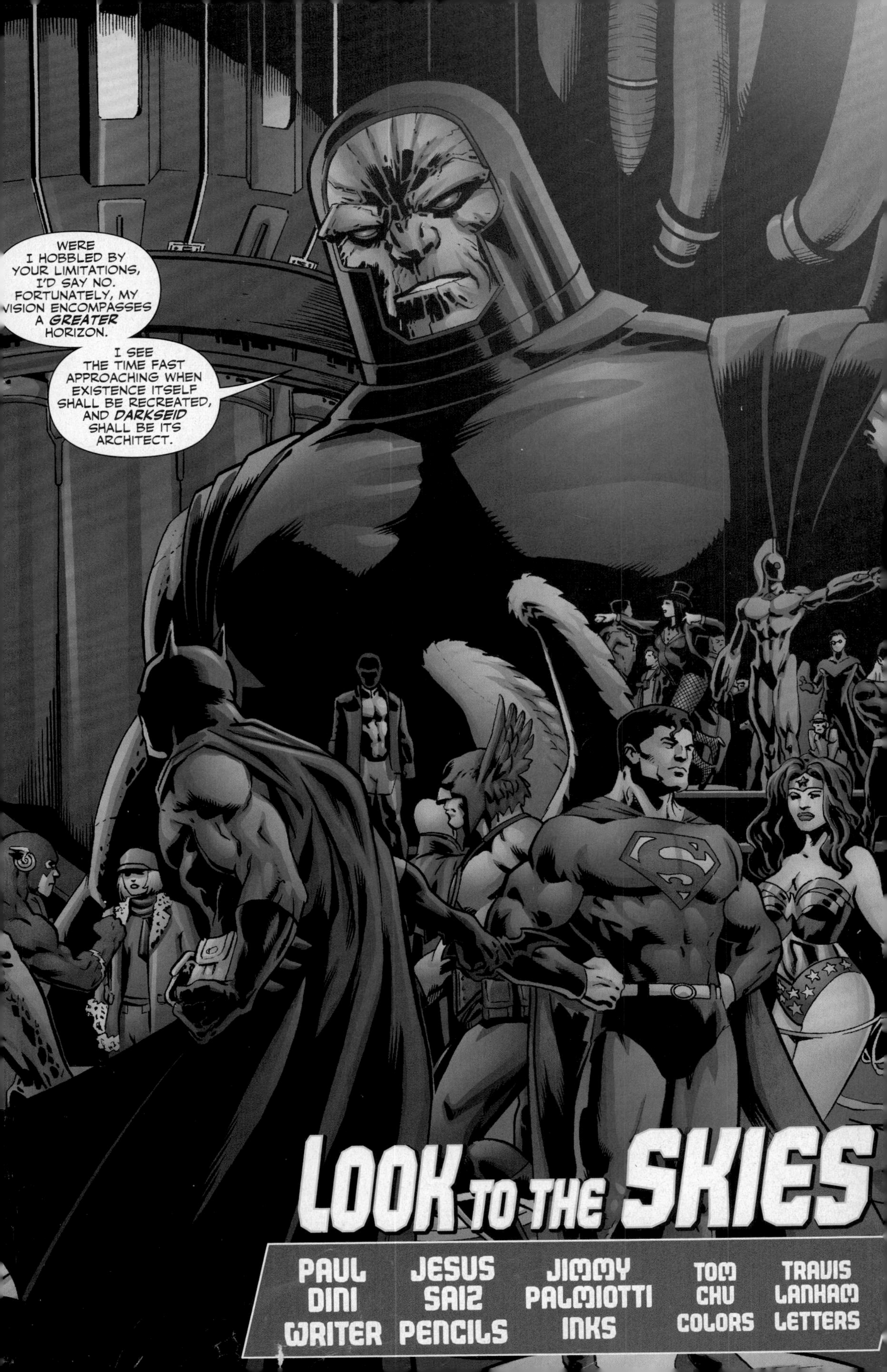
WERE I HOBBLED BY YOUR LIMITATIONS, I'D SAY NO. FORTUNATELY, MY VISION ENCOMPASSES A GREATER HORIZON.
I SEE THE TIME FAST APPROACHING WHEN EXISTENCE ITSELF SHALL BE RECREATED, AND DARKSEID SHALL BE ITS ARCHITECT.
LOOK TO THE SKIES
PAUL DINI WRITER
JESUS SAIZ PENCILS
JIMMY PALMIOTTI INKS
TOM CHU COLORS
TRAVIS LANHAM LETTERS

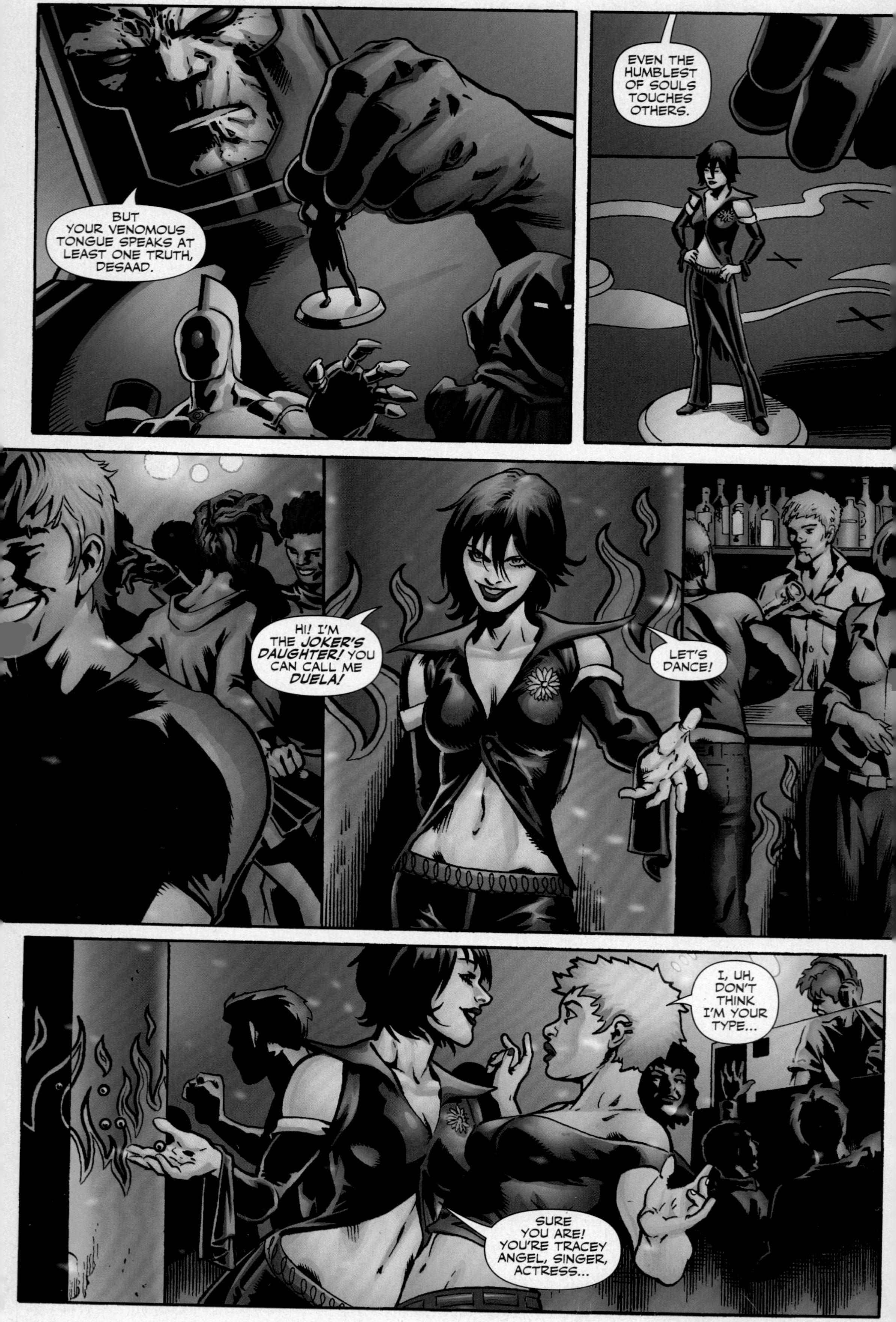
BUT YOUR VENOMOUS TONGUE SPEAKS AT LEAST ONE TRUTH, DESAAD.
EVEN THE HUMBLEST OF SOULS TOUCHES OTHERS.
HI! I'M THE JOKER'S DAUGHTER! YOU CAN CALL ME DUELA!
LET'S DANCE!
I, UH, DON'T THINK I'M YOUR TYPE...
SURE YOU ARE! YOU'RE TRACEY ANGEL, SINGER, ACTRESS...

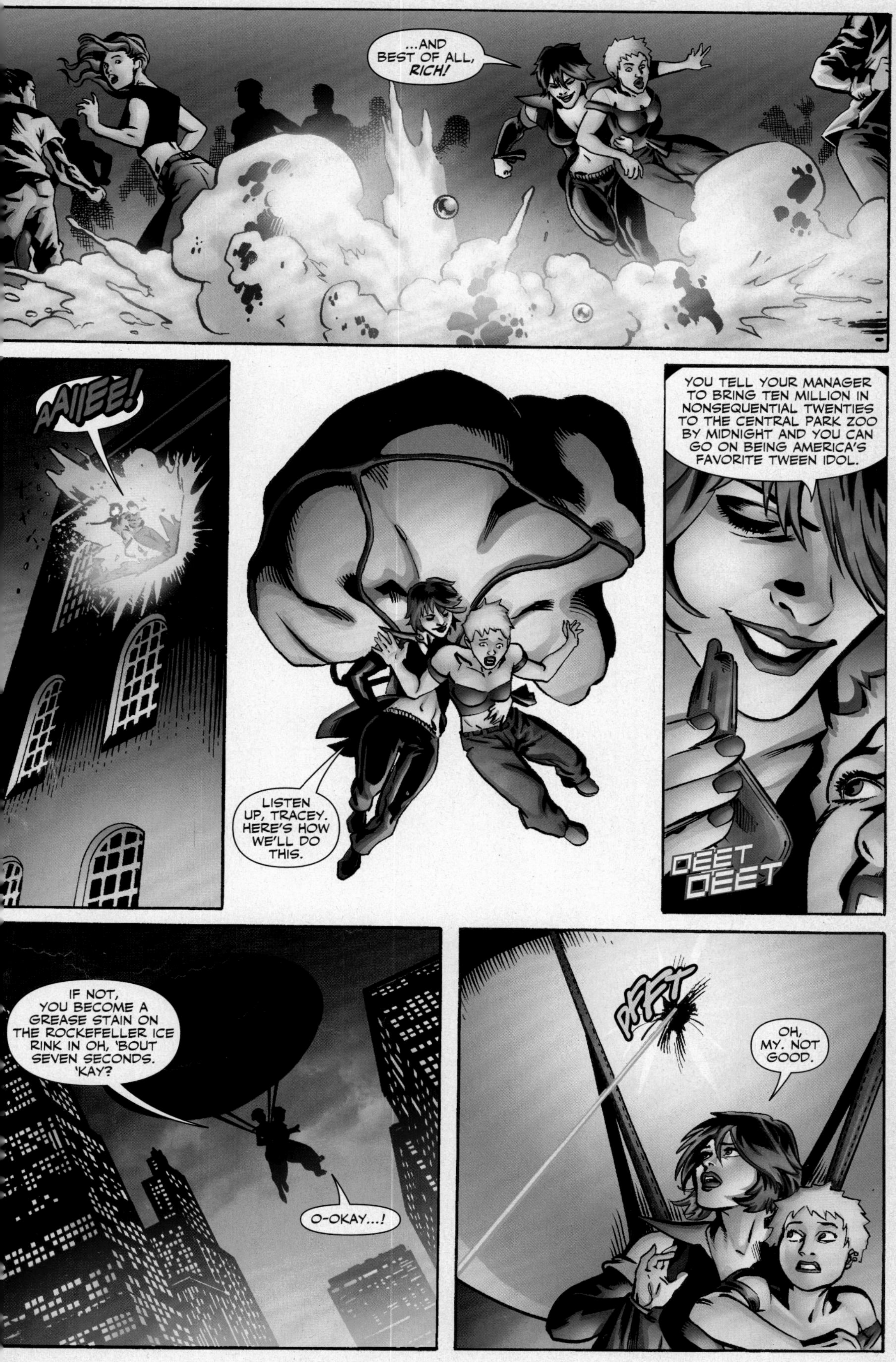
...AND BEST OF ALL, RICH!
AAIIEE!
LISTEN UP, TRACEY. HERE'S HOW WE'LL DO THIS.
YOU TELL YOUR MANAGER TO BRING TEN MILLION IN NONSEQUENTIAL TWENTIES TO THE CENTRAL PARK ZOO BY MIDNIGHT AND YOU CAN GO ON BEING AMERICA'S FAVORITE TWEEN IDOL.
DEET DEET
IF NOT, YOU BECOME A GREASE STAIN ON THE ROCKEFELLER ICE RINK IN OH, 'BOUT SEVEN SECONDS. 'KAY?
O-OKAY...!
PFFT
OH, MY. NOT GOOD.

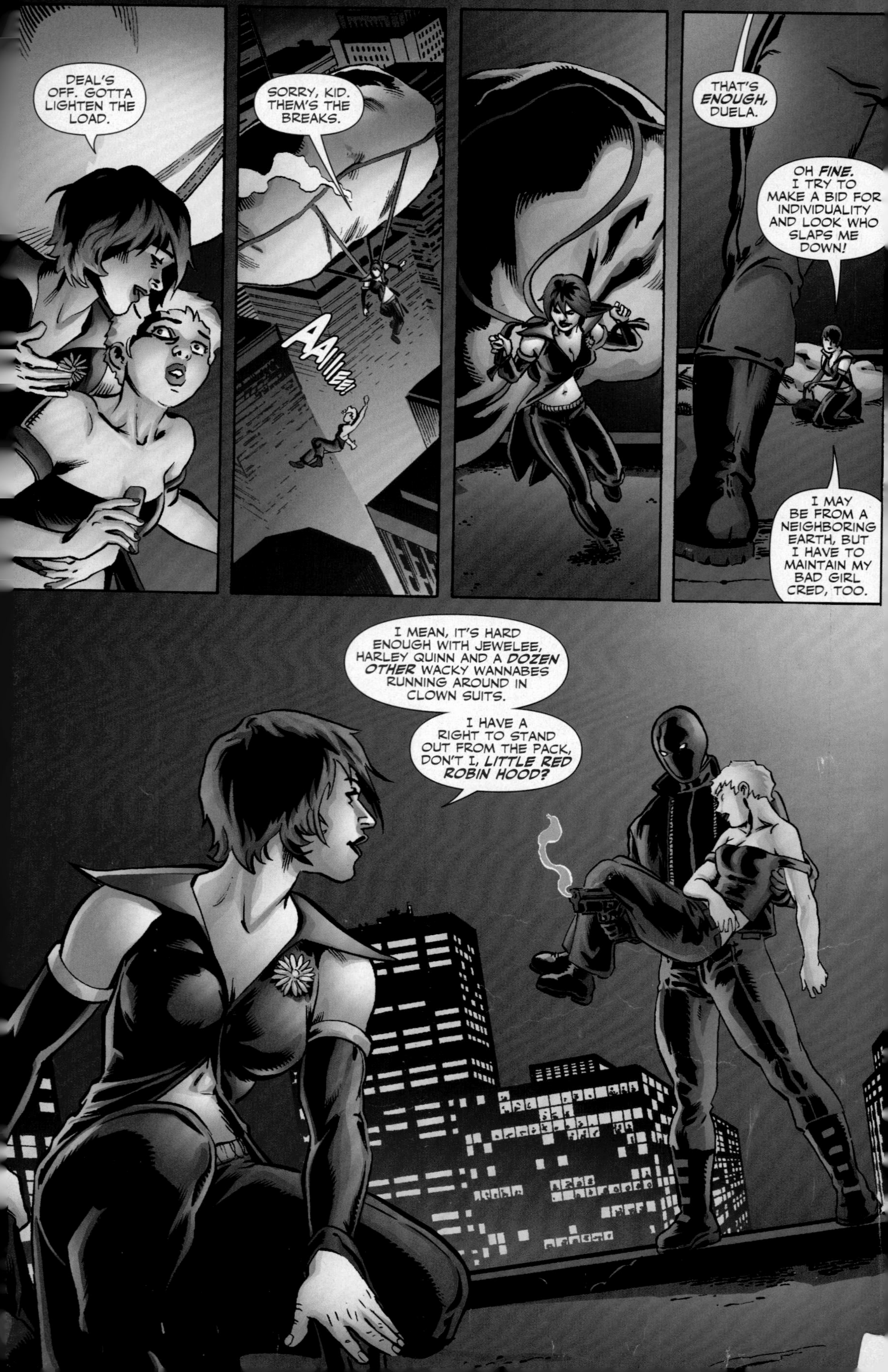
DEAL'S OFF. GOTTA LIGHTEN THE LOAD.
SORRY, KID. THEM'S THE BREAKS.
AAIIIEEE!
THAT'S ENOUGH, DUELA.
OH FINE. I TRY TO MAKE A BID FOR INDIVIDUALITY AND LOOK WHO SLAPS ME DOWN!
I MAY BE FROM A NEIGHBORING EARTH, BUT I HAVE TO MAINTAIN MY BAD GIRL CRED, TOO.
I MEAN, IT'S HARD ENOUGH WITH JEWELEE, HARLEY QUINN AND A DOZEN OTHER WACKY WANNABES RUNNING AROUND IN CLOWN SUITS.
I HAVE A RIGHT TO STAND OUT FROM THE PACK, DON'T I, LITTLE RED ROBIN HOOD?

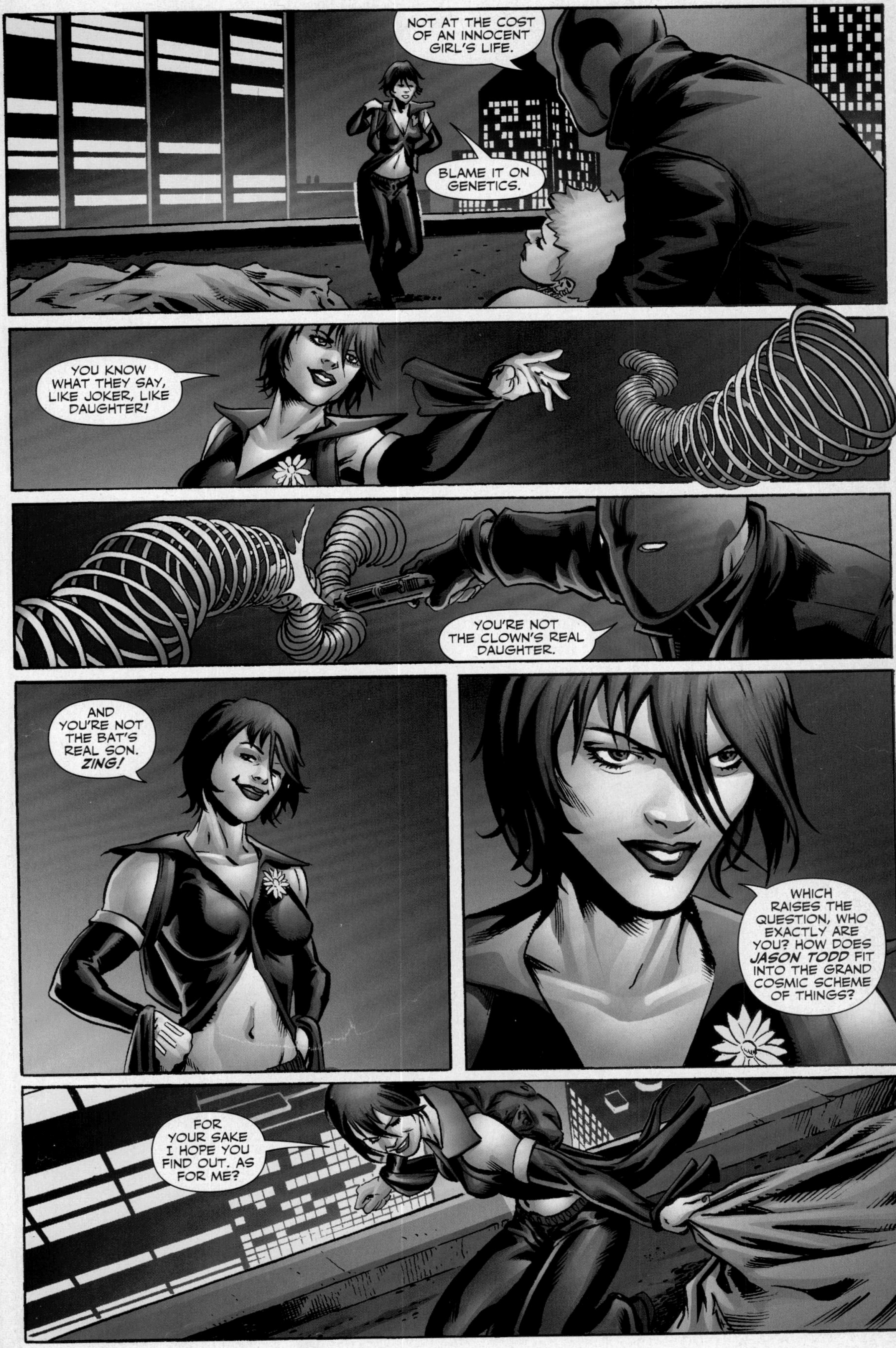
NOT AT THE COST OF AN INNOCENT GIRL'S LIFE.
BLAME IT ON GENETICS.
YOU KNOW WHAT THEY SAY, LIKE JOKER, LIKE DAUGHTER!
YOU'RE NOT THE CLOWN'S REAL DAUGHTER.
AND YOU'RE NOT THE BAT'S REAL SON. ZING!
WHICH RAISES THE QUESTION, WHO EXACTLY ARE YOU? HOW DOES JASON TODD FIT INTO THE GRAND COSMIC SCHEME OF THINGS?
FOR YOUR SAKE I HOPE YOU FIND OUT. AS FOR ME?

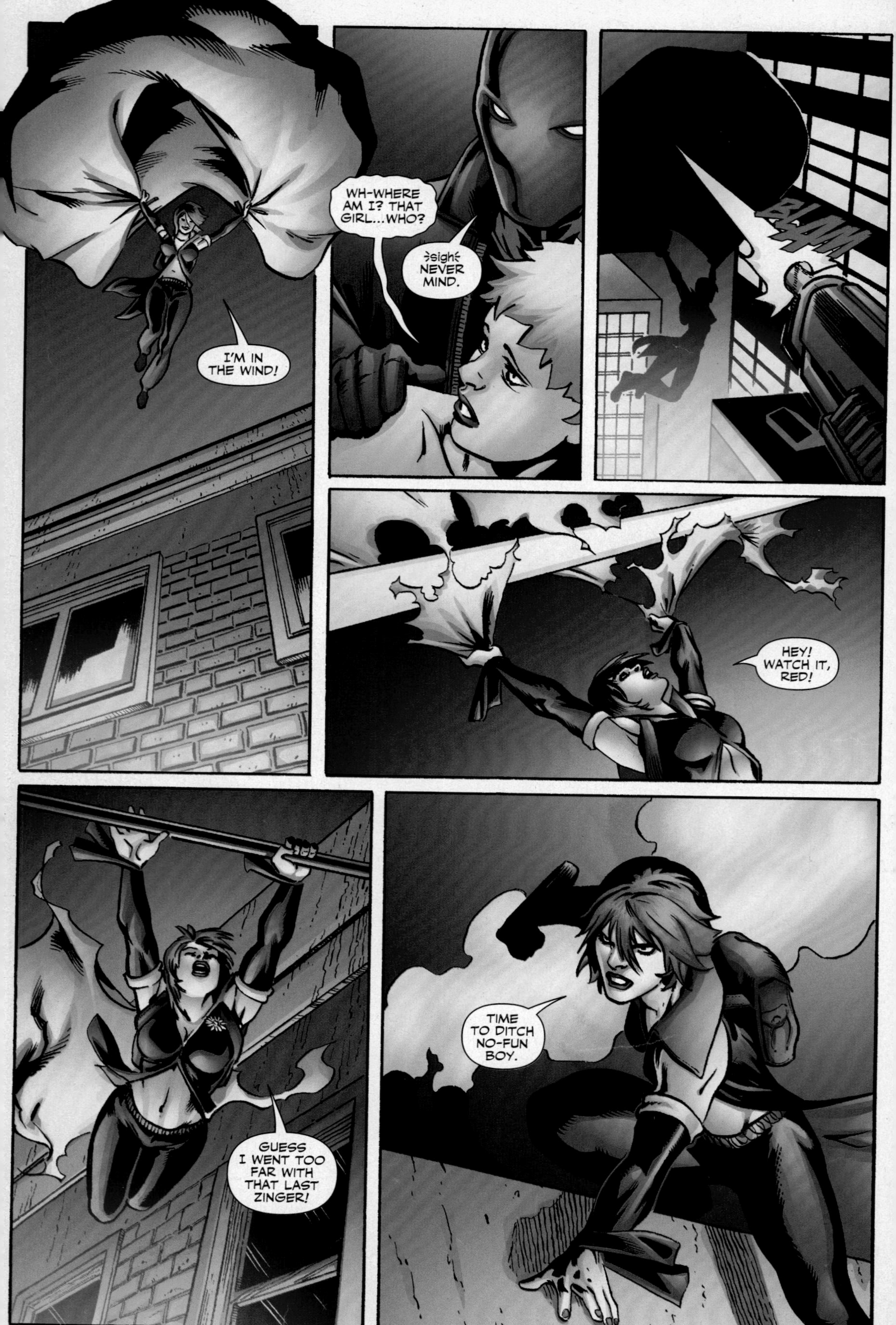
I'M IN THE WIND!
WH-WHERE AM I? THAT GIRL...WHO?
sigh NEVER MIND.
BLAM
HEY! WATCH IT, RED!
GUESS I WENT TOO FAR WITH THAT LAST ZINGER!
TIME TO DITCH NO-FUN BOY.

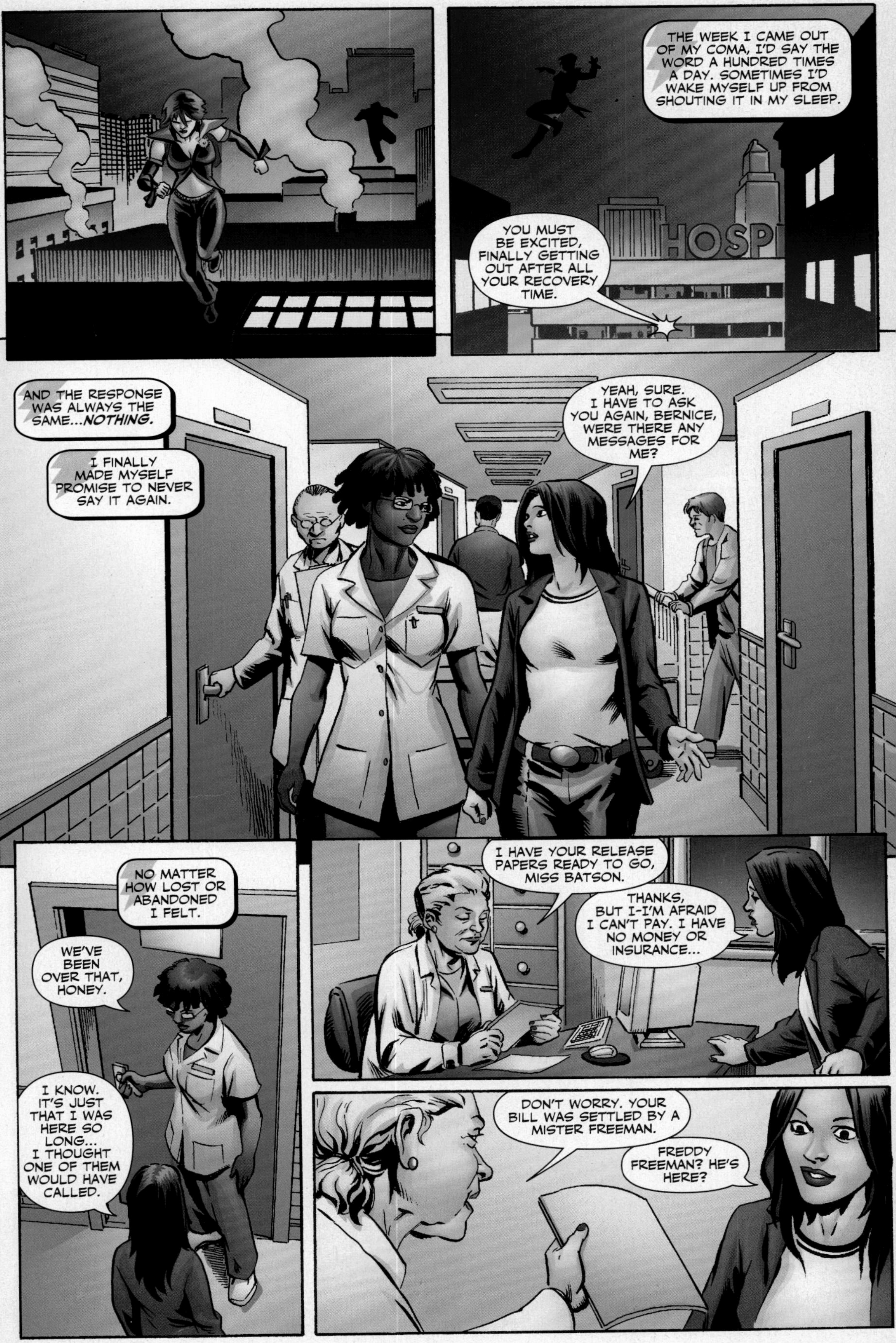
THE WEEK I CAME OUT OF MY COMA, I'D SAY THE WORD A HUNDRED TIMES A DAY. SOMETIMES I'D WAKE MYSELF UP FROM SHOUTING IT IN MY SLEEP.
HOSP
YOU MUST BE EXCITED, FINALLY GETTING OUT AFTER ALL YOUR RECOVERY TIME.
AND THE RESPONSE WAS ALWAYS THE SAME...*NOTHING.*
I FINALLY MADE MYSELF PROMISE TO NEVER SAY IT AGAIN.
YEAH, SURE. I HAVE TO ASK YOU AGAIN, BERNICE, WERE THERE ANY MESSAGES FOR ME?
NO MATTER HOW LOST OR ABANDONED I FELT.
WE'VE BEEN OVER THAT, HONEY.
I KNOW. IT'S JUST THAT I WAS HERE SO LONG... I THOUGHT ONE OF THEM WOULD HAVE CALLED.
I HAVE YOUR RELEASE PAPERS READY TO GO, MISS BATSON.
THANKS, BUT I-I'M AFRAID I CAN'T PAY. I HAVE NO MONEY OR INSURANCE...
DON'T WORRY. YOUR BILL WAS SETTLED BY A MISTER FREEMAN.
FREDDY FREEMAN? HE'S HERE?

HE STOPPED BY THIS AFTERNOON JUST LONG ENOUGH TO MAKE THE PAYMENT.

BUT HE MUST HAVE LEFT SOMETHING FOR ME! A NOTE, A PHONE NUMBER, ANYTHING?

JUST THIS.

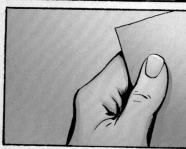

Mary--
Don't try to find me.
F.

SHAZAM.

HEH...

16

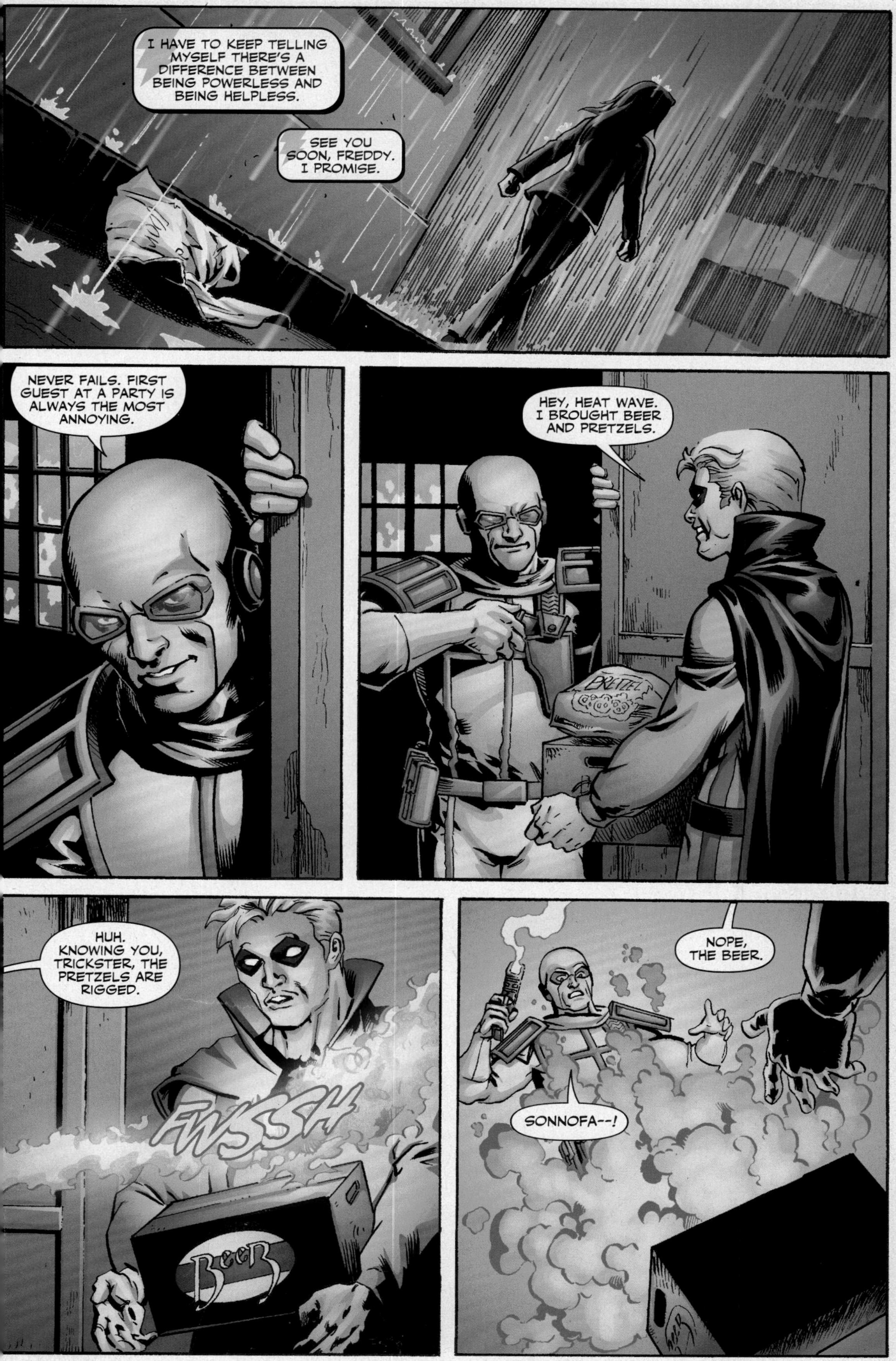
I HAVE TO KEEP TELLING MYSELF THERE'S A DIFFERENCE BETWEEN BEING POWERLESS AND BEING HELPLESS.
SEE YOU SOON, FREDDY. I PROMISE.
NEVER FAILS. FIRST GUEST AT A PARTY IS ALWAYS THE MOST ANNOYING.
HEY, HEAT WAVE. I BROUGHT BEER AND PRETZELS.
PRETZEL
HUH. KNOWING YOU, TRICKSTER, THE PRETZELS ARE RIGGED.
FWSSH
BEER
NOPE, THE BEER.
SONNOFA--!

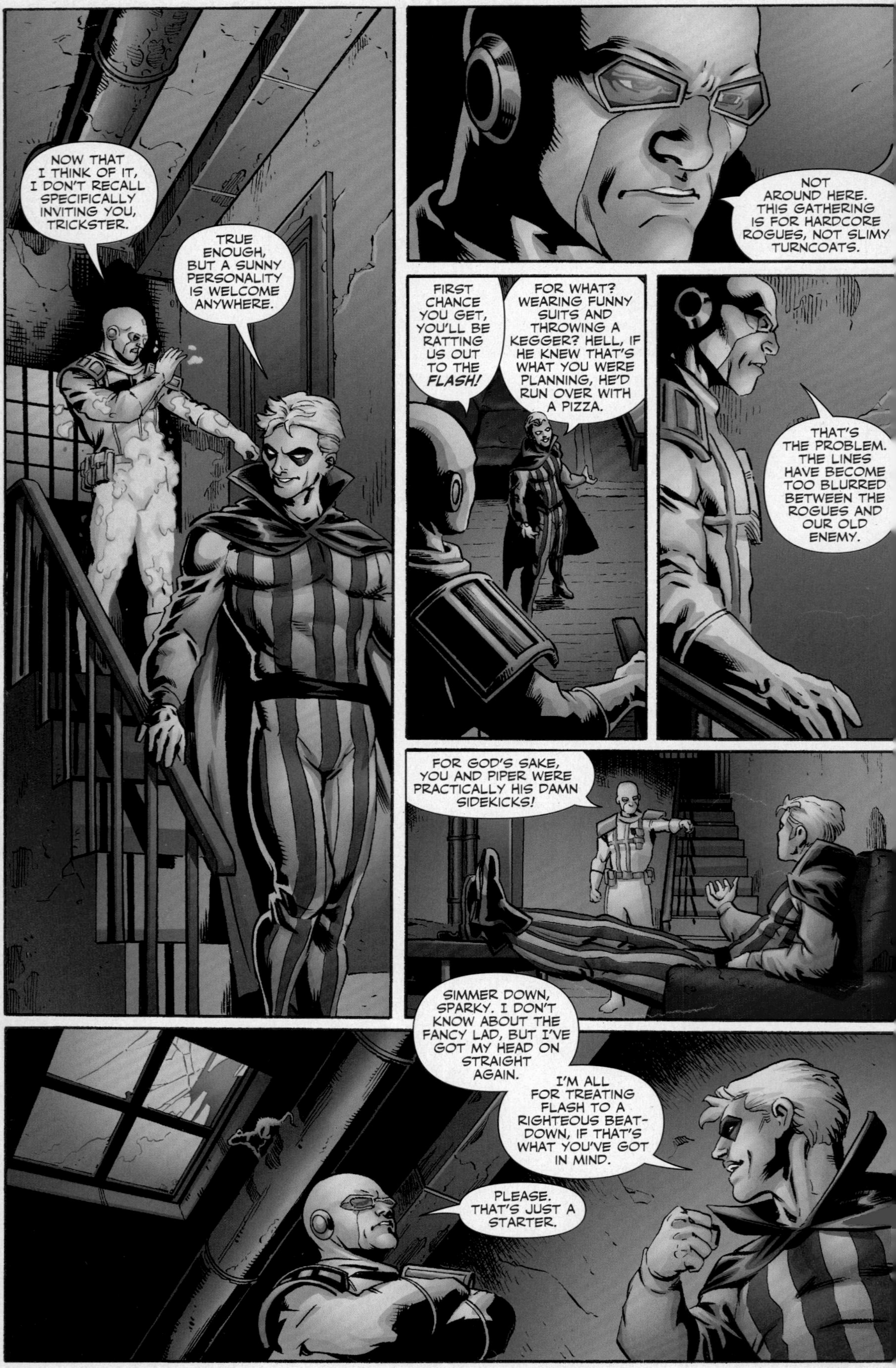
NOW THAT I THINK OF IT, I DON'T RECALL SPECIFICALLY INVITING YOU, TRICKSTER.
TRUE ENOUGH, BUT A SUNNY PERSONALITY IS WELCOME ANYWHERE.
NOT AROUND HERE. THIS GATHERING IS FOR HARDCORE ROGUES, NOT SLIMY TURNCOATS.
FIRST CHANCE YOU GET, YOU'LL BE RATTING US OUT TO THE FLASH!
FOR WHAT? WEARING FUNNY SUITS AND THROWING A KEGGER? HELL, IF HE KNEW THAT'S WHAT YOU WERE PLANNING, HE'D RUN OVER WITH A PIZZA.
THAT'S THE PROBLEM. THE LINES HAVE BECOME TOO BLURRED BETWEEN THE ROGUES AND OUR OLD ENEMY.
FOR GOD'S SAKE, YOU AND PIPER WERE PRACTICALLY HIS DAMN SIDEKICKS!
SIMMER DOWN, SPARKY. I DON'T KNOW ABOUT THE FANCY LAD, BUT I'VE GOT MY HEAD ON STRAIGHT AGAIN.
I'M ALL FOR TREATING FLASH TO A RIGHTEOUS BEAT-DOWN, IF THAT'S WHAT YOU'VE GOT IN MIND.
PLEASE. THAT'S JUST A STARTER.

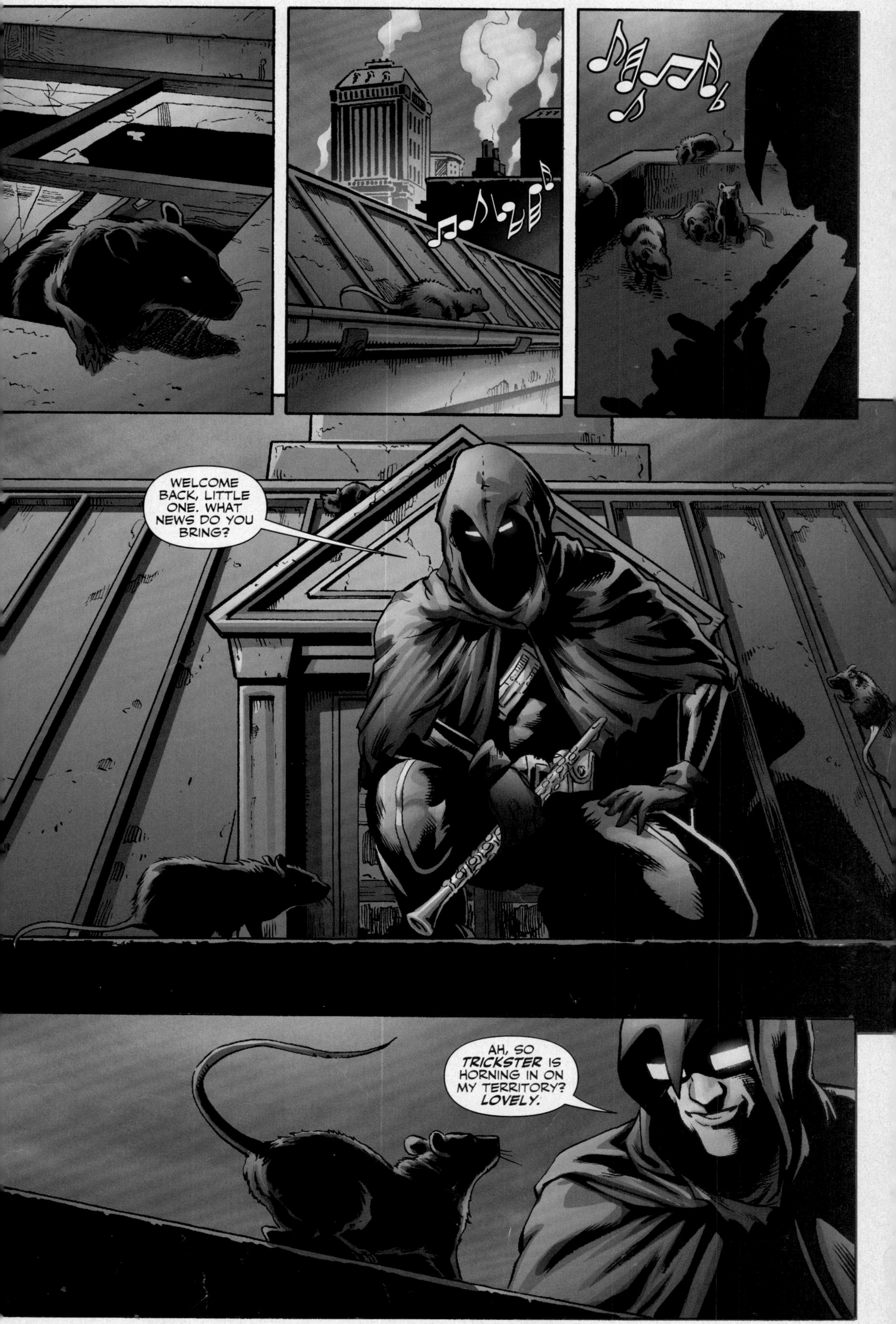
WELCOME BACK, LITTLE ONE. WHAT NEWS DO YOU BRING?
AH, SO *TRICKSTER* IS HORNING IN ON MY TERRITORY? *LOVELY.*

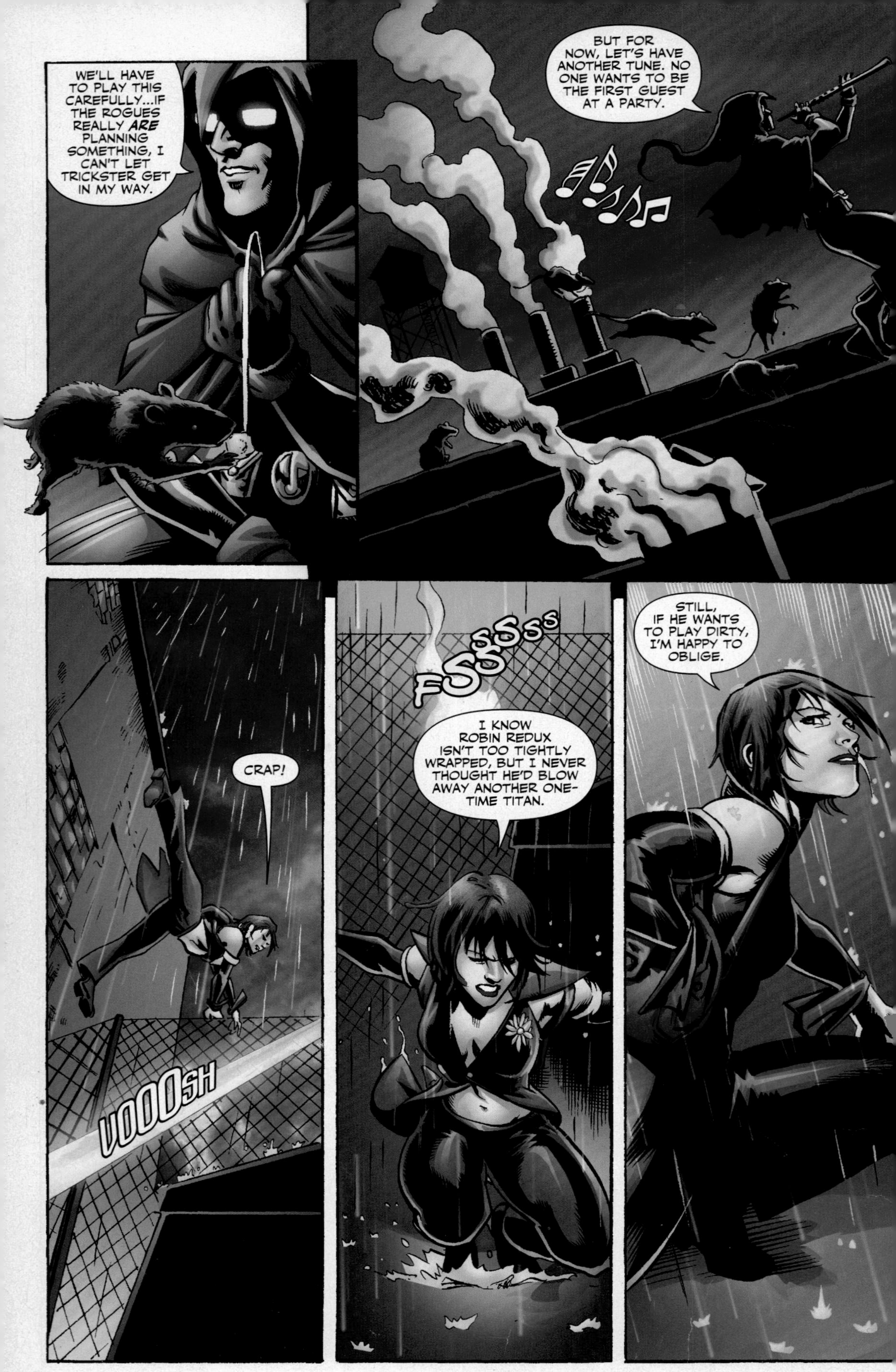
WE'LL HAVE TO PLAY THIS CAREFULLY...IF THE ROGUES REALLY *ARE* PLANNING SOMETHING, I CAN'T LET TRICKSTER GET IN MY WAY.
BUT FOR NOW, LET'S HAVE ANOTHER TUNE. NO ONE WANTS TO BE THE FIRST GUEST AT A PARTY.
CRAP!
VOOOSH
FSSSSS
I KNOW ROBIN REDUX ISN'T TOO TIGHTLY WRAPPED, BUT I NEVER THOUGHT HE'D BLOW AWAY ANOTHER ONE-TIME TITAN.
STILL, IF HE WANTS TO PLAY DIRTY, I'M HAPPY TO OBLIGE.

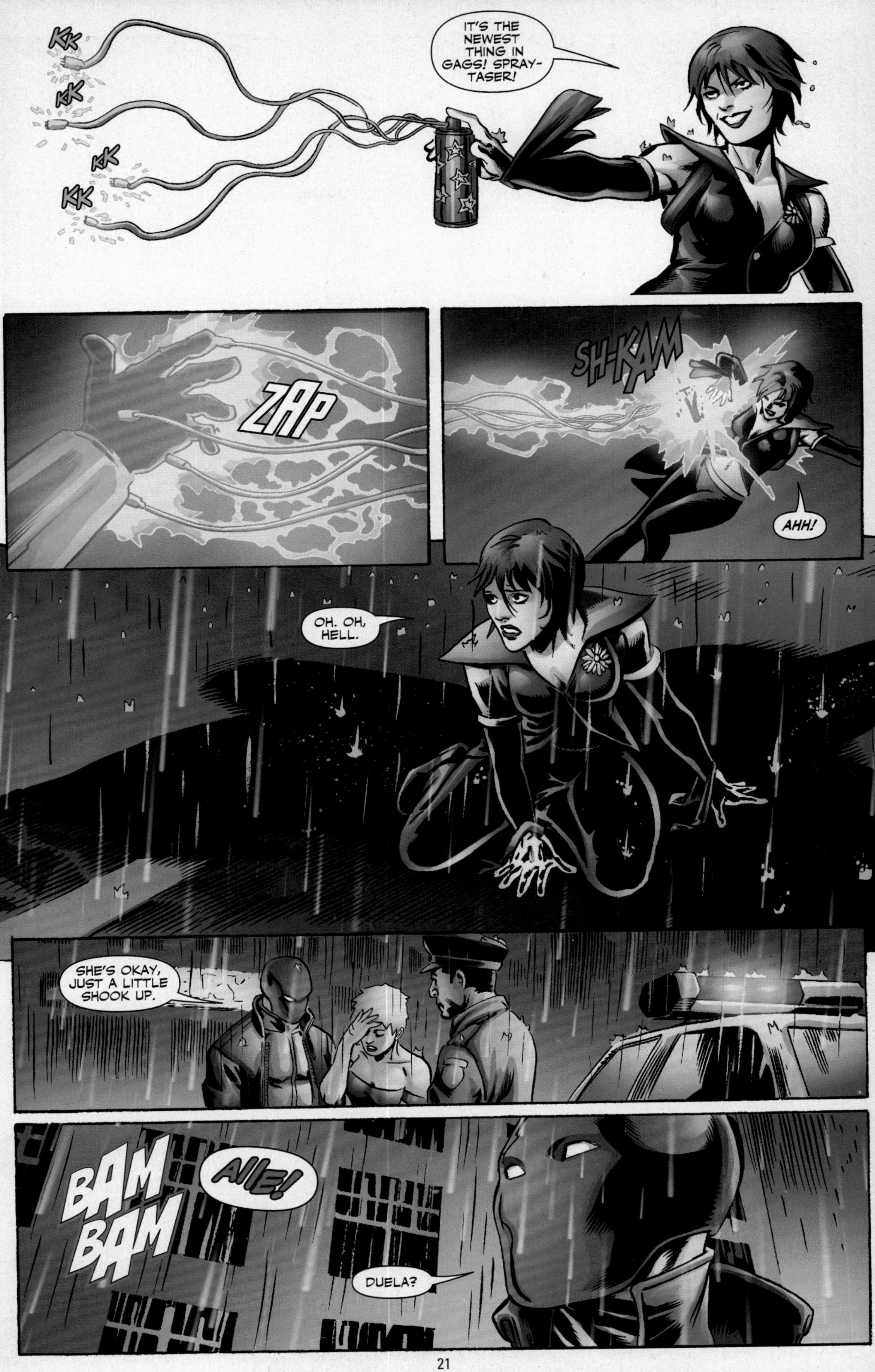
KK
KK
KK
KK
IT'S THE NEWEST THING IN GAGS! SPRAY-TASER!
ZAP
SH-KAM
AHH!
OH. OH, HELL.
SHE'S OKAY, JUST A LITTLE SHOOK UP.
BAM
BAM
AIIE!
DUELA?

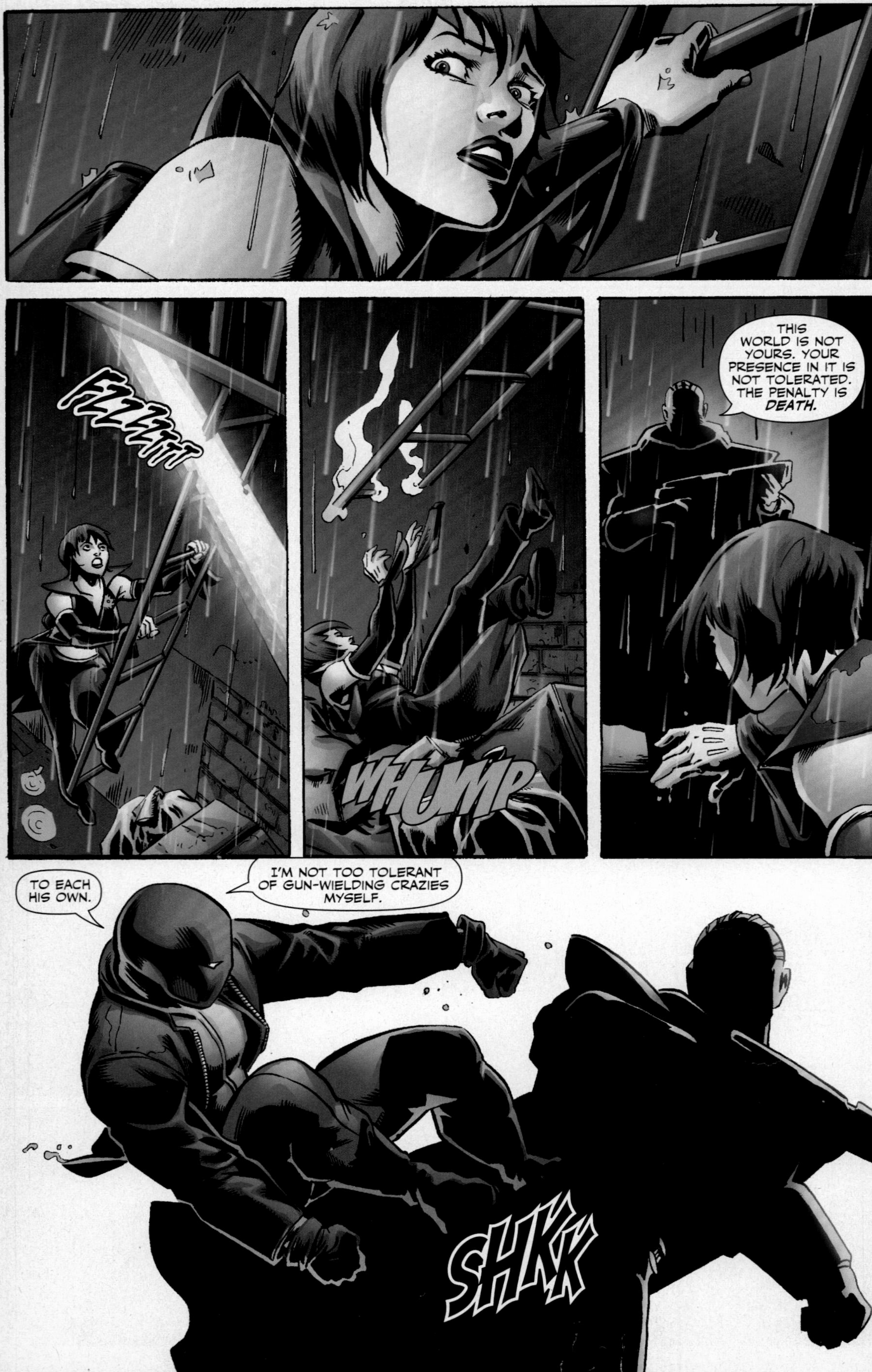
FZZZZTTT
WHUMP
THIS WORLD IS NOT YOURS. YOUR PRESENCE IN IT IS NOT TOLERATED. THE PENALTY IS DEATH.
TO EACH HIS OWN.
I'M NOT TOO TOLERANT OF GUN-WIELDING CRAZIES MYSELF.
SHKK

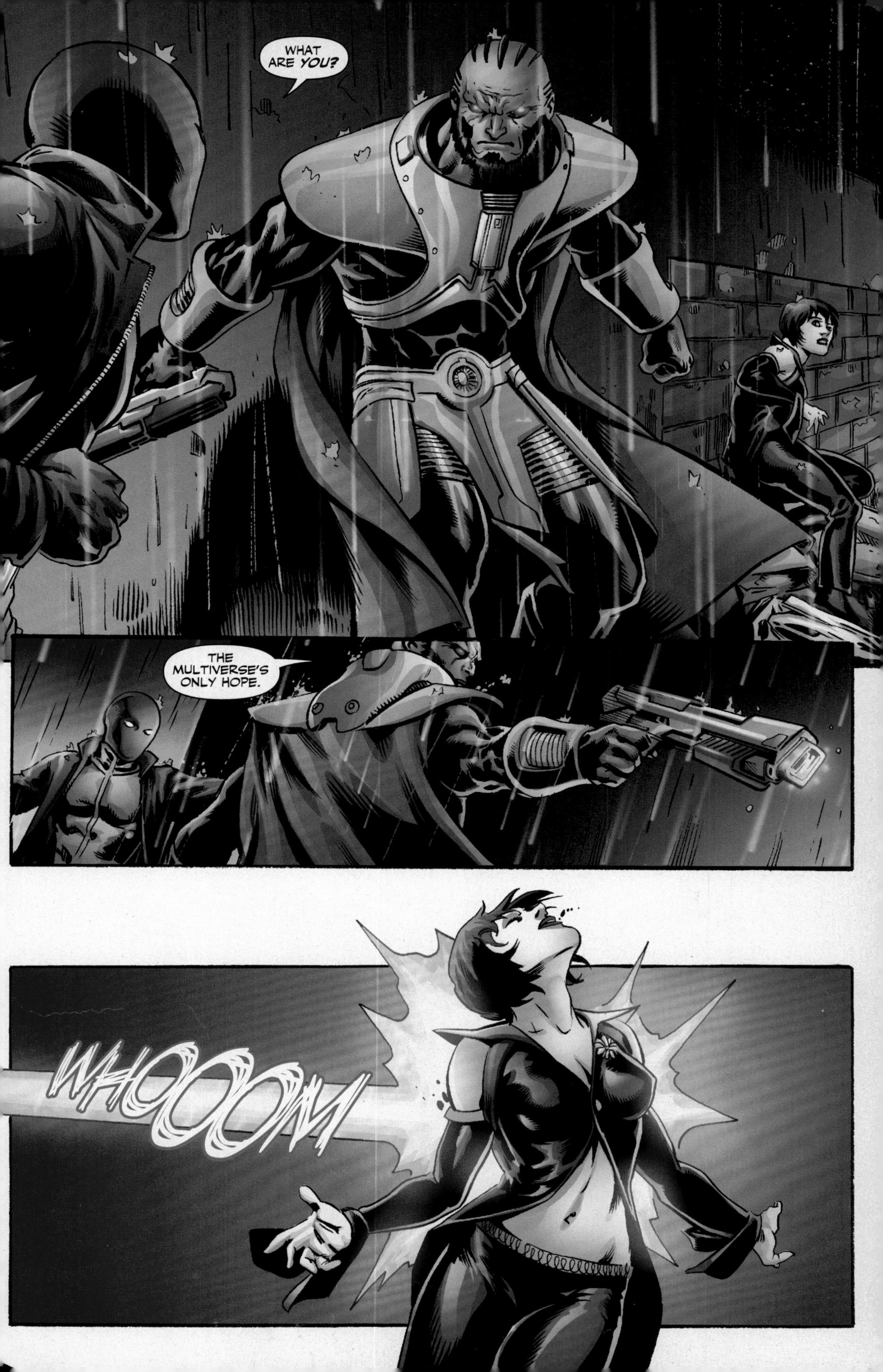
WHAT ARE YOU?
THE MULTIVERSE'S ONLY HOPE.
WHOOOM

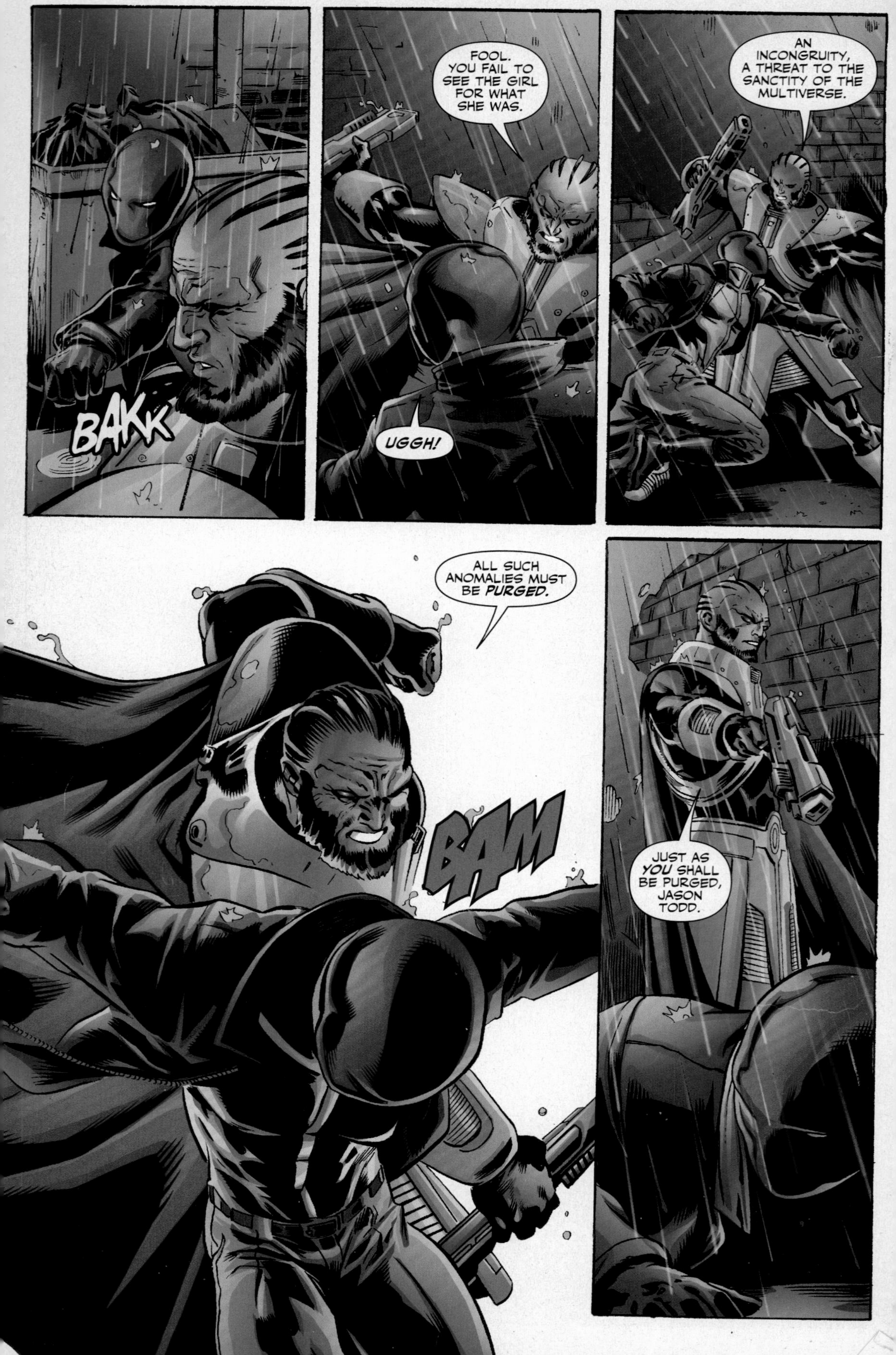
BAKK
FOOL. YOU FAIL TO SEE THE GIRL FOR WHAT SHE WAS.
UGGH!
AN INCONGRUITY, A THREAT TO THE SANCTITY OF THE MULTIVERSE.
ALL SUCH ANOMALIES MUST BE PURGED.
BAM
JUST AS YOU SHALL BE PURGED, JASON TODD.

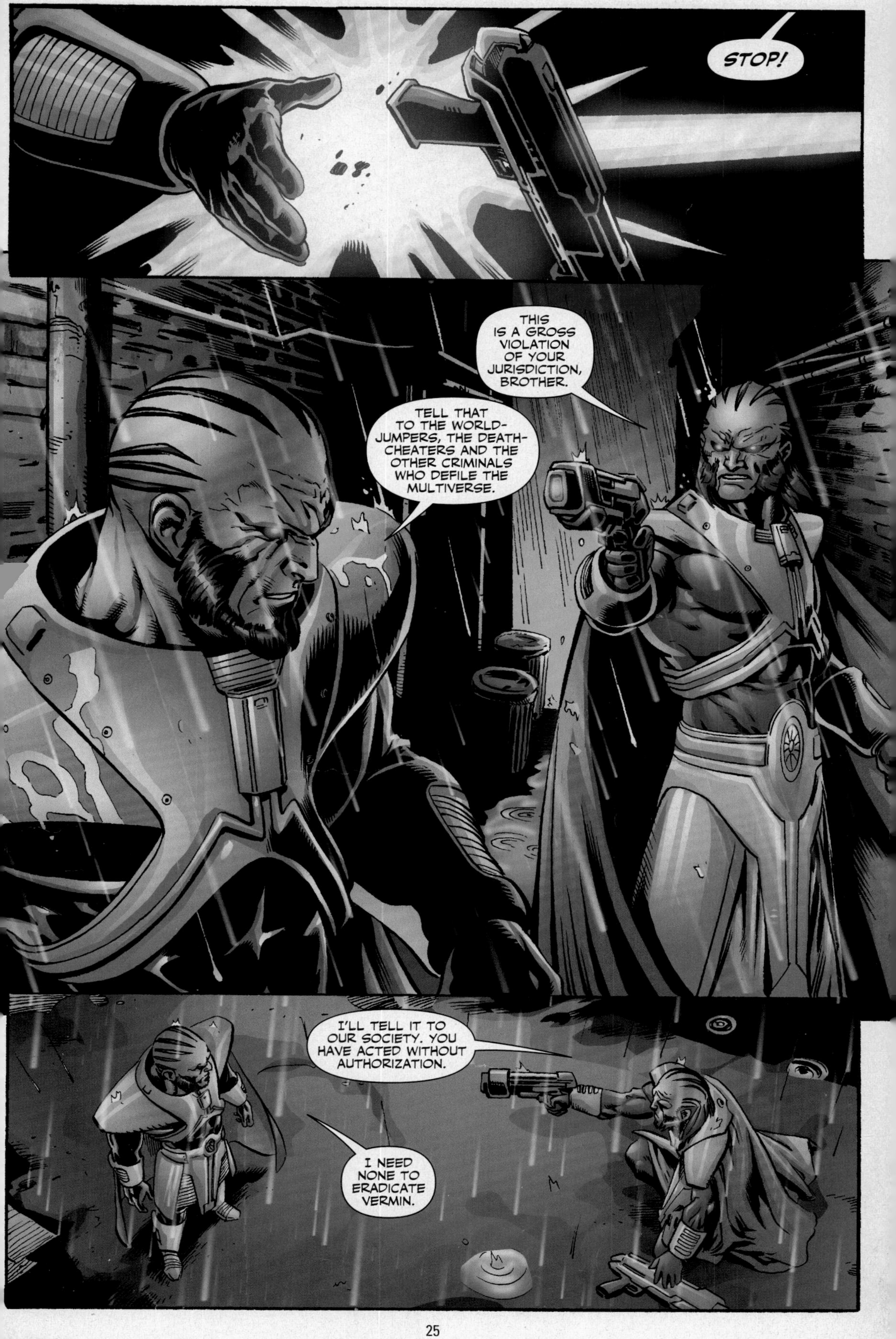
STOP!
THIS IS A GROSS VIOLATION OF YOUR JURISDICTION, BROTHER.
TELL THAT TO THE WORLD-JUMPERS, THE DEATH-CHEATERS AND THE OTHER CRIMINALS WHO DEFILE THE MULTIVERSE.
I'LL TELL IT TO OUR SOCIETY. YOU HAVE ACTED WITHOUT AUTHORIZATION.
I NEED NONE TO ERADICATE VERMIN.

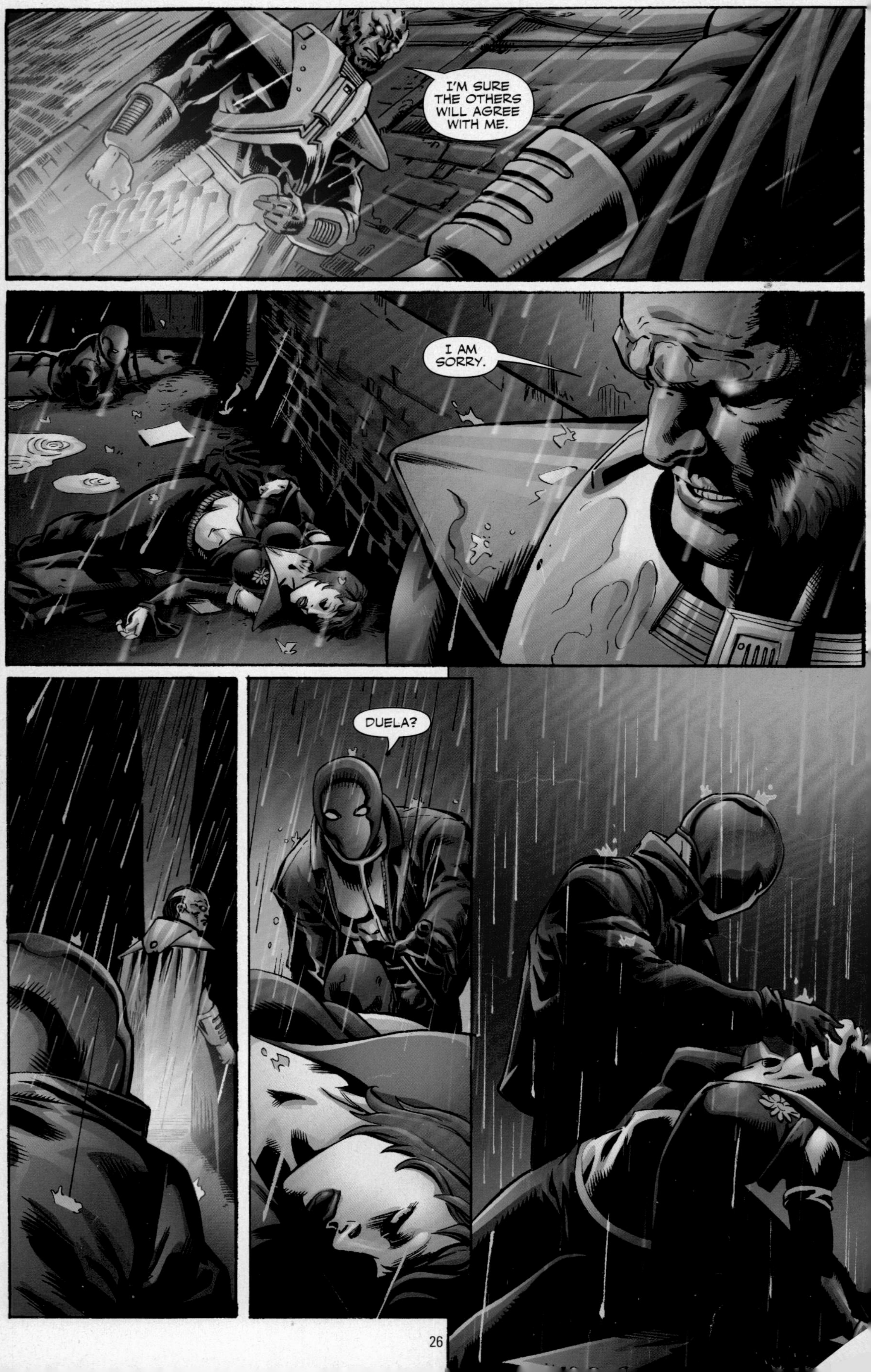
I'M SURE THE OTHERS WILL AGREE WITH ME.
ZZZZZTTT
I AM SORRY.
DUELA?

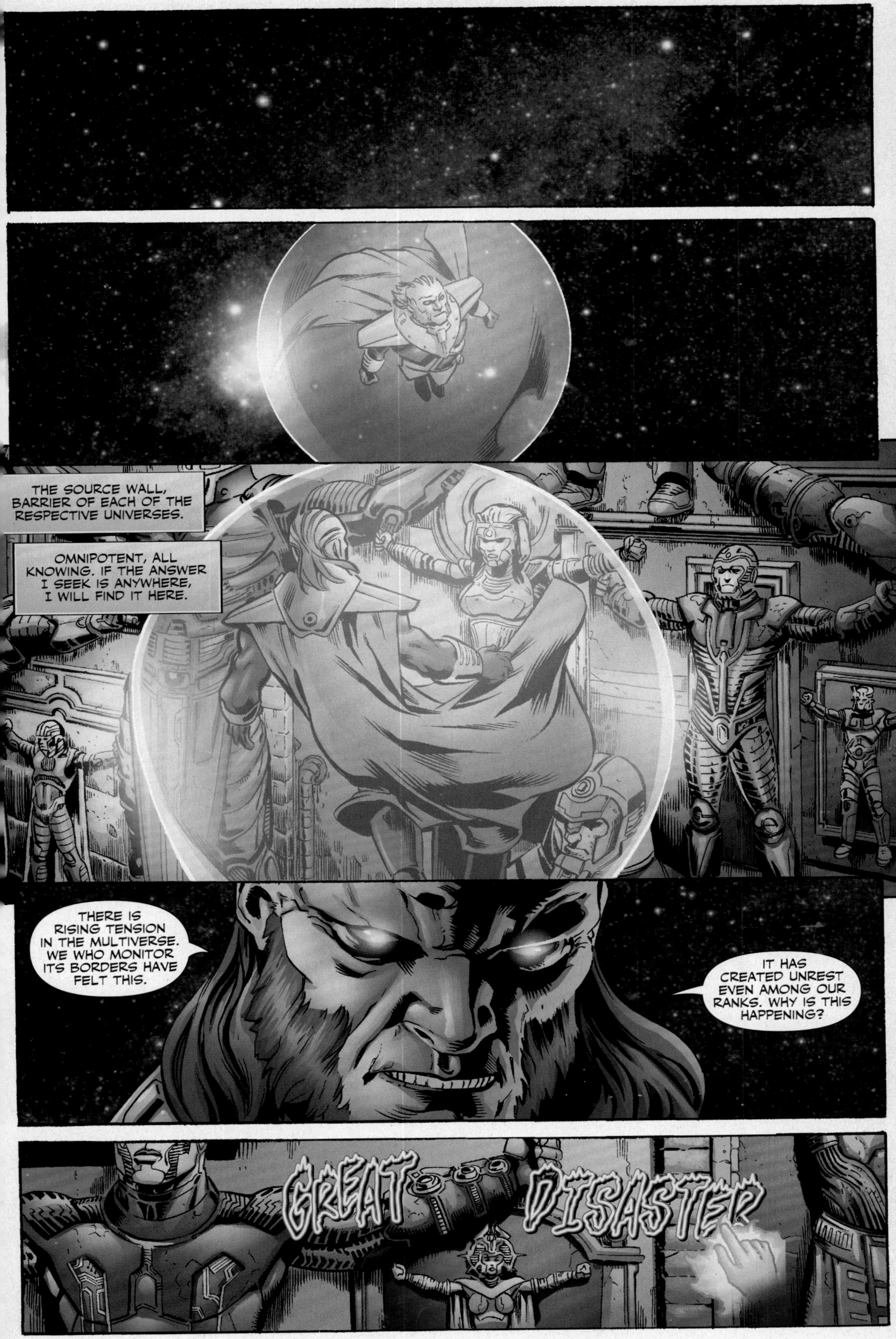
THE SOURCE WALL, BARRIER OF EACH OF THE RESPECTIVE UNIVERSES.
OMNIPOTENT, ALL KNOWING. IF THE ANSWER I SEEK IS ANYWHERE, I WILL FIND IT HERE.
THERE IS RISING TENSION IN THE MULTIVERSE. WE WHO MONITOR ITS BORDERS HAVE FELT THIS.
IT HAS CREATED UNREST EVEN AMONG OUR RANKS. WHY IS THIS HAPPENING?
GREAT DISASTER

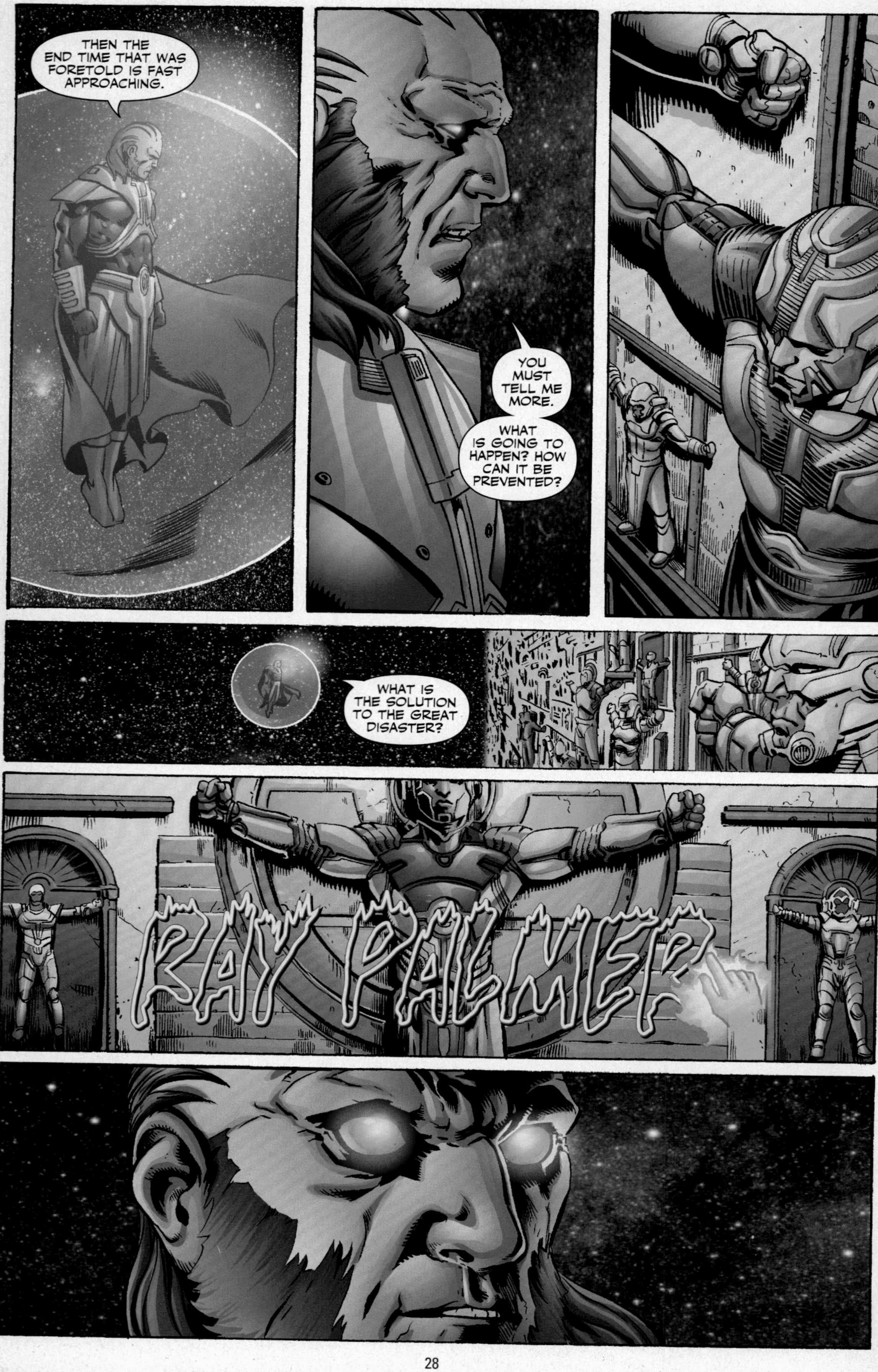
THEN THE END TIME THAT WAS FORETOLD IS FAST APPROACHING.
YOU MUST TELL ME MORE.
WHAT IS GOING TO HAPPEN? HOW CAN IT BE PREVENTED?
WHAT IS THE SOLUTION TO THE GREAT DISASTER?
RAY PALMER

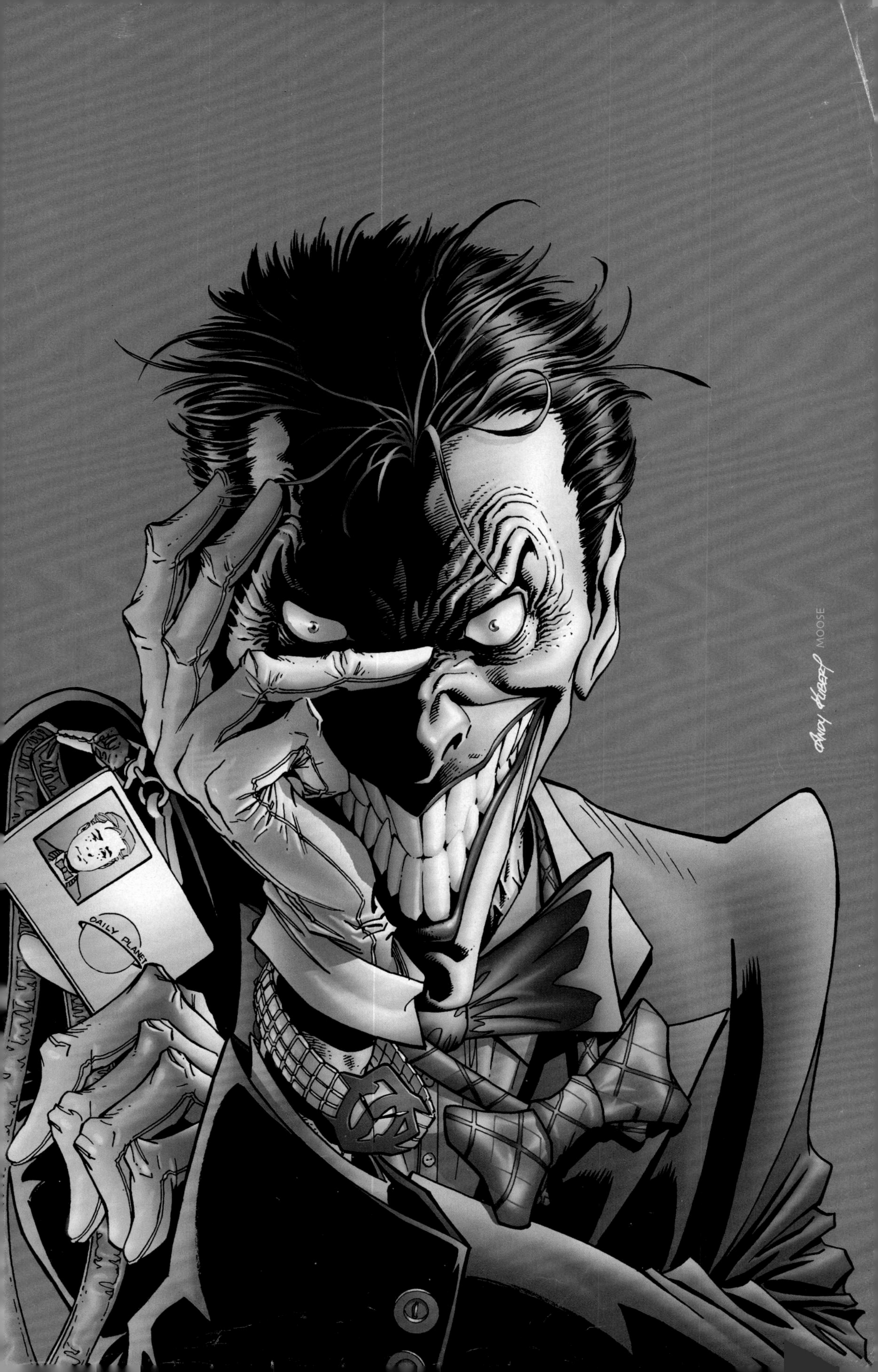
DAILY PLANET
ANDY KUBERT
MOOSE

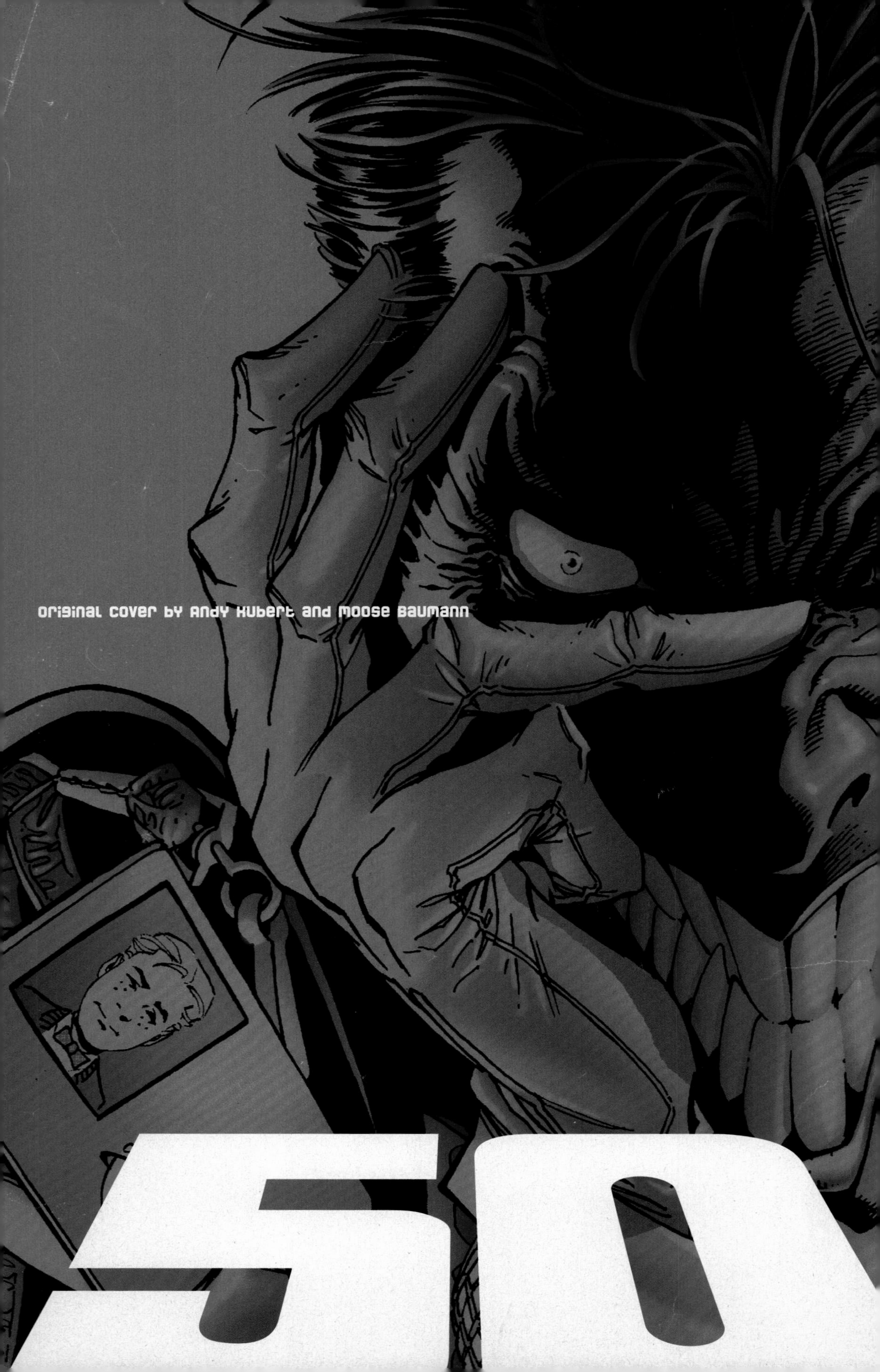
50

original cover by Andy Kubert and Moose Baumann

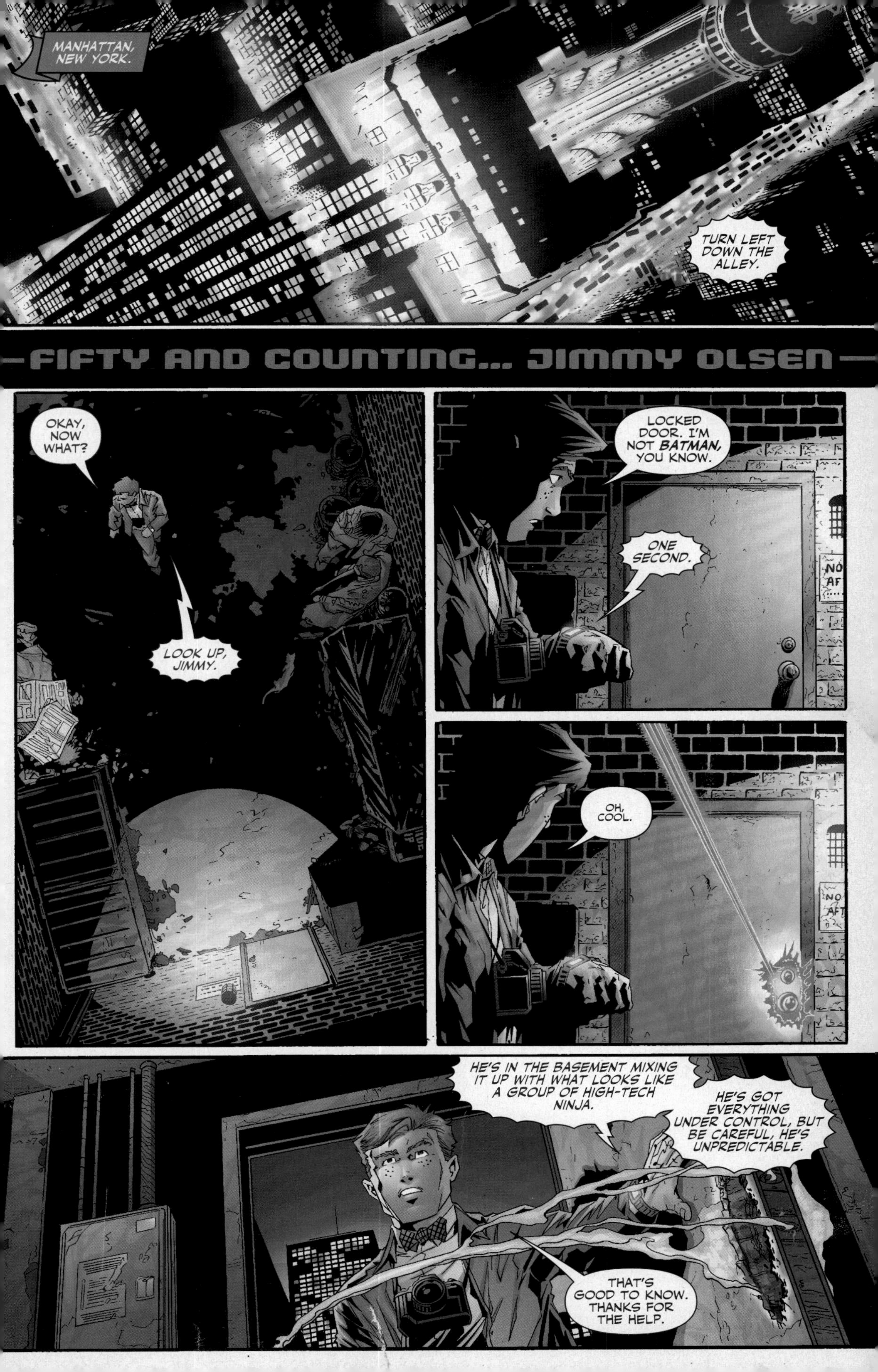
MANHATTAN, NEW YORK.
TURN LEFT DOWN THE ALLEY.
FIFTY AND COUNTING... JIMMY OLSEN
OKAY, NOW WHAT?
LOOK UP, JIMMY.
LOCKED DOOR. I'M NOT BATMAN, YOU KNOW.
ONE SECOND.
OH, COOL.
HE'S IN THE BASEMENT MIXING IT UP WITH WHAT LOOKS LIKE A GROUP OF HIGH-TECH NINJA.
HE'S GOT EVERYTHING UNDER CONTROL, BUT BE CAREFUL, HE'S UNPREDICTABLE.
THAT'S GOOD TO KNOW. THANKS FOR THE HELP.

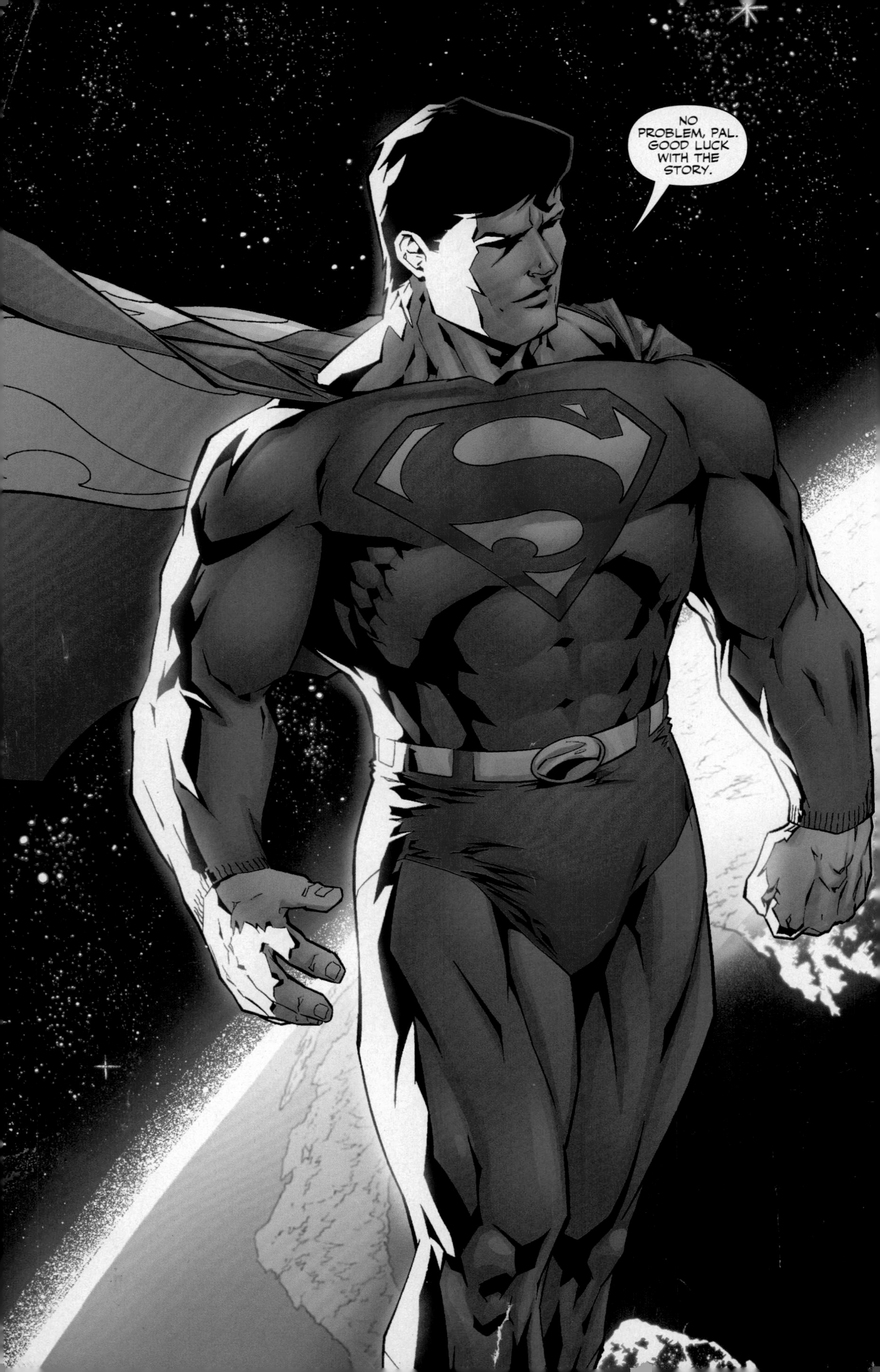
NO PROBLEM, PAL. GOOD LUCK WITH THE STORY.

COUNTDOWN
Last Laugh

PAUL DINI–HEAD WRITER WITH
JIMMY PALMIOTTI & JUSTIN GRAY

J. CALAFIORE–PENCILS   MARK McKENNA–INKS
TOM CHU–COLORS   PAT BROSSEAU–LETTERS

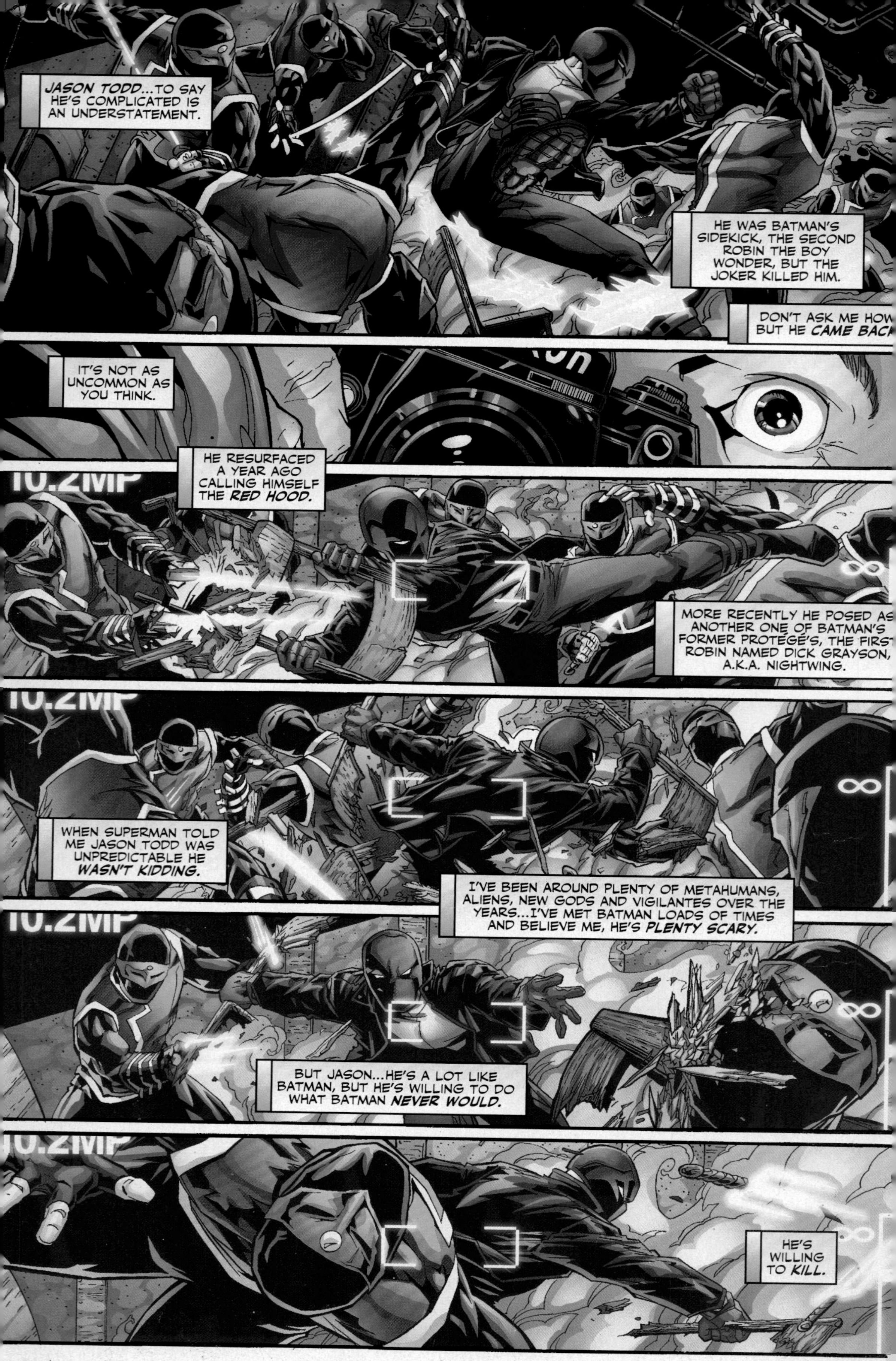
JASON TODD...TO SAY HE'S COMPLICATED IS AN UNDERSTATEMENT.
HE WAS BATMAN'S SIDEKICK, THE SECOND ROBIN THE BOY WONDER, BUT THE JOKER KILLED HIM.
DON'T ASK ME HOW BUT HE CAME BACK
IT'S NOT AS UNCOMMON AS YOU THINK.
HE RESURFACED A YEAR AGO CALLING HIMSELF THE RED HOOD.
10.2MP
MORE RECENTLY HE POSED AS ANOTHER ONE OF BATMAN'S FORMER PROTÉGÉ'S, THE FIRST ROBIN NAMED DICK GRAYSON, A.K.A. NIGHTWING.
10.2MP
WHEN SUPERMAN TOLD ME JASON TODD WAS UNPREDICTABLE HE WASN'T KIDDING.
I'VE BEEN AROUND PLENTY OF METAHUMANS, ALIENS, NEW GODS AND VIGILANTES OVER THE YEARS...I'VE MET BATMAN LOADS OF TIMES AND BELIEVE ME, HE'S PLENTY SCARY.
10.2MP
BUT JASON...HE'S A LOT LIKE BATMAN, BUT HE'S WILLING TO DO WHAT BATMAN NEVER WOULD.
10.2MP
HE'S WILLING TO KILL.

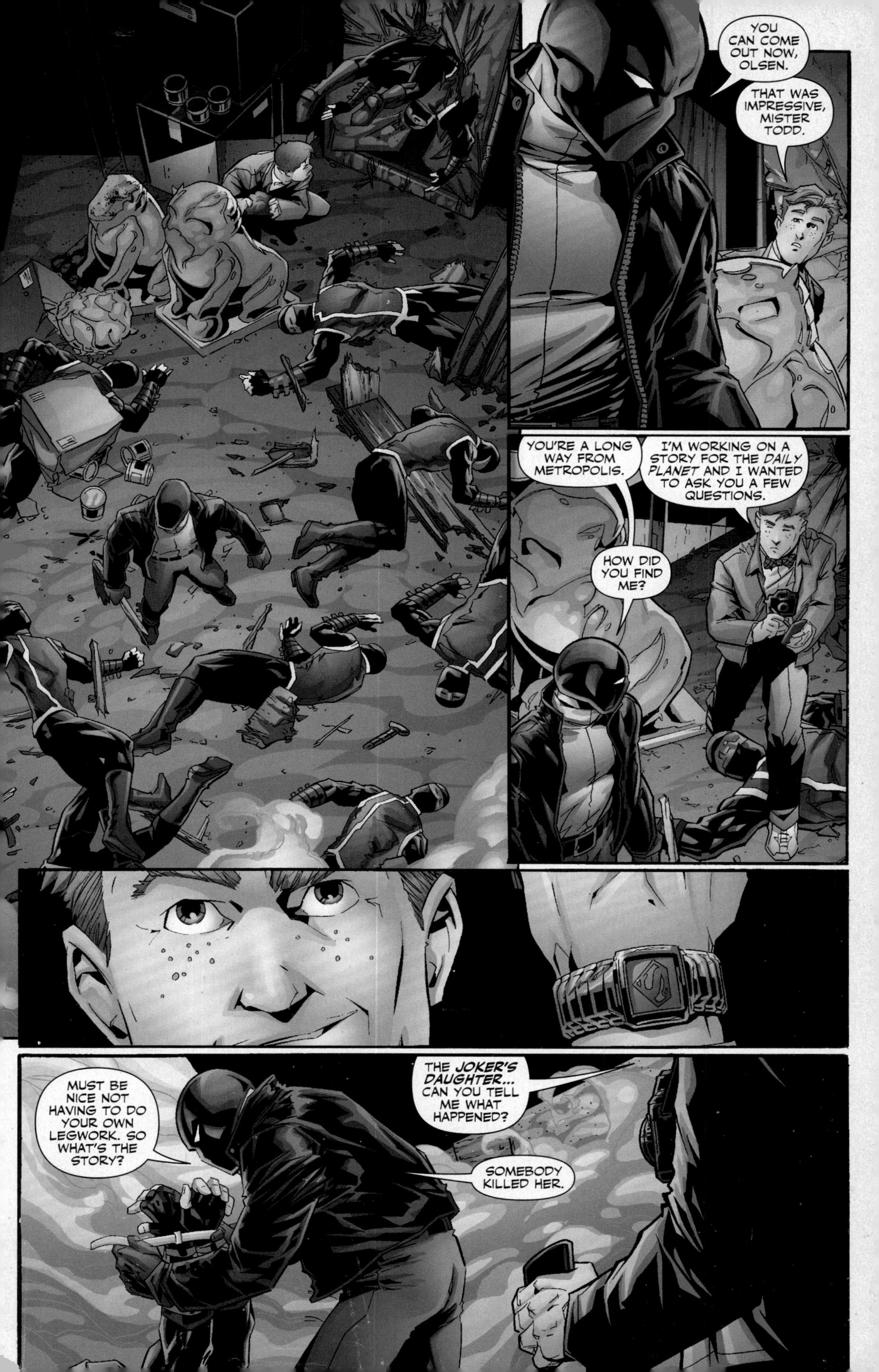
YOU CAN COME OUT NOW, OLSEN.
THAT WAS IMPRESSIVE, MISTER TODD.
YOU'RE A LONG WAY FROM METROPOLIS.
I'M WORKING ON A STORY FOR THE *DAILY PLANET* AND I WANTED TO ASK YOU A FEW QUESTIONS.
HOW DID YOU FIND ME?
MUST BE NICE NOT HAVING TO DO YOUR OWN LEGWORK. SO WHAT'S THE STORY?
THE *JOKER'S DAUGHTER*... CAN YOU TELL ME WHAT HAPPENED?
SOMEBODY KILLED HER.

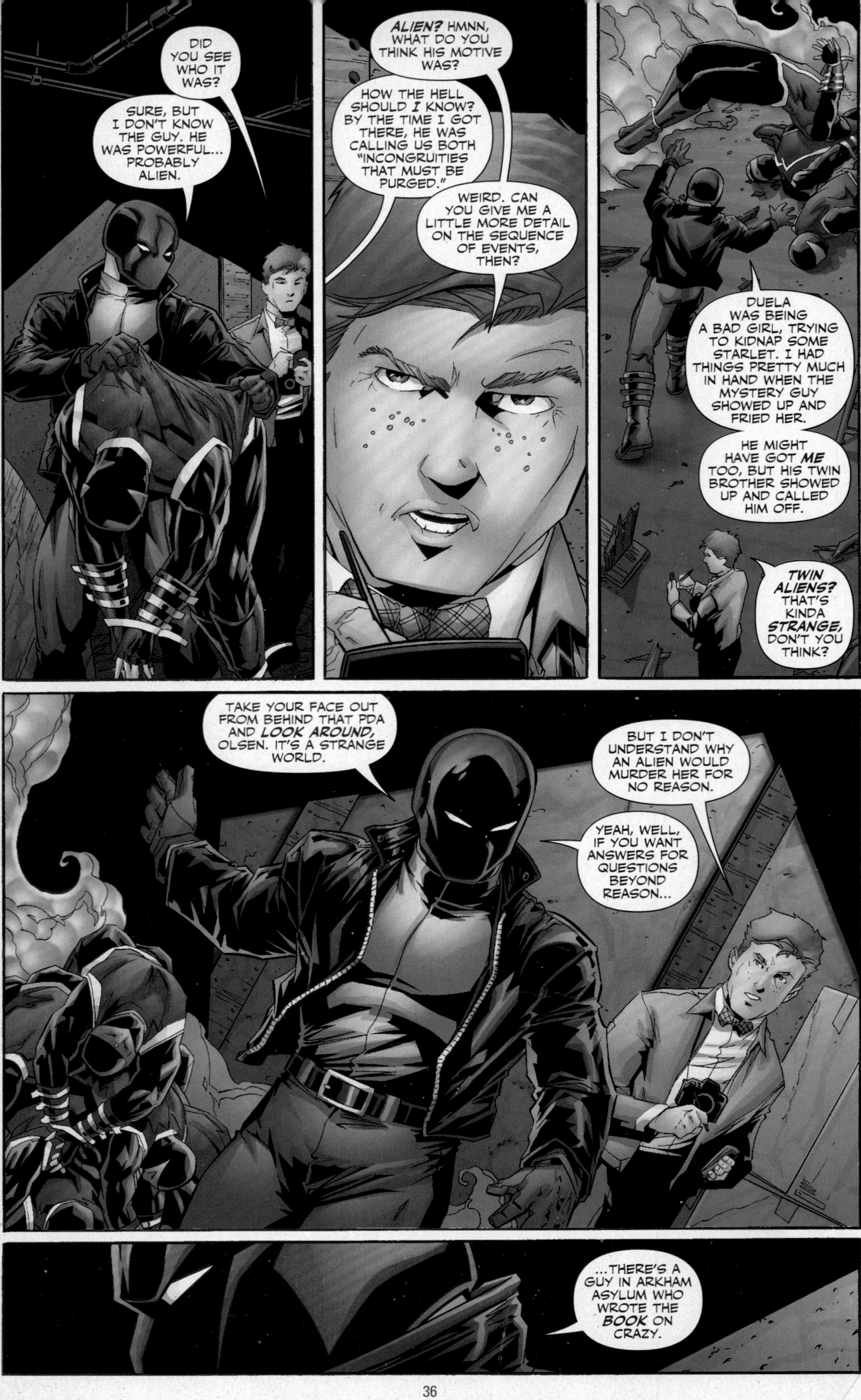

DID YOU SEE WHO IT WAS?
SURE, BUT I DON'T KNOW THE GUY. HE WAS POWERFUL... PROBABLY ALIEN.
ALIEN? HMNN, WHAT DO YOU THINK HIS MOTIVE WAS?
HOW THE HELL SHOULD I KNOW? BY THE TIME I GOT THERE, HE WAS CALLING US BOTH "INCONGRUITIES THAT MUST BE PURGED."
WEIRD. CAN YOU GIVE ME A LITTLE MORE DETAIL ON THE SEQUENCE OF EVENTS, THEN?
DUELA WAS BEING A BAD GIRL, TRYING TO KIDNAP SOME STARLET. I HAD THINGS PRETTY MUCH IN HAND WHEN THE MYSTERY GUY SHOWED UP AND FRIED HER.
HE MIGHT HAVE GOT ME TOO, BUT HIS TWIN BROTHER SHOWED UP AND CALLED HIM OFF.
TWIN ALIENS? THAT'S KINDA STRANGE, DON'T YOU THINK?
TAKE YOUR FACE OUT FROM BEHIND THAT PDA AND LOOK AROUND, OLSEN. IT'S A STRANGE WORLD.
BUT I DON'T UNDERSTAND WHY AN ALIEN WOULD MURDER HER FOR NO REASON.
YEAH, WELL, IF YOU WANT ANSWERS FOR QUESTIONS BEYOND REASON...
...THERE'S A GUY IN ARKHAM ASYLUM WHO WROTE THE BOOK ON CRAZY.

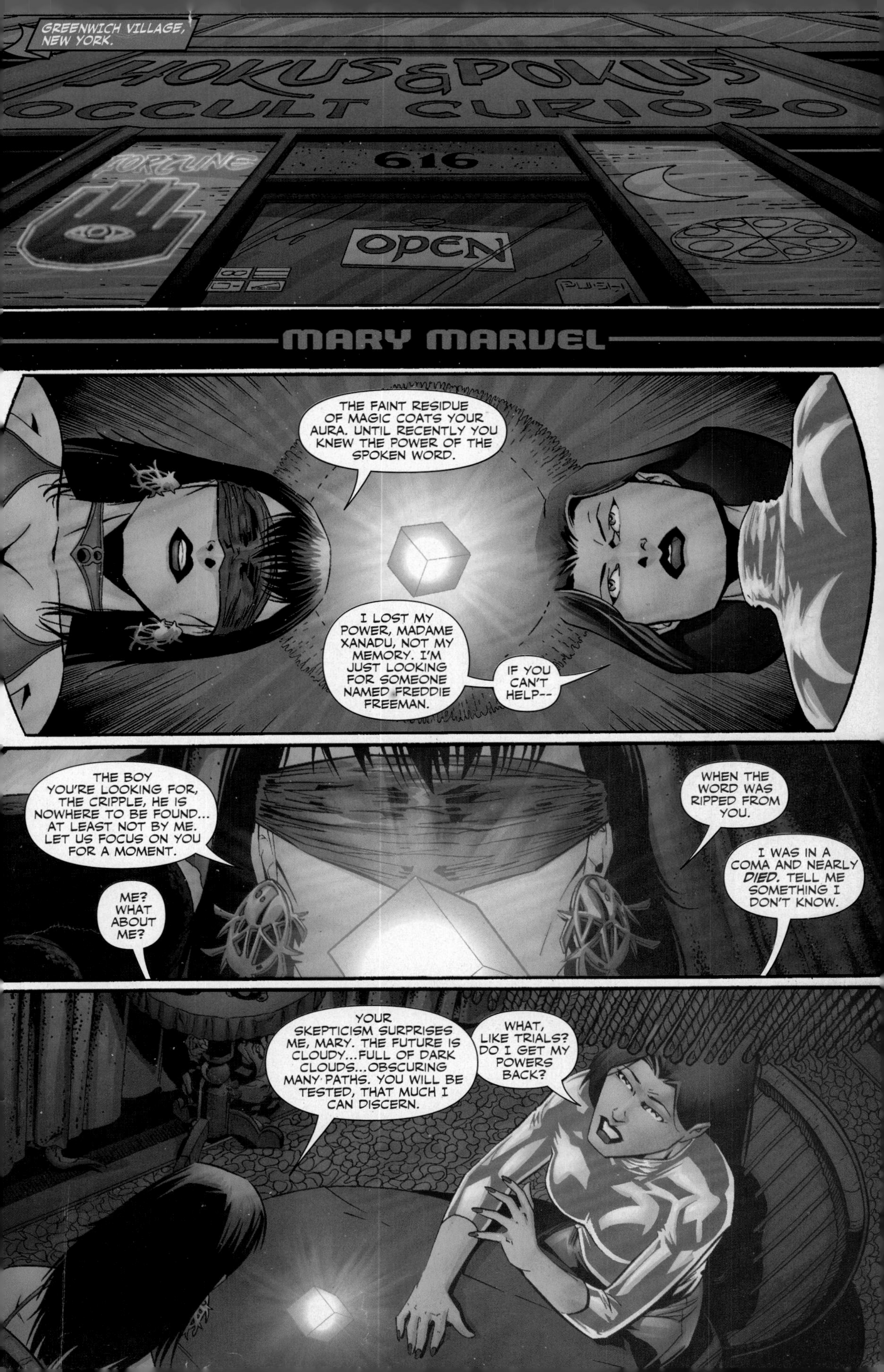
GREENWICH VILLAGE, NEW YORK.
HOKUS & POKUS OCCULT CURIOSO
FORTUNE
616
OPEN
PUSH
MARY MARVEL
THE FAINT RESIDUE OF MAGIC COATS YOUR AURA. UNTIL RECENTLY YOU KNEW THE POWER OF THE SPOKEN WORD.
I LOST MY POWER, MADAME XANADU, NOT MY MEMORY. I'M JUST LOOKING FOR SOMEONE NAMED FREDDIE FREEMAN.
IF YOU CAN'T HELP--
THE BOY YOU'RE LOOKING FOR, THE CRIPPLE, HE IS NOWHERE TO BE FOUND... AT LEAST NOT BY ME. LET US FOCUS ON YOU FOR A MOMENT.
ME? WHAT ABOUT ME?
WHEN THE WORD WAS RIPPED FROM YOU.
I WAS IN A COMA AND NEARLY *DIED.* TELL ME SOMETHING I DON'T KNOW.
YOUR SKEPTICISM SURPRISES ME, MARY. THE FUTURE IS CLOUDY...FULL OF DARK CLOUDS...OBSCURING MANY PATHS. YOU WILL BE TESTED, THAT MUCH I CAN DISCERN.
WHAT, LIKE TRIALS? DO I GET MY POWERS BACK?

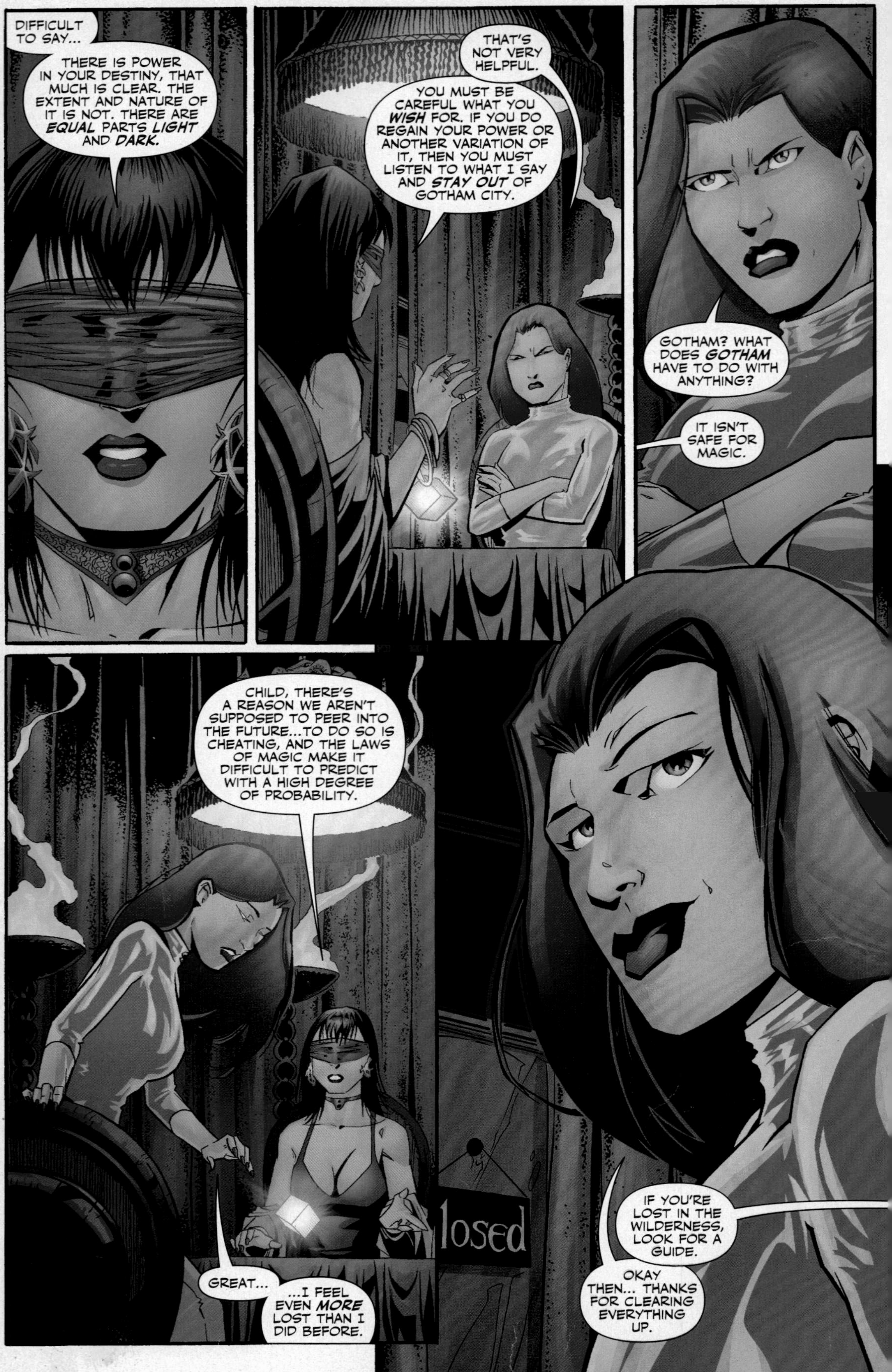
DIFFICULT TO SAY...
THERE IS POWER IN YOUR DESTINY, THAT MUCH IS CLEAR. THE EXTENT AND NATURE OF IT IS NOT. THERE ARE EQUAL PARTS LIGHT AND DARK.
THAT'S NOT VERY HELPFUL.
YOU MUST BE CAREFUL WHAT YOU WISH FOR. IF YOU DO REGAIN YOUR POWER OR ANOTHER VARIATION OF IT, THEN YOU MUST LISTEN TO WHAT I SAY AND STAY OUT OF GOTHAM CITY.
GOTHAM? WHAT DOES GOTHAM HAVE TO DO WITH ANYTHING?
IT ISN'T SAFE FOR MAGIC.
CHILD, THERE'S A REASON WE AREN'T SUPPOSED TO PEER INTO THE FUTURE...TO DO SO IS CHEATING, AND THE LAWS OF MAGIC MAKE IT DIFFICULT TO PREDICT WITH A HIGH DEGREE OF PROBABILITY.
GREAT...
...I FEEL EVEN MORE LOST THAN I DID BEFORE.
losed
IF YOU'RE LOST IN THE WILDERNESS, LOOK FOR A GUIDE.
OKAY THEN... THANKS FOR CLEARING EVERYTHING UP.

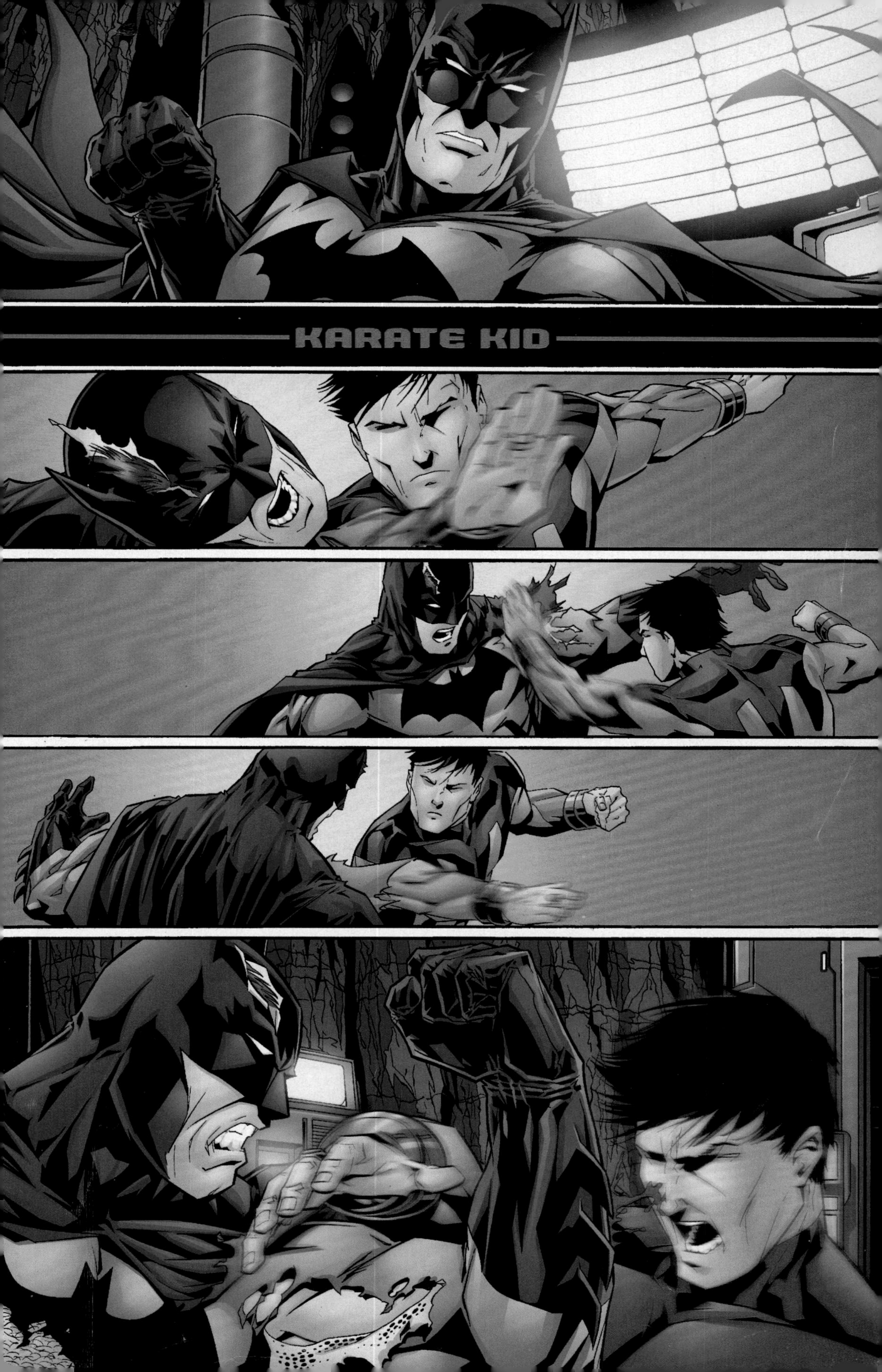
KARATE KID

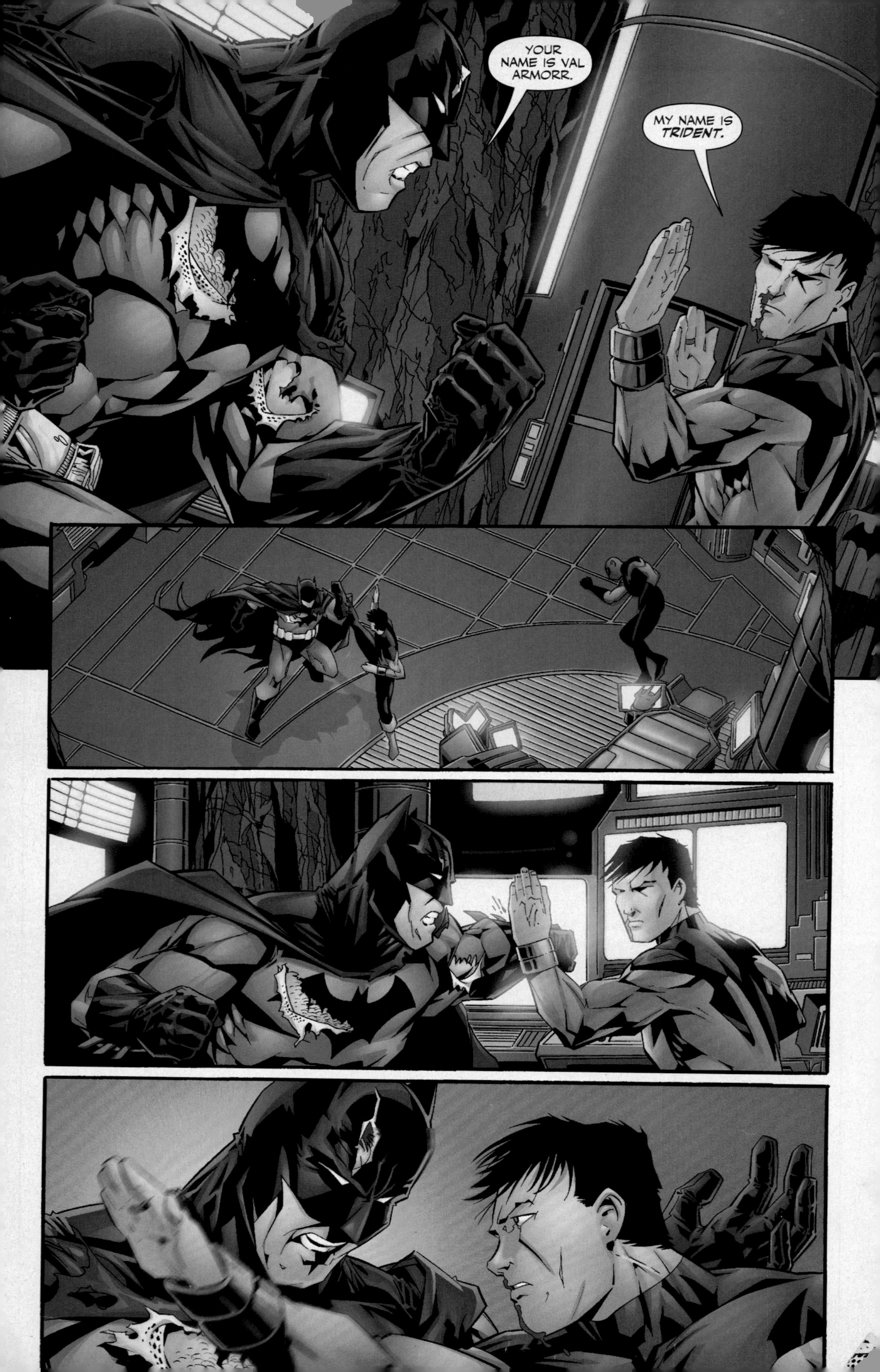
YOUR NAME IS VAL ARMORR.
MY NAME IS TRIDENT.

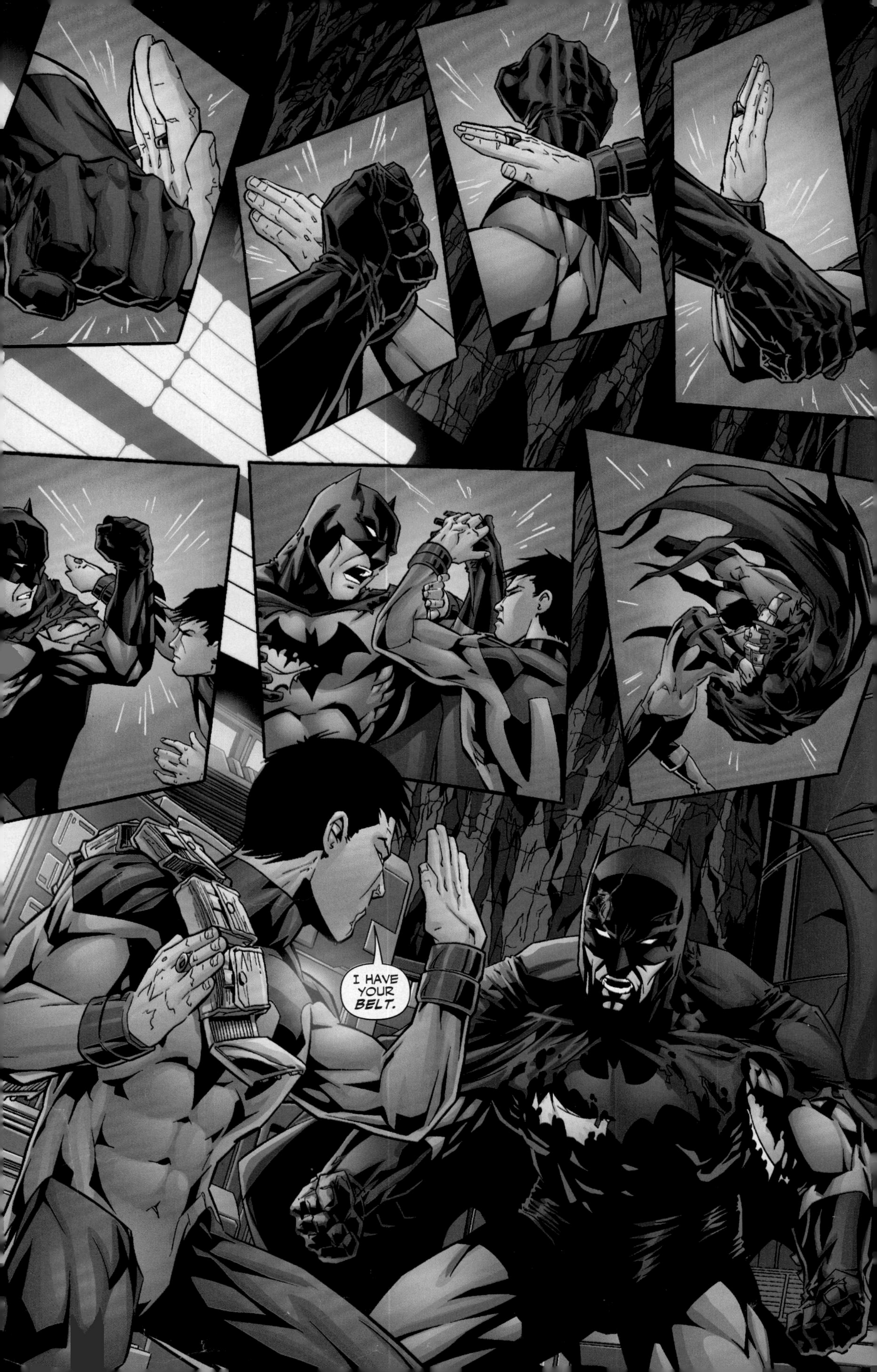
I HAVE YOUR BELT.

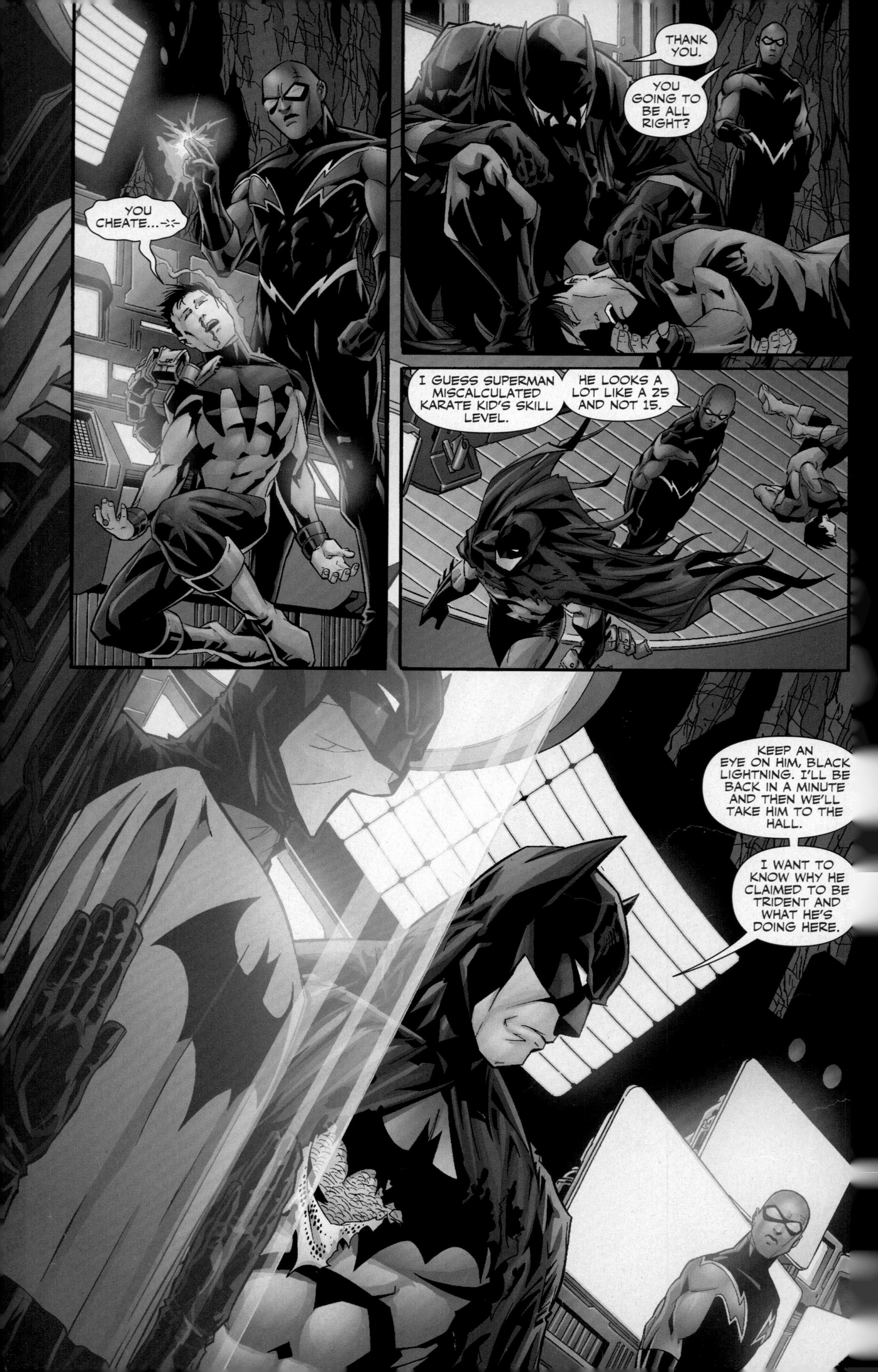

YOU CHEATE...
THANK YOU.
YOU GOING TO BE ALL RIGHT?
I GUESS SUPERMAN MISCALCULATED KARATE KID'S SKILL LEVEL.
HE LOOKS A LOT LIKE A 25 AND NOT 15.
KEEP AN EYE ON HIM, BLACK LIGHTNING. I'LL BE BACK IN A MINUTE AND THEN WE'LL TAKE HIM TO THE HALL.
I WANT TO KNOW WHY HE CLAIMED TO BE TRIDENT AND WHAT HE'S DOING HERE.

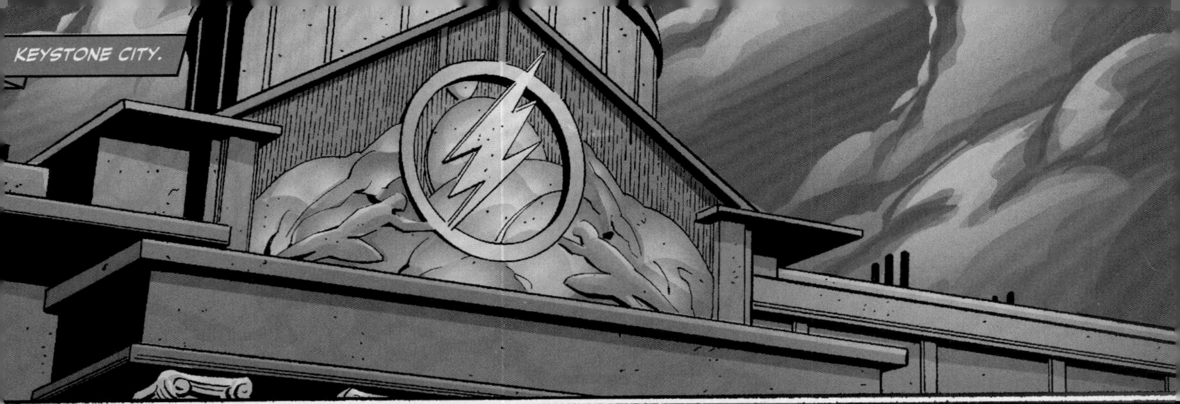
KEYSTONE CITY.

THE ROGUES

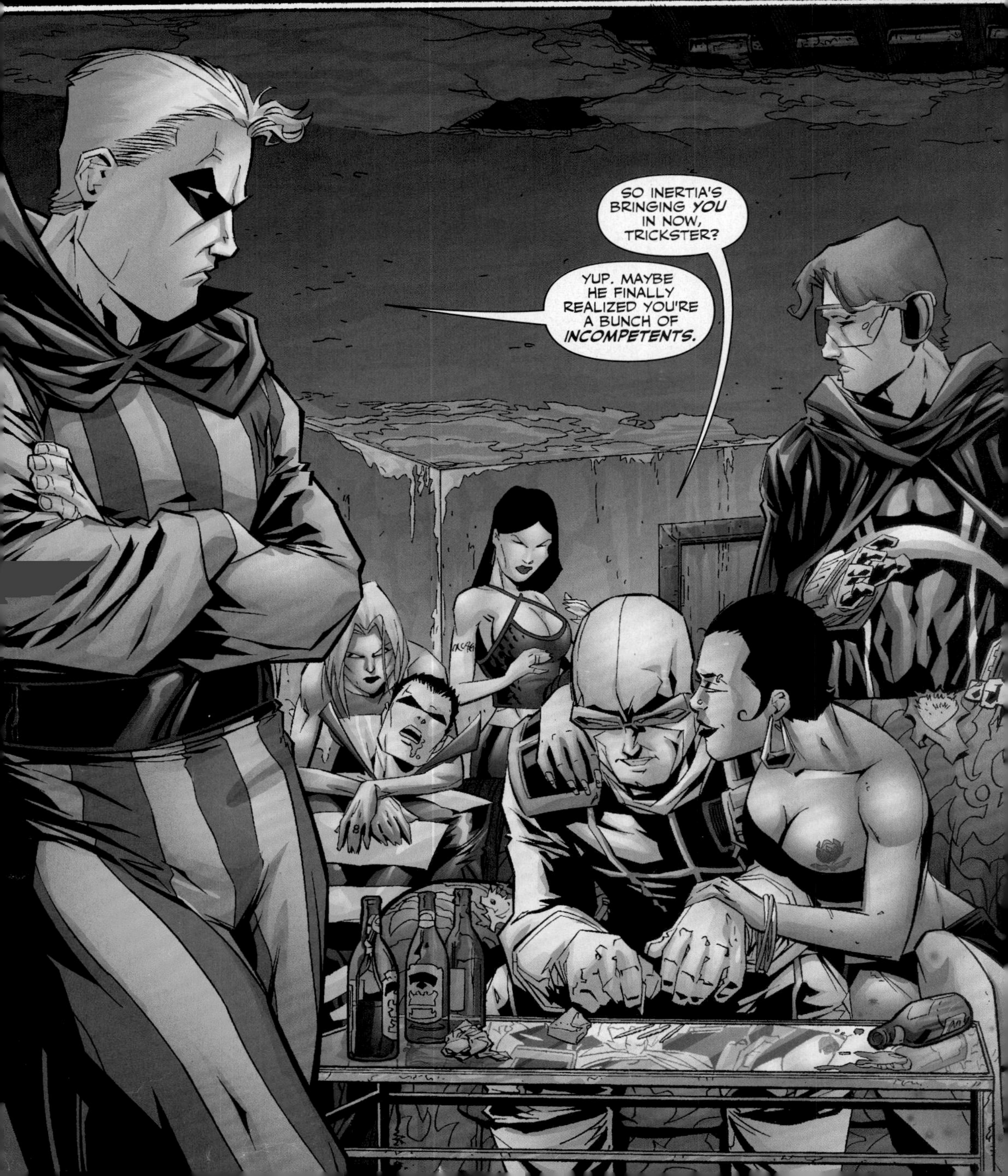
SO INERTIA'S BRINGING YOU IN NOW, TRICKSTER?
YUP. MAYBE HE FINALLY REALIZED YOU'RE A BUNCH OF INCOMPETENTS.

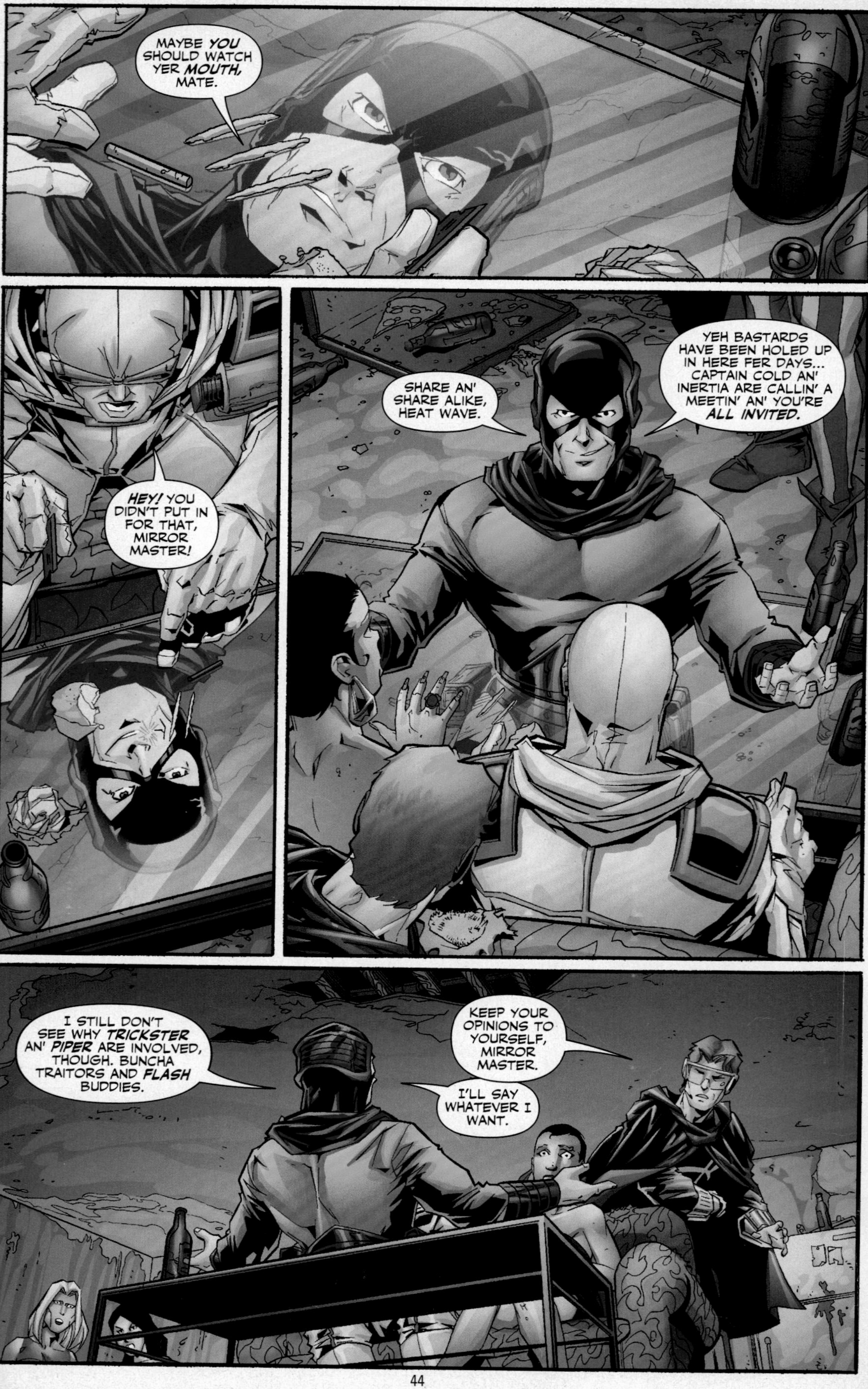
MAYBE YOU SHOULD WATCH YER MOUTH, MATE.
HEY! YOU DIDN'T PUT IN FOR THAT, MIRROR MASTER!
SHARE AN' SHARE ALIKE, HEAT WAVE.
YEH BASTARDS HAVE BEEN HOLED UP IN HERE FER DAYS... CAPTAIN COLD AN' INERTIA ARE CALLIN' A MEETIN' AN' YOU'RE ALL INVITED.
I STILL DON'T SEE WHY TRICKSTER AN' PIPER ARE INVOLVED, THOUGH. BUNCHA TRAITORS AND FLASH BUDDIES.
KEEP YOUR OPINIONS TO YOURSELF, MIRROR MASTER.
I'LL SAY WHATEVER I WANT.

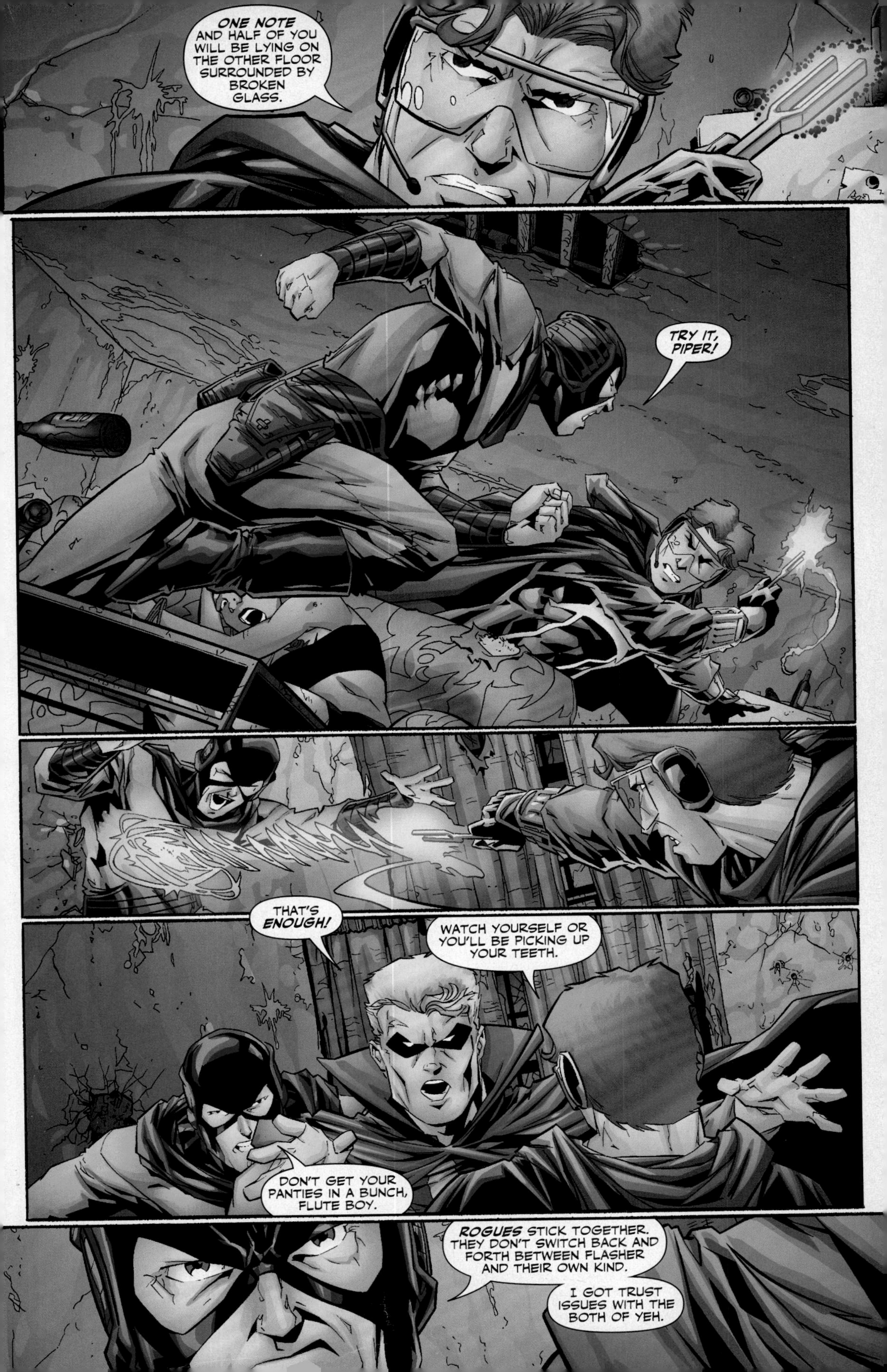
ONE NOTE AND HALF OF YOU WILL BE LYING ON THE OTHER FLOOR SURROUNDED BY BROKEN GLASS.
TRY IT, PIPER!
THAT'S ENOUGH!
WATCH YOURSELF OR YOU'LL BE PICKING UP YOUR TEETH.
DON'T GET YOUR PANTIES IN A BUNCH, FLUTE BOY.
ROGUES STICK TOGETHER. THEY DON'T SWITCH BACK AND FORTH BETWEEN FLASHER AND THEIR OWN KIND.
I GOT TRUST ISSUES WITH THE BOTH OF YEH.

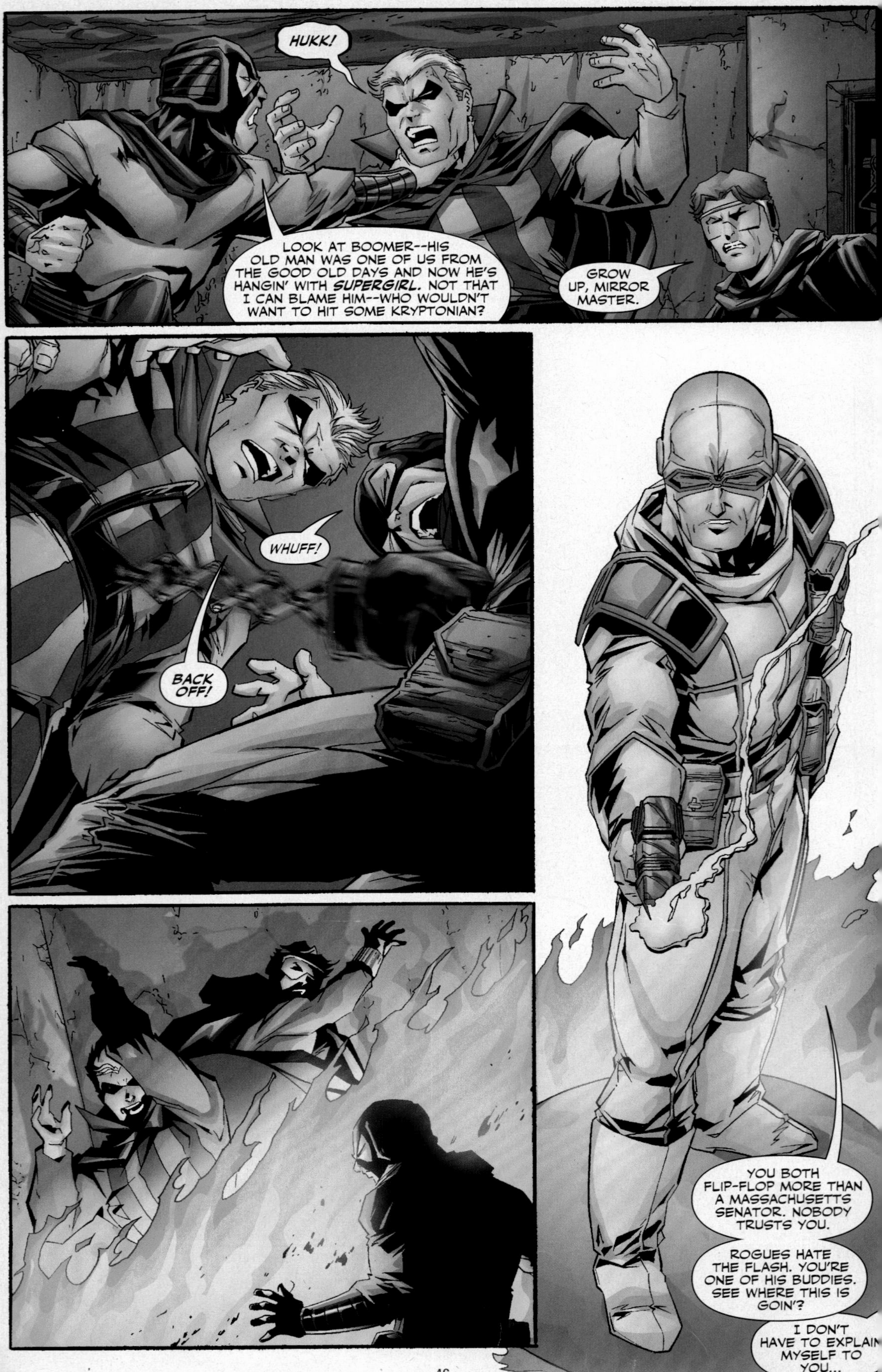
HUKK!
LOOK AT BOOMER--HIS OLD MAN WAS ONE OF US FROM THE GOOD OLD DAYS AND NOW HE'S HANGIN' WITH SUPERGIRL. NOT THAT I CAN BLAME HIM--WHO WOULDN'T WANT TO HIT SOME KRYPTONIAN?
GROW UP, MIRROR MASTER.
WHUFF!
BACK OFF!
YOU BOTH FLIP-FLOP MORE THAN A MASSACHUSETTS SENATOR. NOBODY TRUSTS YOU.
ROGUES HATE THE FLASH. YOU'RE ONE OF HIS BUDDIES. SEE WHERE THIS IS GOIN'?
I DON'T HAVE TO EXPLAIN MYSELF TO YOU...

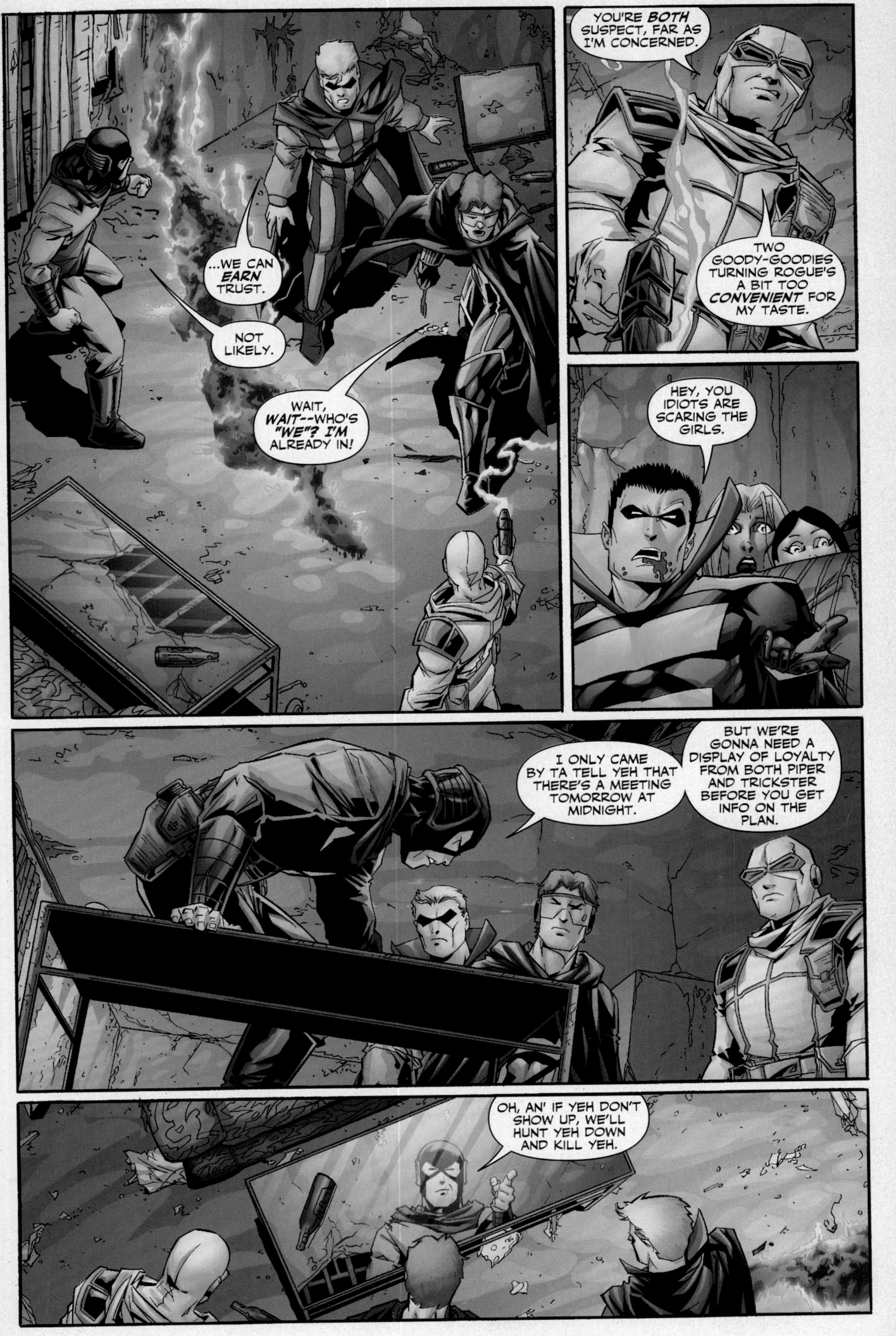
...WE CAN EARN TRUST.
NOT LIKELY.
WAIT, WAIT--WHO'S "WE"? I'M ALREADY IN!
YOU'RE BOTH SUSPECT, FAR AS I'M CONCERNED.
TWO GOODY-GOODIES TURNING ROGUE'S A BIT TOO CONVENIENT FOR MY TASTE.
HEY, YOU IDIOTS ARE SCARING THE GIRLS.
I ONLY CAME BY TA TELL YEH THAT THERE'S A MEETING TOMORROW AT MIDNIGHT.
BUT WE'RE GONNA NEED A DISPLAY OF LOYALTY FROM BOTH PIPER AND TRICKSTER BEFORE YOU GET INFO ON THE PLAN.
OH, AN' IF YEH DON'T SHOW UP, WE'LL HUNT YEH DOWN AND KILL YEH.

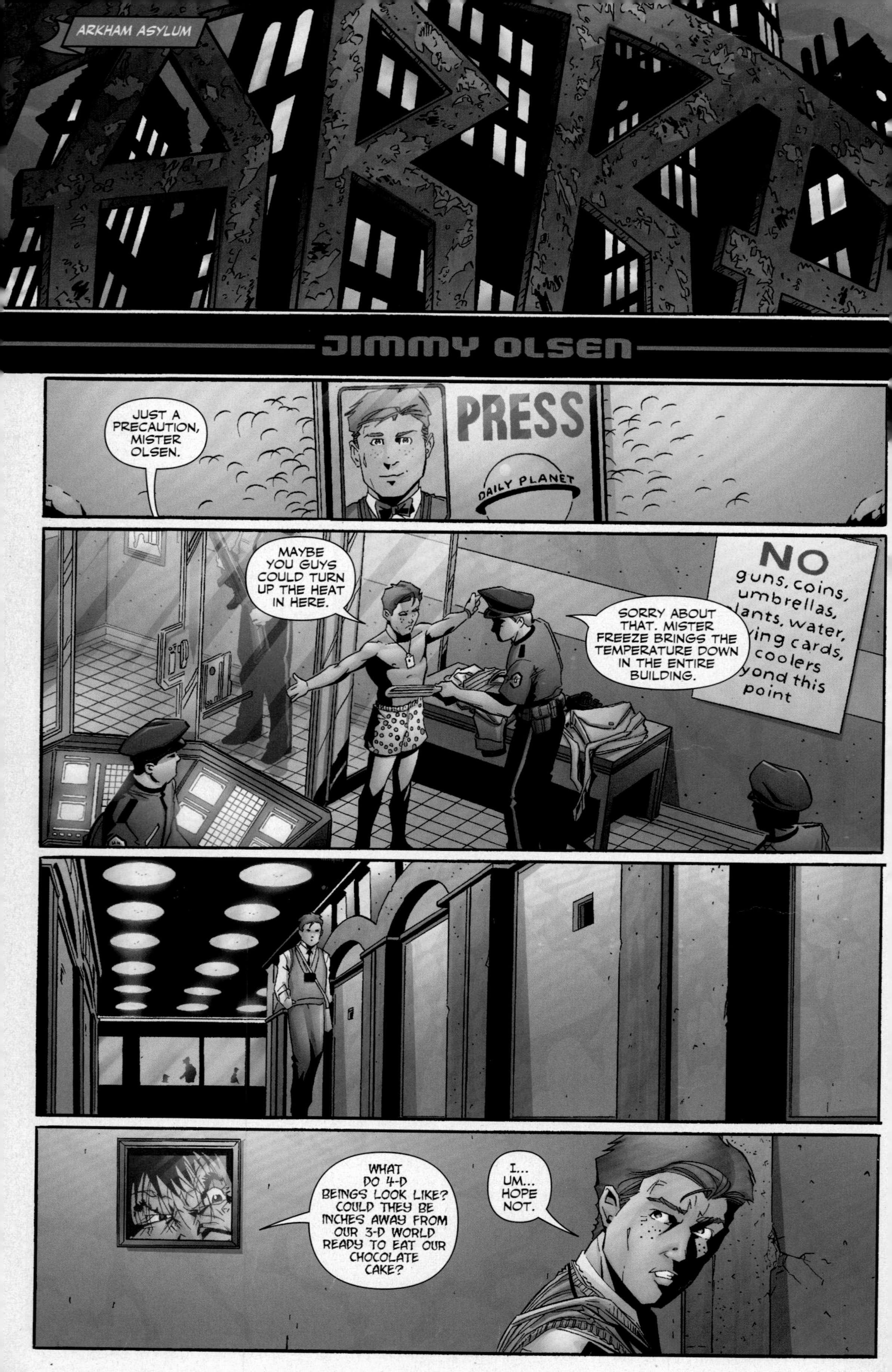
ARKHAM ASYLUM
JIMMY OLSEN
JUST A PRECAUTION, MISTER OLSEN.
PRESS
DAILY PLANET
MAYBE YOU GUYS COULD TURN UP THE HEAT IN HERE.
NO guns, coins, umbrellas, lants, water, ying cards, coolers yond this point
SORRY ABOUT THAT. MISTER FREEZE BRINGS THE TEMPERATURE DOWN IN THE ENTIRE BUILDING.
WHAT DO 4-D BEINGS LOOK LIKE? COULD THEY BE INCHES AWAY FROM OUR 3-D WORLD READY TO EAT OUR CHOCOLATE CAKE?
I... UM... HOPE NOT.

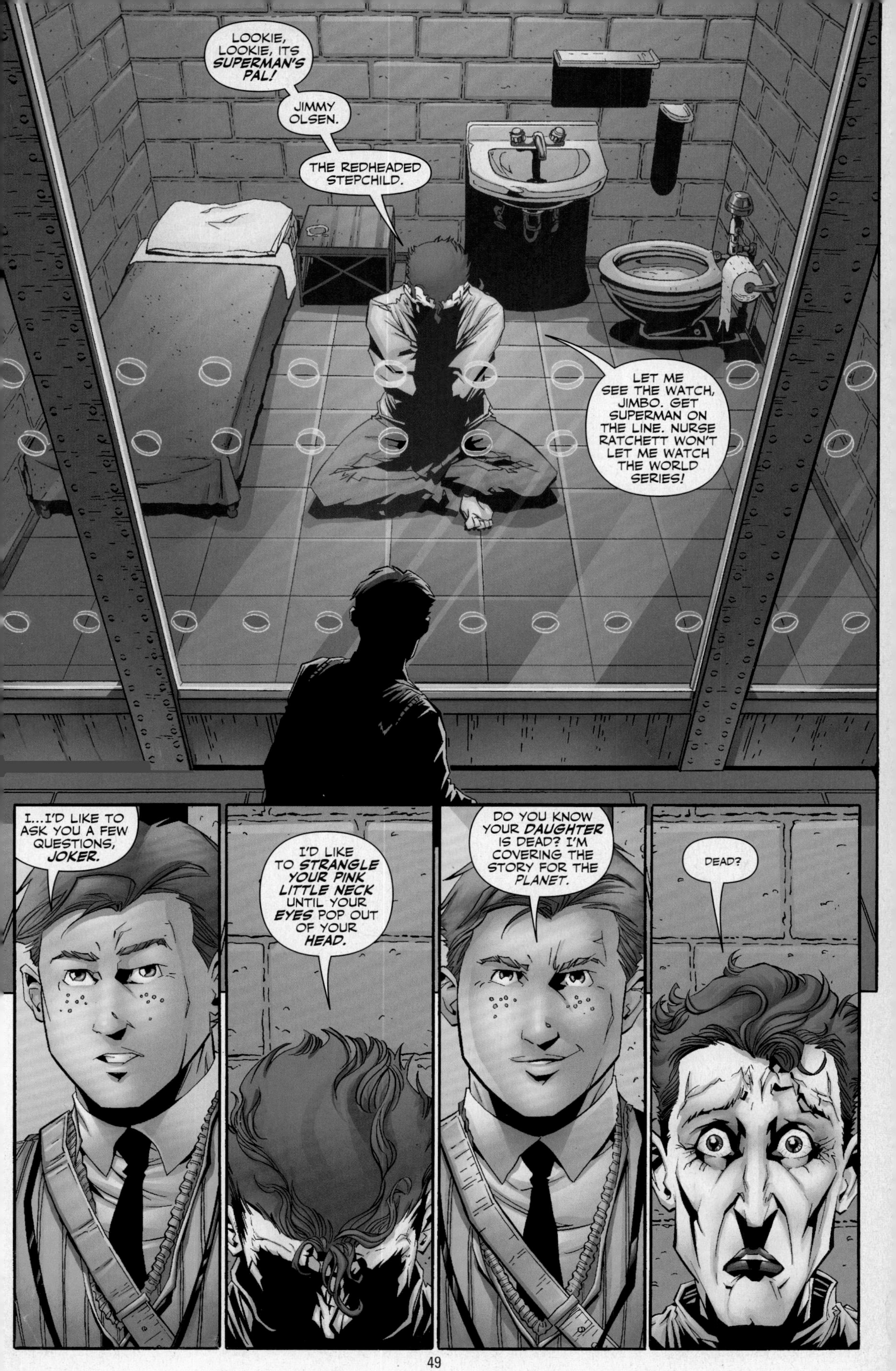
LOOKIE, LOOKIE, ITS SUPERMAN'S PAL!
JIMMY OLSEN.
THE REDHEADED STEPCHILD.
LET ME SEE THE WATCH, JIMBO. GET SUPERMAN ON THE LINE. NURSE RATCHETT WON'T LET ME WATCH THE WORLD SERIES!
I...I'D LIKE TO ASK YOU A FEW QUESTIONS, JOKER.
I'D LIKE TO STRANGLE YOUR PINK LITTLE NECK UNTIL YOUR EYES POP OUT OF YOUR HEAD.
DO YOU KNOW YOUR DAUGHTER IS DEAD? I'M COVERING THE STORY FOR THE PLANET.
DEAD?

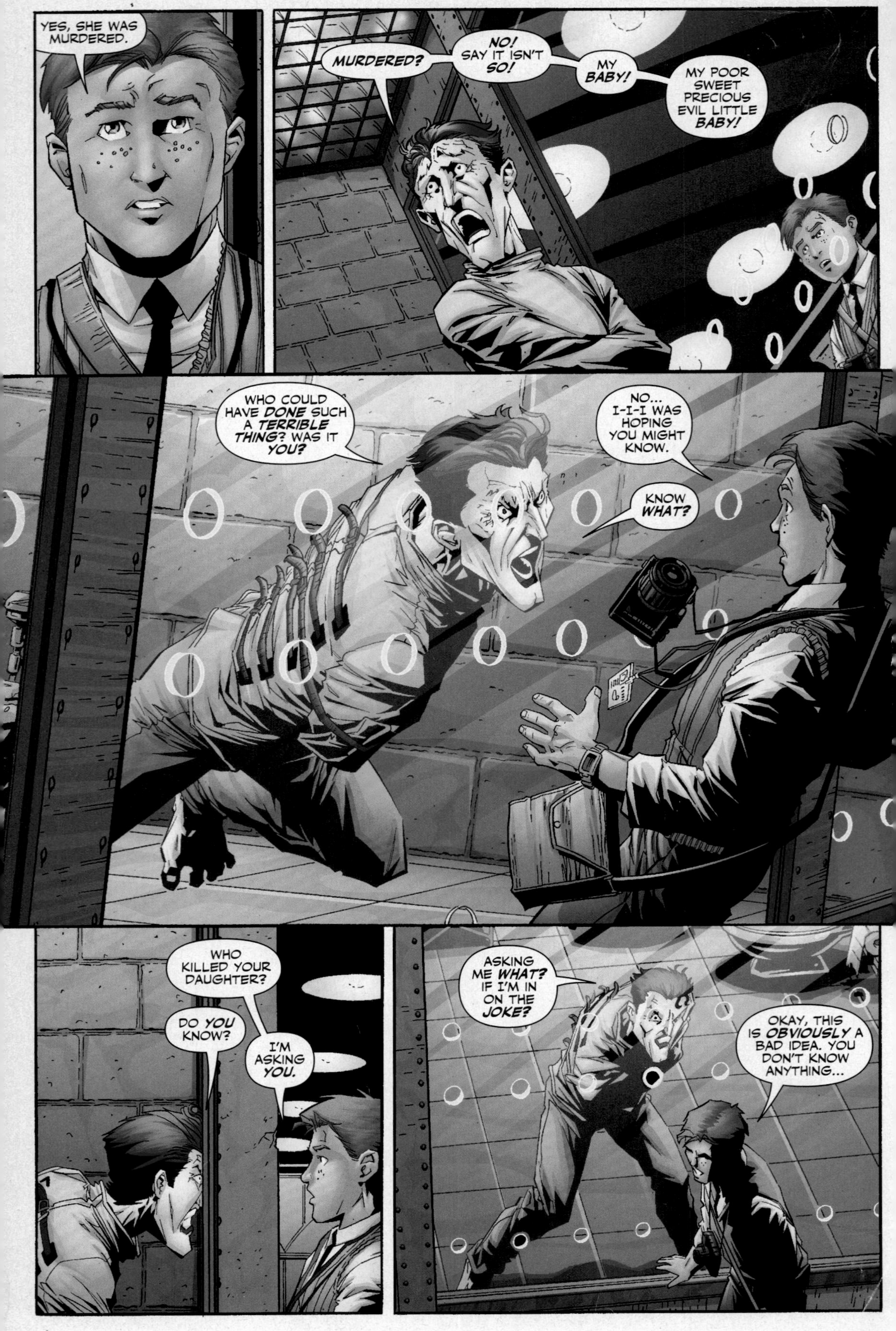
YES, SHE WAS MURDERED.
MURDERED?
NO! SAY IT ISN'T SO!
MY BABY!
MY POOR SWEET PRECIOUS EVIL LITTLE BABY!
WHO COULD HAVE DONE SUCH A TERRIBLE THING? WAS IT YOU?
NO... I-I-I WAS HOPING YOU MIGHT KNOW.
KNOW WHAT?
WHO KILLED YOUR DAUGHTER?
DO YOU KNOW?
I'M ASKING YOU.
ASKING ME WHAT? IF I'M IN ON THE JOKE?
OKAY, THIS IS OBVIOUSLY A BAD IDEA. YOU DON'T KNOW ANYTHING...

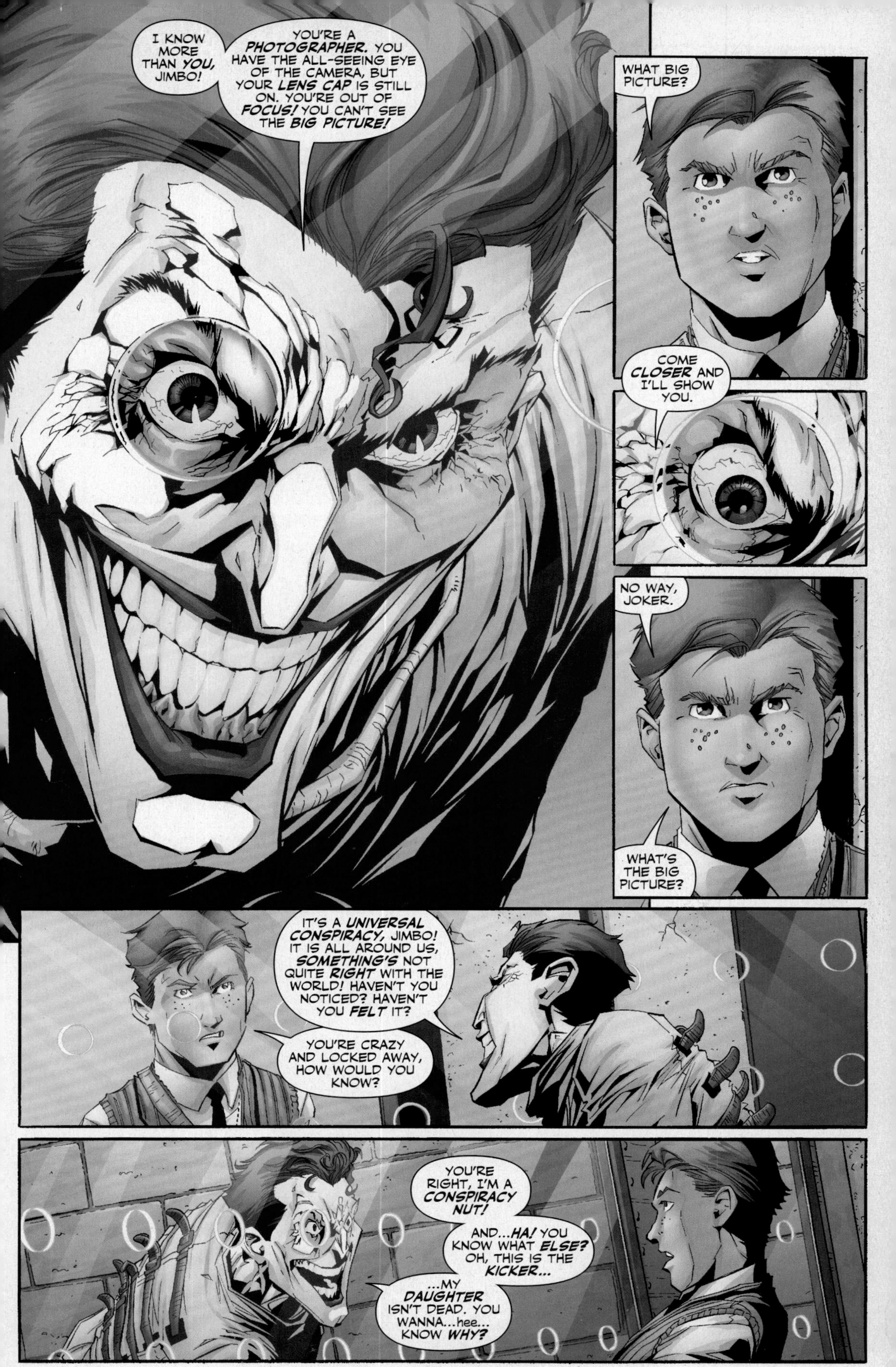
I KNOW MORE THAN YOU, JIMBO!
YOU'RE A PHOTOGRAPHER. YOU HAVE THE ALL-SEEING EYE OF THE CAMERA, BUT YOUR LENS CAP IS STILL ON. YOU'RE OUT OF FOCUS! YOU CAN'T SEE THE BIG PICTURE!
WHAT BIG PICTURE?
COME CLOSER AND I'LL SHOW YOU.
NO WAY, JOKER.
WHAT'S THE BIG PICTURE?
IT'S A UNIVERSAL CONSPIRACY, JIMBO! IT IS ALL AROUND US, SOMETHING'S NOT QUITE RIGHT WITH THE WORLD! HAVEN'T YOU NOTICED? HAVEN'T YOU FELT IT?
YOU'RE CRAZY AND LOCKED AWAY, HOW WOULD YOU KNOW?
YOU'RE RIGHT, I'M A CONSPIRACY NUT!
AND...HA! YOU KNOW WHAT ELSE? OH, THIS IS THE KICKER...
...MY DAUGHTER ISN'T DEAD. YOU WANNA...hee... KNOW WHY?

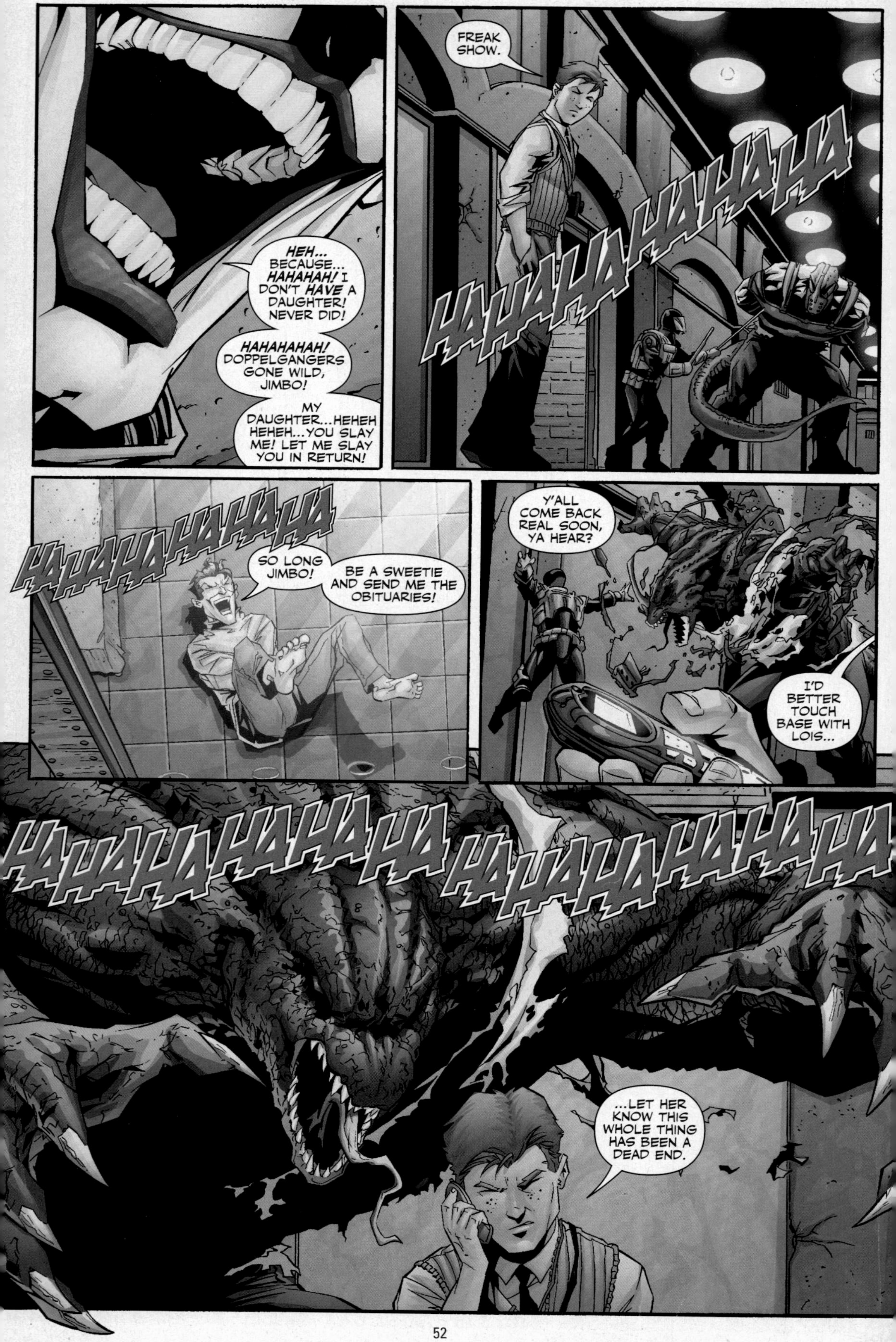
HEH... BECAUSE... HAHAHAH! I DON'T HAVE A DAUGHTER! NEVER DID!
HAHAHAHAH! DOPPELGANGERS GONE WILD, JIMBO!
MY DAUGHTER...HEHEH HEHEH...YOU SLAY ME! LET ME SLAY YOU IN RETURN!
FREAK SHOW.
HAHAHAHAHAHAHA
HAHAHAHAHAHA
SO LONG JIMBO!
BE A SWEETIE AND SEND ME THE OBITUARIES!
Y'ALL COME BACK REAL SOON, YA HEAR?
I'D BETTER TOUCH BASE WITH LOIS...
HAHAHAHAHAHA HAHAHAHAHAHAHA
...LET HER KNOW THIS WHOLE THING HAS BEEN A DEAD END.

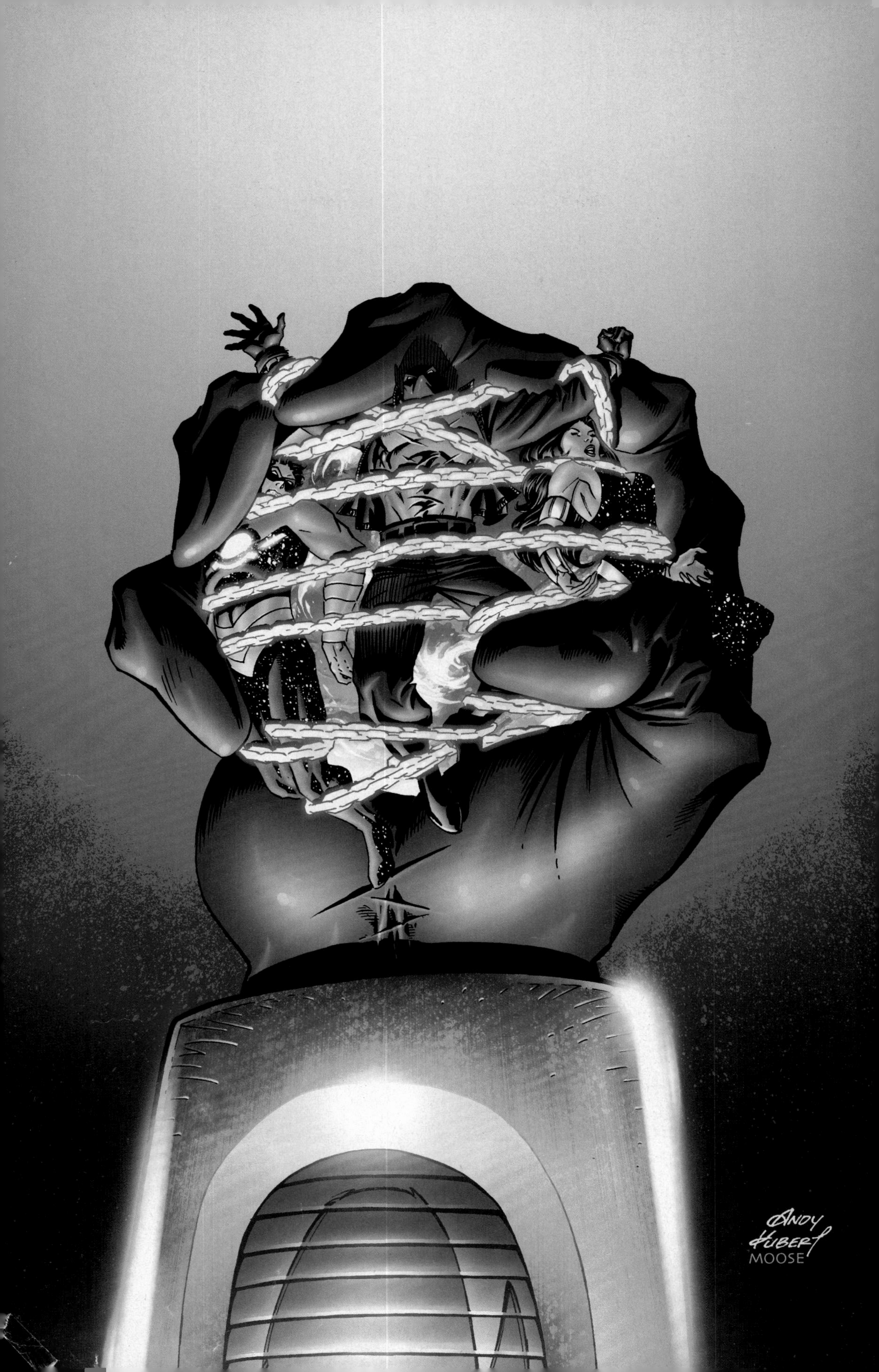
ANDY KUBERT
MOOSE

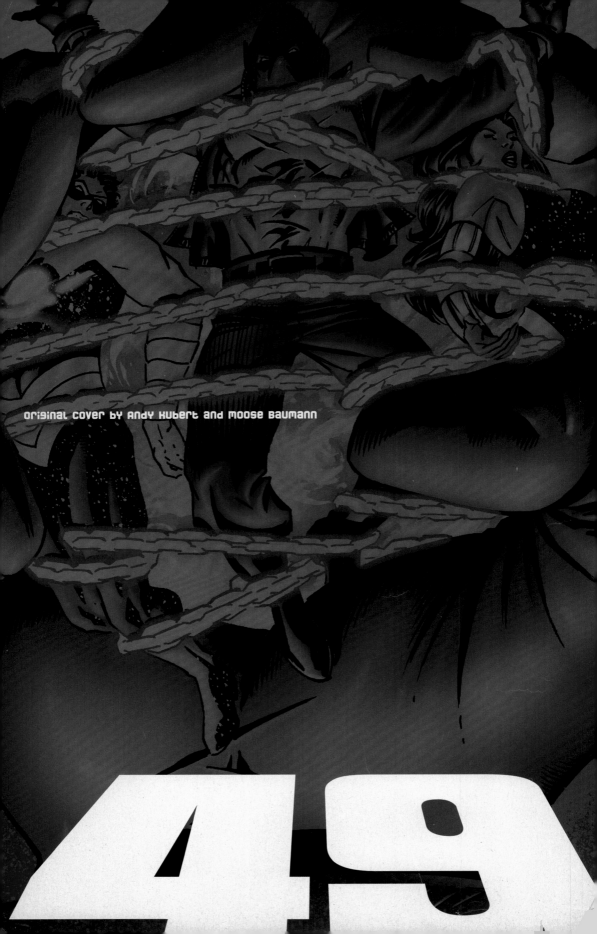

ORIGINAL COVER BY ANDY KUBERT AND MOOSE BAUMANN

49

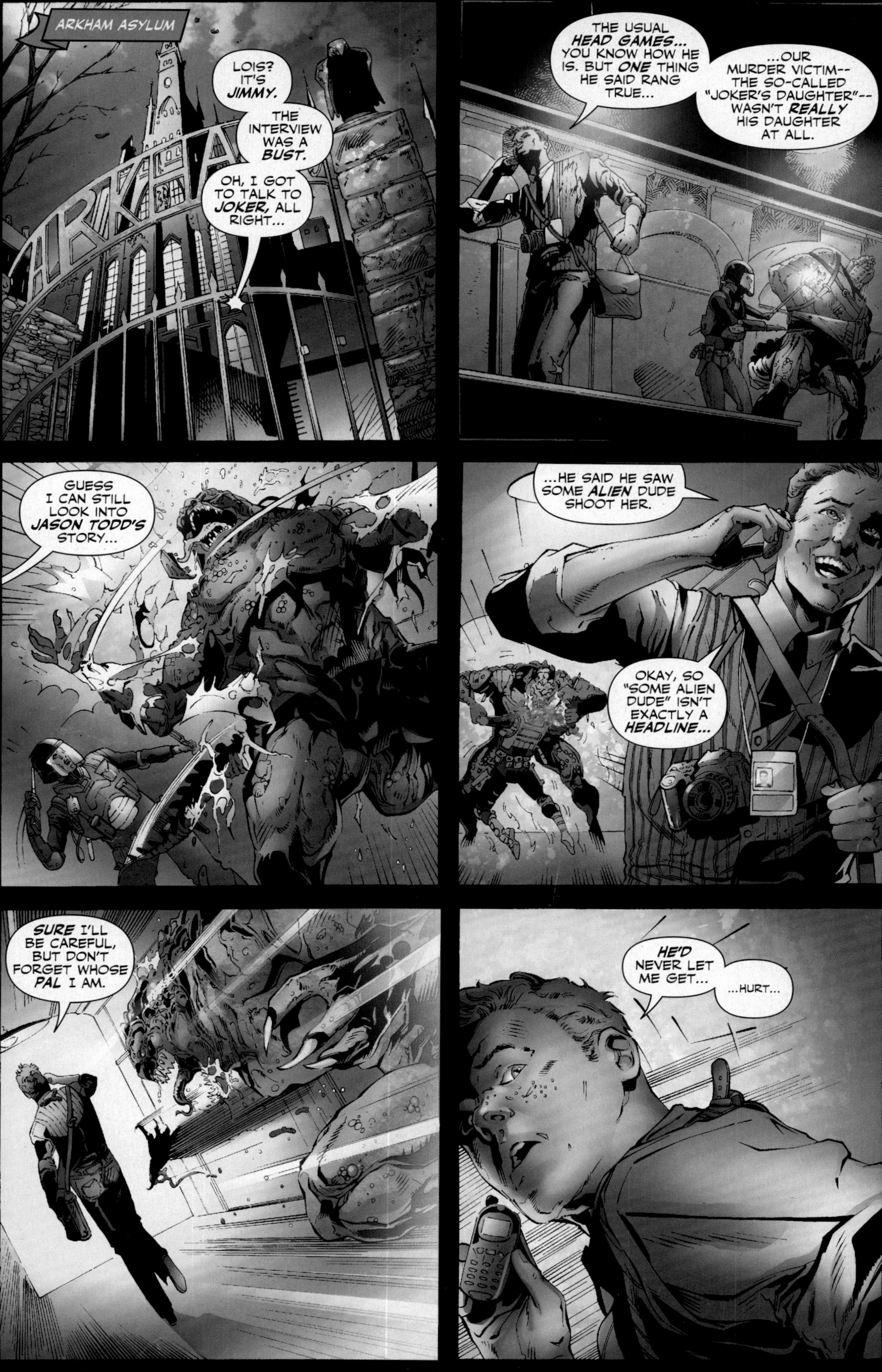
ARKHAM ASYLUM
LOIS? IT'S JIMMY.
THE INTERVIEW WAS A BUST.
OH, I GOT TO TALK TO JOKER, ALL RIGHT...
THE USUAL HEAD GAMES... YOU KNOW HOW HE IS. BUT ONE THING HE SAID RANG TRUE...
...OUR MURDER VICTIM-- THE SO-CALLED "JOKER'S DAUGHTER"-- WASN'T REALLY HIS DAUGHTER AT ALL.
GUESS I CAN STILL LOOK INTO JASON TODD'S STORY...
...HE SAID HE SAW SOME ALIEN DUDE SHOOT HER.
OKAY, SO "SOME ALIEN DUDE" ISN'T EXACTLY A HEADLINE...
SURE I'LL BE CAREFUL, BUT DON'T FORGET WHOSE PAL I AM.
HE'D NEVER LET ME GET...
...HURT...

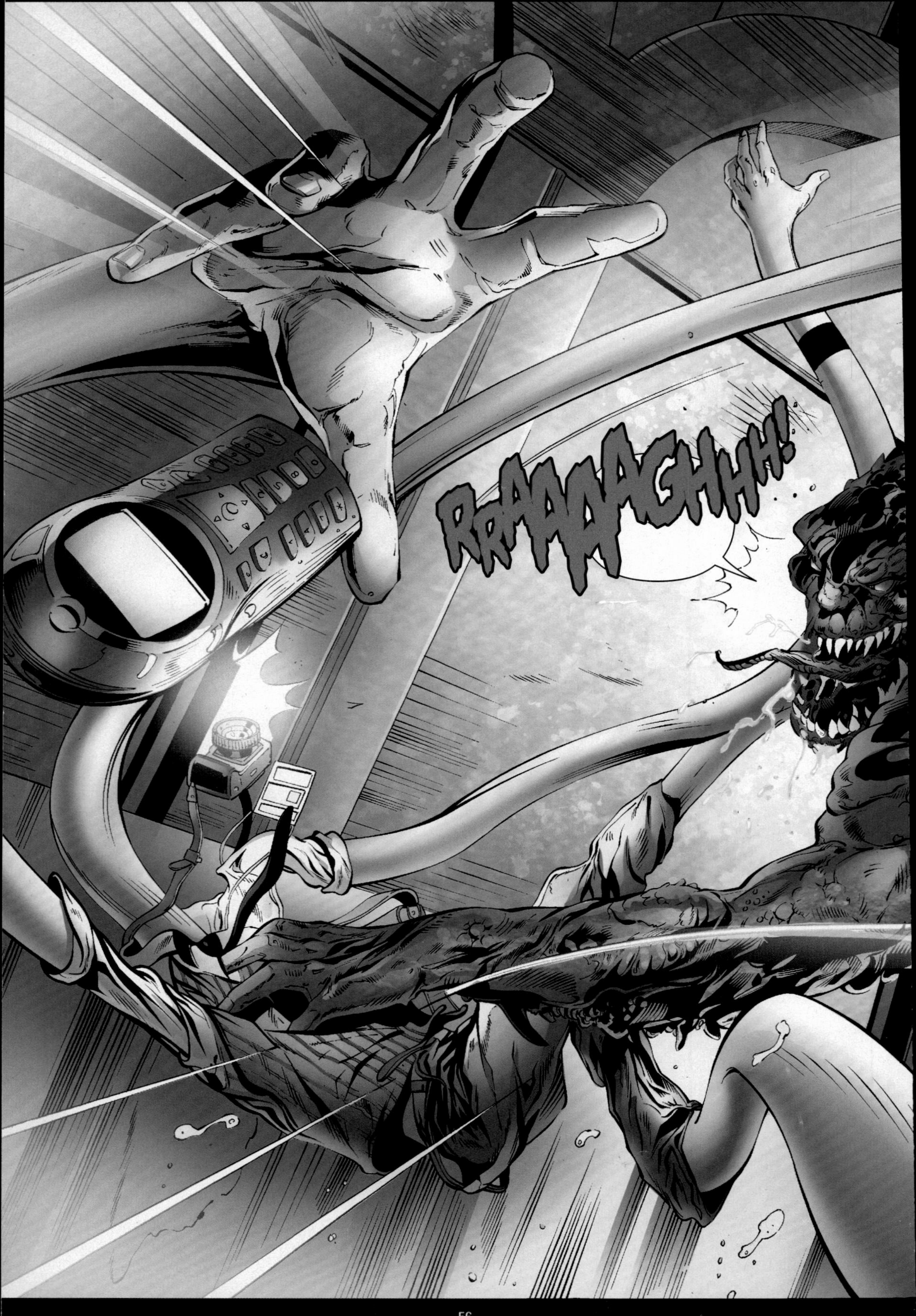
RRAAAAGHHH!

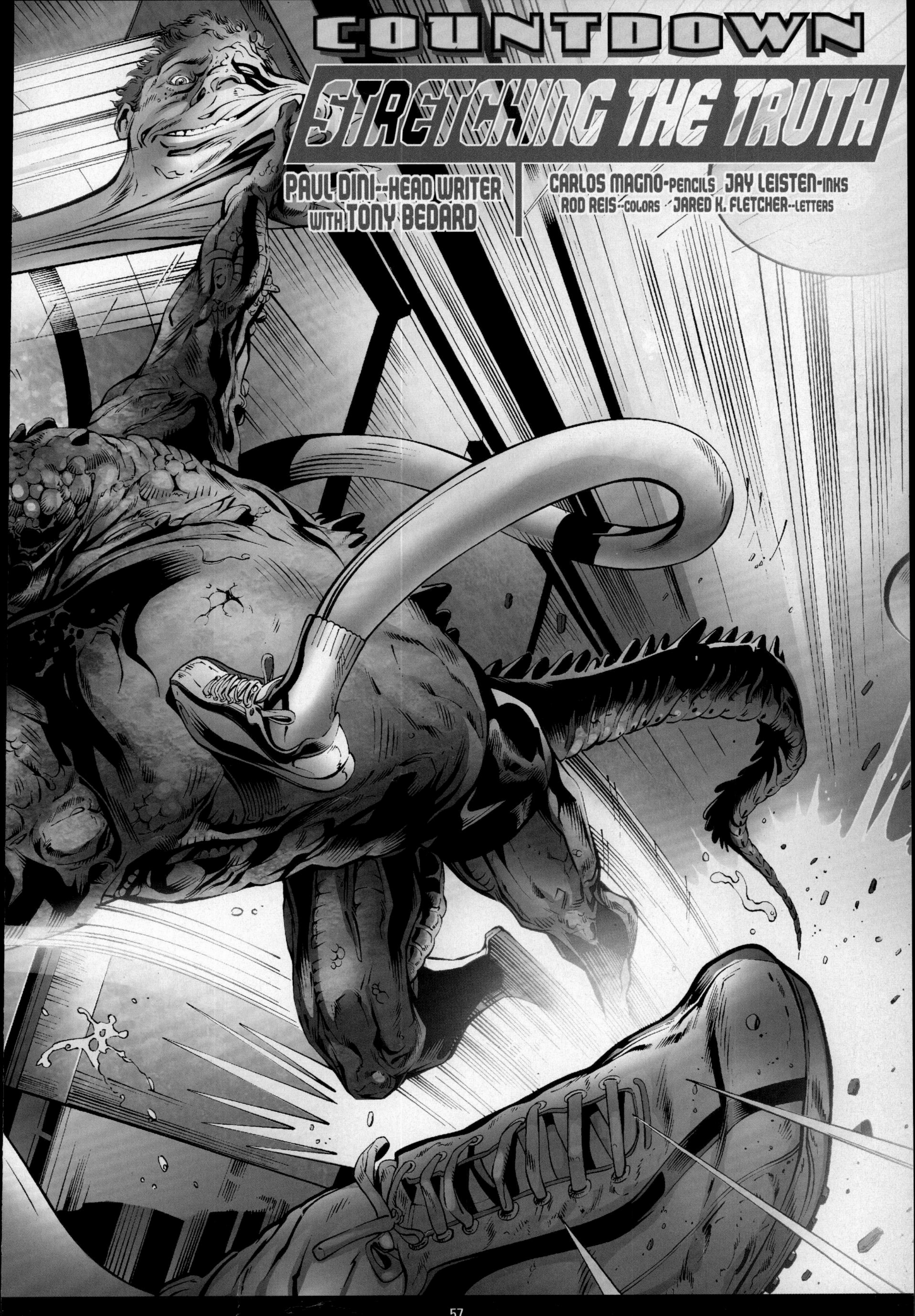
COUNTDOWN
STRETCHING THE TRUTH
PAUL DINI--HEAD WRITER
WITH TONY BEDARD
CARLOS MAGNO-PENCILS JAY LEISTEN-INKS
ROD REIS--COLORS JARED K. FLETCHER--LETTERS

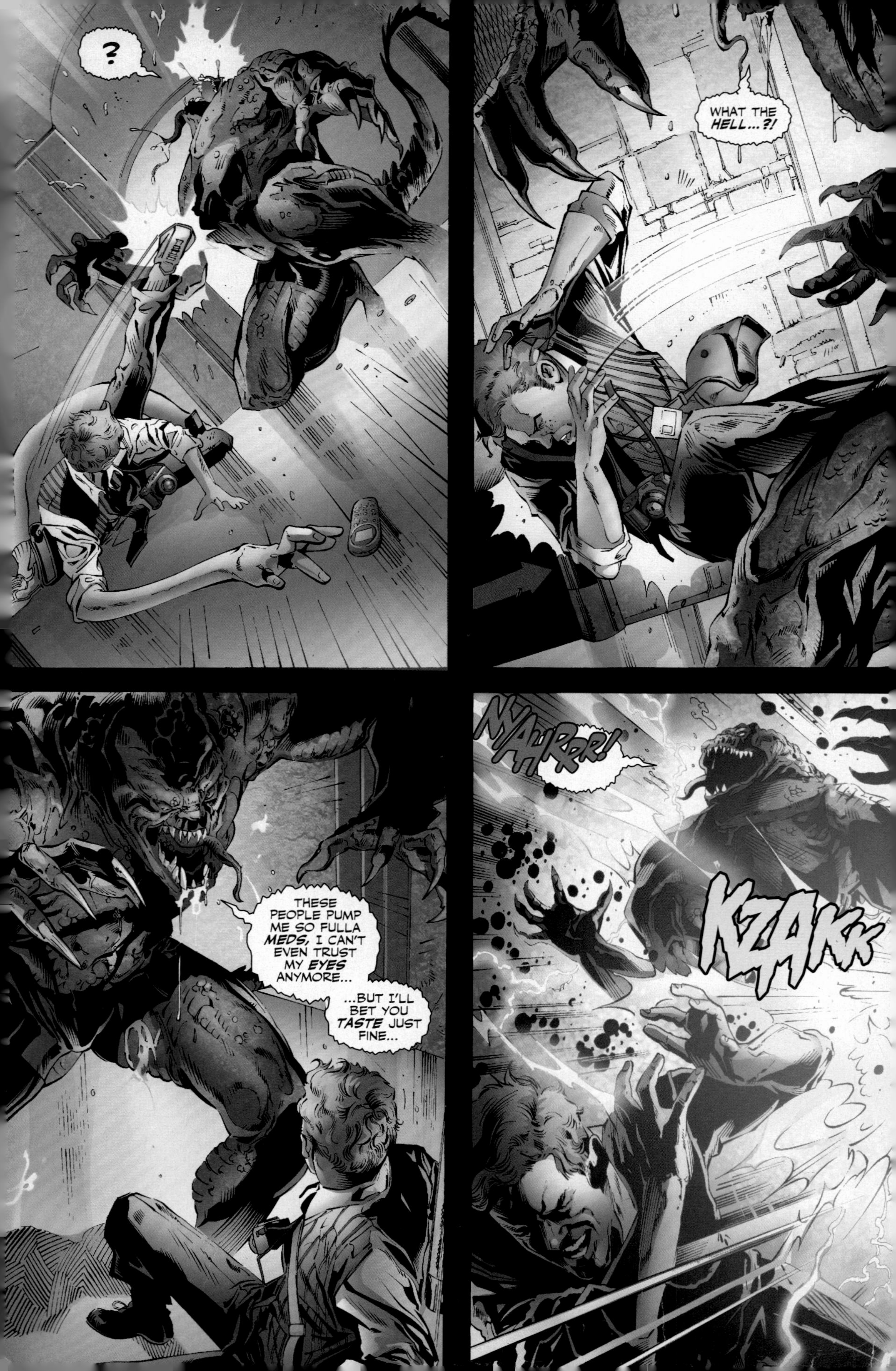
?
WHAT THE HELL...?!
THESE PEOPLE PUMP ME SO FULLA MEDS, I CAN'T EVEN TRUST MY EYES ANYMORE...
...BUT I'LL BET YOU TASTE JUST FINE...
NYAHRRR!
KZAKK

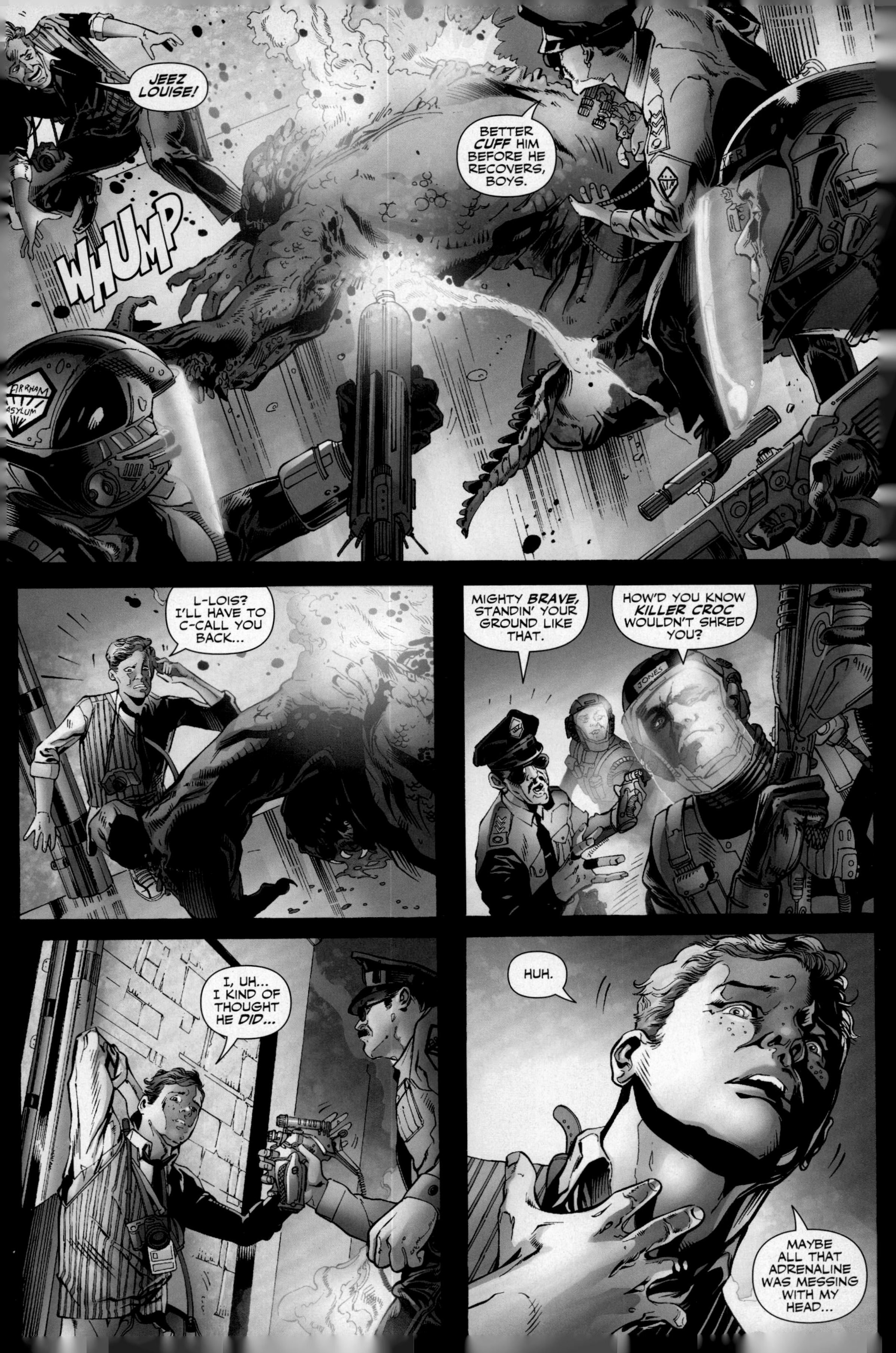
JEEZ LOUISE!
BETTER CUFF HIM BEFORE HE RECOVERS, BOYS.
WHUMP
ARKHAM ASYLUM
L-LOIS? I'LL HAVE TO C-CALL YOU BACK...
MIGHTY BRAVE, STANDIN' YOUR GROUND LIKE THAT.
HOW'D YOU KNOW KILLER CROC WOULDN'T SHRED YOU?
JONES
I, UH... I KIND OF THOUGHT HE DID...
HUH.
MAYBE ALL THAT ADRENALINE WAS MESSING WITH MY HEAD...

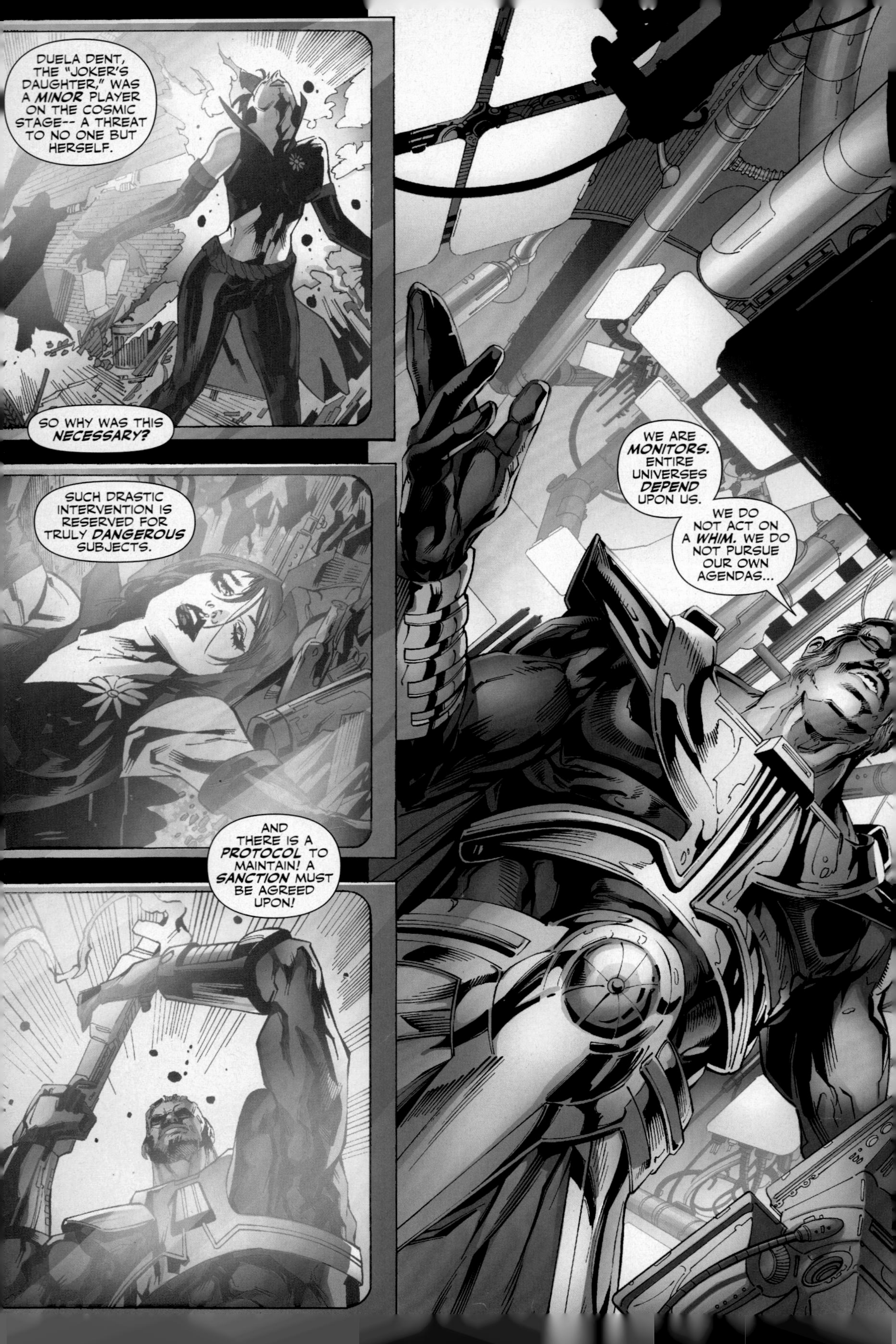
DUELA DENT, THE "JOKER'S DAUGHTER," WAS A MINOR PLAYER ON THE COSMIC STAGE-- A THREAT TO NO ONE BUT HERSELF.
SO WHY WAS THIS NECESSARY?
SUCH DRASTIC INTERVENTION IS RESERVED FOR TRULY DANGEROUS SUBJECTS.
AND THERE IS A PROTOCOL TO MAINTAIN! A SANCTION MUST BE AGREED UPON!
WE ARE MONITORS. ENTIRE UNIVERSES DEPEND UPON US.
WE DO NOT ACT ON A WHIM. WE DO NOT PURSUE OUR OWN AGENDAS...

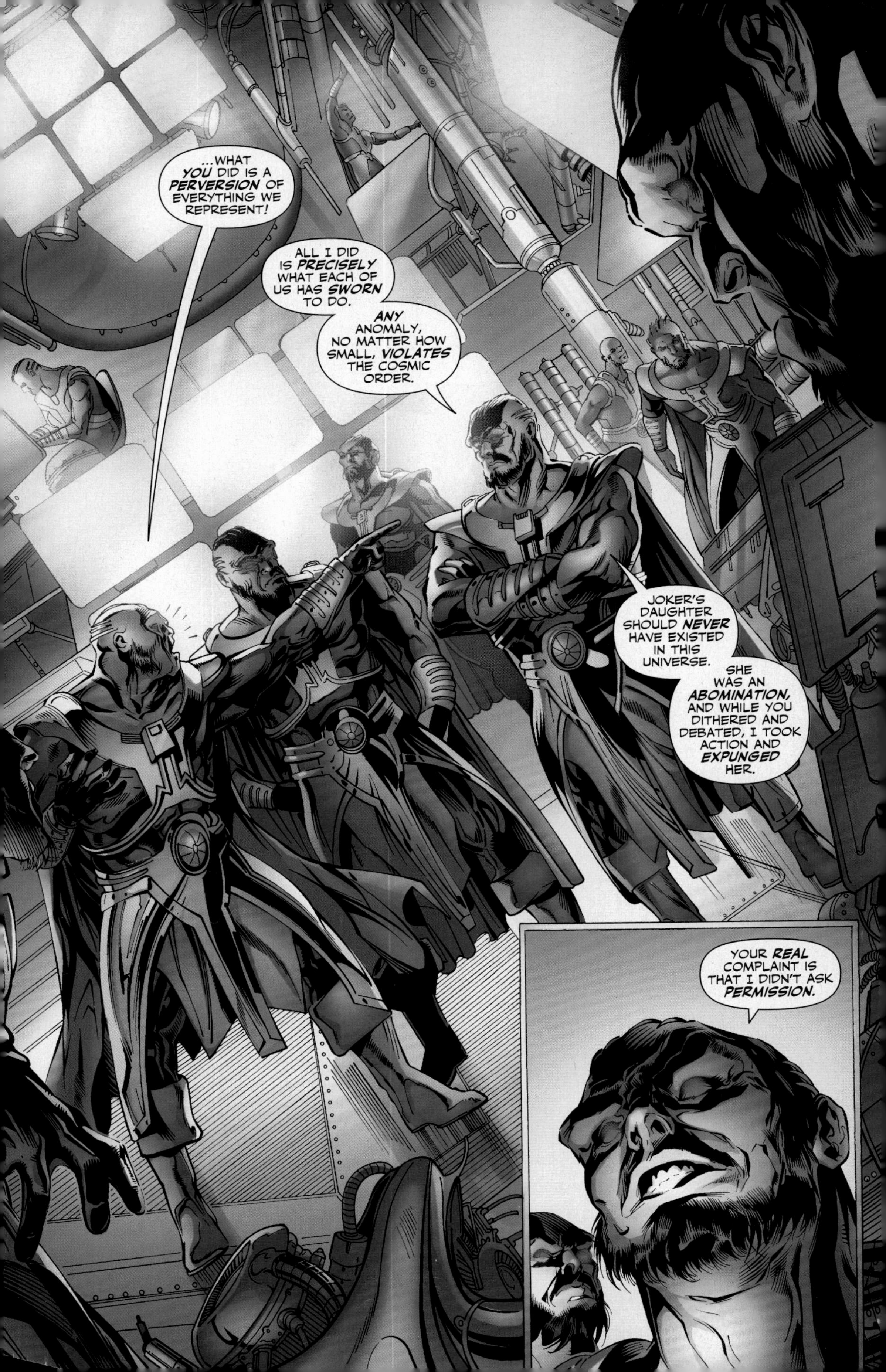
...WHAT YOU DID IS A PERVERSION OF EVERYTHING WE REPRESENT!
ALL I DID IS PRECISELY WHAT EACH OF US HAS SWORN TO DO.
ANY ANOMALY, NO MATTER HOW SMALL, VIOLATES THE COSMIC ORDER.
JOKER'S DAUGHTER SHOULD NEVER HAVE EXISTED IN THIS UNIVERSE.
SHE WAS AN ABOMINATION, AND WHILE YOU DITHERED AND DEBATED, I TOOK ACTION AND EXPUNGED HER.
YOUR REAL COMPLAINT IS THAT I DIDN'T ASK PERMISSION.

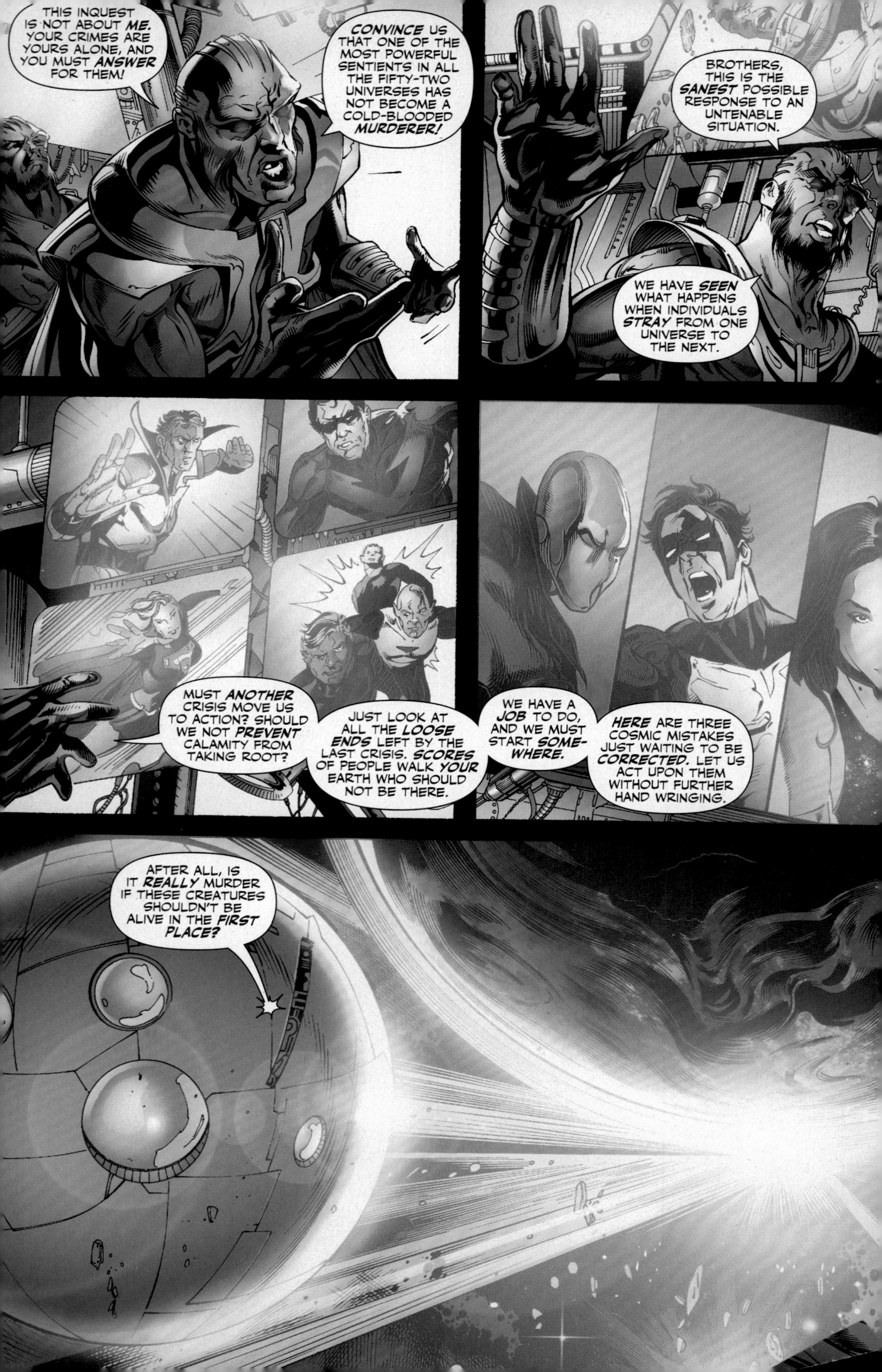
THIS INQUEST IS NOT ABOUT ME. YOUR CRIMES ARE YOURS ALONE, AND YOU MUST ANSWER FOR THEM!
CONVINCE US THAT ONE OF THE MOST POWERFUL SENTIENTS IN ALL THE FIFTY-TWO UNIVERSES HAS NOT BECOME A COLD-BLOODED MURDERER!
BROTHERS, THIS IS THE SANEST POSSIBLE RESPONSE TO AN UNTENABLE SITUATION.
WE HAVE SEEN WHAT HAPPENS WHEN INDIVIDUALS STRAY FROM ONE UNIVERSE TO THE NEXT.
MUST ANOTHER CRISIS MOVE US TO ACTION? SHOULD WE NOT PREVENT CALAMITY FROM TAKING ROOT?
JUST LOOK AT ALL THE LOOSE ENDS LEFT BY THE LAST CRISIS. SCORES OF PEOPLE WALK YOUR EARTH WHO SHOULD NOT BE THERE.
WE HAVE A JOB TO DO, AND WE MUST START SOME-WHERE.
HERE ARE THREE COSMIC MISTAKES JUST WAITING TO BE CORRECTED. LET US ACT UPON THEM WITHOUT FURTHER HAND WRINGING.
AFTER ALL, IS IT REALLY MURDER IF THESE CREATURES SHOULDN'T BE ALIVE IN THE FIRST PLACE?

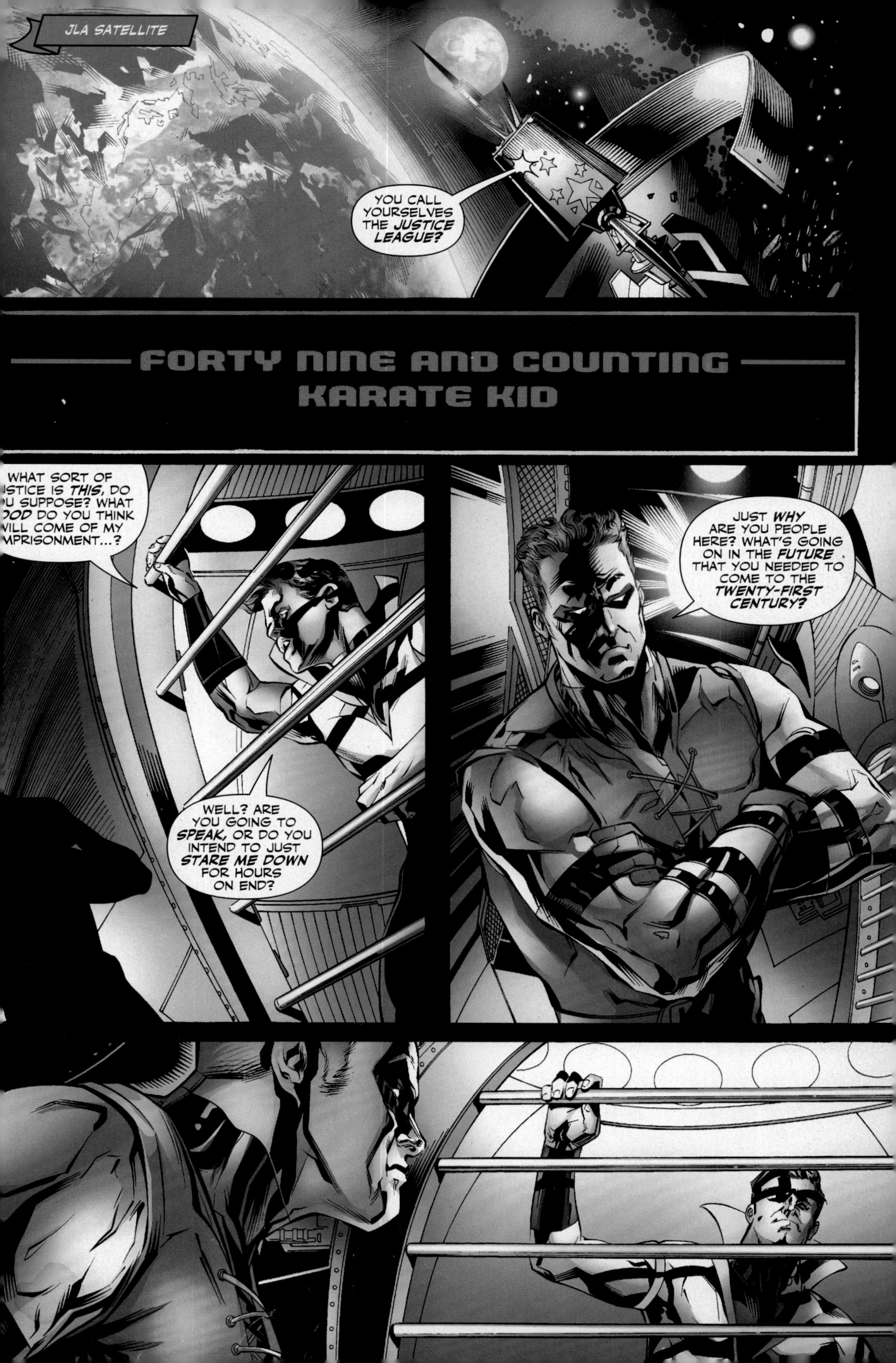

JLA SATELLITE
YOU CALL YOURSELVES THE JUSTICE LEAGUE?
FORTY NINE AND COUNTING
KARATE KID
WHAT SORT OF STICE IS THIS, DO U SUPPOSE? WHAT DOD DO YOU THINK VILL COME OF MY MPRISONMENT...?
WELL? ARE YOU GOING TO SPEAK, OR DO YOU INTEND TO JUST STARE ME DOWN FOR HOURS ON END?
JUST WHY ARE YOU PEOPLE HERE? WHAT'S GOING ON IN THE FUTURE THAT YOU NEEDED TO COME TO THE TWENTY-FIRST CENTURY?

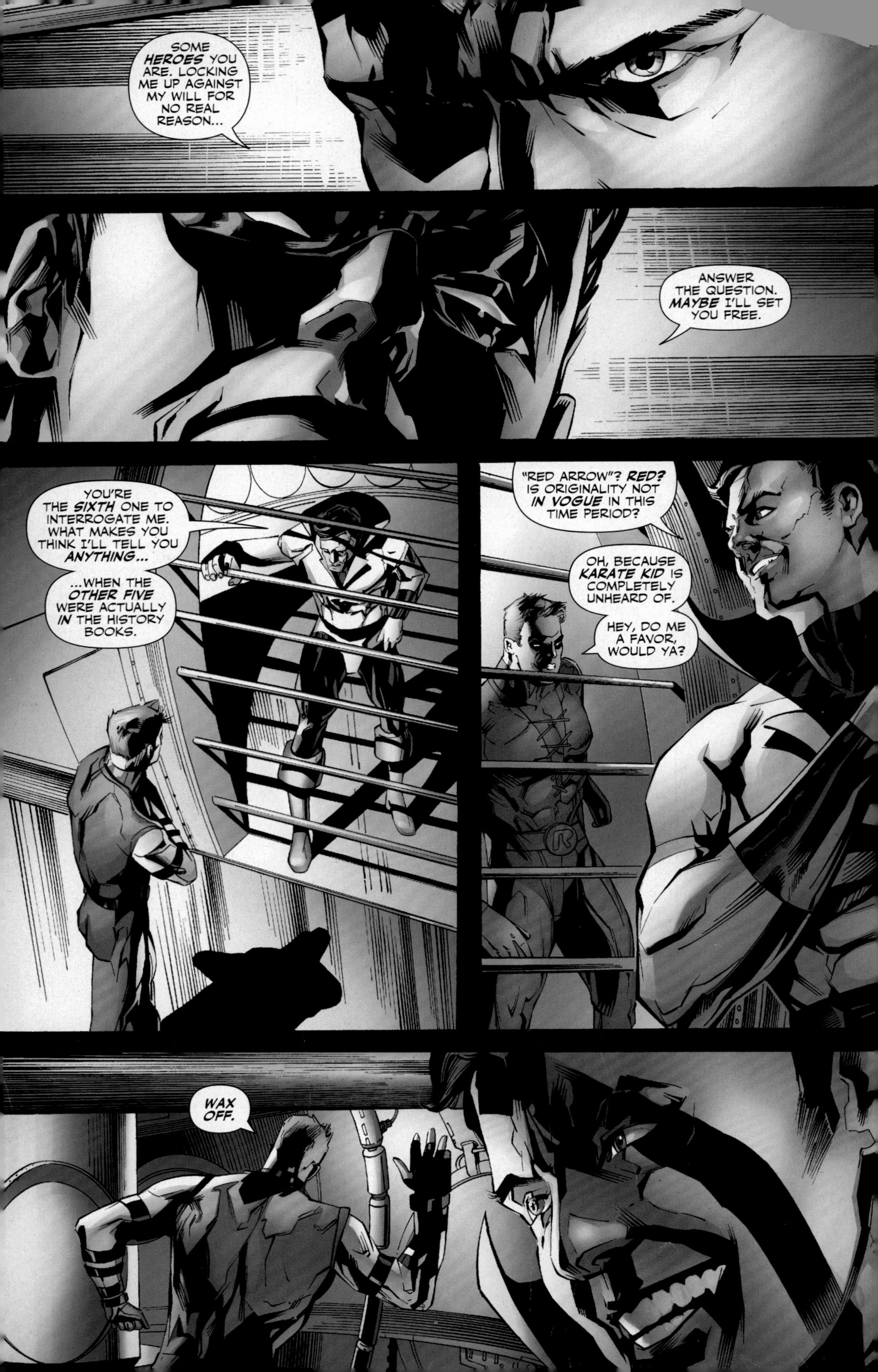
SOME *HEROES* YOU ARE. LOCKING ME UP AGAINST MY WILL FOR NO REAL REASON...
ANSWER THE QUESTION. *MAYBE* I'LL SET YOU FREE.
YOU'RE THE *SIXTH* ONE TO INTERROGATE ME. WHAT MAKES YOU THINK I'LL TELL YOU *ANYTHING*...
...WHEN THE *OTHER FIVE* WERE ACTUALLY *IN* THE HISTORY BOOKS.
"RED ARROW"? *RED?* IS ORIGINALITY NOT *IN VOGUE* IN THIS TIME PERIOD?
OH, BECAUSE *KARATE KID* IS COMPLETELY UNHEARD OF.
HEY, DO ME A FAVOR, WOULD YA?
WAX OFF.

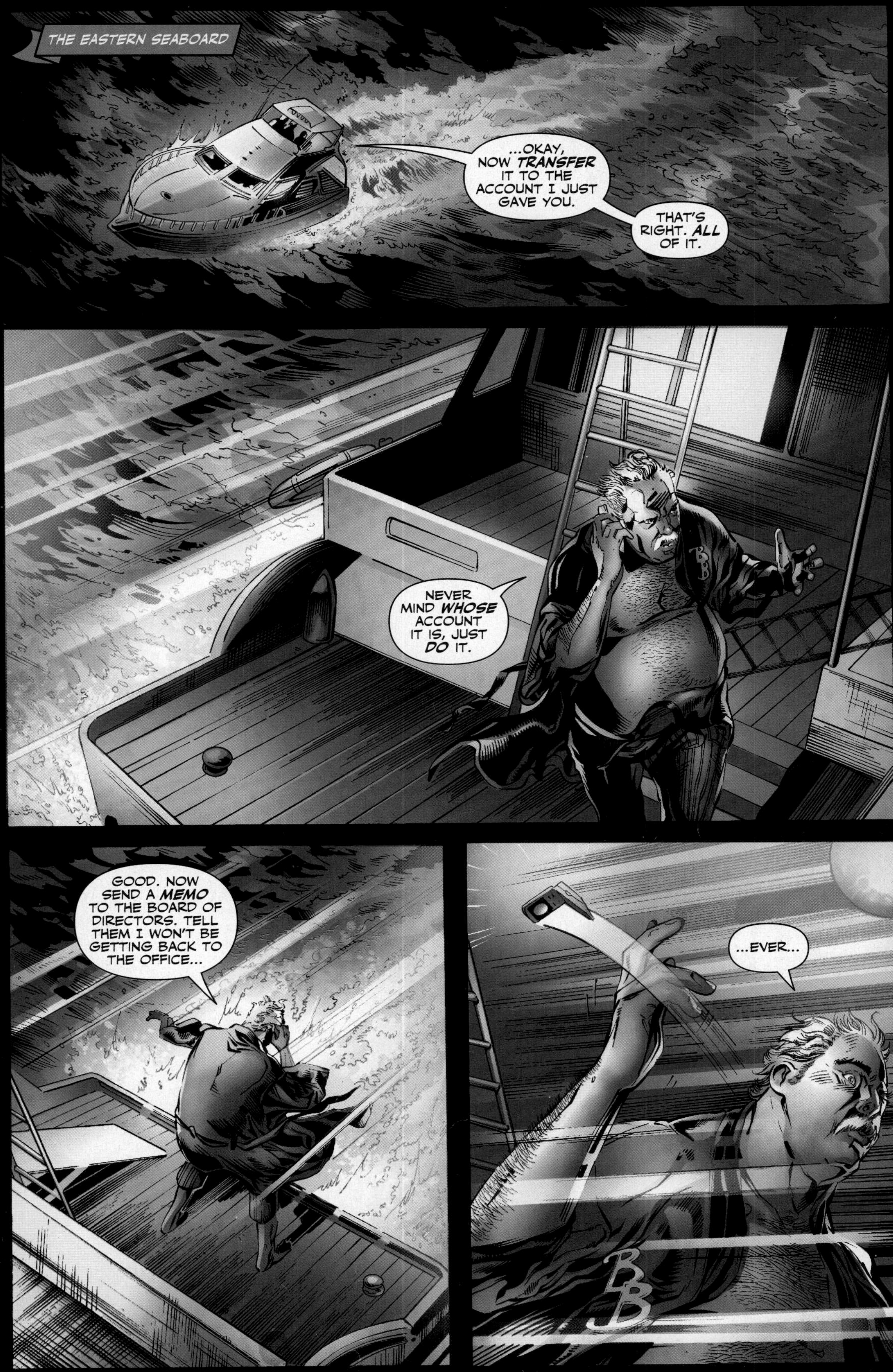
THE EASTERN SEABOARD
...OKAY, NOW TRANSFER IT TO THE ACCOUNT I JUST GAVE YOU.
THAT'S RIGHT. ALL OF IT.
NEVER MIND WHOSE ACCOUNT IT IS, JUST DO IT.
GOOD. NOW SEND A MEMO TO THE BOARD OF DIRECTORS. TELL THEM I WON'T BE GETTING BACK TO THE OFFICE...
...EVER...

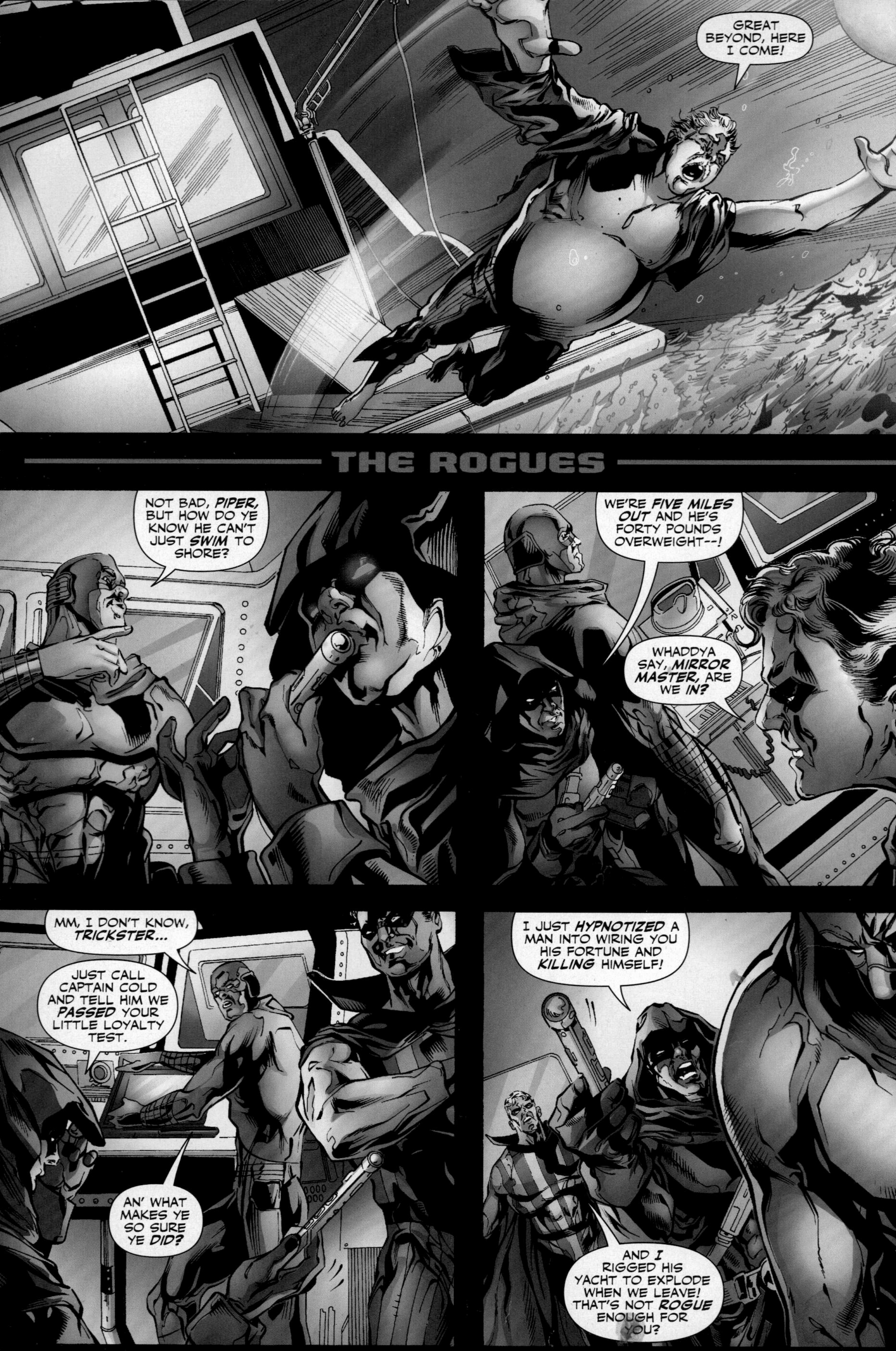
GREAT BEYOND, HERE I COME!
THE ROGUES
NOT BAD, PIPER, BUT HOW DO YE KNOW HE CAN'T JUST SWIM TO SHORE?
WE'RE FIVE MILES OUT AND HE'S FORTY POUNDS OVERWEIGHT--!
WHADDYA SAY, MIRROR MASTER, ARE WE IN?
MM, I DON'T KNOW, TRICKSTER...
JUST CALL CAPTAIN COLD AND TELL HIM WE PASSED YOUR LITTLE LOYALTY TEST.
AN' WHAT MAKES YE SO SURE YE DID?
I JUST HYPNOTIZED A MAN INTO WIRING YOU HIS FORTUNE AND KILLING HIMSELF!
AND I RIGGED HIS YACHT TO EXPLODE WHEN WE LEAVE! THAT'S NOT ROGUE ENOUGH FOR YOU?

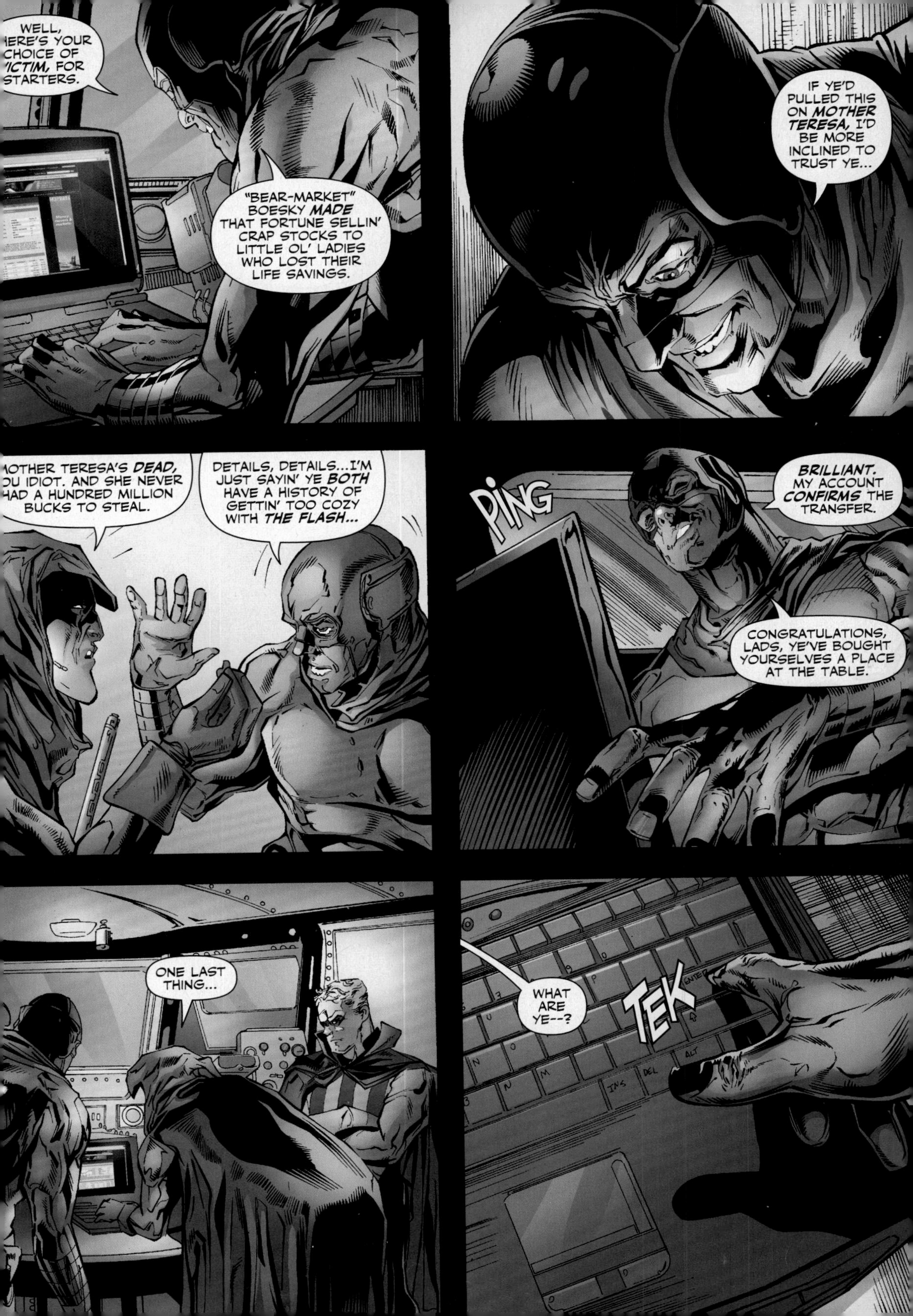

WELL, HERE'S YOUR CHOICE OF VICTIM, FOR STARTERS.
"BEAR-MARKET" BOESKY MADE THAT FORTUNE SELLIN' CRAP STOCKS TO LITTLE OL' LADIES WHO LOST THEIR LIFE SAVINGS.
IF YE'D PULLED THIS ON MOTHER TERESA, I'D BE MORE INCLINED TO TRUST YE...
MOTHER TERESA'S DEAD, YOU IDIOT. AND SHE NEVER HAD A HUNDRED MILLION BUCKS TO STEAL.
DETAILS, DETAILS...I'M JUST SAYIN' YE BOTH HAVE A HISTORY OF GETTIN' TOO COZY WITH THE FLASH...
PING
BRILLIANT. MY ACCOUNT CONFIRMS THE TRANSFER.
CONGRATULATIONS, LADS, YE'VE BOUGHT YOURSELVES A PLACE AT THE TABLE.
ONE LAST THING...
WHAT ARE YE--?
TEK

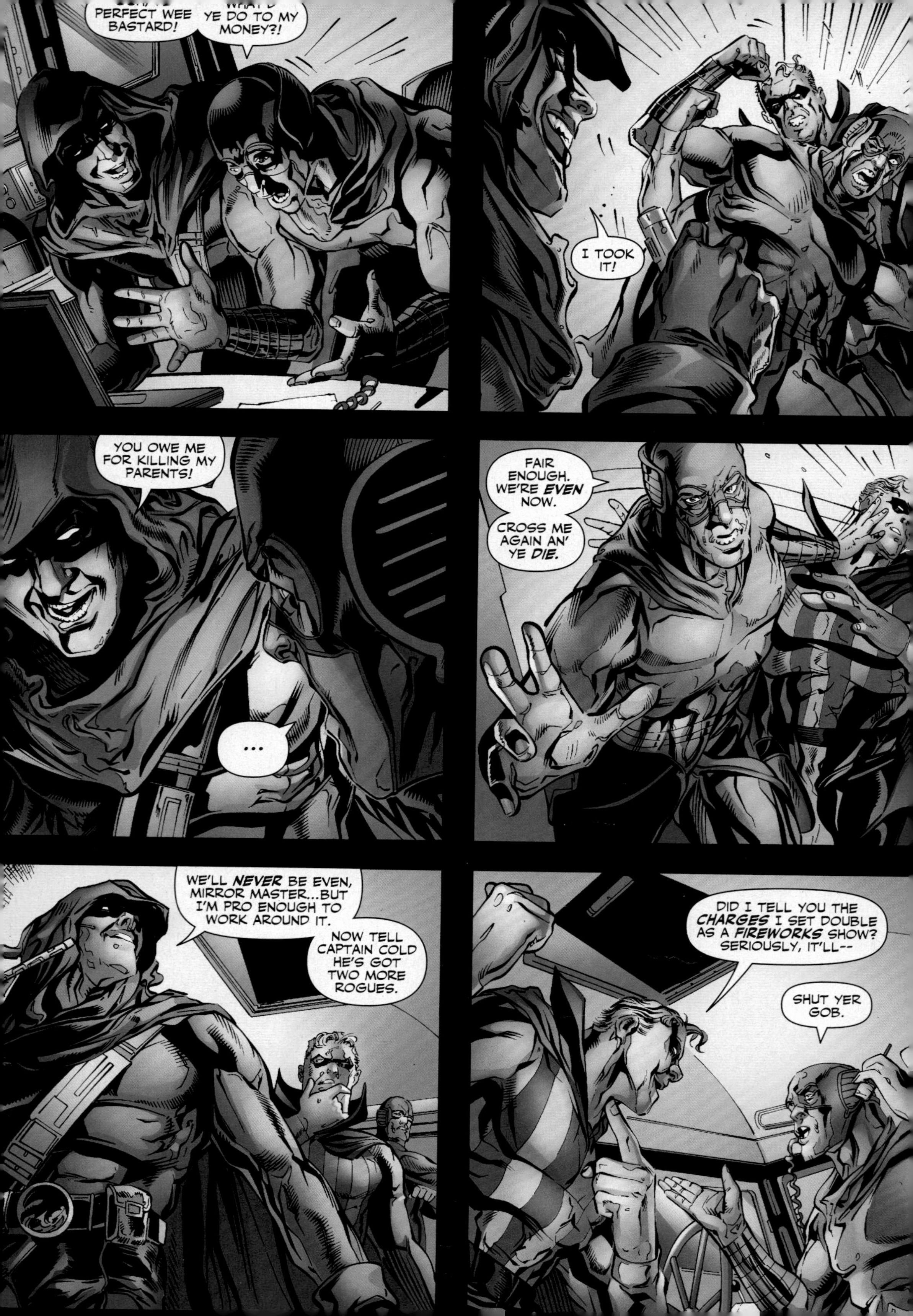

PERFECT WEE BASTARD!
YE DO TO MY MONEY?!
I TOOK IT!
YOU OWE ME FOR KILLING MY PARENTS!
...
FAIR ENOUGH. WE'RE *EVEN* NOW.
CROSS ME AGAIN AN' YE *DIE*.
WE'LL *NEVER* BE EVEN, MIRROR MASTER...BUT I'M PRO ENOUGH TO WORK AROUND IT.
NOW TELL CAPTAIN COLD HE'S GOT TWO MORE ROGUES.
DID I TELL YOU THE *CHARGES* I SET DOUBLE AS A *FIREWORKS* SHOW? SERIOUSLY, IT'LL--
SHUT YER GOB.

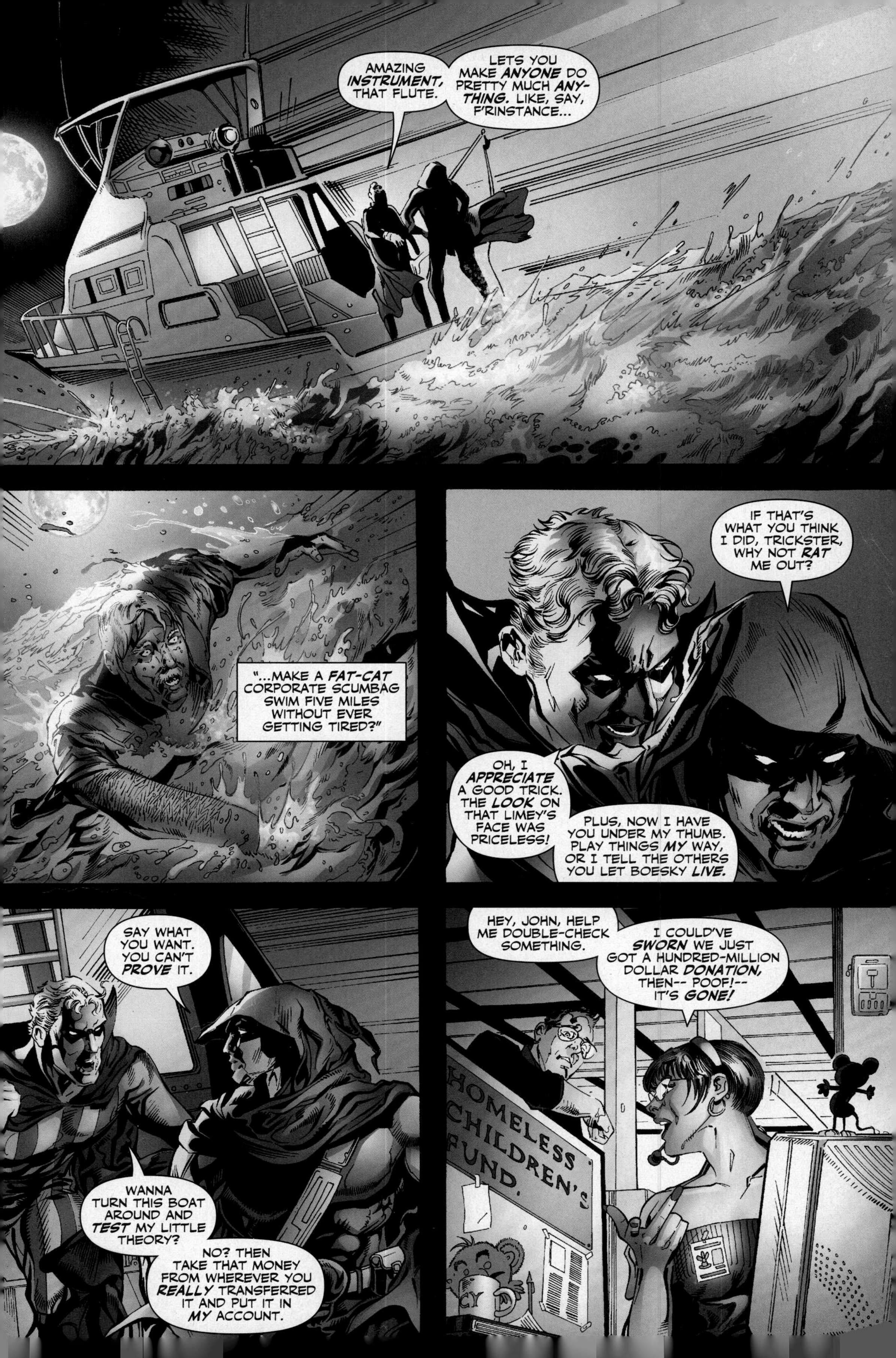

AMAZING INSTRUMENT, THAT FLUTE.
LETS YOU MAKE ANYONE DO PRETTY MUCH ANY-THING. LIKE, SAY, F'RINSTANCE...
"...MAKE A FAT-CAT CORPORATE SCUMBAG SWIM FIVE MILES WITHOUT EVER GETTING TIRED?"
IF THAT'S WHAT YOU THINK I DID, TRICKSTER, WHY NOT RAT ME OUT?
OH, I APPRECIATE A GOOD TRICK. THE LOOK ON THAT LIMEY'S FACE WAS PRICELESS!
PLUS, NOW I HAVE YOU UNDER MY THUMB. PLAY THINGS MY WAY, OR I TELL THE OTHERS YOU LET BOESKY LIVE.
SAY WHAT YOU WANT. YOU CAN'T PROVE IT.
WANNA TURN THIS BOAT AROUND AND TEST MY LITTLE THEORY?
NO? THEN TAKE THAT MONEY FROM WHEREVER YOU REALLY TRANSFERRED IT AND PUT IT IN MY ACCOUNT.
HEY, JOHN, HELP ME DOUBLE-CHECK SOMETHING.
I COULD'VE SWORN WE JUST GOT A HUNDRED-MILLION DOLLAR DONATION, THEN-- POOF!-- IT'S GONE!
HOMELESS CHILDREN'S FUND.

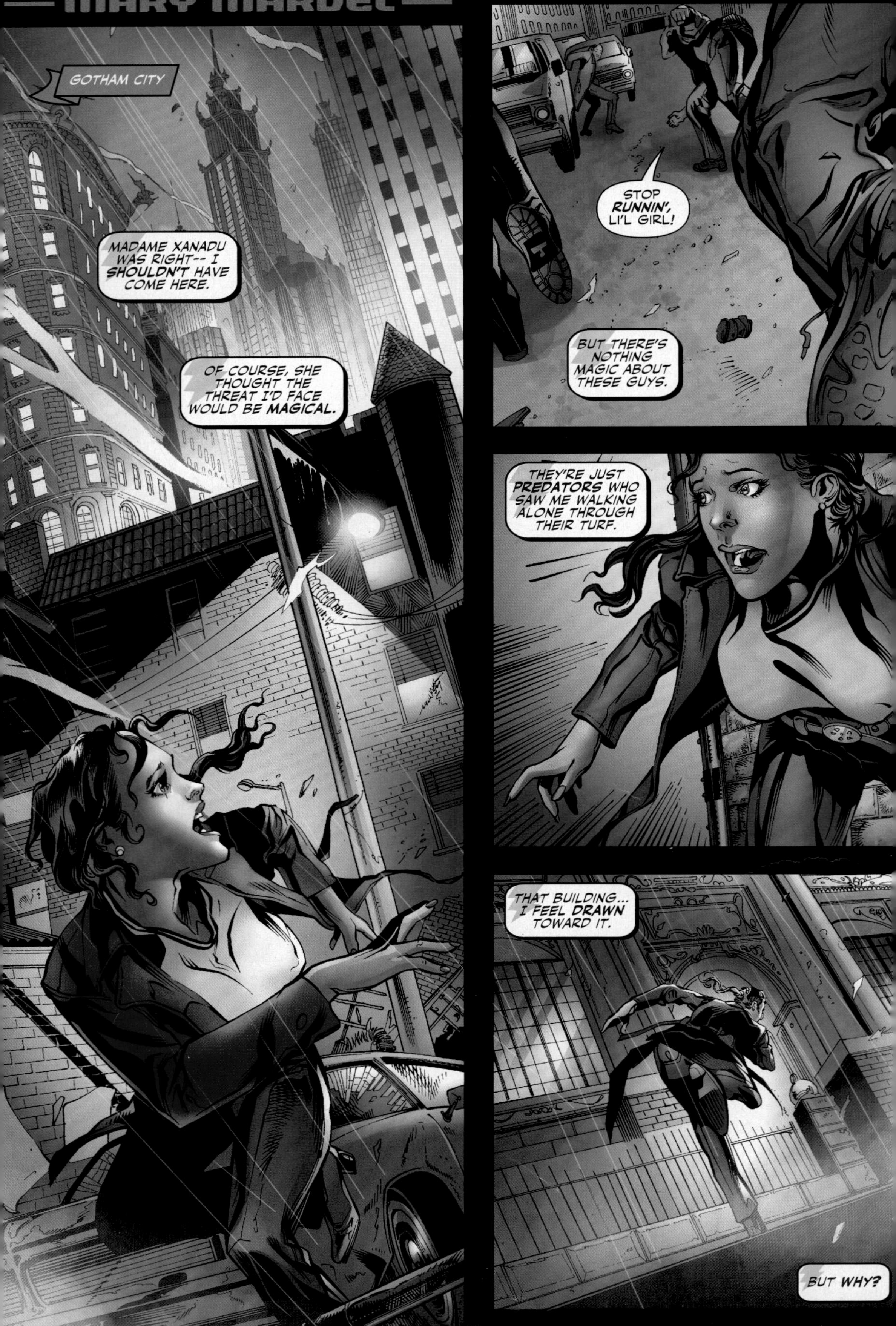
GOTHAM CITY
MADAME XANADU WAS RIGHT-- I SHOULDN'T HAVE COME HERE.
OF COURSE, SHE THOUGHT THE THREAT I'D FACE WOULD BE MAGICAL.
STOP RUNNIN', LI'L GIRL!
BUT THERE'S NOTHING MAGIC ABOUT THESE GUYS.
THEY'RE JUST PREDATORS WHO SAW ME WALKING ALONE THROUGH THEIR TURF.
THAT BUILDING... I FEEL DRAWN TOWARD IT.
BUT WHY?

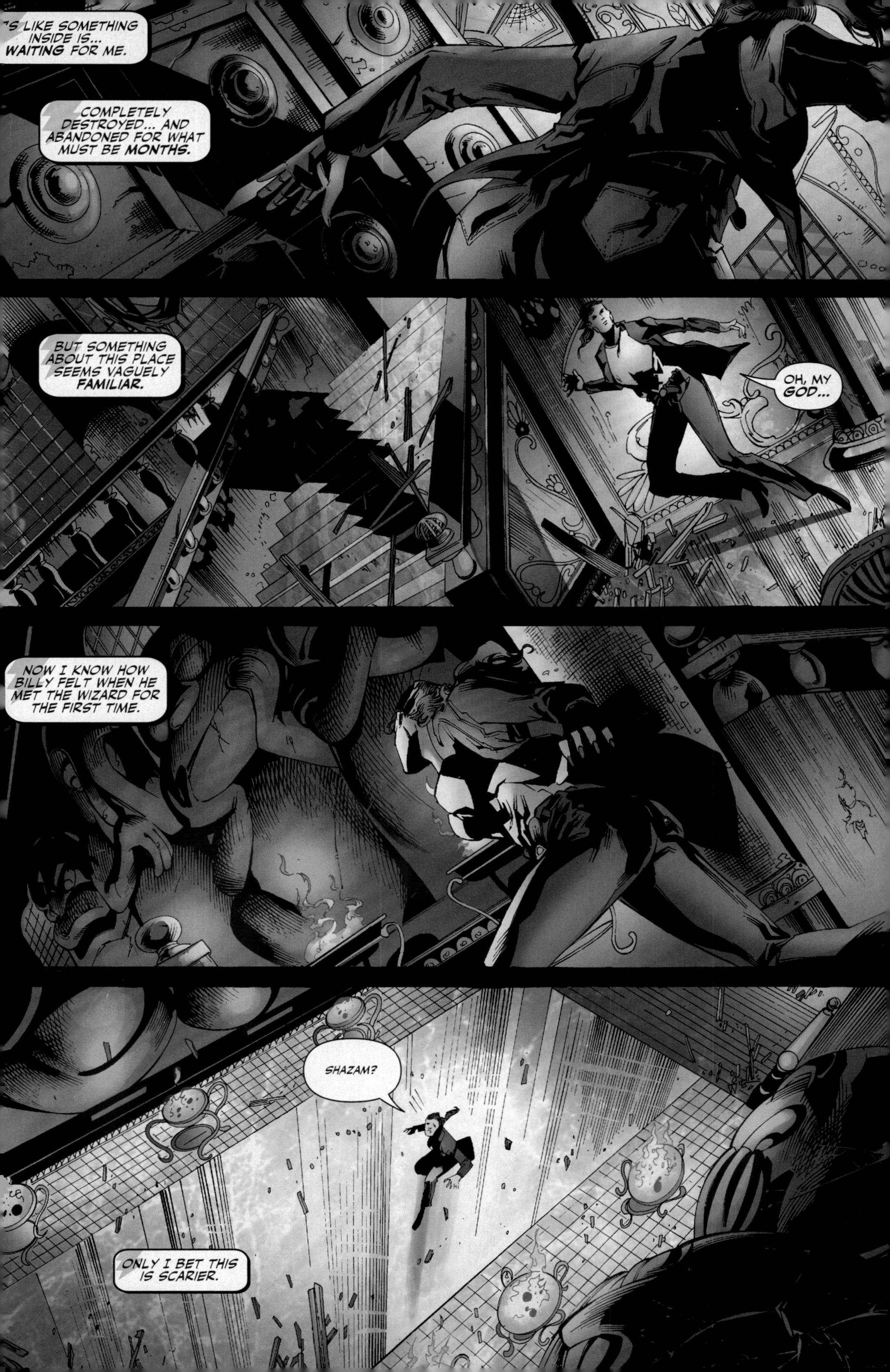
'S LIKE SOMETHING INSIDE IS... WAITING FOR ME.
COMPLETELY DESTROYED... AND ABANDONED FOR WHAT MUST BE MONTHS.
BUT SOMETHING ABOUT THIS PLACE SEEMS VAGUELY FAMILIAR.
OH, MY GOD...
NOW I KNOW HOW BILLY FELT WHEN HE MET THE WIZARD FOR THE FIRST TIME.
SHAZAM?
ONLY I BET THIS IS SCARIER.

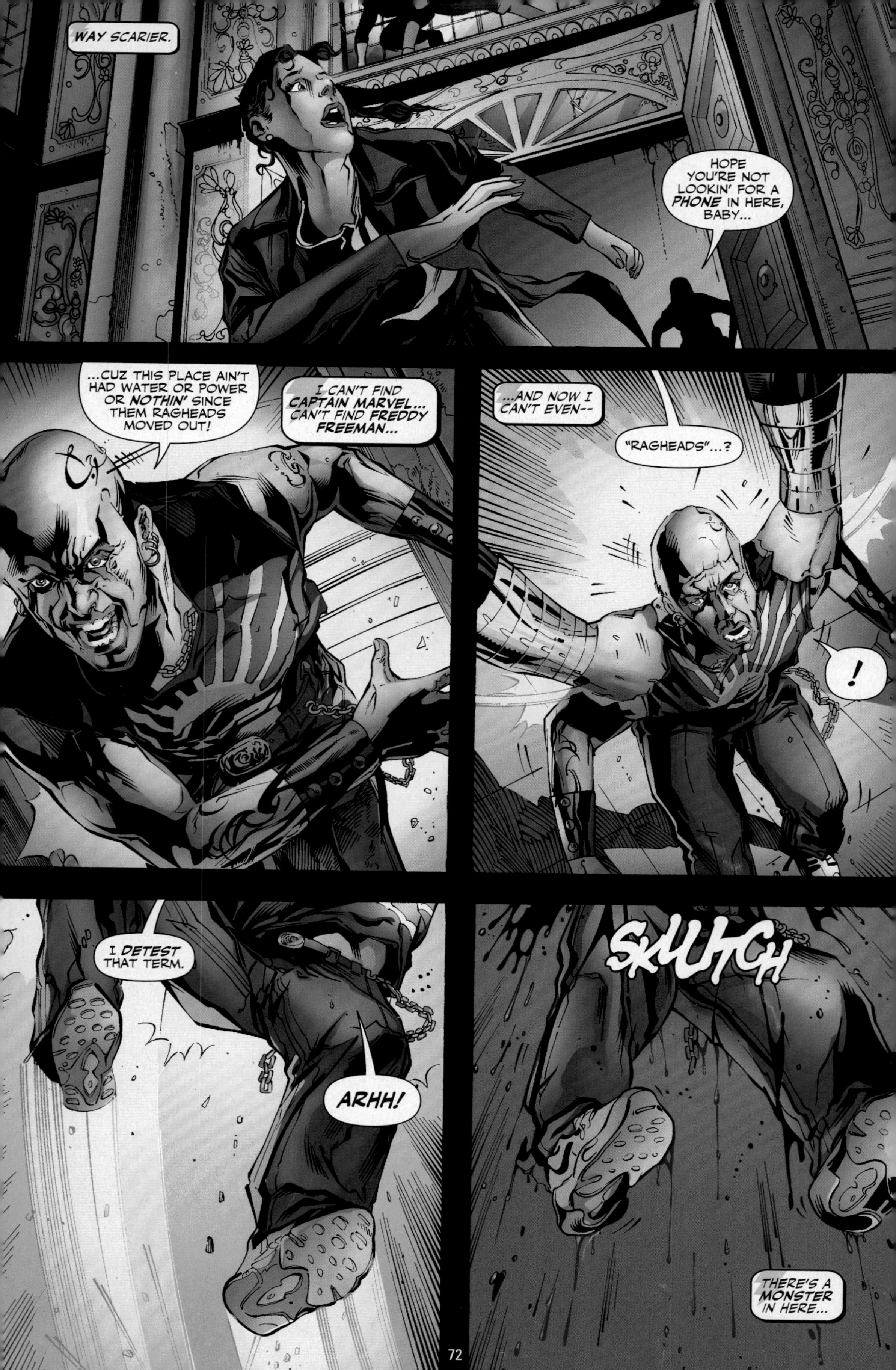
WAY SCARIER.
HOPE YOU'RE NOT LOOKIN' FOR A PHONE IN HERE, BABY...
...CUZ THIS PLACE AIN'T HAD WATER OR POWER OR NOTHIN' SINCE THEM RAGHEADS MOVED OUT!
I CAN'T FIND CAPTAIN MARVEL... CAN'T FIND FREDDY FREEMAN...
...AND NOW I CAN'T EVEN--
"RAGHEADS"...?
!
I DETEST THAT TERM.
ARHH!
SKLUTCH
THERE'S A MONSTER IN HERE...

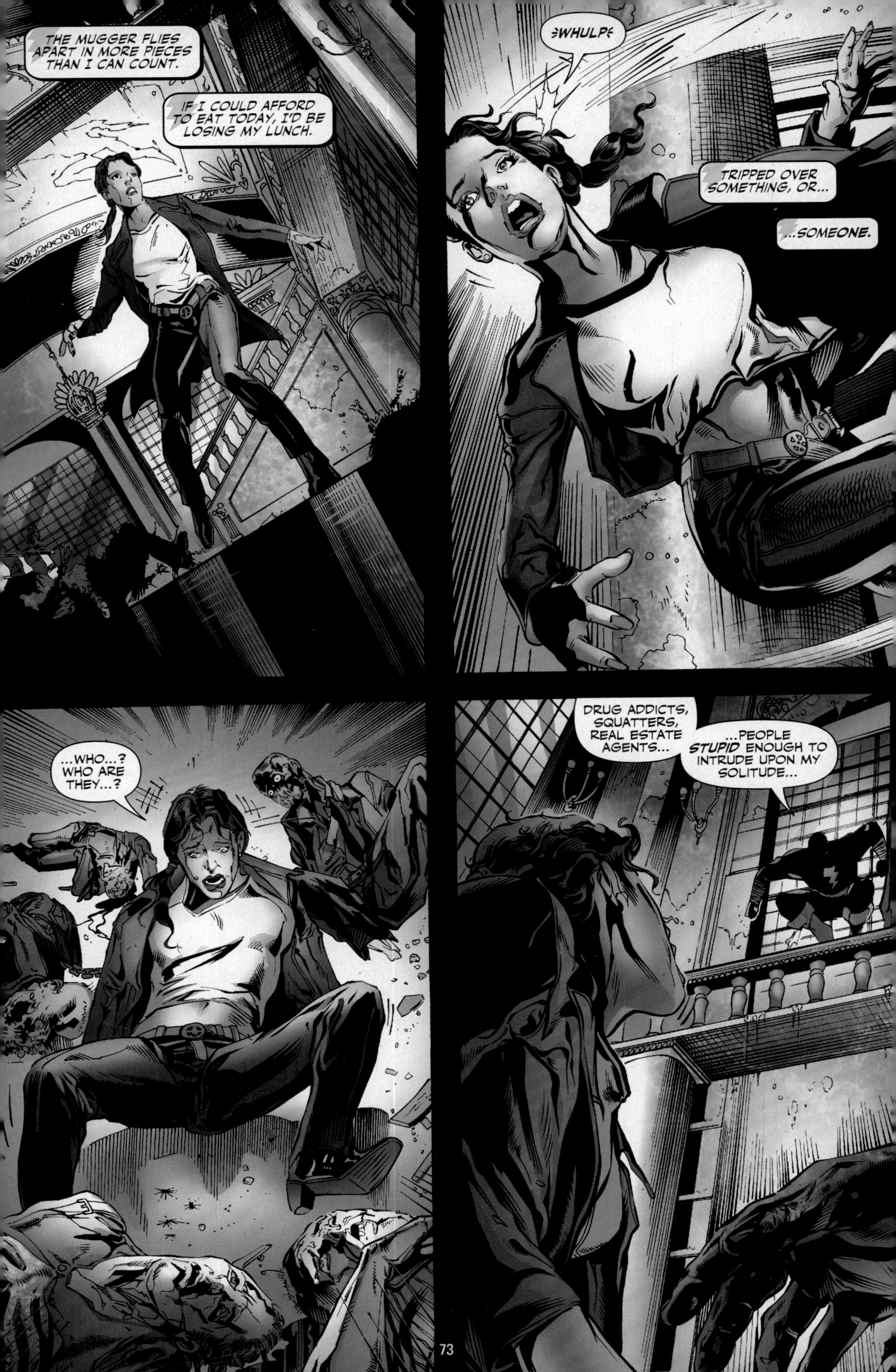
THE MUGGER FLIES APART IN MORE PIECES THAN I CAN COUNT.
IF I COULD AFFORD TO EAT TODAY, I'D BE LOSING MY LUNCH.
WHULP
TRIPPED OVER SOMETHING, OR...
...SOMEONE.
...WHO...? WHO ARE THEY...?
DRUG ADDICTS, SQUATTERS, REAL ESTATE AGENTS...
...PEOPLE STUPID ENOUGH TO INTRUDE UPON MY SOLITUDE...

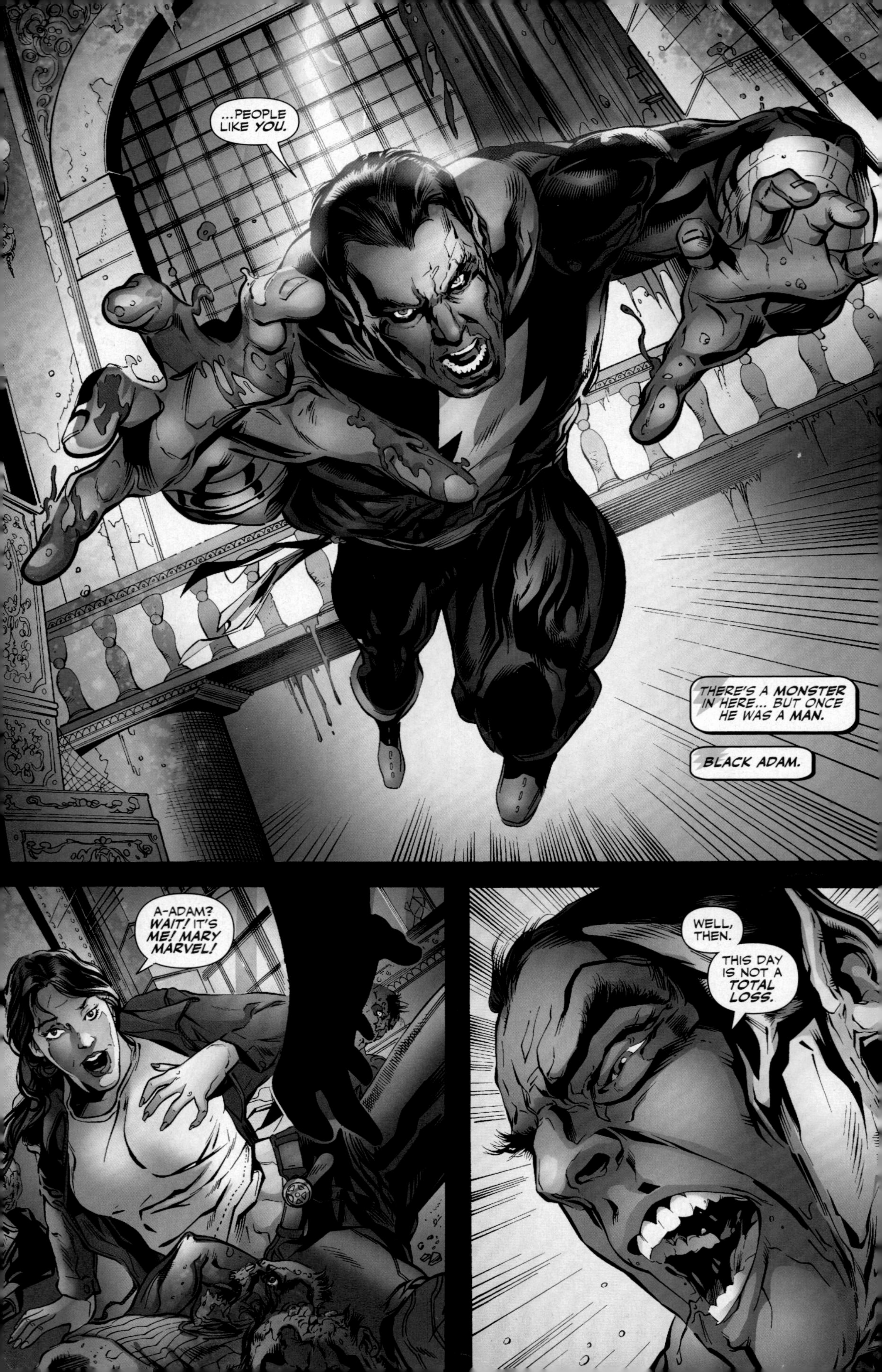
...PEOPLE LIKE YOU.
THERE'S A MONSTER IN HERE... BUT ONCE HE WAS A MAN.
BLACK ADAM.
A-ADAM? WAIT! IT'S ME! MARY MARVEL!
WELL, THEN.
THIS DAY IS NOT A TOTAL LOSS.

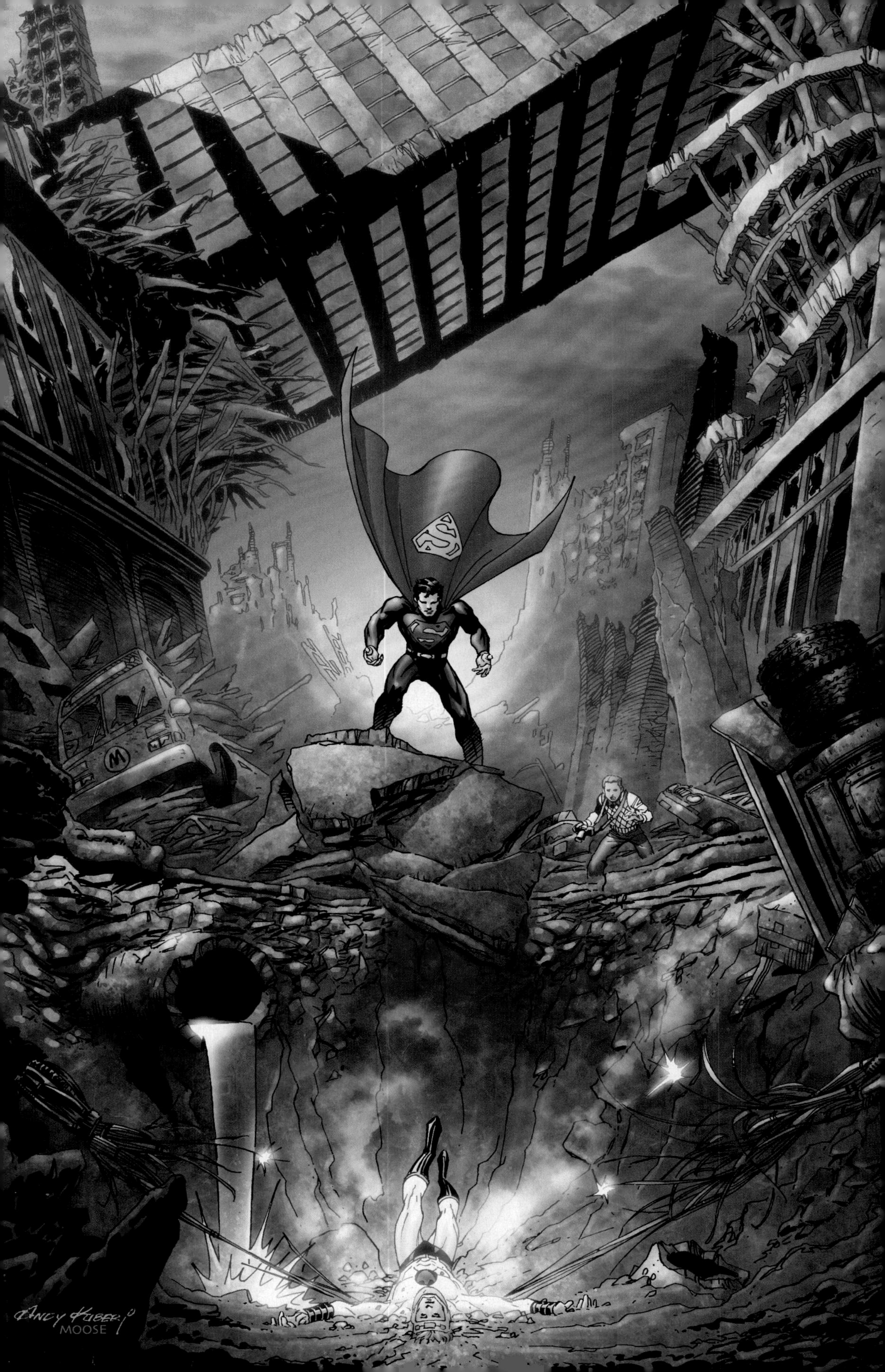
MOOSE

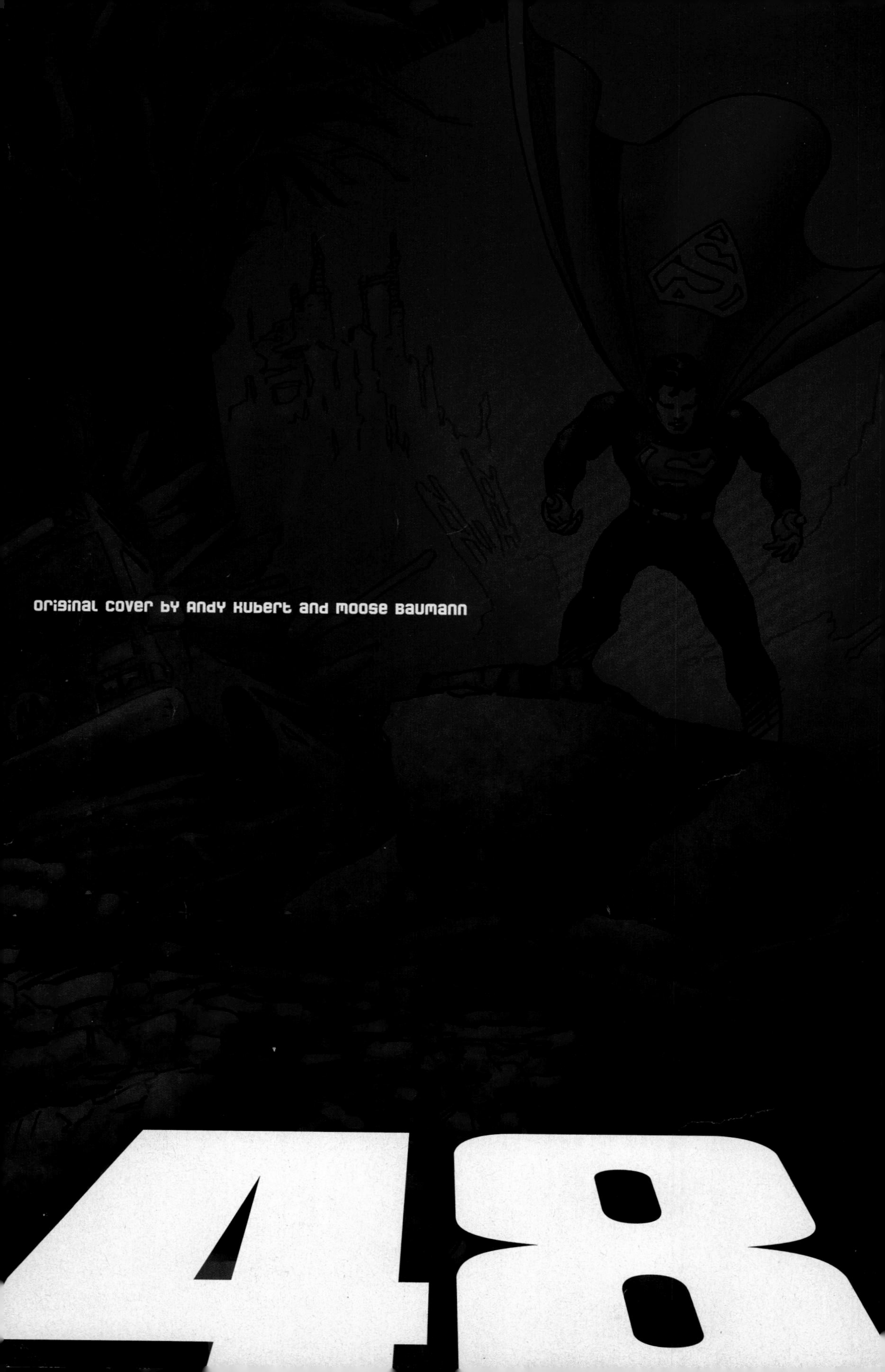
48

original cover by Andy Kubert and Moose Baumann

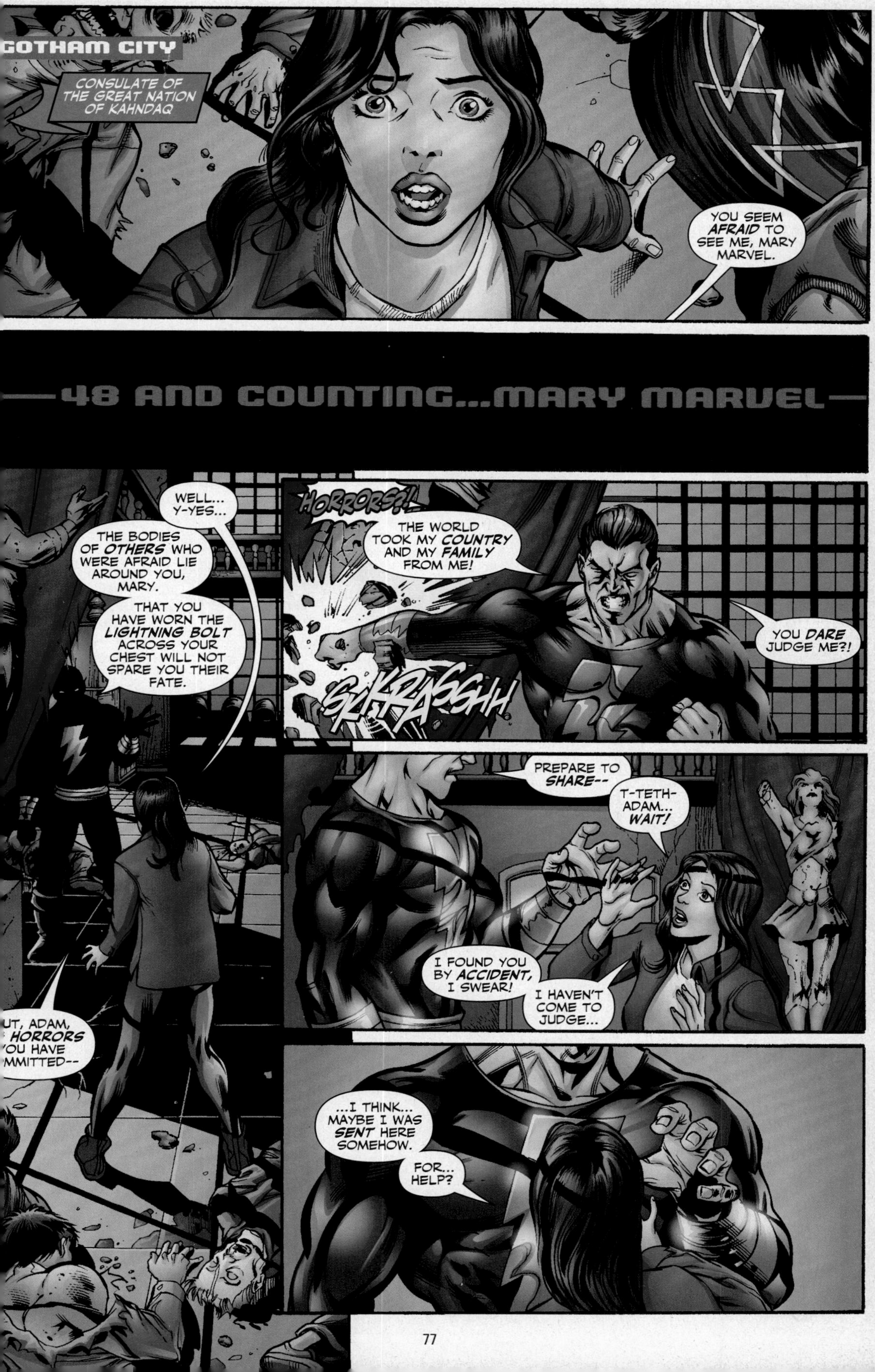
GOTHAM CITY
CONSULATE OF THE GREAT NATION OF KAHNDAQ
YOU SEEM AFRAID TO SEE ME, MARY MARVEL.
—48 AND COUNTING...MARY MARVEL—
WELL... Y-YES...
THE BODIES OF OTHERS WHO WERE AFRAID LIE AROUND YOU, MARY.
THAT YOU HAVE WORN THE LIGHTNING BOLT ACROSS YOUR CHEST WILL NOT SPARE YOU THEIR FATE.
UT, ADAM, HORRORS YOU HAVE MMITTED--
HORRORS?!
THE WORLD TOOK MY COUNTRY AND MY FAMILY FROM ME!
YOU DARE JUDGE ME?!
SKKRASSHH
PREPARE TO SHARE--
T-TETH-ADAM... WAIT!
I FOUND YOU BY ACCIDENT, I SWEAR!
I HAVEN'T COME TO JUDGE...
...I THINK... MAYBE I WAS SENT HERE SOMEHOW.
FOR... HELP?

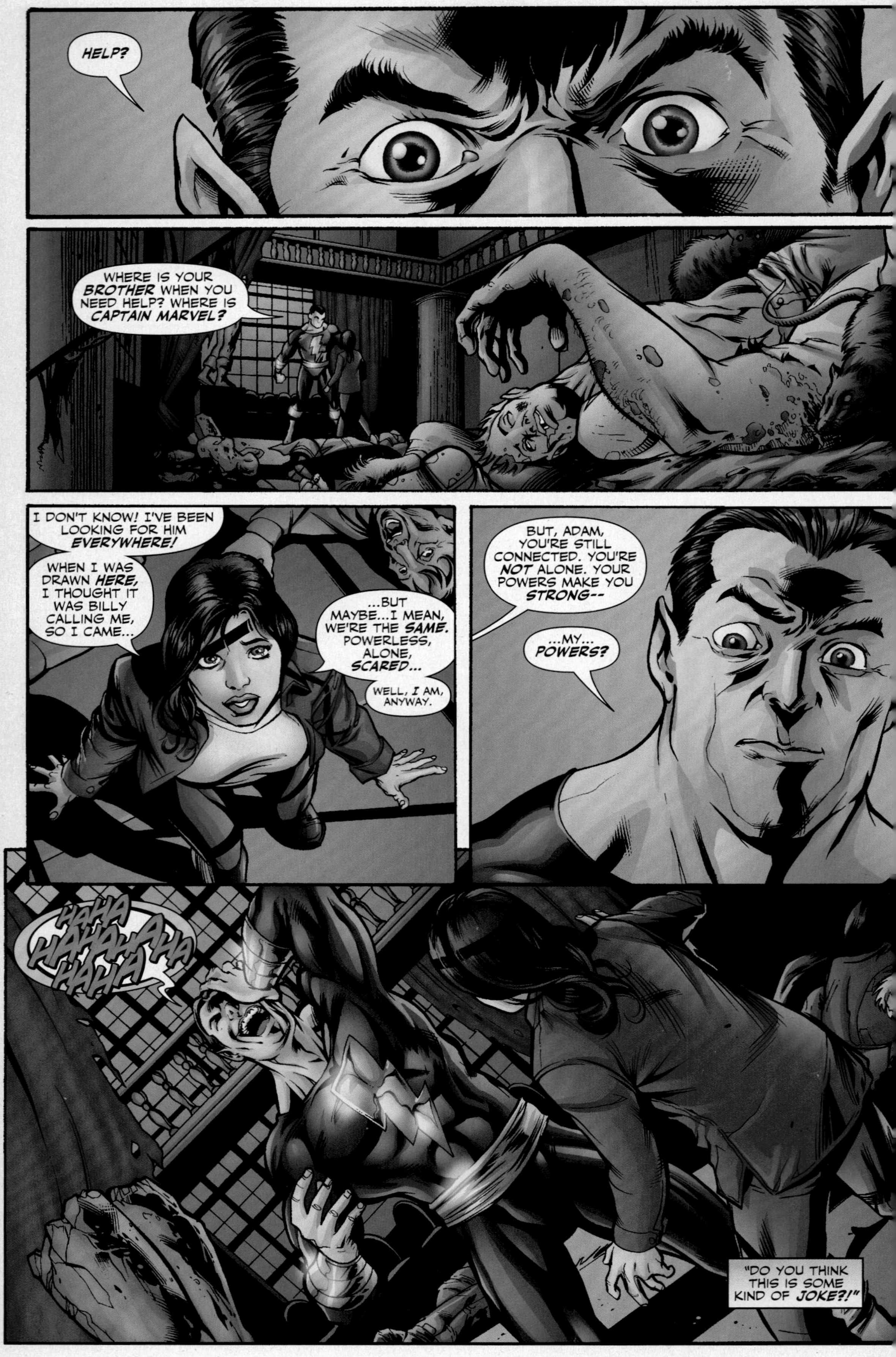
HELP?
WHERE IS YOUR BROTHER WHEN YOU NEED HELP? WHERE IS CAPTAIN MARVEL?
I DON'T KNOW! I'VE BEEN LOOKING FOR HIM EVERYWHERE!
WHEN I WAS DRAWN HERE, I THOUGHT IT WAS BILLY CALLING ME, SO I CAME...
...BUT MAYBE...I MEAN, WE'RE THE SAME. POWERLESS, ALONE, SCARED...
WELL, I AM, ANYWAY.
BUT, ADAM, YOU'RE STILL CONNECTED. YOU'RE NOT ALONE. YOUR POWERS MAKE YOU STRONG--
...MY... POWERS?
HAHA HAHAHAHAHA HAHA
"DO YOU THINK THIS IS SOME KIND OF JOKE?!"

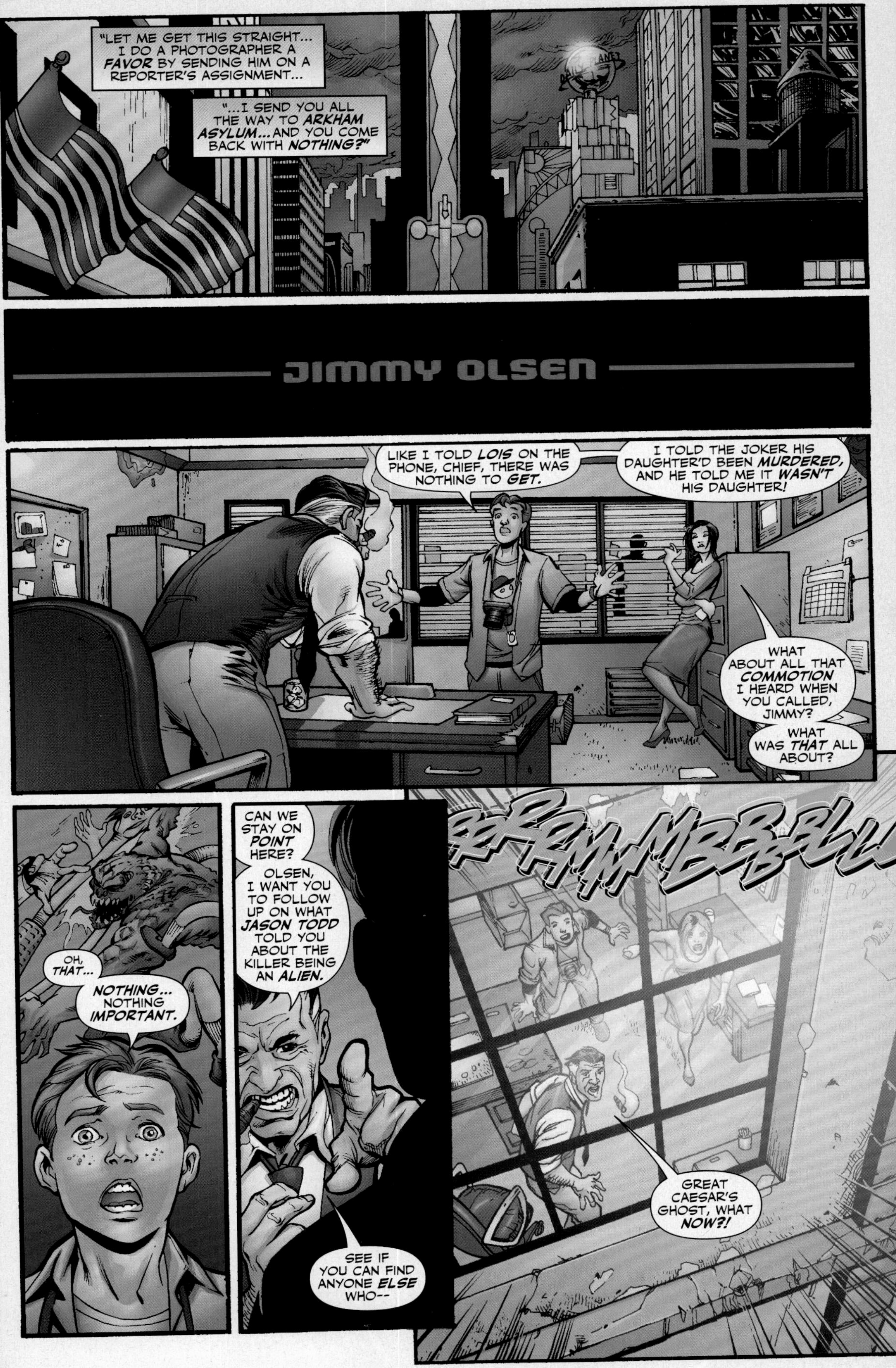
"LET ME GET THIS STRAIGHT... I DO A PHOTOGRAPHER A FAVOR BY SENDING HIM ON A REPORTER'S ASSIGNMENT...
"...I SEND YOU ALL THE WAY TO ARKHAM ASYLUM... AND YOU COME BACK WITH NOTHING?"
JIMMY OLSEN
LIKE I TOLD LOIS ON THE PHONE, CHIEF, THERE WAS NOTHING TO GET.
I TOLD THE JOKER HIS DAUGHTER'D BEEN MURDERED, AND HE TOLD ME IT WASN'T HIS DAUGHTER!
WHAT ABOUT ALL THAT COMMOTION I HEARD WHEN YOU CALLED, JIMMY?
WHAT WAS THAT ALL ABOUT?
OH, THAT...
NOTHING... NOTHING IMPORTANT.
CAN WE STAY ON POINT HERE?
OLSEN, I WANT YOU TO FOLLOW UP ON WHAT JASON TODD TOLD YOU ABOUT THE KILLER BEING AN ALIEN.
SEE IF YOU CAN FIND ANYONE ELSE WHO--
GREAT CAESAR'S GHOST, WHAT NOW?!

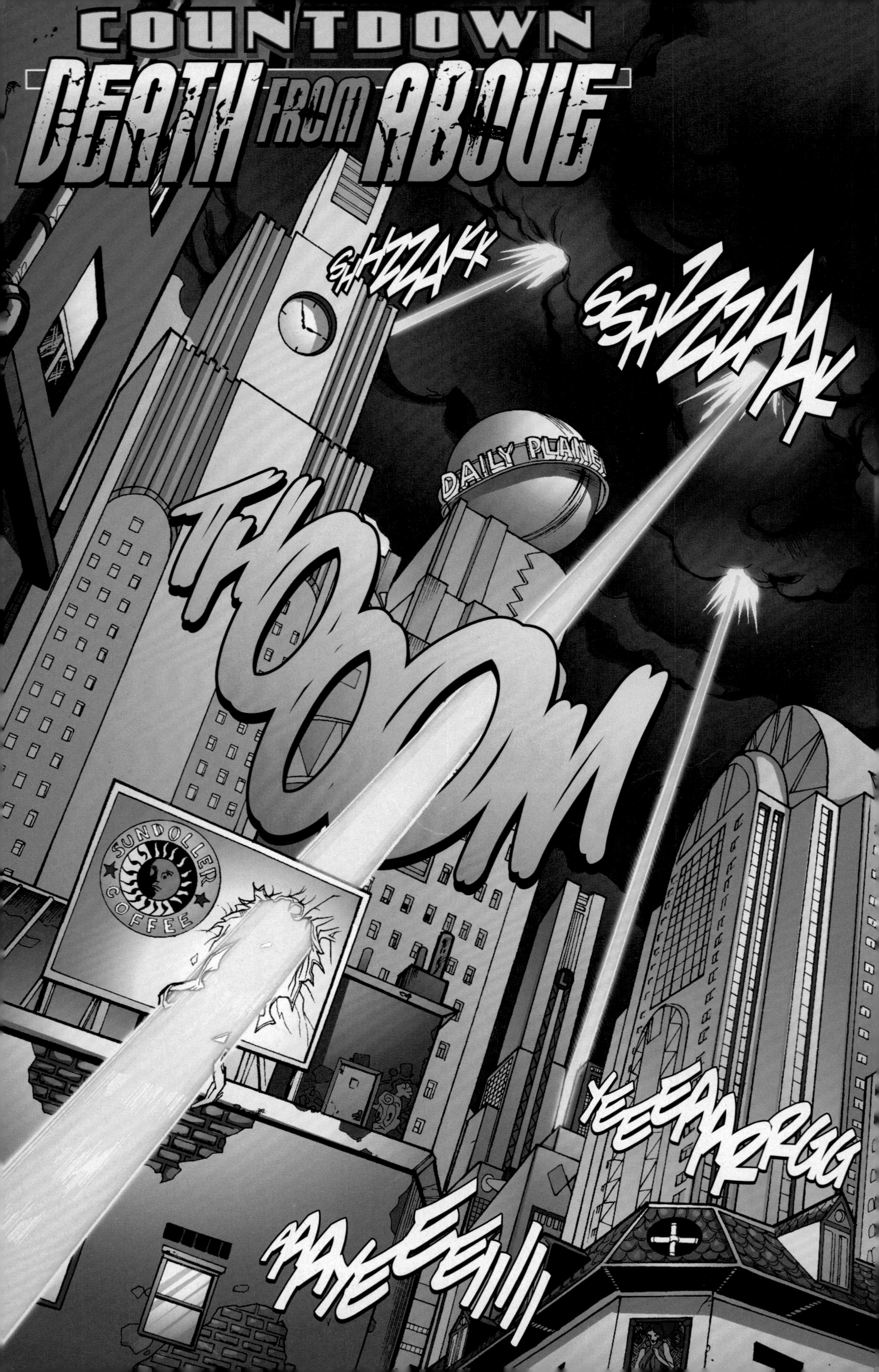
COUNTDOWN
DEATH FROM ABOVE
SHZZZAKK
SSHZZZAAK
DAILY PLANE
THOOOM
SUNDOLLER COFFEE
YEEEAARRGG
AAAYEEEIII

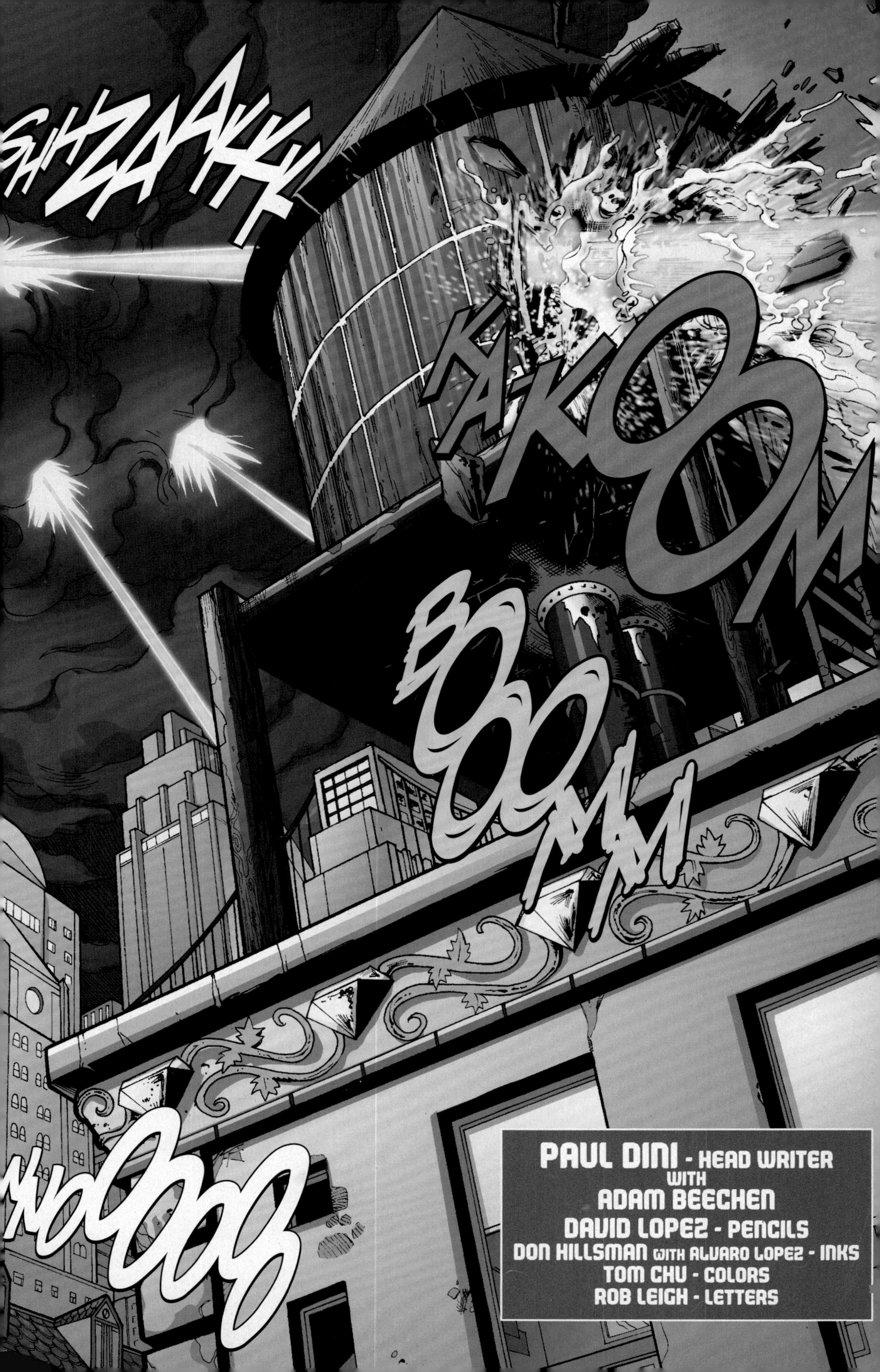
SHZAAKK
KA-KOOM
BOOOM
PAUL DINI - HEAD WRITER
WITH
ADAM BEECHEN
DAVID LOPEZ - PENCILS
DON HILLSMAN WITH ALVARO LOPEZ - INKS
TOM CHU - COLORS
ROB LEIGH - LETTERS

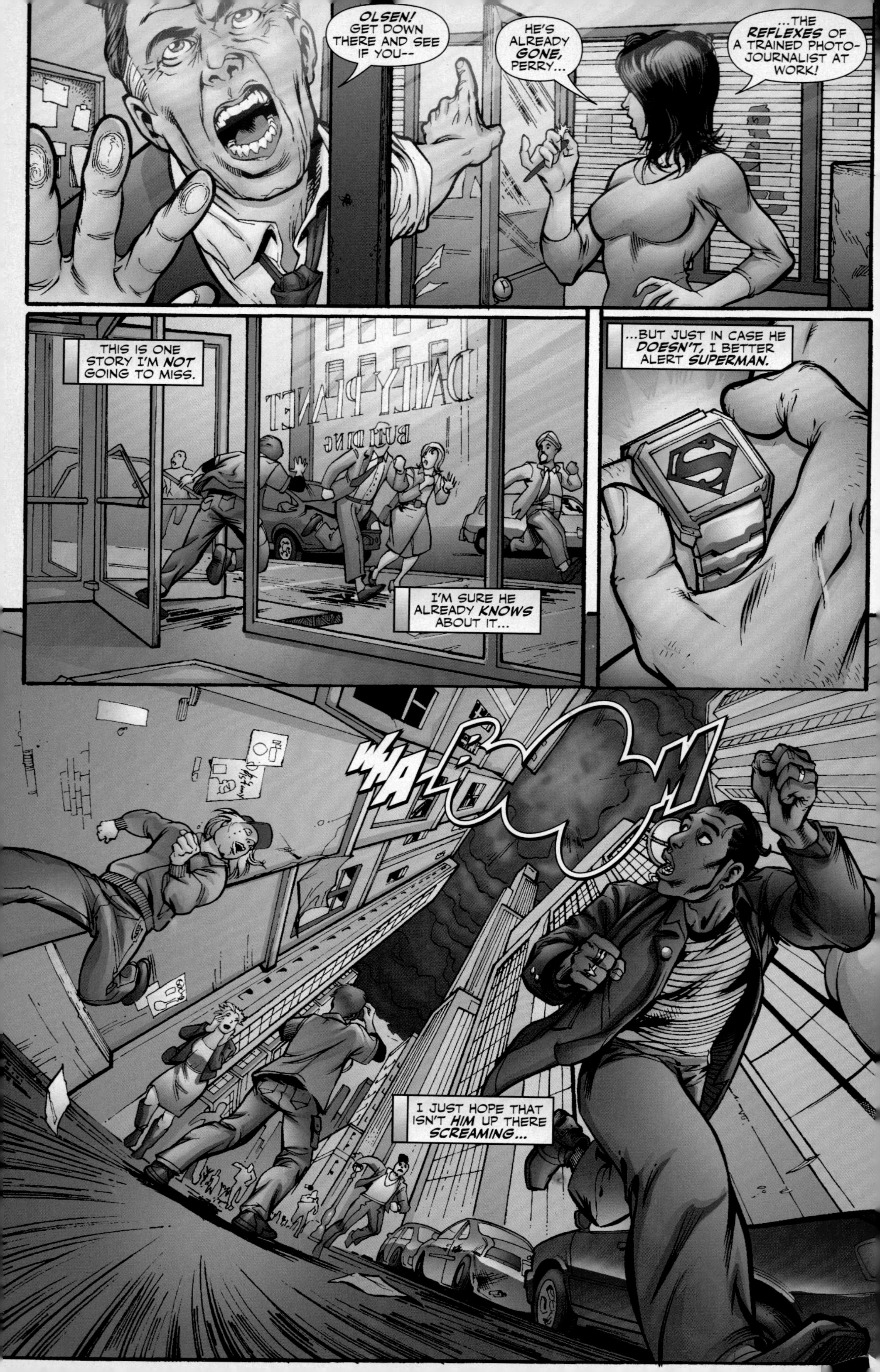
OLSEN! GET DOWN THERE AND SEE IF YOU--
HE'S ALREADY GONE, PERRY...
...THE REFLEXES OF A TRAINED PHOTO-JOURNALIST AT WORK!
THIS IS ONE STORY I'M NOT GOING TO MISS.
DAILY PLANET BUILDING
I'M SURE HE ALREADY KNOWS ABOUT IT...
...BUT JUST IN CASE HE DOESN'T, I BETTER ALERT SUPERMAN.
WHA-BOOM
I JUST HOPE THAT ISN'T HIM UP THERE SCREAMING...

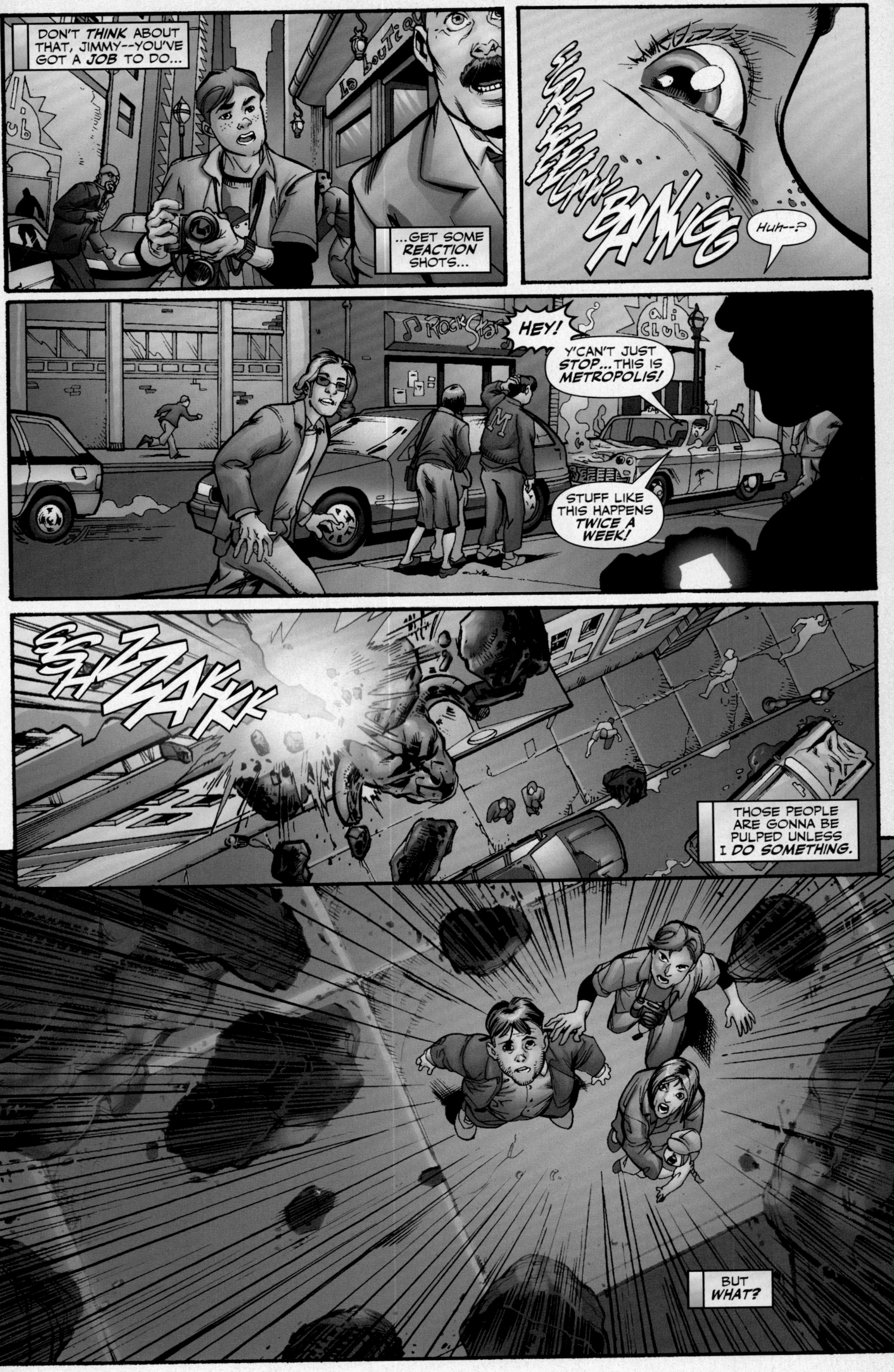
DON'T THINK ABOUT THAT, JIMMY--YOU'VE GOT A JOB TO DO...
La Bouti
...GET SOME REACTION SHOTS...
BANGG
Huh--?
RockStar
ali club
HEY!
Y'CAN'T JUST STOP... THIS IS METROPOLIS!
STUFF LIKE THIS HAPPENS TWICE A WEEK!
THOSE PEOPLE ARE GONNA BE PULPED UNLESS I DO SOMETHING.
BUT WHAT?

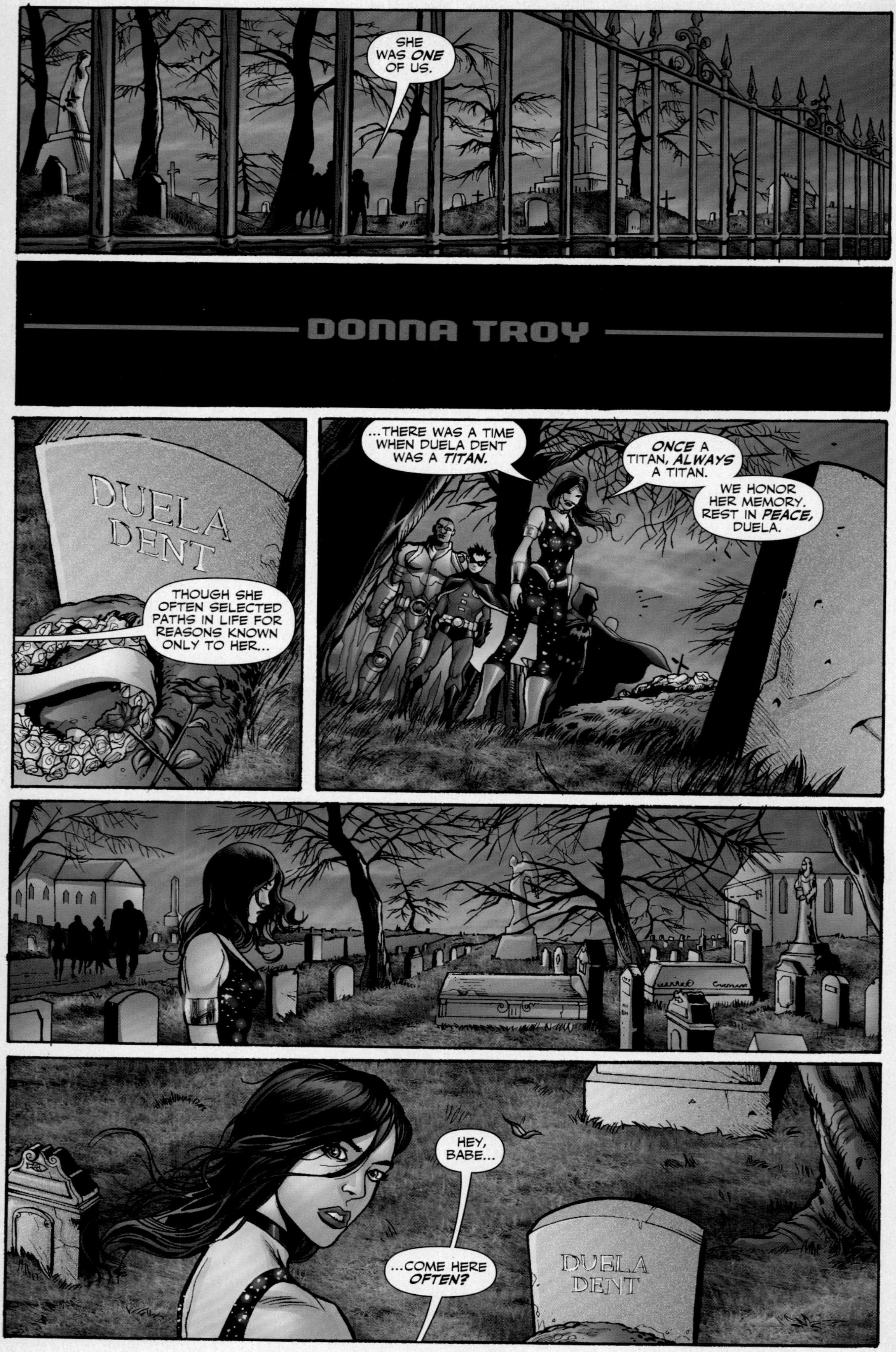

SHE WAS ONE OF US.
DONNA TROY
DUELA DENT
THOUGH SHE OFTEN SELECTED PATHS IN LIFE FOR REASONS KNOWN ONLY TO HER...
...THERE WAS A TIME WHEN DUELA DENT WAS A TITAN.
ONCE A TITAN, ALWAYS A TITAN.
WE HONOR HER MEMORY. REST IN PEACE, DUELA.
HEY, BABE...
...COME HERE OFTEN?
DUELA DENT

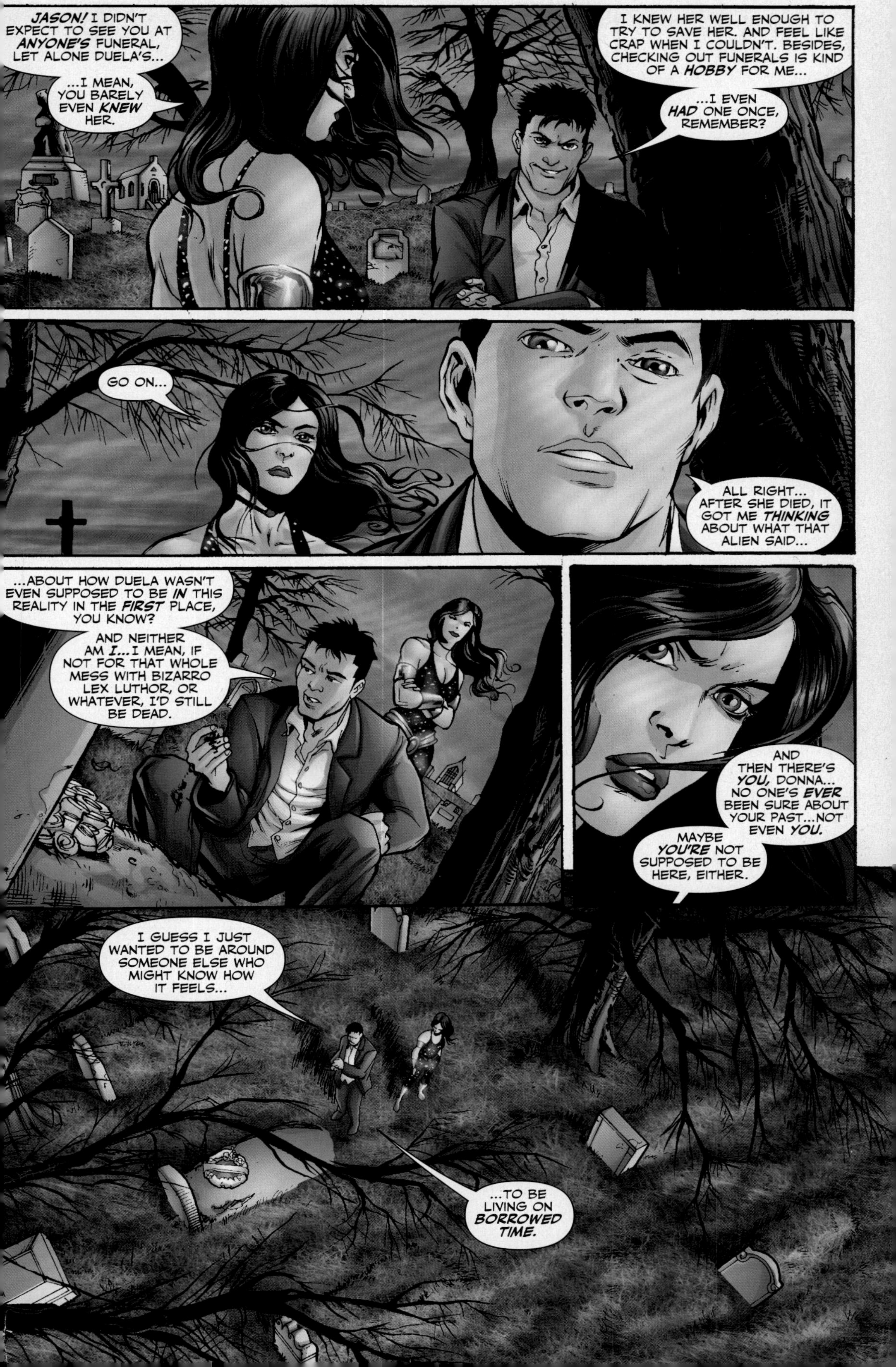
JASON! I DIDN'T EXPECT TO SEE YOU AT ANYONE'S FUNERAL, LET ALONE DUELA'S...
...I MEAN, YOU BARELY EVEN KNEW HER.
I KNEW HER WELL ENOUGH TO TRY TO SAVE HER. AND FEEL LIKE CRAP WHEN I COULDN'T. BESIDES, CHECKING OUT FUNERALS IS KIND OF A HOBBY FOR ME...
...I EVEN HAD ONE ONCE, REMEMBER?
GO ON...
ALL RIGHT... AFTER SHE DIED, IT GOT ME THINKING ABOUT WHAT THAT ALIEN SAID...
...ABOUT HOW DUELA WASN'T EVEN SUPPOSED TO BE IN THIS REALITY IN THE FIRST PLACE, YOU KNOW?
AND NEITHER AM I...I MEAN, IF NOT FOR THAT WHOLE MESS WITH BIZARRO LEX LUTHOR, OR WHATEVER, I'D STILL BE DEAD.
AND THEN THERE'S YOU, DONNA... NO ONE'S EVER BEEN SURE ABOUT YOUR PAST...NOT EVEN YOU.
MAYBE YOU'RE NOT SUPPOSED TO BE HERE, EITHER.
I GUESS I JUST WANTED TO BE AROUND SOMEONE ELSE WHO MIGHT KNOW HOW IT FEELS...
...TO BE LIVING ON BORROWED TIME.

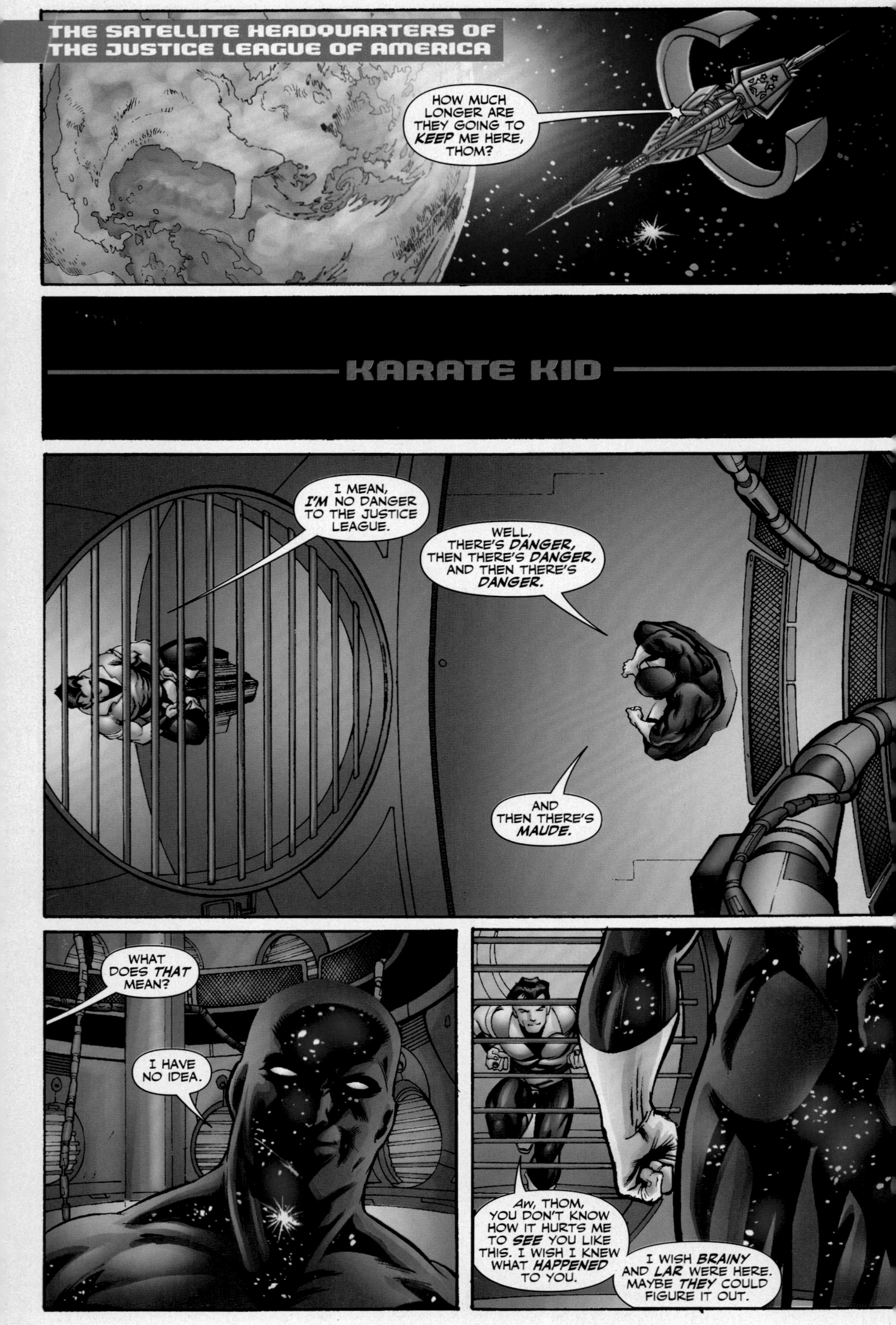

THE SATELLITE HEADQUARTERS OF THE JUSTICE LEAGUE OF AMERICA
HOW MUCH LONGER ARE THEY GOING TO KEEP ME HERE, THOM?
KARATE KID
I MEAN, I'M NO DANGER TO THE JUSTICE LEAGUE.
WELL, THERE'S DANGER, THEN THERE'S DANGER, AND THEN THERE'S DANGER.
AND THEN THERE'S MAUDE.
WHAT DOES THAT MEAN?
I HAVE NO IDEA.
AW, THOM, YOU DON'T KNOW HOW IT HURTS ME TO SEE YOU LIKE THIS. I WISH I KNEW WHAT HAPPENED TO YOU.
I WISH BRAINY AND LAR WERE HERE. MAYBE THEY COULD FIGURE IT OUT.

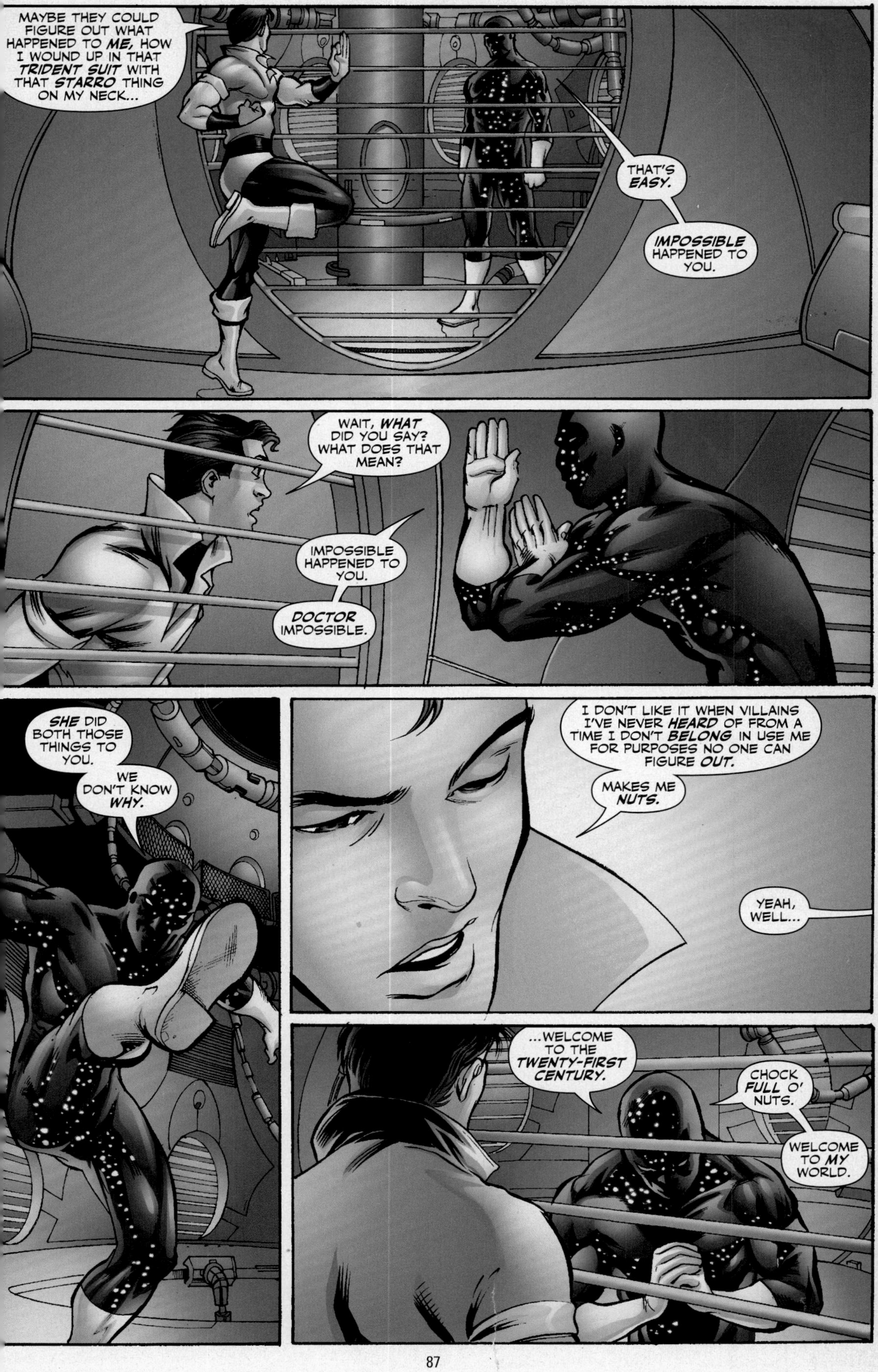
MAYBE THEY COULD FIGURE OUT WHAT HAPPENED TO *ME,* HOW I WOUND UP IN THAT *TRIDENT SUIT* WITH THAT *STARRO* THING ON MY NECK...
THAT'S *EASY.*
IMPOSSIBLE HAPPENED TO YOU.
WAIT, *WHAT* DID YOU SAY? WHAT DOES THAT MEAN?
IMPOSSIBLE HAPPENED TO YOU.
DOCTOR IMPOSSIBLE.
SHE DID BOTH THOSE THINGS TO YOU.
WE DON'T KNOW *WHY.*
I DON'T LIKE IT WHEN VILLAINS I'VE NEVER *HEARD* OF FROM A TIME I DON'T *BELONG* IN USE ME FOR PURPOSES NO ONE CAN FIGURE *OUT.*
MAKES ME *NUTS.*
YEAH, WELL...
...WELCOME TO THE *TWENTY-FIRST CENTURY.*
CHOCK *FULL* O' NUTS.
WELCOME TO *MY* WORLD.

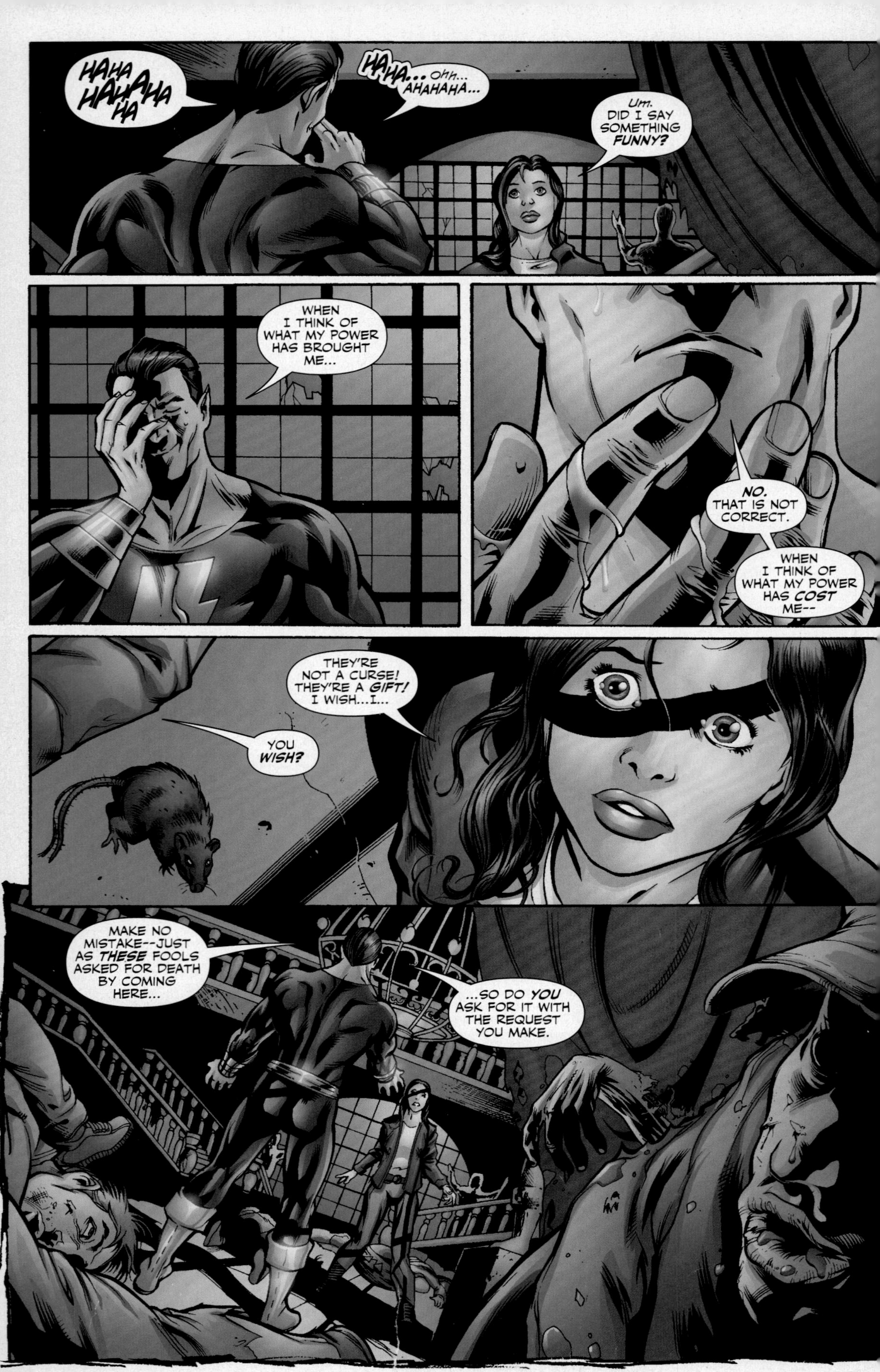
HAHA HAHAHAHA HA
HAHA... Ohh... AHAHAHA...
Um. DID I SAY SOMETHING FUNNY?
WHEN I THINK OF WHAT MY POWER HAS BROUGHT ME...
NO. THAT IS NOT CORRECT.
WHEN I THINK OF WHAT MY POWER HAS COST ME--
THEY'RE NOT A CURSE! THEY'RE A GIFT! I WISH...I...
YOU WISH?
MAKE NO MISTAKE--JUST AS THESE FOOLS ASKED FOR DEATH BY COMING HERE...
...SO DO YOU ASK FOR IT WITH THE REQUEST YOU MAKE.

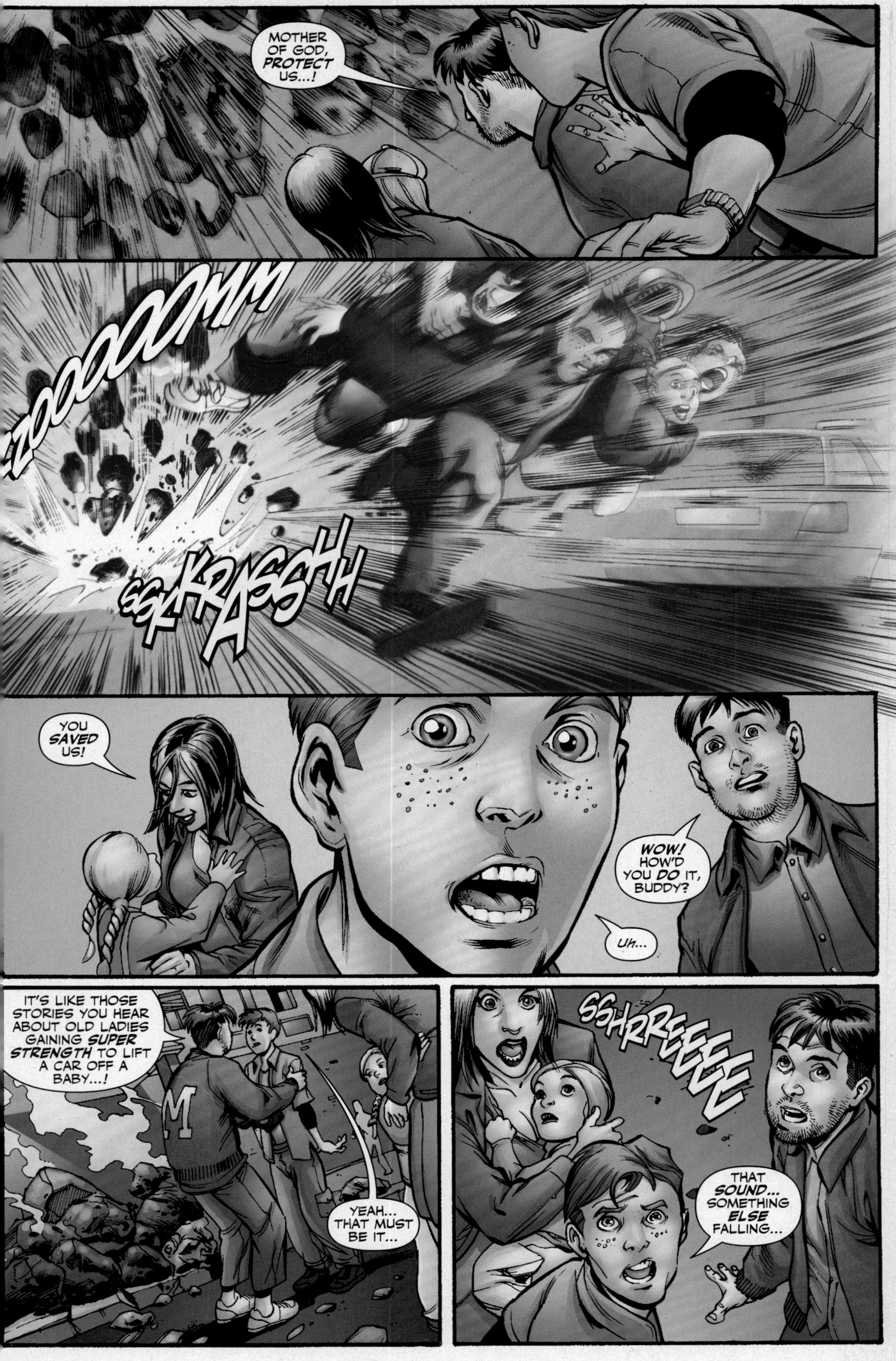
MOTHER OF GOD, PROTECT US...!
ZOOOOOOMM
SSKKRASSHH
YOU SAVED US!
WOW! HOW'D YOU DO IT, BUDDY?
Uh...
IT'S LIKE THOSE STORIES YOU HEAR ABOUT OLD LADIES GAINING SUPER STRENGTH TO LIFT A CAR OFF A BABY...!
YEAH... THAT MUST BE IT...
SSHRREEEEE
THAT SOUND... SOMETHING ELSE FALLING...

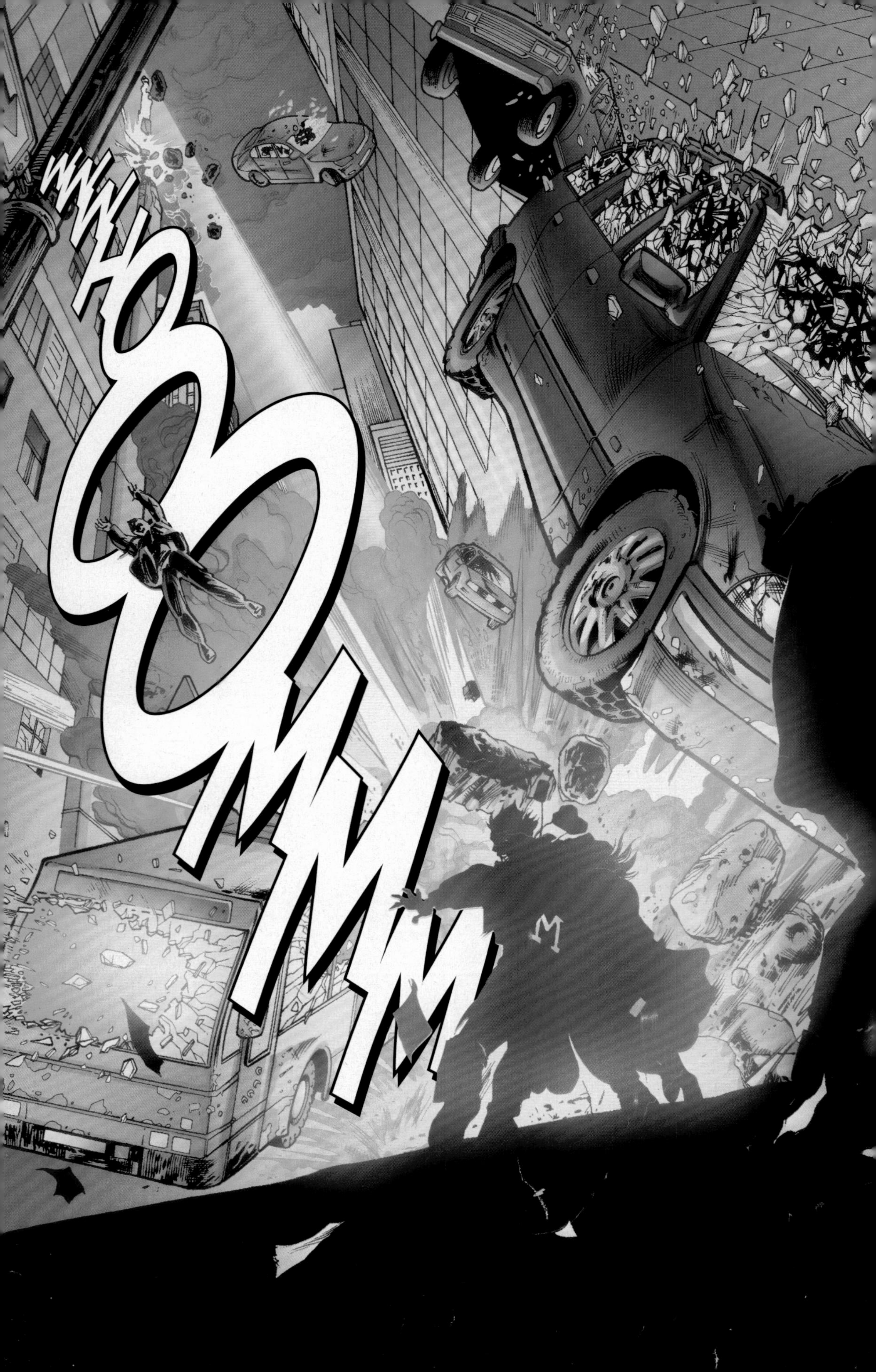
WHOOOMMMM

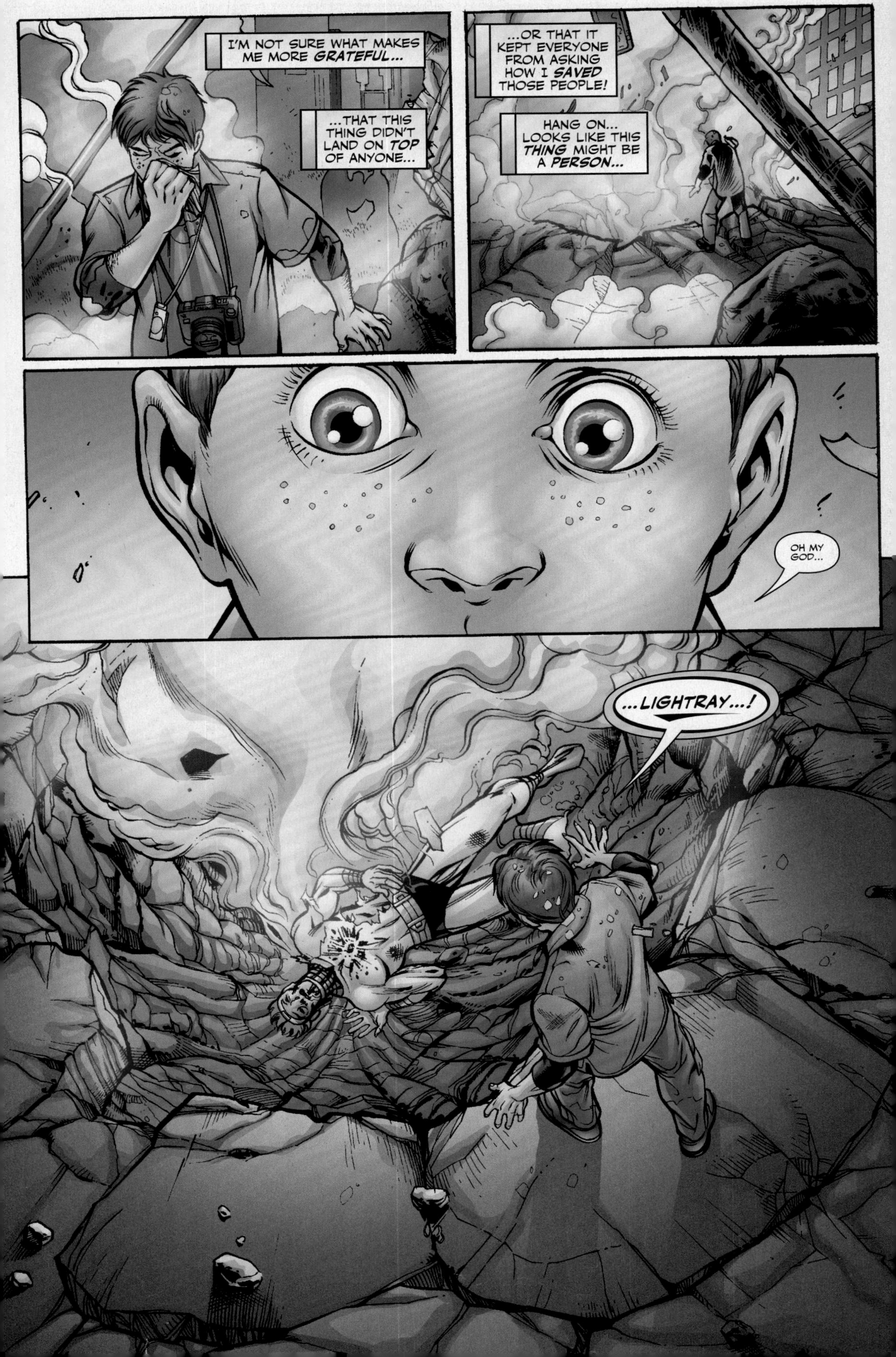
I'M NOT SURE WHAT MAKES ME MORE GRATEFUL...
...THAT THIS THING DIDN'T LAND ON TOP OF ANYONE...
...OR THAT IT KEPT EVERYONE FROM ASKING HOW I SAVED THOSE PEOPLE!
HANG ON... LOOKS LIKE THIS THING MIGHT BE A PERSON...
OH MY GOD...
...LIGHTRAY...!

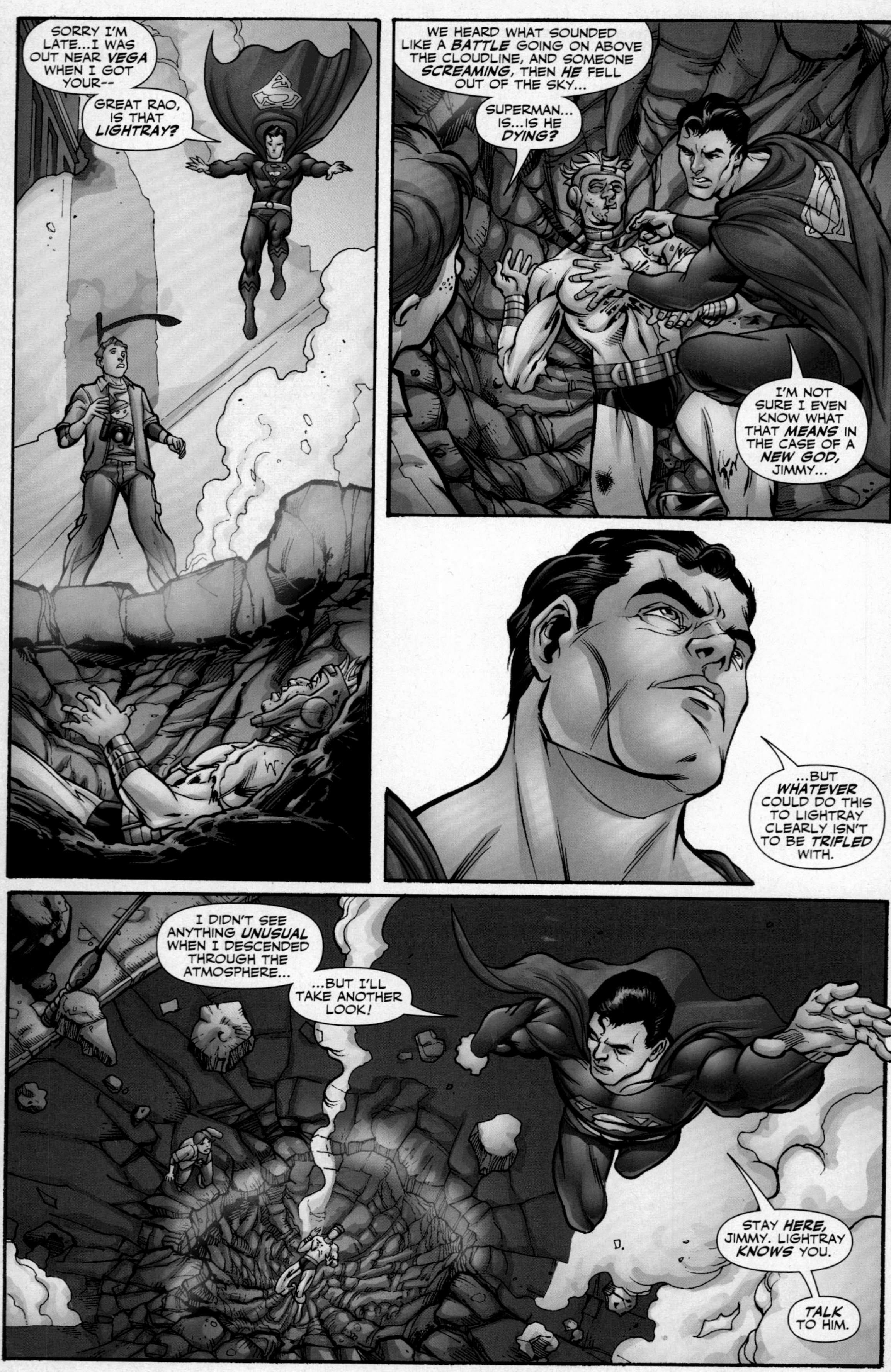
SORRY I'M LATE...I WAS OUT NEAR VEGA WHEN I GOT YOUR--
GREAT RAO, IS THAT LIGHTRAY?
WE HEARD WHAT SOUNDED LIKE A BATTLE GOING ON ABOVE THE CLOUDLINE, AND SOMEONE SCREAMING, THEN HE FELL OUT OF THE SKY...
SUPERMAN... IS...IS HE DYING?
I'M NOT SURE I EVEN KNOW WHAT THAT MEANS IN THE CASE OF A NEW GOD, JIMMY...
...BUT WHATEVER COULD DO THIS TO LIGHTRAY CLEARLY ISN'T TO BE TRIFLED WITH.
I DIDN'T SEE ANYTHING UNUSUAL WHEN I DESCENDED THROUGH THE ATMOSPHERE...
...BUT I'LL TAKE ANOTHER LOOK!
STAY HERE, JIMMY. LIGHTRAY KNOWS YOU.
TALK TO HIM.

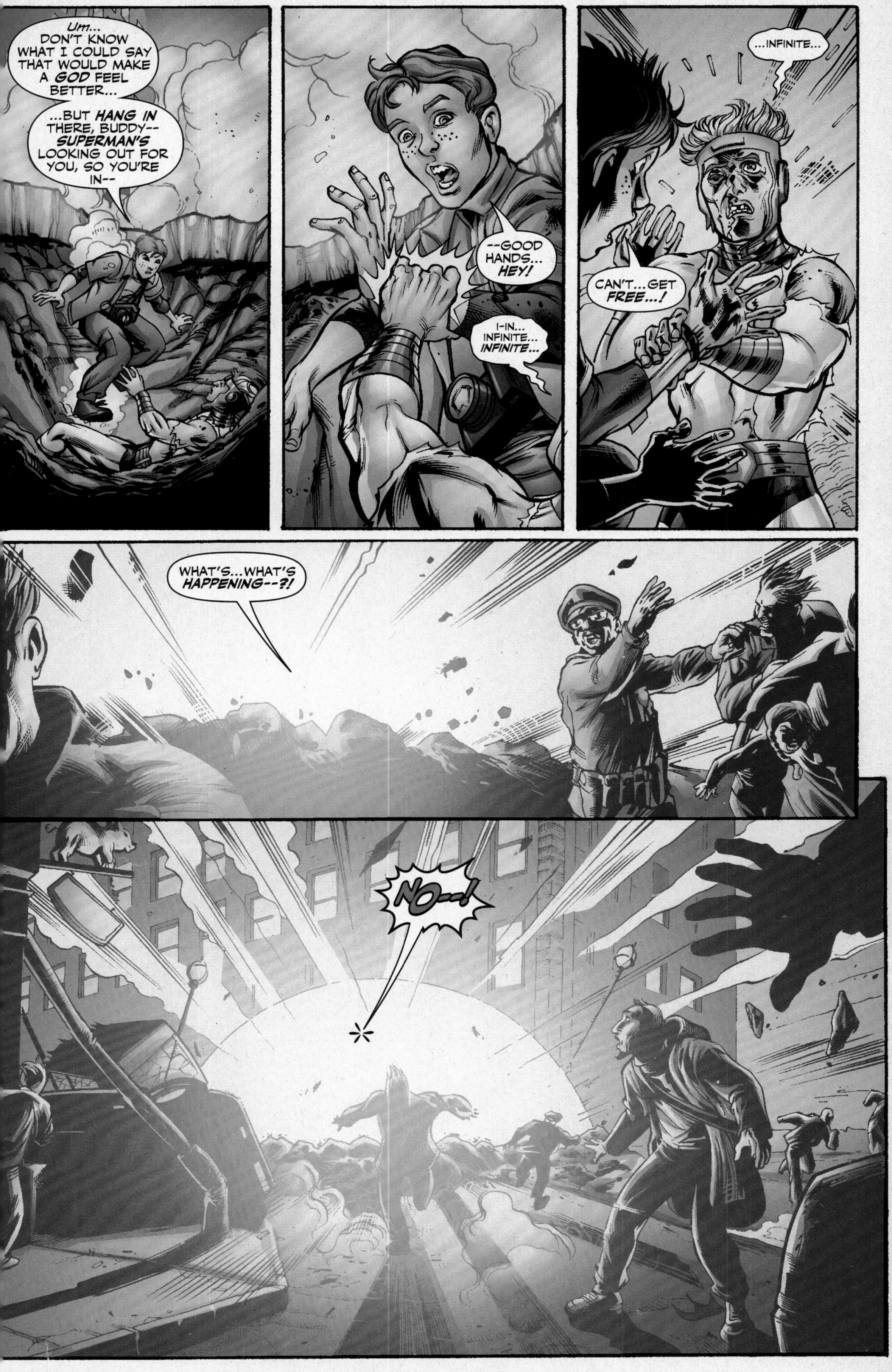
Um... DON'T KNOW WHAT I COULD SAY THAT WOULD MAKE A GOD FEEL BETTER...
...BUT HANG IN THERE, BUDDY-- SUPERMAN'S LOOKING OUT FOR YOU, SO YOU'RE IN--
--GOOD HANDS... HEY!
I-IN... INFINITE... INFINITE...
...INFINITE...
CAN'T...GET FREE...!
WHAT'S...WHAT'S HAPPENING--?!
NO--!

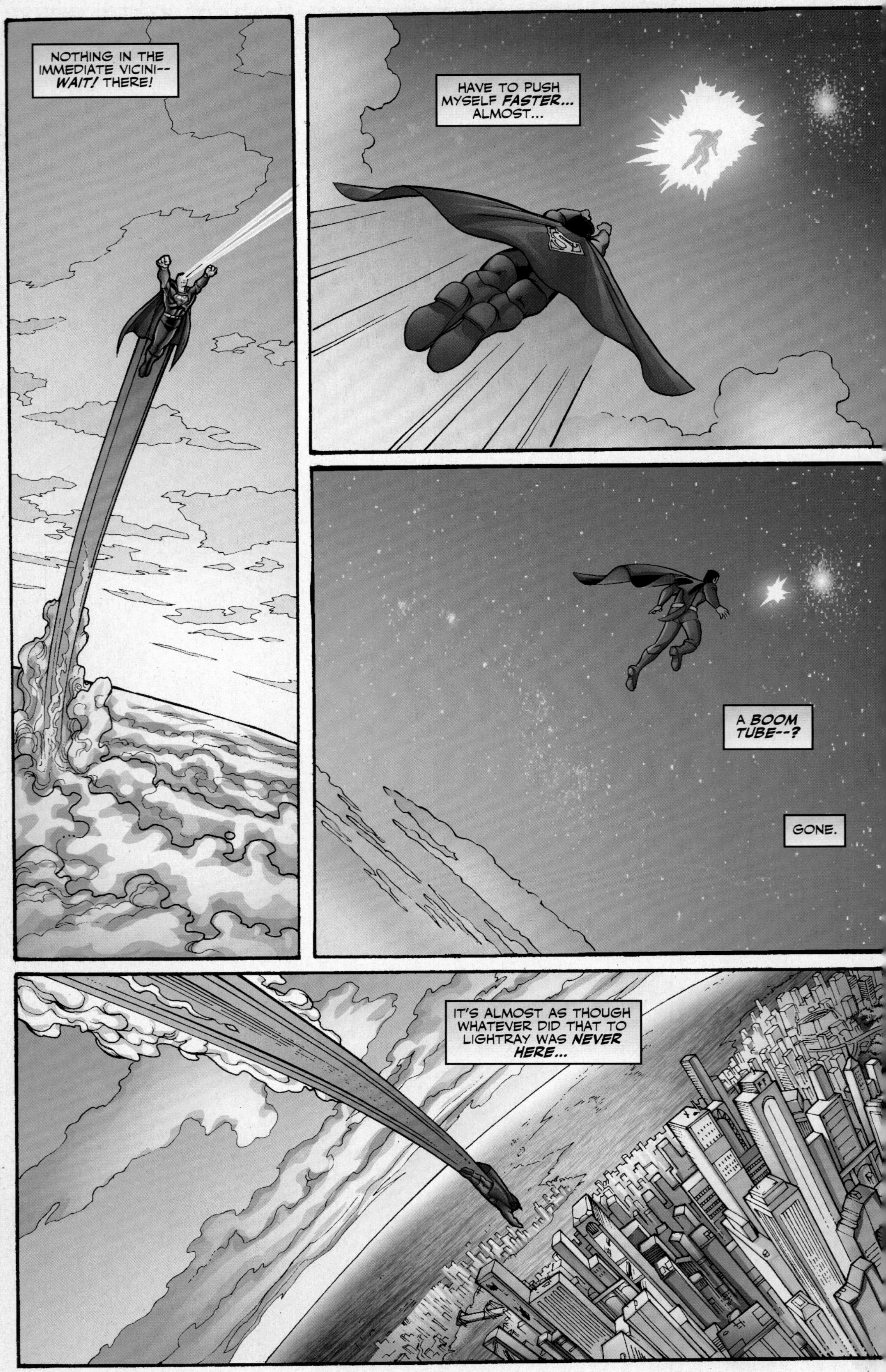
NOTHING IN THE IMMEDIATE VICINI-- *WAIT!* THERE!
HAVE TO PUSH MYSELF *FASTER...* ALMOST...
A *BOOM TUBE--?*
GONE.
IT'S ALMOST AS THOUGH WHATEVER DID THAT TO LIGHTRAY WAS *NEVER HERE...*

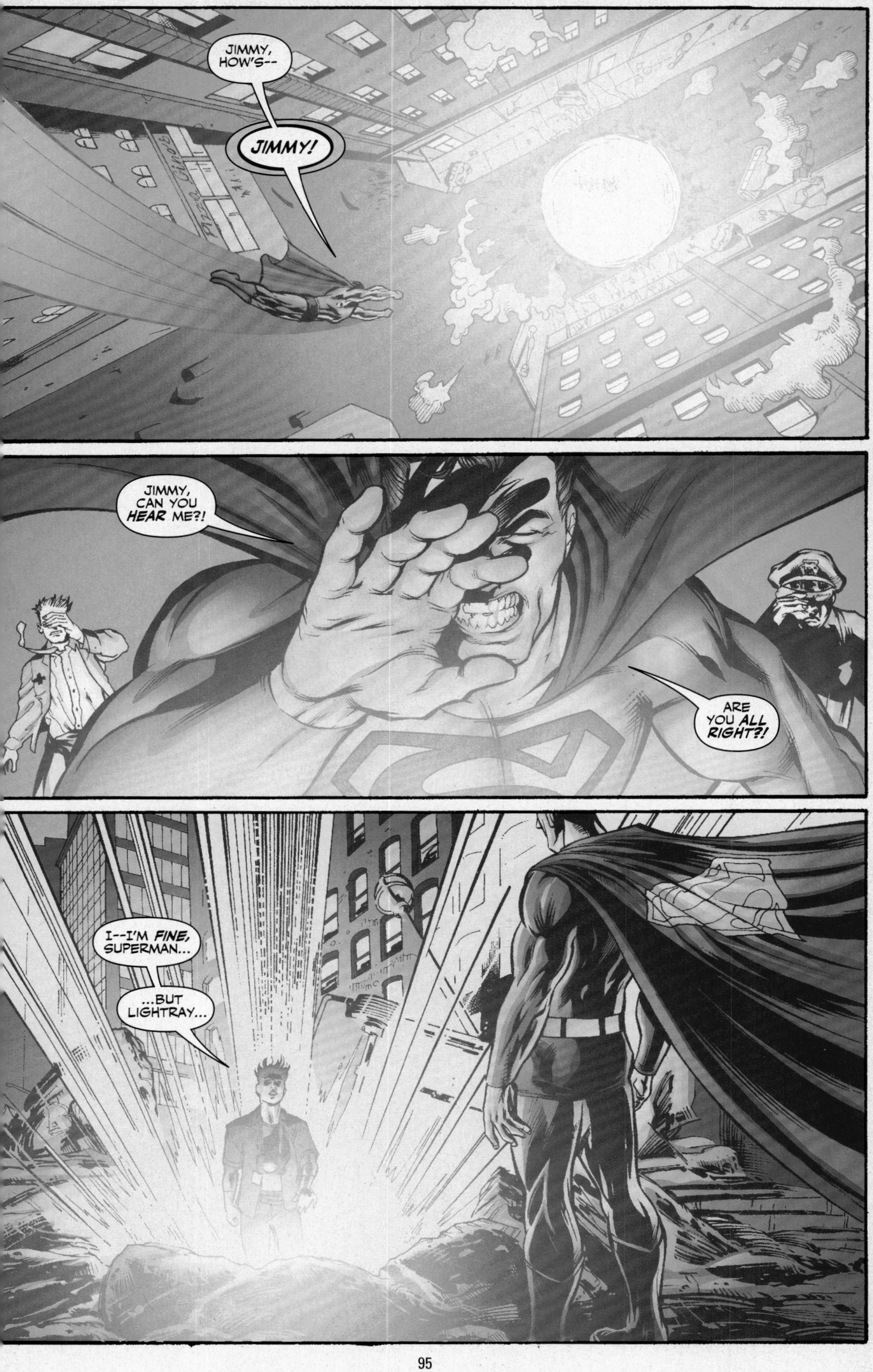
JIMMY, HOW'S--
JIMMY!
JIMMY, CAN YOU HEAR ME?!
ARE YOU ALL RIGHT?!
I--I'M FINE, SUPERMAN...
...BUT LIGHTRAY...

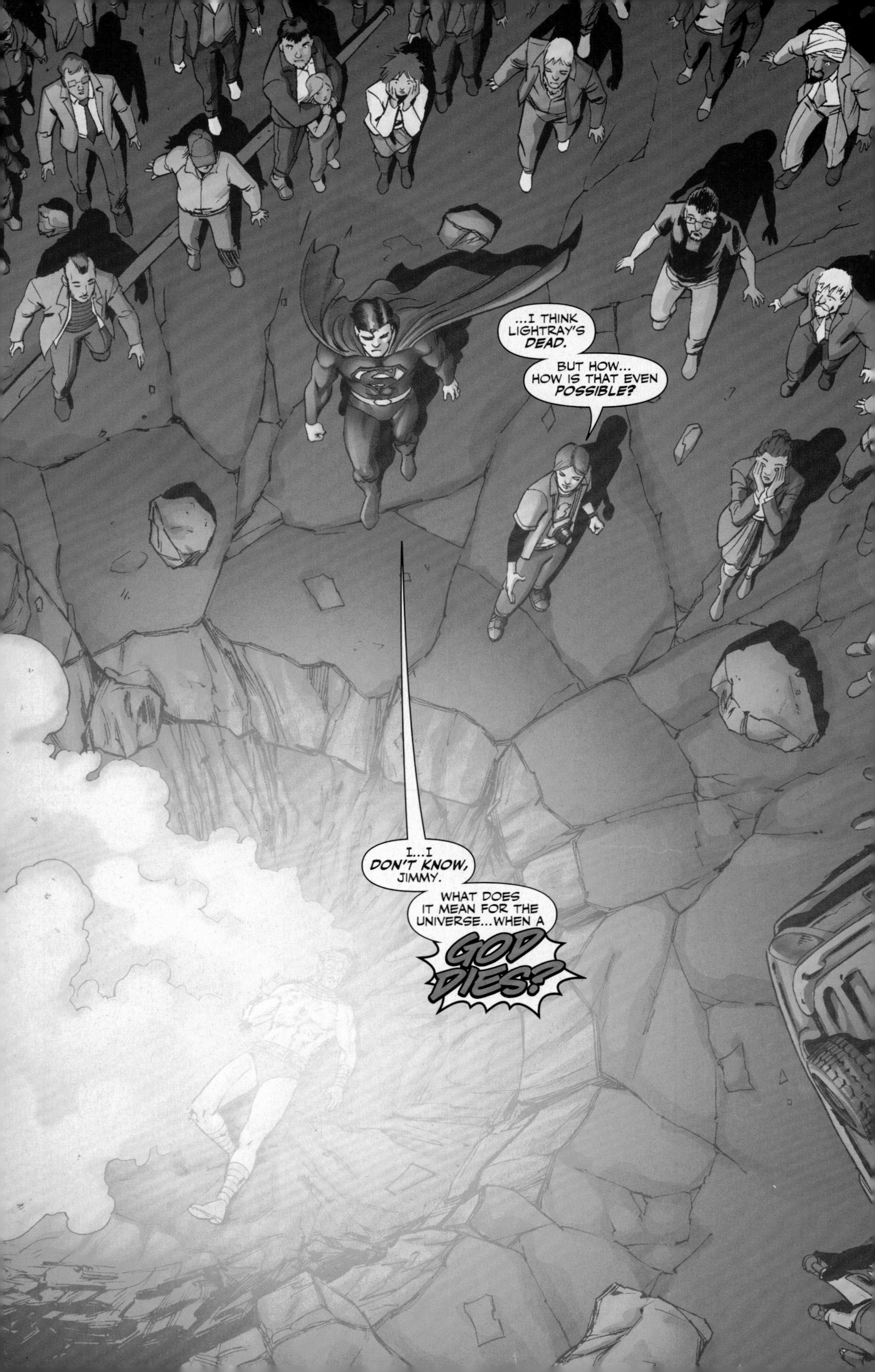
...I THINK LIGHTRAY'S *DEAD.*
BUT HOW... HOW IS THAT EVEN *POSSIBLE?*
I...I *DON'T KNOW,* JIMMY.
WHAT DOES IT MEAN FOR THE UNIVERSE...WHEN A
GOD DIES?

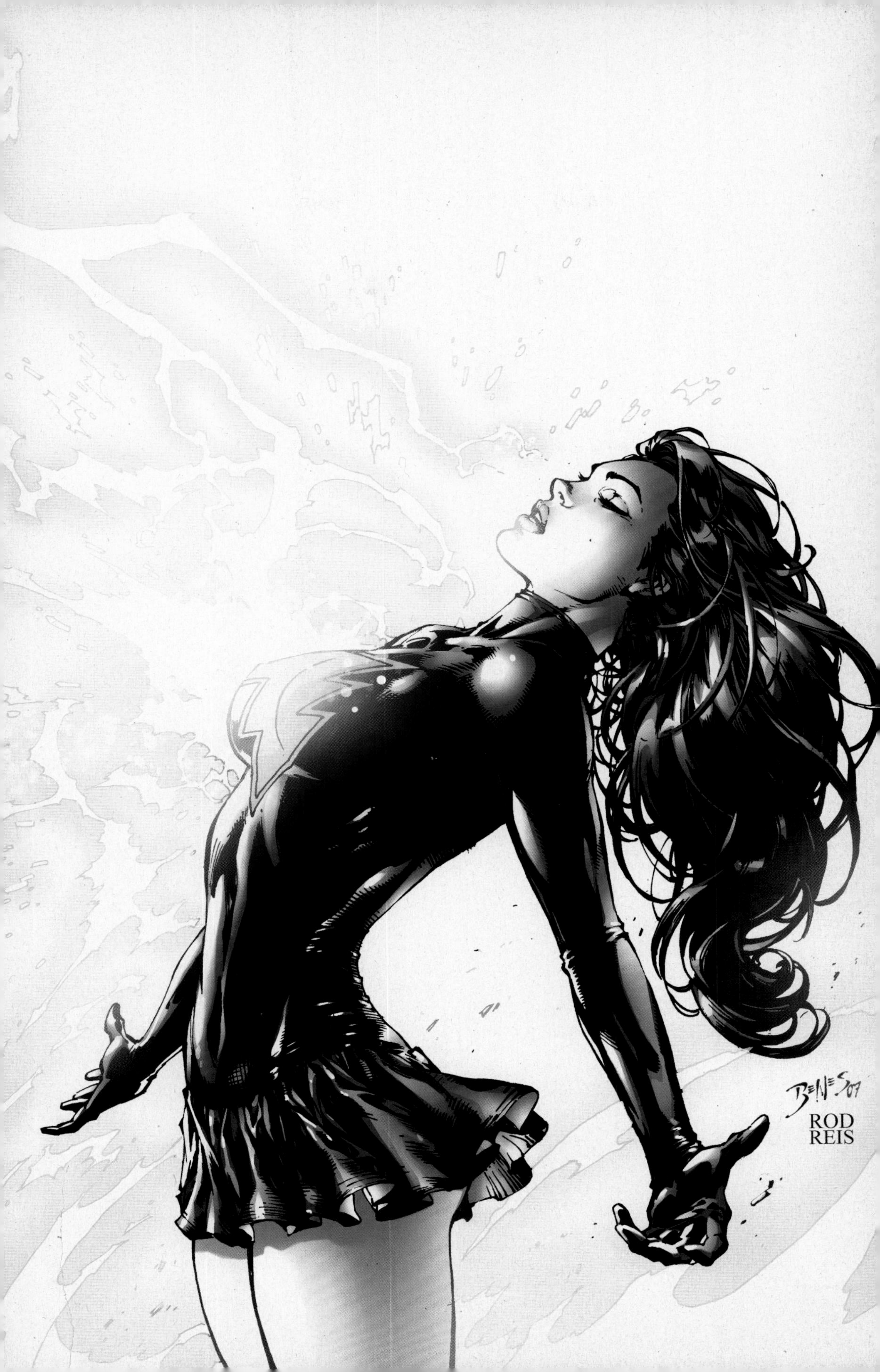
ROD
REIS

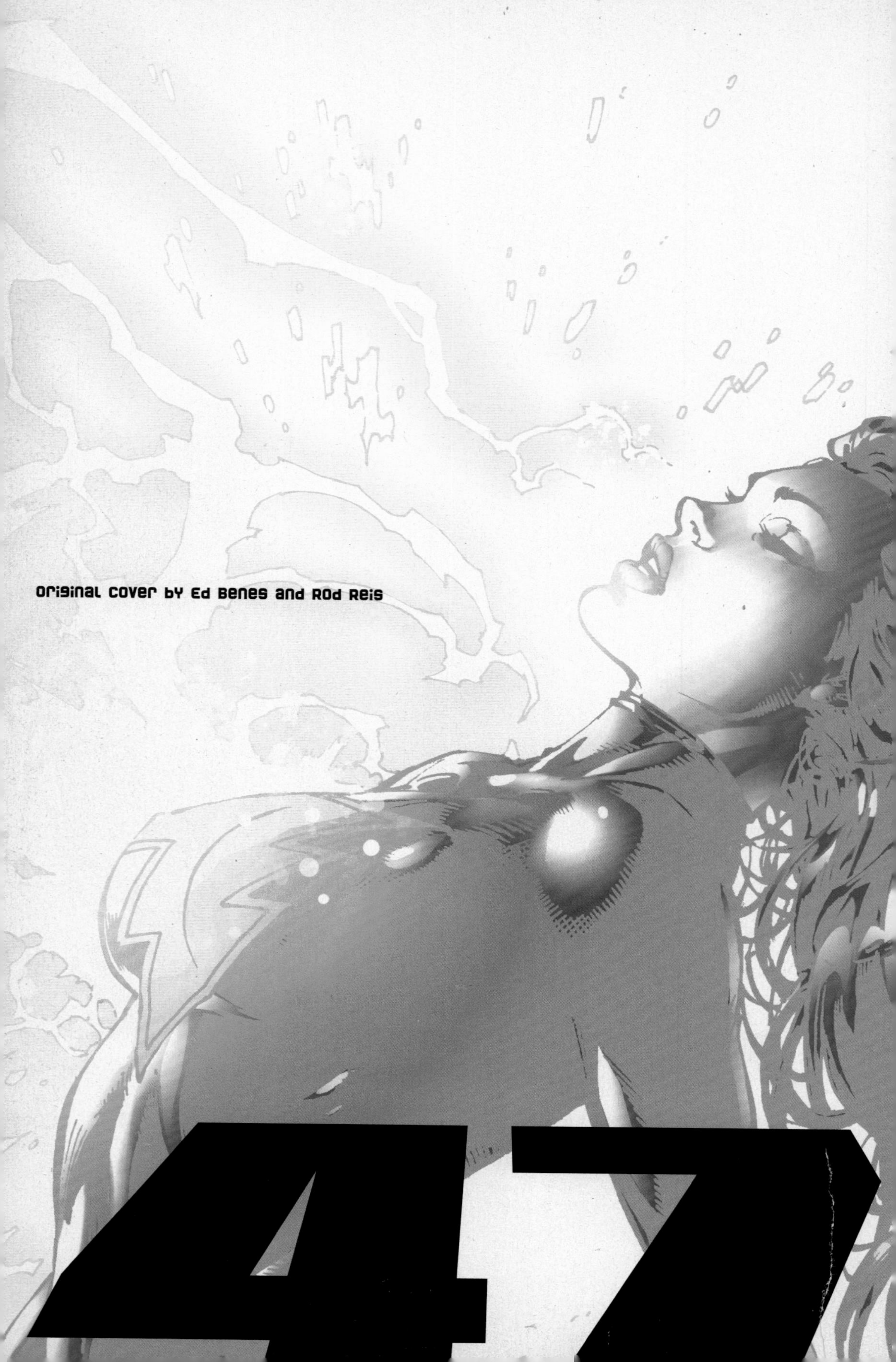

original cover by Ed Benes and Rod Reis

47

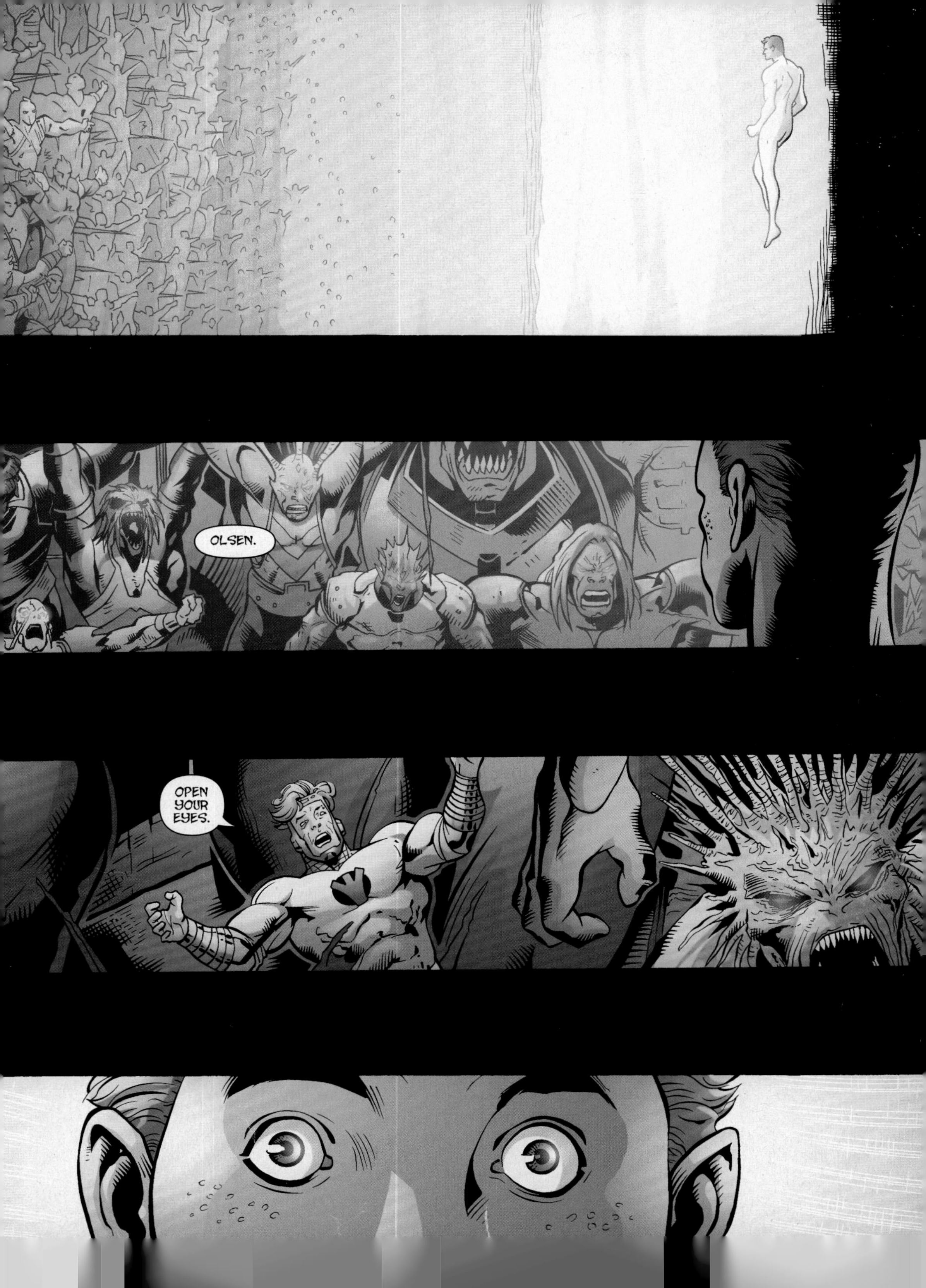
OLSEN.
OPEN YOUR EYES.

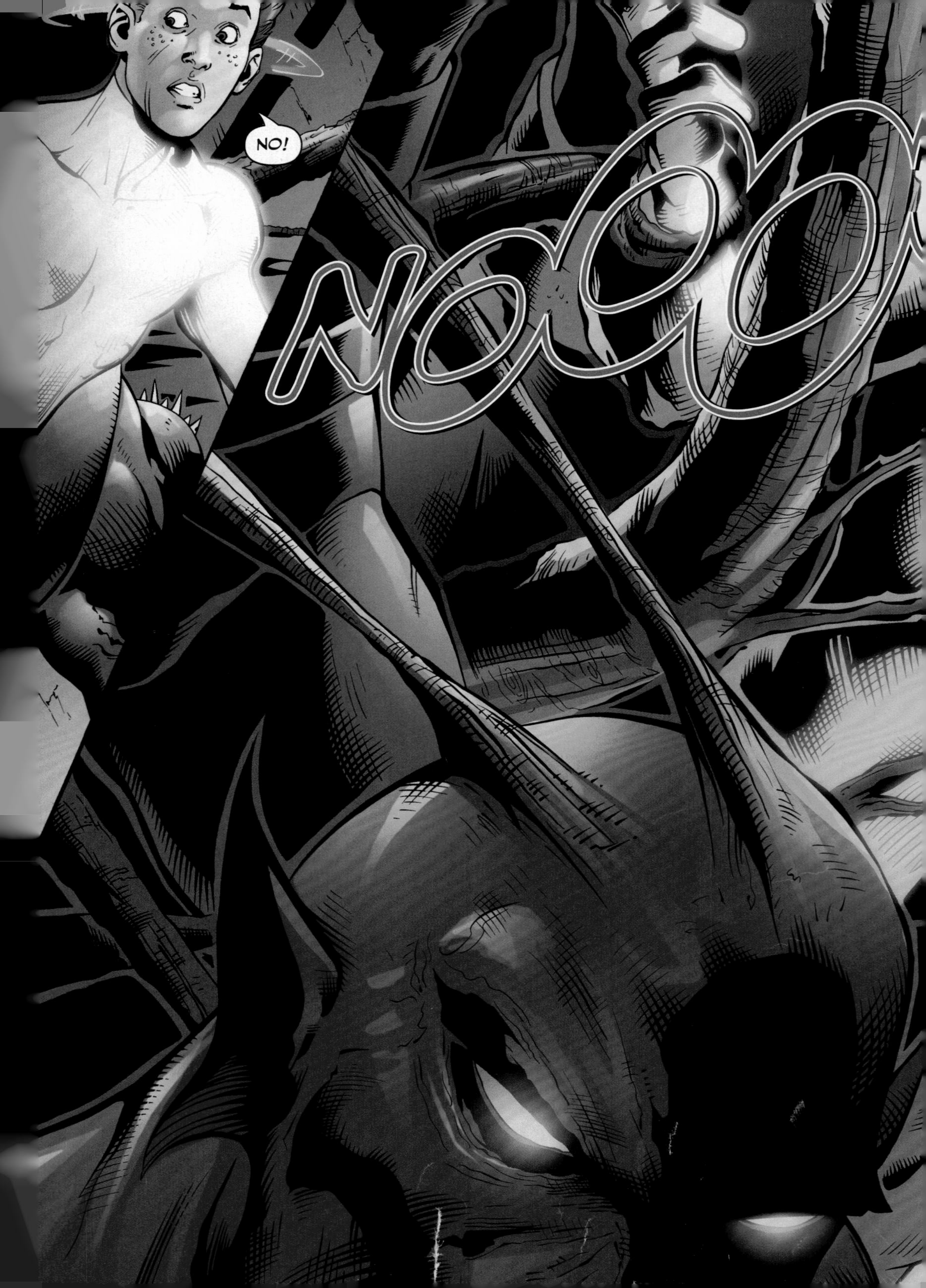
NO!
NOOOO

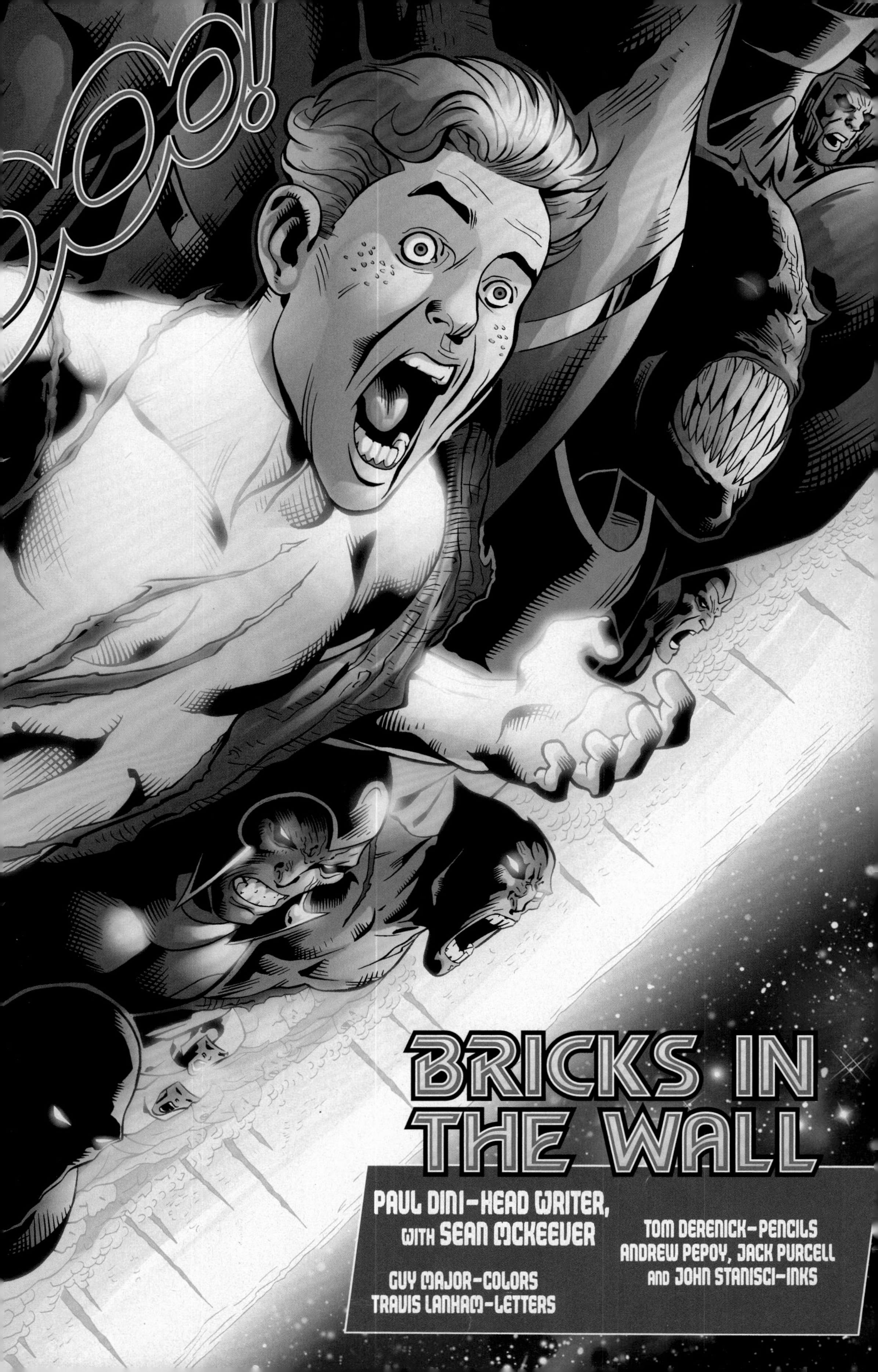

...OOO!
BRICKS IN THE WALL
PAUL DINI–HEAD WRITER, WITH SEAN MCKEEVER
TOM DERENICK–PENCILS
ANDREW PEPOY, JACK PURCELL AND JOHN STANISCI–INKS
GUY MAJOR–COLORS
TRAVIS LANHAM–LETTERS

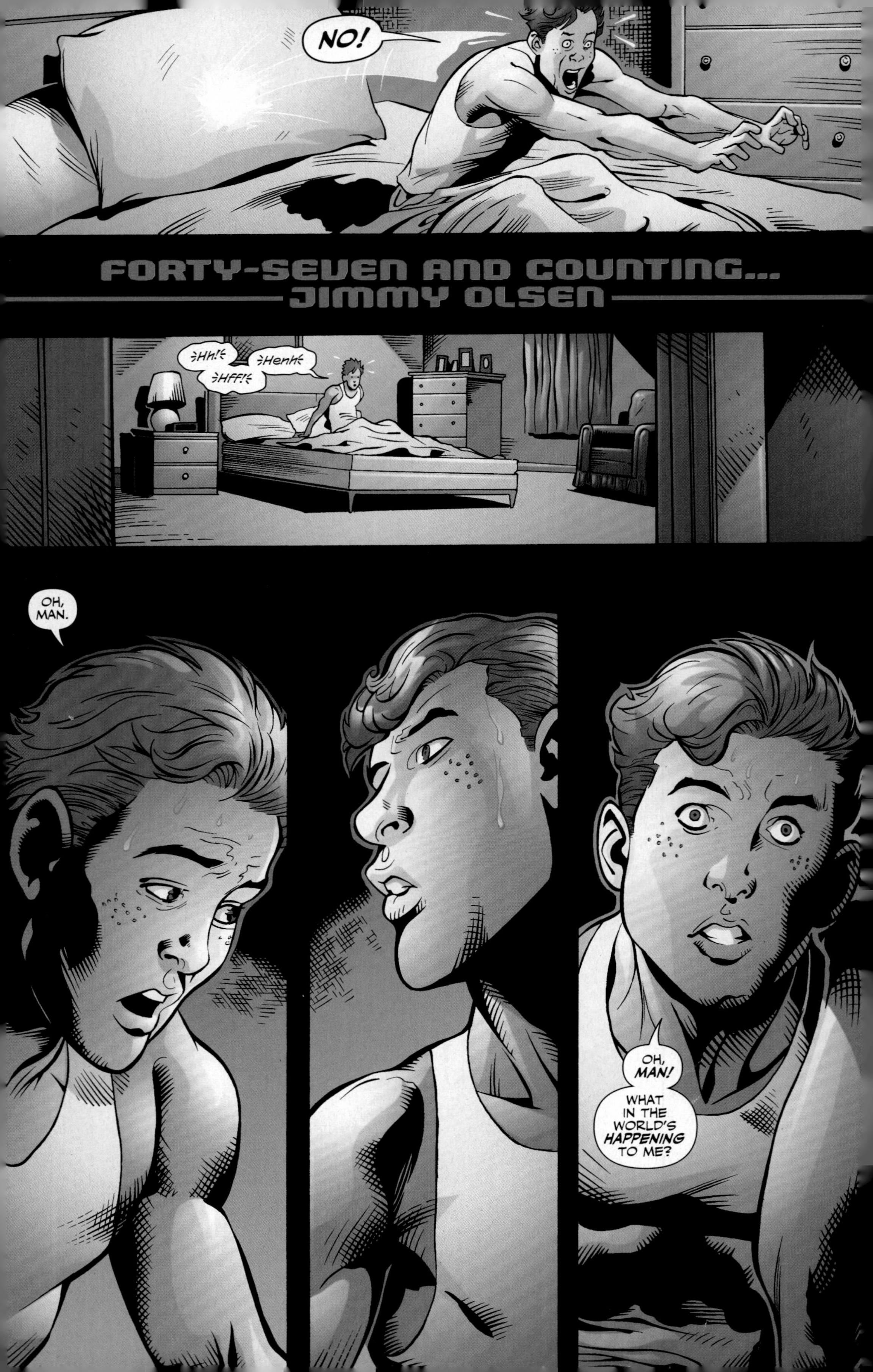
NO!
FORTY-SEVEN AND COUNTING...
JIMMY OLSEN
Hh!
Hff!
Henh
OH, MAN.
OH, MAN!
WHAT IN THE WORLD'S HAPPENING TO ME?

METROPOLIS.

DAILY ☆ STAR —
EVEN GODS DIE !!!

GOTHAM GAZETTE
COP KILLER STILL AT LARGE!

UH-OH.

EWSWEEK — IME — ANDYO

VISION — TEEN

-ASIA- — WOMEN

WELL — FITNESS FORM

I'M IN *SUCH* DEEP--

UNIVERSE — HER

SCIENTIFIC UNIVERSE

SWI

HOLLY ROBINSON

HEY, BABY, '*SUP!*

LOOK LIKE YOU *NEW* IN TOWN. NEED A *JOB?* NEED A PLACE TO *STAY?*

GET LOST.

HEY, YOU KNOW, I GOT *LOADSA* WORK FOR A GIRL'S INTO *FETISH* STUFF LIKE THAT!

YEAH...

...*NOW* WE'RE TALKIN'--

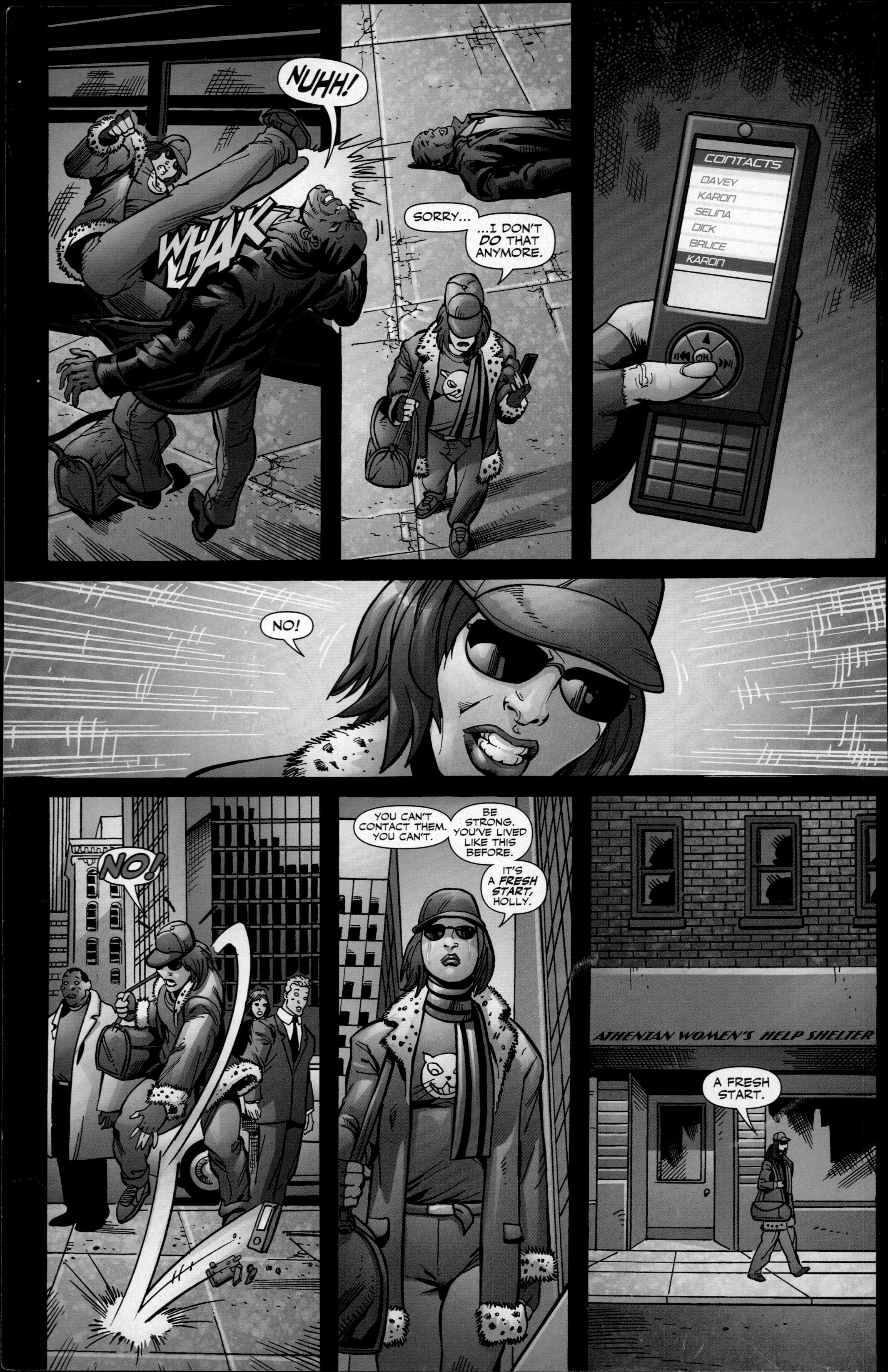
NUHH!
WHAK
SORRY...
...I DON'T DO THAT ANYMORE.
CONTACTS
DAVEY
KARON
SELINA
DICK
BRUCE
KARON
OK
NO!
NO!
YOU CAN'T CONTACT THEM. YOU CAN'T.
BE STRONG. YOU'VE LIVED LIKE THIS BEFORE.
IT'S A FRESH START, HOLLY.
ATHENIAN WOMEN'S HELP SHELTER
A FRESH START.

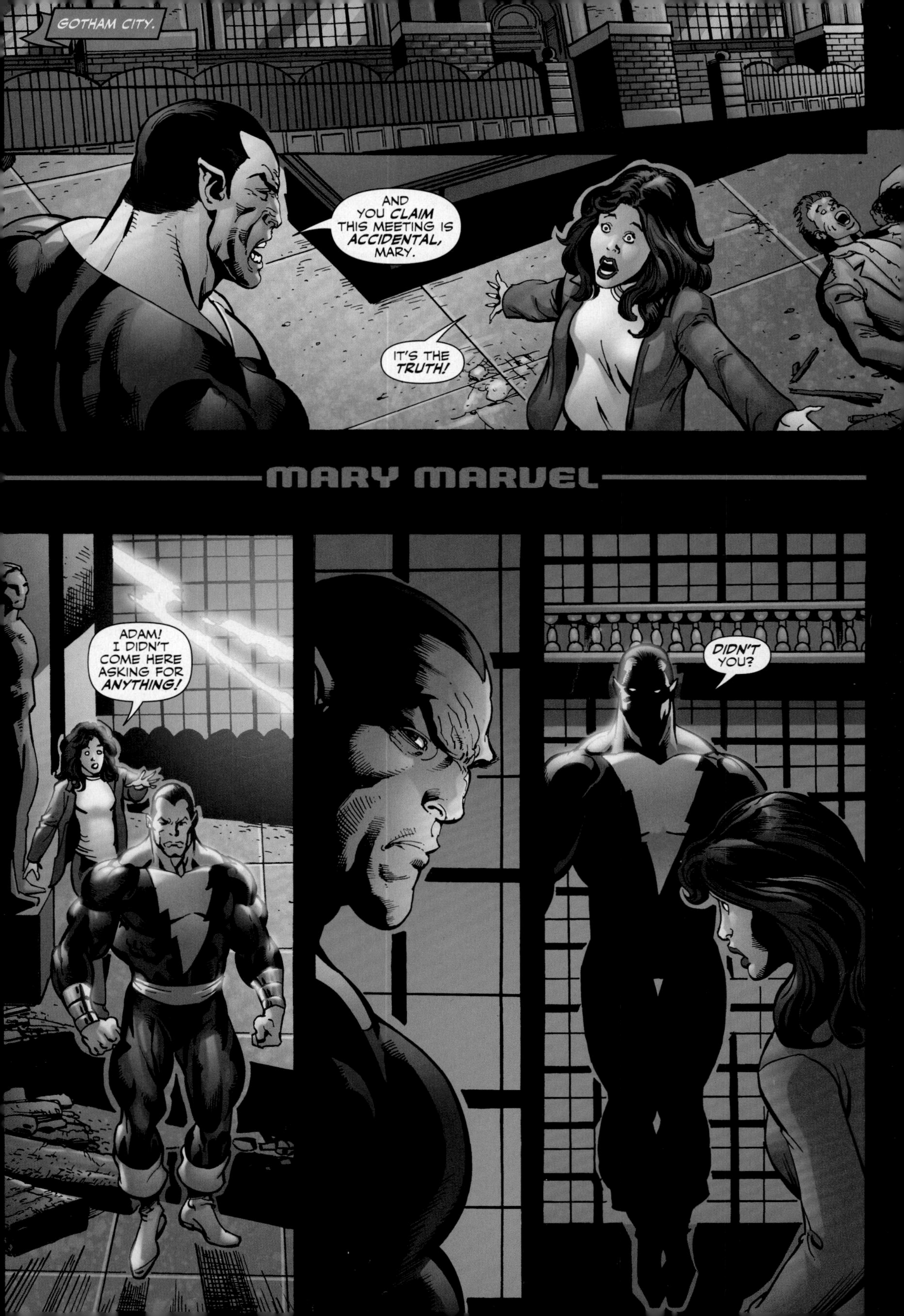
GOTHAM CITY.
AND YOU CLAIM THIS MEETING IS ACCIDENTAL, MARY.
IT'S THE TRUTH!
MARY MARVEL
ADAM! I DIDN'T COME HERE ASKING FOR ANYTHING!
DIDN'T YOU?

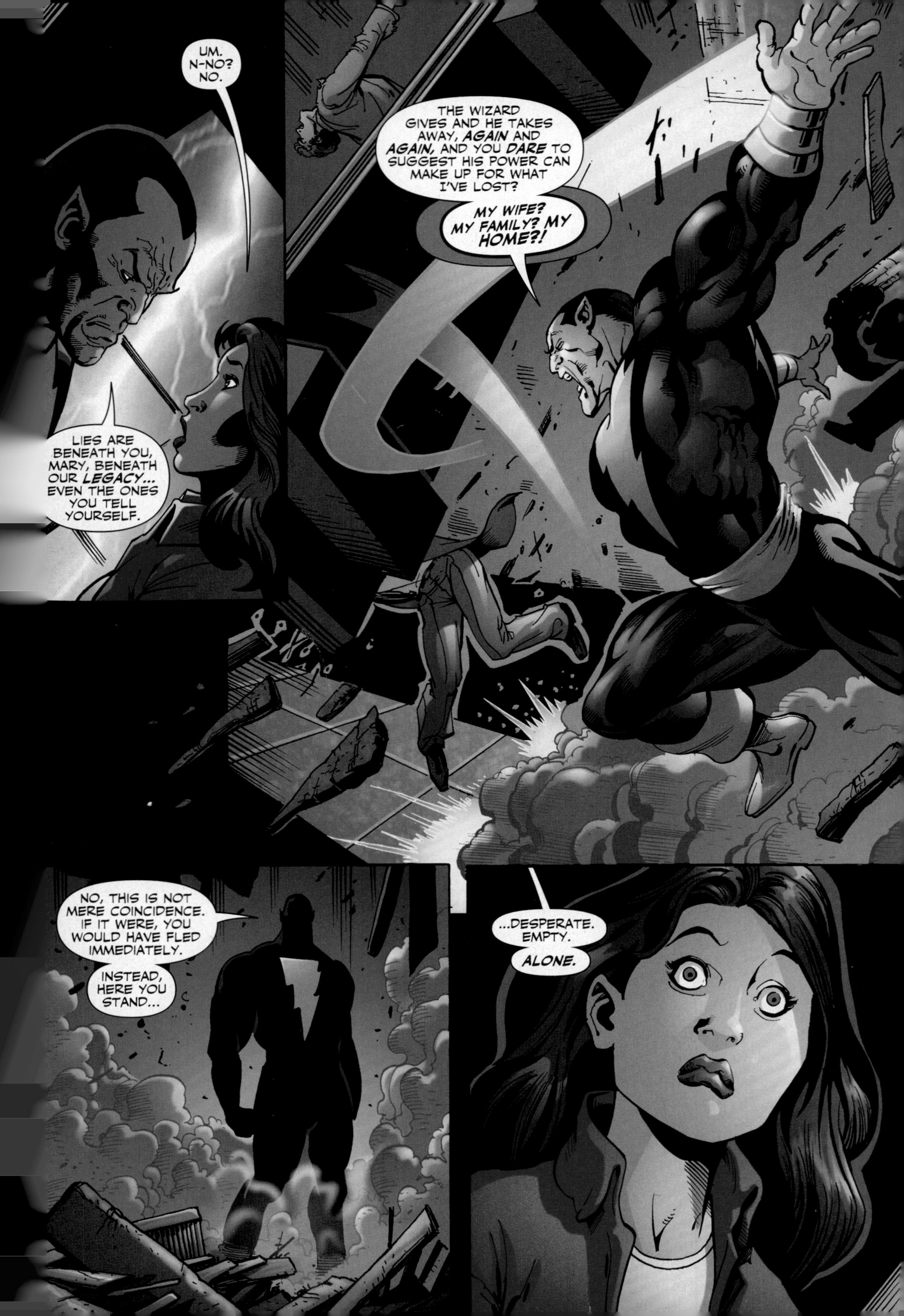
UM. N-NO? NO.
LIES ARE BENEATH YOU, MARY, BENEATH OUR *LEGACY*... EVEN THE ONES YOU TELL YOURSELF.
THE WIZARD GIVES AND HE TAKES AWAY, *AGAIN* AND *AGAIN*, AND YOU *DARE* TO SUGGEST HIS POWER CAN MAKE UP FOR WHAT I'VE LOST?
MY WIFE? MY FAMILY? MY HOME?!
NO, THIS IS NOT MERE COINCIDENCE. IF IT WERE, YOU WOULD HAVE FLED IMMEDIATELY.
INSTEAD, HERE YOU STAND...
...DESPERATE. EMPTY.
ALONE.

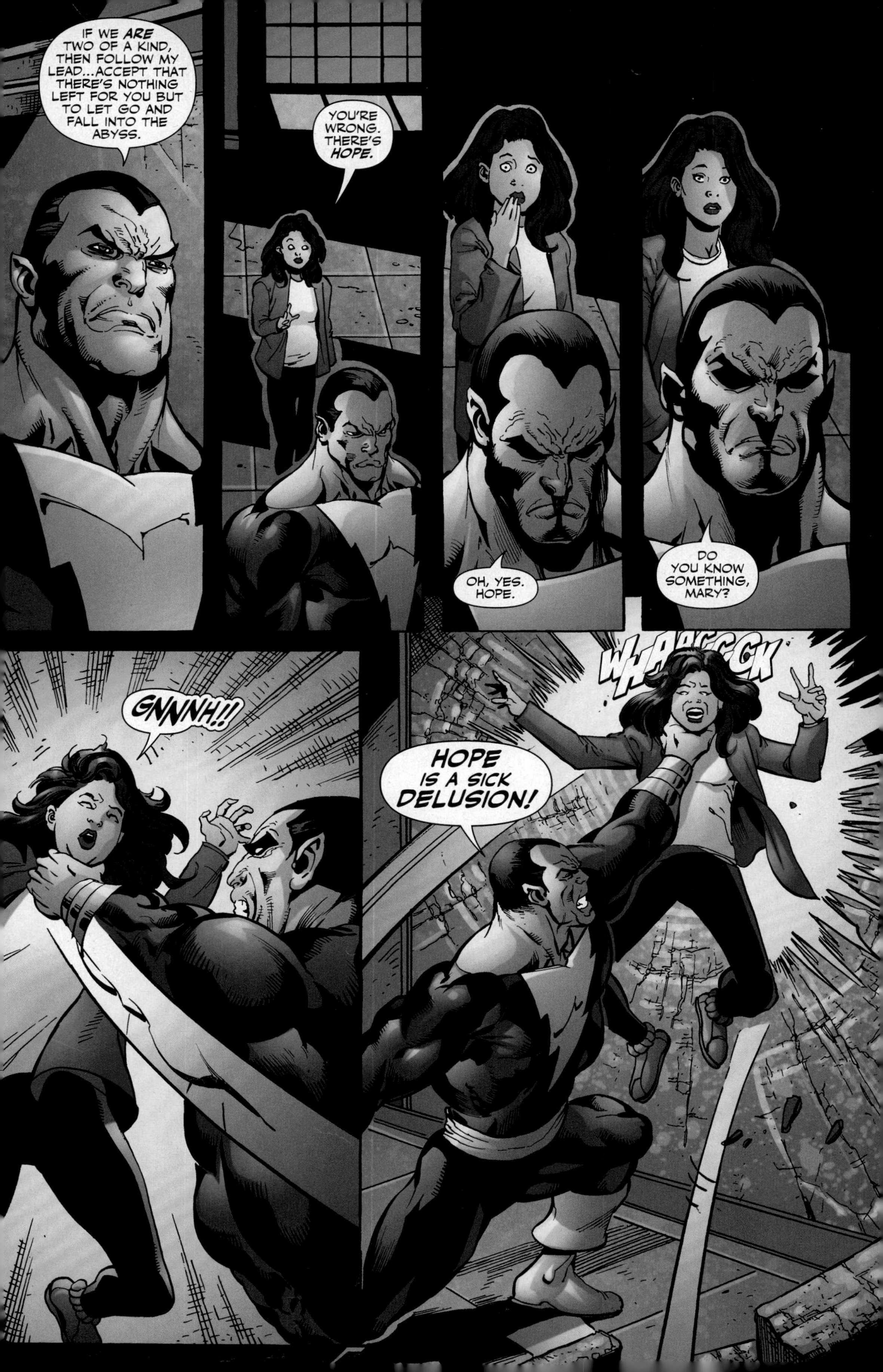

IF WE ARE TWO OF A KIND, THEN FOLLOW MY LEAD...ACCEPT THAT THERE'S NOTHING LEFT FOR YOU BUT TO LET GO AND FALL INTO THE ABYSS.
YOU'RE WRONG. THERE'S HOPE.
OH, YES. HOPE.
DO YOU KNOW SOMETHING, MARY?
GNNNH!!
WHAAACCK
HOPE IS A SICK DELUSION!

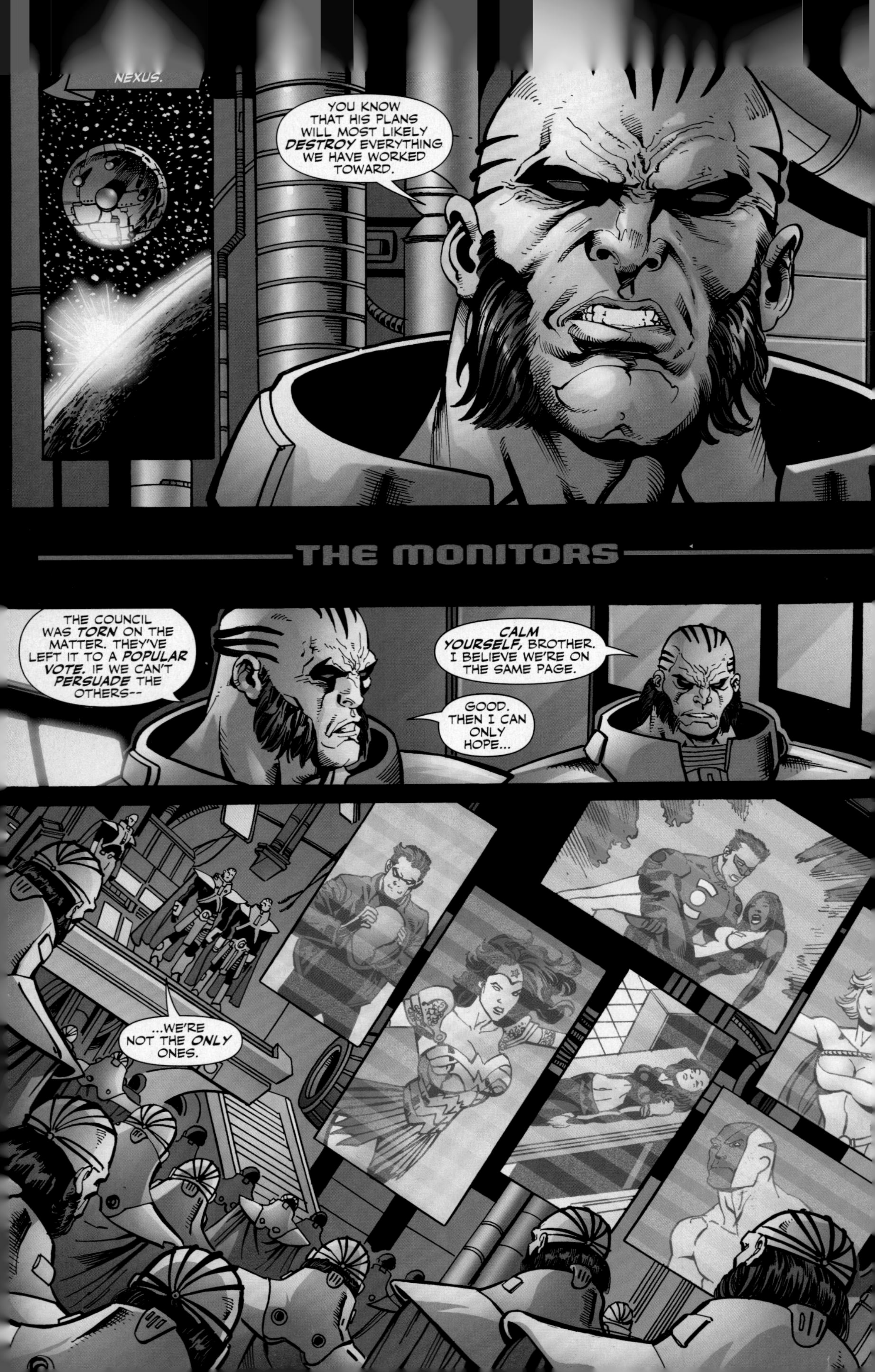
NEXUS.
YOU KNOW THAT HIS PLANS WILL MOST LIKELY DESTROY EVERYTHING WE HAVE WORKED TOWARD.
THE MONITORS
THE COUNCIL WAS TORN ON THE MATTER. THEY'VE LEFT IT TO A POPULAR VOTE. IF WE CAN'T PERSUADE THE OTHERS--
CALM YOURSELF, BROTHER. I BELIEVE WE'RE ON THE SAME PAGE.
GOOD. THEN I CAN ONLY HOPE...
...WE'RE NOT THE ONLY ONES.

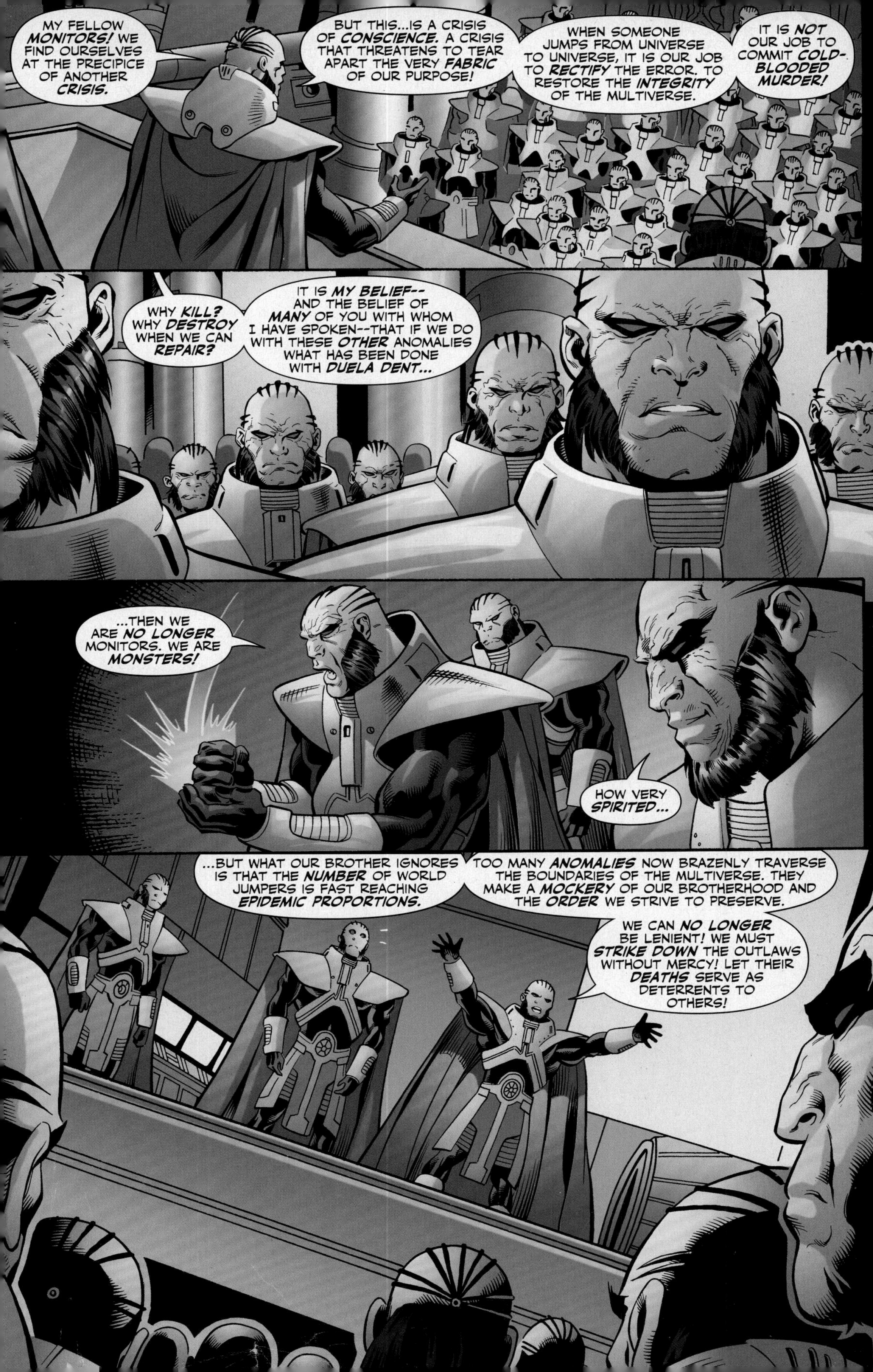
MY FELLOW MONITORS! WE FIND OURSELVES AT THE PRECIPICE OF ANOTHER CRISIS.
BUT THIS...IS A CRISIS OF CONSCIENCE. A CRISIS THAT THREATENS TO TEAR APART THE VERY FABRIC OF OUR PURPOSE!
WHEN SOMEONE JUMPS FROM UNIVERSE TO UNIVERSE, IT IS OUR JOB TO RECTIFY THE ERROR. TO RESTORE THE INTEGRITY OF THE MULTIVERSE.
IT IS NOT OUR JOB TO COMMIT COLD-BLOODED MURDER!
WHY KILL? WHY DESTROY WHEN WE CAN REPAIR?
IT IS MY BELIEF-- AND THE BELIEF OF MANY OF YOU WITH WHOM I HAVE SPOKEN--THAT IF WE DO WITH THESE OTHER ANOMALIES WHAT HAS BEEN DONE WITH DUELA DENT...
...THEN WE ARE NO LONGER MONITORS. WE ARE MONSTERS!
HOW VERY SPIRITED...
...BUT WHAT OUR BROTHER IGNORES IS THAT THE NUMBER OF WORLD JUMPERS IS FAST REACHING EPIDEMIC PROPORTIONS.
TOO MANY ANOMALIES NOW BRAZENLY TRAVERSE THE BOUNDARIES OF THE MULTIVERSE. THEY MAKE A MOCKERY OF OUR BROTHERHOOD AND THE ORDER WE STRIVE TO PRESERVE.
WE CAN NO LONGER BE LENIENT! WE MUST STRIKE DOWN THE OUTLAWS WITHOUT MERCY! LET THEIR DEATHS SERVE AS DETERRENTS TO OTHERS!

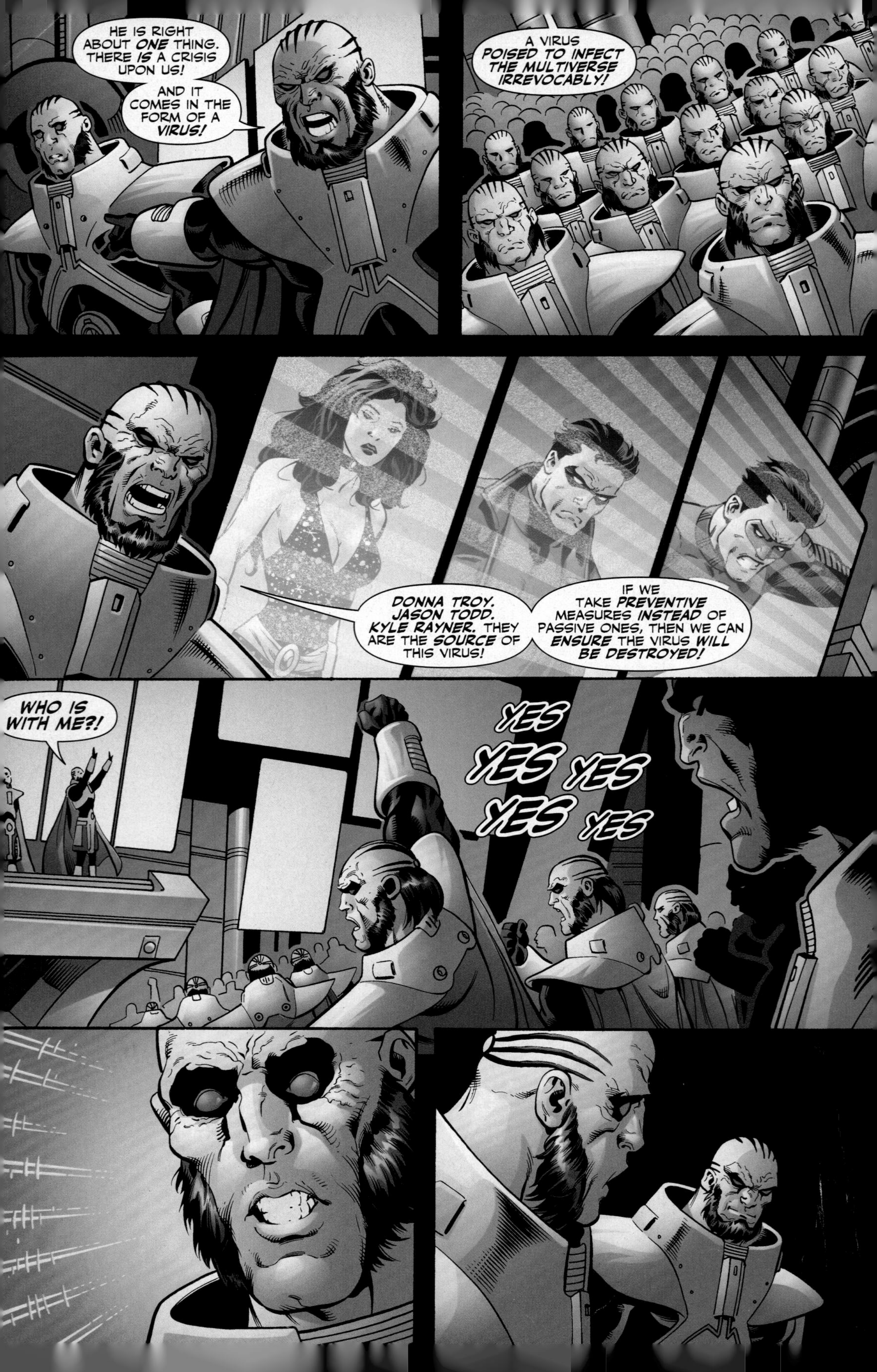
HE IS RIGHT ABOUT ONE THING. THERE IS A CRISIS UPON US!
AND IT COMES IN THE FORM OF A VIRUS!
A VIRUS POISED TO INFECT THE MULTIVERSE IRREVOCABLY!
DONNA TROY. JASON TODD. KYLE RAYNER. THEY ARE THE SOURCE OF THIS VIRUS!
IF WE TAKE PREVENTIVE MEASURES INSTEAD OF PASSIVE ONES, THEN WE CAN ENSURE THE VIRUS WILL BE DESTROYED!
WHO IS WITH ME?!
YES
YES YES
YES YES

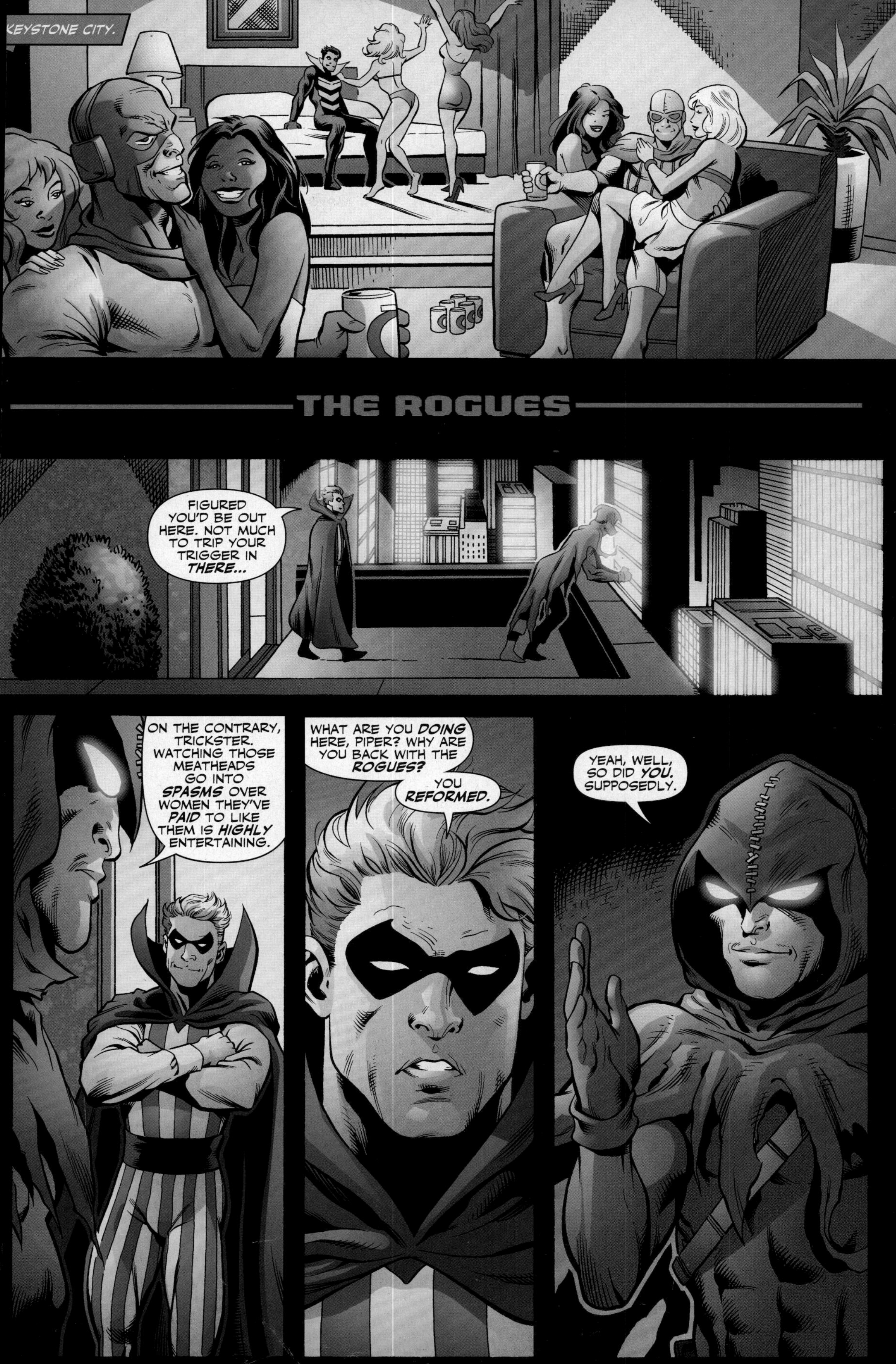
KEYSTONE CITY.
THE ROGUES
FIGURED YOU'D BE OUT HERE. NOT MUCH TO TRIP YOUR TRIGGER IN THERE...
ON THE CONTRARY, TRICKSTER. WATCHING THOSE MEATHEADS GO INTO SPASMS OVER WOMEN THEY'VE PAID TO LIKE THEM IS HIGHLY ENTERTAINING.
WHAT ARE YOU DOING HERE, PIPER? WHY ARE YOU BACK WITH THE ROGUES?
YOU REFORMED.
YEAH, WELL, SO DID YOU. SUPPOSEDLY.

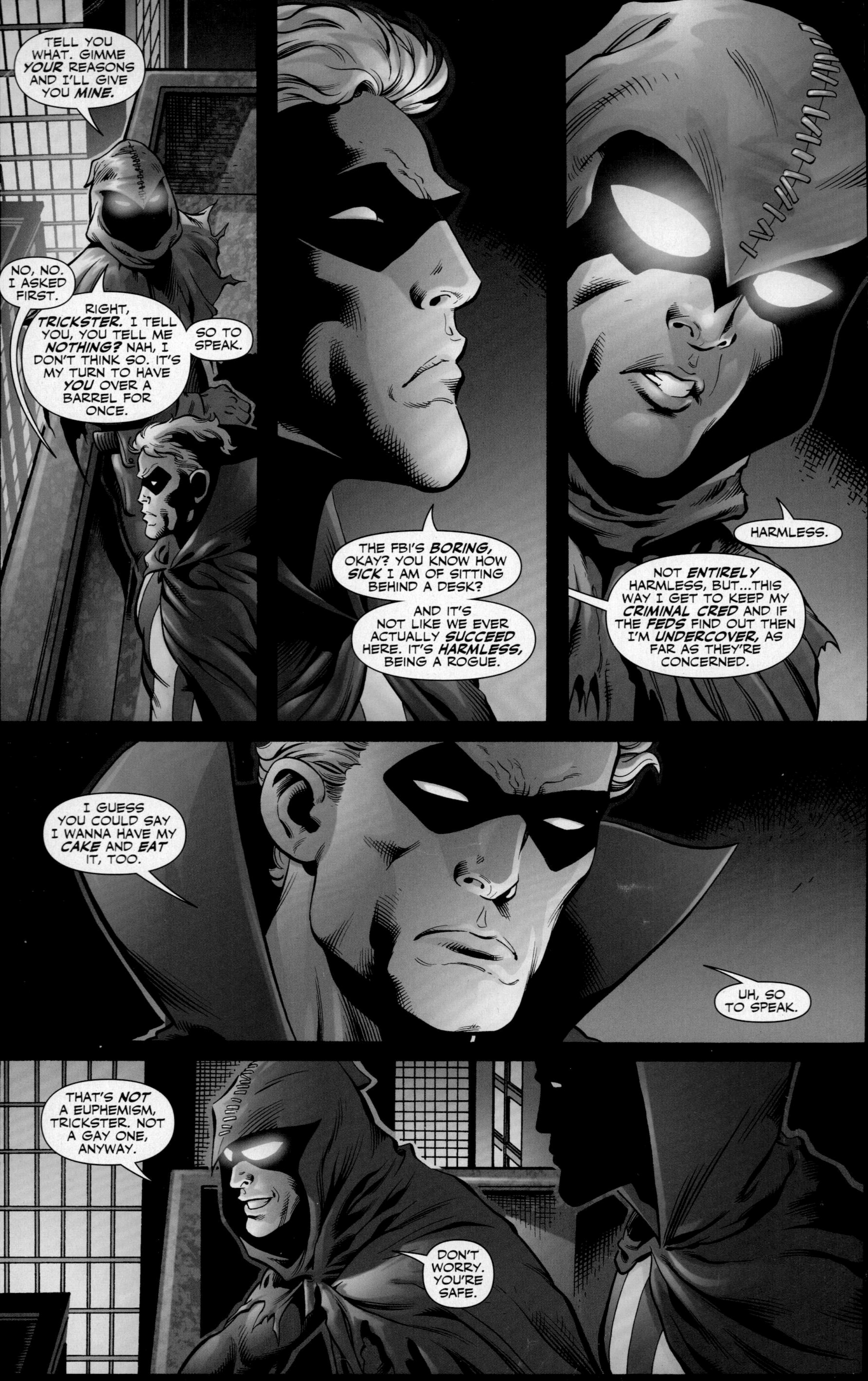

TELL YOU WHAT. GIMME YOUR REASONS AND I'LL GIVE YOU MINE.
NO, NO. I ASKED FIRST.
RIGHT, TRICKSTER. I TELL YOU, YOU TELL ME NOTHING? NAH, I DON'T THINK SO. IT'S MY TURN TO HAVE YOU OVER A BARREL FOR ONCE.
SO TO SPEAK.
THE FBI'S BORING, OKAY? YOU KNOW HOW SICK I AM OF SITTING BEHIND A DESK?
AND IT'S NOT LIKE WE EVER ACTUALLY SUCCEED HERE. IT'S HARMLESS, BEING A ROGUE.
HARMLESS.
NOT ENTIRELY HARMLESS, BUT...THIS WAY I GET TO KEEP MY CRIMINAL CRED AND IF THE FEDS FIND OUT THEN I'M UNDERCOVER, AS FAR AS THEY'RE CONCERNED.
I GUESS YOU COULD SAY I WANNA HAVE MY CAKE AND EAT IT, TOO.
UH, SO TO SPEAK.
THAT'S NOT A EUPHEMISM, TRICKSTER. NOT A GAY ONE, ANYWAY.
DON'T WORRY. YOU'RE SAFE.

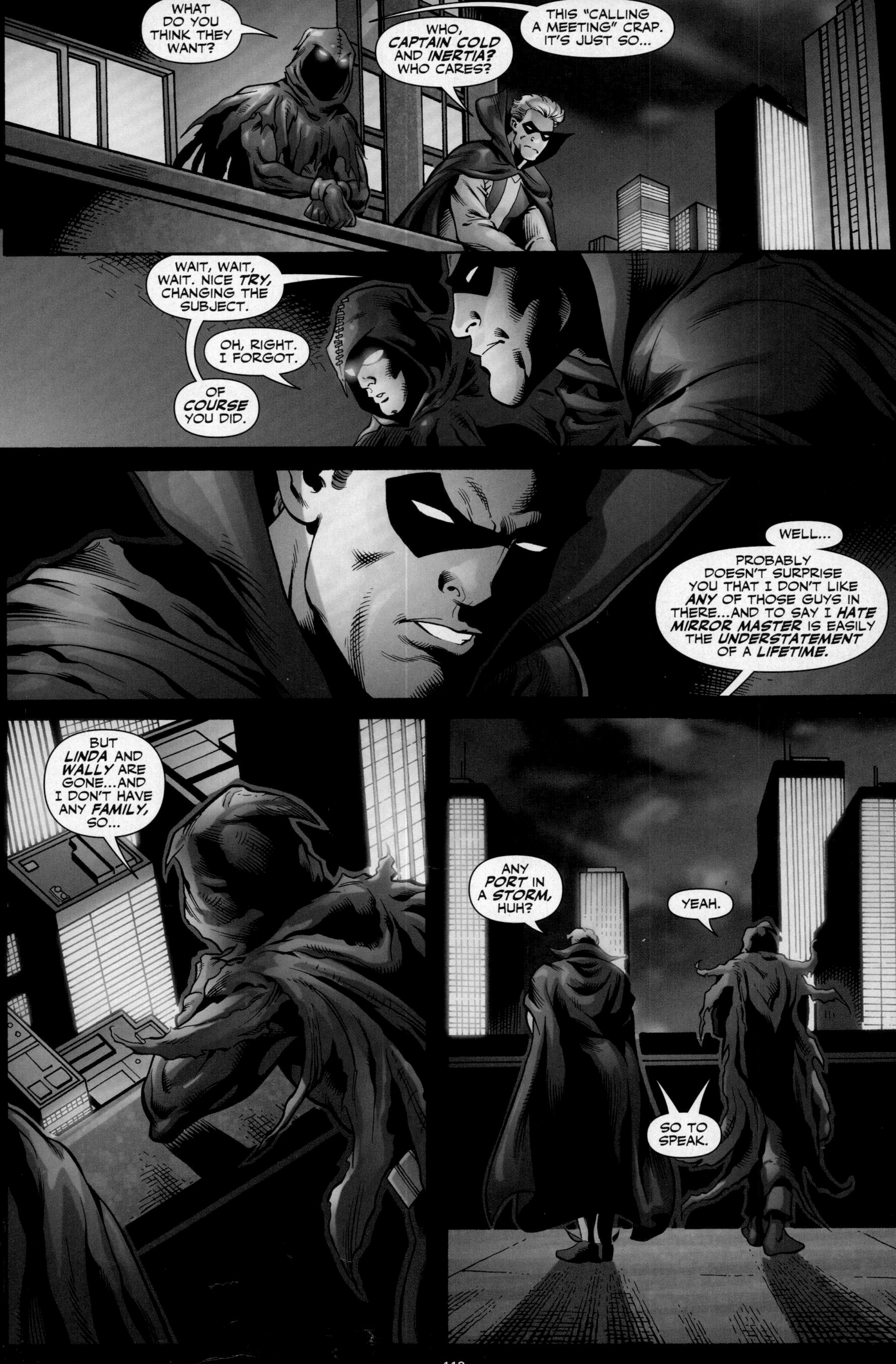
WHAT DO YOU THINK THEY WANT?
WHO, CAPTAIN COLD AND INERTIA? WHO CARES?
THIS "CALLING A MEETING" CRAP. IT'S JUST SO...
WAIT, WAIT, WAIT. NICE TRY, CHANGING THE SUBJECT.
OH, RIGHT. I FORGOT.
OF COURSE YOU DID.
WELL...
PROBABLY DOESN'T SURPRISE YOU THAT I DON'T LIKE ANY OF THOSE GUYS IN THERE...AND TO SAY I HATE MIRROR MASTER IS EASILY THE UNDERSTATEMENT OF A LIFETIME.
BUT LINDA AND WALLY ARE GONE...AND I DON'T HAVE ANY FAMILY, SO...
ANY PORT IN A STORM, HUH?
YEAH.
SO TO SPEAK.

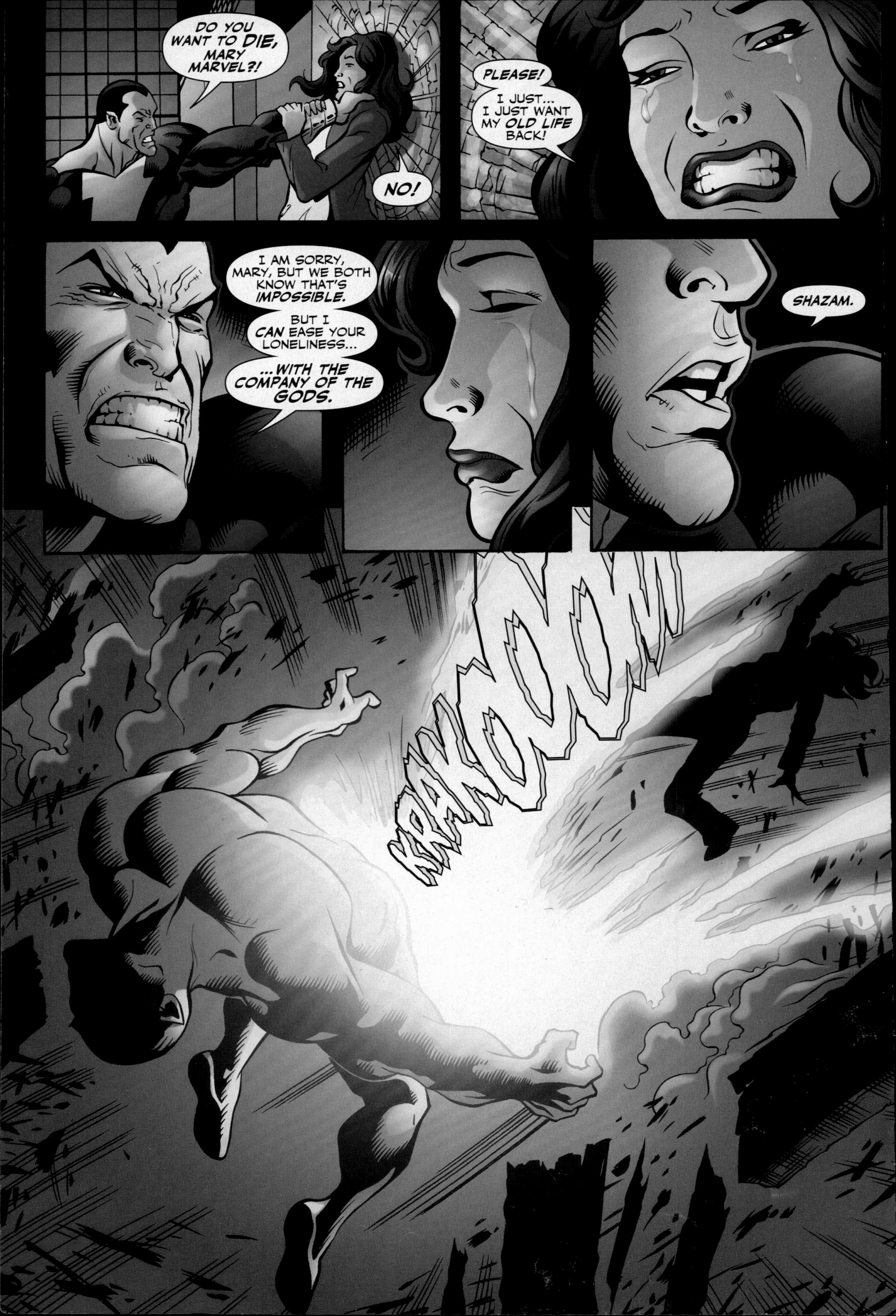
DO YOU WANT TO DIE, MARY MARVEL?!
NO!
PLEASE!
I JUST... I JUST WANT MY OLD LIFE BACK!
I AM SORRY, MARY, BUT WE BOTH KNOW THAT'S IMPOSSIBLE.
BUT I CAN EASE YOUR LONELINESS...
...WITH THE COMPANY OF THE GODS.
SHAZAM.
KRAKOOOM

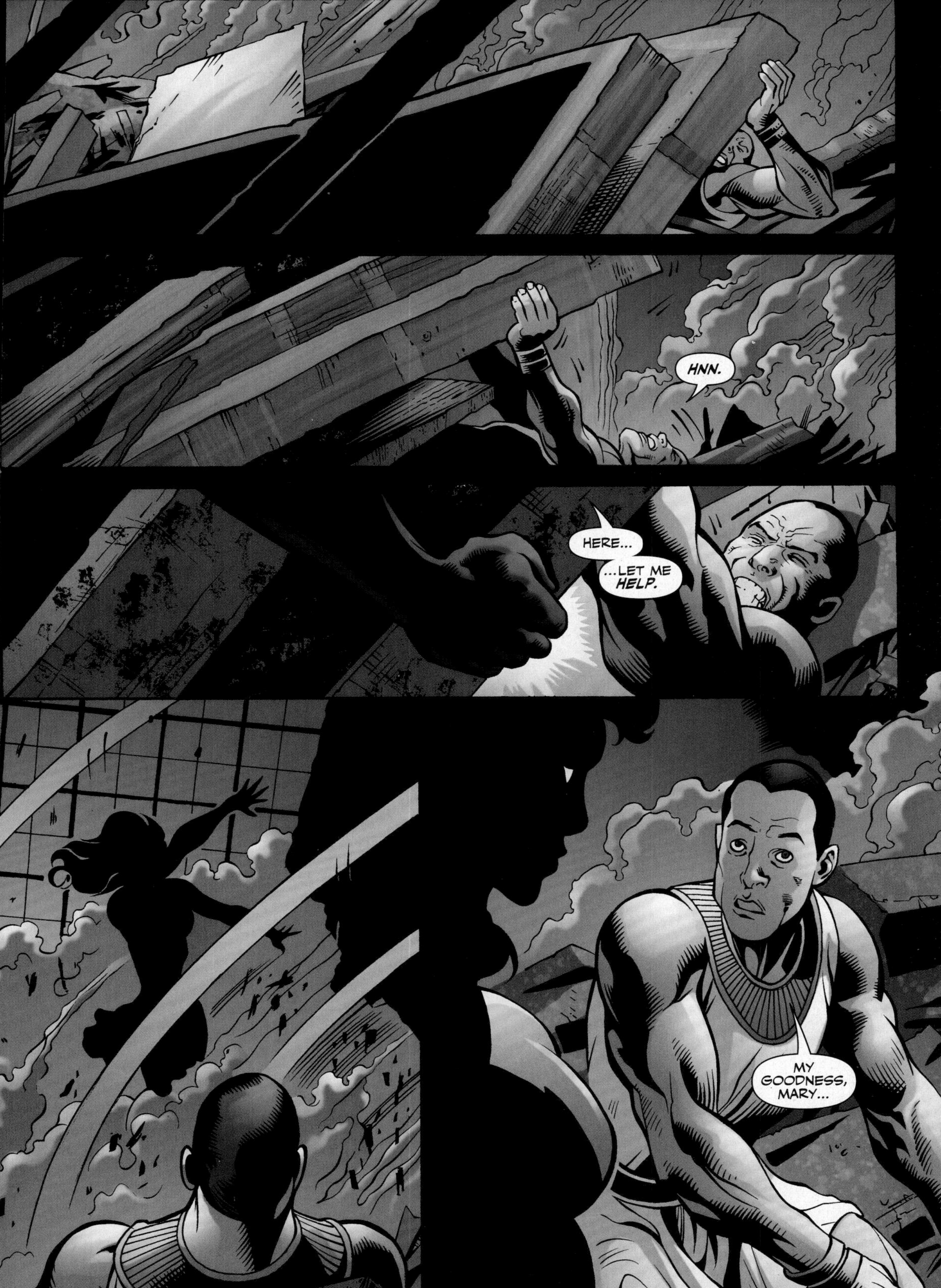
HNN.
HERE...
...LET ME HELP.
MY GOODNESS, MARY...

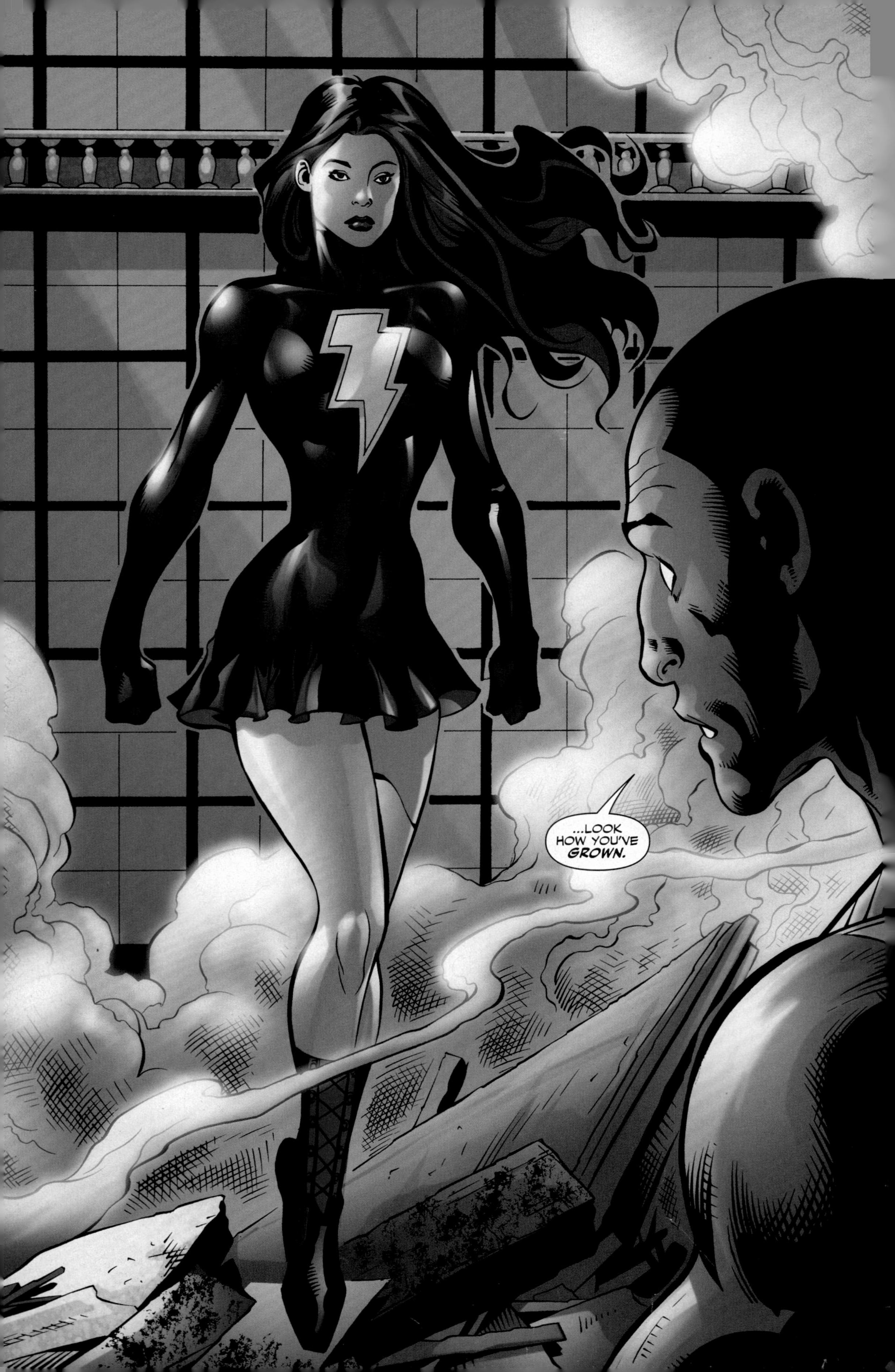
...LOOK HOW YOU'VE GROWN.

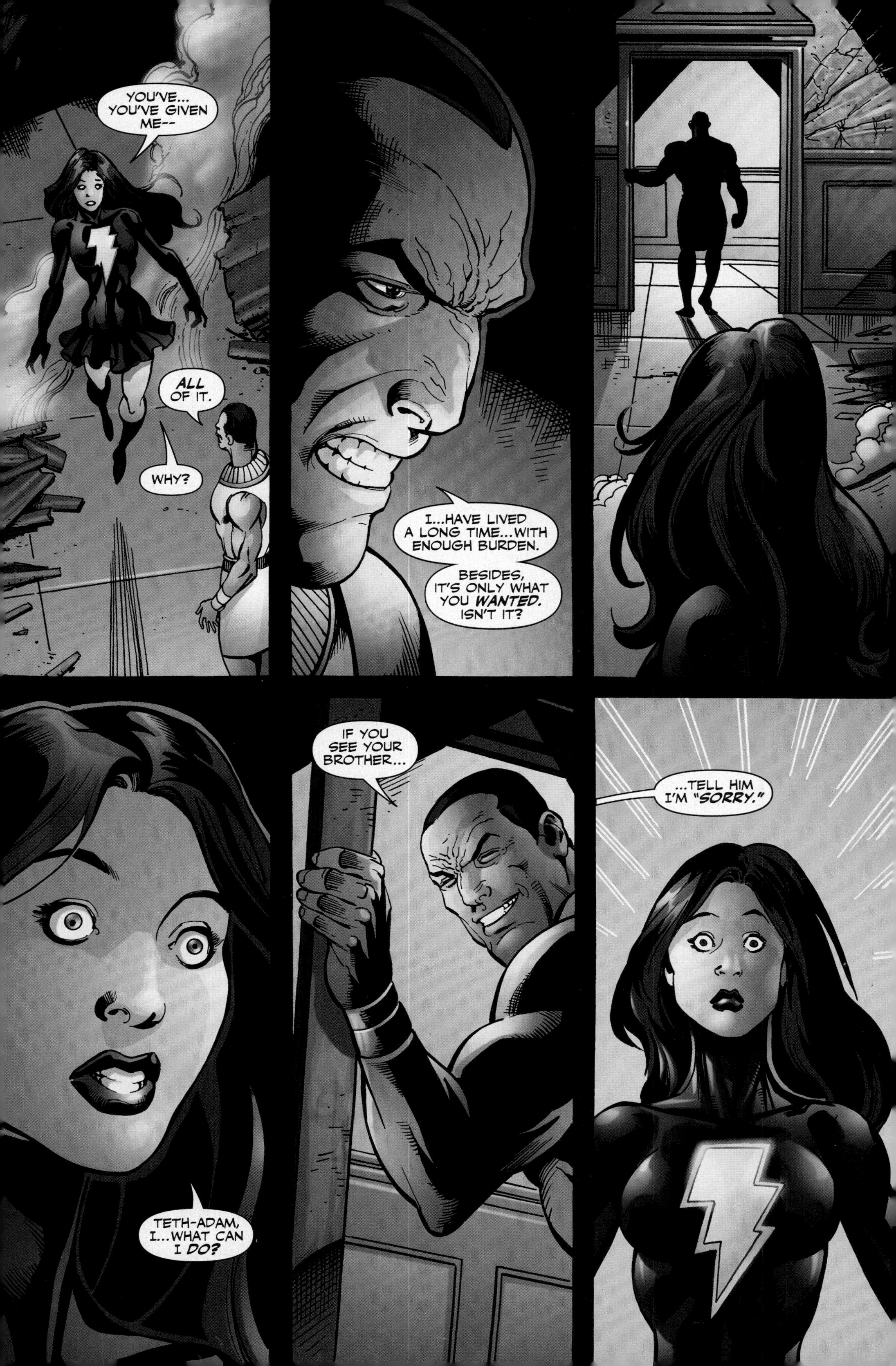
YOU'VE... YOU'VE GIVEN ME--
ALL OF IT.
WHY?
I...HAVE LIVED A LONG TIME...WITH ENOUGH BURDEN.
BESIDES, IT'S ONLY WHAT YOU WANTED. ISN'T IT?
TETH-ADAM, I...WHAT CAN I DO?
IF YOU SEE YOUR BROTHER...
...TELL HIM I'M "SORRY."

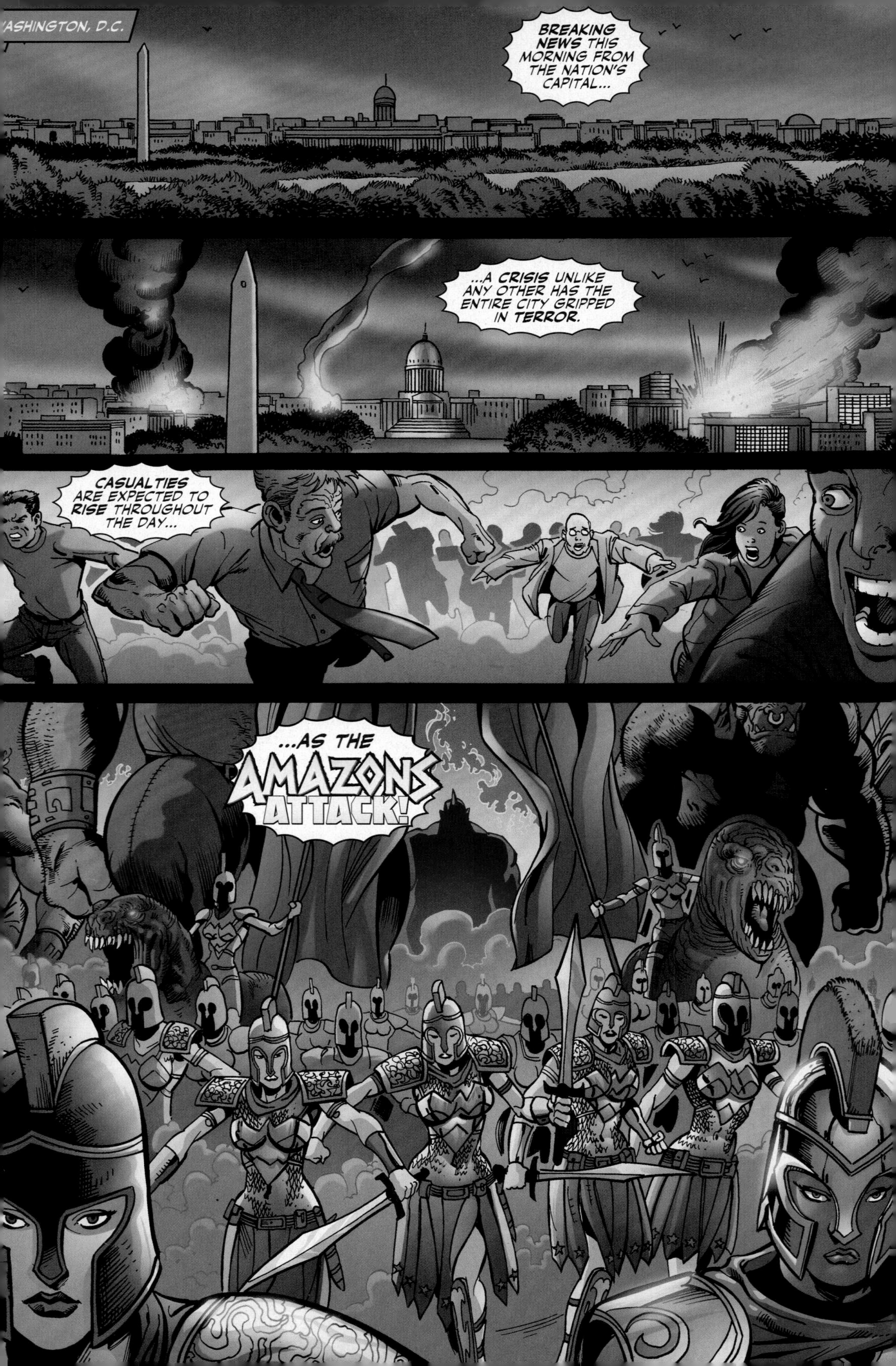
WASHINGTON, D.C.
BREAKING NEWS THIS MORNING FROM THE NATION'S CAPITAL...
...A CRISIS UNLIKE ANY OTHER HAS THE ENTIRE CITY GRIPPED IN TERROR.
CASUALTIES ARE EXPECTED TO RISE THROUGHOUT THE DAY...
...AS THE
AMAZONS ATTACK!

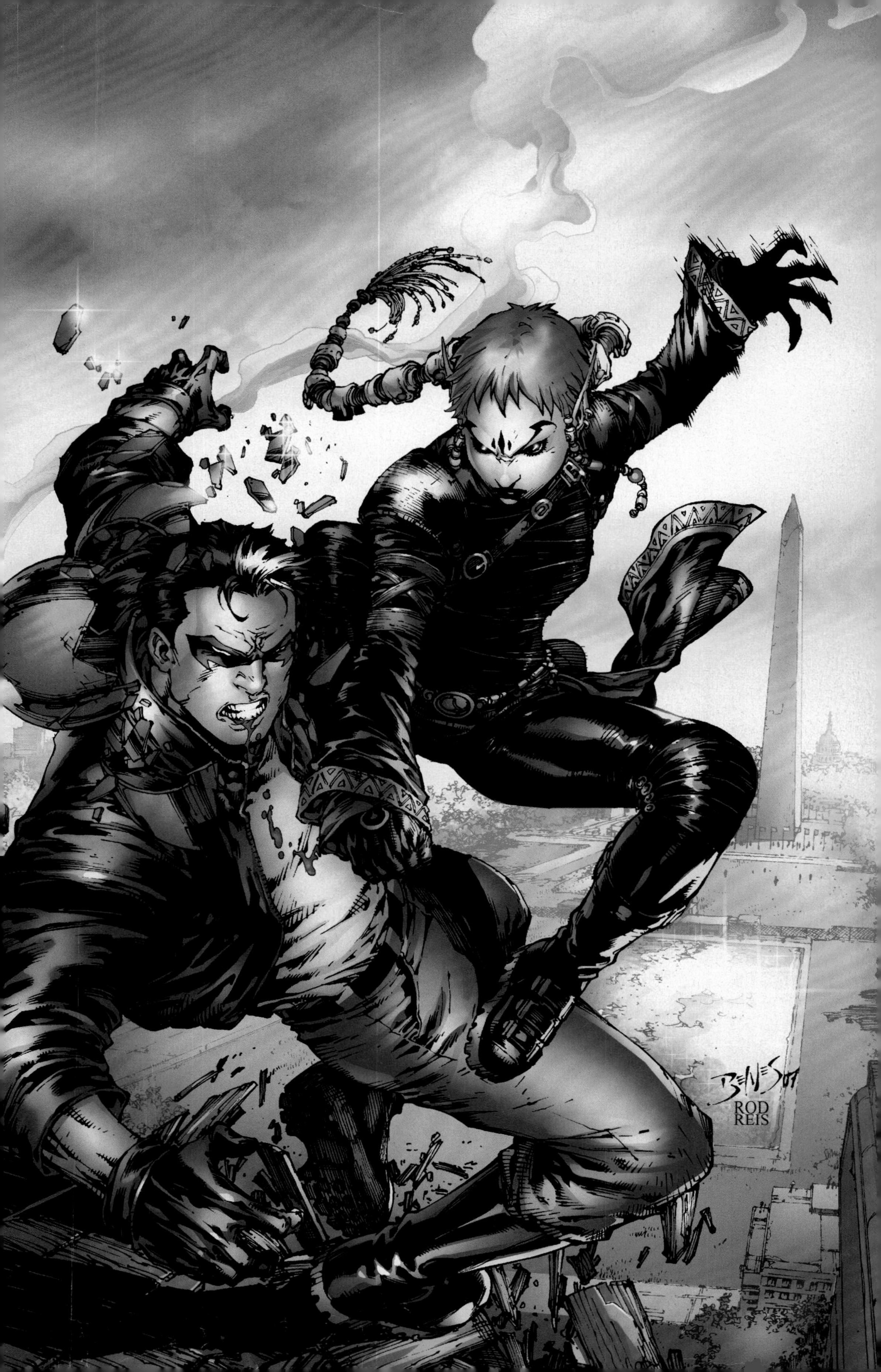
ROD
REIS

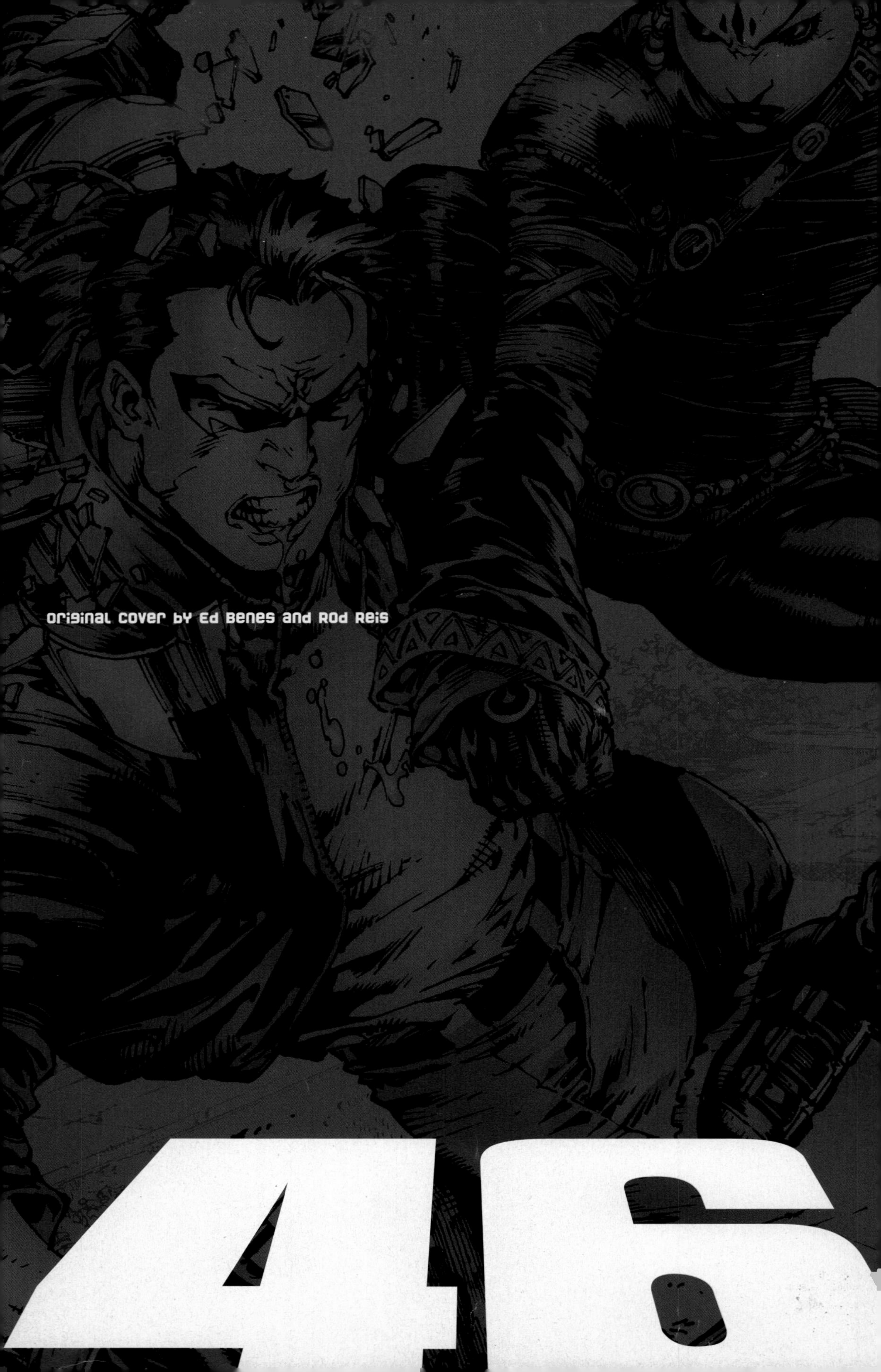

original cover by Ed Benes and Rod Reis

46

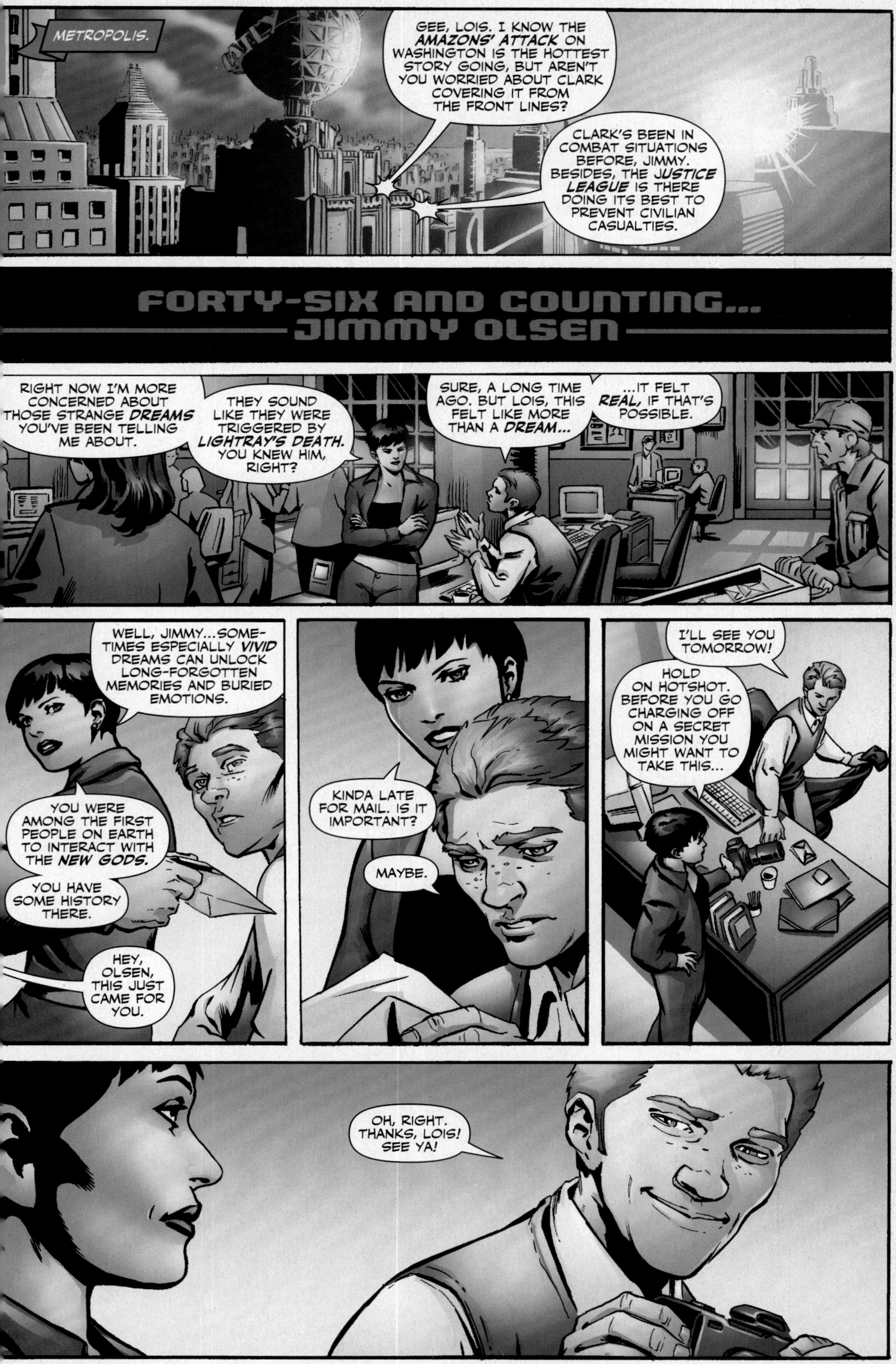
METROPOLIS.
GEE, LOIS. I KNOW THE AMAZONS' ATTACK ON WASHINGTON IS THE HOTTEST STORY GOING, BUT AREN'T YOU WORRIED ABOUT CLARK COVERING IT FROM THE FRONT LINES?
CLARK'S BEEN IN COMBAT SITUATIONS BEFORE, JIMMY. BESIDES, THE JUSTICE LEAGUE IS THERE DOING ITS BEST TO PREVENT CIVILIAN CASUALTIES.
FORTY-SIX AND COUNTING... JIMMY OLSEN
RIGHT NOW I'M MORE CONCERNED ABOUT THOSE STRANGE DREAMS YOU'VE BEEN TELLING ME ABOUT.
THEY SOUND LIKE THEY WERE TRIGGERED BY LIGHTRAY'S DEATH. YOU KNEW HIM, RIGHT?
SURE, A LONG TIME AGO. BUT LOIS, THIS FELT LIKE MORE THAN A DREAM...
...IT FELT REAL, IF THAT'S POSSIBLE.
WELL, JIMMY...SOME-TIMES ESPECIALLY VIVID DREAMS CAN UNLOCK LONG-FORGOTTEN MEMORIES AND BURIED EMOTIONS.
YOU WERE AMONG THE FIRST PEOPLE ON EARTH TO INTERACT WITH THE NEW GODS.
YOU HAVE SOME HISTORY THERE.
HEY, OLSEN, THIS JUST CAME FOR YOU.
KINDA LATE FOR MAIL. IS IT IMPORTANT?
MAYBE.
I'LL SEE YOU TOMORROW!
HOLD ON HOTSHOT. BEFORE YOU GO CHARGING OFF ON A SECRET MISSION YOU MIGHT WANT TO TAKE THIS...
OH, RIGHT. THANKS, LOIS! SEE YA!

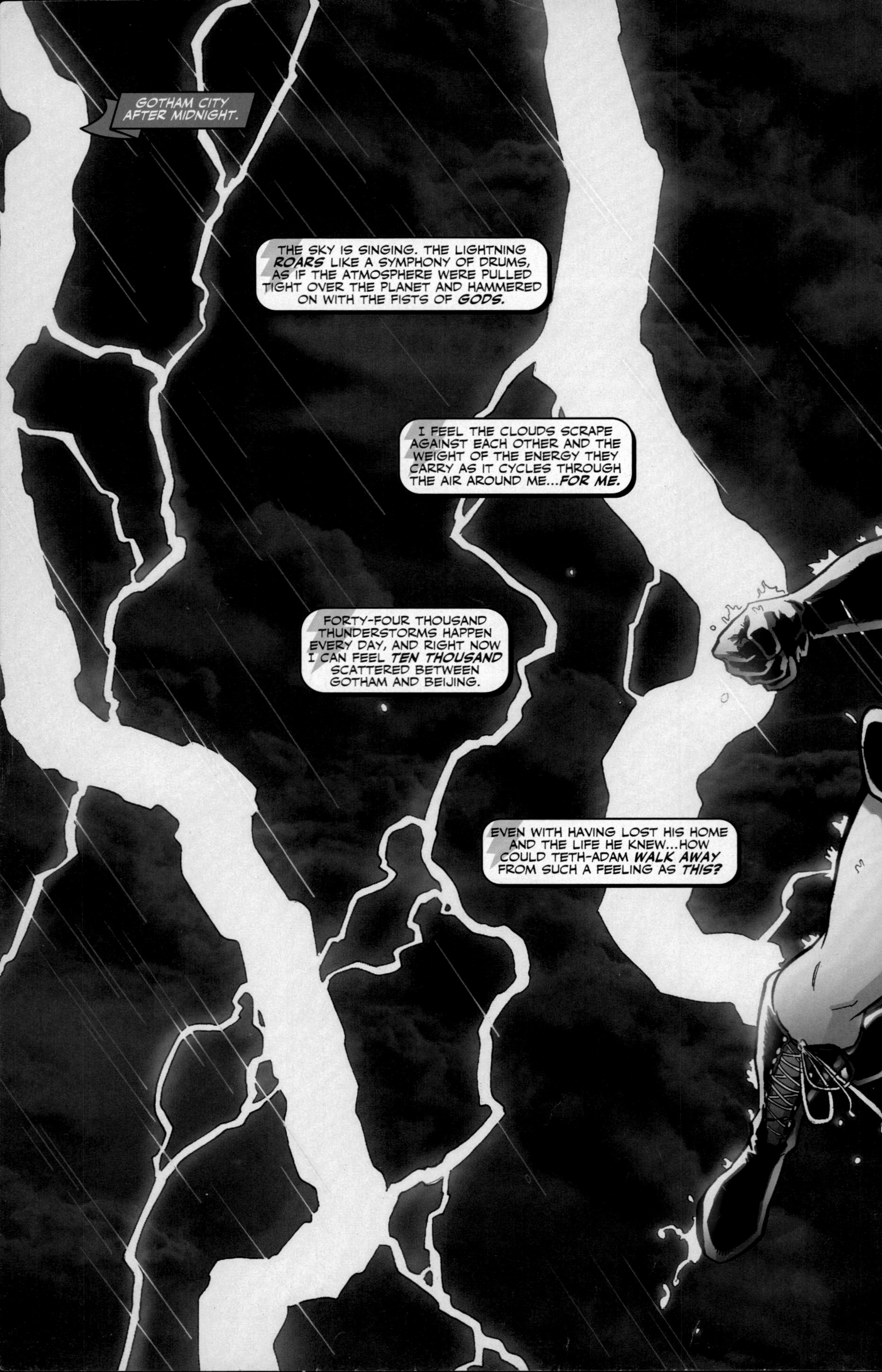
GOTHAM CITY AFTER MIDNIGHT.
THE SKY IS SINGING. THE LIGHTNING ROARS LIKE A SYMPHONY OF DRUMS, AS IF THE ATMOSPHERE WERE PULLED TIGHT OVER THE PLANET AND HAMMERED ON WITH THE FISTS OF GODS.
I FEEL THE CLOUDS SCRAPE AGAINST EACH OTHER AND THE WEIGHT OF THE ENERGY THEY CARRY AS IT CYCLES THROUGH THE AIR AROUND ME...FOR ME.
FORTY-FOUR THOUSAND THUNDERSTORMS HAPPEN EVERY DAY, AND RIGHT NOW I CAN FEEL TEN THOUSAND SCATTERED BETWEEN GOTHAM AND BEIJING.
EVEN WITH HAVING LOST HIS HOME AND THE LIFE HE KNEW...HOW COULD TETH-ADAM WALK AWAY FROM SUCH A FEELING AS THIS?

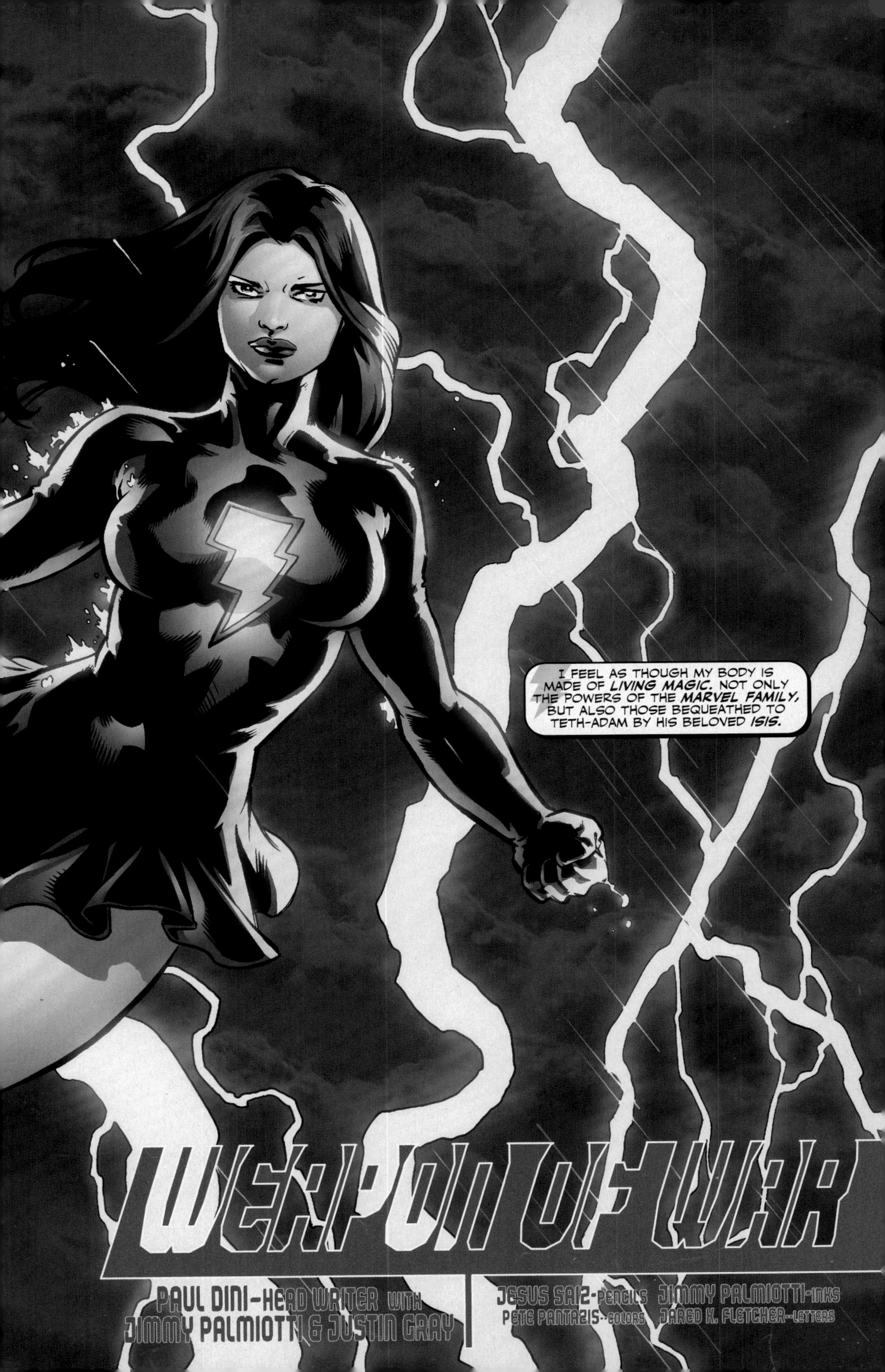
I FEEL AS THOUGH MY BODY IS MADE OF LIVING MAGIC. NOT ONLY THE POWERS OF THE MARVEL FAMILY, BUT ALSO THOSE BEQUEATHED TO TETH-ADAM BY HIS BELOVED ISIS.
WEAPON OF WAR
PAUL DINI-HEAD WRITER WITH JIMMY PALMIOTTI & JUSTIN GRAY
JESUS SAIZ-PENCILS JIMMY PALMIOTTI-INKS
PETE PANTAZIS--COLORS JARED K. FLETCHER--LETTERS

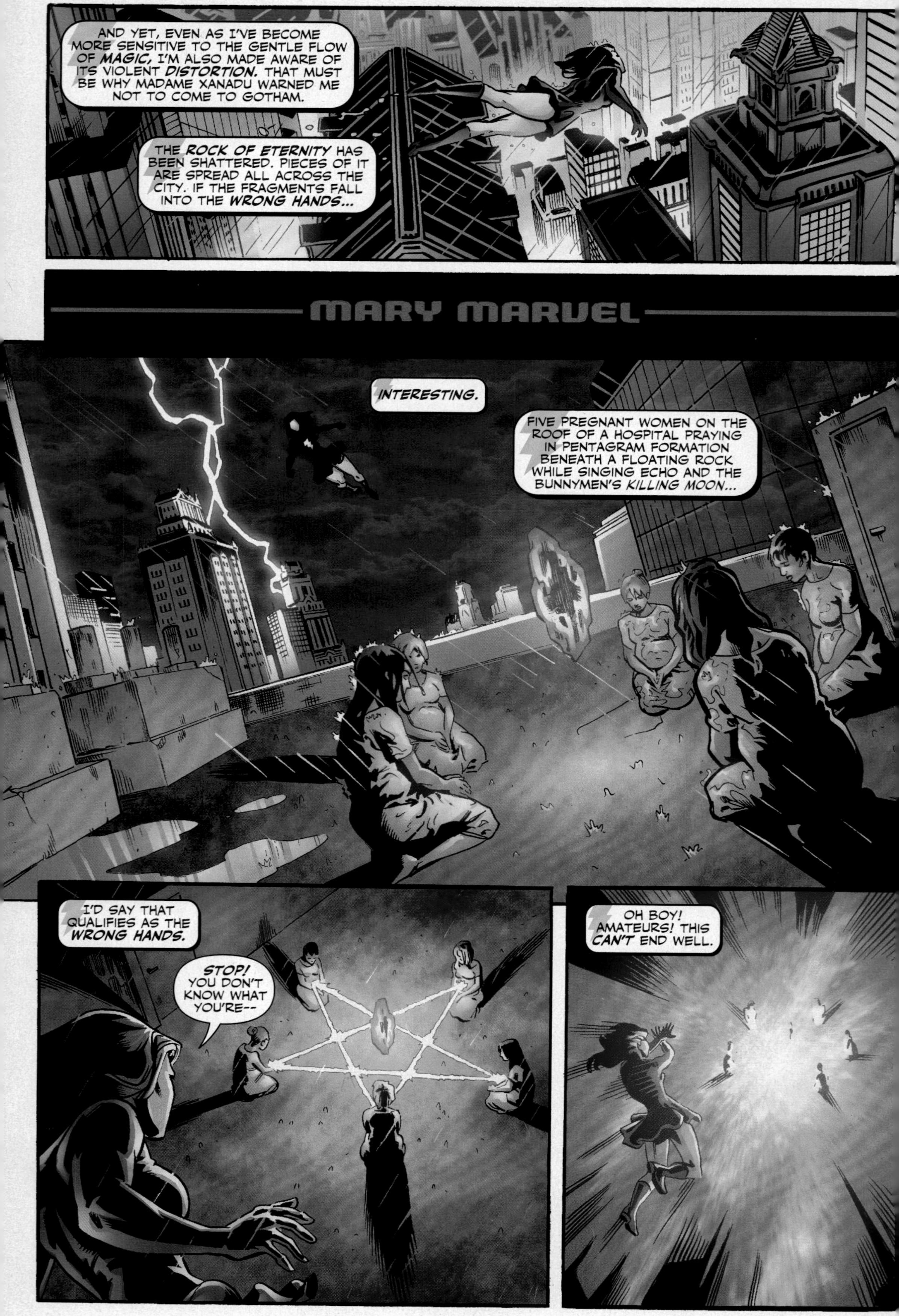
AND YET, EVEN AS I'VE BECOME MORE SENSITIVE TO THE GENTLE FLOW OF MAGIC, I'M ALSO MADE AWARE OF ITS VIOLENT DISTORTION. THAT MUST BE WHY MADAME XANADU WARNED ME NOT TO COME TO GOTHAM.
THE ROCK OF ETERNITY HAS BEEN SHATTERED. PIECES OF IT ARE SPREAD ALL ACROSS THE CITY. IF THE FRAGMENTS FALL INTO THE WRONG HANDS...
MARY MARVEL
INTERESTING.
FIVE PREGNANT WOMEN ON THE ROOF OF A HOSPITAL PRAYING IN PENTAGRAM FORMATION BENEATH A FLOATING ROCK WHILE SINGING ECHO AND THE BUNNYMEN'S KILLING MOON...
I'D SAY THAT QUALIFIES AS THE WRONG HANDS.
STOP! YOU DON'T KNOW WHAT YOU'RE--
OH BOY! AMATEURS! THIS CAN'T END WELL.

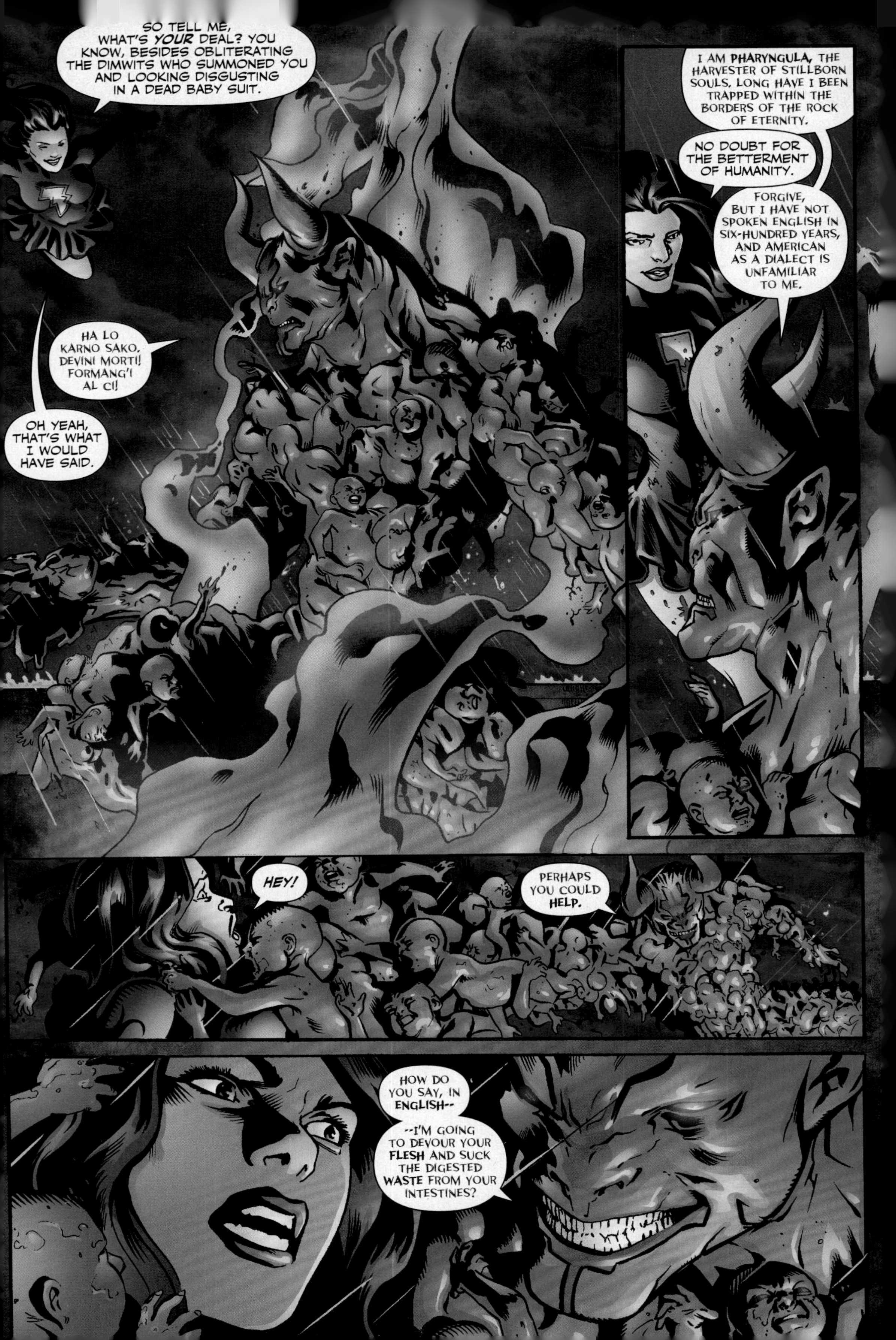
SO TELL ME, WHAT'S YOUR DEAL? YOU KNOW, BESIDES OBLITERATING THE DIMWITS WHO SUMMONED YOU AND LOOKING DISGUSTING IN A DEAD BABY SUIT.
HA LO KARNO SAKO, DEVINI MORTI! FORMANG'I AL CI!
OH YEAH, THAT'S WHAT I WOULD HAVE SAID.
I AM PHARYNGULA, THE HARVESTER OF STILLBORN SOULS. LONG HAVE I BEEN TRAPPED WITHIN THE BORDERS OF THE ROCK OF ETERNITY.
NO DOUBT FOR THE BETTERMENT OF HUMANITY.
FORGIVE, BUT I HAVE NOT SPOKEN ENGLISH IN SIX-HUNDRED YEARS, AND AMERICAN AS A DIALECT IS UNFAMILIAR TO ME.
HEY!
PERHAPS YOU COULD HELP.
HOW DO YOU SAY, IN ENGLISH--
--I'M GOING TO DEVOUR YOUR FLESH AND SUCK THE DIGESTED WASTE FROM YOUR INTESTINES?

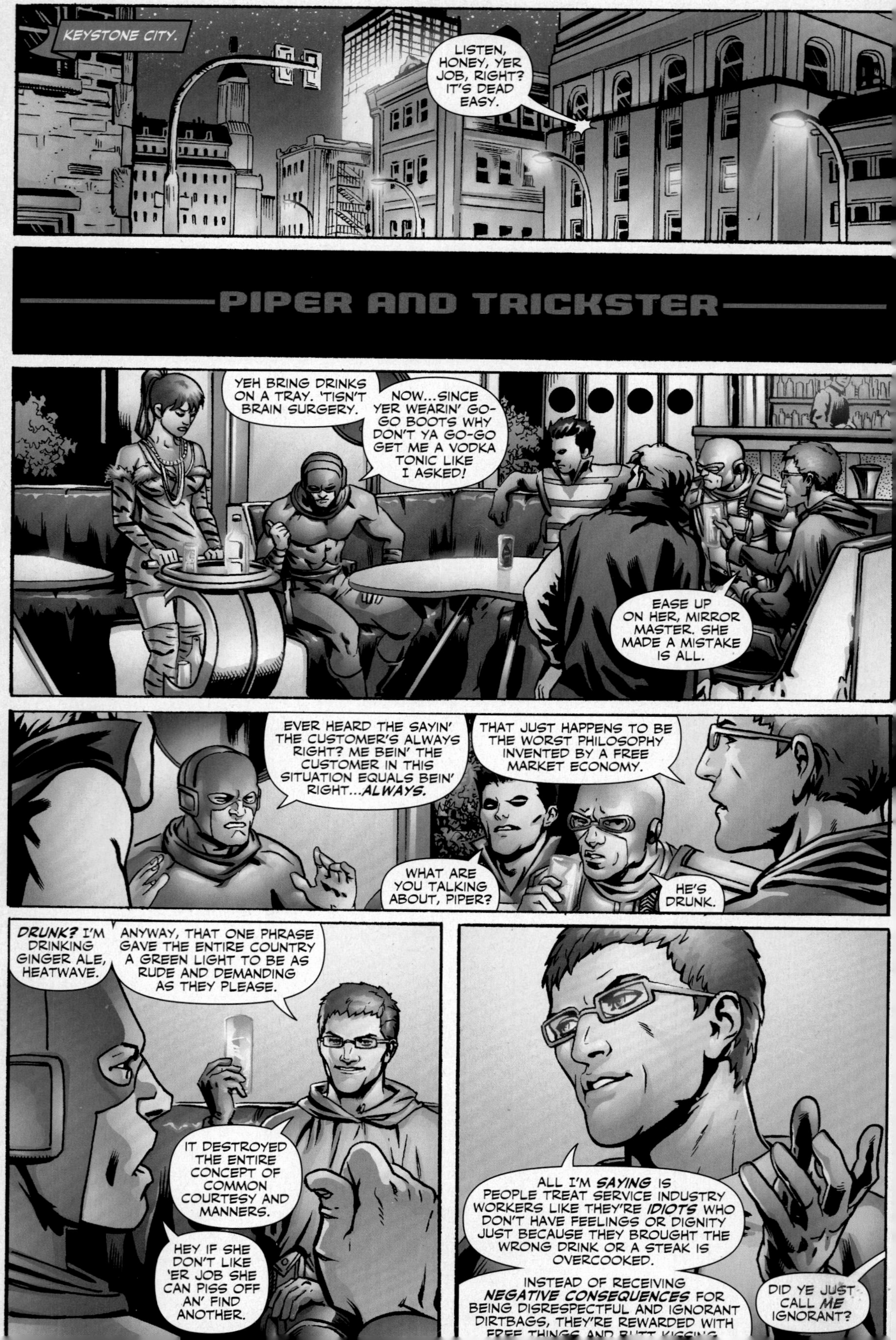
KEYSTONE CITY.
LISTEN, HONEY, YER JOB, RIGHT? IT'S DEAD EASY.
PIPER AND TRICKSTER
YEH BRING DRINKS ON A TRAY. 'TISN'T BRAIN SURGERY.
NOW...SINCE YER WEARIN' GO-GO BOOTS WHY DON'T YA GO-GO GET ME A VODKA TONIC LIKE I ASKED!
EASE UP ON HER, MIRROR MASTER. SHE MADE A MISTAKE IS ALL.
EVER HEARD THE SAYIN' THE CUSTOMER'S ALWAYS RIGHT? ME BEIN' THE CUSTOMER IN THIS SITUATION EQUALS BEIN' RIGHT...ALWAYS.
THAT JUST HAPPENS TO BE THE WORST PHILOSOPHY INVENTED BY A FREE MARKET ECONOMY.
WHAT ARE YOU TALKING ABOUT, PIPER?
HE'S DRUNK.
DRUNK? I'M DRINKING GINGER ALE, HEATWAVE.
ANYWAY, THAT ONE PHRASE GAVE THE ENTIRE COUNTRY A GREEN LIGHT TO BE AS RUDE AND DEMANDING AS THEY PLEASE.
IT DESTROYED THE ENTIRE CONCEPT OF COMMON COURTESY AND MANNERS.
HEY IF SHE DON'T LIKE 'ER JOB SHE CAN PISS OFF AN' FIND ANOTHER.
ALL I'M SAYING IS PEOPLE TREAT SERVICE INDUSTRY WORKERS LIKE THEY'RE IDIOTS WHO DON'T HAVE FEELINGS OR DIGNITY JUST BECAUSE THEY BROUGHT THE WRONG DRINK OR A STEAK IS OVERCOOKED.
INSTEAD OF RECEIVING NEGATIVE CONSEQUENCES FOR BEING DISRESPECTFUL AND IGNORANT DIRTBAGS, THEY'RE REWARDED WITH
DID YE JUST CALL ME IGNORANT?

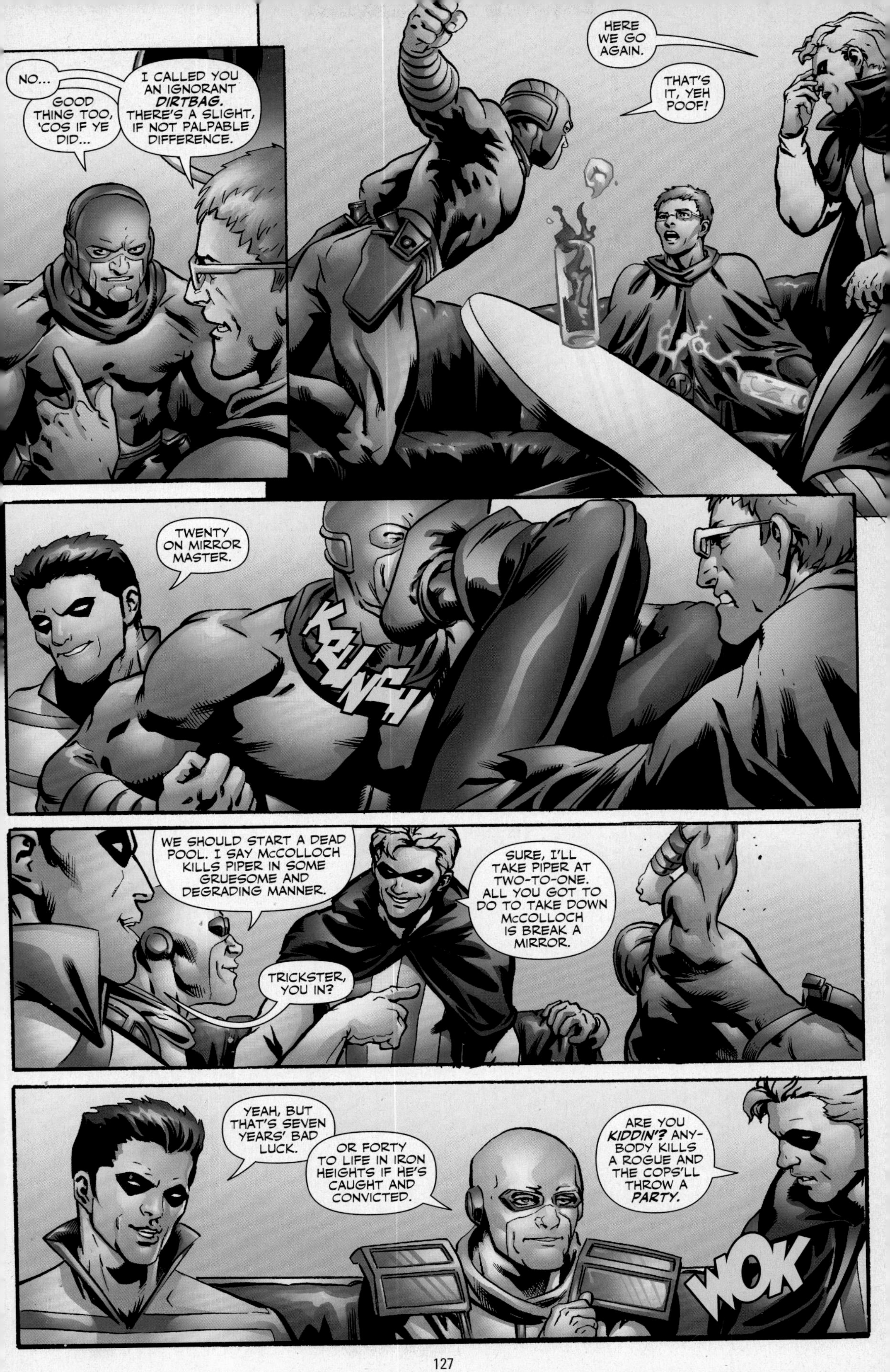
NO...
GOOD THING TOO, 'COS IF YE DID...
I CALLED YOU AN IGNORANT DIRTBAG. THERE'S A SLIGHT, IF NOT PALPABLE DIFFERENCE.
HERE WE GO AGAIN.
THAT'S IT, YEH POOF!
TWENTY ON MIRROR MASTER.
KRUNCH
WE SHOULD START A DEAD POOL. I SAY McCOLLOCH KILLS PIPER IN SOME GRUESOME AND DEGRADING MANNER.
TRICKSTER, YOU IN?
SURE, I'LL TAKE PIPER AT TWO-TO-ONE. ALL YOU GOT TO DO TO TAKE DOWN McCOLLOCH IS BREAK A MIRROR.
YEAH, BUT THAT'S SEVEN YEARS' BAD LUCK.
OR FORTY TO LIFE IN IRON HEIGHTS IF HE'S CAUGHT AND CONVICTED.
ARE YOU KIDDIN'? ANYBODY KILLS A ROGUE AND THE COPS'LL THROW A PARTY.
WOK

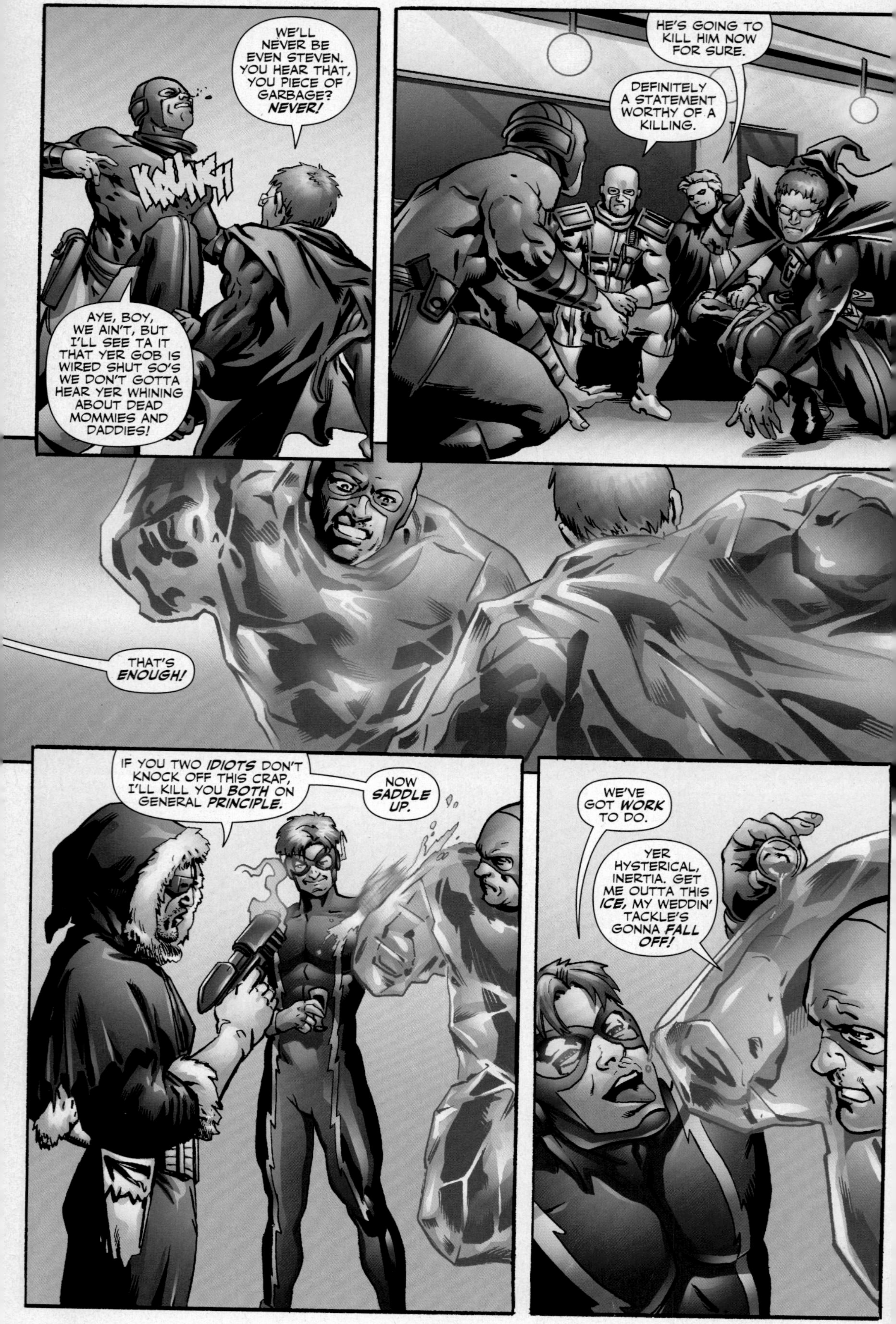
WE'LL NEVER BE EVEN STEVEN. YOU HEAR THAT, YOU PIECE OF GARBAGE? NEVER!
KRUNCH
AYE, BOY, WE AIN'T, BUT I'LL SEE TA IT THAT YER GOB IS WIRED SHUT SO'S WE DON'T GOTTA HEAR YER WHINING ABOUT DEAD MOMMIES AND DADDIES!
HE'S GOING TO KILL HIM NOW FOR SURE.
DEFINITELY A STATEMENT WORTHY OF A KILLING.
THAT'S ENOUGH!
IF YOU TWO IDIOTS DON'T KNOCK OFF THIS CRAP, I'LL KILL YOU BOTH ON GENERAL PRINCIPLE.
NOW SADDLE UP.
WE'VE GOT WORK TO DO.
YER HYSTERICAL, INERTIA. GET ME OUTTA THIS ICE, MY WEDDIN' TACKLE'S GONNA FALL OFF!

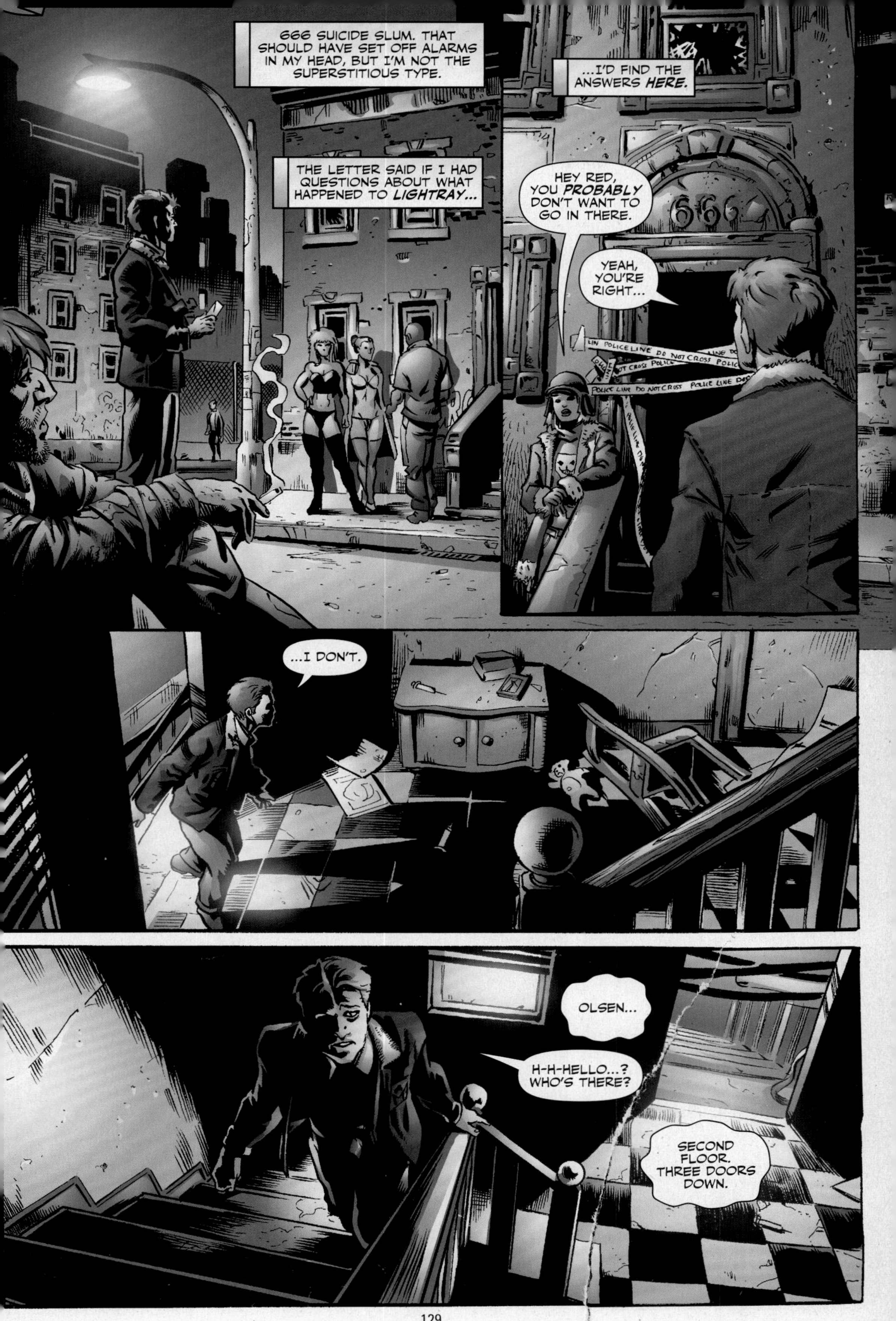
666 SUICIDE SLUM. THAT SHOULD HAVE SET OFF ALARMS IN MY HEAD, BUT I'M NOT THE SUPERSTITIOUS TYPE.
THE LETTER SAID IF I HAD QUESTIONS ABOUT WHAT HAPPENED TO LIGHTRAY...
...I'D FIND THE ANSWERS HERE.
666
HEY RED, YOU PROBABLY DON'T WANT TO GO IN THERE.
YEAH, YOU'RE RIGHT...
POLICE LINE DO NOT CROSS
...I DON'T.
OLSEN...
H-H-HELLO...? WHO'S THERE?
SECOND FLOOR. THREE DOORS DOWN.

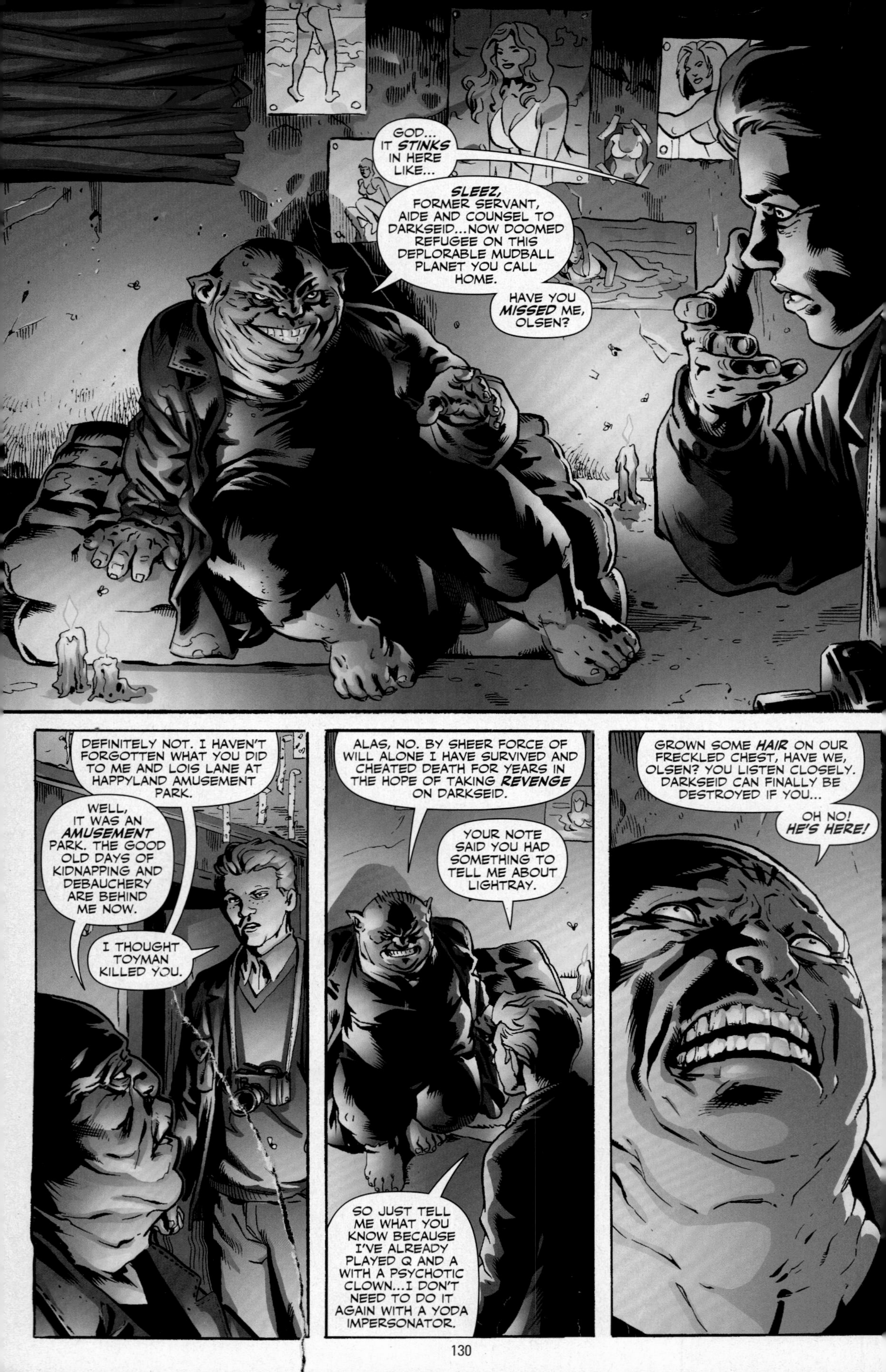
GOD... IT STINKS IN HERE LIKE...
SLEEZ, FORMER SERVANT, AIDE AND COUNSEL TO DARKSEID...NOW DOOMED REFUGEE ON THIS DEPLORABLE MUDBALL PLANET YOU CALL HOME.
HAVE YOU MISSED ME, OLSEN?
DEFINITELY NOT. I HAVEN'T FORGOTTEN WHAT YOU DID TO ME AND LOIS LANE AT HAPPYLAND AMUSEMENT PARK.
WELL, IT WAS AN AMUSEMENT PARK. THE GOOD OLD DAYS OF KIDNAPPING AND DEBAUCHERY ARE BEHIND ME NOW.
I THOUGHT TOYMAN KILLED YOU.
ALAS, NO. BY SHEER FORCE OF WILL ALONE I HAVE SURVIVED AND CHEATED DEATH FOR YEARS IN THE HOPE OF TAKING REVENGE ON DARKSEID.
YOUR NOTE SAID YOU HAD SOMETHING TO TELL ME ABOUT LIGHTRAY.
SO JUST TELL ME WHAT YOU KNOW BECAUSE I'VE ALREADY PLAYED Q AND A WITH A PSYCHOTIC CLOWN...I DON'T NEED TO DO IT AGAIN WITH A YODA IMPERSONATOR.
GROWN SOME HAIR ON OUR FRECKLED CHEST, HAVE WE, OLSEN? YOU LISTEN CLOSELY. DARKSEID CAN FINALLY BE DESTROYED IF YOU...
OH NO! HE'S HERE!

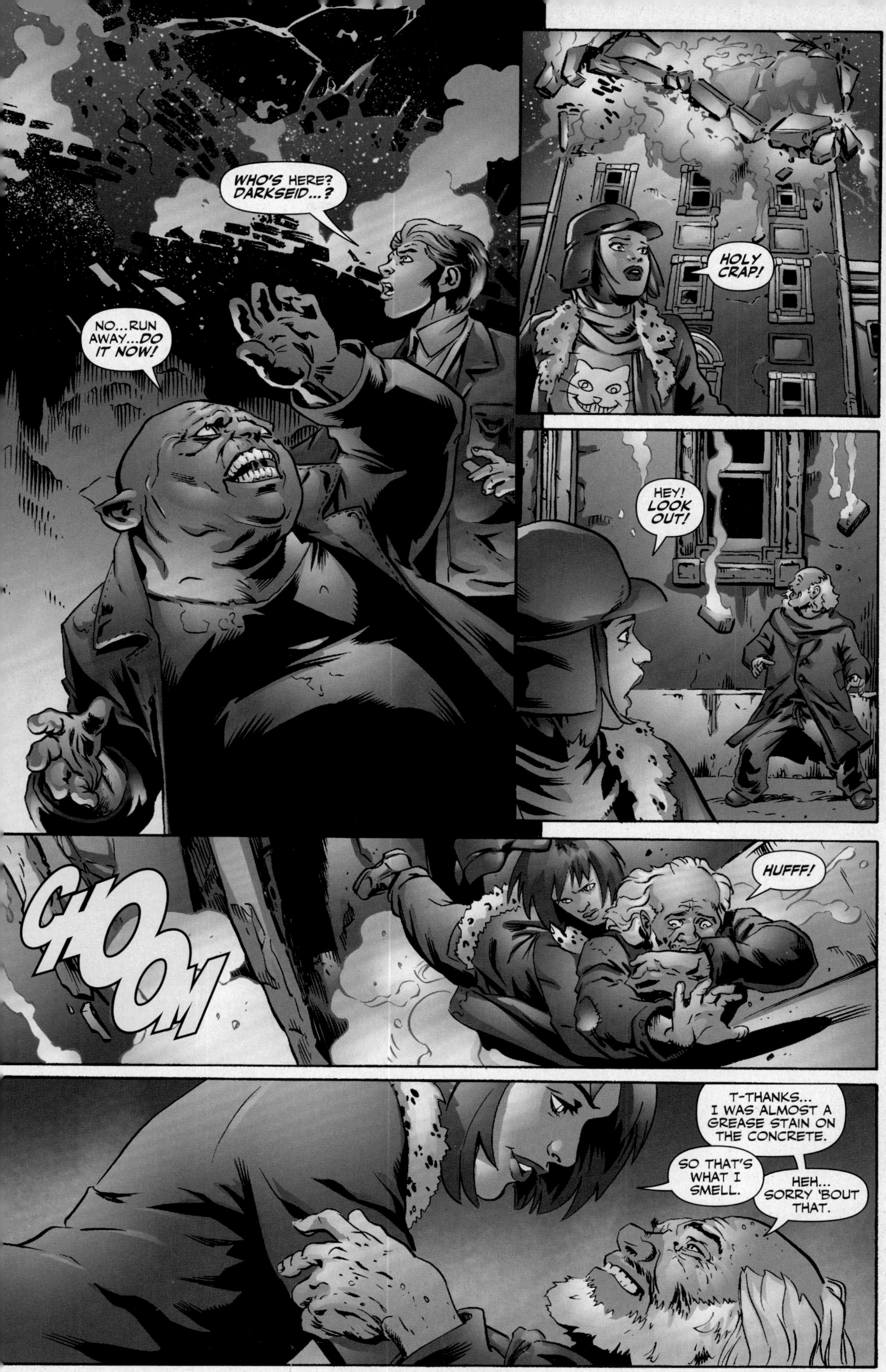
WHO'S HERE? DARKSEID...?
NO...RUN AWAY...DO IT NOW!
HOLY CRAP!
HEY! LOOK OUT!
GHOOM
HUFFF!
T-THANKS... I WAS ALMOST A GREASE STAIN ON THE CONCRETE.
SO THAT'S WHAT I SMELL.
HEH... SORRY 'BOUT THAT.

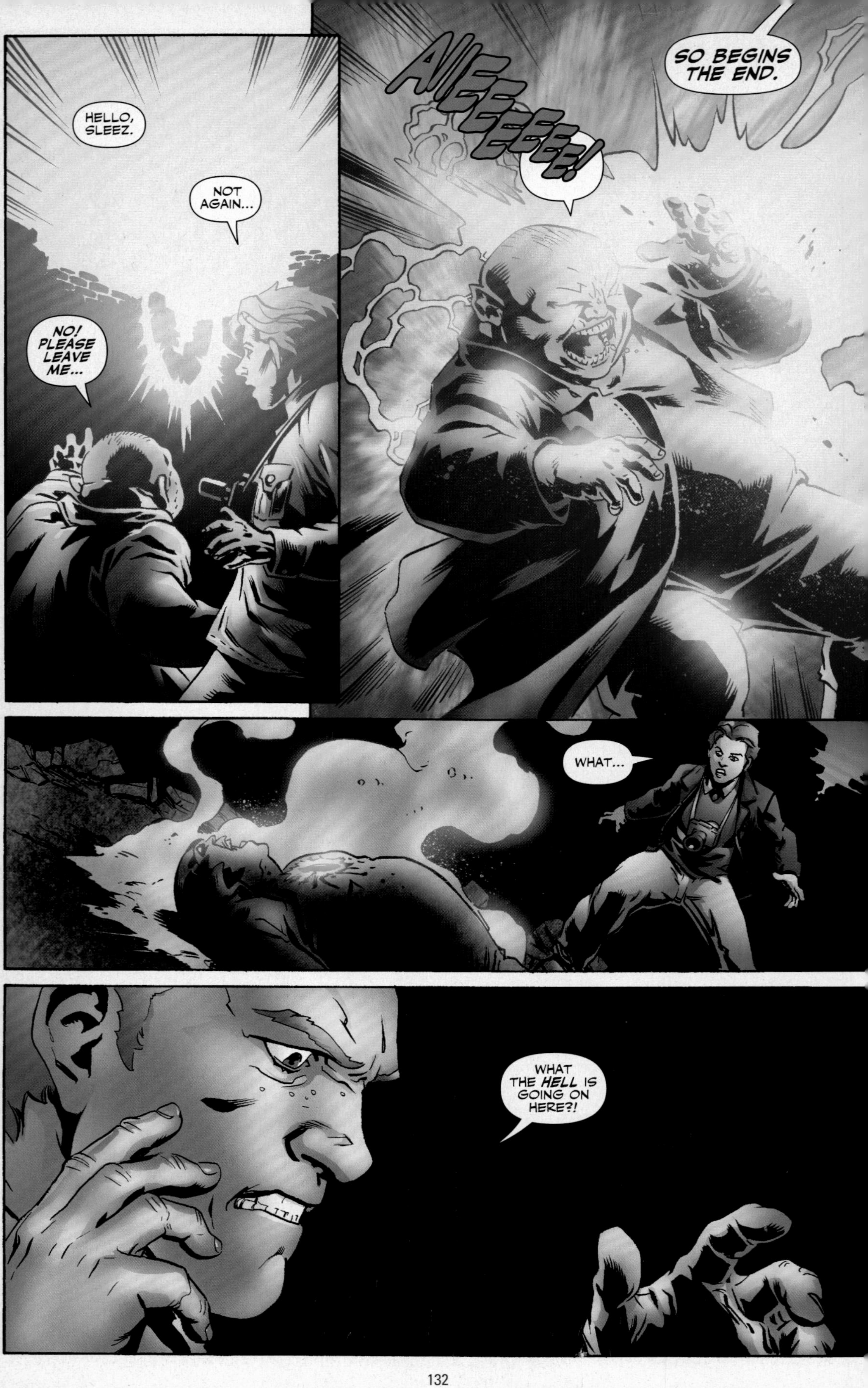
HELLO, SLEEZ.
NOT AGAIN...
NO! PLEASE LEAVE ME...
SO BEGINS THE END.
AIIEEEEEEE!
WHAT...
WHAT THE HELL IS GOING ON HERE?!

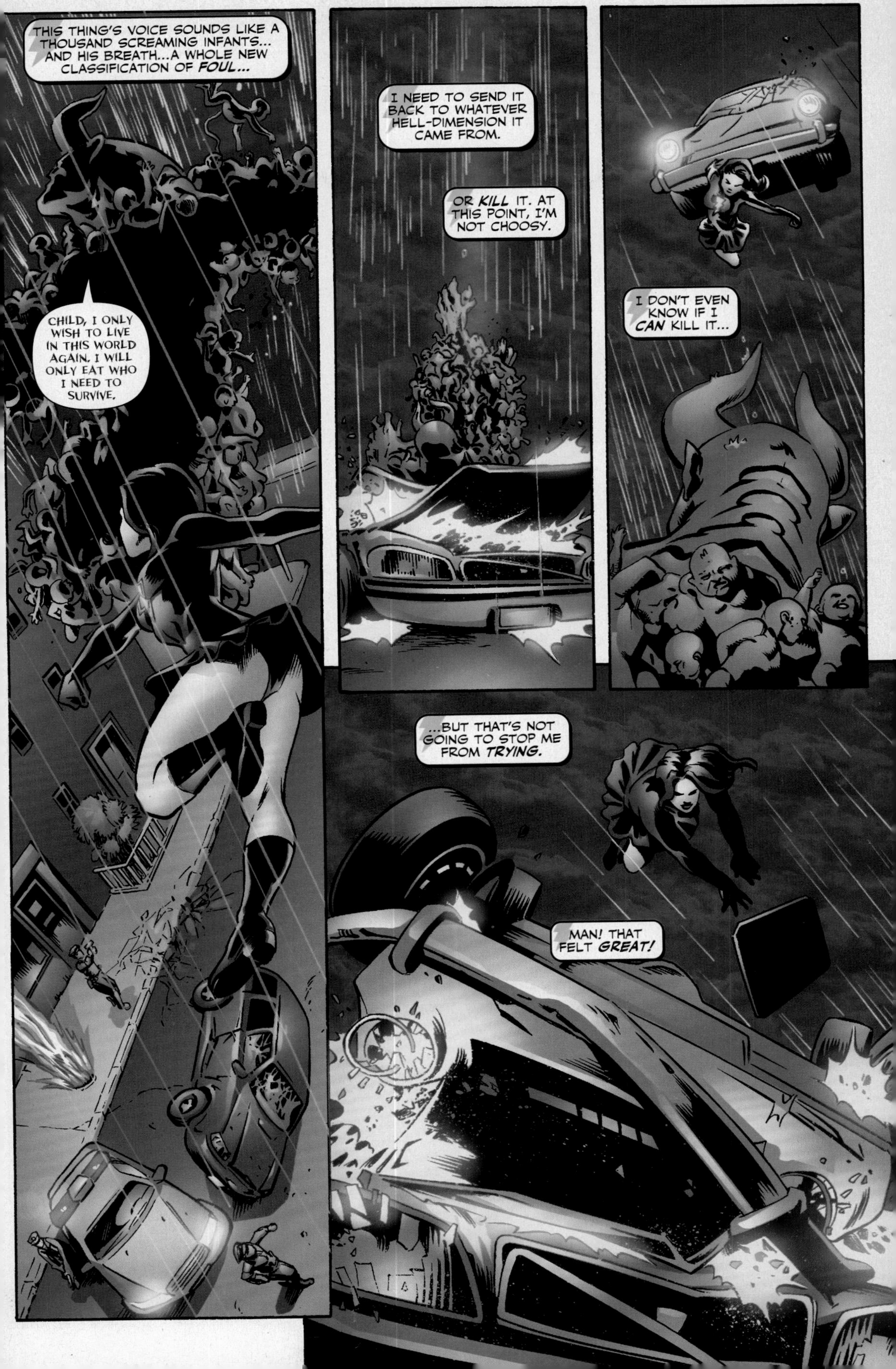
THIS THING'S VOICE SOUNDS LIKE A THOUSAND SCREAMING INFANTS... AND HIS BREATH...A WHOLE NEW CLASSIFICATION OF FOUL...
CHILD, I ONLY WISH TO LIVE IN THIS WORLD AGAIN. I WILL ONLY EAT WHO I NEED TO SURVIVE.
I NEED TO SEND IT BACK TO WHATEVER HELL-DIMENSION IT CAME FROM.
OR KILL IT. AT THIS POINT, I'M NOT CHOOSY.
I DON'T EVEN KNOW IF I CAN KILL IT...
...BUT THAT'S NOT GOING TO STOP ME FROM TRYING.
MAN! THAT FELT GREAT!

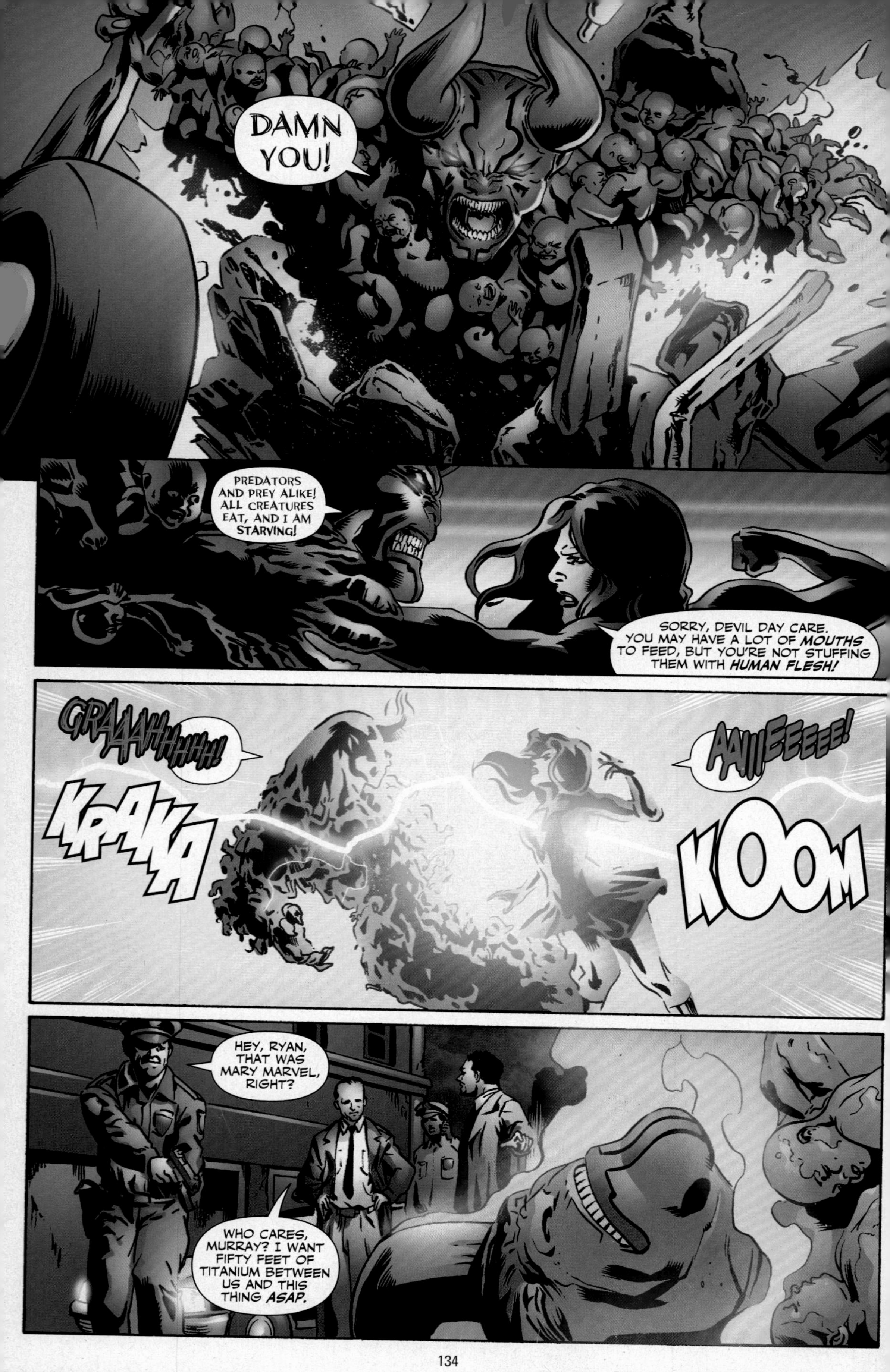
DAMN YOU!
PREDATORS AND PREY ALIKE! ALL CREATURES EAT, AND I AM STARVING!
SORRY, DEVIL DAY CARE. YOU MAY HAVE A LOT OF MOUTHS TO FEED, BUT YOU'RE NOT STUFFING THEM WITH HUMAN FLESH!
GRAAAHHHHH!
AAIIIEEEEE!
KRAKA
KOOM
HEY, RYAN, THAT WAS MARY MARVEL, RIGHT?
WHO CARES, MURRAY? I WANT FIFTY FEET OF TITANIUM BETWEEN US AND THIS THING ASAP.

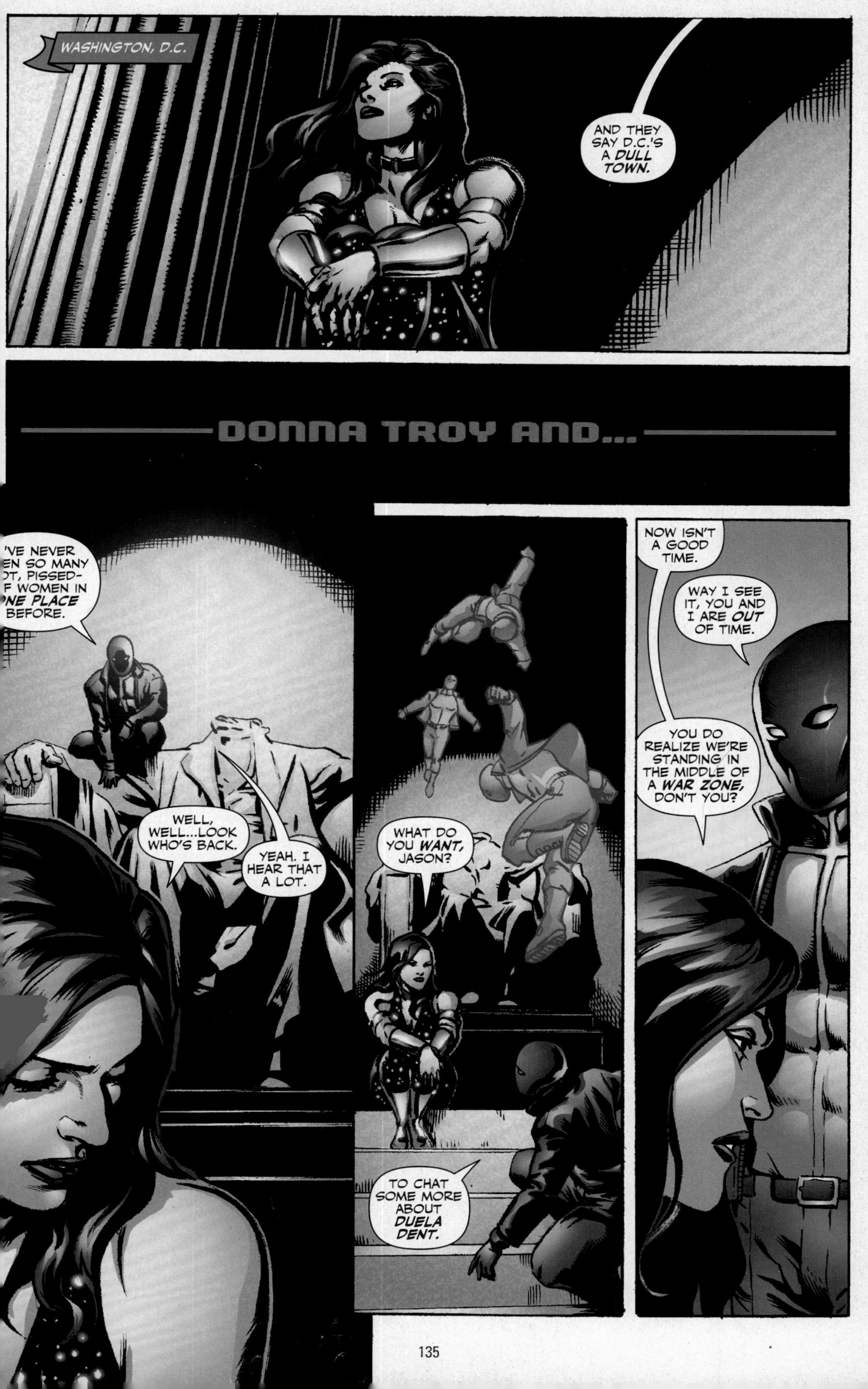
WASHINGTON, D.C.
AND THEY SAY D.C.'S A DULL TOWN.
DONNA TROY AND...
'VE NEVER EN SO MANY OT, PISSED- F WOMEN IN NE PLACE BEFORE.
WELL, WELL...LOOK WHO'S BACK.
YEAH. I HEAR THAT A LOT.
WHAT DO YOU WANT, JASON?
TO CHAT SOME MORE ABOUT DUELA DENT.
NOW ISN'T A GOOD TIME.
WAY I SEE IT, YOU AND I ARE OUT OF TIME.
YOU DO REALIZE WE'RE STANDING IN THE MIDDLE OF A WAR ZONE, DON'T YOU?

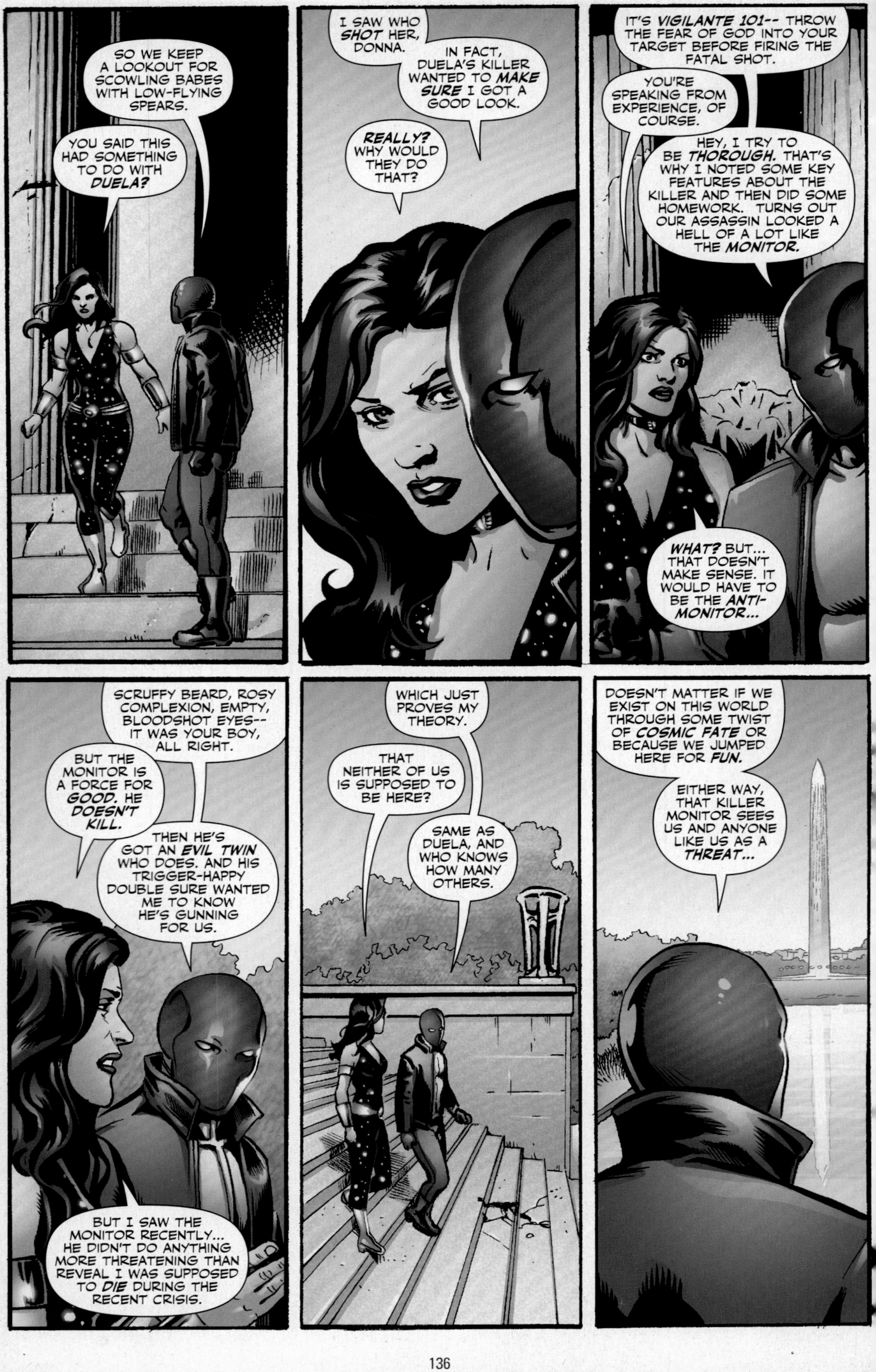
SO WE KEEP A LOOKOUT FOR SCOWLING BABES WITH LOW-FLYING SPEARS.
YOU SAID THIS HAD SOMETHING TO DO WITH DUELA?
I SAW WHO SHOT HER, DONNA.
IN FACT, DUELA'S KILLER WANTED TO MAKE SURE I GOT A GOOD LOOK.
REALLY? WHY WOULD THEY DO THAT?
IT'S VIGILANTE 101-- THROW THE FEAR OF GOD INTO YOUR TARGET BEFORE FIRING THE FATAL SHOT.
YOU'RE SPEAKING FROM EXPERIENCE, OF COURSE.
HEY, I TRY TO BE THOROUGH. THAT'S WHY I NOTED SOME KEY FEATURES ABOUT THE KILLER AND THEN DID SOME HOMEWORK. TURNS OUT OUR ASSASSIN LOOKED A HELL OF A LOT LIKE THE MONITOR.
WHAT? BUT... THAT DOESN'T MAKE SENSE. IT WOULD HAVE TO BE THE ANTI-MONITOR...
SCRUFFY BEARD, ROSY COMPLEXION, EMPTY, BLOODSHOT EYES-- IT WAS YOUR BOY, ALL RIGHT.
BUT THE MONITOR IS A FORCE FOR GOOD. HE DOESN'T KILL.
THEN HE'S GOT AN EVIL TWIN WHO DOES. AND HIS TRIGGER-HAPPY DOUBLE SURE WANTED ME TO KNOW HE'S GUNNING FOR US.
BUT I SAW THE MONITOR RECENTLY... HE DIDN'T DO ANYTHING MORE THREATENING THAN REVEAL I WAS SUPPOSED TO DIE DURING THE RECENT CRISIS.
WHICH JUST PROVES MY THEORY.
THAT NEITHER OF US IS SUPPOSED TO BE HERE?
SAME AS DUELA, AND WHO KNOWS HOW MANY OTHERS.
DOESN'T MATTER IF WE EXIST ON THIS WORLD THROUGH SOME TWIST OF COSMIC FATE OR BECAUSE WE JUMPED HERE FOR FUN.
EITHER WAY, THAT KILLER MONITOR SEES US AND ANYONE LIKE US AS A THREAT...

...AND THAT'S EARNED US A SLOT ON THE COSMIC HIT LIST.

I BELIEVE WE *UNDERESTIMATED* JASON TODD.

OBVIOUSLY.

COURSE OF ACTION?

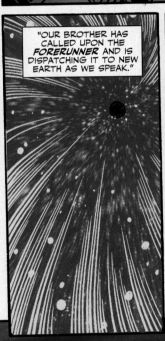

"OUR BROTHER HAS CALLED UPON THE *FORERUNNER* AND IS DISPATCHING IT TO NEW EARTH AS WE SPEAK."

EXCELLENT.

"THE FORERUNNER WAS CHOSEN TO BE OUR SWORD, THE *WEAPON* REQUIRED SHOULD THE NEED ARISE.

"OUR ZEALOUS BROTHER WOULD HAVE BEEN WISE TO EMPLOY FORERUNNER AGAINST DUELA DENT INSTEAD OF ELIMINATING HER *HIMSELF.*

"HAVE *FAITH* IN WHAT MUST BE DONE, BROTHERS."

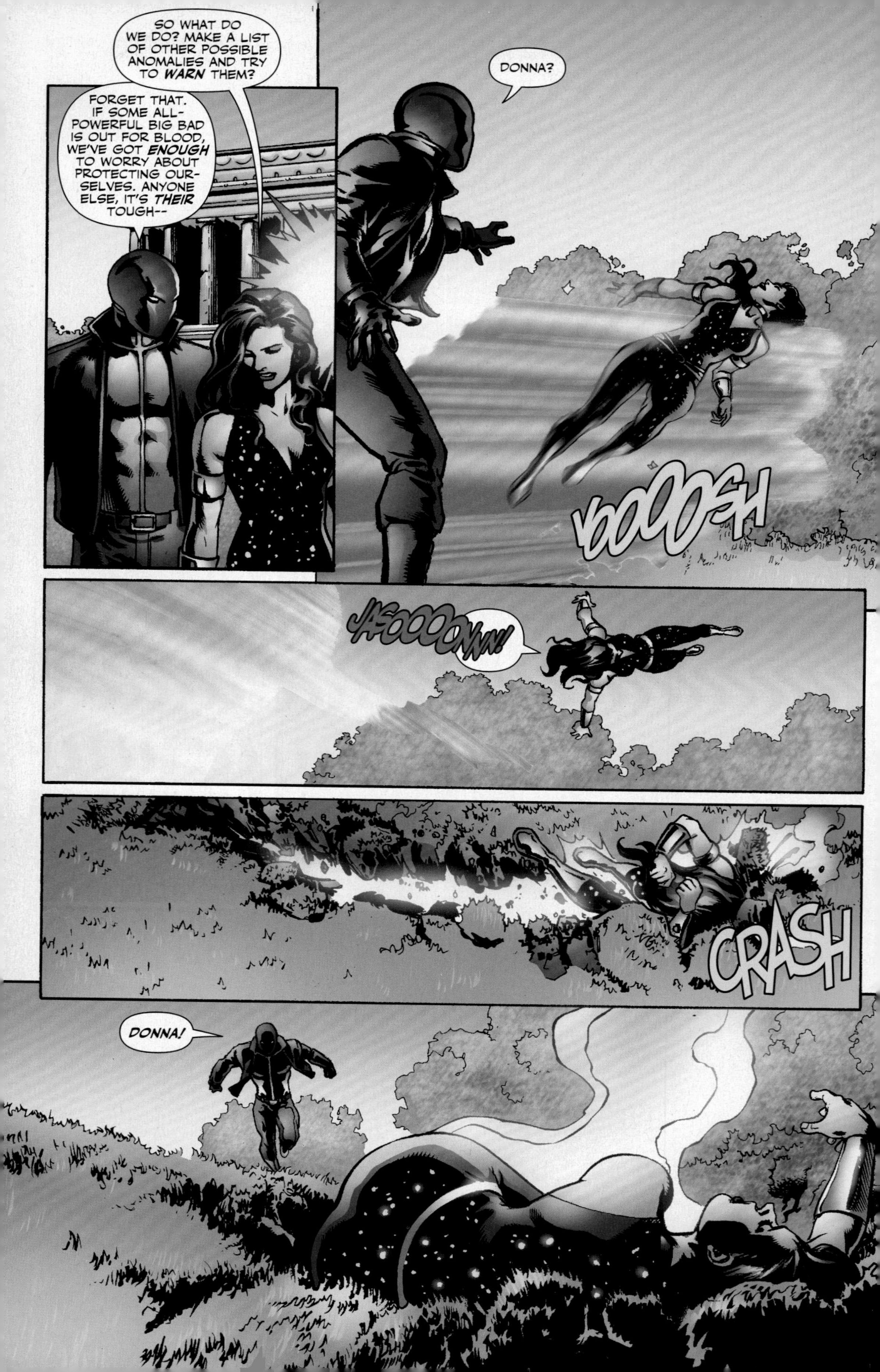
SO WHAT DO WE DO? MAKE A LIST OF OTHER POSSIBLE ANOMALIES AND TRY TO *WARN* THEM?
FORGET THAT. IF SOME ALL-POWERFUL BIG BAD IS OUT FOR BLOOD, WE'VE GOT *ENOUGH* TO WORRY ABOUT PROTECTING OURSELVES. ANYONE ELSE, IT'S *THEIR* TOUGH--
DONNA?
VOOOOSH
JASOOOONNN!
CRASH
DONNA!

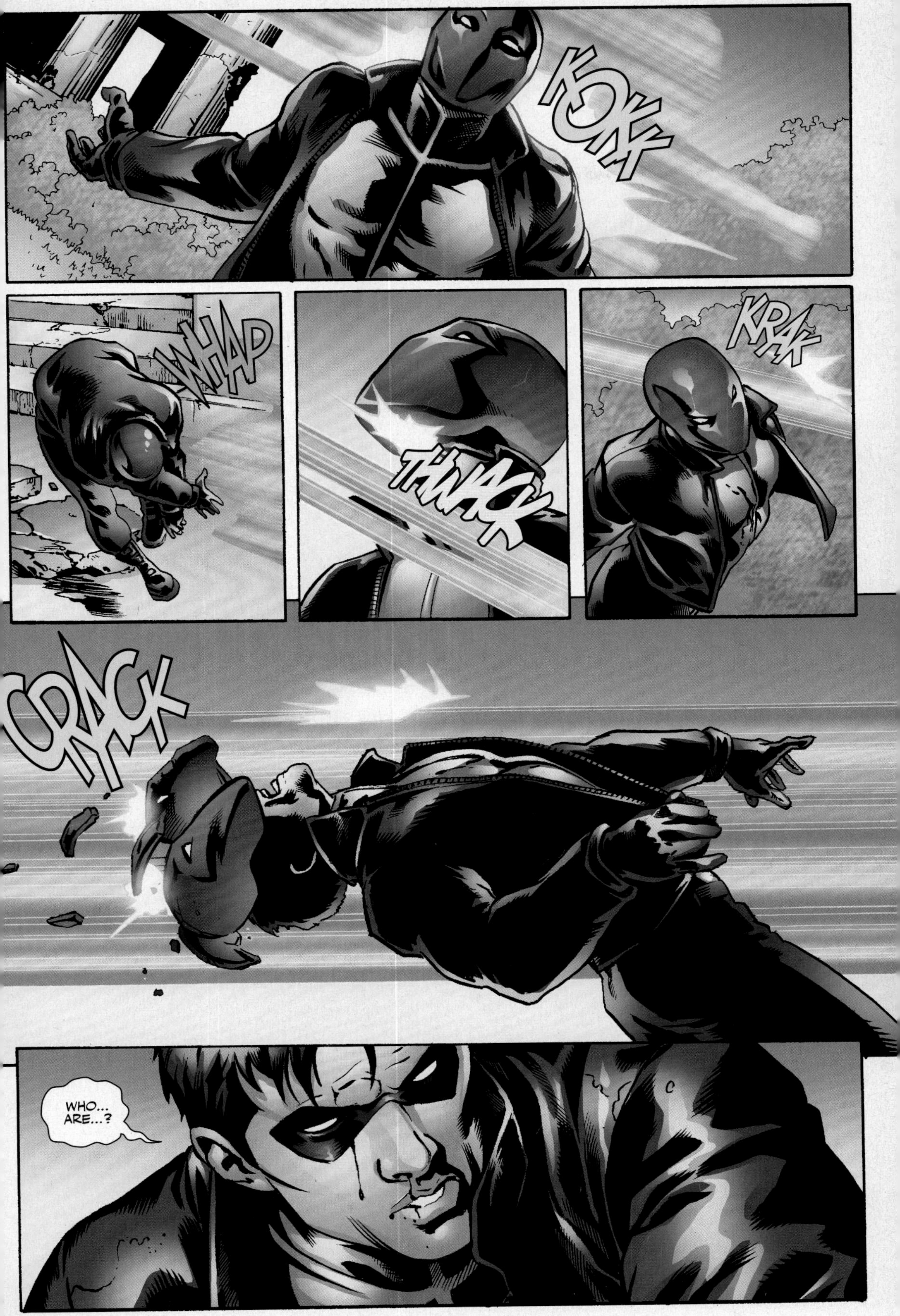
KOKK
WHAP
THWACK
KRAK
CRACK
WHO... ARE...?

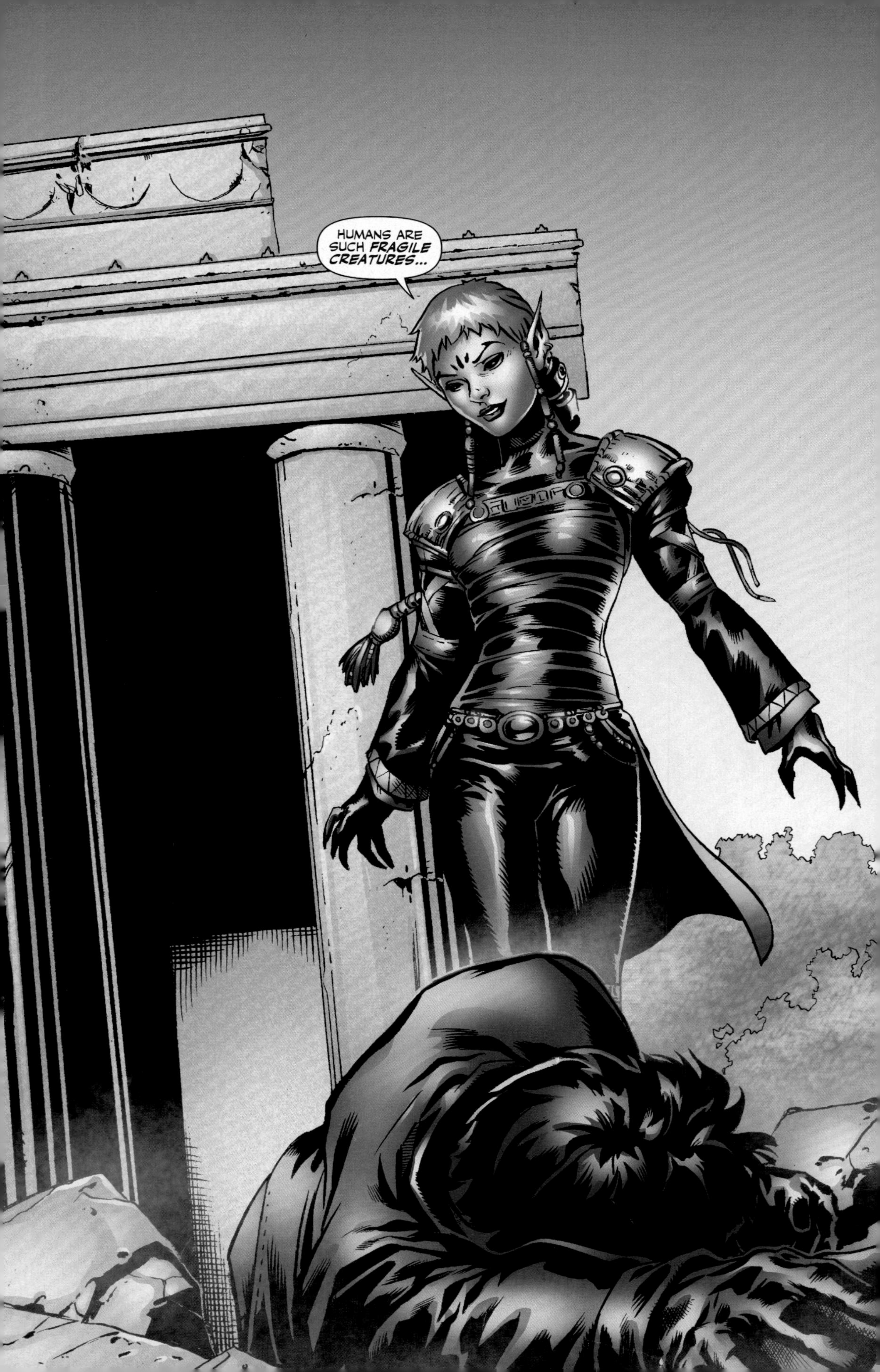
HUMANS ARE SUCH FRAGILE CREATURES...

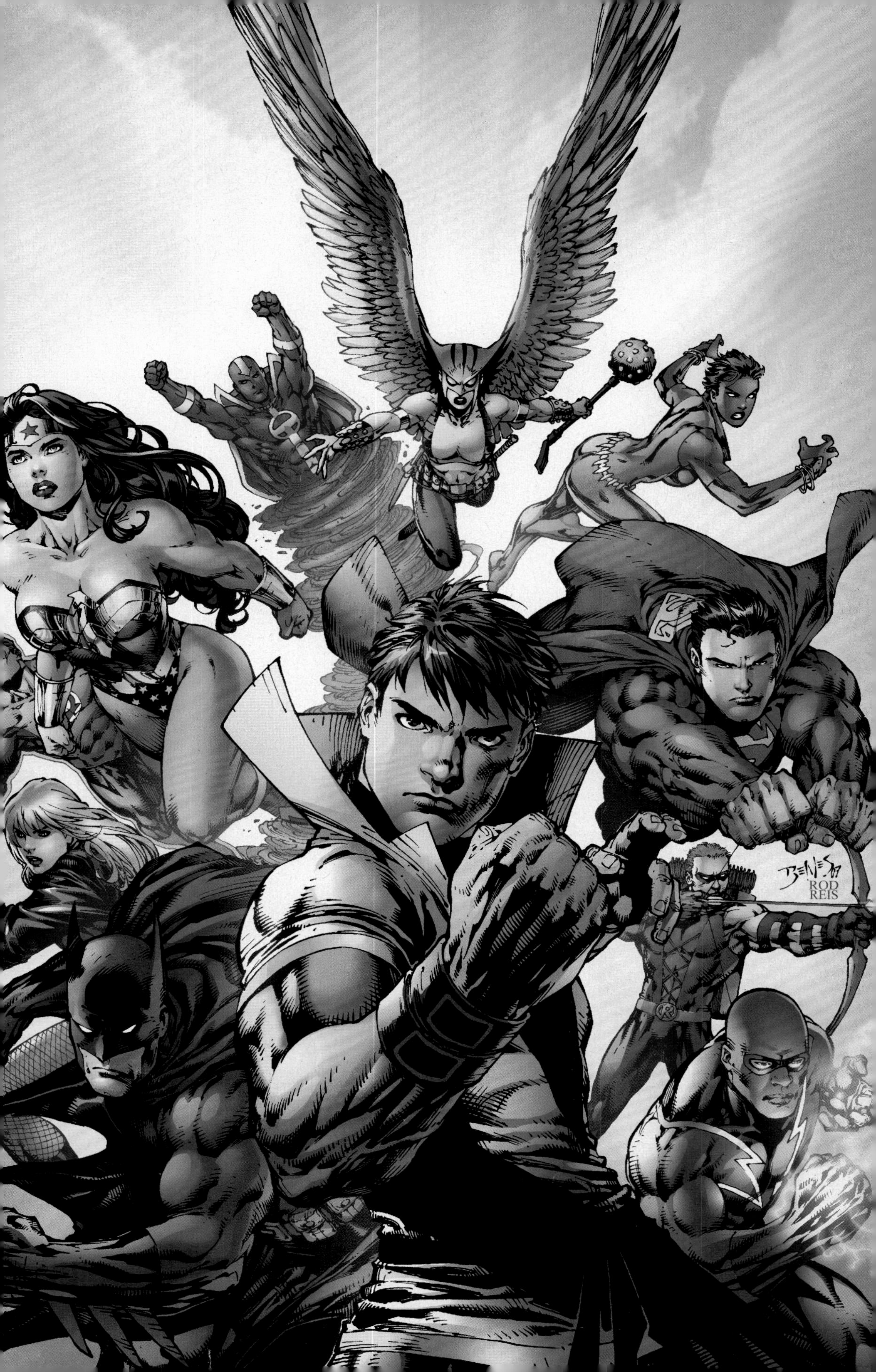
BENES 07
ROD
REIS

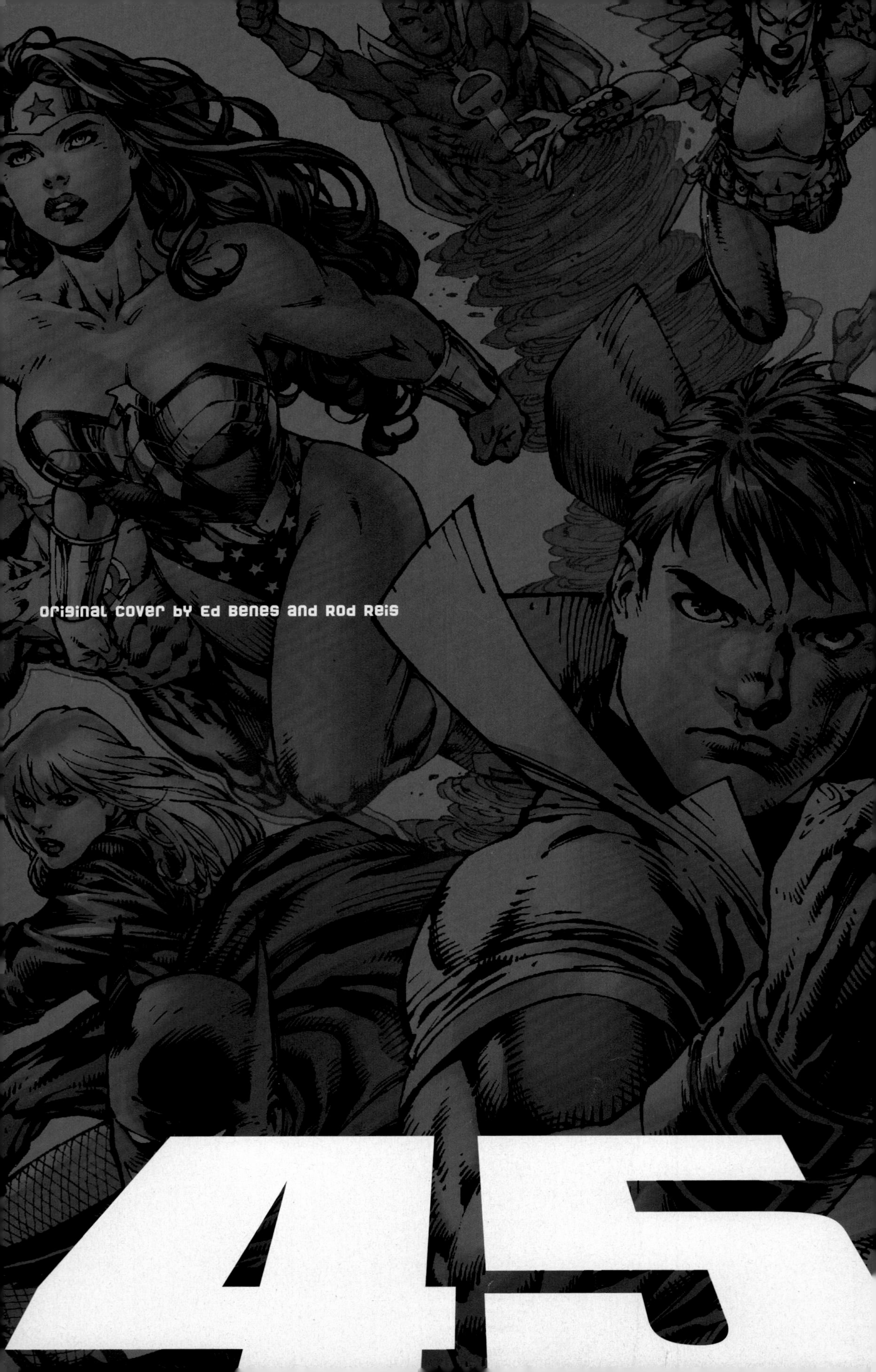
Original cover by Ed Benes and Rod Reis
45

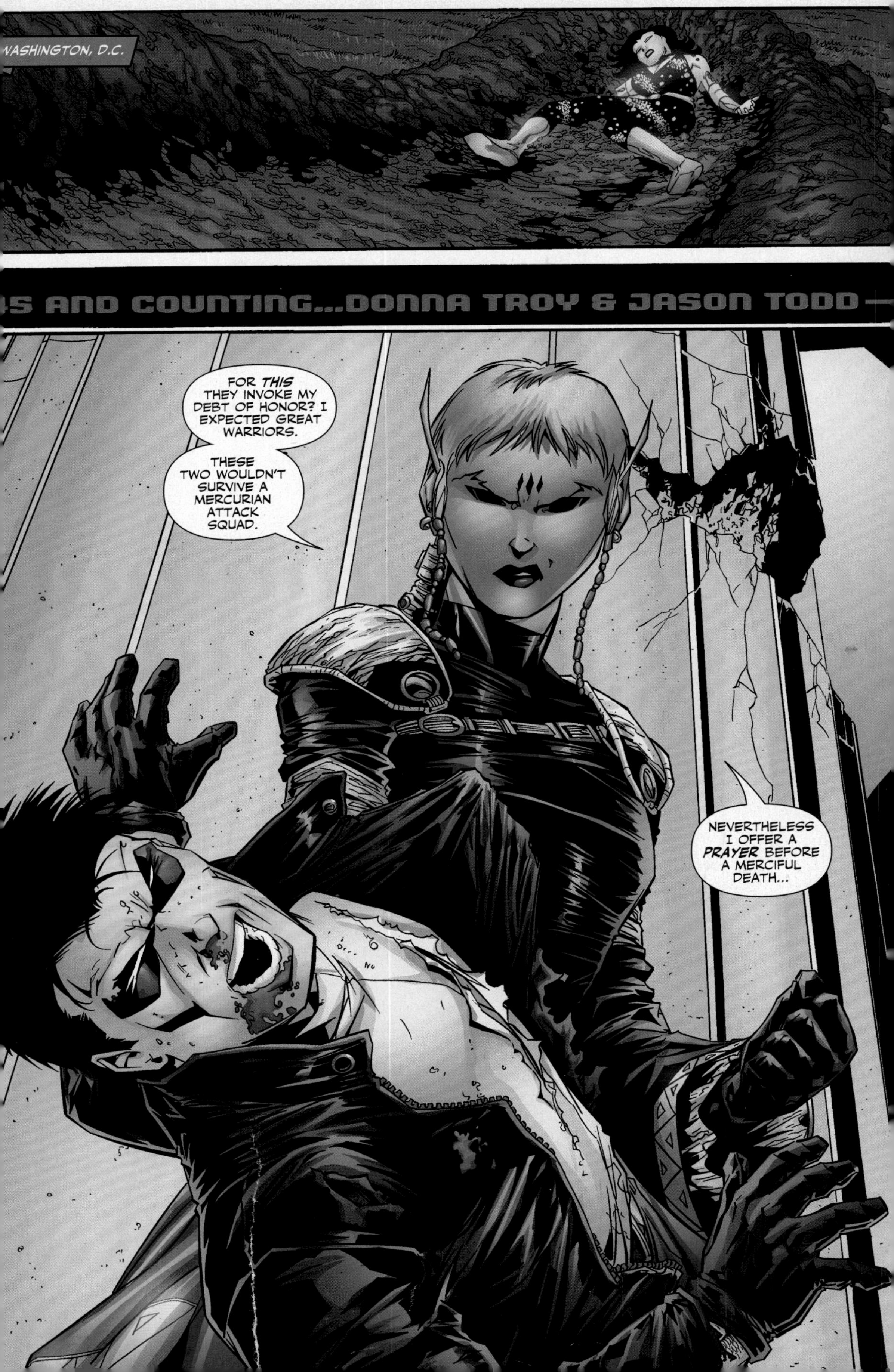

WASHINGTON, D.C.
45 AND COUNTING...DONNA TROY & JASON TODD—
FOR THIS THEY INVOKE MY DEBT OF HONOR? I EXPECTED GREAT WARRIORS.
THESE TWO WOULDN'T SURVIVE A MERCURIAN ATTACK SQUAD.
NEVERTHELESS I OFFER A PRAYER BEFORE A MERCIFUL DEATH...

MONITOR DUTY!

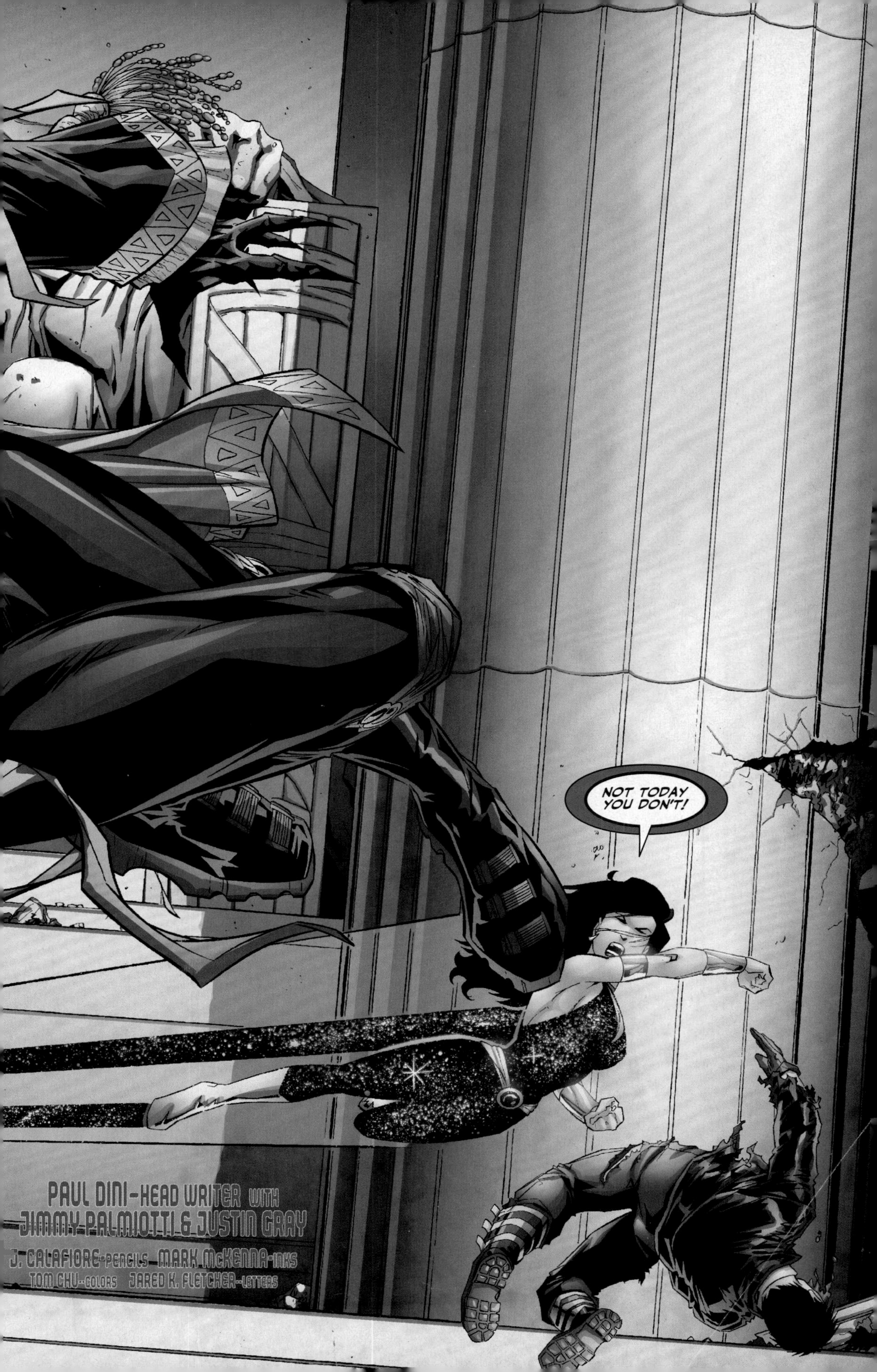
NOT TODAY YOU DON'T!
PAUL DINI–HEAD WRITER WITH
JIMMY PALMIOTTI & JUSTIN GRAY
J. CALAFIORE–PENCILS MARK McKENNA–INKS
TOM CHU–COLORS JARED K. FLETCHER–LETTERS

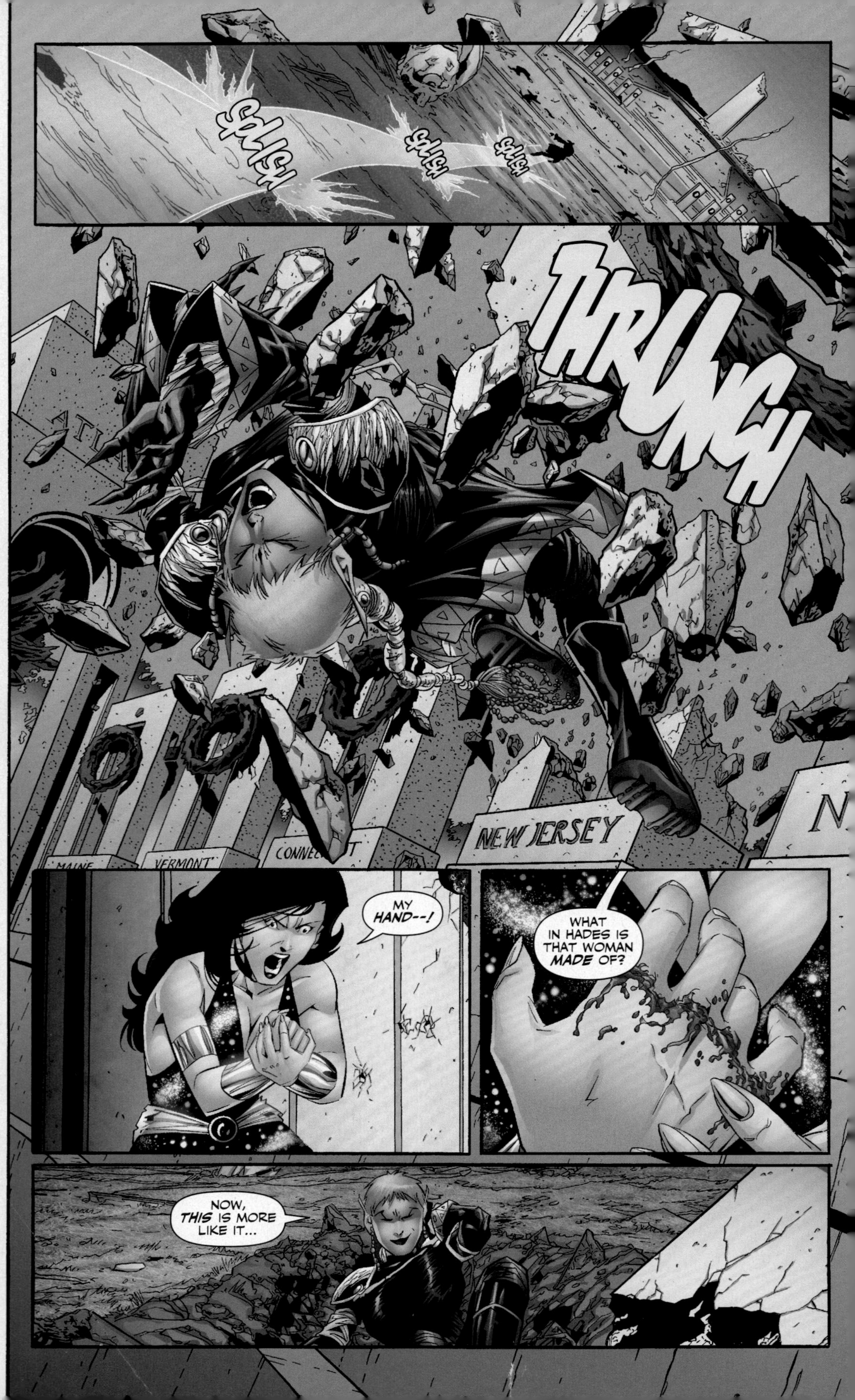
SPLISH
SPLISH
SPLISH
THRUNCH
NEW JERSEY
CONNECTICUT
VERMONT
MAINE
MY HAND--!
WHAT IN HADES IS THAT WOMAN MADE OF?
NOW, THIS IS MORE LIKE IT...

TESTING, TESTING...

STUPID THING BETTER WORK.

LORD KNOWS I FEEL LIKE AN *IDIOT* TALKING TO MYSELF, BUT MISS LANE SAYS IT HELPS HER PULL A STORY TOGETHER...

METROPOLIS P.D.

METROPOLIS P.D. - CRIME SCENE

JIMMY OLSEN

≹KLIK≹ LORD KNOWS I FEEL LIKE AN IDIOT-- ≹KLIK≹

HEH.

OKAY...ALL I'VE GOT SO FAR IS A STRING OF FREAKY INCIDENTS, BUT MY GUT SAYS THEY'RE CONNECTED-- INCLUDING WHAT HAPPENED *HERE.*

DO NOT CROSS POLICE

NOT CROSS POLICE LINE DO NOT CROSS POLICE LINE DO N

POLICE LINE DO NOT CROSS POLICE LINE DO NOT CROSS P

CROSS POLICE LINE DO NOT CROSS POLICE LIN

THIS WAS HOME TO ONE OF THE *NEW GODS*--A ...RST-CLASS DIRTBAG ...AMED *SLEEZ* WHO'D BEEN KICKED OFF APOKOLIPS.

SLEEZ PROMISED ME *INFO* CONCERNING THE MURDER OF A FELLOW NEW GOD NAMED *LIGHTRAY.*

HM. BETTER SPELL OUT *WHO* THE NEW GODS ARE, IF I WANT THIS TO MAKE SENSE WHEN IT HITS THE FRONT PAGE...

POLICE LINE DO NOT CR...

DO NOT CROSS POLICE

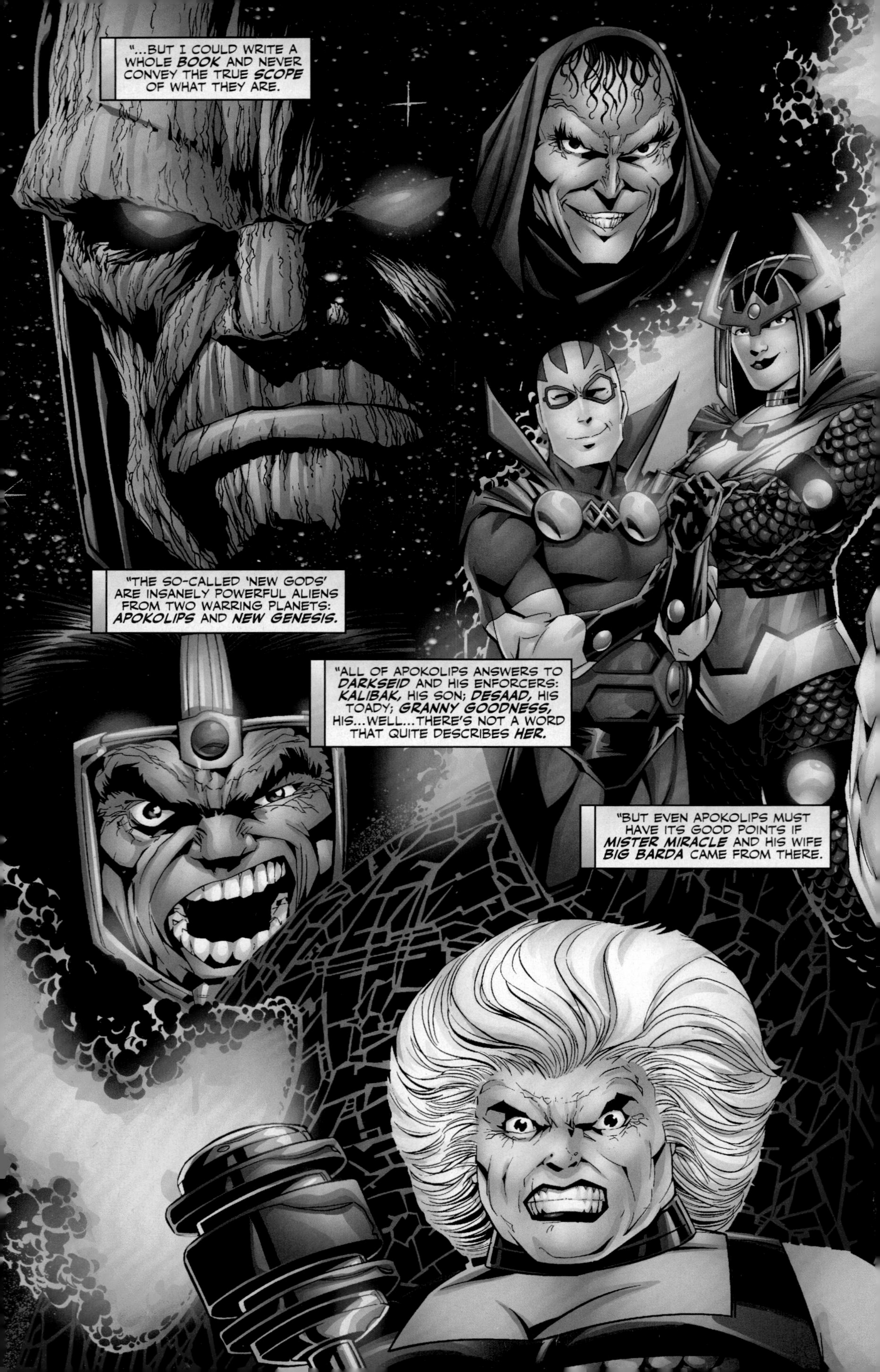
"...BUT I COULD WRITE A WHOLE *BOOK* AND NEVER CONVEY THE TRUE *SCOPE* OF WHAT THEY ARE.
"THE SO-CALLED 'NEW GODS' ARE INSANELY POWERFUL ALIENS FROM TWO WARRING PLANETS: *APOKOLIPS* AND *NEW GENESIS.*
"ALL OF APOKOLIPS ANSWERS TO *DARKSEID* AND HIS ENFORCERS: *KALIBAK,* HIS SON; *DESAAD,* HIS TOADY; *GRANNY GOODNESS,* HIS...WELL...THERE'S NOT A WORD THAT QUITE DESCRIBES *HER.*
"BUT EVEN APOKOLIPS MUST HAVE ITS GOOD POINTS IF *MISTER MIRACLE* AND HIS WIFE *BIG BARDA* CAME FROM THERE.

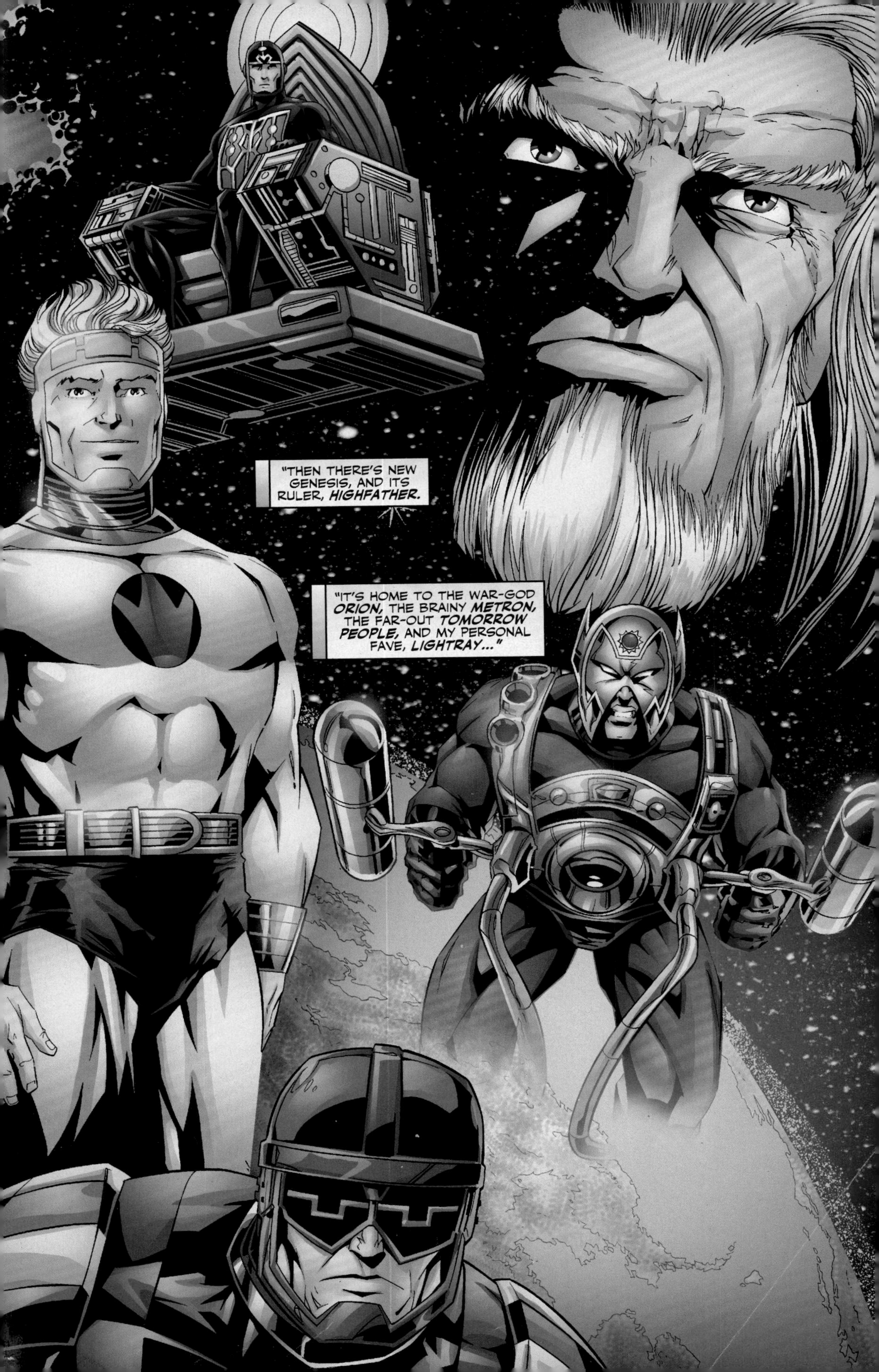
"THEN THERE'S NEW GENESIS, AND ITS RULER, HIGHFATHER.
"IT'S HOME TO THE WAR-GOD ORION, THE BRAINY METRON, THE FAR-OUT TOMORROW PEOPLE, AND MY PERSONAL FAVE, LIGHTRAY..."

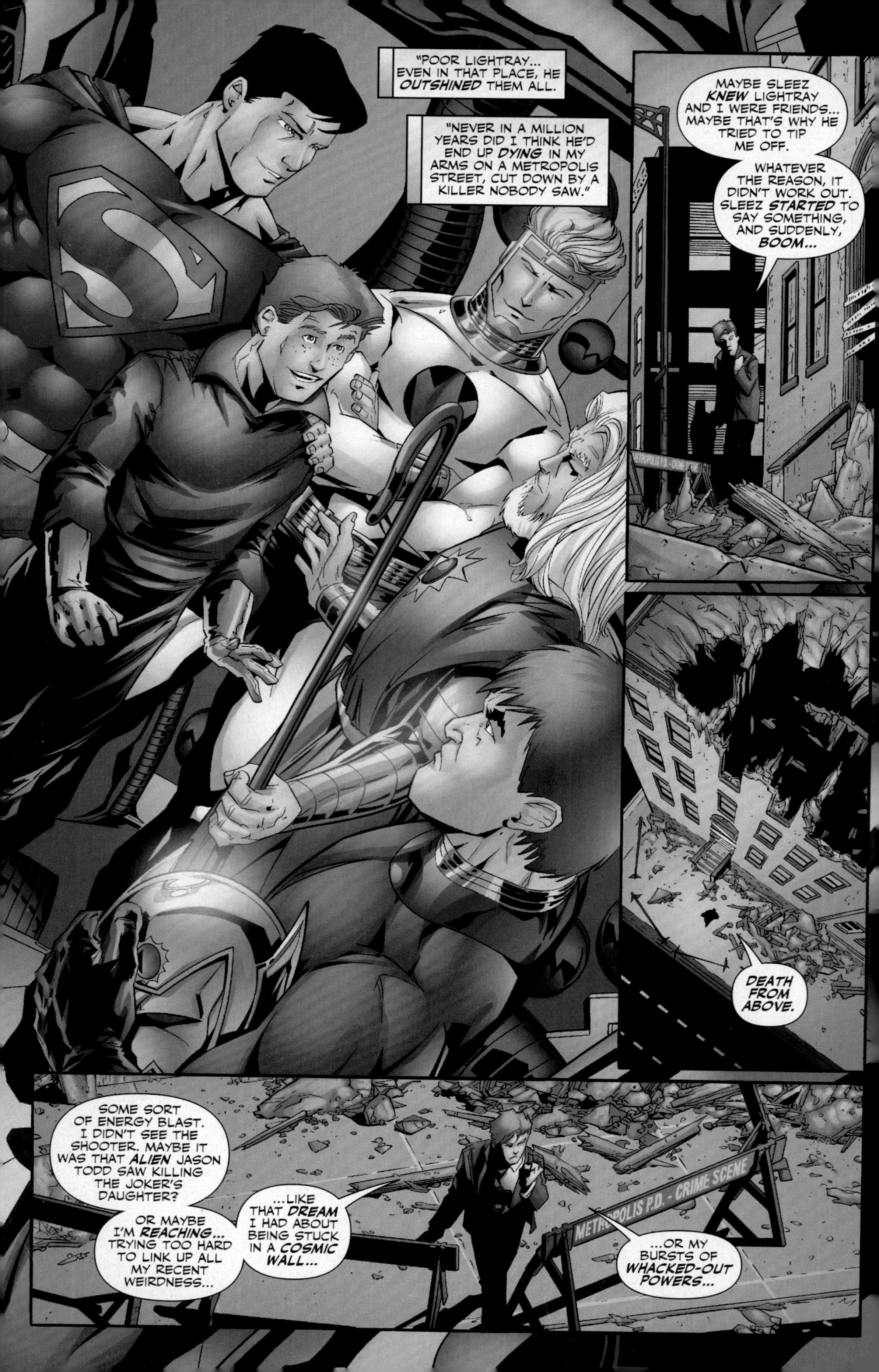
"POOR LIGHTRAY... EVEN IN THAT PLACE, HE OUTSHINED THEM ALL.
"NEVER IN A MILLION YEARS DID I THINK HE'D END UP DYING IN MY ARMS ON A METROPOLIS STREET, CUT DOWN BY A KILLER NOBODY SAW."
MAYBE SLEEZ KNEW LIGHTRAY AND I WERE FRIENDS... MAYBE THAT'S WHY HE TRIED TO TIP ME OFF.
WHATEVER THE REASON, IT DIDN'T WORK OUT. SLEEZ STARTED TO SAY SOMETHING, AND SUDDENLY, BOOM...
DEATH FROM ABOVE.
SOME SORT OF ENERGY BLAST. I DIDN'T SEE THE SHOOTER. MAYBE IT WAS THAT ALIEN JASON TODD SAW KILLING THE JOKER'S DAUGHTER?
OR MAYBE I'M REACHING... TRYING TOO HARD TO LINK UP ALL MY RECENT WEIRDNESS...
...LIKE THAT DREAM I HAD ABOUT BEING STUCK IN A COSMIC WALL...
...OR MY BURSTS OF WHACKED-OUT POWERS...
METROPOLIS P.D. - CRIME SCENE

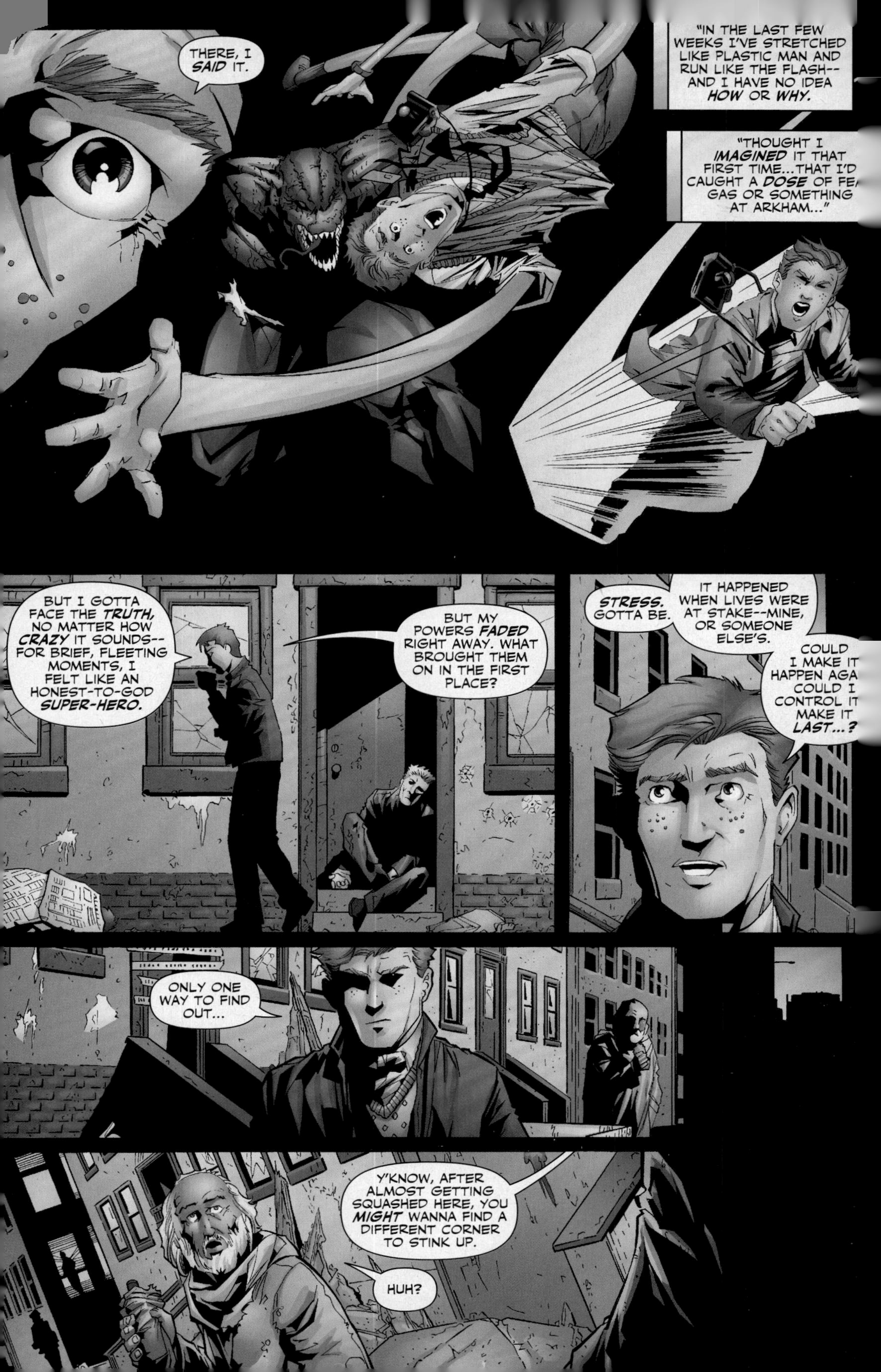

THERE, I SAID IT.
"IN THE LAST FEW WEEKS I'VE STRETCHED LIKE PLASTIC MAN AND RUN LIKE THE FLASH-- AND I HAVE NO IDEA HOW OR WHY.
"THOUGHT I IMAGINED IT THAT FIRST TIME...THAT I'D CAUGHT A DOSE OF FE GAS OR SOMETHING AT ARKHAM..."
BUT I GOTTA FACE THE TRUTH, NO MATTER HOW CRAZY IT SOUNDS-- FOR BRIEF, FLEETING MOMENTS, I FELT LIKE AN HONEST-TO-GOD SUPER-HERO.
BUT MY POWERS FADED RIGHT AWAY. WHAT BROUGHT THEM ON IN THE FIRST PLACE?
STRESS. GOTTA BE.
IT HAPPENED WHEN LIVES WERE AT STAKE--MINE, OR SOMEONE ELSE'S.
COULD I MAKE IT HAPPEN AGA COULD I CONTROL IT MAKE IT LAST...?
ONLY ONE WAY TO FIND OUT...
Y'KNOW, AFTER ALMOST GETTING SQUASHED HERE, YOU MIGHT WANNA FIND A DIFFERENT CORNER TO STINK UP.
HUH?

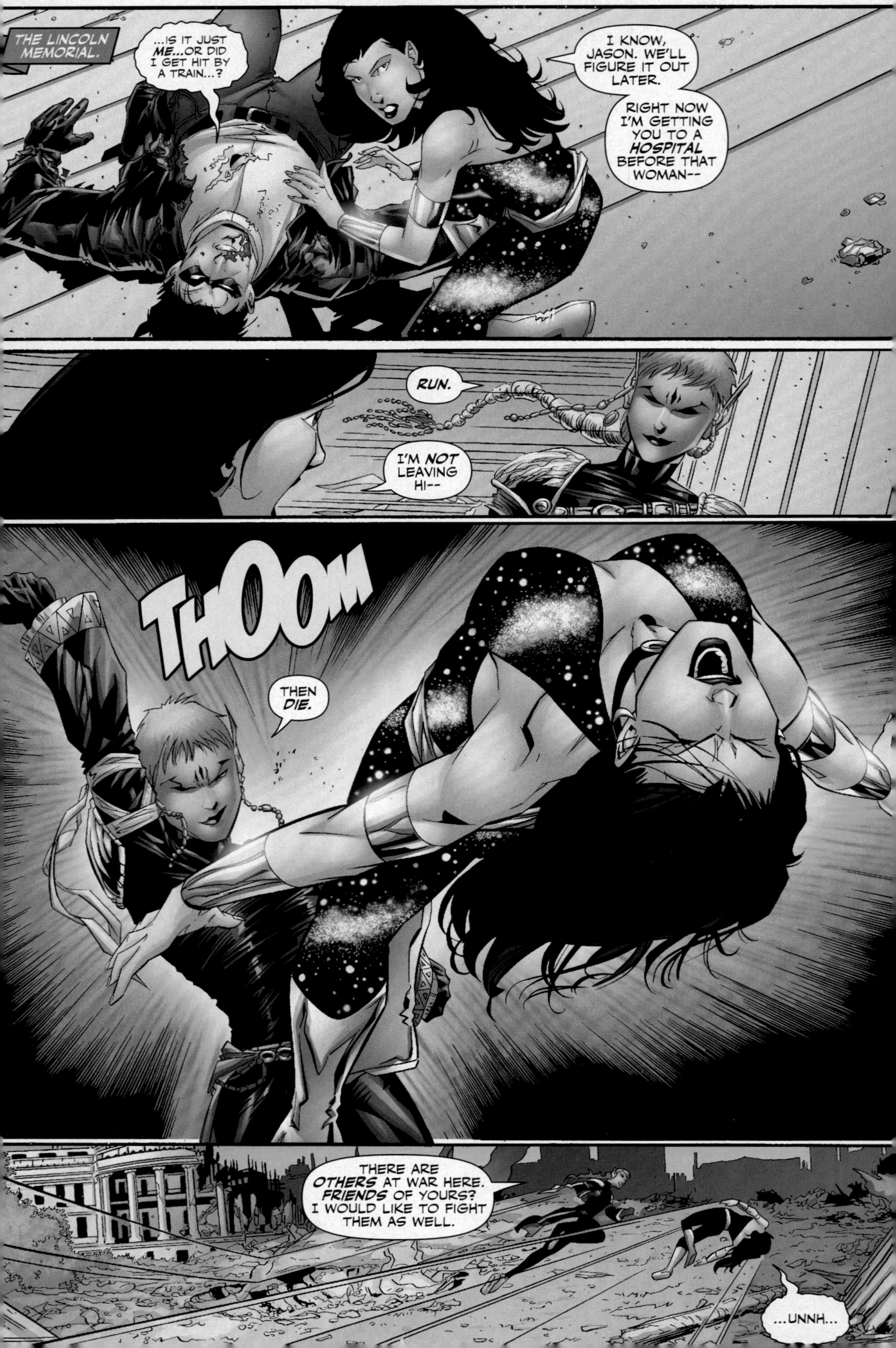
THE LINCOLN MEMORIAL.
...IS IT JUST ME...OR DID I GET HIT BY A TRAIN...?
I KNOW, JASON. WE'LL FIGURE IT OUT LATER.
RIGHT NOW I'M GETTING YOU TO A HOSPITAL BEFORE THAT WOMAN--
RUN.
I'M NOT LEAVING HI--
THOOM
THEN DIE.
THERE ARE OTHERS AT WAR HERE. FRIENDS OF YOURS? I WOULD LIKE TO FIGHT THEM AS WELL.
...UNNH...

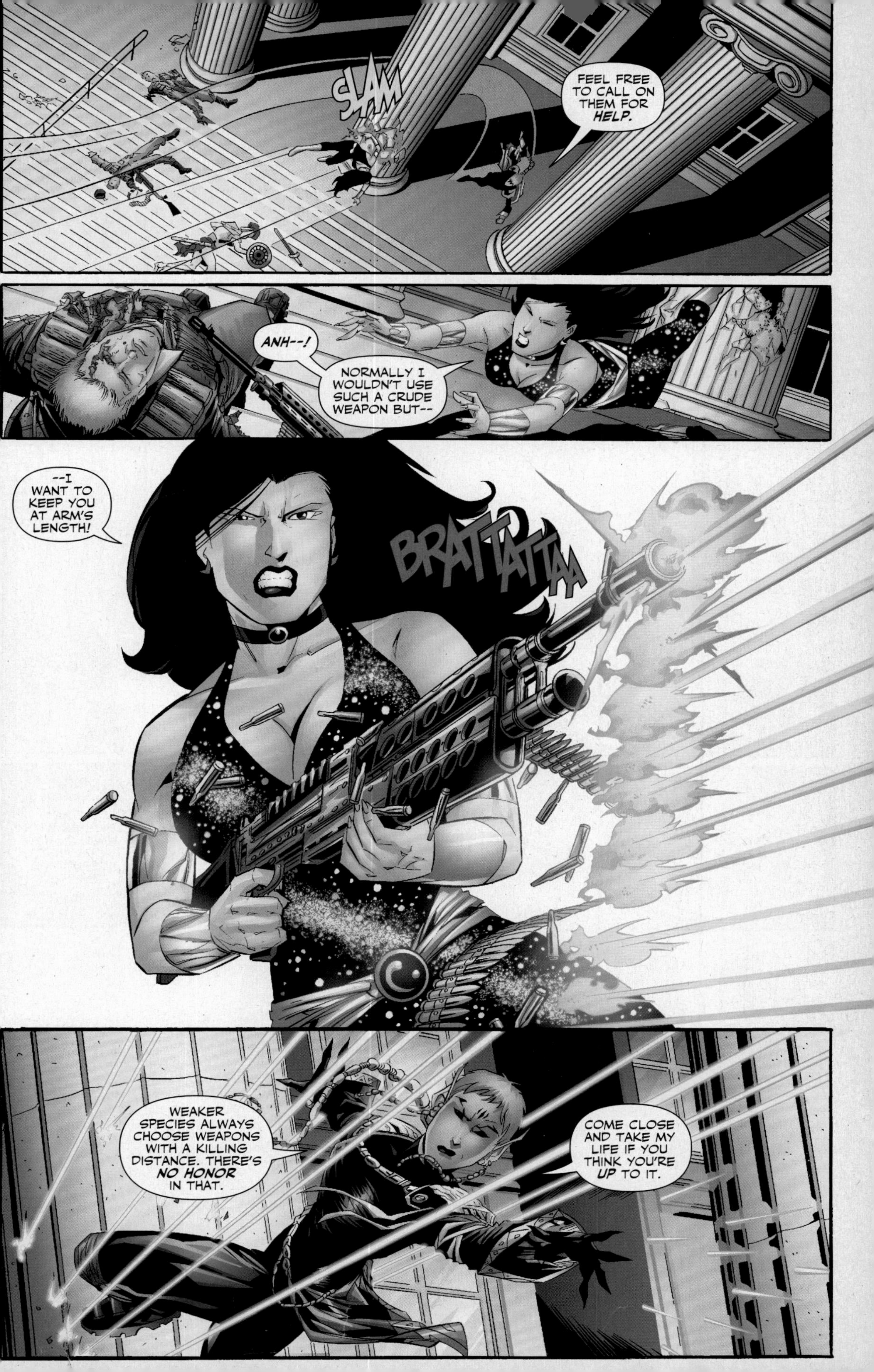
SLAM
FEEL FREE TO CALL ON THEM FOR HELP.
ANH--!
NORMALLY I WOULDN'T USE SUCH A CRUDE WEAPON BUT--
--I WANT TO KEEP YOU AT ARM'S LENGTH!
BRATTATTAA
WEAKER SPECIES ALWAYS CHOOSE WEAPONS WITH A KILLING DISTANCE. THERE'S NO HONOR IN THAT.
COME CLOSE AND TAKE MY LIFE IF YOU THINK YOU'RE UP TO IT.

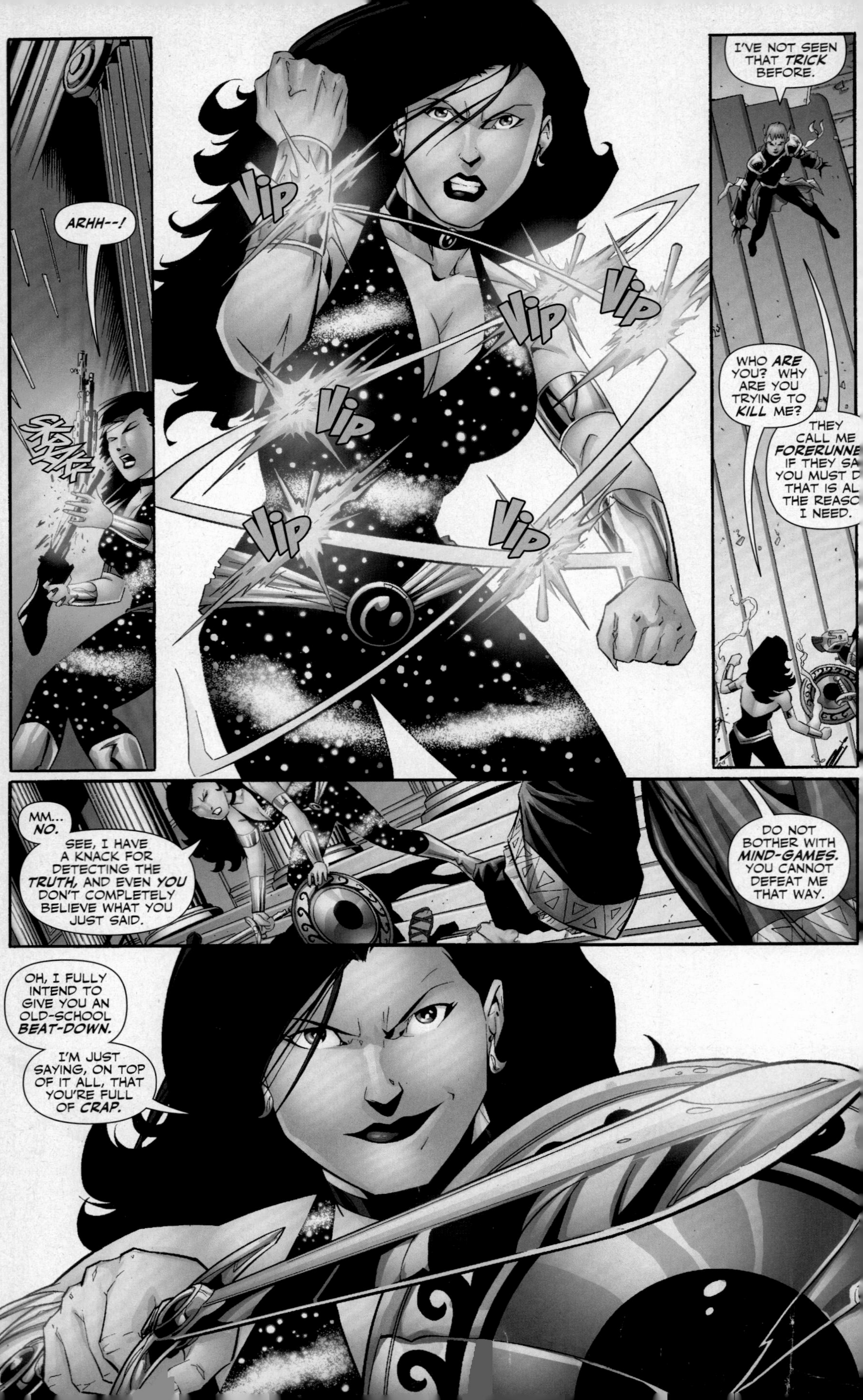
ARHH--!
SKRAK
VIP
VIP
VIP
VIP
VIP
VIP
I'VE NOT SEEN THAT TRICK BEFORE.
WHO ARE YOU? WHY ARE YOU TRYING TO KILL ME?
THEY CALL ME FORERUNNE IF THEY SA YOU MUST D THAT IS AL THE REASO I NEED.
MM... NO.
SEE, I HAVE A KNACK FOR DETECTING THE TRUTH, AND EVEN YOU DON'T COMPLETELY BELIEVE WHAT YOU JUST SAID.
DO NOT BOTHER WITH MIND-GAMES. YOU CANNOT DEFEAT ME THAT WAY.
OH, I FULLY INTEND TO GIVE YOU AN OLD-SCHOOL BEAT-DOWN.
I'M JUST SAYING, ON TOP OF IT ALL, THAT YOU'RE FULL OF CRAP.

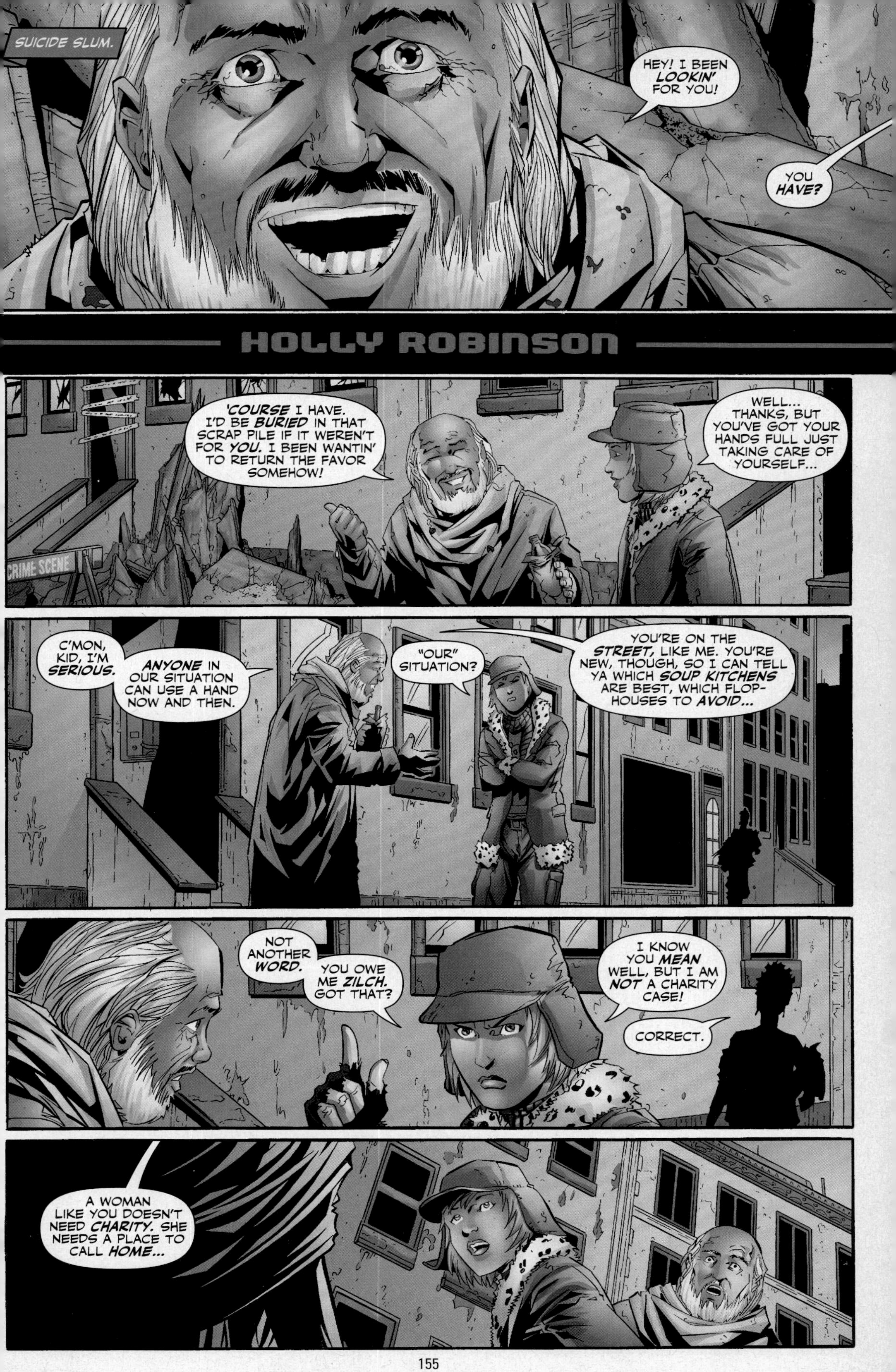
SUICIDE SLUM.
HEY! I BEEN LOOKIN' FOR YOU!
YOU HAVE?
HOLLY ROBINSON
'COURSE I HAVE. I'D BE BURIED IN THAT SCRAP PILE IF IT WEREN'T FOR YOU. I BEEN WANTIN' TO RETURN THE FAVOR SOMEHOW!
WELL... THANKS, BUT YOU'VE GOT YOUR HANDS FULL JUST TAKING CARE OF YOURSELF...
CRIME SCENE
C'MON, KID, I'M SERIOUS.
ANYONE IN OUR SITUATION CAN USE A HAND NOW AND THEN.
"OUR" SITUATION?
YOU'RE ON THE STREET, LIKE ME. YOU'RE NEW, THOUGH, SO I CAN TELL YA WHICH SOUP KITCHENS ARE BEST, WHICH FLOP-HOUSES TO AVOID...
NOT ANOTHER WORD.
YOU OWE ME ZILCH. GOT THAT?
I KNOW YOU MEAN WELL, BUT I AM NOT A CHARITY CASE!
CORRECT.
A WOMAN LIKE YOU DOESN'T NEED CHARITY. SHE NEEDS A PLACE TO CALL HOME...

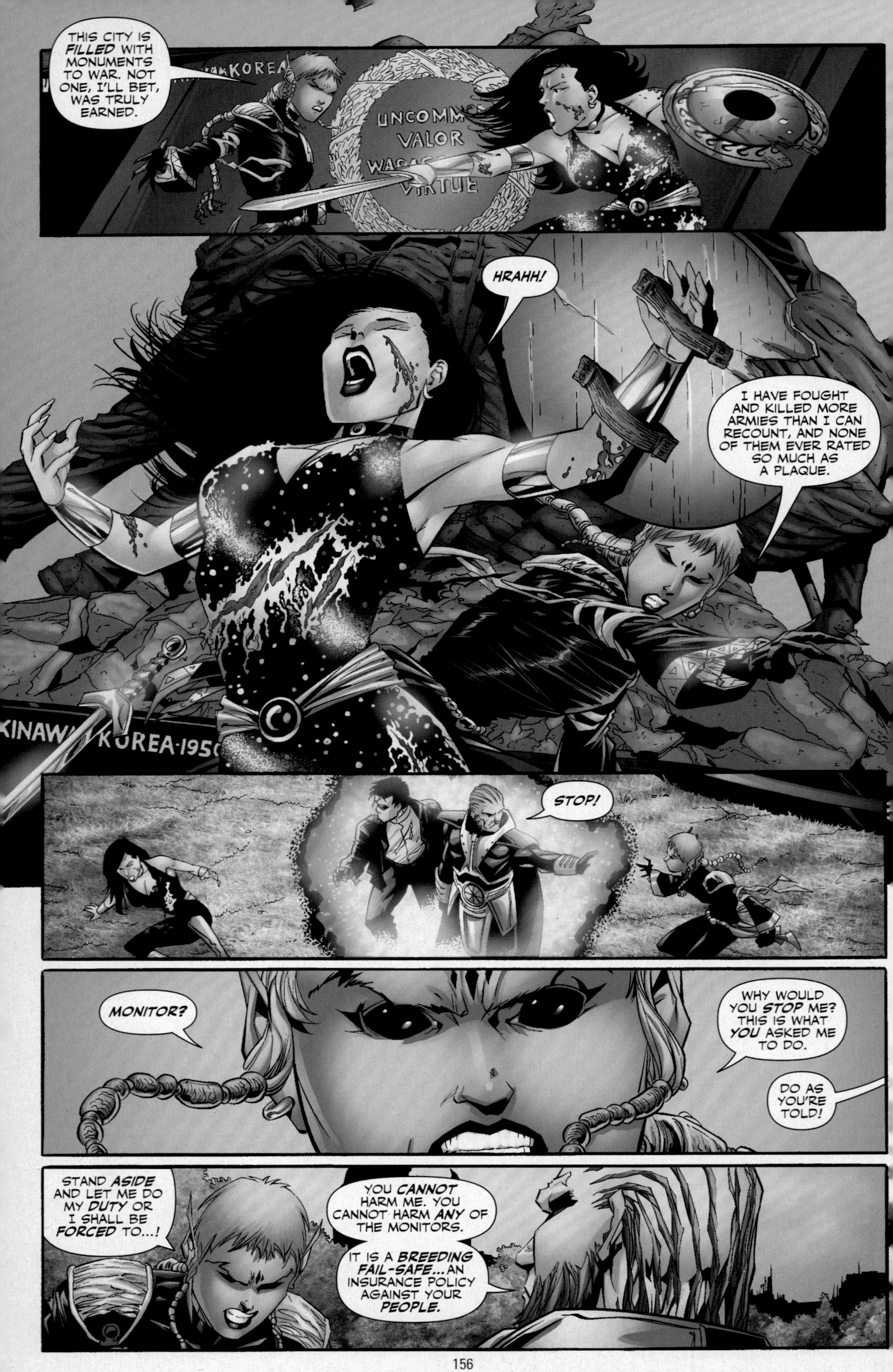
THIS CITY IS FILLED WITH MONUMENTS TO WAR. NOT ONE, I'LL BET, WAS TRULY EARNED.
KOREA
UNCOMM VALOR
VIRTUE
HRAHH!
I HAVE FOUGHT AND KILLED MORE ARMIES THAN I CAN RECOUNT, AND NONE OF THEM EVER RATED SO MUCH AS A PLAQUE.
KOREA-1950
STOP!
MONITOR?
WHY WOULD YOU STOP ME? THIS IS WHAT YOU ASKED ME TO DO.
DO AS YOU'RE TOLD!
STAND ASIDE AND LET ME DO MY DUTY OR I SHALL BE FORCED TO...!
YOU CANNOT HARM ME. YOU CANNOT HARM ANY OF THE MONITORS.
IT IS A BREEDING FAIL-SAFE... AN INSURANCE POLICY AGAINST YOUR PEOPLE.

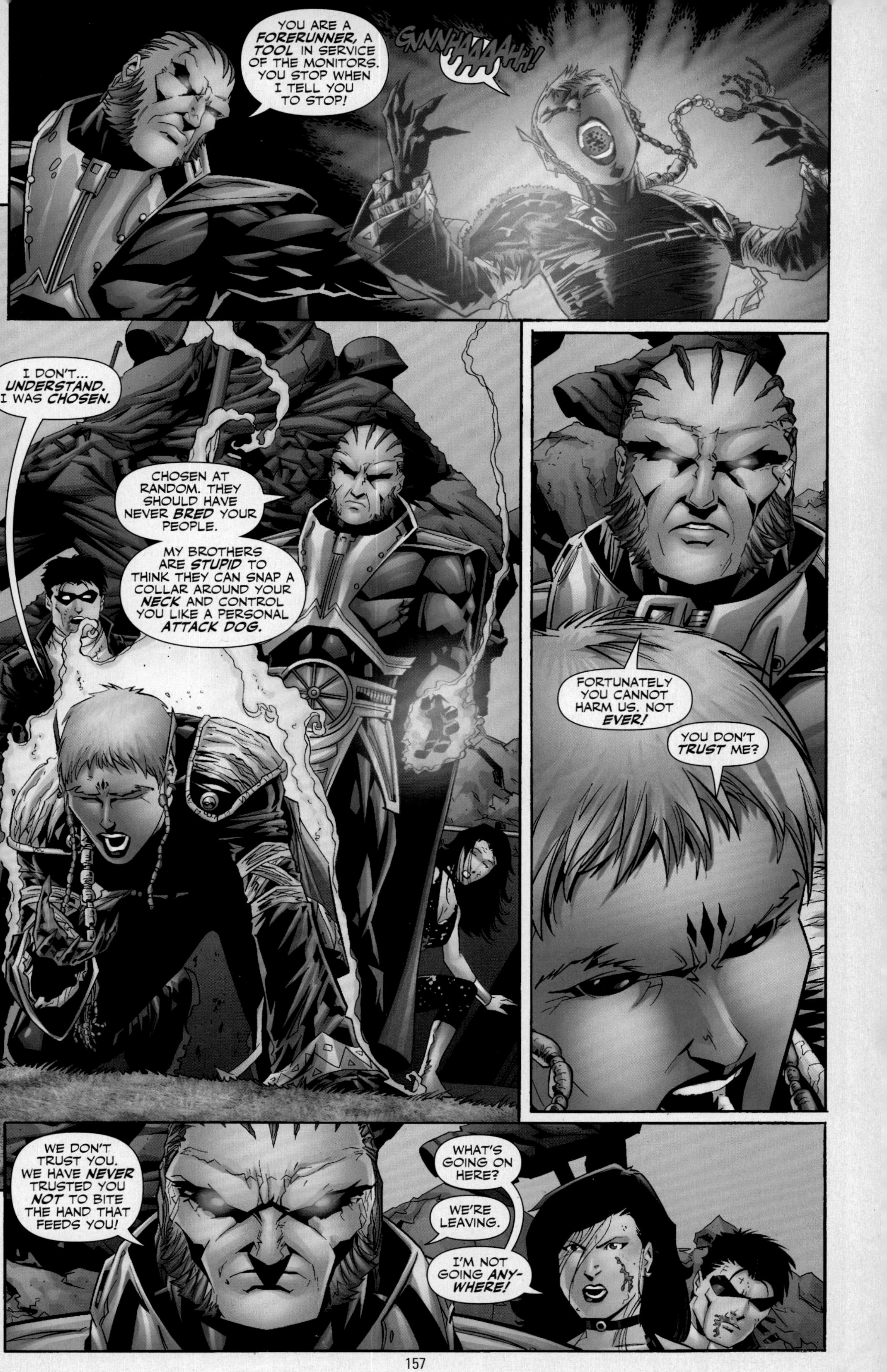

YOU ARE A FORERUNNER, A TOOL IN SERVICE OF THE MONITORS. YOU STOP WHEN I TELL YOU TO STOP!
GNNHAAAAHH!
I DON'T... UNDERSTAND. I WAS CHOSEN.
CHOSEN AT RANDOM. THEY SHOULD HAVE NEVER BRED YOUR PEOPLE.
MY BROTHERS ARE STUPID TO THINK THEY CAN SNAP A COLLAR AROUND YOUR NECK AND CONTROL YOU LIKE A PERSONAL ATTACK DOG.
FORTUNATELY YOU CANNOT HARM US. NOT EVER!
YOU DON'T TRUST ME?
WE DON'T TRUST YOU. WE HAVE NEVER TRUSTED YOU NOT TO BITE THE HAND THAT FEEDS YOU!
WHAT'S GOING ON HERE?
WE'RE LEAVING.
I'M NOT GOING ANY-WHERE!

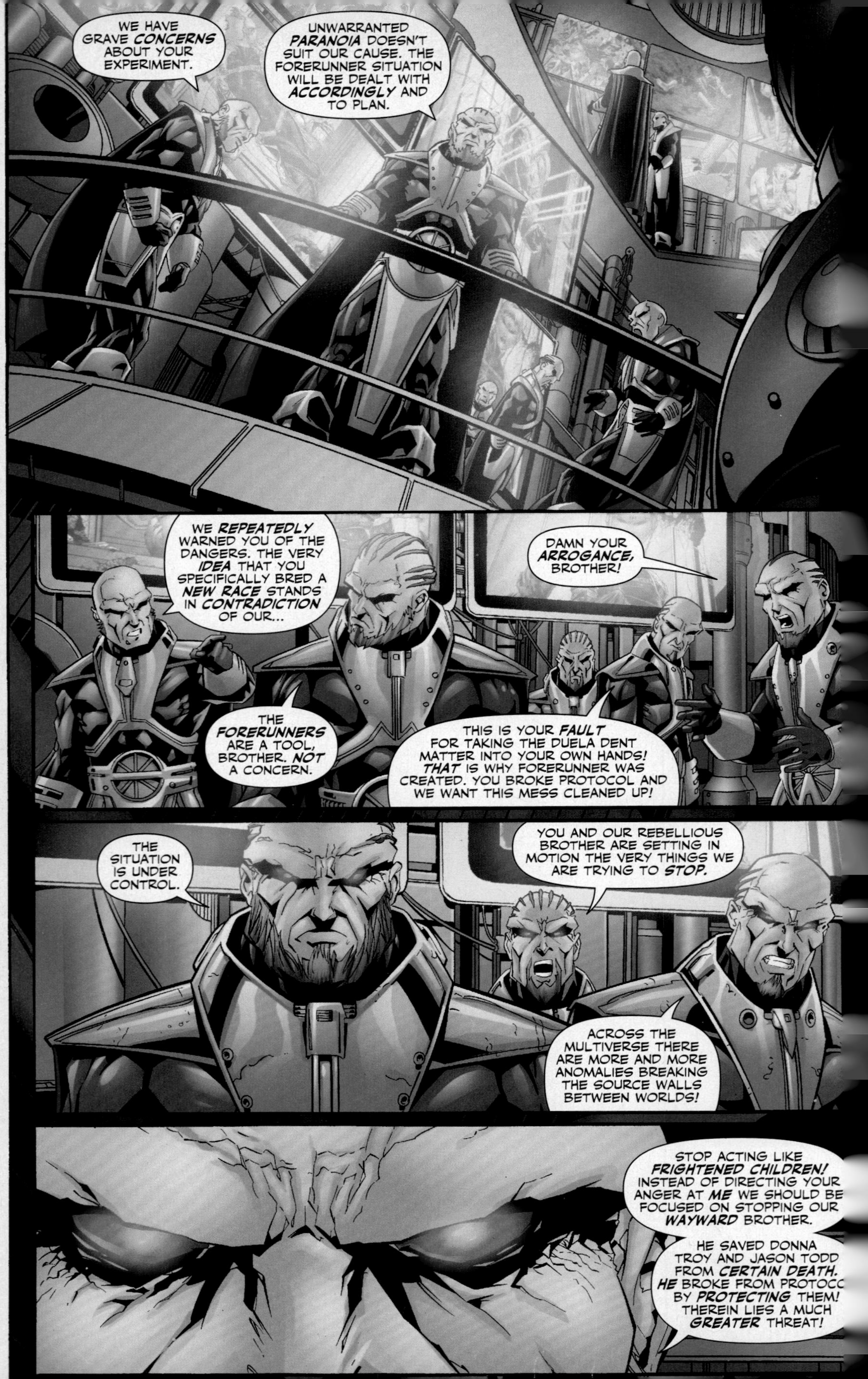
WE HAVE GRAVE CONCERNS ABOUT YOUR EXPERIMENT.
UNWARRANTED PARANOIA DOESN'T SUIT OUR CAUSE. THE FORERUNNER SITUATION WILL BE DEALT WITH ACCORDINGLY AND TO PLAN.
WE REPEATEDLY WARNED YOU OF THE DANGERS. THE VERY IDEA THAT YOU SPECIFICALLY BRED A NEW RACE STANDS IN CONTRADICTION OF OUR...
DAMN YOUR ARROGANCE, BROTHER!
THE FORERUNNERS ARE A TOOL, BROTHER. NOT A CONCERN.
THIS IS YOUR FAULT FOR TAKING THE DUELA DENT MATTER INTO YOUR OWN HANDS! THAT IS WHY FORERUNNER WAS CREATED. YOU BROKE PROTOCOL AND WE WANT THIS MESS CLEANED UP!
THE SITUATION IS UNDER CONTROL.
YOU AND OUR REBELLIOUS BROTHER ARE SETTING IN MOTION THE VERY THINGS WE ARE TRYING TO STOP.
ACROSS THE MULTIVERSE THERE ARE MORE AND MORE ANOMALIES BREAKING THE SOURCE WALLS BETWEEN WORLDS!
STOP ACTING LIKE FRIGHTENED CHILDREN! INSTEAD OF DIRECTING YOUR ANGER AT ME WE SHOULD BE FOCUSED ON STOPPING OUR WAYWARD BROTHER.
HE SAVED DONNA TROY AND JASON TODD FROM CERTAIN DEATH. HE BROKE FROM PROTOCO BY PROTECTING THEM! THEREIN LIES A MUCH GREATER THREAT!

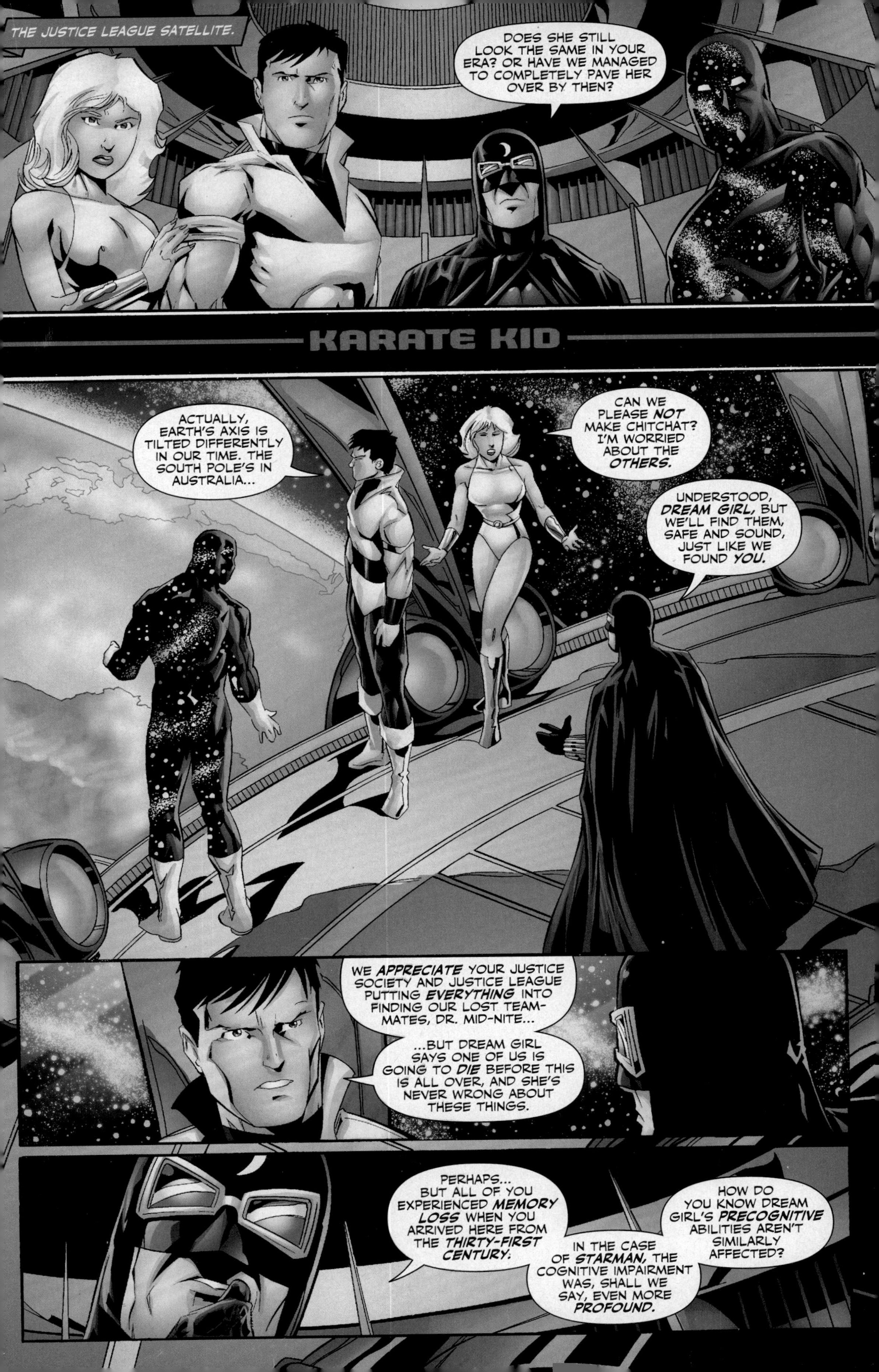
THE JUSTICE LEAGUE SATELLITE.
DOES SHE STILL LOOK THE SAME IN YOUR ERA? OR HAVE WE MANAGED TO COMPLETELY PAVE HER OVER BY THEN?
KARATE KID
ACTUALLY, EARTH'S AXIS IS TILTED DIFFERENTLY IN OUR TIME. THE SOUTH POLE'S IN AUSTRALIA...
CAN WE PLEASE NOT MAKE CHITCHAT? I'M WORRIED ABOUT THE OTHERS.
UNDERSTOOD, DREAM GIRL, BUT WE'LL FIND THEM, SAFE AND SOUND, JUST LIKE WE FOUND YOU.
WE APPRECIATE YOUR JUSTICE SOCIETY AND JUSTICE LEAGUE PUTTING EVERYTHING INTO FINDING OUR LOST TEAM-MATES, DR. MID-NITE...
...BUT DREAM GIRL SAYS ONE OF US IS GOING TO DIE BEFORE THIS IS ALL OVER, AND SHE'S NEVER WRONG ABOUT THESE THINGS.
PERHAPS... BUT ALL OF YOU EXPERIENCED MEMORY LOSS WHEN YOU ARRIVED HERE FROM THE THIRTY-FIRST CENTURY.
IN THE CASE OF STARMAN, THE COGNITIVE IMPAIRMENT WAS, SHALL WE SAY, EVEN MORE PROFOUND.
HOW DO YOU KNOW DREAM GIRL'S PRECOGNITIVE ABILITIES AREN'T SIMILARLY AFFECTED?

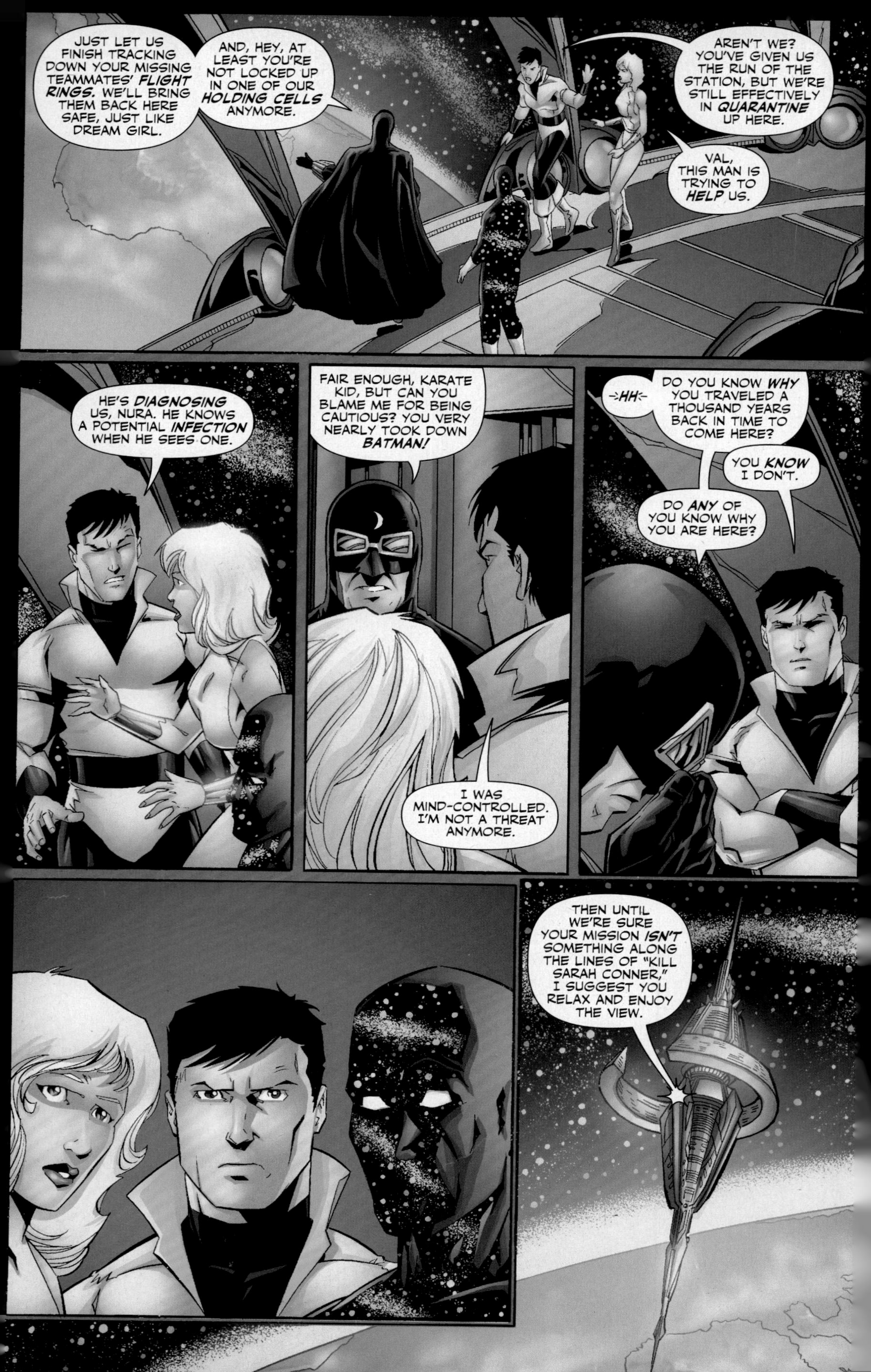
JUST LET US FINISH TRACKING DOWN YOUR MISSING TEAMMATES' FLIGHT RINGS. WE'LL BRING THEM BACK HERE SAFE, JUST LIKE DREAM GIRL.
AND, HEY, AT LEAST YOU'RE NOT LOCKED UP IN ONE OF OUR HOLDING CELLS ANYMORE.
AREN'T WE? YOU'VE GIVEN US THE RUN OF THE STATION, BUT WE'RE STILL EFFECTIVELY IN QUARANTINE UP HERE.
VAL, THIS MAN IS TRYING TO HELP US.
HE'S DIAGNOSING US, NURA. HE KNOWS A POTENTIAL INFECTION WHEN HE SEES ONE.
FAIR ENOUGH, KARATE KID, BUT CAN YOU BLAME ME FOR BEING CAUTIOUS? YOU VERY NEARLY TOOK DOWN BATMAN!
I WAS MIND-CONTROLLED. I'M NOT A THREAT ANYMORE.
HH
DO YOU KNOW WHY YOU TRAVELED A THOUSAND YEARS BACK IN TIME TO COME HERE?
YOU KNOW I DON'T.
DO ANY OF YOU KNOW WHY YOU ARE HERE?
THEN UNTIL WE'RE SURE YOUR MISSION ISN'T SOMETHING ALONG THE LINES OF "KILL SARAH CONNER," I SUGGEST YOU RELAX AND ENJOY THE VIEW.

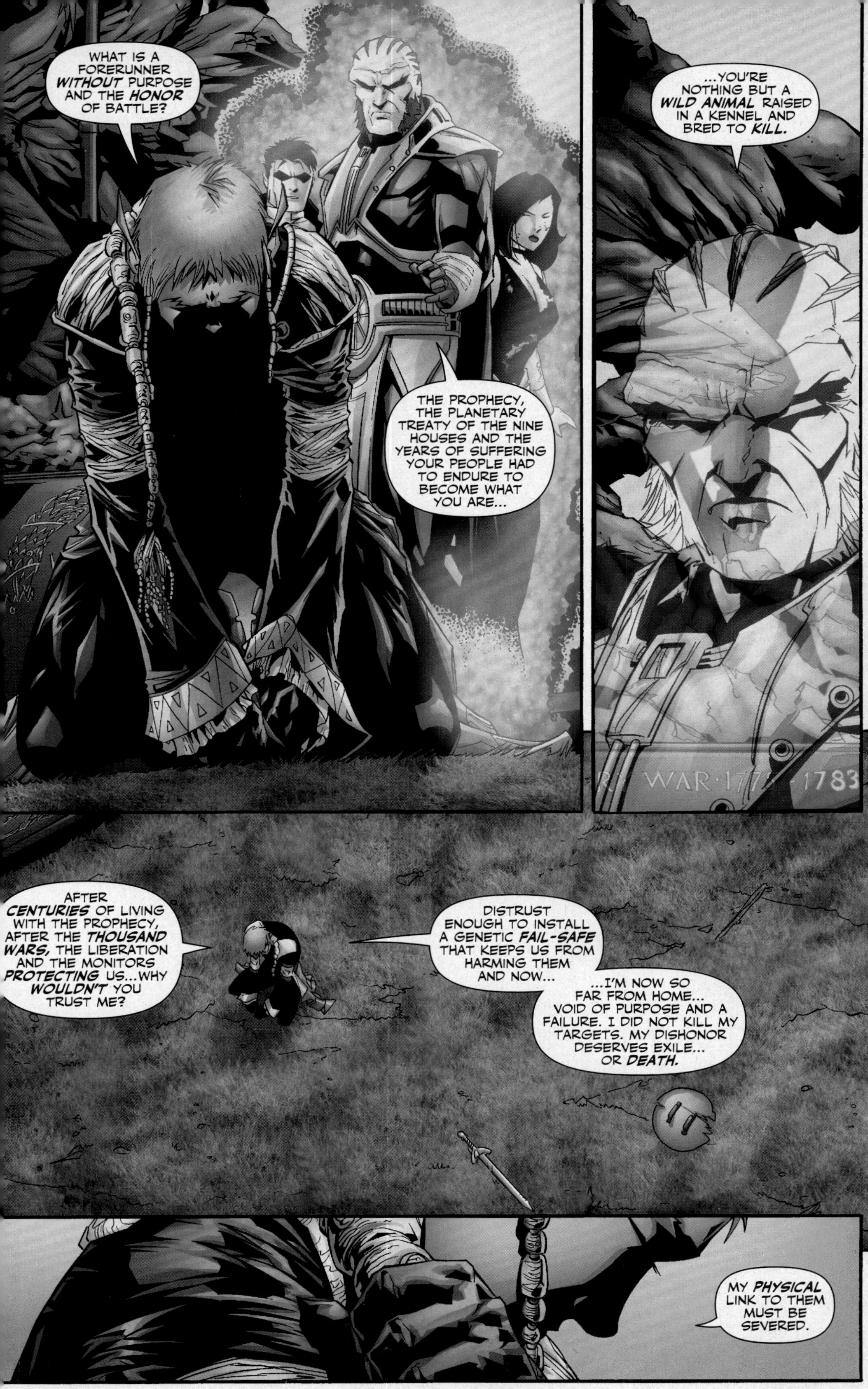

WHAT IS A FORERUNNER WITHOUT PURPOSE AND THE HONOR OF BATTLE?
THE PROPHECY, THE PLANETARY TREATY OF THE NINE HOUSES AND THE YEARS OF SUFFERING YOUR PEOPLE HAD TO ENDURE TO BECOME WHAT YOU ARE...
...YOU'RE NOTHING BUT A WILD ANIMAL RAISED IN A KENNEL AND BRED TO KILL.
AFTER CENTURIES OF LIVING WITH THE PROPHECY, AFTER THE THOUSAND WARS, THE LIBERATION AND THE MONITORS PROTECTING US...WHY WOULDN'T YOU TRUST ME?
DISTRUST ENOUGH TO INSTALL A GENETIC FAIL-SAFE THAT KEEPS US FROM HARMING THEM AND NOW...
...I'M NOW SO FAR FROM HOME... VOID OF PURPOSE AND A FAILURE. I DID NOT KILL MY TARGETS. MY DISHONOR DESERVES EXILE... OR DEATH.
MY PHYSICAL LINK TO THEM MUST BE SEVERED.

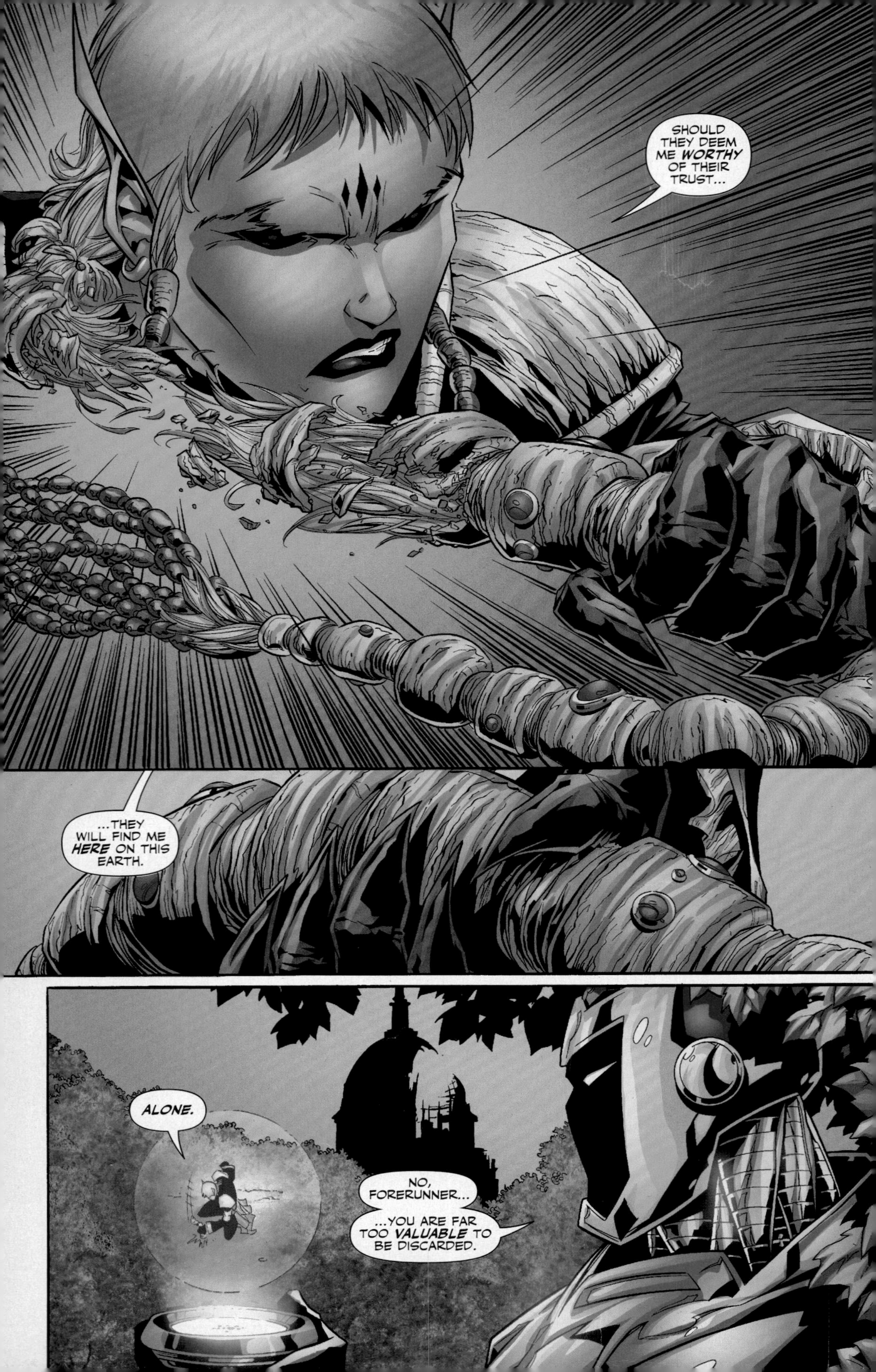
SHOULD THEY DEEM ME WORTHY OF THEIR TRUST...
...THEY WILL FIND ME HERE ON THIS EARTH.
ALONE.
NO, FORERUNNER...
...YOU ARE FAR TOO VALUABLE TO BE DISCARDED.

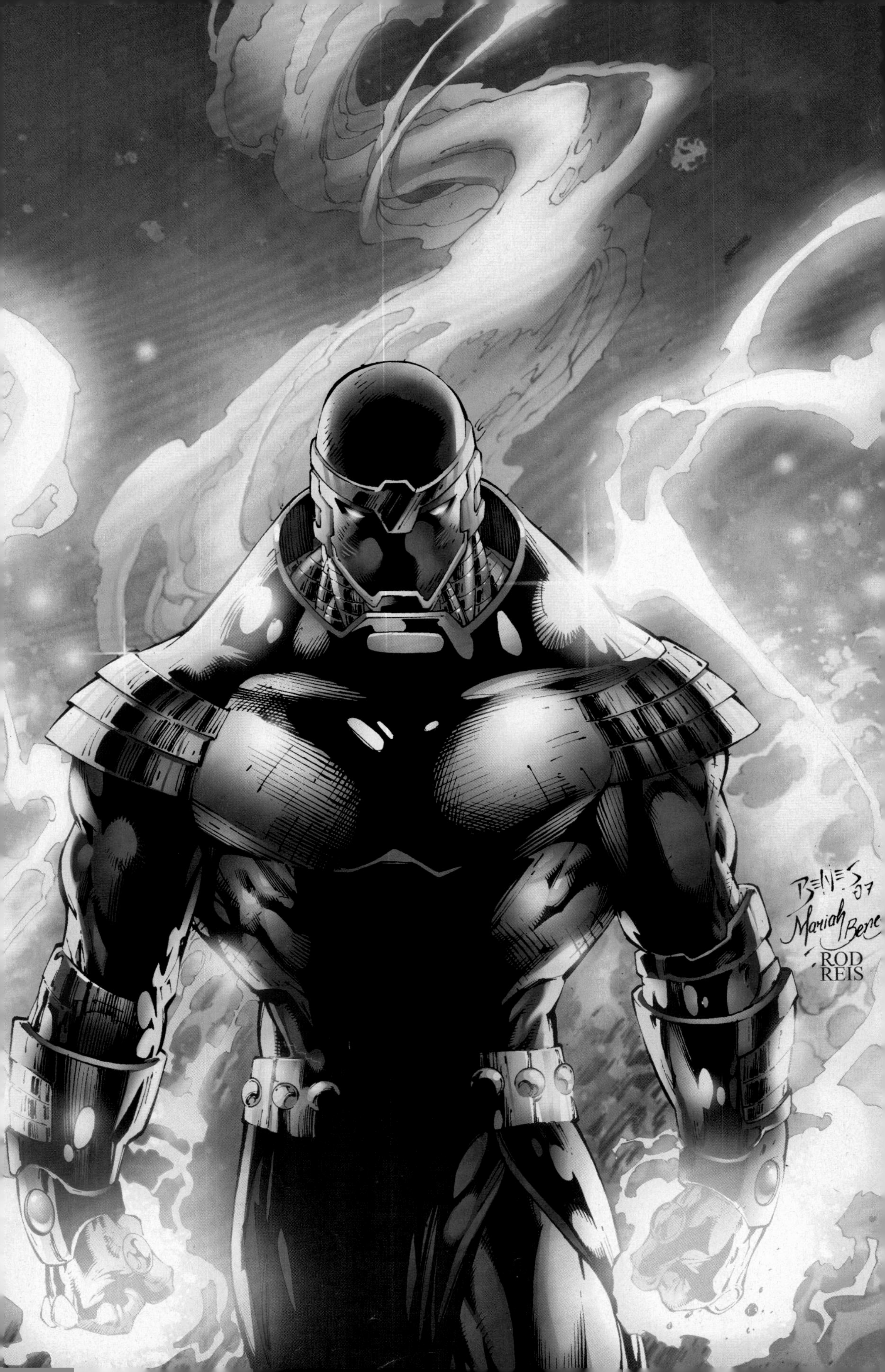
BENES '07
Mariah Benes
ROD REIS

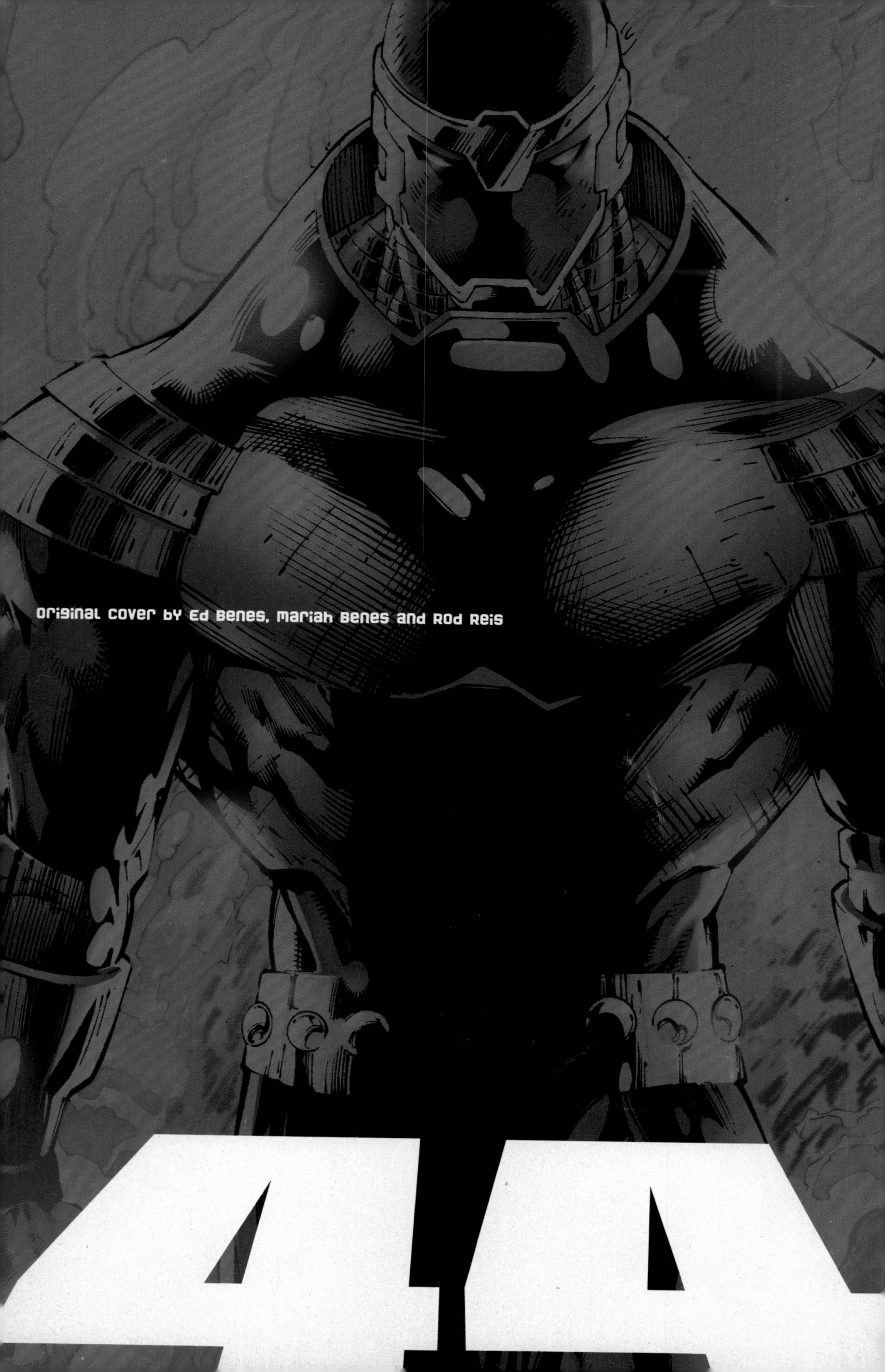
44

Original cover by Ed Benes, Mariah Benes and Rod Reis

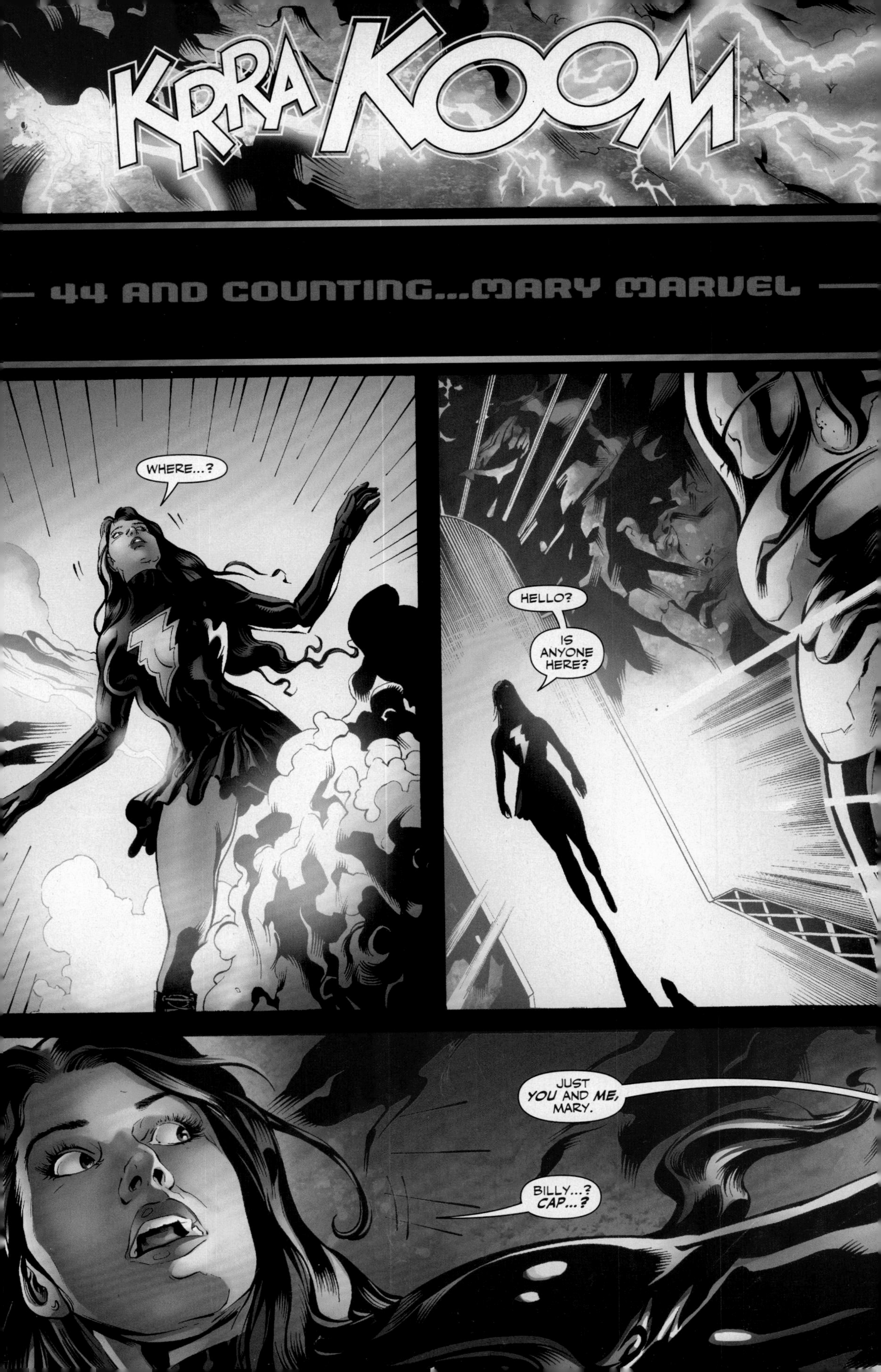
KRRA KOOM
44 AND COUNTING...MARY MARVEL
WHERE...?
HELLO?
IS ANYONE HERE?
JUST *YOU AND ME,* MARY.
BILLY...? *CAP...?*

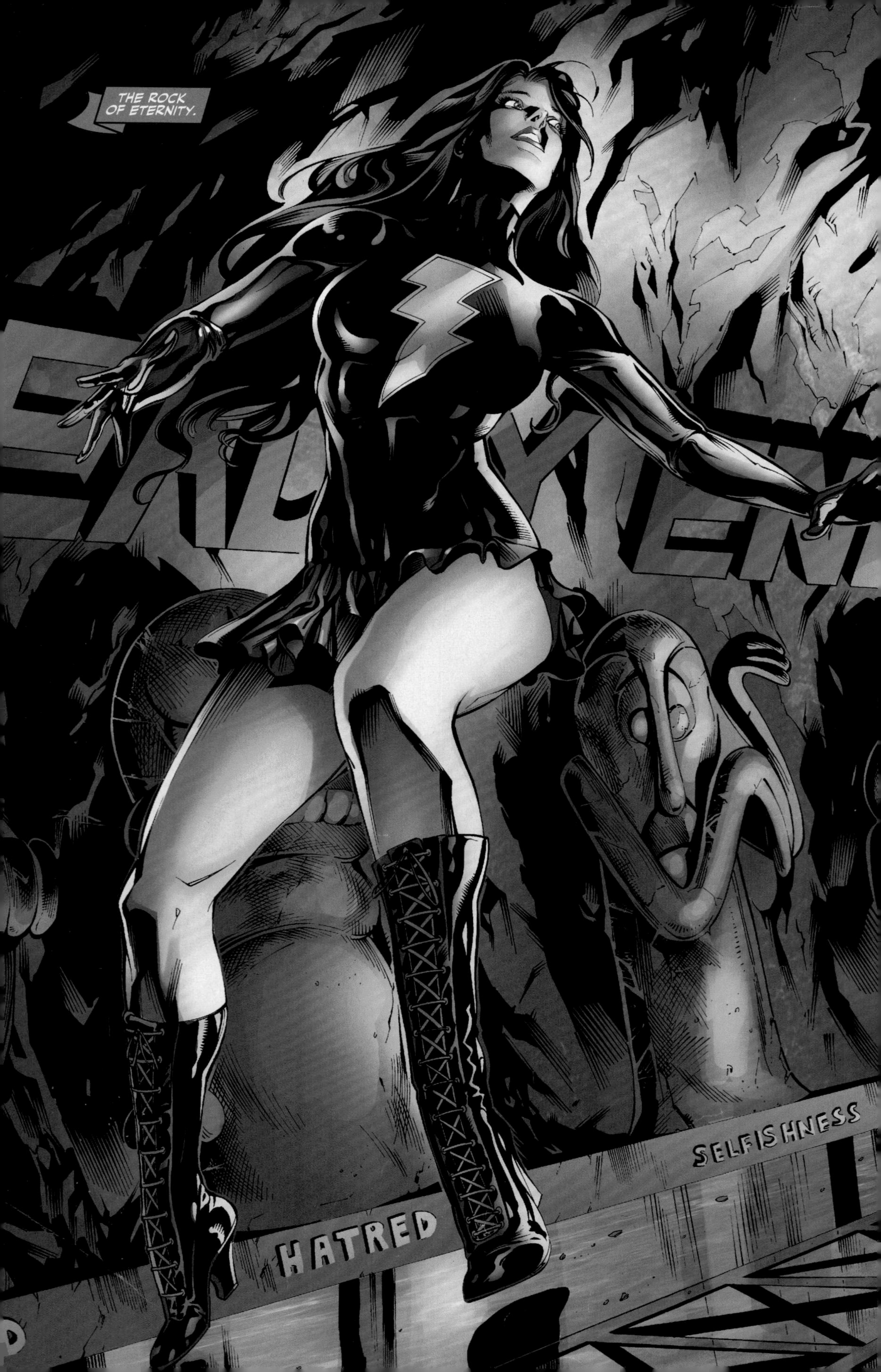
THE ROCK OF ETERNITY.
SELFISHNESS
HATRED

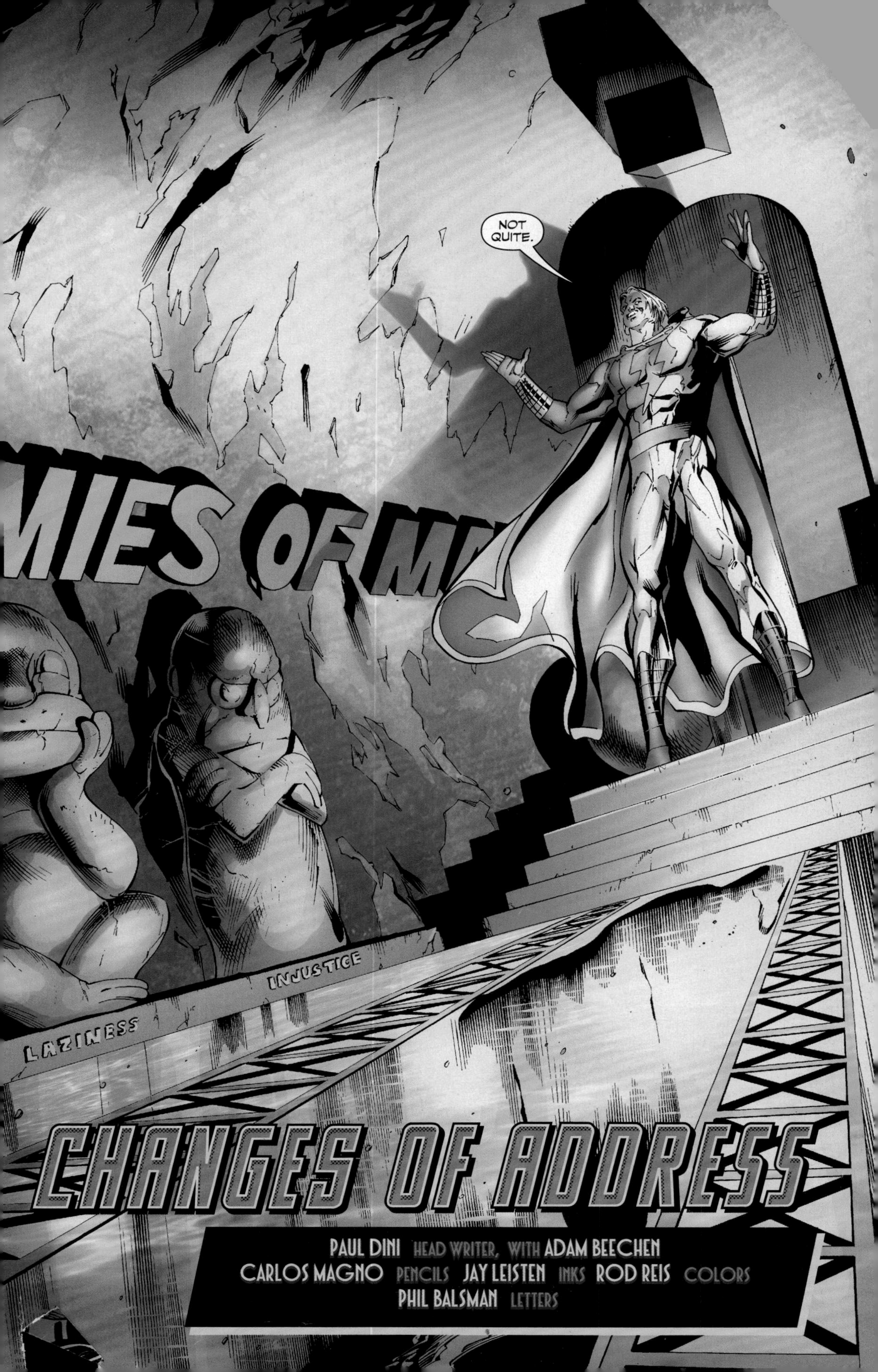

NOT QUITE.
MIES OF MI
INJUSTICE
LAZINESS
CHANGES OF ADDRESS
PAUL DINI HEAD WRITER, WITH ADAM BEECHEN
CARLOS MAGNO PENCILS JAY LEISTEN INKS ROD REIS COLORS
PHIL BALSMAN LETTERS

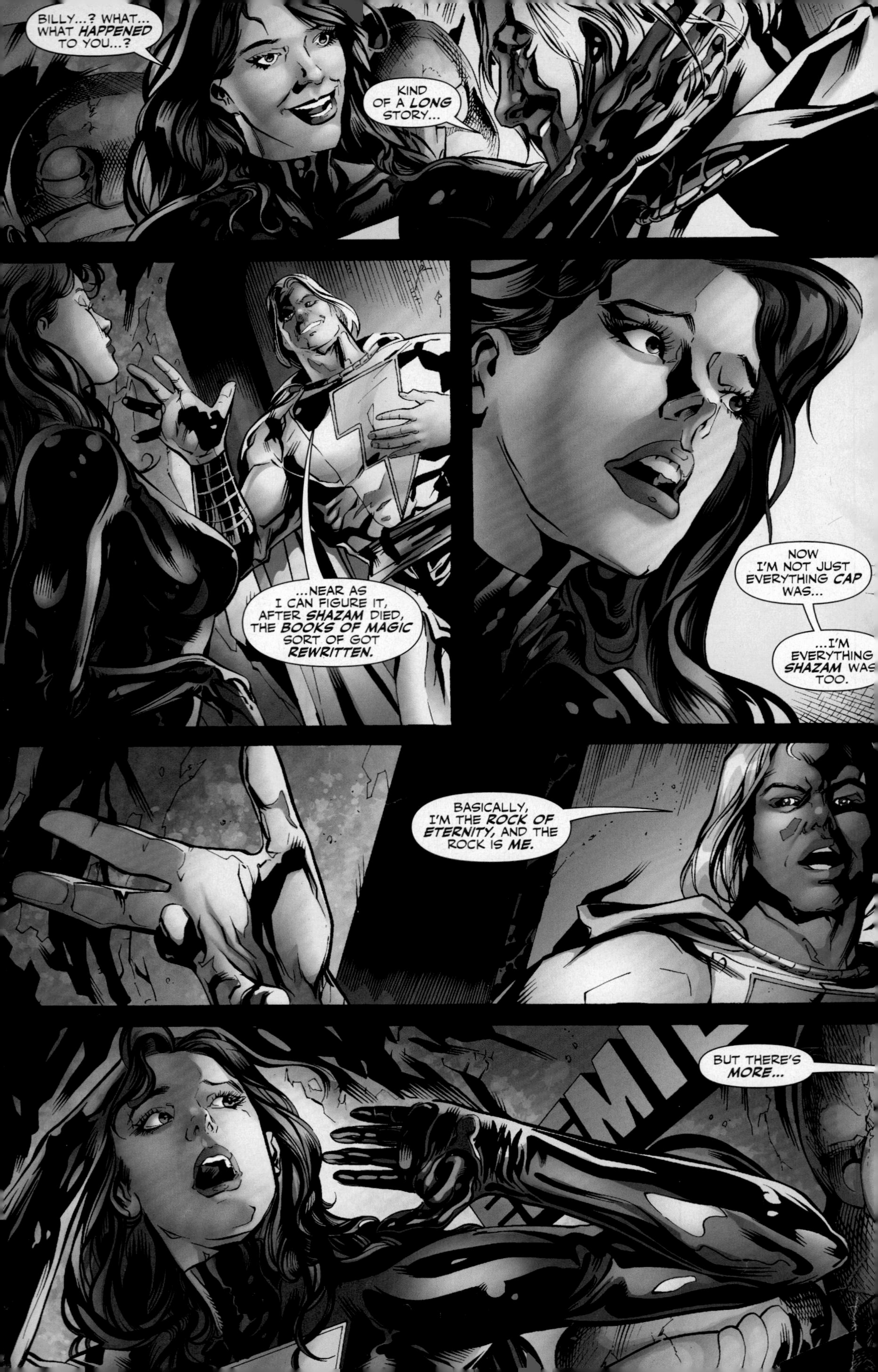
BILLY...? WHAT... WHAT HAPPENED TO YOU...?
KIND OF A LONG STORY...
...NEAR AS I CAN FIGURE IT, AFTER SHAZAM DIED, THE BOOKS OF MAGIC SORT OF GOT REWRITTEN.
NOW I'M NOT JUST EVERYTHING CAP WAS...
...I'M EVERYTHING SHAZAM WAS TOO.
BASICALLY, I'M THE ROCK OF ETERNITY, AND THE ROCK IS ME.
BUT THERE'S MORE...

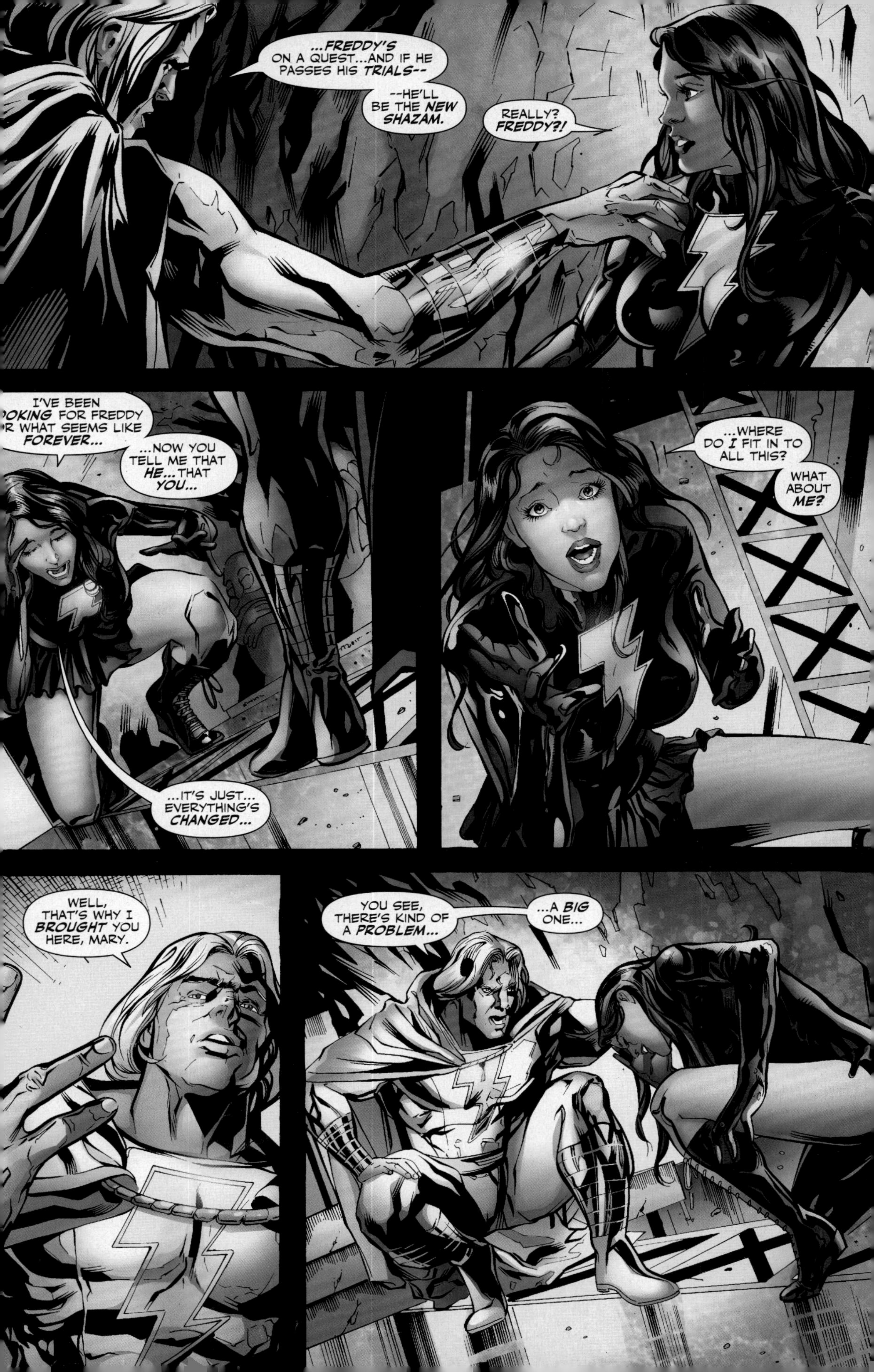

...FREDDY'S ON A QUEST...AND IF HE PASSES HIS TRIALS--
--HE'LL BE THE NEW SHAZAM.
REALLY? FREDDY?!
I'VE BEEN OOKING FOR FREDDY R WHAT SEEMS LIKE FOREVER...
...NOW YOU TELL ME THAT HE...THAT YOU...
...IT'S JUST... EVERYTHING'S CHANGED...
...WHERE DO I FIT IN TO ALL THIS?
WHAT ABOUT ME?
WELL, THAT'S WHY I BROUGHT YOU HERE, MARY.
YOU SEE, THERE'S KIND OF A PROBLEM...
...A BIG ONE...

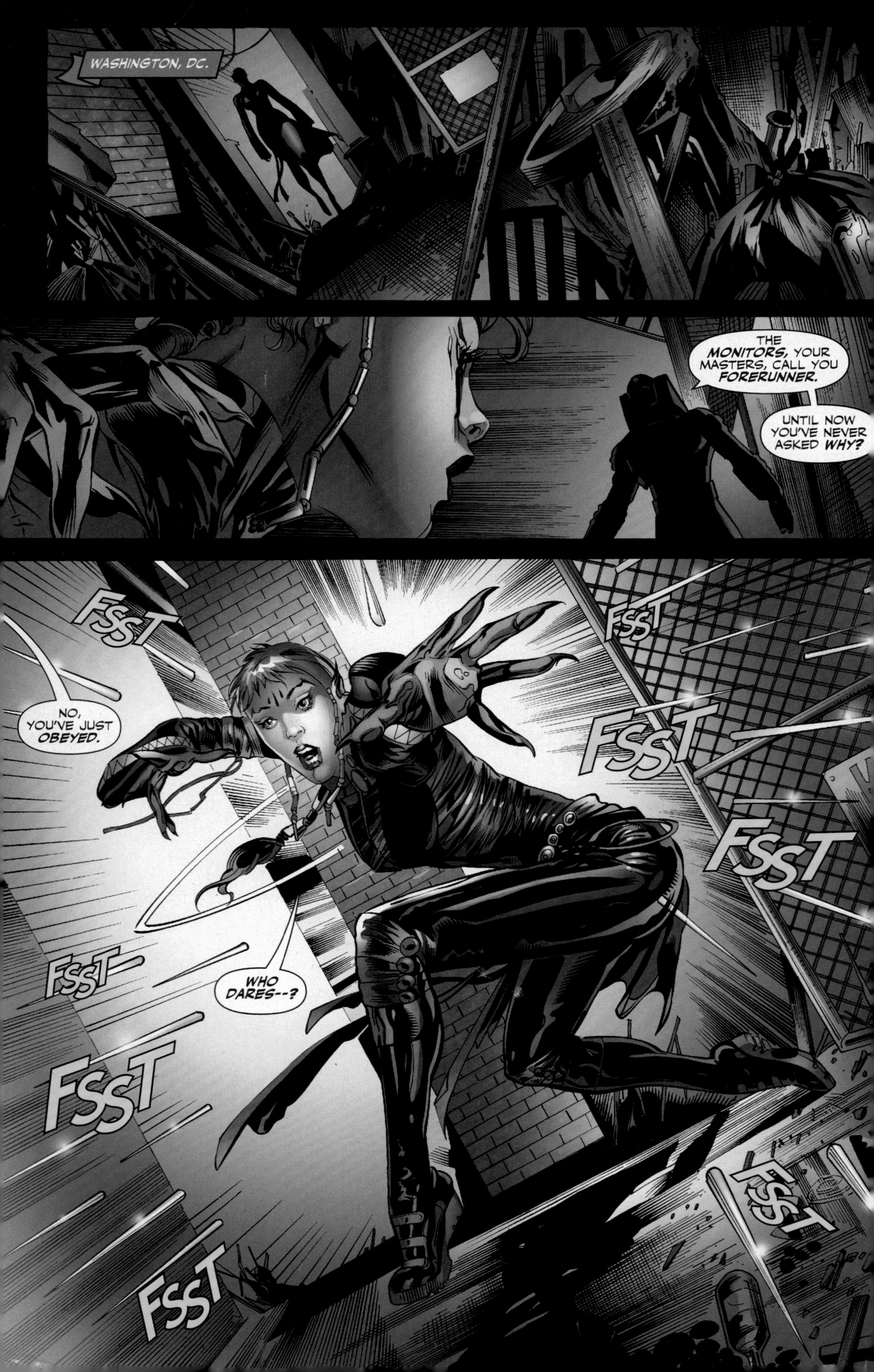
WASHINGTON, DC.
THE MONITORS, YOUR MASTERS, CALL YOU FORERUNNER.
UNTIL NOW YOU'VE NEVER ASKED WHY?
FSST
FSST
NO, YOU'VE JUST OBEYED.
FSST
FSST
FSST
WHO DARES--?
FSST
FSST
FSST

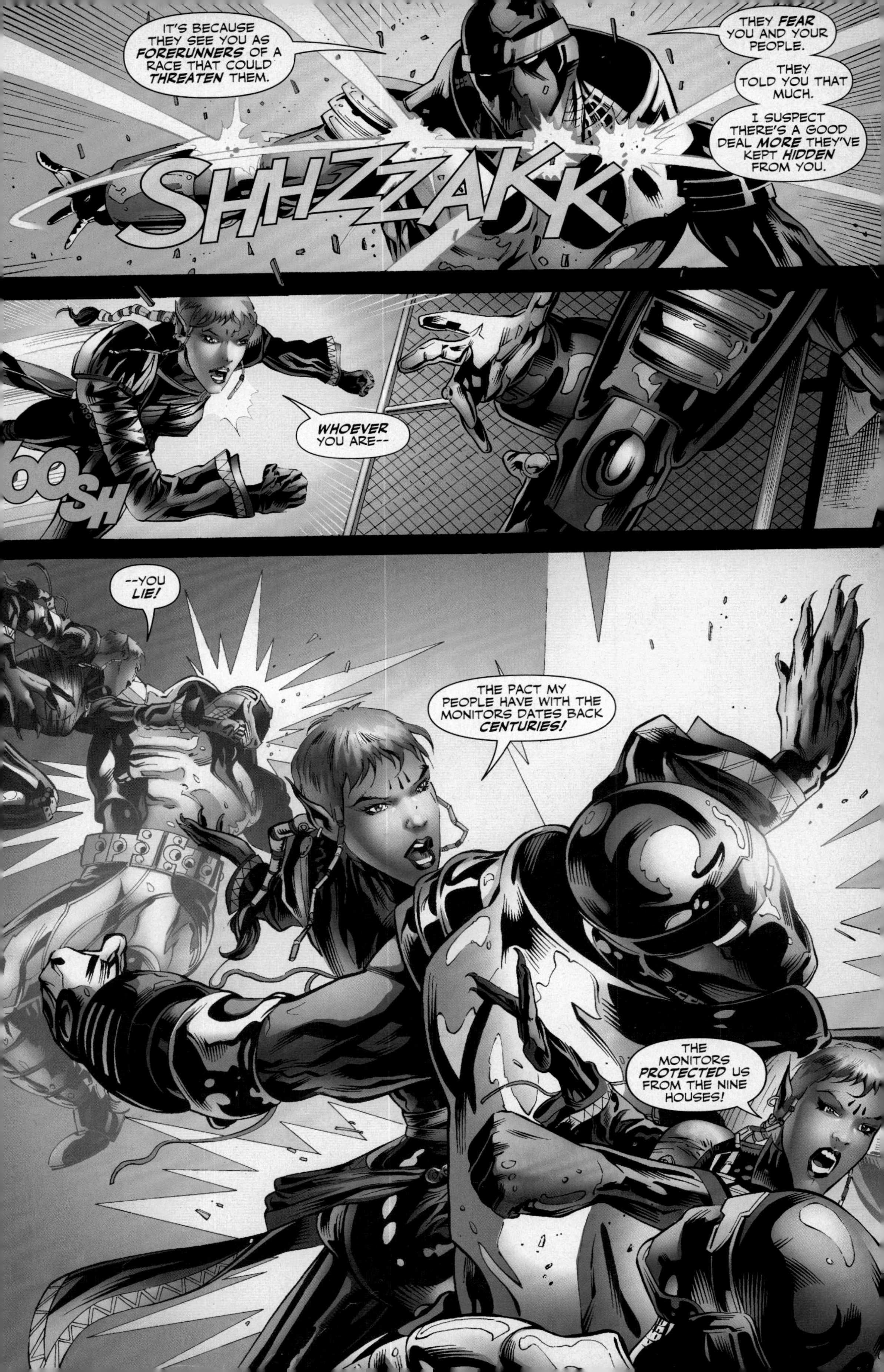

IT'S BECAUSE THEY SEE YOU AS FORERUNNERS OF A RACE THAT COULD THREATEN THEM.
THEY FEAR YOU AND YOUR PEOPLE.
THEY TOLD YOU THAT MUCH.
I SUSPECT THERE'S A GOOD DEAL MORE THEY'VE KEPT HIDDEN FROM YOU.
SHHZZAKK
WHOEVER YOU ARE--
OOSH
--YOU LIE!
THE PACT MY PEOPLE HAVE WITH THE MONITORS DATES BACK CENTURIES!
THE MONITORS PROTECTED US FROM THE NINE HOUSES!

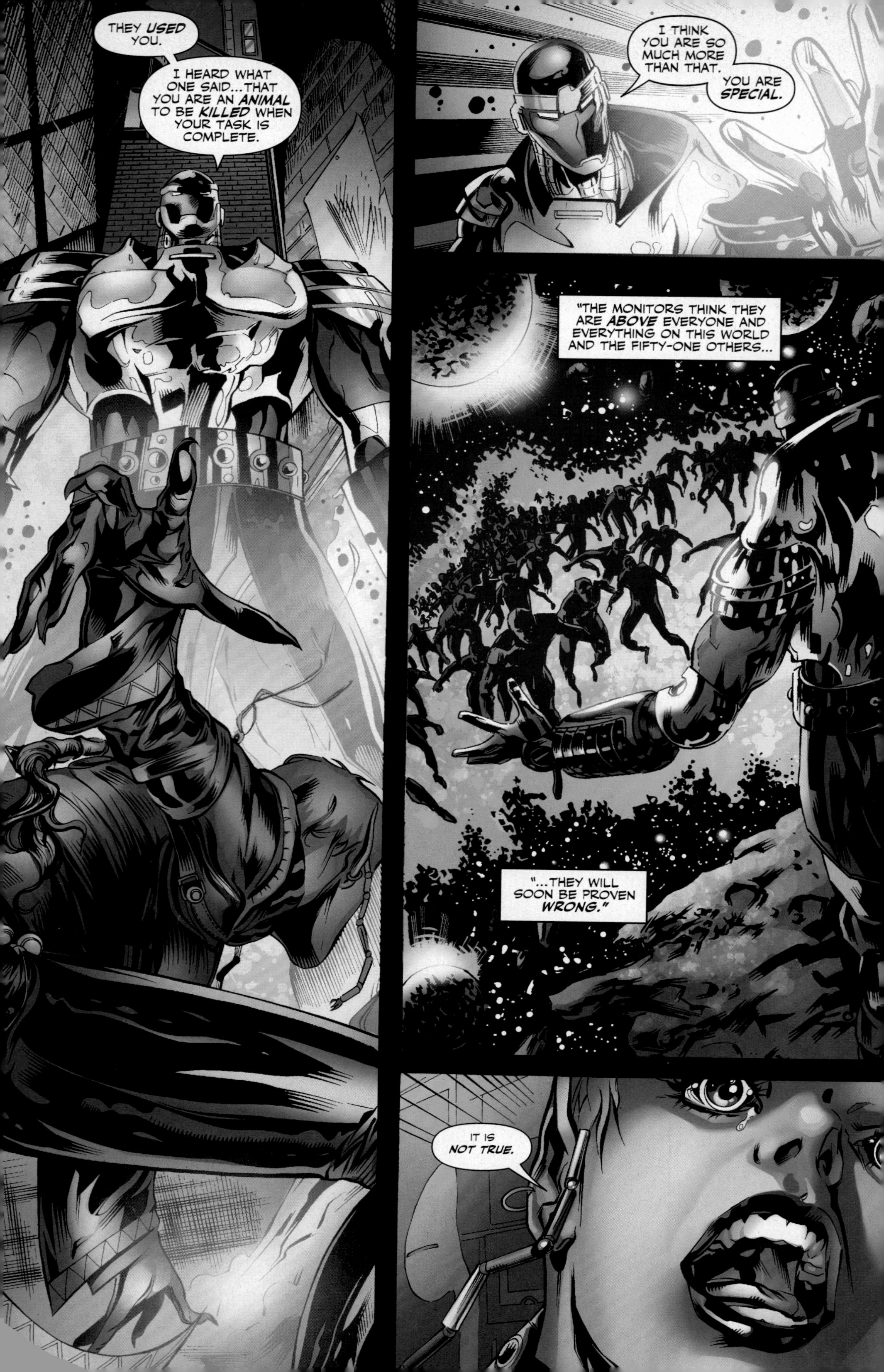
THEY USED YOU.
I HEARD WHAT ONE SAID...THAT YOU ARE AN ANIMAL TO BE KILLED WHEN YOUR TASK IS COMPLETE.
I THINK YOU ARE SO MUCH MORE THAN THAT.
YOU ARE SPECIAL.
"THE MONITORS THINK THEY ARE ABOVE EVERYONE AND EVERYTHING ON THIS WORLD AND THE FIFTY-ONE OTHERS...
"...THEY WILL SOON BE PROVEN WRONG."
IT IS NOT TRUE.

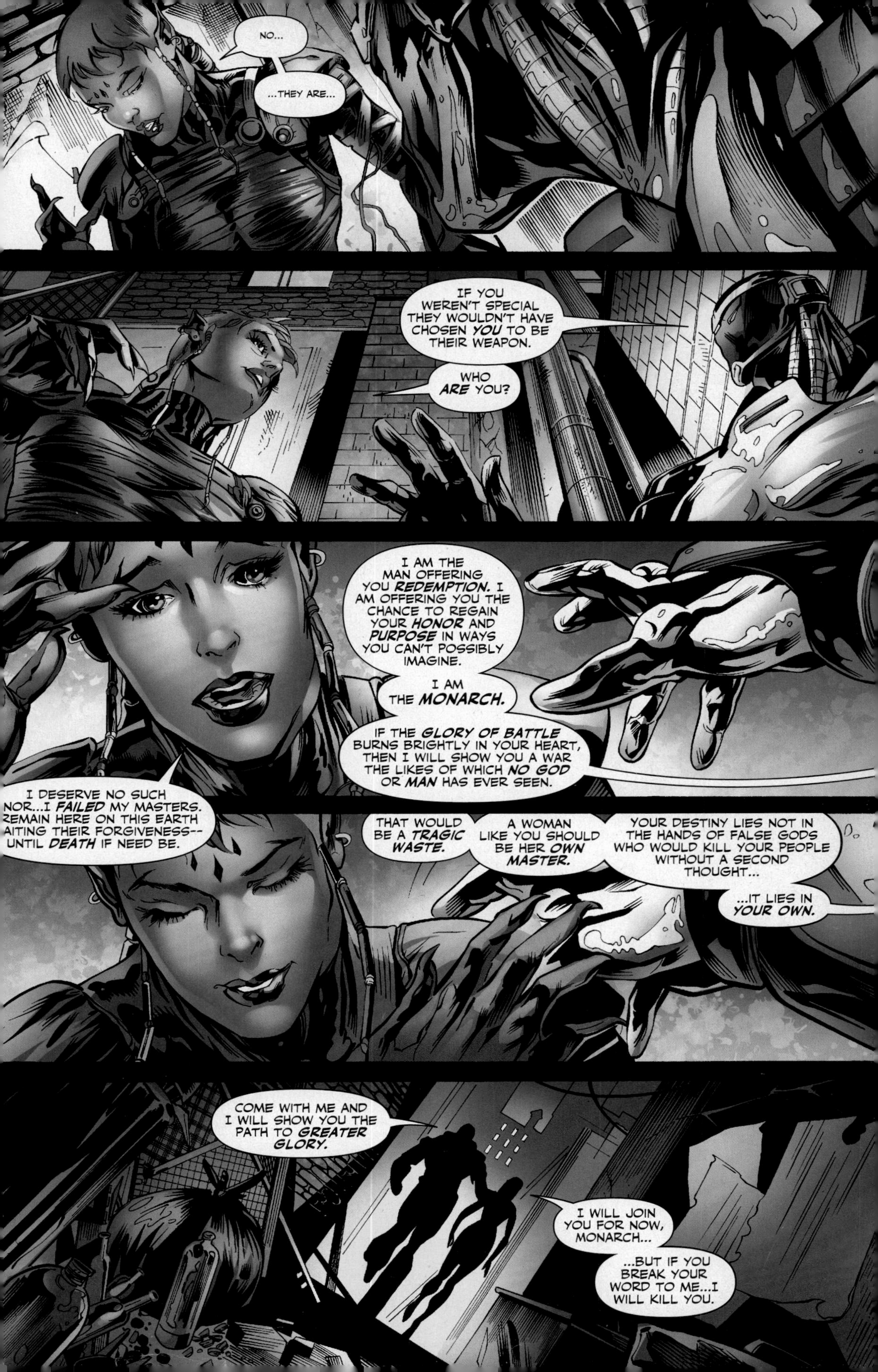
NO...
...THEY ARE...
IF YOU WEREN'T SPECIAL THEY WOULDN'T HAVE CHOSEN YOU TO BE THEIR WEAPON.
WHO ARE YOU?
I AM THE MAN OFFERING YOU REDEMPTION. I AM OFFERING YOU THE CHANCE TO REGAIN YOUR HONOR AND PURPOSE IN WAYS YOU CAN'T POSSIBLY IMAGINE.
I AM THE MONARCH.
IF THE GLORY OF BATTLE BURNS BRIGHTLY IN YOUR HEART, THEN I WILL SHOW YOU A WAR THE LIKES OF WHICH NO GOD OR MAN HAS EVER SEEN.
I DESERVE NO SUCH NOR...I FAILED MY MASTERS. REMAIN HERE ON THIS EARTH AITING THEIR FORGIVENESS-- UNTIL DEATH IF NEED BE.
THAT WOULD BE A TRAGIC WASTE.
A WOMAN LIKE YOU SHOULD BE HER OWN MASTER.
YOUR DESTINY LIES NOT IN THE HANDS OF FALSE GODS WHO WOULD KILL YOUR PEOPLE WITHOUT A SECOND THOUGHT...
...IT LIES IN YOUR OWN.
COME WITH ME AND I WILL SHOW YOU THE PATH TO GREATER GLORY.
I WILL JOIN YOU FOR NOW, MONARCH...
...BUT IF YOU BREAK YOUR WORD TO ME...I WILL KILL YOU.

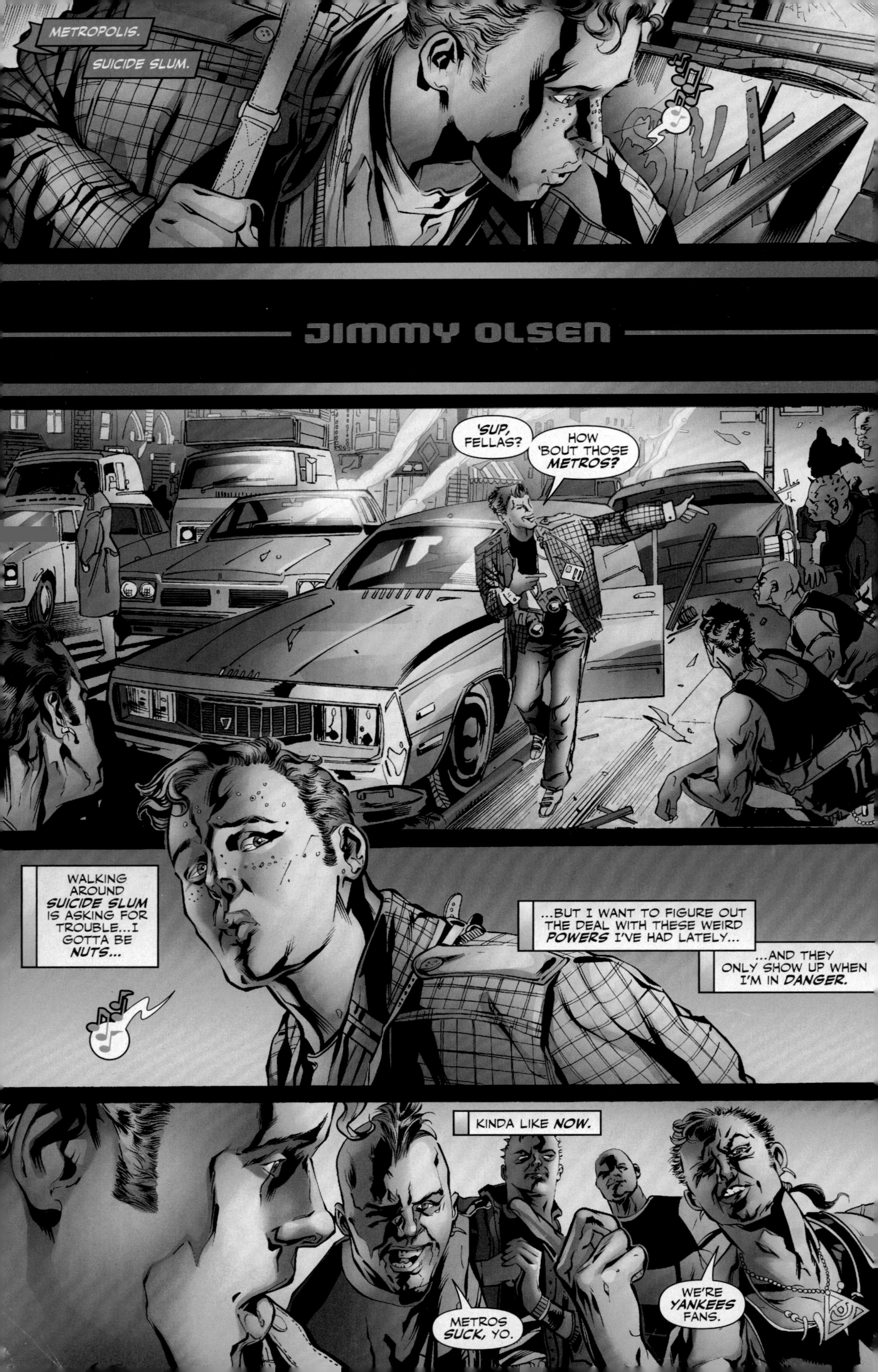
METROPOLIS.
SUICIDE SLUM.
JIMMY OLSEN
'SUP, FELLAS?
HOW 'BOUT THOSE METROS?
WALKING AROUND SUICIDE SLUM IS ASKING FOR TROUBLE...I GOTTA BE NUTS...
...BUT I WANT TO FIGURE OUT THE DEAL WITH THESE WEIRD POWERS I'VE HAD LATELY...
...AND THEY ONLY SHOW UP WHEN I'M IN DANGER.
KINDA LIKE NOW.
METROS SUCK, YO.
WE'RE YANKEES FANS.

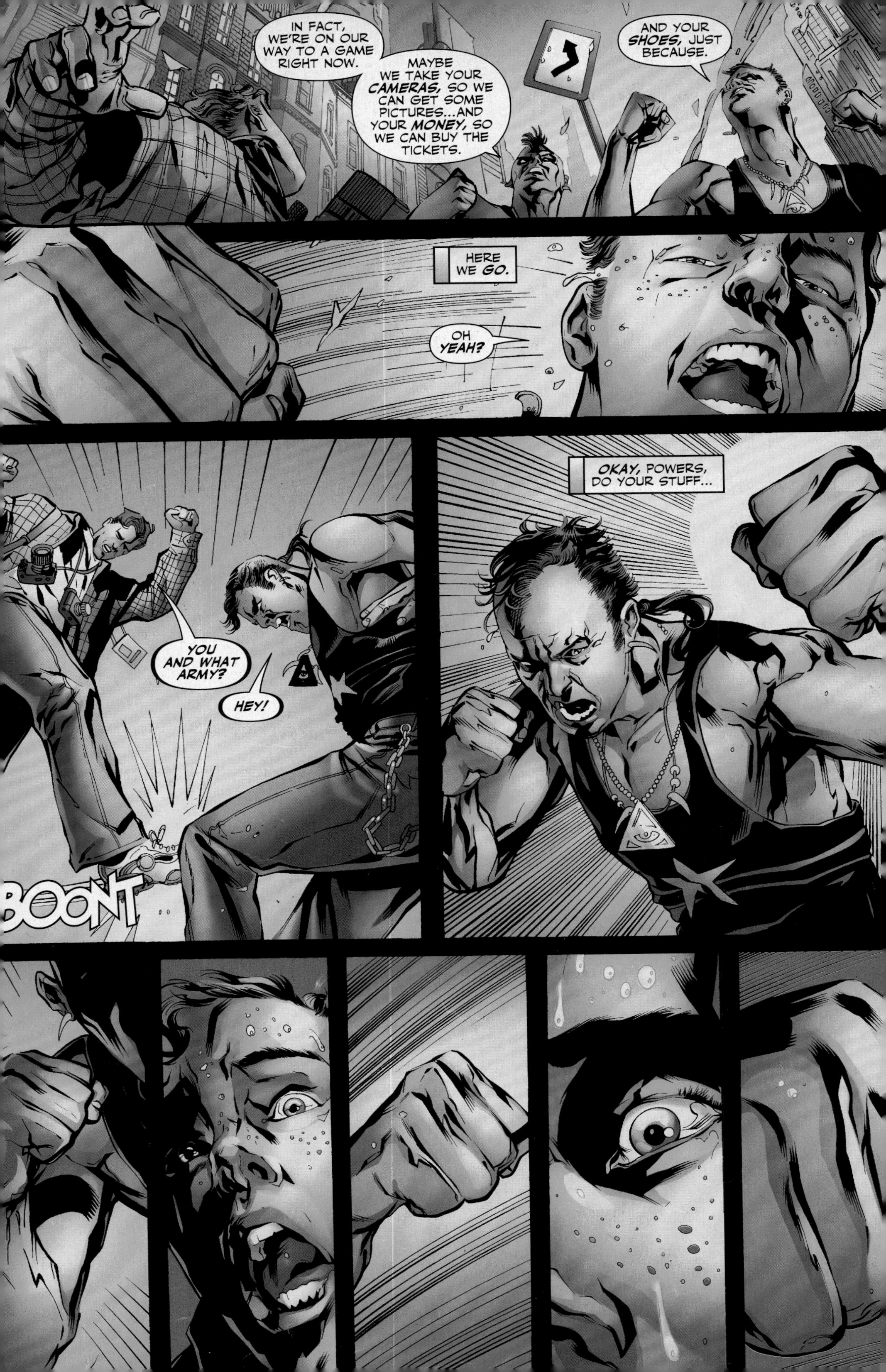
IN FACT, WE'RE ON OUR WAY TO A GAME RIGHT NOW.
MAYBE WE TAKE YOUR CAMERAS, SO WE CAN GET SOME PICTURES...AND YOUR MONEY, SO WE CAN BUY THE TICKETS.
AND YOUR SHOES, JUST BECAUSE.
HERE WE GO.
OH YEAH?
YOU AND WHAT ARMY?
HEY!
BOONT
OKAY, POWERS, DO YOUR STUFF...

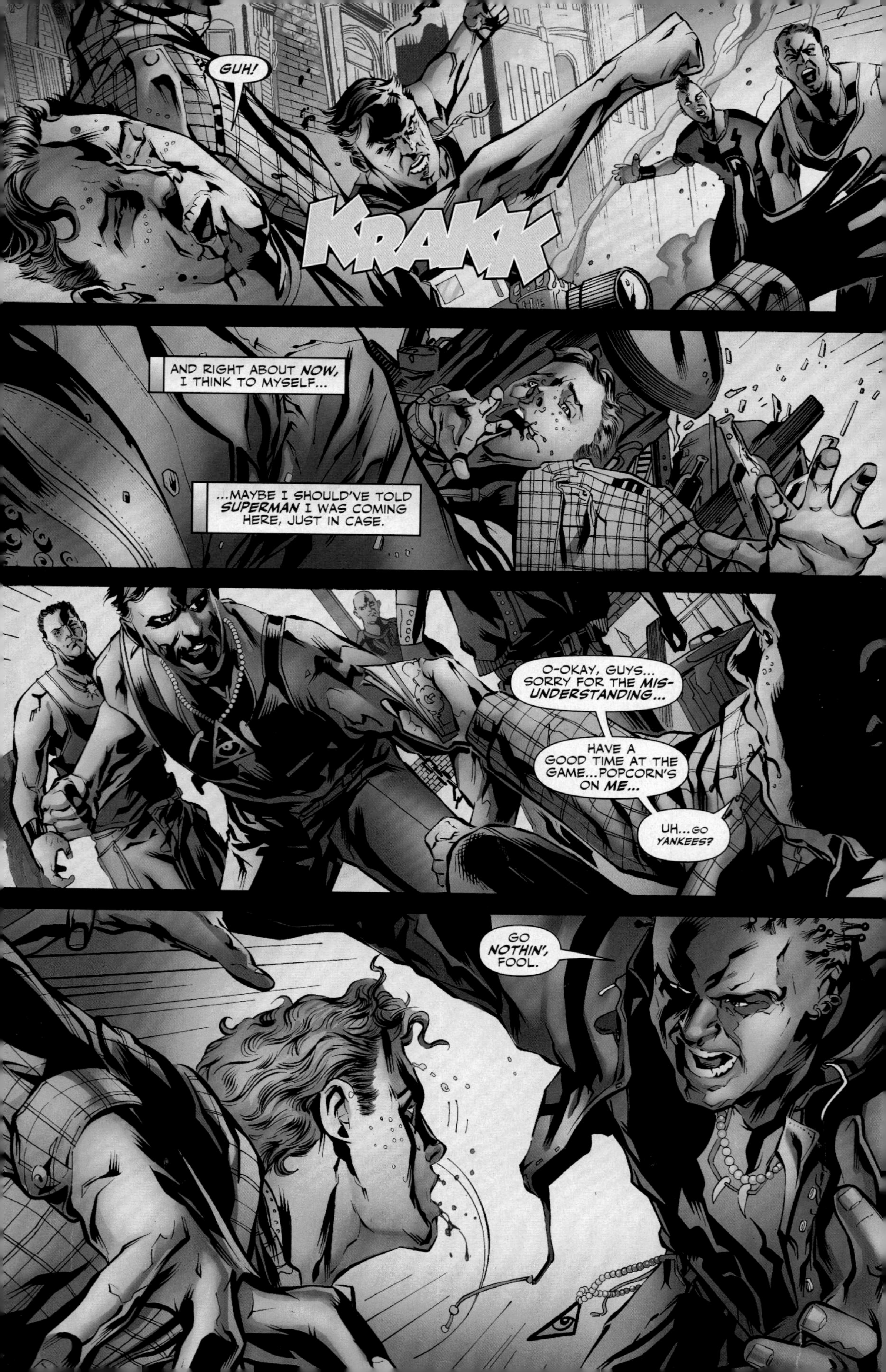
GUH!
KRAKK
AND RIGHT ABOUT NOW, I THINK TO MYSELF...
...MAYBE I SHOULD'VE TOLD SUPERMAN I WAS COMING HERE, JUST IN CASE.
O-OKAY, GUYS... SORRY FOR THE MIS-UNDERSTANDING...
HAVE A GOOD TIME AT THE GAME...POPCORN'S ON ME...
UH...GO YANKEES?
GO NOTHIN', FOOL.

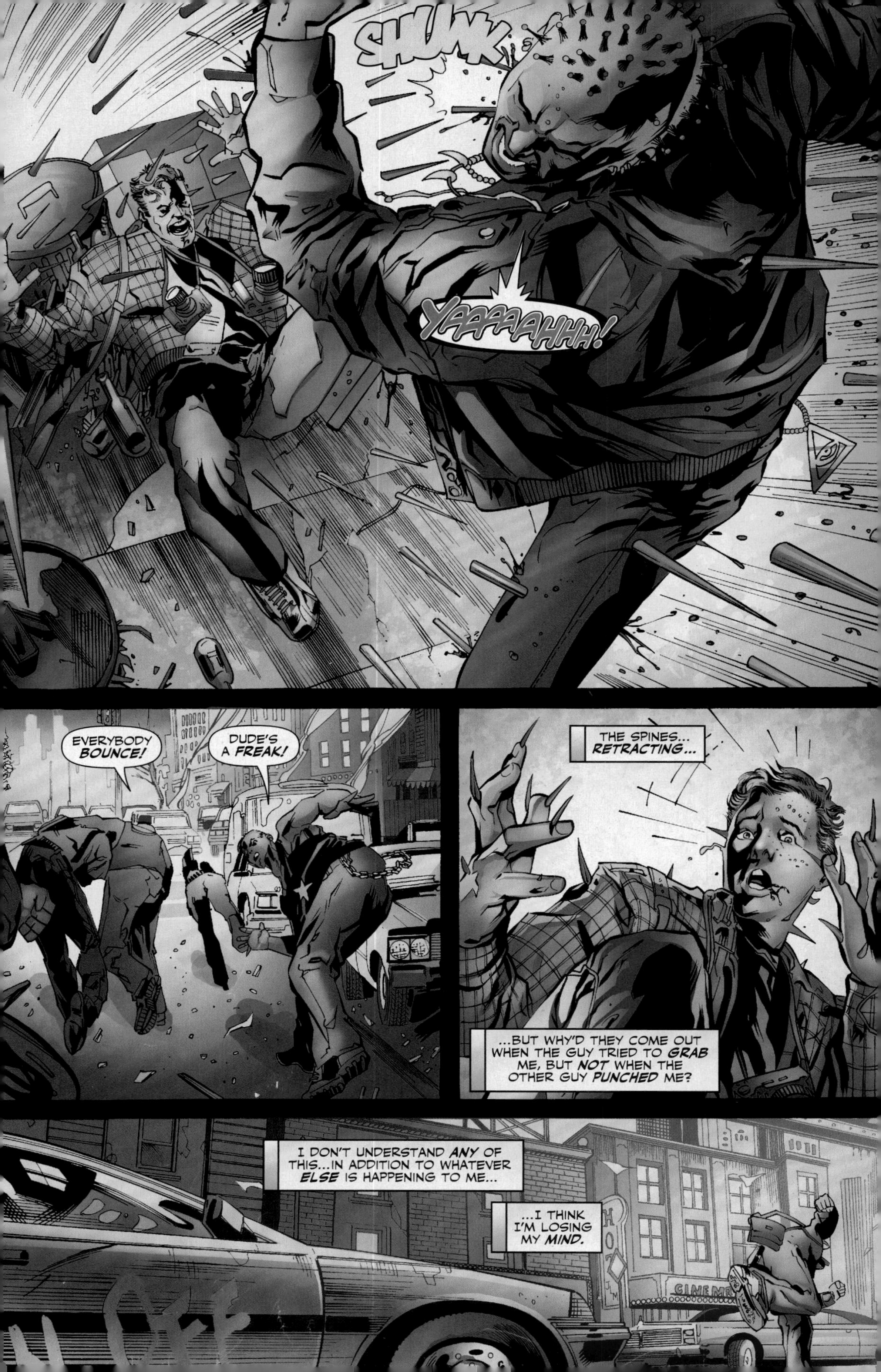
SHUNK
YAAAAAHHH!
EVERYBODY BOUNCE!
DUDE'S A FREAK!
THE SPINES... RETRACTING...
...BUT WHY'D THEY COME OUT WHEN THE GUY TRIED TO GRAB ME, BUT NOT WHEN THE OTHER GUY PUNCHED ME?
I DON'T UNDERSTAND ANY OF THIS...IN ADDITION TO WHATEVER ELSE IS HAPPENING TO ME...
...I THINK I'M LOSING MY MIND.

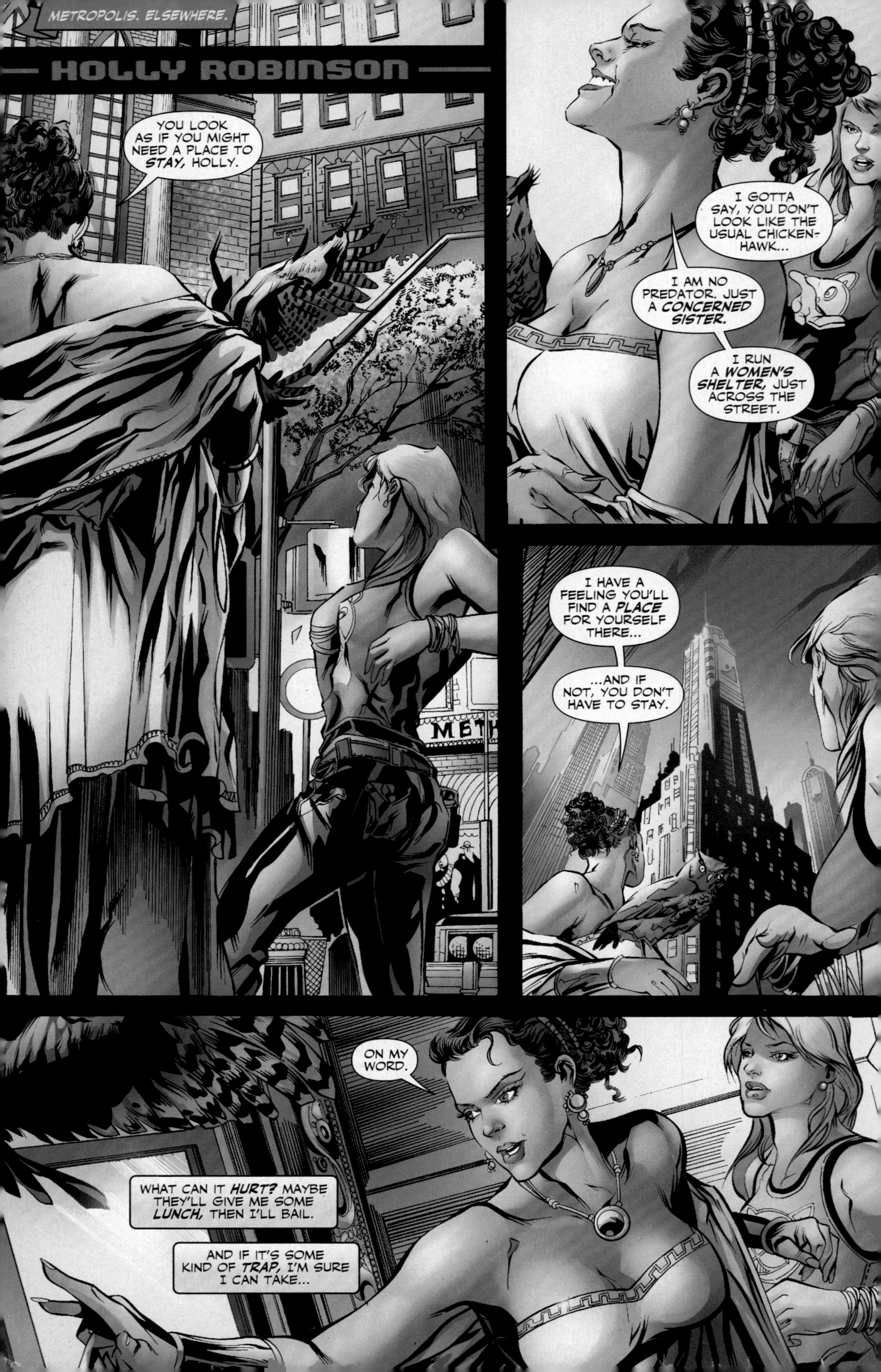
METROPOLIS. ELSEWHERE.
HOLLY ROBINSON
YOU LOOK AS IF YOU MIGHT NEED A PLACE TO STAY, HOLLY.
I GOTTA SAY, YOU DON'T LOOK LIKE THE USUAL CHICKEN-HAWK...
I AM NO PREDATOR. JUST A CONCERNED SISTER.
I RUN A WOMEN'S SHELTER, JUST ACROSS THE STREET.
I HAVE A FEELING YOU'LL FIND A PLACE FOR YOURSELF THERE...
...AND IF NOT, YOU DON'T HAVE TO STAY.
ON MY WORD.
WHAT CAN IT HURT? MAYBE THEY'LL GIVE ME SOME LUNCH, THEN I'LL BAIL.
AND IF IT'S SOME KIND OF TRAP, I'M SURE I CAN TAKE...

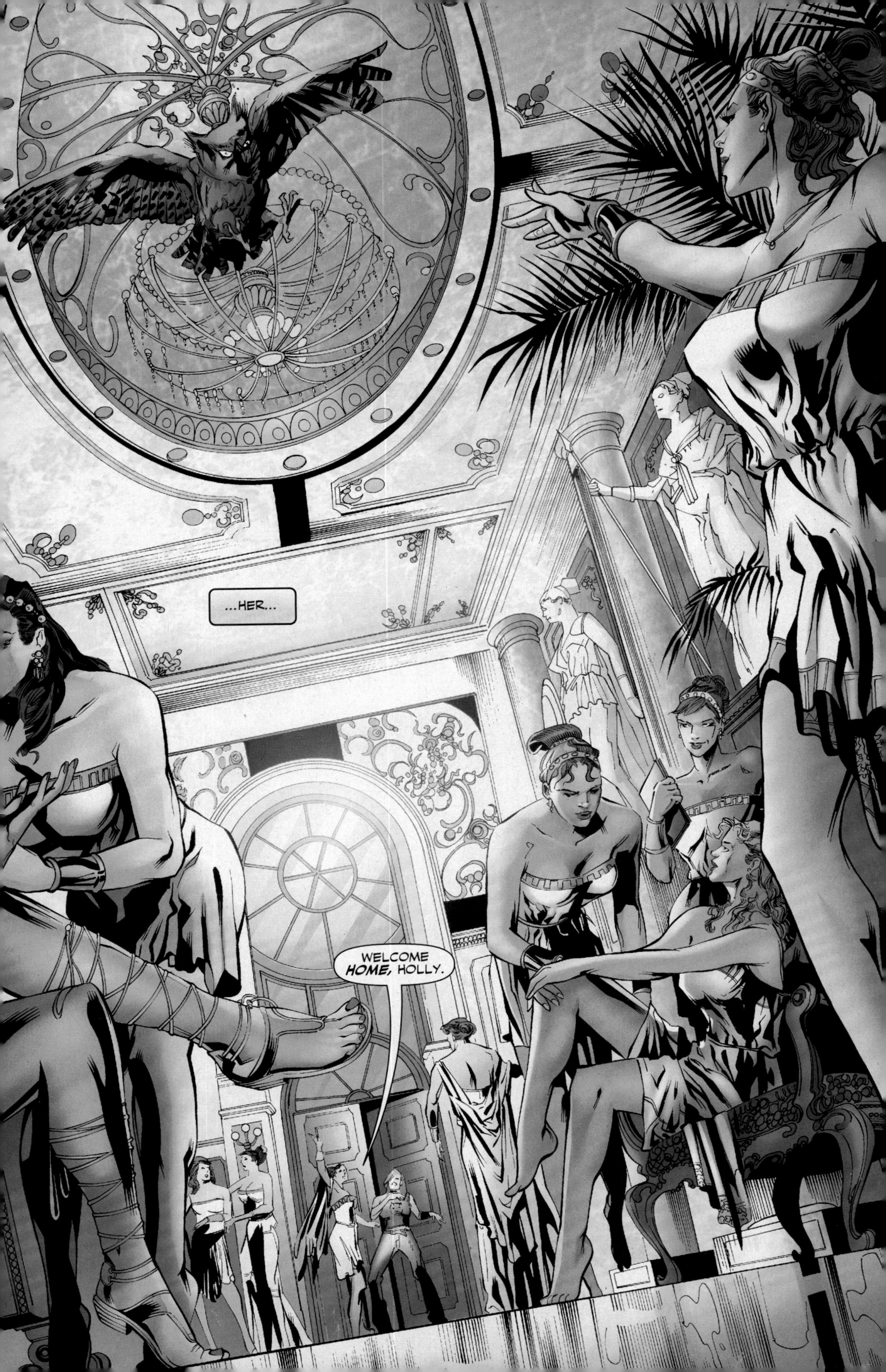
...HER...
WELCOME HOME, HOLLY.

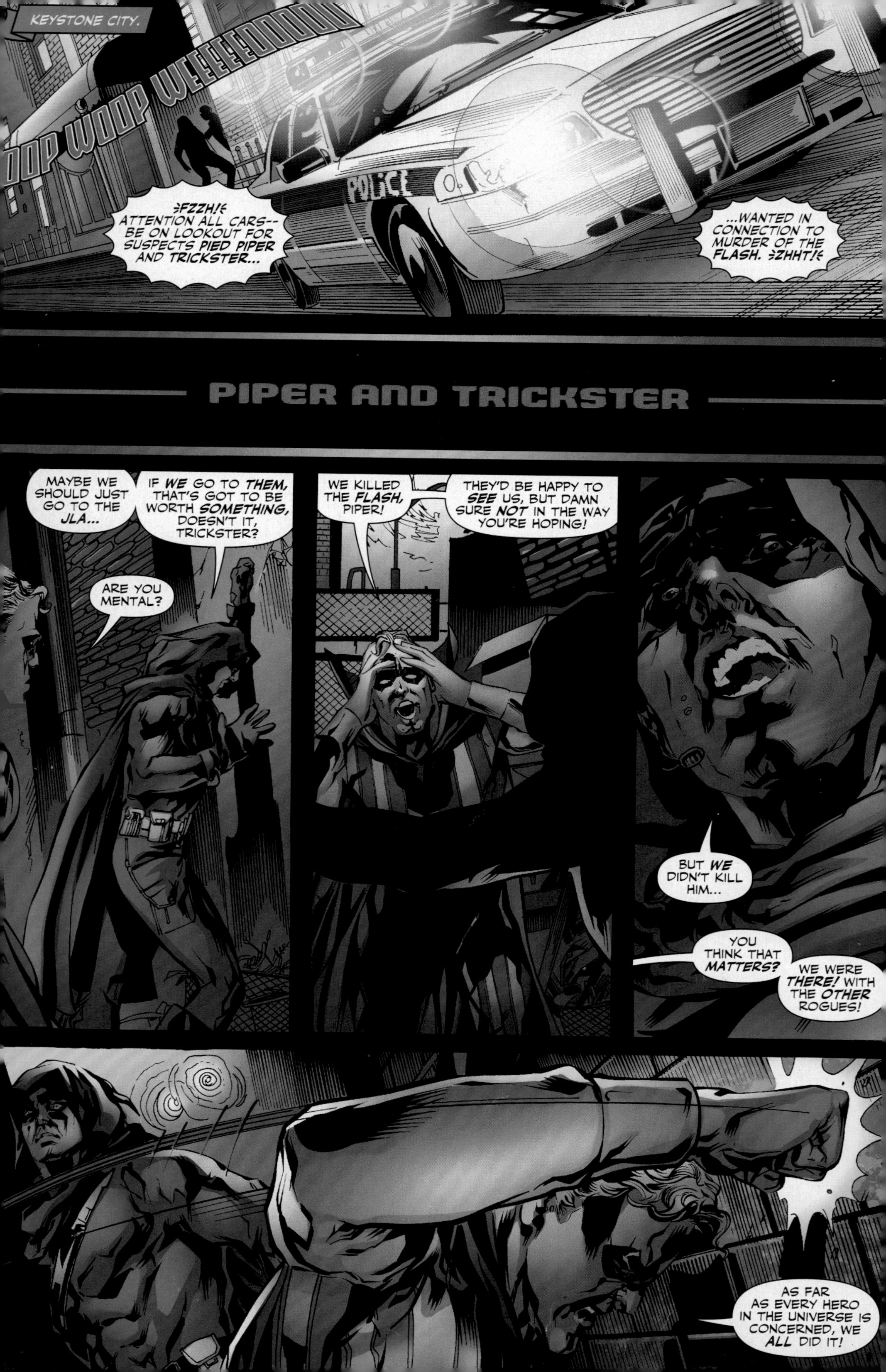
KEYSTONE CITY.
OOP WOOP WEEEEEOOOOU
POLICE
⋟FZZH!⋞ ATTENTION ALL CARS-- BE ON LOOKOUT FOR SUSPECTS PIED PIPER AND TRICKSTER...
...WANTED IN CONNECTION TO MURDER OF THE FLASH. ⋟ZHHT!⋞
PIPER AND TRICKSTER
MAYBE WE SHOULD JUST GO TO THE JLA...
IF WE GO TO THEM, THAT'S GOT TO BE WORTH SOMETHING, DOESN'T IT, TRICKSTER?
ARE YOU MENTAL?
WE KILLED THE FLASH, PIPER!
THEY'D BE HAPPY TO SEE US, BUT DAMN SURE NOT IN THE WAY YOU'RE HOPING!
BUT WE DIDN'T KILL HIM...
YOU THINK THAT MATTERS?
WE WERE THERE! WITH THE OTHER ROGUES!
AS FAR AS EVERY HERO IN THE UNIVERSE IS CONCERNED, WE ALL DID IT!

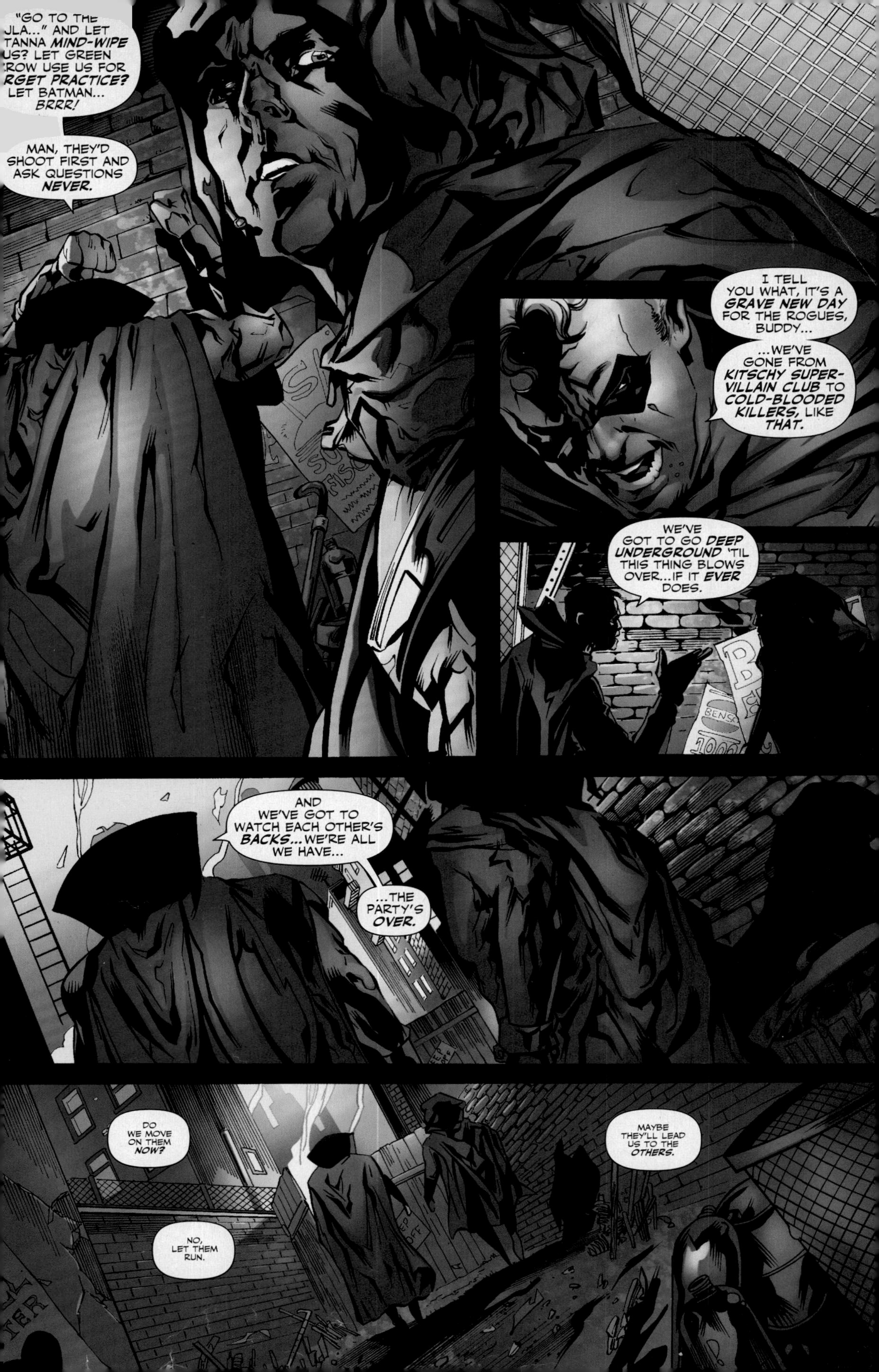
"GO TO THE JLA..." AND LET TANNA MIND-WIPE US? LET GREEN ROW USE US FOR RGET PRACTICE? LET BATMAN... BRRR!
MAN, THEY'D SHOOT FIRST AND ASK QUESTIONS NEVER.
I TELL YOU WHAT, IT'S A GRAVE NEW DAY FOR THE ROGUES, BUDDY...
...WE'VE GONE FROM KITSCHY SUPER-VILLAIN CLUB TO COLD-BLOODED KILLERS, LIKE THAT.
WE'VE GOT TO GO DEEP UNDERGROUND 'TIL THIS THING BLOWS OVER...IF IT EVER DOES.
AND WE'VE GOT TO WATCH EACH OTHER'S BACKS...WE'RE ALL WE HAVE...
...THE PARTY'S OVER.
DO WE MOVE ON THEM NOW?
NO, LET THEM RUN.
MAYBE THEY'LL LEAD US TO THE OTHERS.

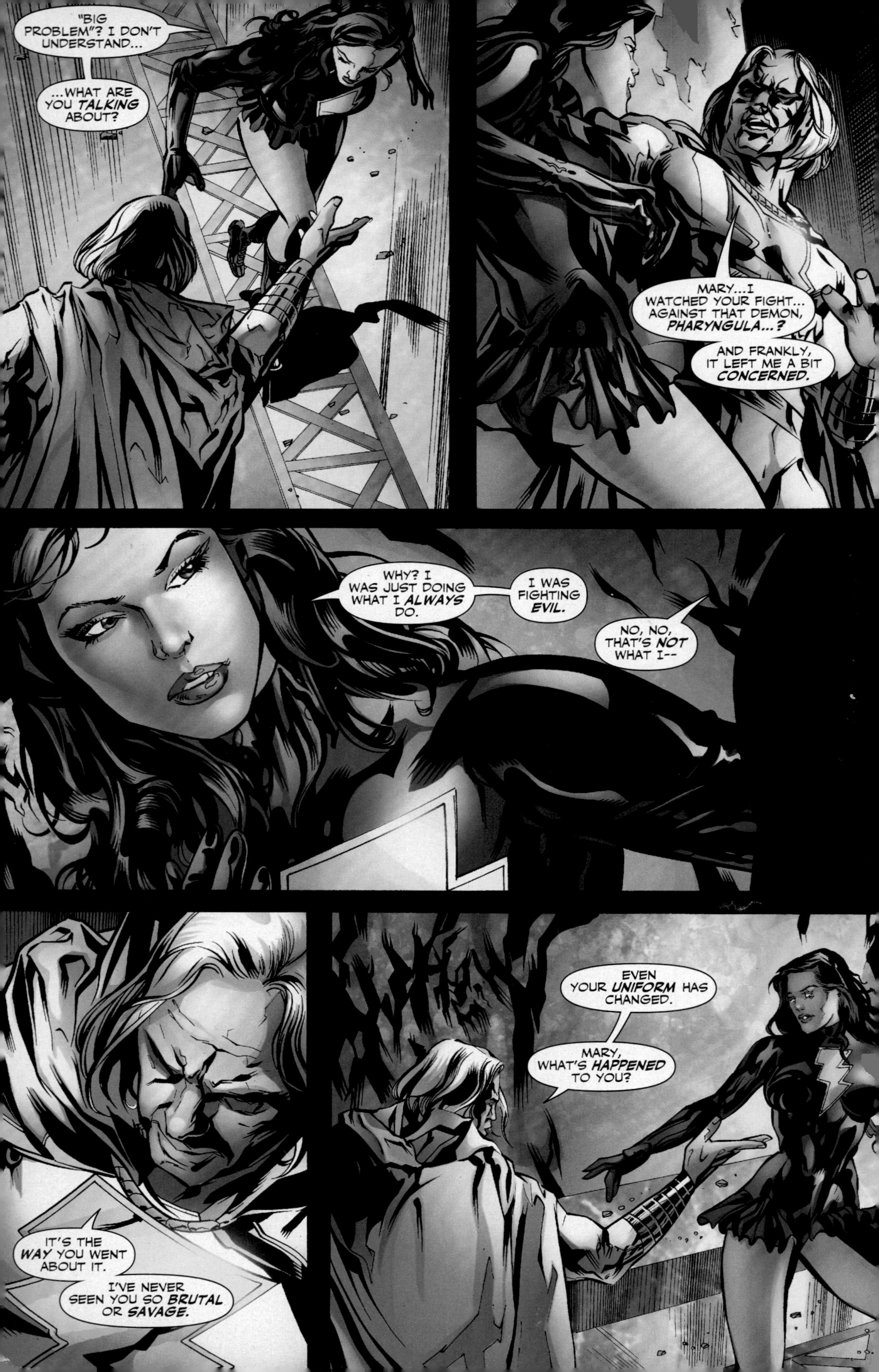
"BIG PROBLEM"? I DON'T UNDERSTAND...
...WHAT ARE YOU TALKING ABOUT?
MARY...I WATCHED YOUR FIGHT... AGAINST THAT DEMON, PHARYNGULA...?
AND FRANKLY, IT LEFT ME A BIT CONCERNED.
WHY? I WAS JUST DOING WHAT I ALWAYS DO.
I WAS FIGHTING EVIL.
NO, NO, THAT'S NOT WHAT I--
IT'S THE WAY YOU WENT ABOUT IT.
I'VE NEVER SEEN YOU SO BRUTAL OR SAVAGE.
EVEN YOUR UNIFORM HAS CHANGED.
MARY, WHAT'S HAPPENED TO YOU?

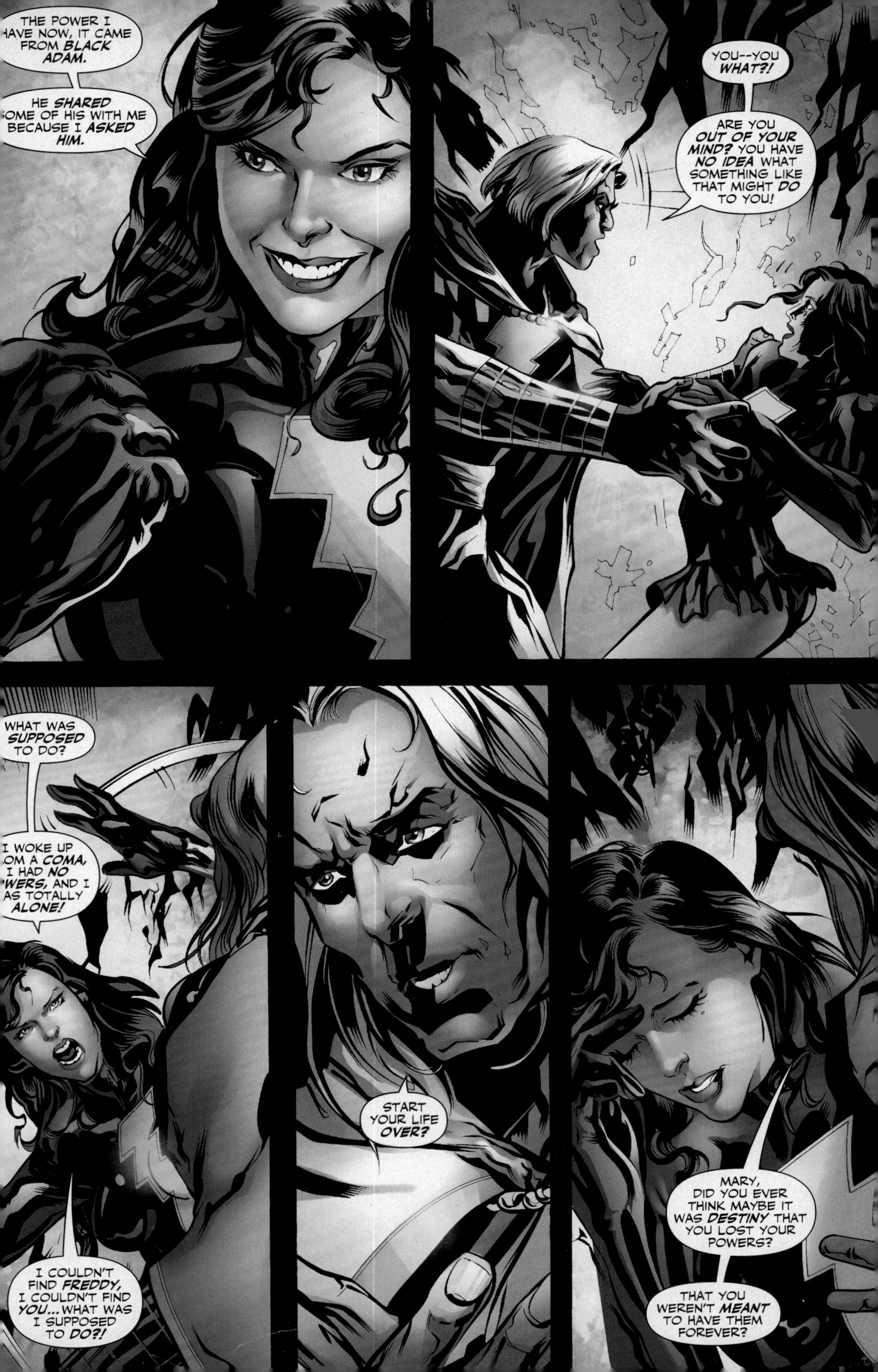
THE POWER I HAVE NOW, IT CAME FROM BLACK ADAM.
HE SHARED SOME OF HIS WITH ME BECAUSE I ASKED HIM.
YOU--YOU WHAT?!
ARE YOU OUT OF YOUR MIND? YOU HAVE NO IDEA WHAT SOMETHING LIKE THAT MIGHT DO TO YOU!
WHAT WAS SUPPOSED TO DO?
I WOKE UP OM A COMA, I HAD NO WERS, AND I AS TOTALLY ALONE!
I COULDN'T FIND FREDDY, I COULDN'T FIND YOU... WHAT WAS I SUPPOSED TO DO?!
START YOUR LIFE OVER?
MARY, DID YOU EVER THINK MAYBE IT WAS DESTINY THAT YOU LOST YOUR POWERS?
THAT YOU WEREN'T MEANT TO HAVE THEM FOREVER?

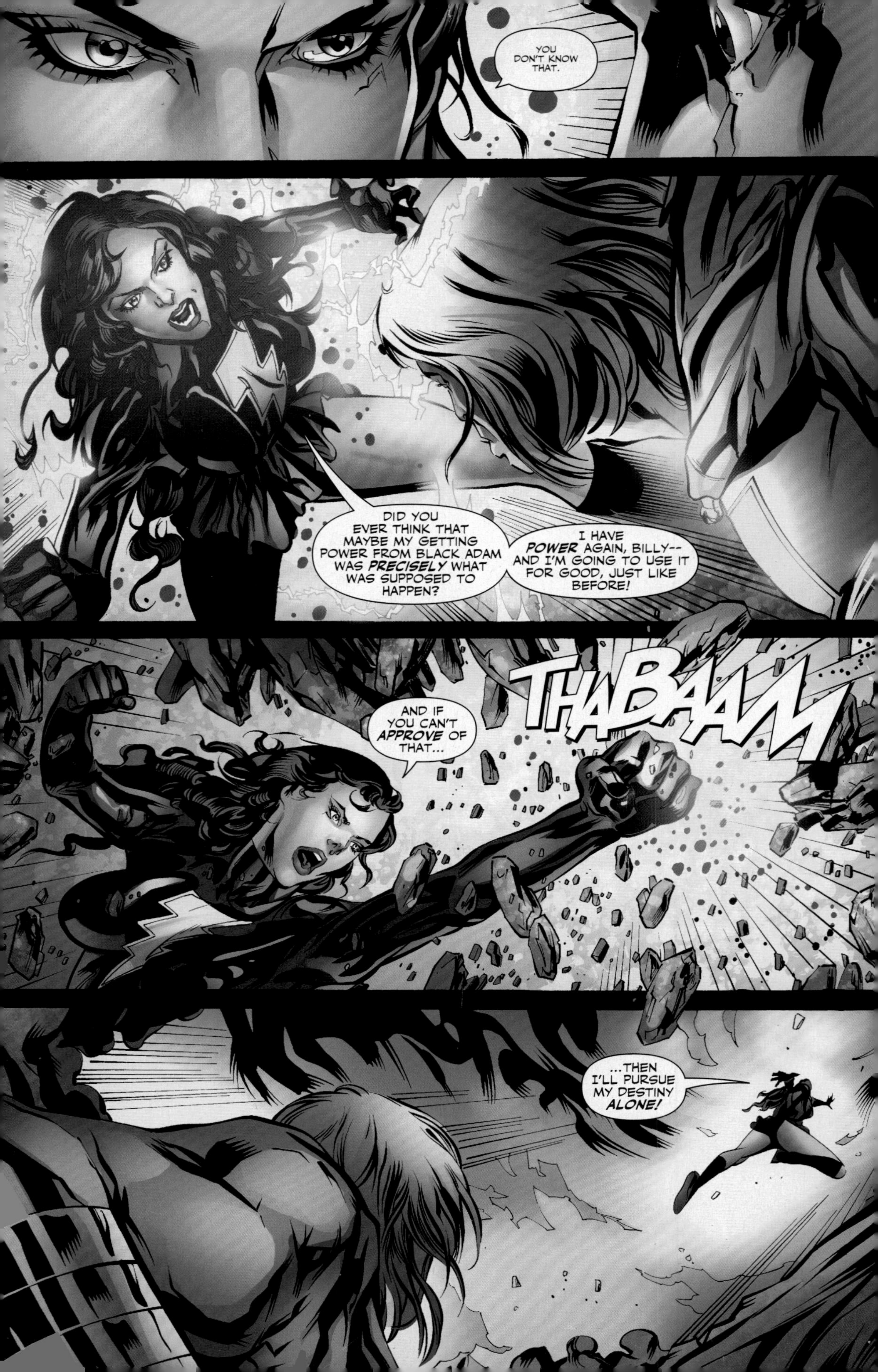
YOU DON'T KNOW THAT.
DID YOU EVER THINK THAT MAYBE MY GETTING POWER FROM BLACK ADAM WAS *PRECISELY* WHAT WAS SUPPOSED TO HAPPEN?
I HAVE *POWER* AGAIN, BILLY-- AND I'M GOING TO USE IT FOR GOOD, JUST LIKE BEFORE!
THABAAM
AND IF YOU CAN'T *APPROVE* OF THAT...
...THEN I'LL PURSUE MY DESTINY *ALONE!*

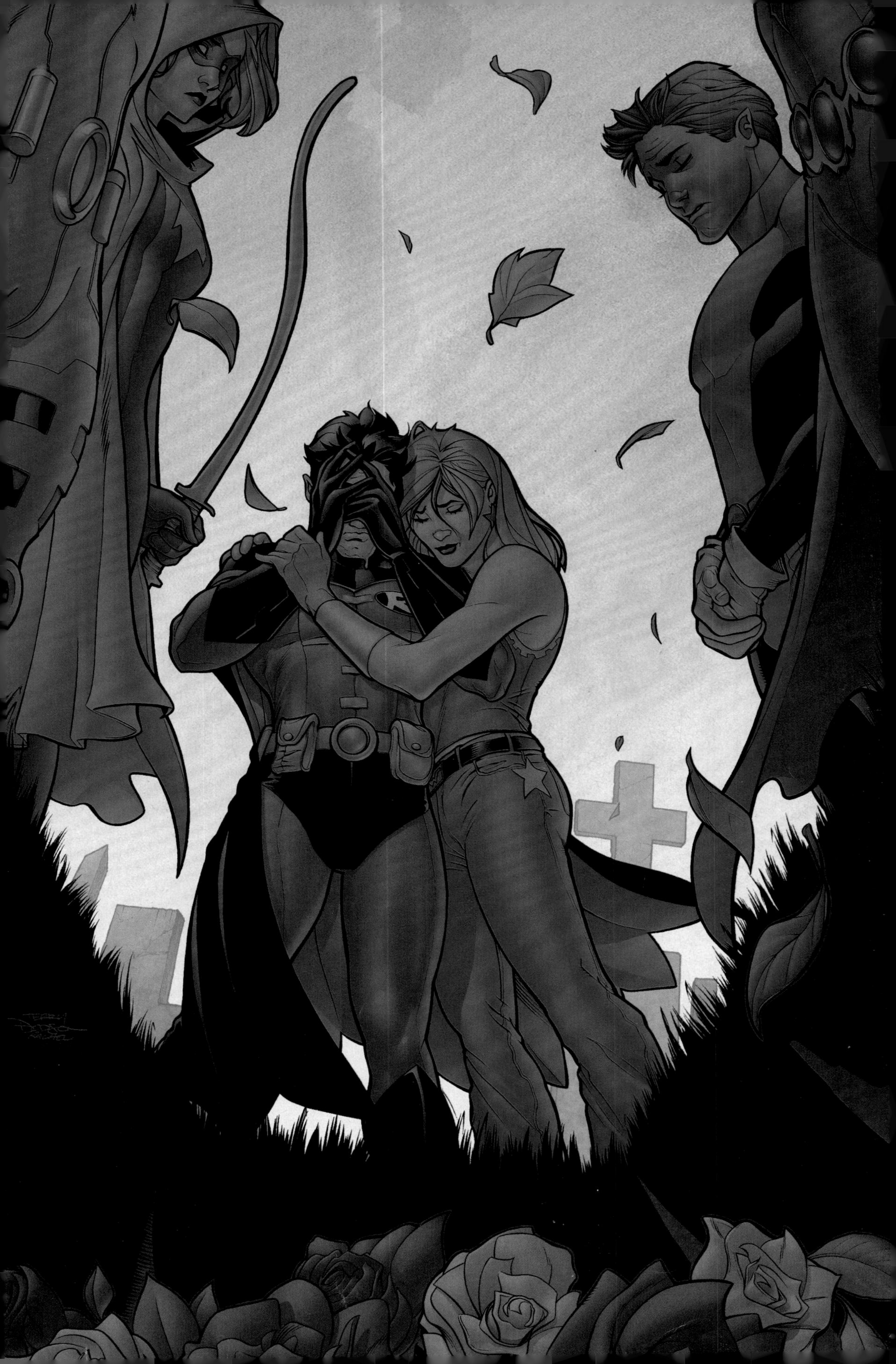

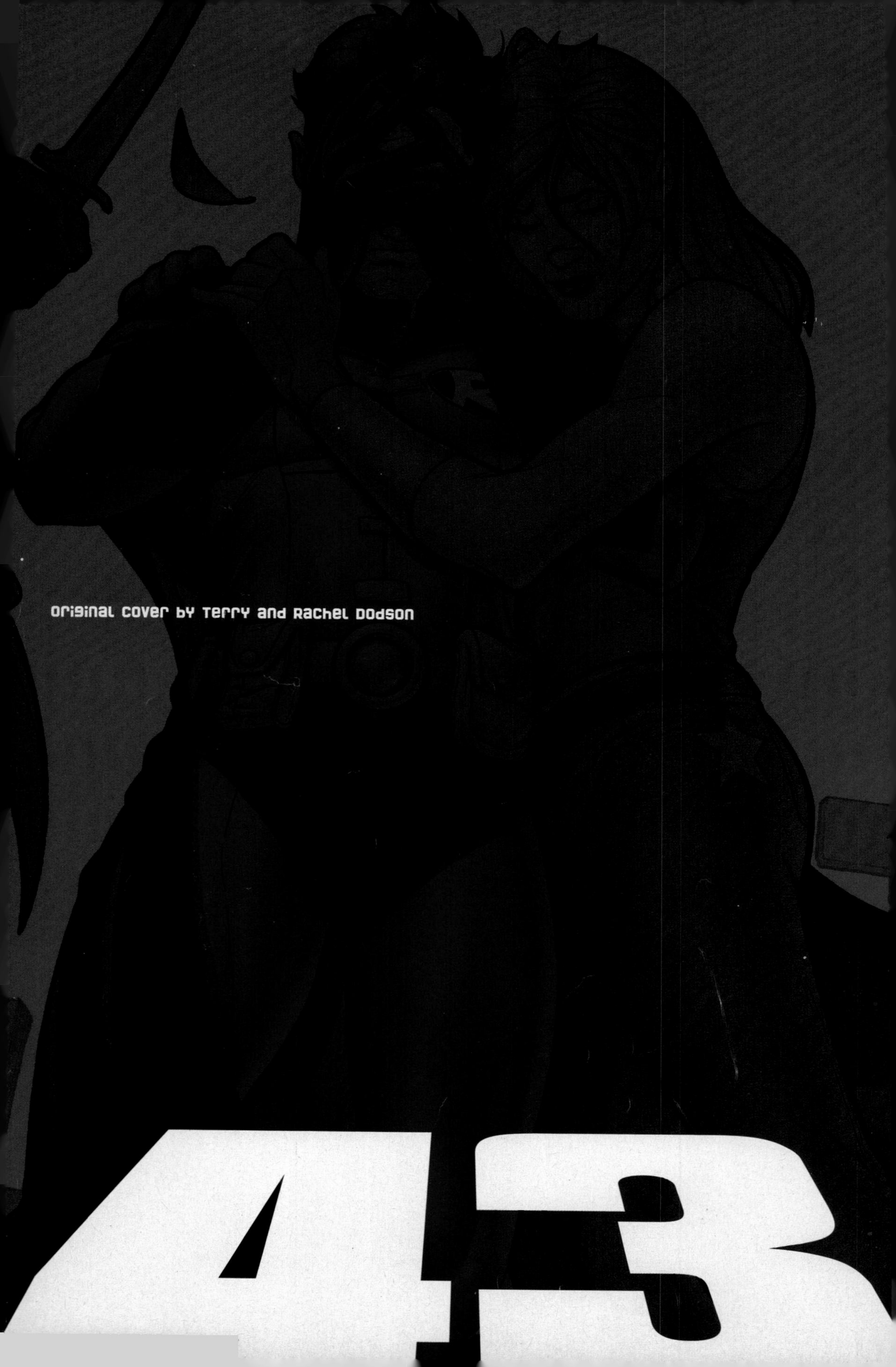
43

original cover by Terry and Rachel Dodson

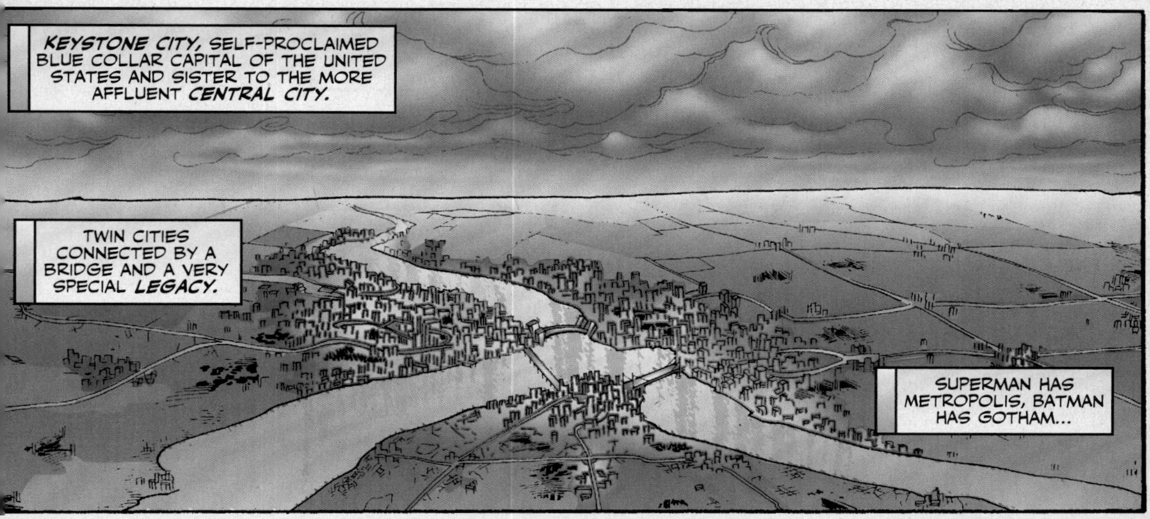
KEYSTONE CITY, SELF-PROCLAIMED BLUE COLLAR CAPITAL OF THE UNITED STATES AND SISTER TO THE MORE AFFLUENT CENTRAL CITY.
TWIN CITIES CONNECTED BY A BRIDGE AND A VERY SPECIAL LEGACY.
SUPERMAN HAS METROPOLIS, BATMAN HAS GOTHAM...

WEEK 43 AND COUNTING
JIMMY OLSEN

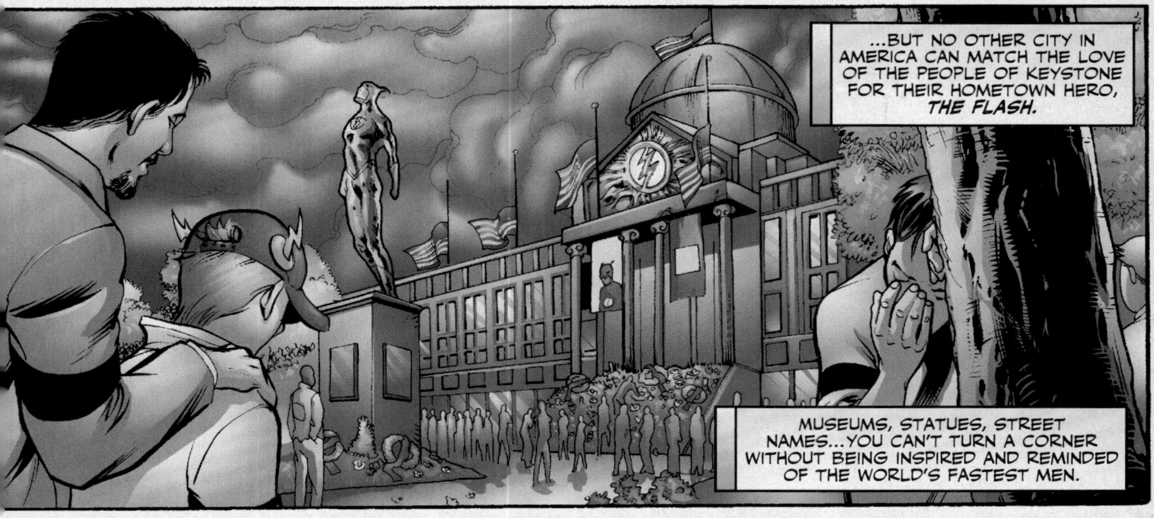
...BUT NO OTHER CITY IN AMERICA CAN MATCH THE LOVE OF THE PEOPLE OF KEYSTONE FOR THEIR HOMETOWN HERO, THE FLASH.
MUSEUMS, STATUES, STREET NAMES...YOU CAN'T TURN A CORNER WITHOUT BEING INSPIRED AND REMINDED OF THE WORLD'S FASTEST MEN.

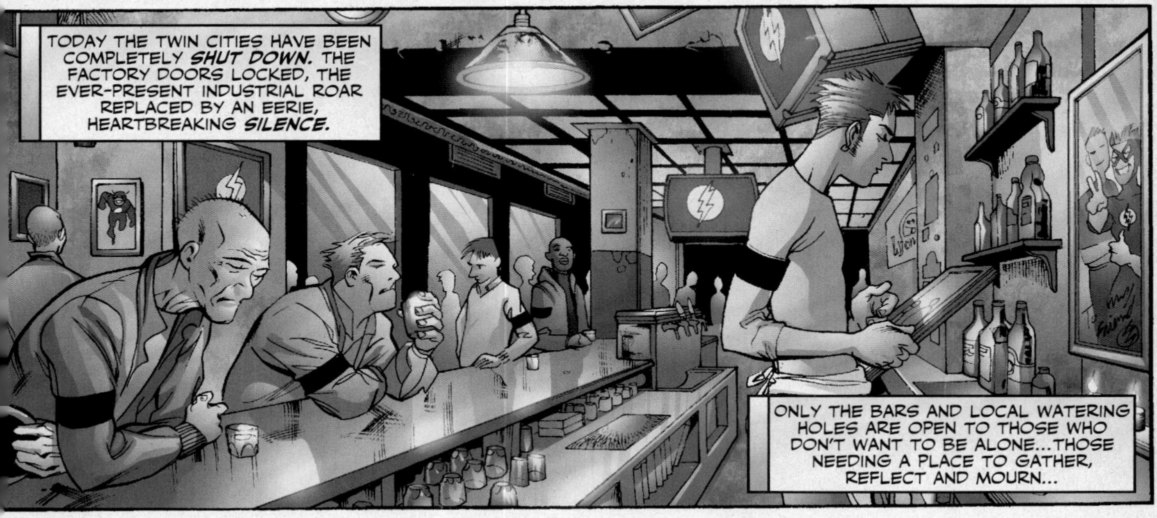
TODAY THE TWIN CITIES HAVE BEEN COMPLETELY SHUT DOWN. THE FACTORY DOORS LOCKED, THE EVER-PRESENT INDUSTRIAL ROAR REPLACED BY AN EERIE, HEARTBREAKING SILENCE.
ONLY THE BARS AND LOCAL WATERING HOLES ARE OPEN TO THOSE WHO DON'T WANT TO BE ALONE...THOSE NEEDING A PLACE TO GATHER, REFLECT AND MOURN...

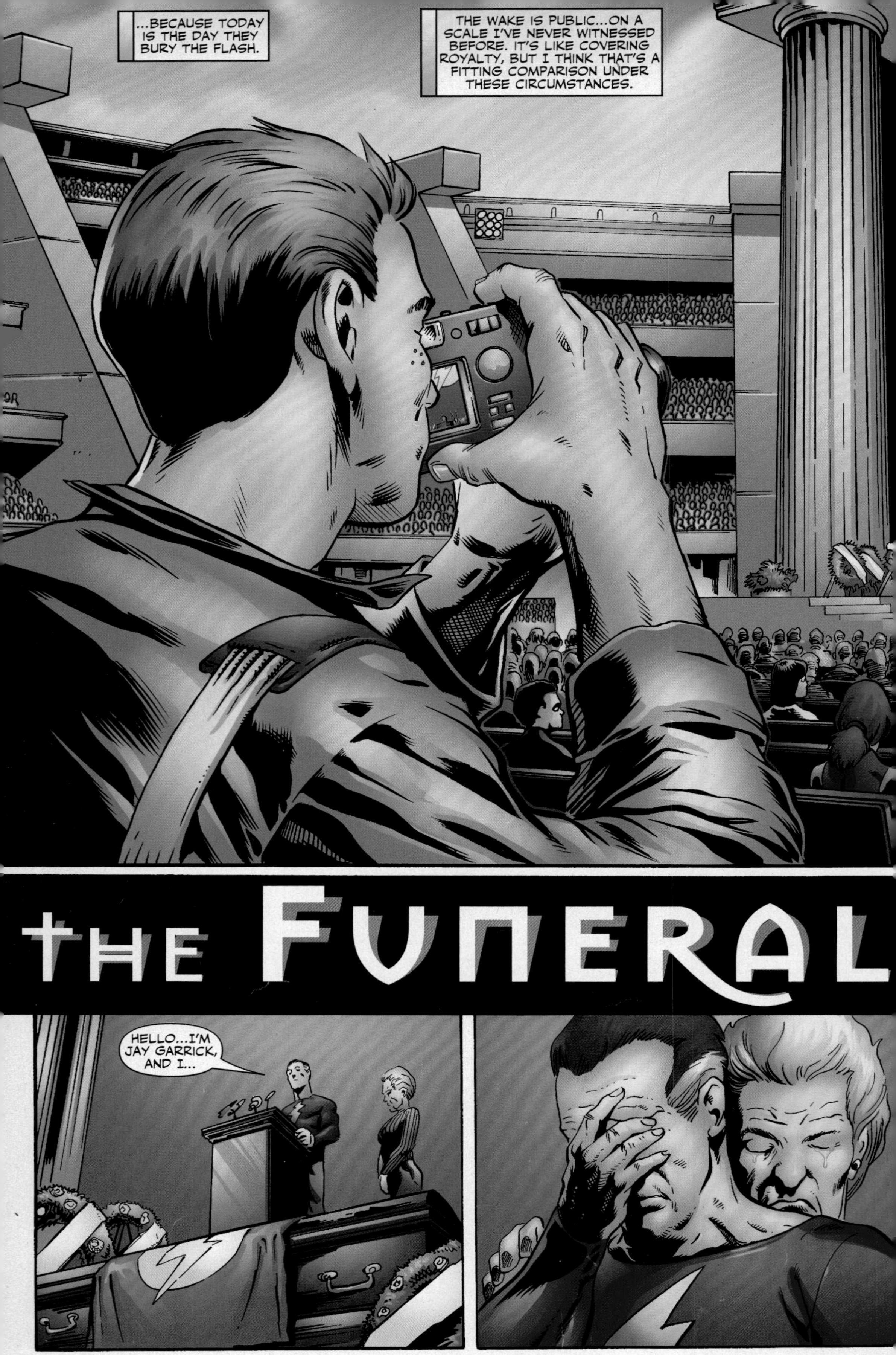
...BECAUSE TODAY IS THE DAY THEY BURY THE FLASH.
THE WAKE IS PUBLIC...ON A SCALE I'VE NEVER WITNESSED BEFORE. IT'S LIKE COVERING ROYALTY, BUT I THINK THAT'S A FITTING COMPARISON UNDER THESE CIRCUMSTANCES.
THE FUNERAL
HELLO...I'M JAY GARRICK, AND I...

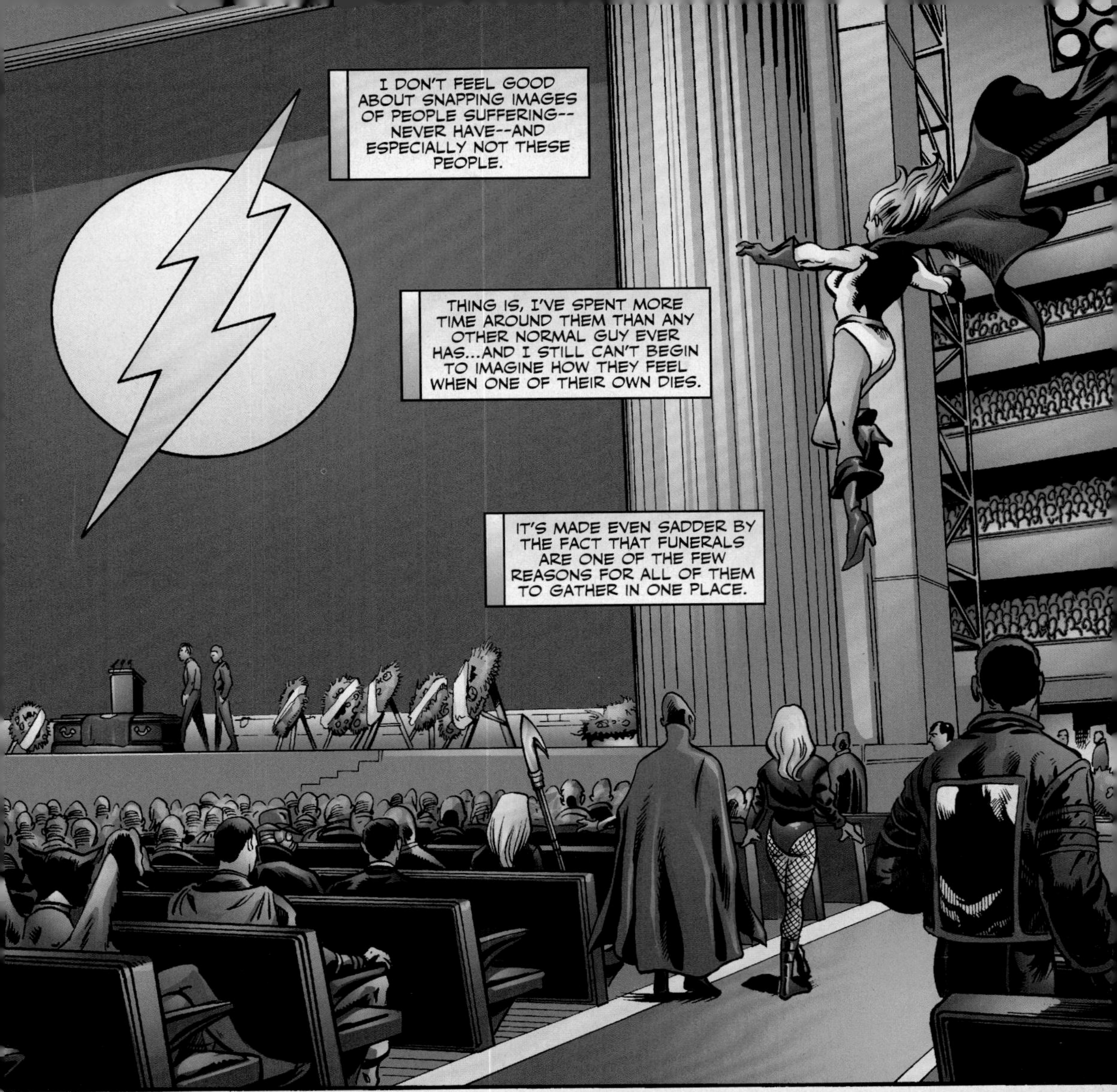
I DON'T FEEL GOOD ABOUT SNAPPING IMAGES OF PEOPLE SUFFERING-- NEVER HAVE--AND ESPECIALLY NOT THESE PEOPLE.
THING IS, I'VE SPENT MORE TIME AROUND THEM THAN ANY OTHER NORMAL GUY EVER HAS...AND I STILL CAN'T BEGIN TO IMAGINE HOW THEY FEEL WHEN ONE OF THEIR OWN DIES.
IT'S MADE EVEN SADDER BY THE FACT THAT FUNERALS ARE ONE OF THE FEW REASONS FOR ALL OF THEM TO GATHER IN ONE PLACE.

PAUL DINI - HEAD WRITER, WITH JIMMY PALMIOTTI & JUSTIN GRAY
MANUEL GARCIA W/DAVID LOPEZ - PENCILS JIMMY PALMIOTTI W/DON HILLSMAN - INK
PETE PANTAZIS - COLORS KEN LOPEZ - LETTERS

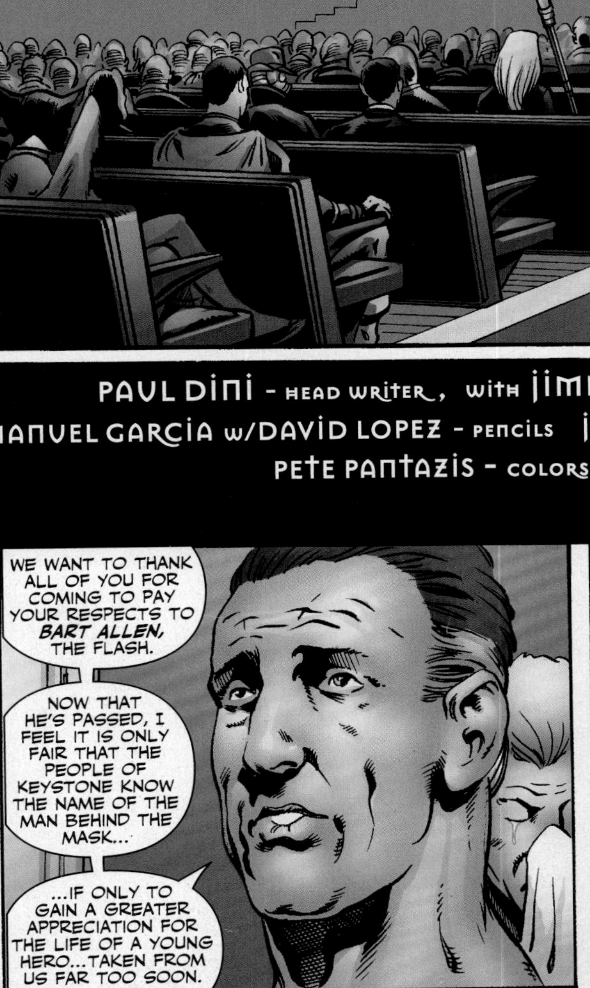
WE WANT TO THANK ALL OF YOU FOR COMING TO PAY YOUR RESPECTS TO *BART ALLEN,* THE FLASH.
NOW THAT HE'S PASSED, I FEEL IT IS ONLY FAIR THAT THE PEOPLE OF KEYSTONE KNOW THE NAME OF THE MAN BEHIND THE MASK...
...IF ONLY TO GAIN A GREATER APPRECIATION FOR THE LIFE OF A YOUNG HERO...TAKEN FROM US FAR TOO SOON.

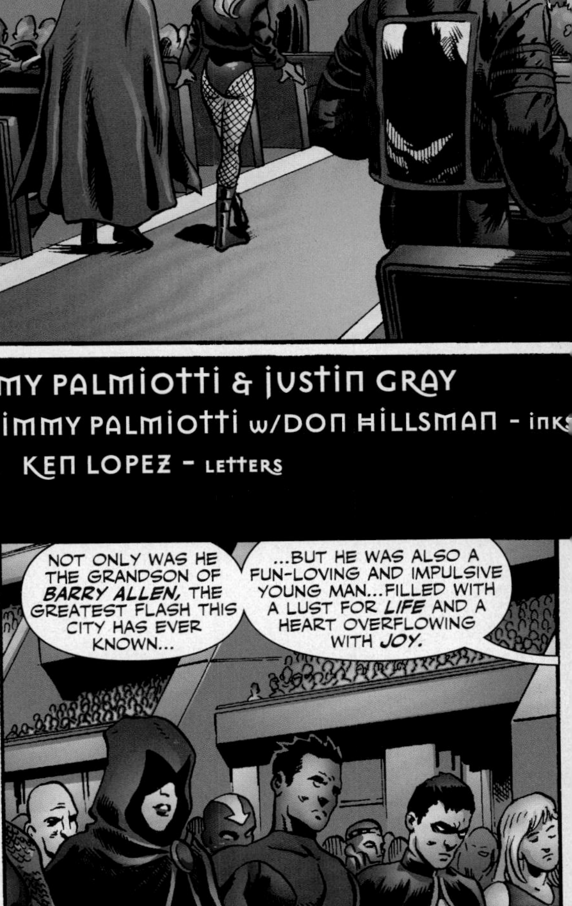
NOT ONLY WAS HE THE GRANDSON OF *BARRY ALLEN,* THE GREATEST FLASH THIS CITY HAS EVER KNOWN...
...BUT HE WAS ALSO A FUN-LOVING AND IMPULSIVE YOUNG MAN...FILLED WITH A LUST FOR *LIFE* AND A HEART OVERFLOWING WITH *JOY.*

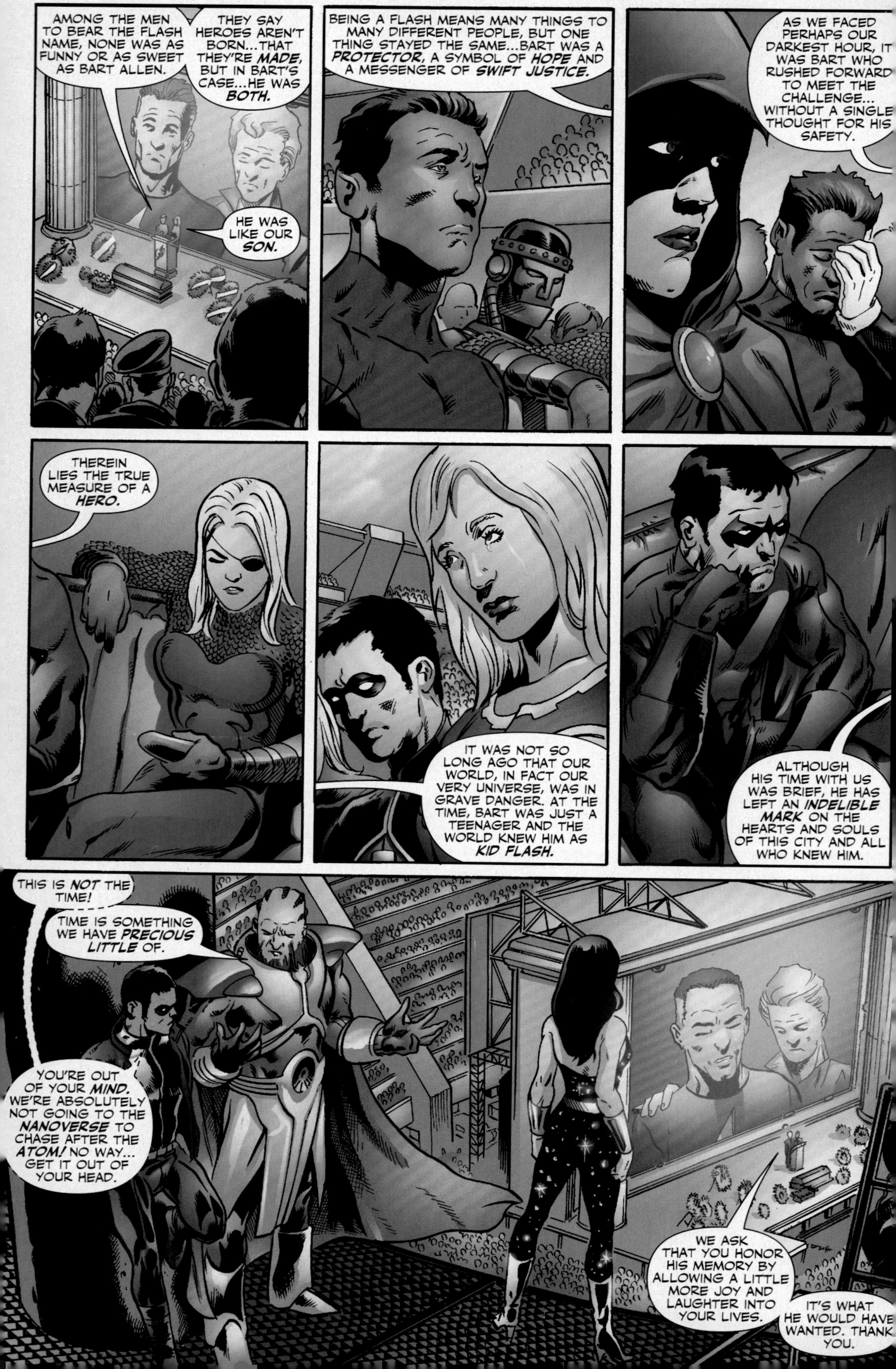
AMONG THE MEN TO BEAR THE FLASH NAME, NONE WAS AS FUNNY OR AS SWEET AS BART ALLEN.
THEY SAY HEROES AREN'T BORN...THAT THEY'RE *MADE,* BUT IN BART'S CASE...HE WAS *BOTH.*
HE WAS LIKE OUR *SON.*
BEING A FLASH MEANS MANY THINGS TO MANY DIFFERENT PEOPLE, BUT ONE THING STAYED THE SAME...BART WAS A *PROTECTOR,* A SYMBOL OF *HOPE* AND A MESSENGER OF *SWIFT JUSTICE.*
AS WE FACED PERHAPS OUR DARKEST HOUR, IT WAS BART WHO RUSHED FORWARD TO MEET THE CHALLENGE... WITHOUT A SINGLE THOUGHT FOR HIS SAFETY.
THEREIN LIES THE TRUE MEASURE OF A *HERO.*
IT WAS NOT SO LONG AGO THAT OUR WORLD, IN FACT OUR VERY UNIVERSE, WAS IN GRAVE DANGER. AT THE TIME, BART WAS JUST A TEENAGER AND THE WORLD KNEW HIM AS *KID FLASH.*
ALTHOUGH HIS TIME WITH US WAS BRIEF, HE HAS LEFT AN *INDELIBLE MARK* ON THE HEARTS AND SOULS OF THIS CITY AND ALL WHO KNEW HIM.
THIS IS *NOT* THE TIME!
TIME IS SOMETHING WE HAVE *PRECIOUS LITTLE* OF.
YOU'RE OUT OF YOUR *MIND.* WE'RE ABSOLUTELY NOT GOING TO THE *NANOVERSE* TO CHASE AFTER THE *ATOM!* NO WAY... GET IT OUT OF YOUR HEAD.
WE ASK THAT YOU HONOR HIS MEMORY BY ALLOWING A LITTLE MORE JOY AND LAUGHTER INTO YOUR LIVES.
IT'S WHAT HE WOULD HAVE WANTED. THANK YOU.

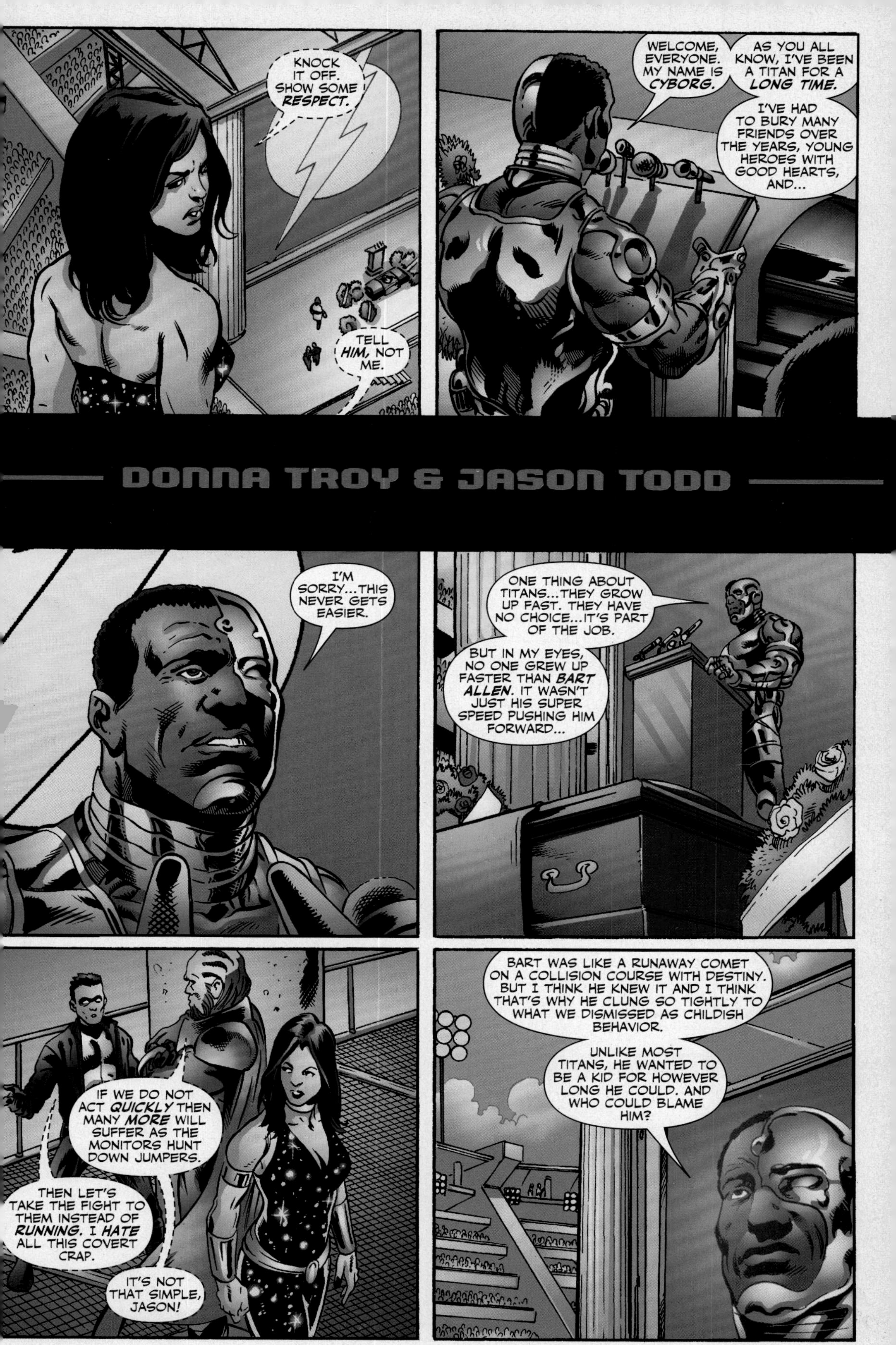
KNOCK IT OFF. SHOW SOME RESPECT.
TELL HIM, NOT ME.
WELCOME, EVERYONE. MY NAME IS CYBORG.
AS YOU ALL KNOW, I'VE BEEN A TITAN FOR A LONG TIME.
I'VE HAD TO BURY MANY FRIENDS OVER THE YEARS, YOUNG HEROES WITH GOOD HEARTS, AND...
DONNA TROY & JASON TODD
I'M SORRY...THIS NEVER GETS EASIER.
ONE THING ABOUT TITANS...THEY GROW UP FAST. THEY HAVE NO CHOICE...IT'S PART OF THE JOB.
BUT IN MY EYES, NO ONE GREW UP FASTER THAN BART ALLEN. IT WASN'T JUST HIS SUPER SPEED PUSHING HIM FORWARD...
IF WE DO NOT ACT QUICKLY THEN MANY MORE WILL SUFFER AS THE MONITORS HUNT DOWN JUMPERS.
THEN LET'S TAKE THE FIGHT TO THEM INSTEAD OF RUNNING. I HATE ALL THIS COVERT CRAP.
IT'S NOT THAT SIMPLE, JASON!
BART WAS LIKE A RUNAWAY COMET ON A COLLISION COURSE WITH DESTINY. BUT I THINK HE KNEW IT AND I THINK THAT'S WHY HE CLUNG SO TIGHTLY TO WHAT WE DISMISSED AS CHILDISH BEHAVIOR.
UNLIKE MOST TITANS, HE WANTED TO BE A KID FOR HOWEVER LONG HE COULD. AND WHO COULD BLAME HIM?

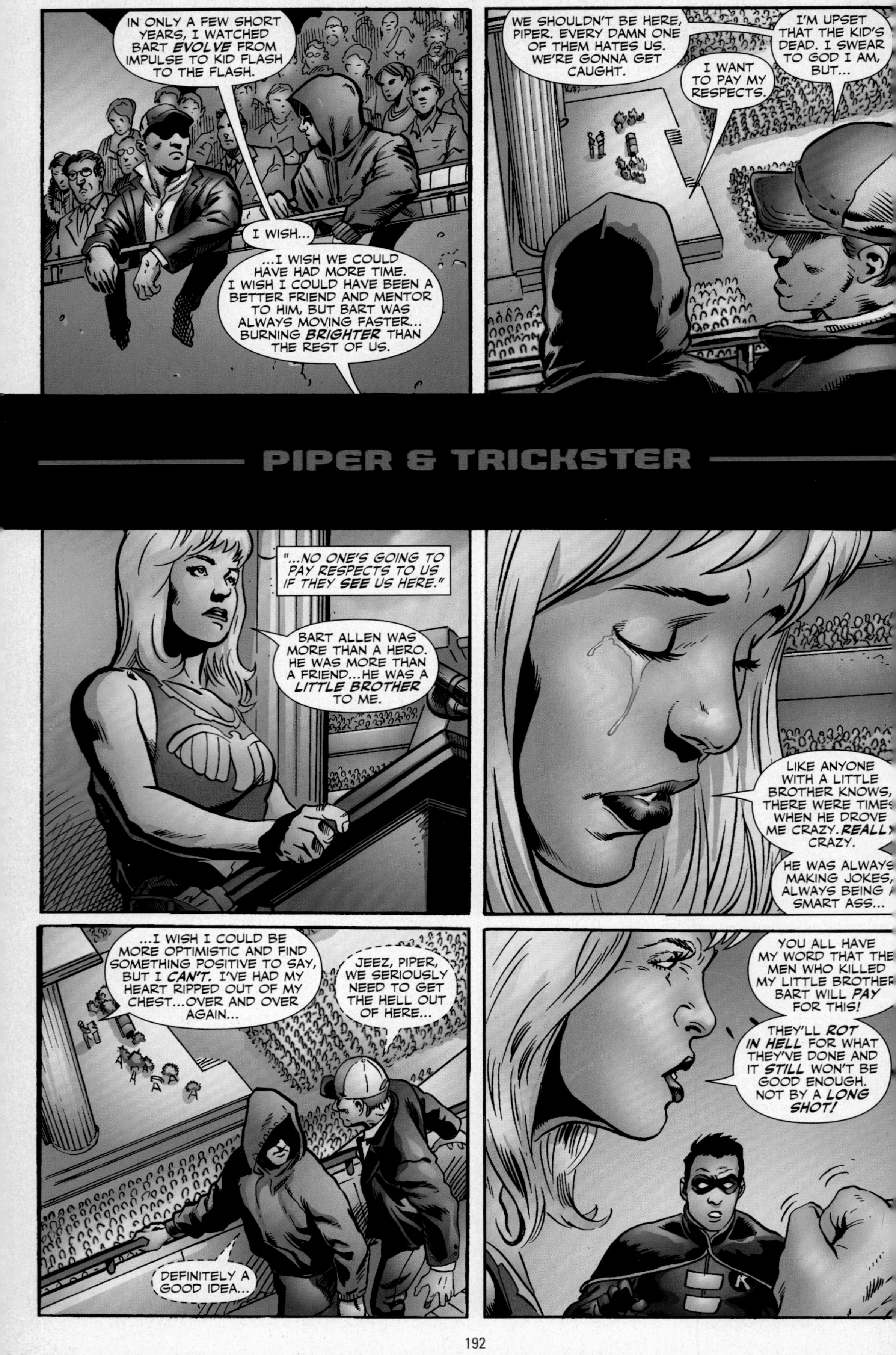

IN ONLY A FEW SHORT YEARS, I WATCHED BART EVOLVE FROM IMPULSE TO KID FLASH TO THE FLASH.
I WISH...
...I WISH WE COULD HAVE HAD MORE TIME. I WISH I COULD HAVE BEEN A BETTER FRIEND AND MENTOR TO HIM, BUT BART WAS ALWAYS MOVING FASTER... BURNING BRIGHTER THAN THE REST OF US.
WE SHOULDN'T BE HERE, PIPER. EVERY DAMN ONE OF THEM HATES US. WE'RE GONNA GET CAUGHT.
I WANT TO PAY MY RESPECTS.
I'M UPSET THAT THE KID'S DEAD. I SWEAR TO GOD I AM, BUT...
PIPER & TRICKSTER
"...NO ONE'S GOING TO PAY RESPECTS TO US IF THEY SEE US HERE."
BART ALLEN WAS MORE THAN A HERO. HE WAS MORE THAN A FRIEND...HE WAS A LITTLE BROTHER TO ME.
LIKE ANYONE WITH A LITTLE BROTHER KNOWS, THERE WERE TIMES WHEN HE DROVE ME CRAZY. REALLY CRAZY.
HE WAS ALWAYS MAKING JOKES, ALWAYS BEING A SMART ASS...
...I WISH I COULD BE MORE OPTIMISTIC AND FIND SOMETHING POSITIVE TO SAY, BUT I CAN'T. I'VE HAD MY HEART RIPPED OUT OF MY CHEST...OVER AND OVER AGAIN...
JEEZ, PIPER, WE SERIOUSLY NEED TO GET THE HELL OUT OF HERE...
DEFINITELY A GOOD IDEA...
YOU ALL HAVE MY WORD THAT THE MEN WHO KILLED MY LITTLE BROTHER BART WILL PAY FOR THIS!
THEY'LL ROT IN HELL FOR WHAT THEY'VE DONE AND IT STILL WON'T BE GOOD ENOUGH. NOT BY A LONG SHOT!

THEY'LL BE HUNTED DOWN LIKE ANIMALS AND *PUNISHED.* MAY THE GODS HELP THEM IF *I'M* THE ONE TO FIND THEM FIRST!

THAT'S IT-- WE'RE *DONE,* PIPER. THIS PARTNERSHIP OR WHATEVER YOU WANT TO CALL IT IS *DISSOLVED!*

FINE BY ME!

I'M SORRY...BART DESERVED A BETTER SPEECH...

HE SHOULD STILL BE HERE...IF HE HAD MORE TIME HE WOULD HAVE BEEN THE GREATEST FLASH KEYSTONE AND CENTRAL CITY EVER HAD.

I KNOW.

YOU GO YOUR WAY AND I'LL GO MINE. THAT'S ALL I'M SAYING.

YOU WANNA *GO...THEN GO.* NO ONE'S STOPPING YOU.

IF WE SPLIT UP, MAYBE WE HAVE A CHANCE...WE CAN ALWAYS HOPE SOME OTHER WORLD-THREATENING OCCURRENCE HAPPENS AND THEY *FORGET* ABOUT US.

I'D RATHER HAUL IN THE ROGUES AND DUMP THEIR BODIES AT WONDER GIRL'S FEET. YOU HEARD HER...

THAT LOOK ON HER FACE...I'M NOT GOING TO BE ABLE TO SLEEP TONIGHT.

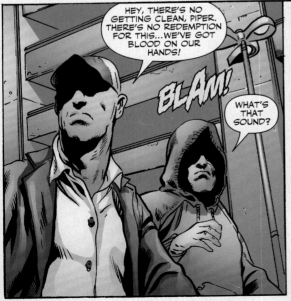

HEY, THERE'S NO GETTING CLEAN, PIPER. THERE'S NO REDEMPTION FOR THIS...WE'VE GOT BLOOD ON OUR HANDS!

BLAM!

WHAT'S THAT SOUND?

BLAM!

SOMEONE'S *SHOOTING* AT US?!

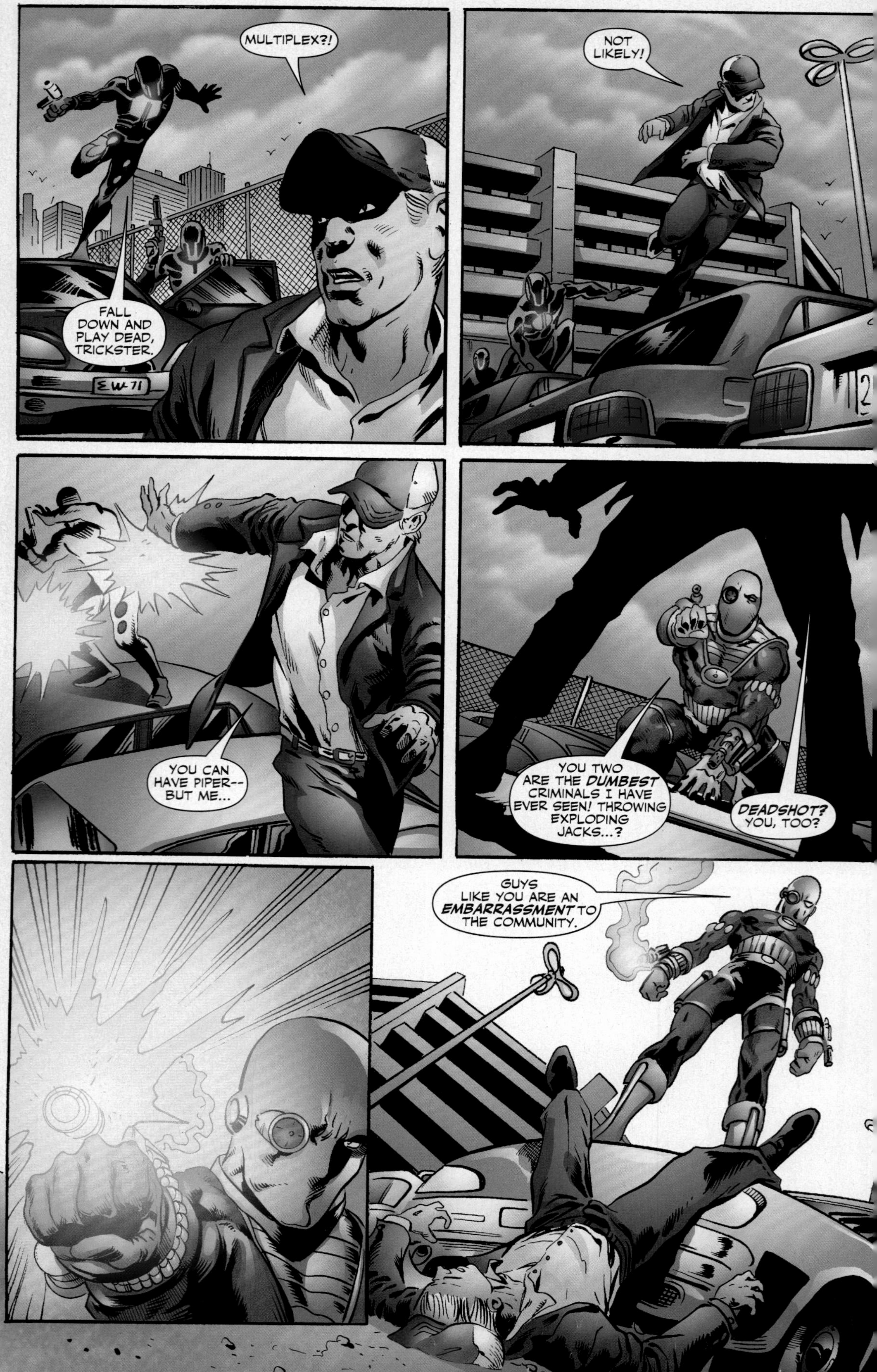
MULTIPLEX?!
FALL DOWN AND PLAY DEAD, TRICKSTER.
NOT LIKELY!
YOU CAN HAVE PIPER-- BUT ME...
DEADSHOT? YOU, TOO?
YOU TWO ARE THE DUMBEST CRIMINALS I HAVE EVER SEEN! THROWING EXPLODING JACKS...?
GUYS LIKE YOU ARE AN EMBARRASSMENT TO THE COMMUNITY.

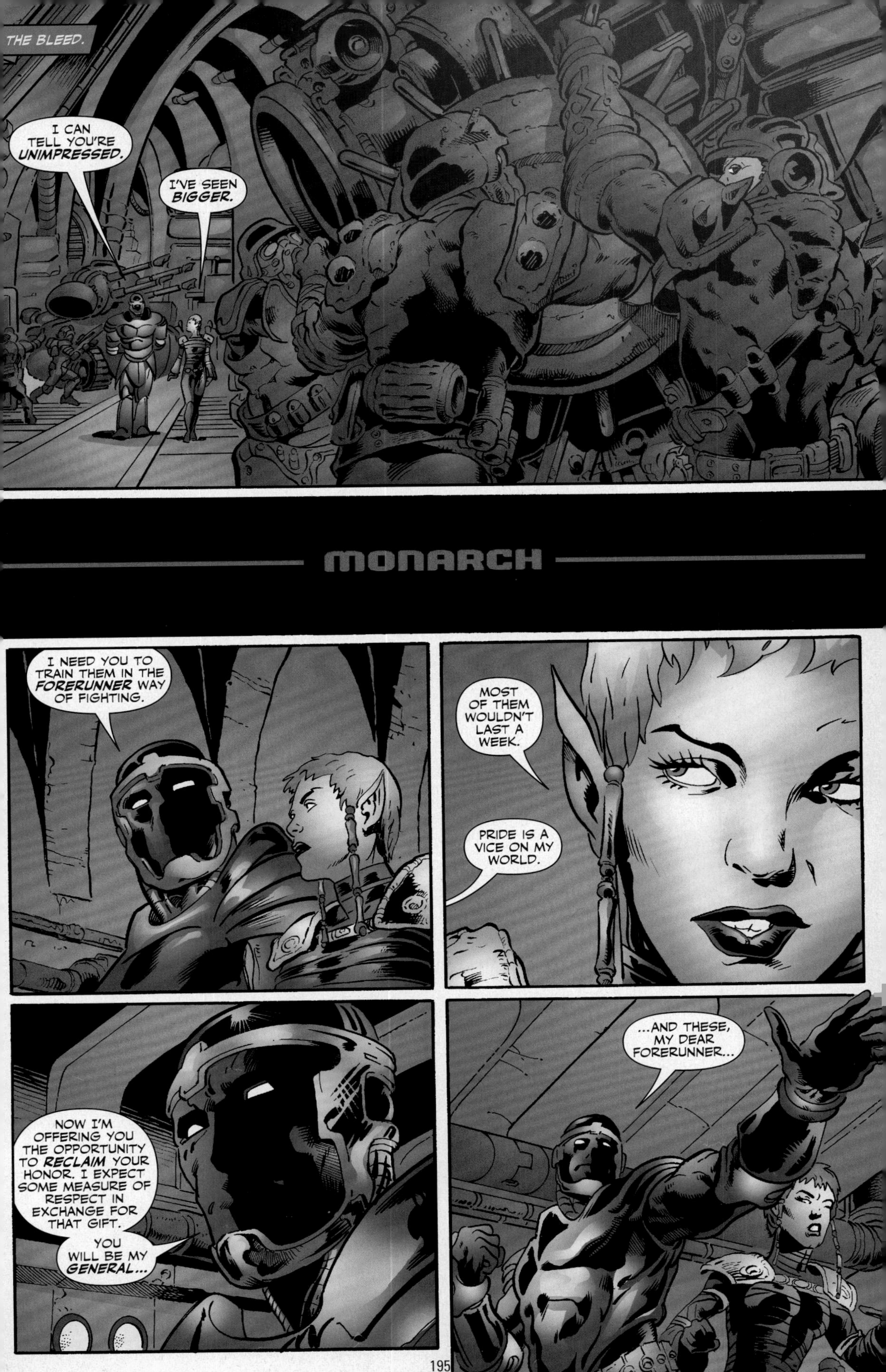
THE BLEED.
I CAN TELL YOU'RE UNIMPRESSED.
I'VE SEEN BIGGER.
MONARCH
I NEED YOU TO TRAIN THEM IN THE FORERUNNER WAY OF FIGHTING.
MOST OF THEM WOULDN'T LAST A WEEK.
PRIDE IS A VICE ON MY WORLD.
NOW I'M OFFERING YOU THE OPPORTUNITY TO RECLAIM YOUR HONOR. I EXPECT SOME MEASURE OF RESPECT IN EXCHANGE FOR THAT GIFT.
YOU WILL BE MY GENERAL...
...AND THESE, MY DEAR FORERUNNER...

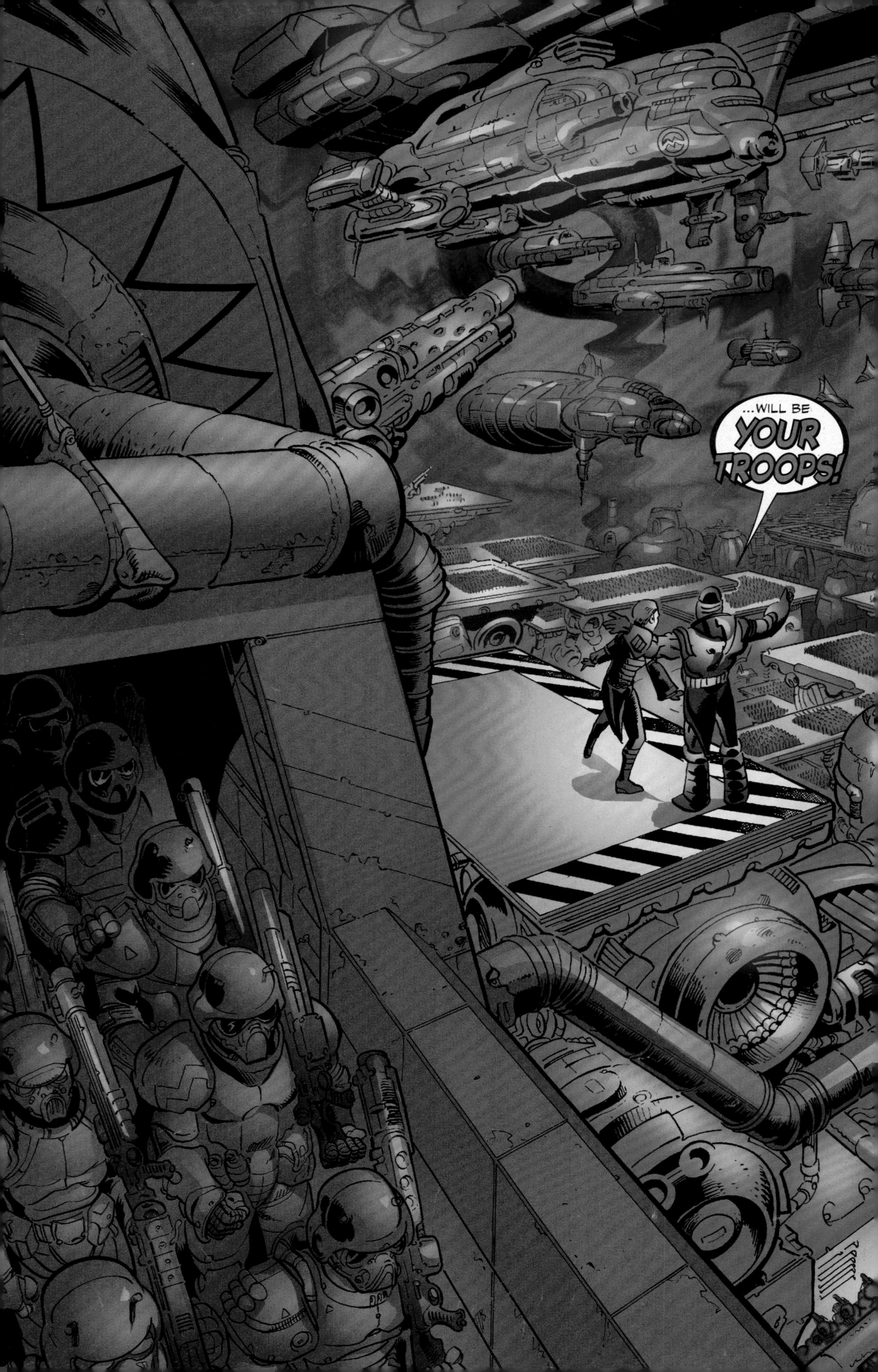
...WILL BE YOUR TROOPS!

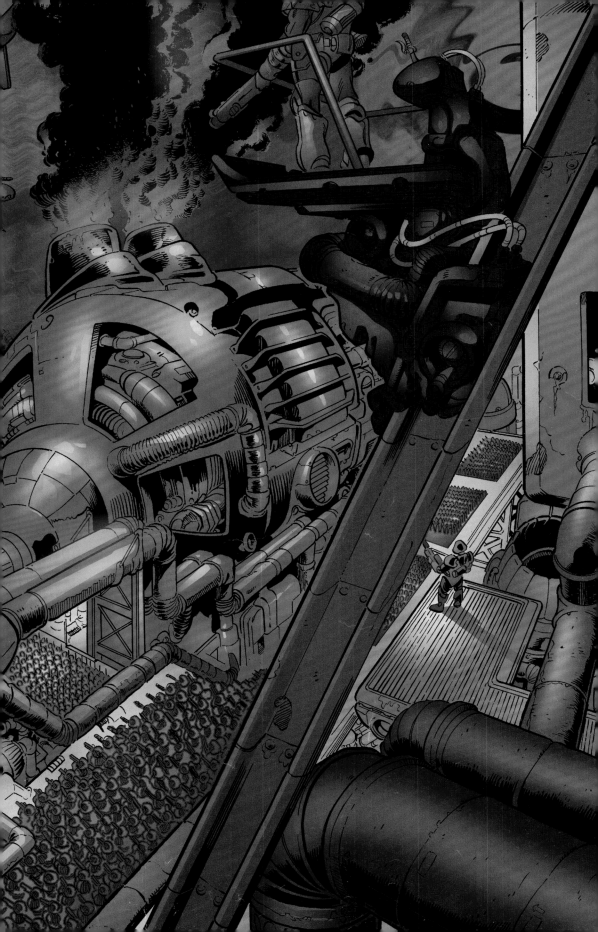

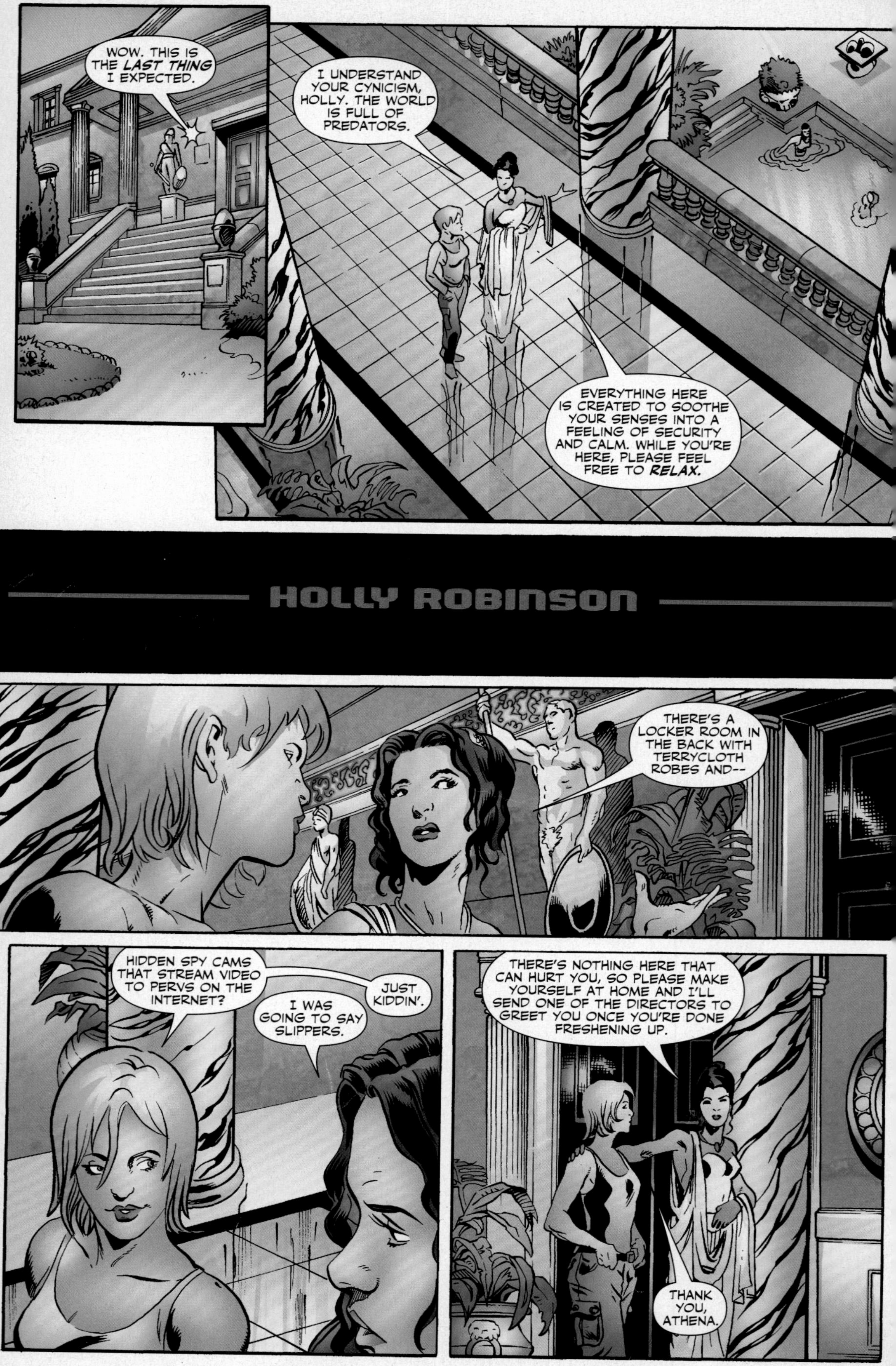
WOW. THIS IS THE LAST THING I EXPECTED.
I UNDERSTAND YOUR CYNICISM, HOLLY. THE WORLD IS FULL OF PREDATORS.
EVERYTHING HERE IS CREATED TO SOOTHE YOUR SENSES INTO A FEELING OF SECURITY AND CALM. WHILE YOU'RE HERE, PLEASE FEEL FREE TO RELAX.
HOLLY ROBINSON
THERE'S A LOCKER ROOM IN THE BACK WITH TERRYCLOTH ROBES AND--
HIDDEN SPY CAMS THAT STREAM VIDEO TO PERVS ON THE INTERNET?
JUST KIDDIN'.
I WAS GOING TO SAY SLIPPERS.
THERE'S NOTHING HERE THAT CAN HURT YOU, SO PLEASE MAKE YOURSELF AT HOME AND I'LL SEND ONE OF THE DIRECTORS TO GREET YOU ONCE YOU'RE DONE FRESHENING UP.
THANK YOU, ATHENA.

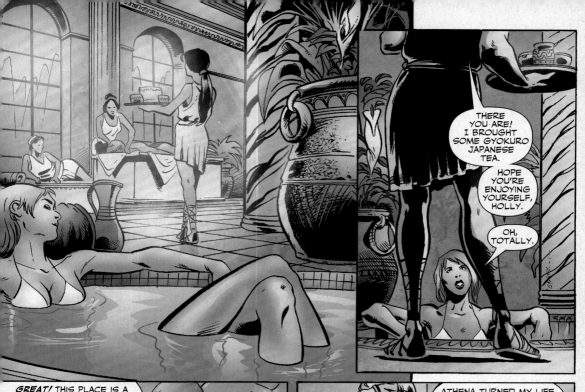

THERE YOU ARE! I BROUGHT SOME GYOKURO JAPANESE TEA.

HOPE YOU'RE ENJOYING YOURSELF, HOLLY.

OH, TOTALLY.

GREAT! THIS PLACE IS A GODSEND--IT SAVED MY LIFE AND JUST ABOUT EVERY OTHER WOMAN'S IN HERE. I TELL YOU, HONEY, BEFORE I GOT HERE I WAS A *REAL MESS*...

...AND TRUST ME, THAT'S THE *UNDERSTATEMENT* OF THE YEAR.

THANKS.

ATHENA TURNED MY LIFE AROUND. SHE TAUGHT ME TO RESPECT AND LOVE ME FOR ME, YOU KNOW?

I WAS THE KIND OF GIRL THAT ALWAYS NEEDED A MAN, EVEN IF HE WAS THE *WORST* POSSIBLE EXAMPLE OF THE SPECIES. MY LAST BOYFRIEND WAS A REAL *MANIAC*.

UHH... I'M NOT REALLY HERE BECAUSE OF...

HONEY, YOU DON'T HAVE TO TALK ABOUT IT IF YOU DON'T WANT TO. THIS IS A PRESSURE-FREE ZONE.

OH GOSH, WHERE ARE MY *MANNERS*? I DIDN'T INTRODUCE MYSELF. I'M *HARLEEN QUINZEL*.

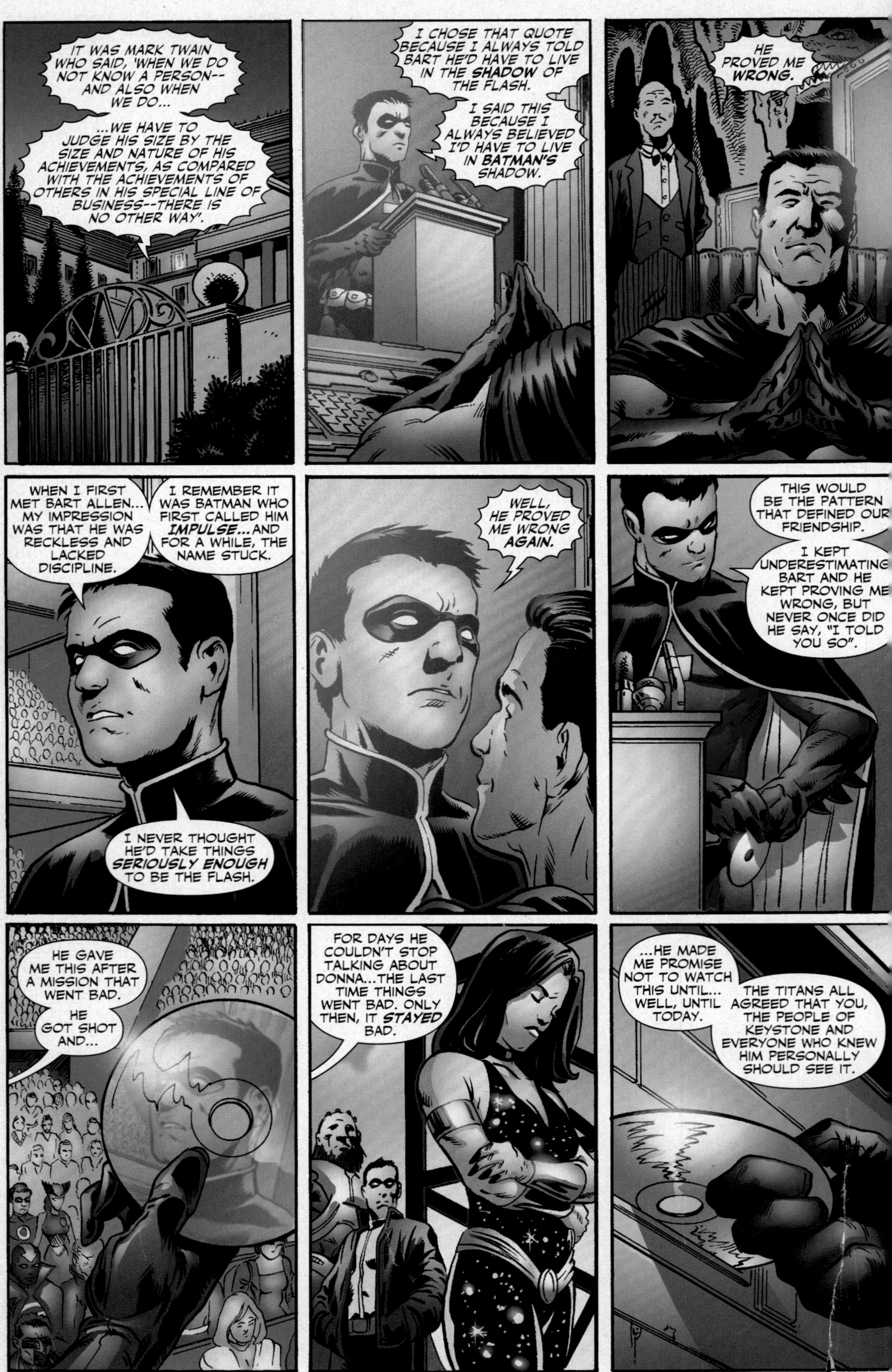
IT WAS MARK TWAIN WHO SAID, 'WHEN WE DO NOT KNOW A PERSON--AND ALSO WHEN WE DO...
...WE HAVE TO JUDGE HIS SIZE BY THE SIZE AND NATURE OF HIS ACHIEVEMENTS, AS COMPARED WITH THE ACHIEVEMENTS OF OTHERS IN HIS SPECIAL LINE OF BUSINESS--THERE IS NO OTHER WAY'.
I CHOSE THAT QUOTE BECAUSE I ALWAYS TOLD BART HE'D HAVE TO LIVE IN THE SHADOW OF THE FLASH.
I SAID THIS BECAUSE I ALWAYS BELIEVED I'D HAVE TO LIVE IN BATMAN'S SHADOW.
HE PROVED ME WRONG.
WHEN I FIRST MET BART ALLEN... MY IMPRESSION WAS THAT HE WAS RECKLESS AND LACKED DISCIPLINE.
I REMEMBER IT WAS BATMAN WHO FIRST CALLED HIM IMPULSE...AND FOR A WHILE, THE NAME STUCK.
I NEVER THOUGHT HE'D TAKE THINGS SERIOUSLY ENOUGH TO BE THE FLASH.
WELL, HE PROVED ME WRONG AGAIN.
THIS WOULD BE THE PATTERN THAT DEFINED OUR FRIENDSHIP.
I KEPT UNDERESTIMATING BART AND HE KEPT PROVING ME WRONG, BUT NEVER ONCE DID HE SAY, "I TOLD YOU SO".
HE GAVE ME THIS AFTER A MISSION THAT WENT BAD.
HE GOT SHOT AND...
FOR DAYS HE COULDN'T STOP TALKING ABOUT DONNA...THE LAST TIME THINGS WENT BAD. ONLY THEN, IT STAYED BAD.
...HE MADE ME PROMISE NOT TO WATCH THIS UNTIL... WELL, UNTIL TODAY.
THE TITANS ALL AGREED THAT YOU, THE PEOPLE OF KEYSTONE AND EVERYONE WHO KNEW HIM PERSONALLY SHOULD SEE IT.

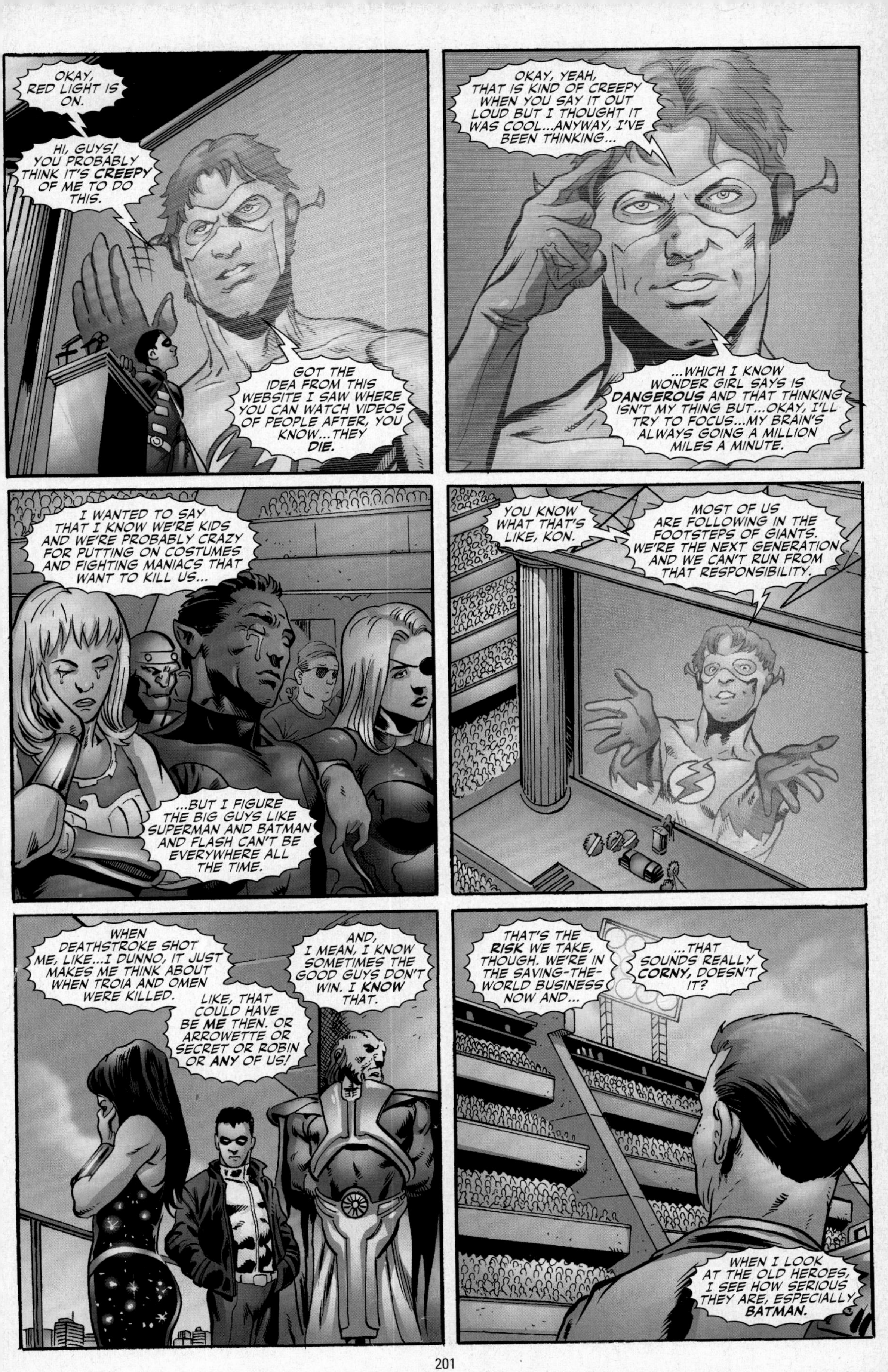
OKAY, RED LIGHT IS ON.
HI, GUYS! YOU PROBABLY THINK IT'S CREEPY OF ME TO DO THIS.
GOT THE IDEA FROM THIS WEBSITE I SAW WHERE YOU CAN WATCH VIDEOS OF PEOPLE AFTER, YOU KNOW...THEY DIE.
OKAY, YEAH, THAT IS KIND OF CREEPY WHEN YOU SAY IT OUT LOUD BUT I THOUGHT IT WAS COOL...ANYWAY, I'VE BEEN THINKING...
...WHICH I KNOW WONDER GIRL SAYS IS DANGEROUS AND THAT THINKING ISN'T MY THING BUT...OKAY, I'LL TRY TO FOCUS...MY BRAIN'S ALWAYS GOING A MILLION MILES A MINUTE.
I WANTED TO SAY THAT I KNOW WE'RE KIDS AND WE'RE PROBABLY CRAZY FOR PUTTING ON COSTUMES AND FIGHTING MANIACS THAT WANT TO KILL US...
...BUT I FIGURE THE BIG GUYS LIKE SUPERMAN AND BATMAN AND FLASH CAN'T BE EVERYWHERE ALL THE TIME.
YOU KNOW WHAT THAT'S LIKE, KON.
MOST OF US ARE FOLLOWING IN THE FOOTSTEPS OF GIANTS. WE'RE THE NEXT GENERATION AND WE CAN'T RUN FROM THAT RESPONSIBILITY.
WHEN DEATHSTROKE SHOT ME, LIKE...I DUNNO, IT JUST MAKES ME THINK ABOUT WHEN TROIA AND OMEN WERE KILLED.
LIKE, THAT COULD HAVE BE ME THEN. OR ARROWETTE OR SECRET OR ROBIN OR ANY OF US!
AND, I MEAN, I KNOW SOMETIMES THE GOOD GUYS DON'T WIN. I KNOW THAT.
THAT'S THE RISK WE TAKE, THOUGH. WE'RE IN THE SAVING-THE-WORLD BUSINESS NOW AND...
...THAT SOUNDS REALLY CORNY, DOESN'T IT?
WHEN I LOOK AT THE OLD HEROES, I SEE HOW SERIOUS THEY ARE, ESPECIALLY BATMAN.

GEEZ, COULD HE **LIGHTEN UP** EVERY ONCE IN A WHILE OR WHAT?

ROBIN, PLEASE DON'T TELL HIM I SAID THAT.

ANYWAY, IF FOR SOME REASON I SHOULD GET KILLED IN THE FLASH TRADITION OF SAVING THE UNIVERSE FROM SOME CRISIS OR KICKING DARKSEID'S BUTT...

...I DON'T WANT YOU TO FORGET HOW MUCH FUN I HAD BEING ALIVE OR HOW LUCKY I AM TO HAVE YOU GUYS AS MY FRIENDS.

AND MAKE SURE SOMEONE TELLS WALLY, IF HE CAN'T BE HERE TO SEE THIS, THAT IT'S **OKAY.** I MEAN, HE **IS** A HUGE BUTTHEAD, BUT HE WAS ALSO A GREAT TEACHER AND IT'S NOT HIS FAULT THAT BAD THINGS HAPPEN.

I KNOW WONDER GIRL IS STILL HURTING, EVEN THOUGH SHE'S ALL TOUGH AND WOULD NEVER SAY IT. HER IDEA TO START A NEW TITANS?

IT'S **AWESOME!** BEST IDEA **EVER!** BECAUSE WE CAN'T EVER GIVE UP HOPE. THAT'S NOT WHAT WE DO.

I KNOW I WON'T REGRET A SINGLE MOMENT, AND IF I'M SUPER LUCKY, THEN SOMEDAY I'LL BE THE FLASH JUST LIKE MY GRANDFATHER BARRY.

SURE I'LL NEVER BE AS **GOOD** AS HE WAS, BUT I OWE IT TO HIM AND THE PEOPLE OF KEYSTONE TO AT LEAST **TRY.**

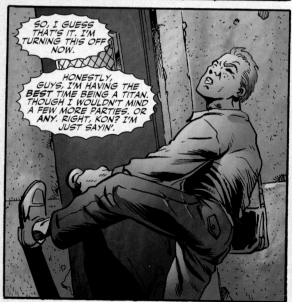

SO, I GUESS THAT'S IT. I'M TURNING THIS OFF NOW.

HONESTLY, GUYS, I'M HAVING THE **BEST** TIME BEING A TITAN. THOUGH I WOULDN'T MIND A FEW MORE PARTIES. OR ANY. RIGHT, KON? I'M JUST SAYIN'.

NOW THAT IT'S OVER, CAN WE TALK ABOUT THE NANOVERSE...

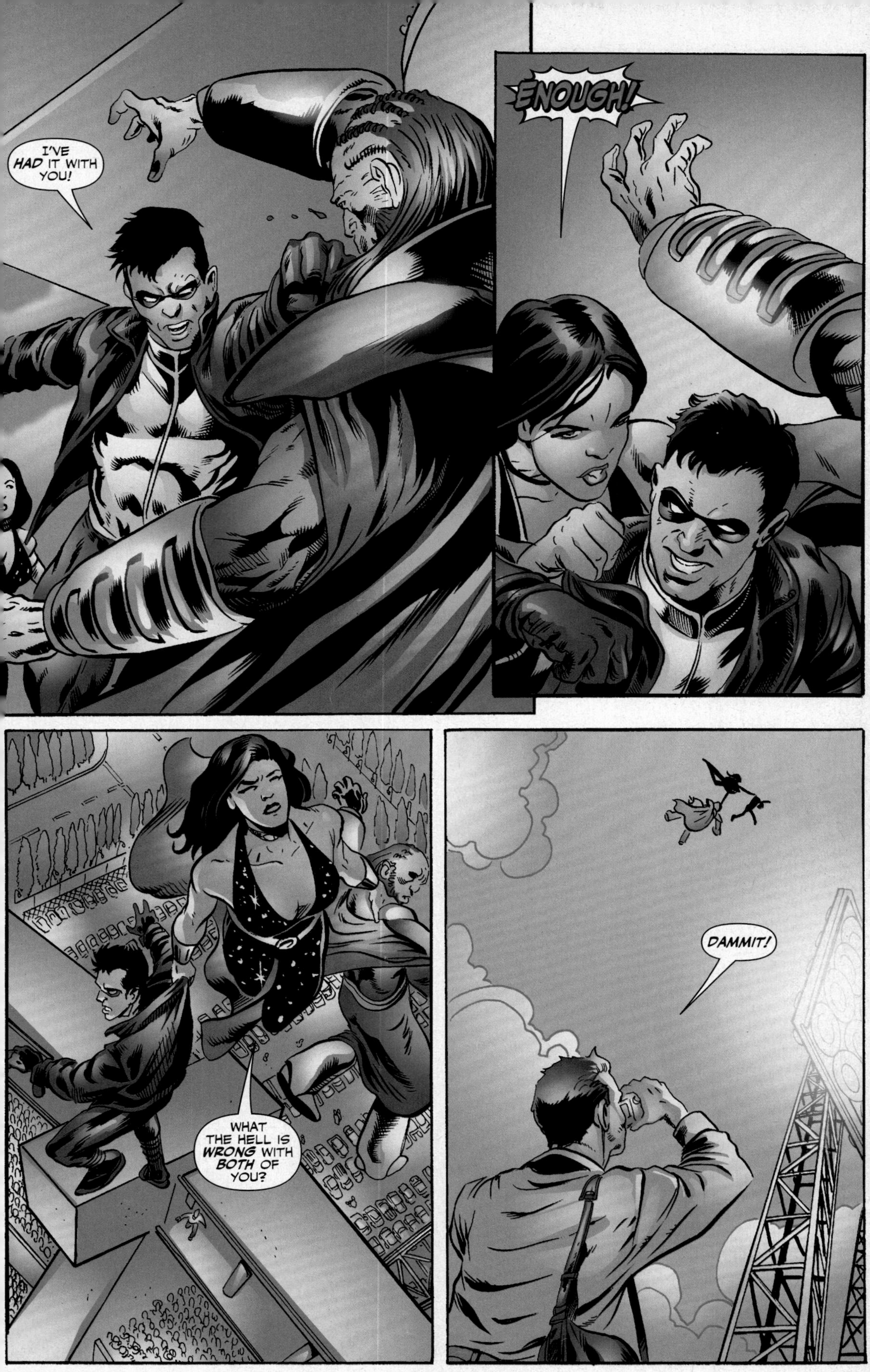
I'VE HAD IT WITH YOU!
ENOUGH!
WHAT THE HELL IS WRONG WITH BOTH OF YOU?
DAMMIT!

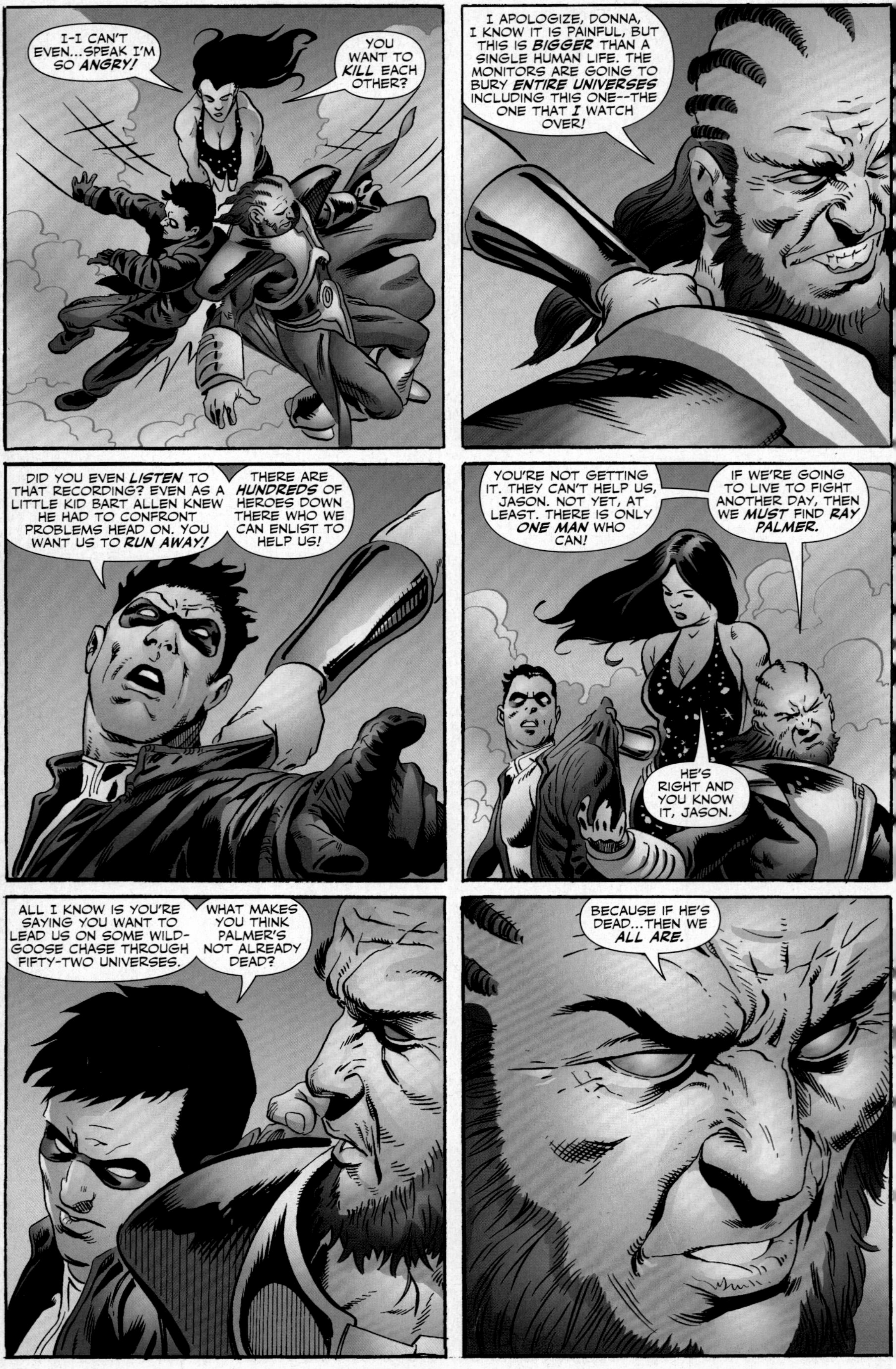
I-I CAN'T EVEN...SPEAK I'M SO ANGRY!
YOU WANT TO KILL EACH OTHER?
I APOLOGIZE, DONNA, I KNOW IT IS PAINFUL, BUT THIS IS BIGGER THAN A SINGLE HUMAN LIFE. THE MONITORS ARE GOING TO BURY ENTIRE UNIVERSES INCLUDING THIS ONE--THE ONE THAT I WATCH OVER!
DID YOU EVEN LISTEN TO THAT RECORDING? EVEN AS A LITTLE KID BART ALLEN KNEW HE HAD TO CONFRONT PROBLEMS HEAD ON. YOU WANT US TO RUN AWAY!
THERE ARE HUNDREDS OF HEROES DOWN THERE WHO WE CAN ENLIST TO HELP US!
YOU'RE NOT GETTING IT. THEY CAN'T HELP US, JASON. NOT YET, AT LEAST. THERE IS ONLY ONE MAN WHO CAN!
IF WE'RE GOING TO LIVE TO FIGHT ANOTHER DAY, THEN WE MUST FIND RAY PALMER.
HE'S RIGHT AND YOU KNOW IT, JASON.
ALL I KNOW IS YOU'RE SAYING YOU WANT TO LEAD US ON SOME WILD-GOOSE CHASE THROUGH FIFTY-TWO UNIVERSES.
WHAT MAKES YOU THINK PALMER'S NOT ALREADY DEAD?
BECAUSE IF HE'S DEAD...THEN WE ALL ARE.

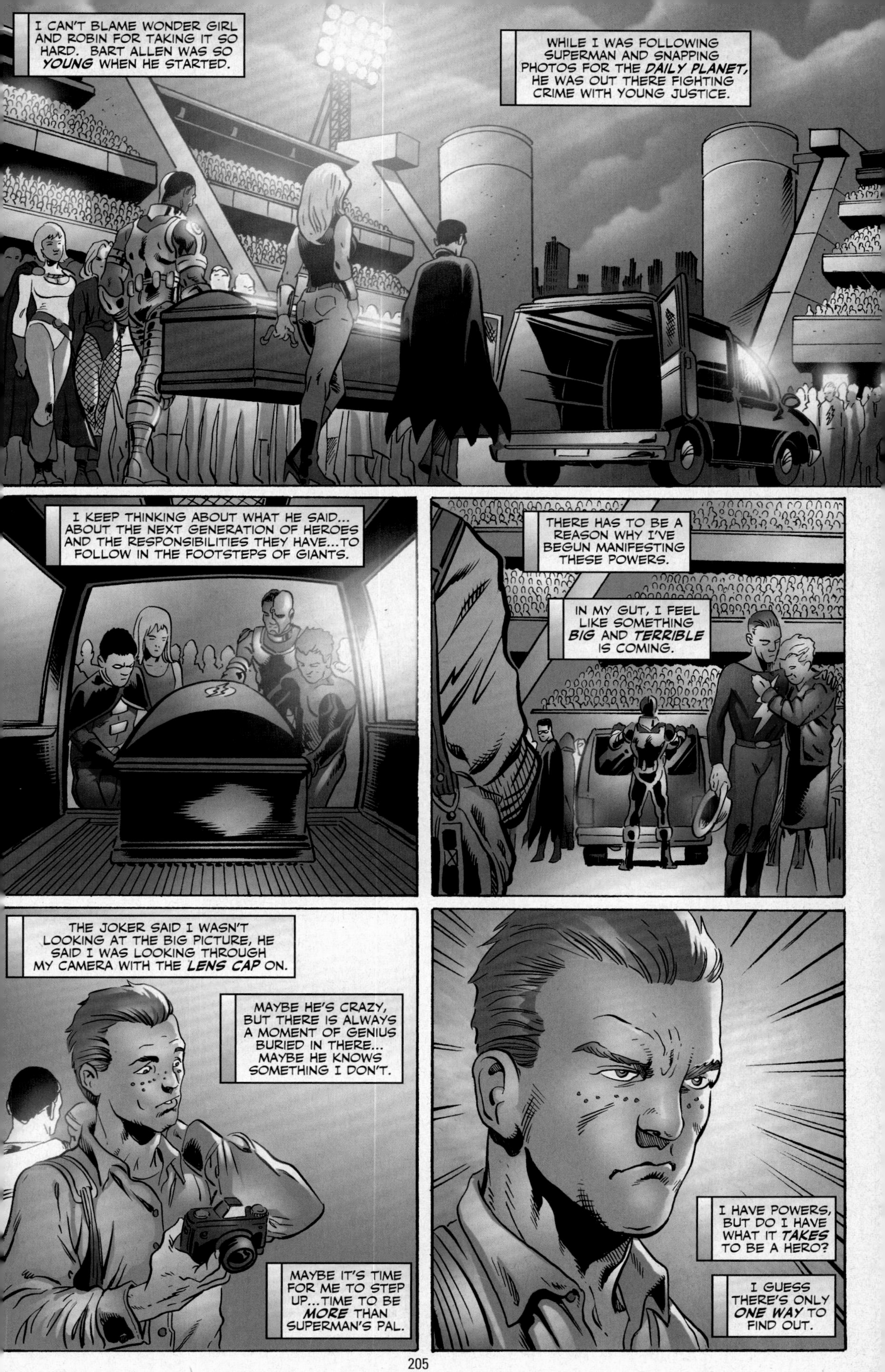
I CAN'T BLAME WONDER GIRL AND ROBIN FOR TAKING IT SO HARD. BART ALLEN WAS SO *YOUNG* WHEN HE STARTED.
WHILE I WAS FOLLOWING SUPERMAN AND SNAPPING PHOTOS FOR THE *DAILY PLANET,* HE WAS OUT THERE FIGHTING CRIME WITH YOUNG JUSTICE.
I KEEP THINKING ABOUT WHAT HE SAID... ABOUT THE NEXT GENERATION OF HEROES AND THE RESPONSIBILITIES THEY HAVE...TO FOLLOW IN THE FOOTSTEPS OF GIANTS.
THERE HAS TO BE A REASON WHY I'VE BEGUN MANIFESTING THESE POWERS.
IN MY GUT, I FEEL LIKE SOMETHING *BIG* AND *TERRIBLE* IS COMING.
THE JOKER SAID I WASN'T LOOKING AT THE BIG PICTURE, HE SAID I WAS LOOKING THROUGH MY CAMERA WITH THE *LENS CAP* ON.
MAYBE HE'S CRAZY, BUT THERE IS ALWAYS A MOMENT OF GENIUS BURIED IN THERE... MAYBE HE KNOWS SOMETHING I DON'T.
MAYBE IT'S TIME FOR ME TO STEP UP...TIME TO BE *MORE* THAN SUPERMAN'S PAL.
I HAVE POWERS, BUT DO I HAVE WHAT IT *TAKES* TO BE A HERO?
I GUESS THERE'S ONLY *ONE WAY* TO FIND OUT.

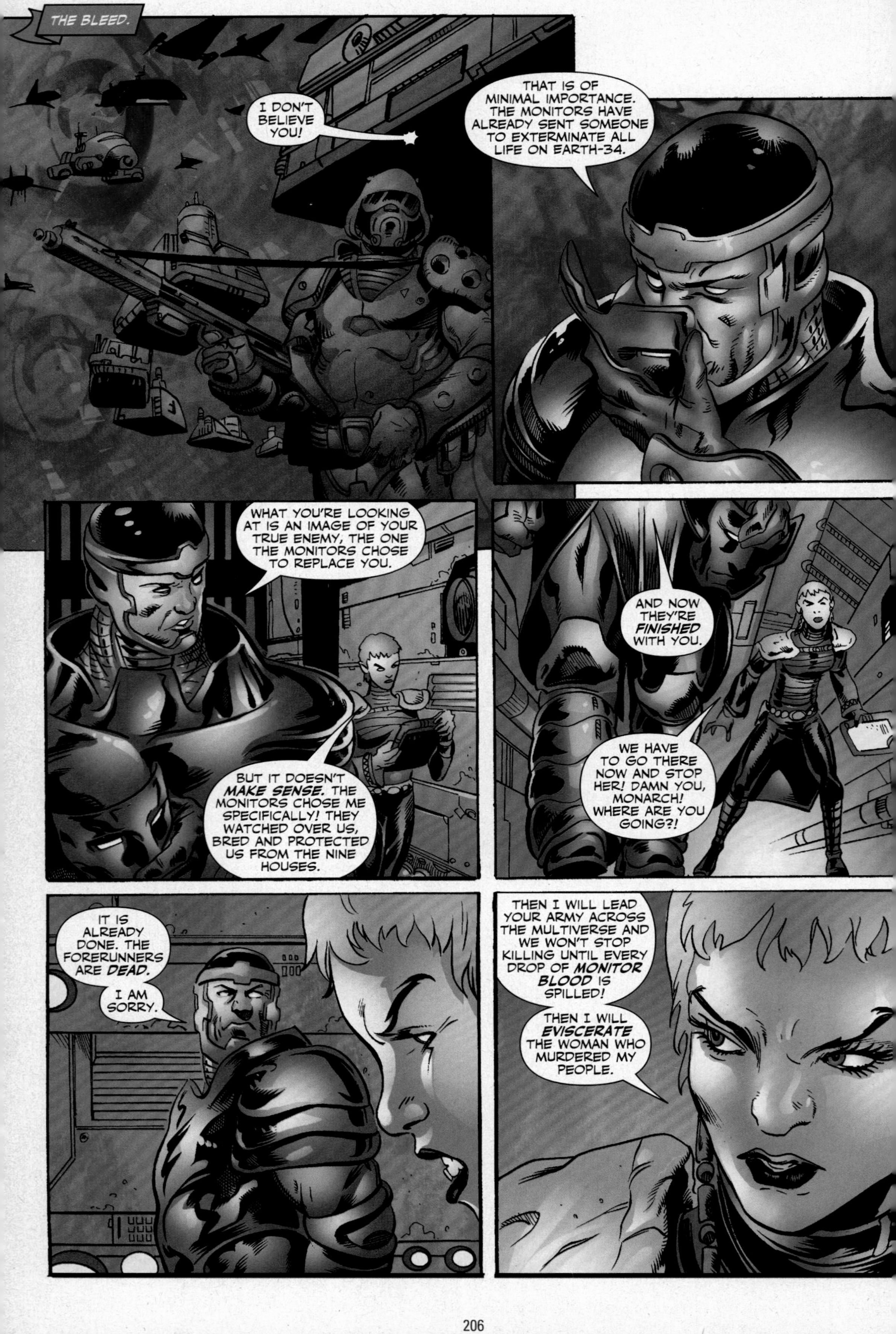
THE BLEED.
I DON'T BELIEVE YOU!
THAT IS OF MINIMAL IMPORTANCE. THE MONITORS HAVE ALREADY SENT SOMEONE TO EXTERMINATE ALL LIFE ON EARTH-34.
WHAT YOU'RE LOOKING AT IS AN IMAGE OF YOUR TRUE ENEMY, THE ONE THE MONITORS CHOSE TO REPLACE YOU.
BUT IT DOESN'T MAKE SENSE. THE MONITORS CHOSE ME SPECIFICALLY! THEY WATCHED OVER US, BRED AND PROTECTED US FROM THE NINE HOUSES.
AND NOW THEY'RE FINISHED WITH YOU.
WE HAVE TO GO THERE NOW AND STOP HER! DAMN YOU, MONARCH! WHERE ARE YOU GOING?!
IT IS ALREADY DONE. THE FORERUNNERS ARE DEAD.
I AM SORRY.
THEN I WILL LEAD YOUR ARMY ACROSS THE MULTIVERSE AND WE WON'T STOP KILLING UNTIL EVERY DROP OF MONITOR BLOOD IS SPILLED!
THEN I WILL EVISCERATE THE WOMAN WHO MURDERED MY PEOPLE.

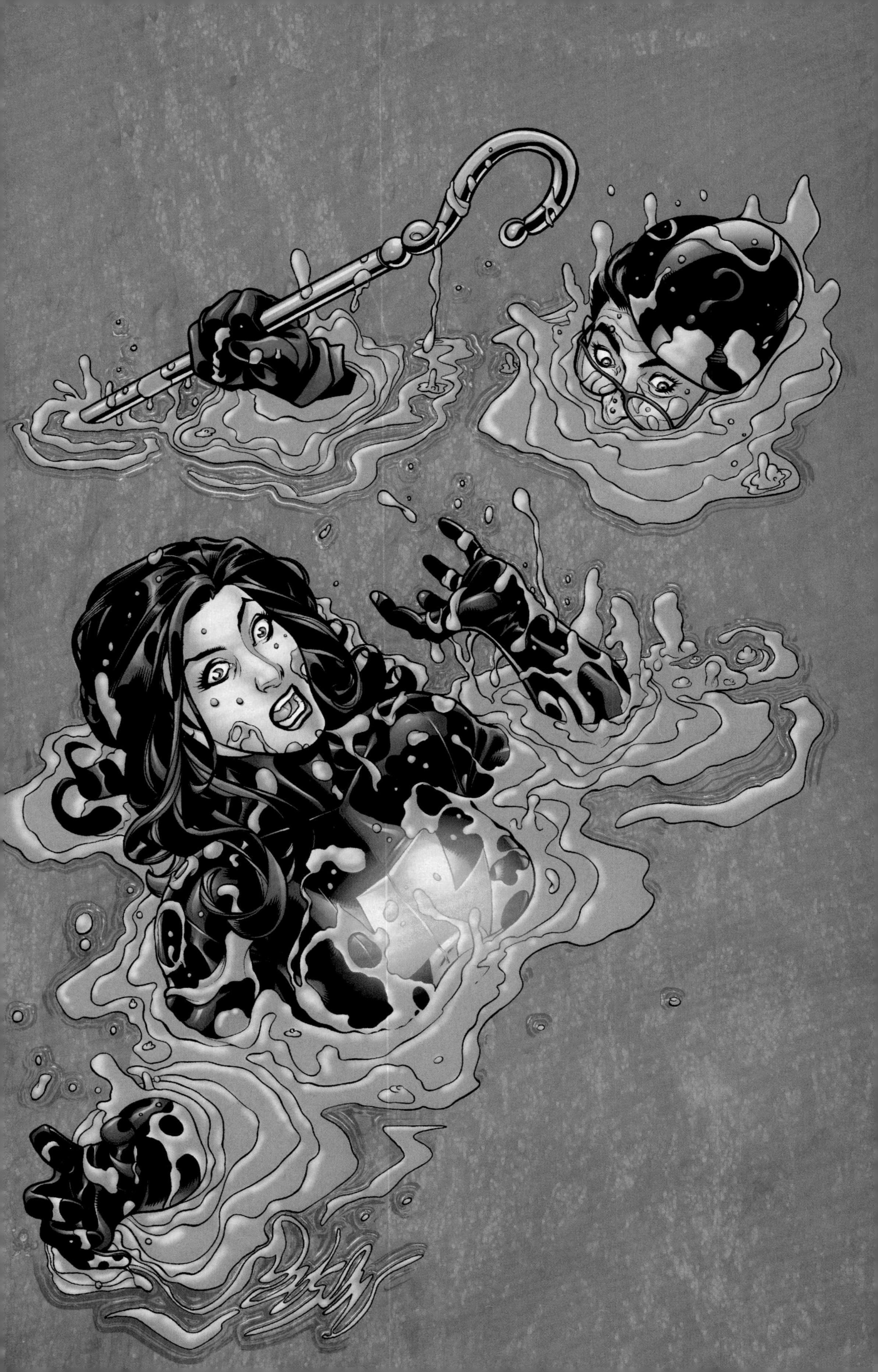

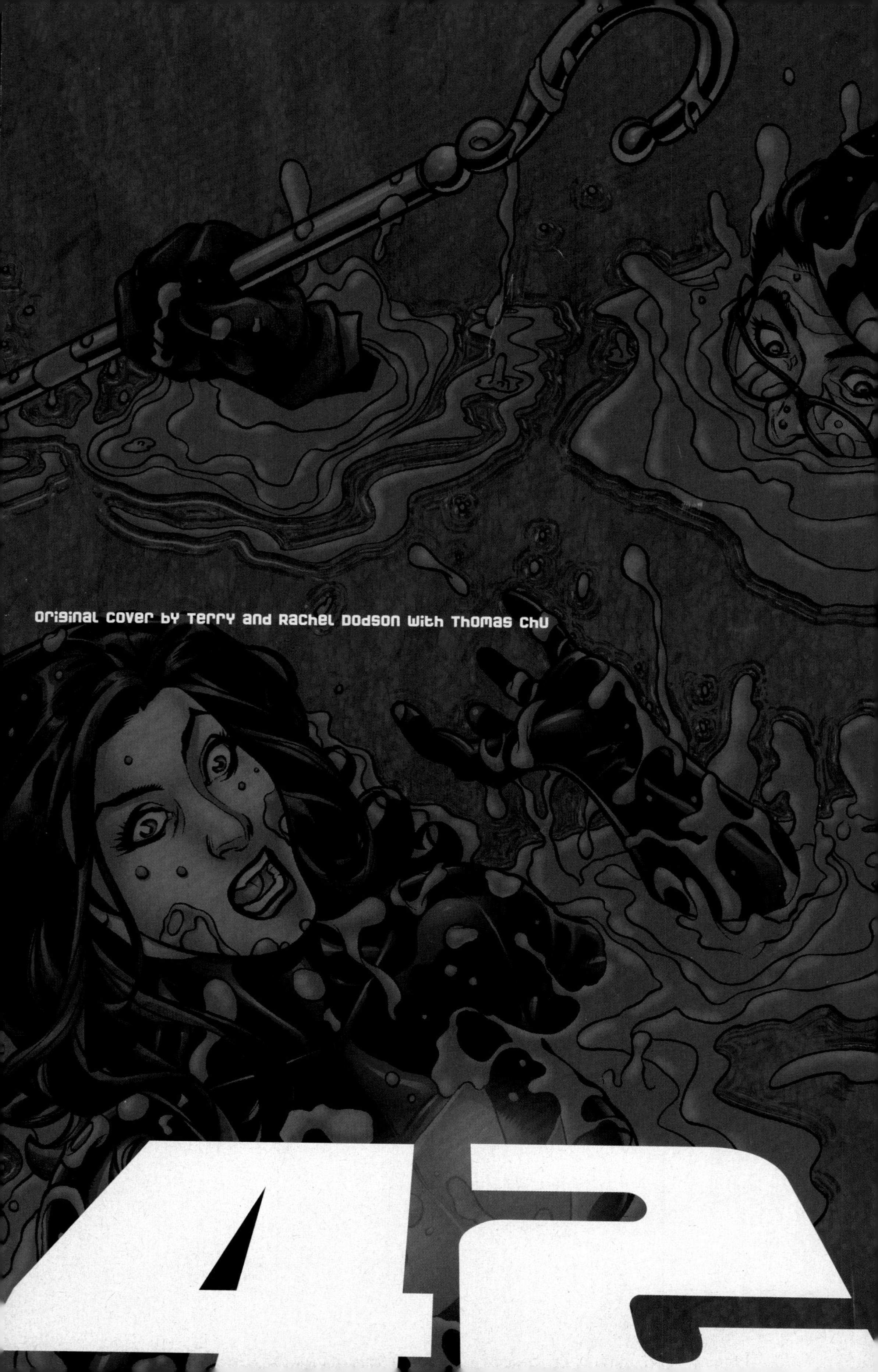
42

Original cover by Terry and Rachel Dodson with Thomas Chu

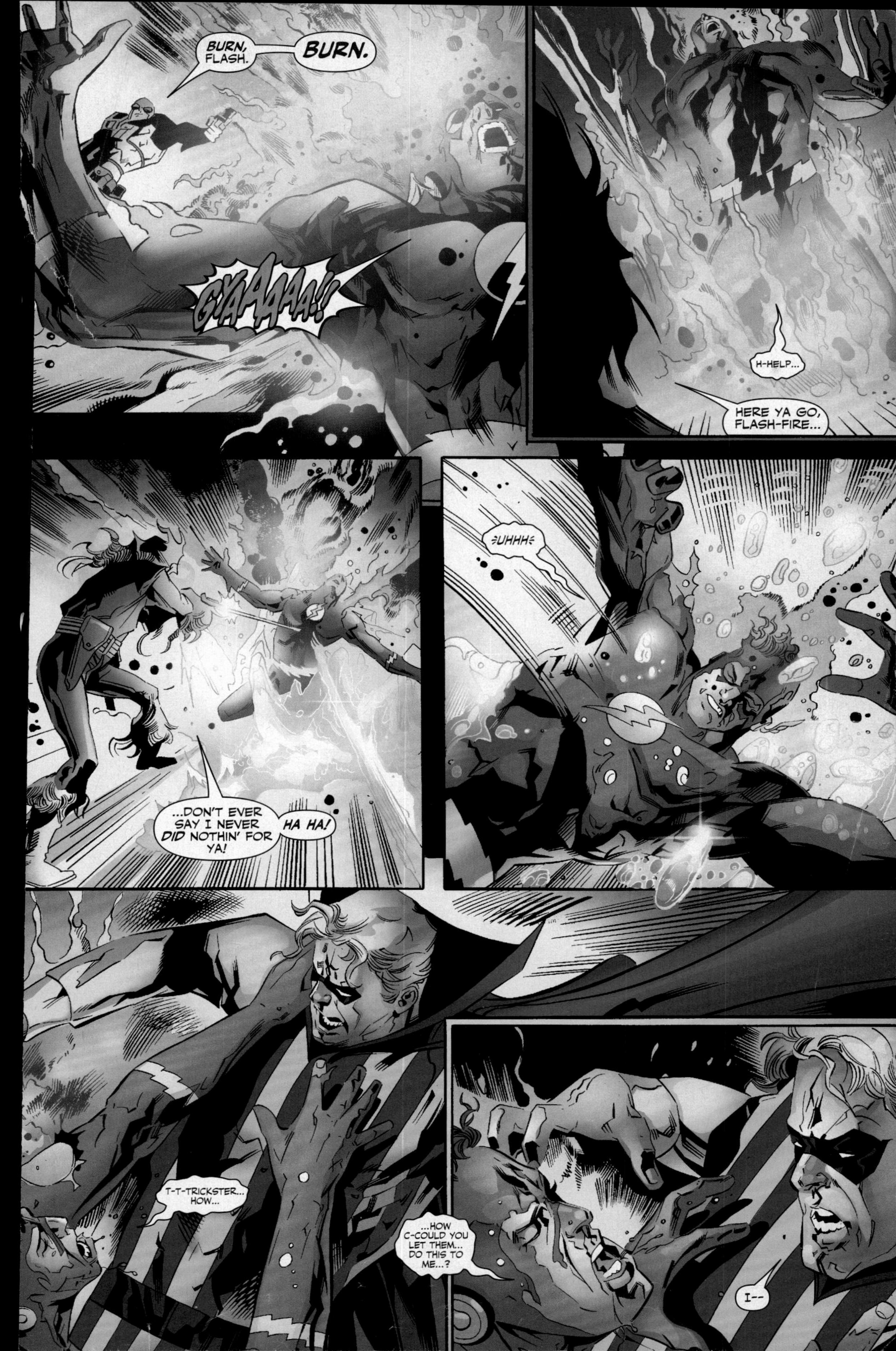
BURN, FLASH.
BURN.
GYAAAAA!!
H-HELP...
HERE YA GO, FLASH-FIRE...
...DON'T EVER SAY I NEVER DID NOTHIN' FOR YA!
HA HA!
UHHH
T-T-TRICKSTER... HOW...
...HOW C-COULD YOU LET THEM... DO THIS TO ME...?
I--

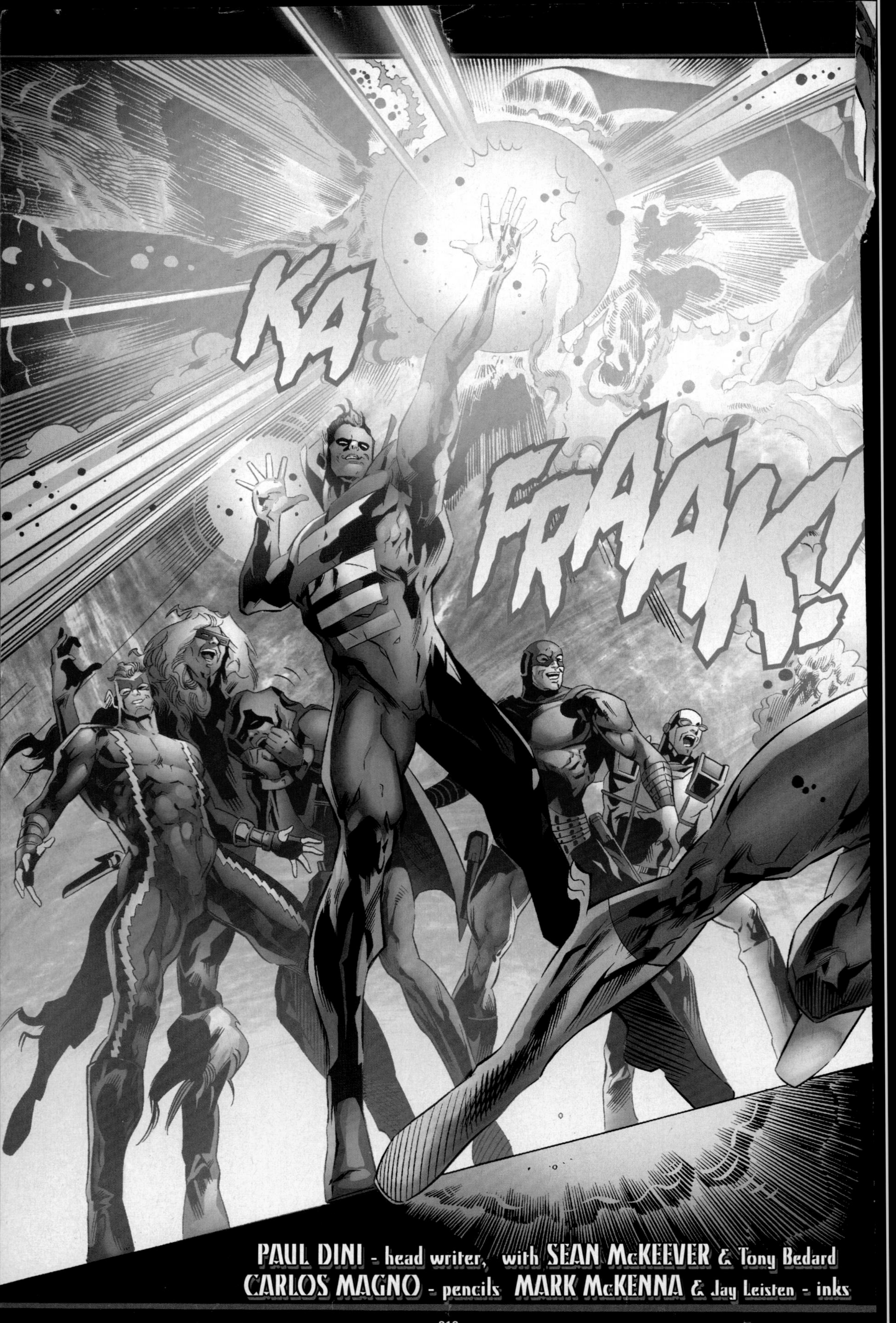
KA
FRAAK!
PAUL DINI - head writer, with SEAN McKEEVER & Tony Bedard
CARLOS MAGNO - pencils MARK McKENNA & Jay Leisten - inks

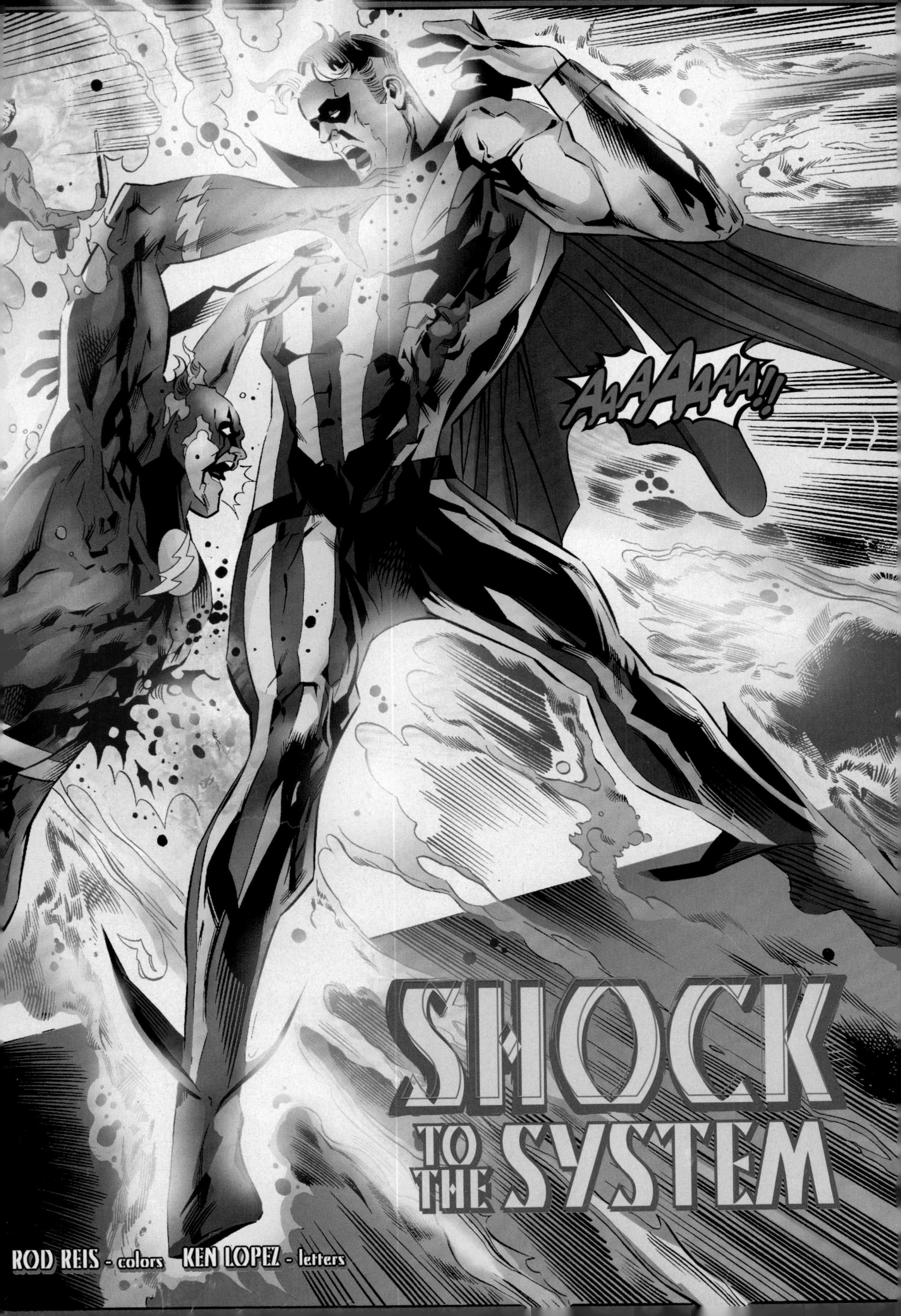
AAAAAAA!!
SHOCK TO THE SYSTEM
ROD REIS - colors KEN LOPEZ - letters

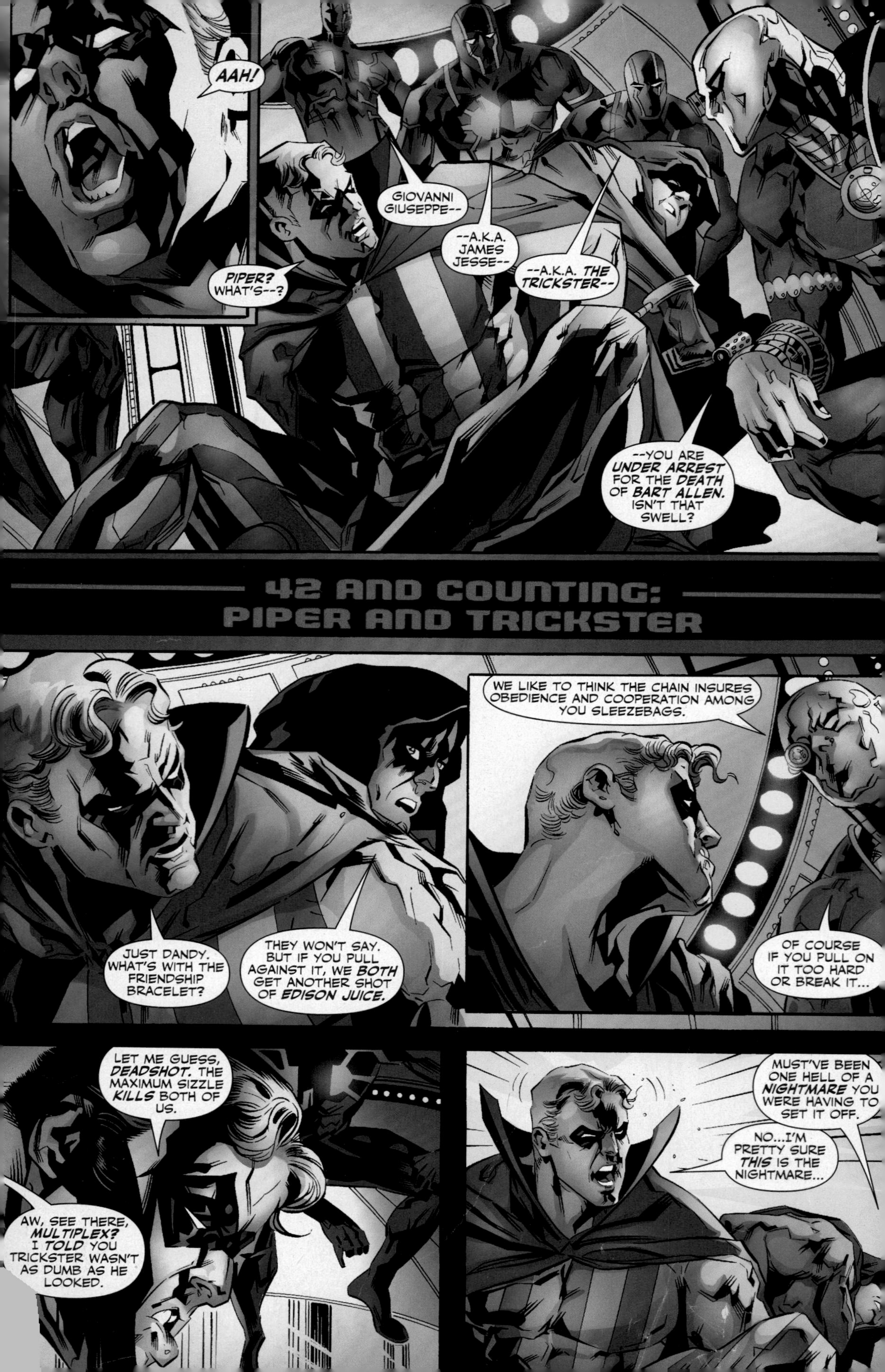
AAH!
PIPER? WHAT'S--?
GIOVANNI GIUSEPPE--
--A.K.A. JAMES JESSE--
--A.K.A. THE TRICKSTER--
--YOU ARE UNDER ARREST FOR THE DEATH OF BART ALLEN. ISN'T THAT SWELL?
42 AND COUNTING: PIPER AND TRICKSTER
JUST DANDY. WHAT'S WITH THE FRIENDSHIP BRACELET?
THEY WON'T SAY. BUT IF YOU PULL AGAINST IT, WE BOTH GET ANOTHER SHOT OF EDISON JUICE.
WE LIKE TO THINK THE CHAIN INSURES OBEDIENCE AND COOPERATION AMONG YOU SLEEZEBAGS.
OF COURSE IF YOU PULL ON IT TOO HARD OR BREAK IT...
LET ME GUESS, DEADSHOT. THE MAXIMUM SIZZLE KILLS BOTH OF US.
AW, SEE THERE, MULTIPLEX? I TOLD YOU TRICKSTER WASN'T AS DUMB AS HE LOOKED.
MUST'VE BEEN ONE HELL OF A NIGHTMARE YOU WERE HAVING TO SET IT OFF.
NO...I'M PRETTY SURE THIS IS THE NIGHTMARE...

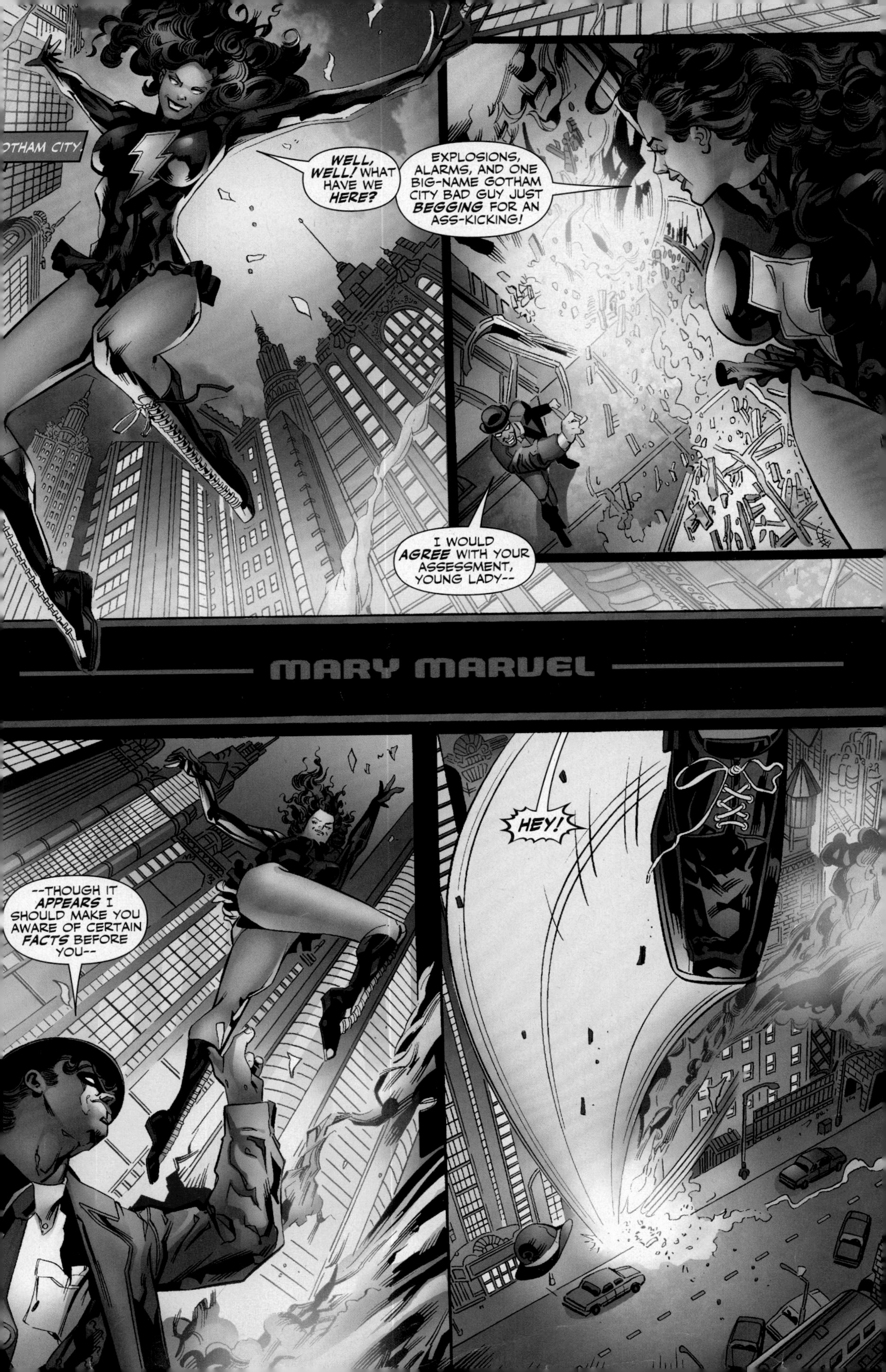
OTHAM CITY.
WELL, WELL! WHAT HAVE WE HERE?
EXPLOSIONS, ALARMS, AND ONE BIG-NAME GOTHAM CITY BAD GUY JUST BEGGING FOR AN ASS-KICKING!
I WOULD AGREE WITH YOUR ASSESSMENT, YOUNG LADY--
MARY MARVEL
--THOUGH IT APPEARS I SHOULD MAKE YOU AWARE OF CERTAIN FACTS BEFORE YOU--
HEY!

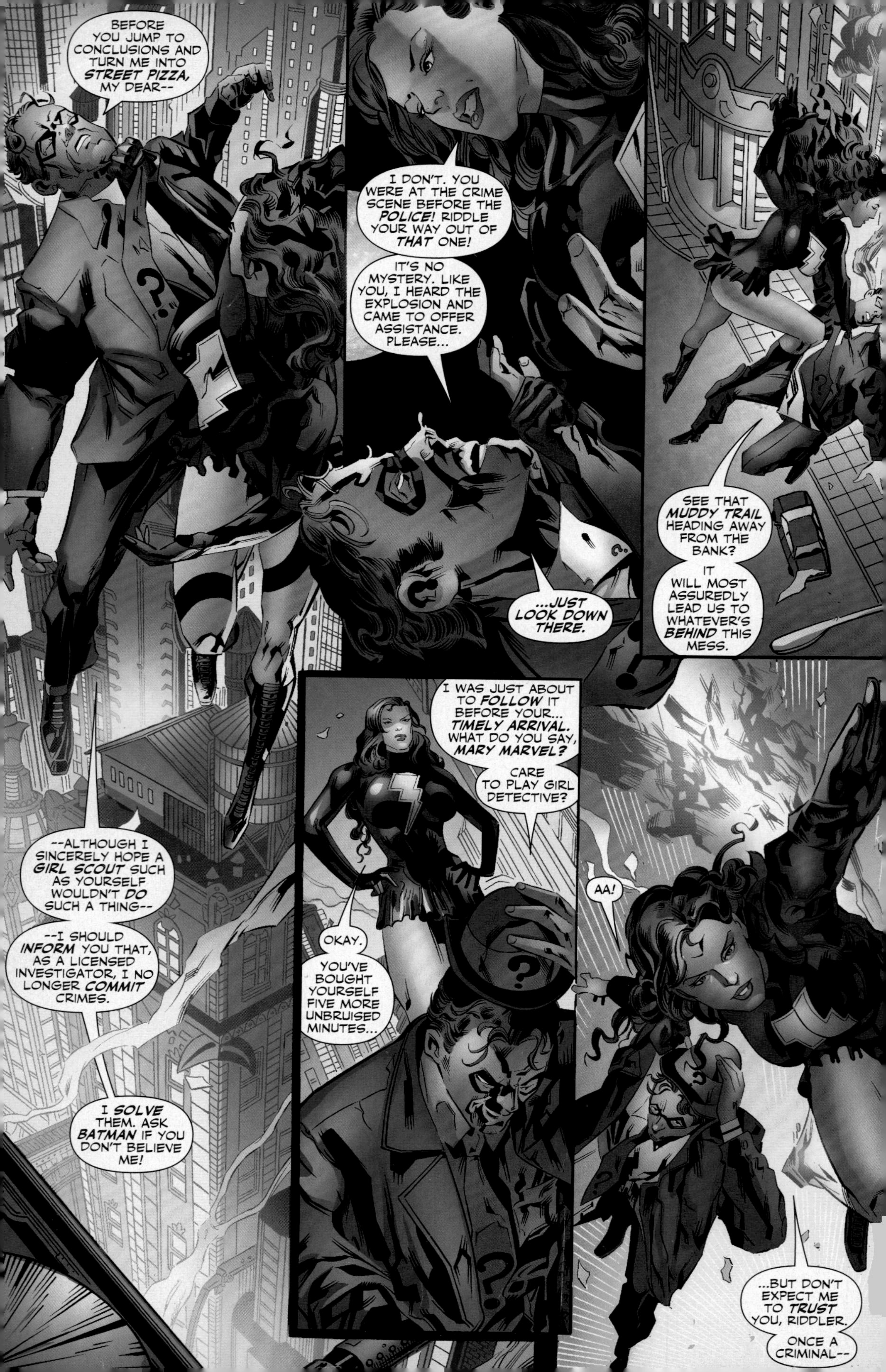
BEFORE YOU JUMP TO CONCLUSIONS AND TURN ME INTO STREET PIZZA, MY DEAR--
I DON'T. YOU WERE AT THE CRIME SCENE BEFORE THE POLICE! RIDDLE YOUR WAY OUT OF THAT ONE!
IT'S NO MYSTERY. LIKE YOU, I HEARD THE EXPLOSION AND CAME TO OFFER ASSISTANCE. PLEASE...
...JUST LOOK DOWN THERE.
SEE THAT MUDDY TRAIL HEADING AWAY FROM THE BANK?
IT WILL MOST ASSUREDLY LEAD US TO WHATEVER'S BEHIND THIS MESS.
--ALTHOUGH I SINCERELY HOPE A GIRL SCOUT SUCH AS YOURSELF WOULDN'T DO SUCH A THING--
--I SHOULD INFORM YOU THAT, AS A LICENSED INVESTIGATOR, I NO LONGER COMMIT CRIMES.
I SOLVE THEM. ASK BATMAN IF YOU DON'T BELIEVE ME!
I WAS JUST ABOUT TO FOLLOW IT BEFORE YOUR... TIMELY ARRIVAL. WHAT DO YOU SAY, MARY MARVEL?
CARE TO PLAY GIRL DETECTIVE?
OKAY.
YOU'VE BOUGHT YOURSELF FIVE MORE UNBRUISED MINUTES...
AA!
...BUT DON'T EXPECT ME TO TRUST YOU, RIDDLER.
ONCE A CRIMINAL--

METROPOLIS.

--ALWAYS A CRIMINAL. ISN'T THAT RIGHT, *HARLEY?*

HARLEEN QUINZEL, THANK YOU. I'VE GOT A NEW LOOK AND A NEW ATTITUDE. HARLEY QUINN IS *BEHIND* ME NOW.

HOLLY ROBINSON

FORGIVE ME IF I'M JUST A *LITTLE* BIT SKEPTICAL, "HARLEEN".

AREN'T YOU SUPPOSED TO BE IN *ARKHAM* FOR THE UMPTEENTH TIME?

I'M *CURED*, HOLLY. RELEASED AND READY TO BE A PRODUCTIVE MEMBER OF SOCIETY AGAIN...

...EXCEPT SOCIETY WOULDN'T HAVE ANYTHING TO *DO* WITH ME. I LEFT GOTHAM... BUMMED AROUND FOR A WHILE...

..BUT OTHER THAN A STINT IN THE *SECRET SIX*--

--I WAS DIRECTIONLESS, ALONE...

...AND THEN *ATHENA* CAME TO ME.

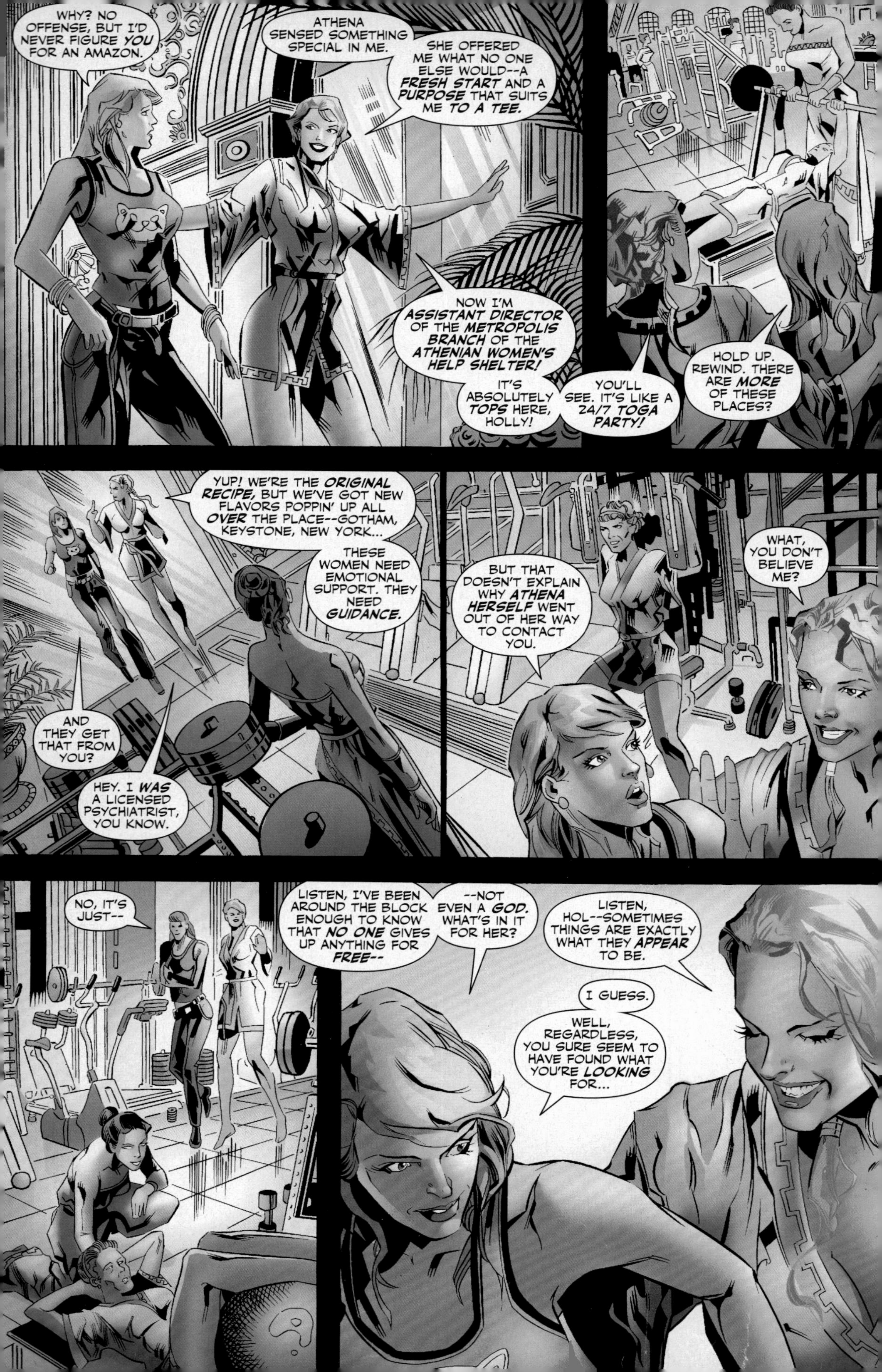
WHY? NO OFFENSE, BUT I'D NEVER FIGURE YOU FOR AN AMAZON.
ATHENA SENSED SOMETHING SPECIAL IN ME.
SHE OFFERED ME WHAT NO ONE ELSE WOULD--A FRESH START AND A PURPOSE THAT SUITS ME TO A TEE.
NOW I'M ASSISTANT DIRECTOR OF THE METROPOLIS BRANCH OF THE ATHENIAN WOMEN'S HELP SHELTER!
IT'S ABSOLUTELY TOPS HERE, HOLLY!
YOU'LL SEE. IT'S LIKE A 24/7 TOGA PARTY!
HOLD UP. REWIND. THERE ARE MORE OF THESE PLACES?
YUP! WE'RE THE ORIGINAL RECIPE, BUT WE'VE GOT NEW FLAVORS POPPIN' UP ALL OVER THE PLACE--GOTHAM, KEYSTONE, NEW YORK...
THESE WOMEN NEED EMOTIONAL SUPPORT. THEY NEED GUIDANCE.
AND THEY GET THAT FROM YOU?
HEY. I WAS A LICENSED PSYCHIATRIST, YOU KNOW.
BUT THAT DOESN'T EXPLAIN WHY ATHENA HERSELF WENT OUT OF HER WAY TO CONTACT YOU.
WHAT, YOU DON'T BELIEVE ME?
NO, IT'S JUST--
LISTEN, I'VE BEEN AROUND THE BLOCK ENOUGH TO KNOW THAT NO ONE GIVES UP ANYTHING FOR FREE--
--NOT EVEN A GOD. WHAT'S IN IT FOR HER?
LISTEN, HOL--SOMETIMES THINGS ARE EXACTLY WHAT THEY APPEAR TO BE.
I GUESS.
WELL, REGARDLESS, YOU SURE SEEM TO HAVE FOUND WHAT YOU'RE LOOKING FOR...

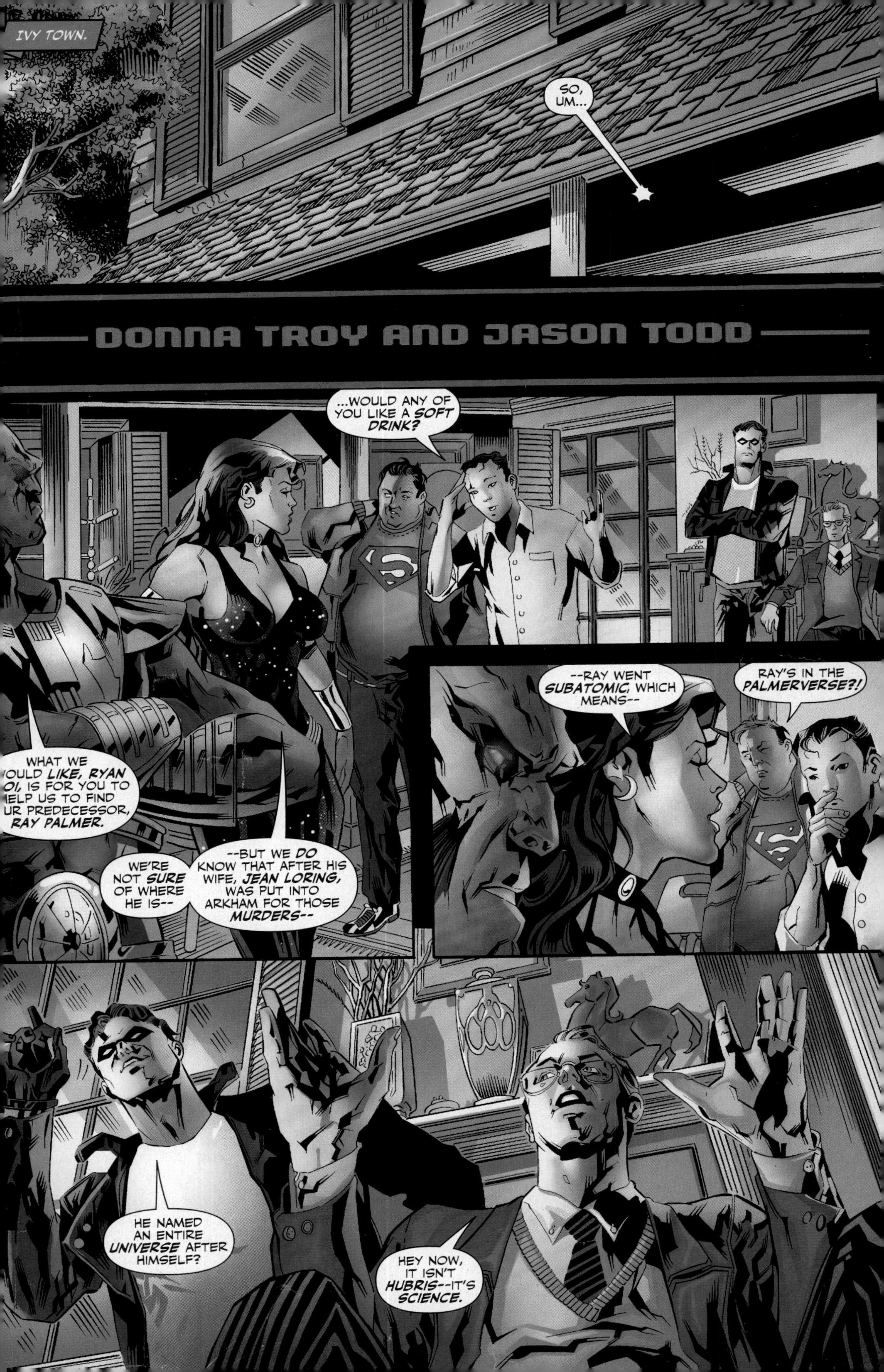
IVY TOWN.
SO, UM...
DONNA TROY AND JASON TODD
...WOULD ANY OF YOU LIKE A SOFT DRINK?
WHAT WE WOULD LIKE, RYAN CHOI, IS FOR YOU TO HELP US TO FIND YOUR PREDECESSOR, RAY PALMER.
WE'RE NOT SURE OF WHERE HE IS--
--BUT WE DO KNOW THAT AFTER HIS WIFE, JEAN LORING, WAS PUT INTO ARKHAM FOR THOSE MURDERS--
--RAY WENT SUBATOMIC, WHICH MEANS--
RAY'S IN THE PALMERVERSE?!
HE NAMED AN ENTIRE UNIVERSE AFTER HIMSELF?
HEY NOW, IT ISN'T HUBRIS--IT'S SCIENCE.

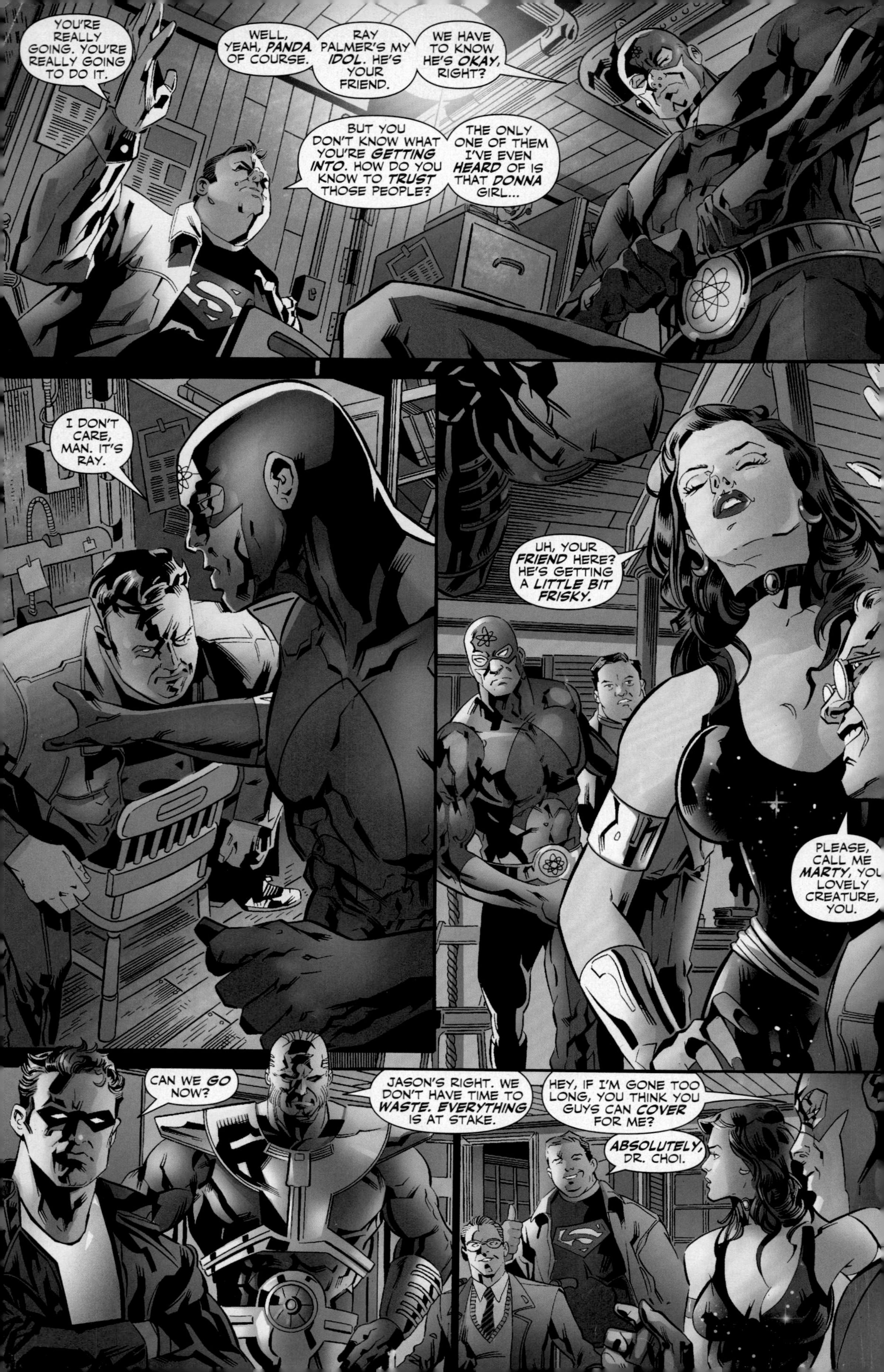
YOU'RE REALLY GOING. YOU'RE REALLY GOING TO DO IT.
WELL, YEAH, PANDA. OF COURSE.
RAY PALMER'S MY IDOL. HE'S YOUR FRIEND.
WE HAVE TO KNOW HE'S OKAY, RIGHT?
BUT YOU DON'T KNOW WHAT YOU'RE GETTING INTO. HOW DO YOU KNOW TO TRUST THOSE PEOPLE?
THE ONLY ONE OF THEM I'VE EVEN HEARD OF IS THAT DONNA GIRL...
I DON'T CARE, MAN. IT'S RAY.
UH, YOUR FRIEND HERE? HE'S GETTING A LITTLE BIT FRISKY.
PLEASE, CALL ME MARTY, YOU LOVELY CREATURE, YOU.
CAN WE GO NOW?
JASON'S RIGHT. WE DON'T HAVE TIME TO WASTE. EVERYTHING IS AT STAKE.
HEY, IF I'M GONE TOO LONG, YOU THINK YOU GUYS CAN COVER FOR ME?
ABSOLUTELY, DR. CHOI.

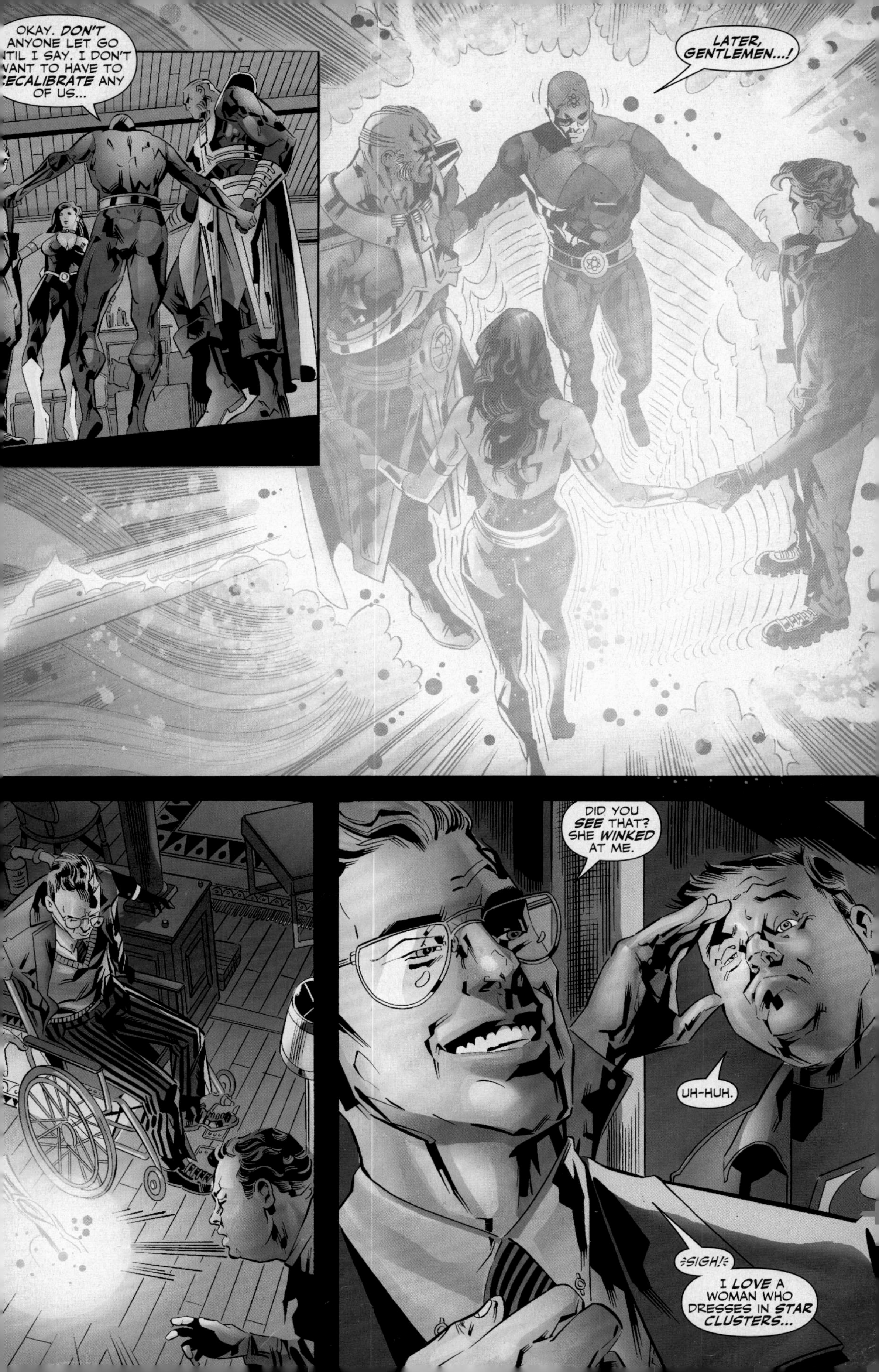
OKAY. DON'T ANYONE LET GO UNTIL I SAY. I DON'T WANT TO HAVE TO RECALIBRATE ANY OF US...
LATER, GENTLEMEN...!
DID YOU SEE THAT? SHE WINKED AT ME.
UH-HUH.
SIGH!
I LOVE A WOMAN WHO DRESSES IN STAR CLUSTERS...

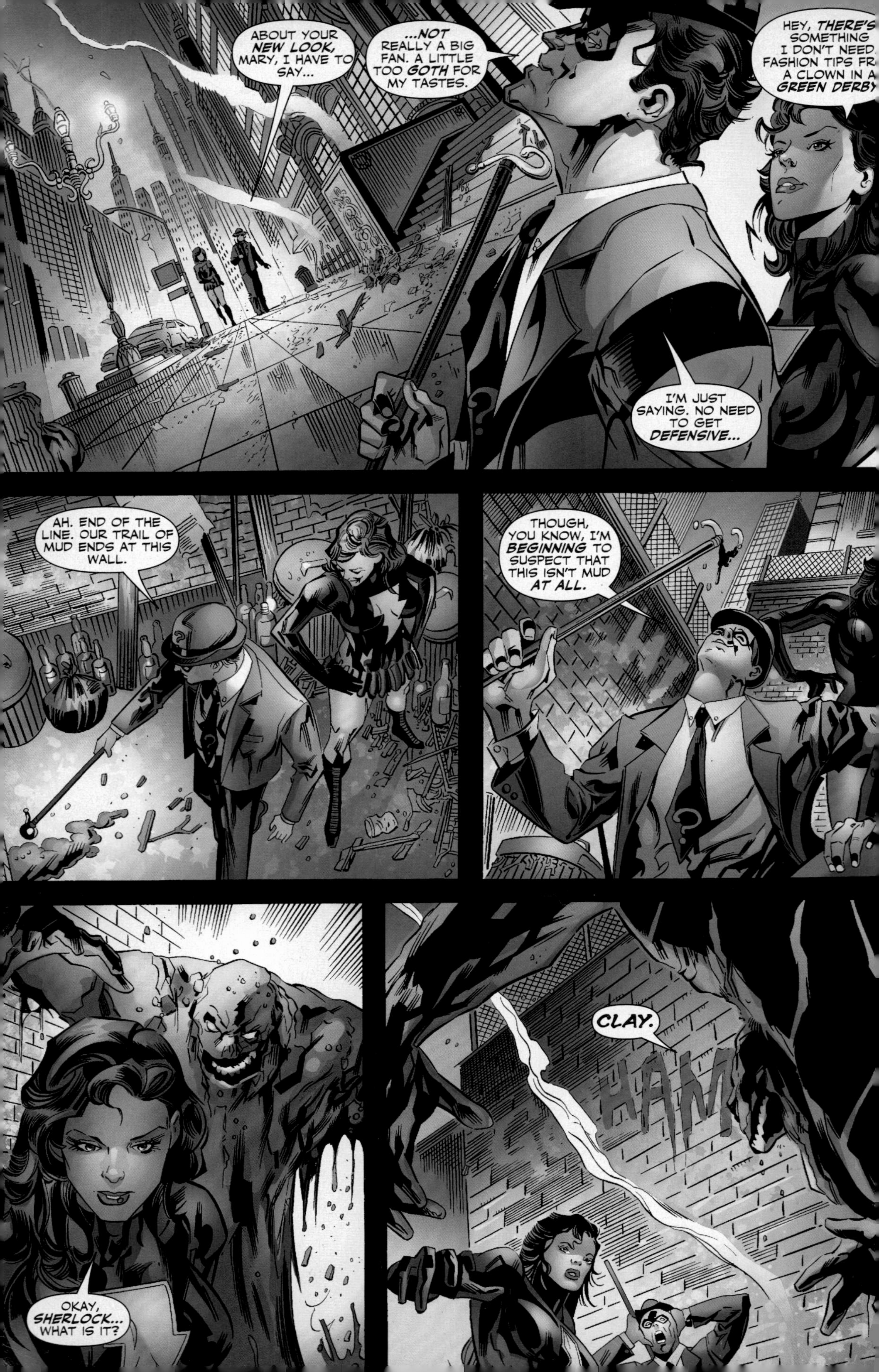

ABOUT YOUR NEW LOOK, MARY, I HAVE TO SAY...
...NOT REALLY A BIG FAN. A LITTLE TOO GOTH FOR MY TASTES.
HEY, THERE'S SOMETHING I DON'T NEED FASHION TIPS FR A CLOWN IN A GREEN DERBY
I'M JUST SAYING. NO NEED TO GET DEFENSIVE...
AH. END OF THE LINE. OUR TRAIL OF MUD ENDS AT THIS WALL.
THOUGH, YOU KNOW, I'M BEGINNING TO SUSPECT THAT THIS ISN'T MUD AT ALL.
OKAY, SHERLOCK... WHAT IS IT?
CLAY.
HAM

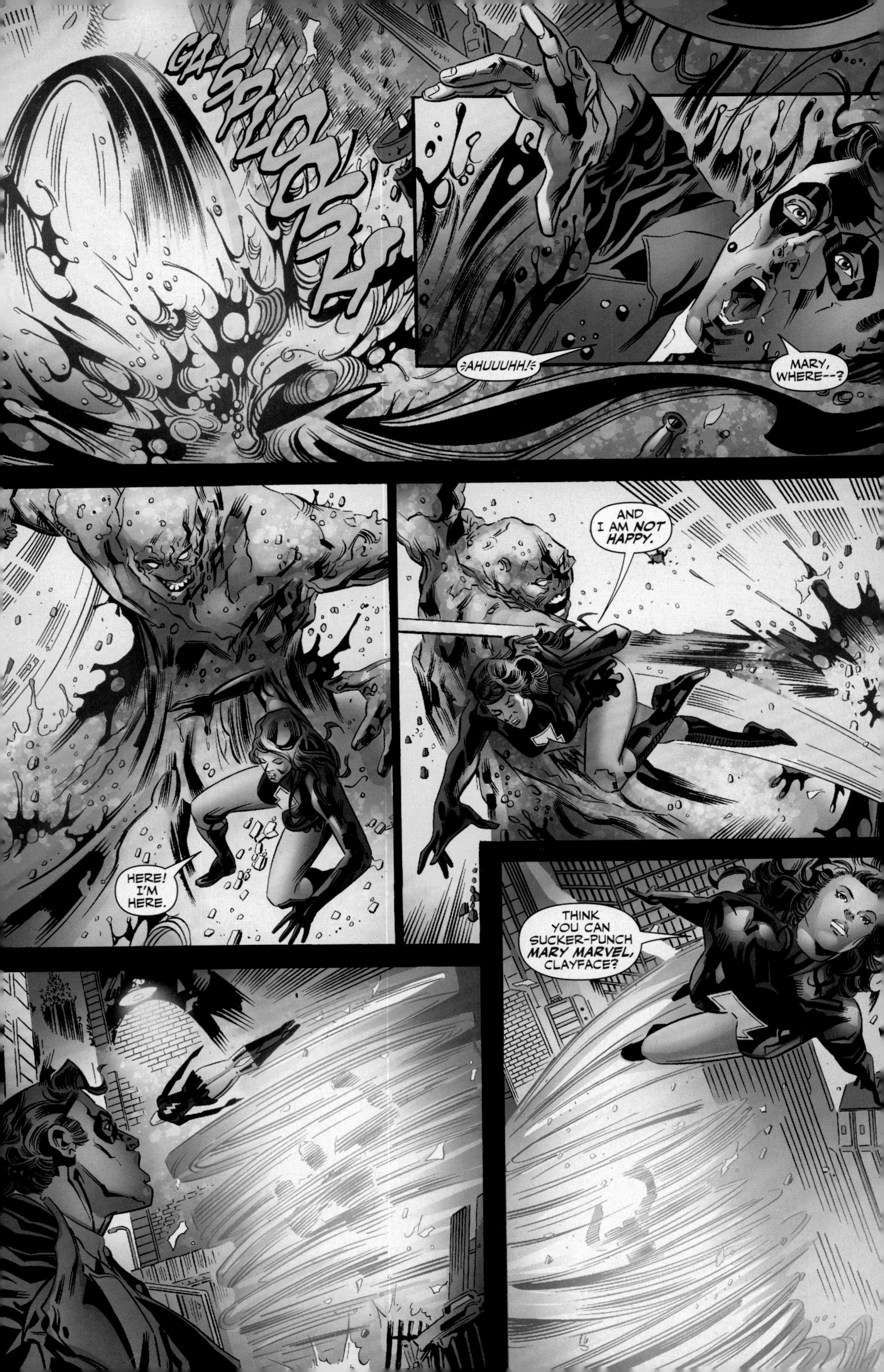
GA-SPLOOOOSH
AHUUUHH!
MARY, WHERE--?
HERE! I'M HERE.
AND I AM NOT HAPPY.
THINK YOU CAN SUCKER-PUNCH MARY MARVEL, CLAYFACE?

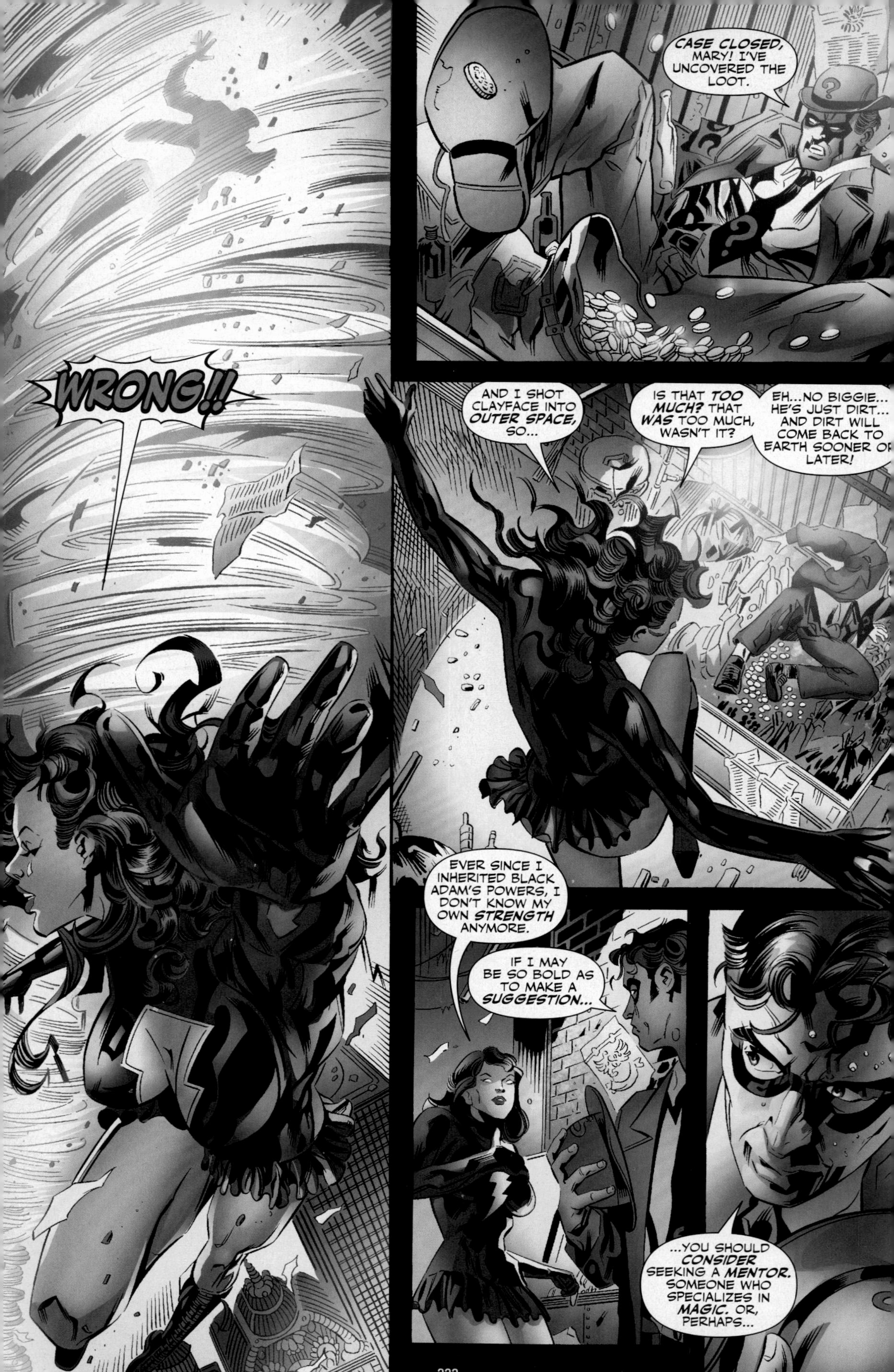
WRONG!!
CASE CLOSED, MARY! I'VE UNCOVERED THE LOOT.
AND I SHOT CLAYFACE INTO OUTER SPACE, SO...
IS THAT TOO MUCH? THAT WAS TOO MUCH, WASN'T IT?
EH...NO BIGGIE... HE'S JUST DIRT... AND DIRT WILL COME BACK TO EARTH SOONER OR LATER!
EVER SINCE I INHERITED BLACK ADAM'S POWERS, I DON'T KNOW MY OWN STRENGTH ANYMORE.
IF I MAY BE SO BOLD AS TO MAKE A SUGGESTION...
...YOU SHOULD CONSIDER SEEKING A MENTOR. SOMEONE WHO SPECIALIZES IN MAGIC. OR, PERHAPS...

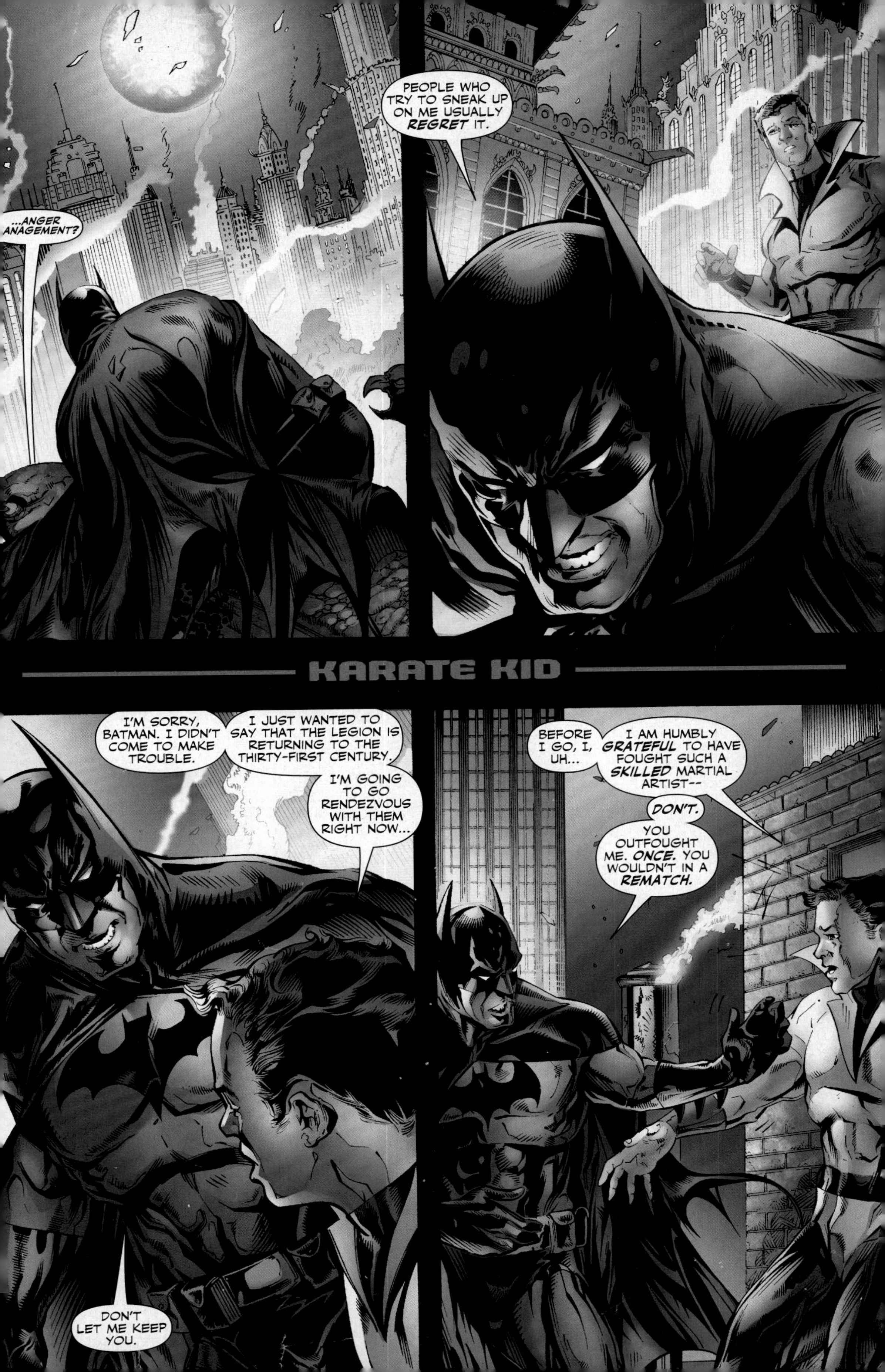
...ANGER ANAGEMENT?
PEOPLE WHO TRY TO SNEAK UP ON ME USUALLY *REGRET* IT.
KARATE KID
I'M SORRY, BATMAN. I DIDN'T COME TO MAKE TROUBLE.
I JUST WANTED TO SAY THAT THE LEGION IS RETURNING TO THE THIRTY-FIRST CENTURY.
I'M GOING TO GO RENDEZVOUS WITH THEM RIGHT NOW...
DON'T LET ME KEEP YOU.
BEFORE I GO, I, UH...
I AM HUMBLY *GRATEFUL* TO HAVE FOUGHT SUCH A *SKILLED* MARTIAL ARTIST--
DON'T.
YOU OUTFOUGHT ME. *ONCE.* YOU WOULDN'T IN A *REMATCH.*

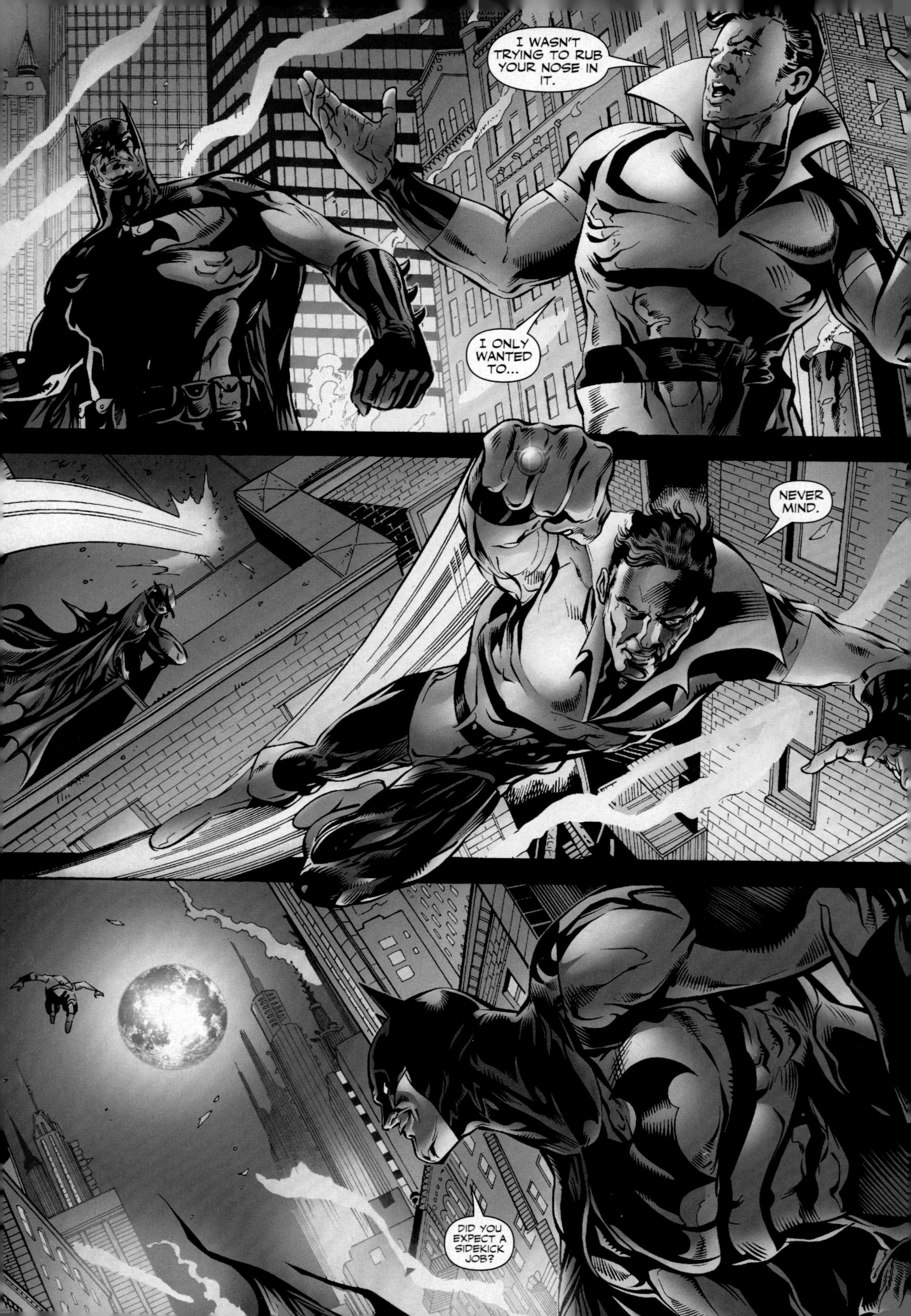
I WASN'T TRYING TO RUB YOUR NOSE IN IT.
I ONLY WANTED TO...
NEVER MIND.
DID YOU EXPECT A SIDEKICK JOB?

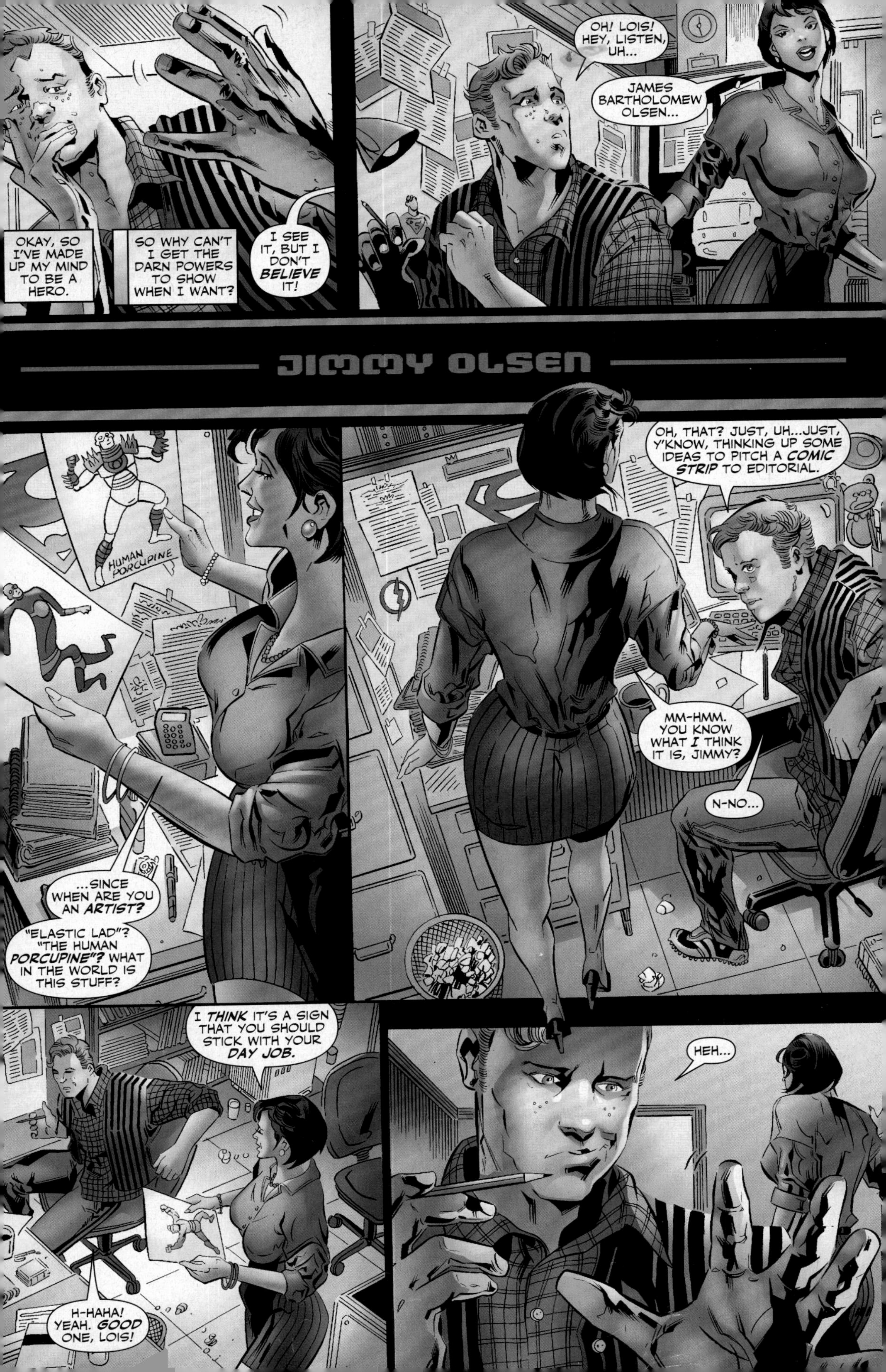
OKAY, SO I'VE MADE UP MY MIND TO BE A HERO.
SO WHY CAN'T I GET THE DARN POWERS TO SHOW WHEN I WANT?
I SEE IT, BUT I DON'T BELIEVE IT!
OH! LOIS! HEY, LISTEN, UH...
JAMES BARTHOLOMEW OLSEN...
JIMMY OLSEN
HUMAN PORCUPINE
...SINCE WHEN ARE YOU AN ARTIST?
"ELASTIC LAD"? "THE HUMAN PORCUPINE"? WHAT IN THE WORLD IS THIS STUFF?
OH, THAT? JUST, UH...JUST, Y'KNOW, THINKING UP SOME IDEAS TO PITCH A COMIC STRIP TO EDITORIAL.
MM-HMM. YOU KNOW WHAT I THINK IT IS, JIMMY?
N-NO...
I THINK IT'S A SIGN THAT YOU SHOULD STICK WITH YOUR DAY JOB.
H-HAHA! YEAH. GOOD ONE, LOIS!
HEH...

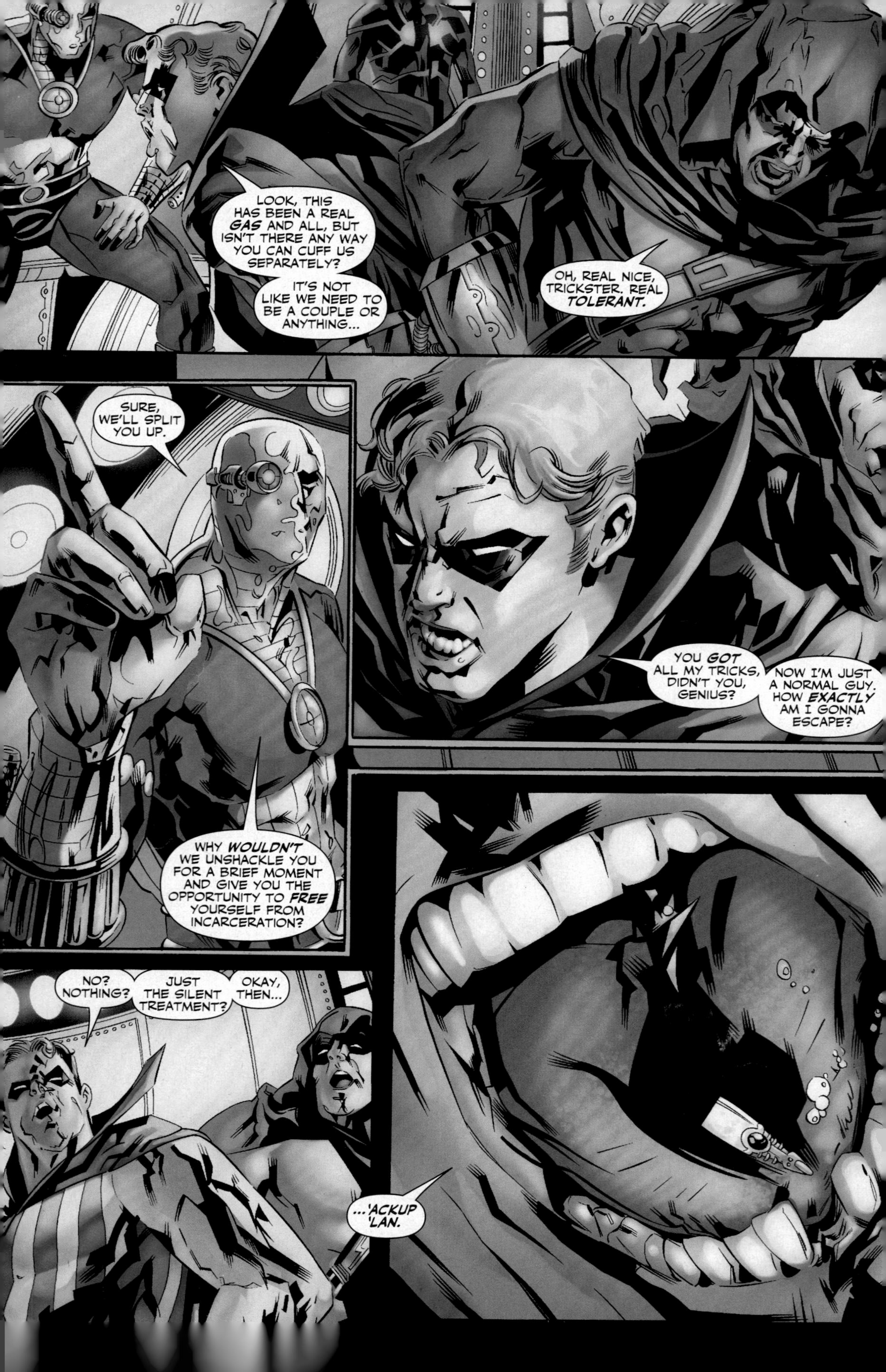
LOOK, THIS HAS BEEN A REAL GAS AND ALL, BUT ISN'T THERE ANY WAY YOU CAN CUFF US SEPARATELY?
IT'S NOT LIKE WE NEED TO BE A COUPLE OR ANYTHING...
OH, REAL NICE, TRICKSTER. REAL TOLERANT.
SURE, WE'LL SPLIT YOU UP.
WHY WOULDN'T WE UNSHACKLE YOU FOR A BRIEF MOMENT AND GIVE YOU THE OPPORTUNITY TO FREE YOURSELF FROM INCARCERATION?
YOU GOT ALL MY TRICKS, DIDN'T YOU, GENIUS?
NOW I'M JUST A NORMAL GUY. HOW EXACTLY AM I GONNA ESCAPE?
NO? NOTHING?
JUST THE SILENT TREATMENT?
OKAY, THEN...
...'ACKUP 'LAN.

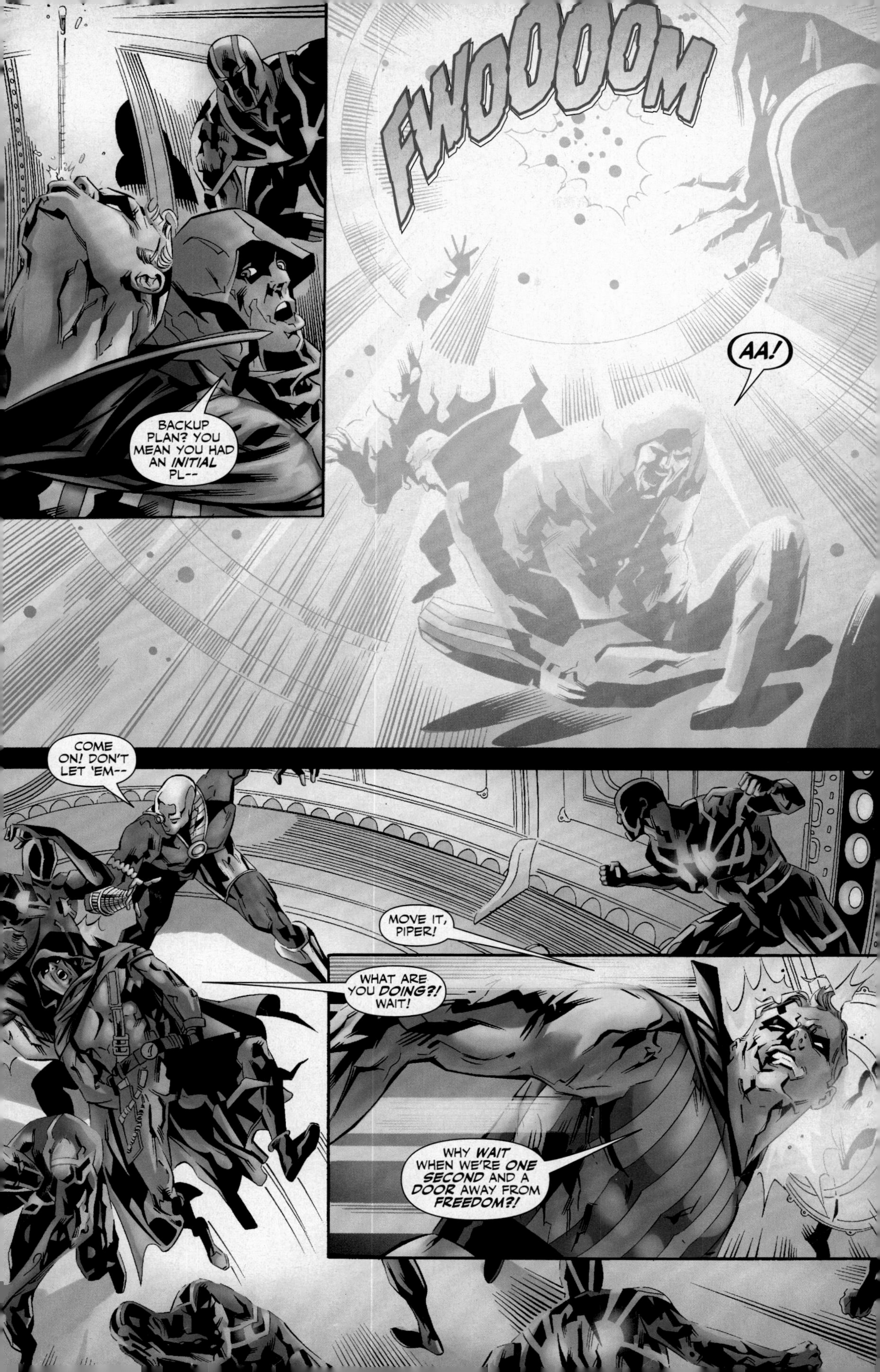
BACKUP PLAN? YOU MEAN YOU HAD AN *INITIAL* PL--
FWOOOOM
AA!
COME ON! DON'T LET 'EM--
MOVE IT, PIPER!
WHAT ARE YOU *DOING?!* WAIT!
WHY *WAIT* WHEN WE'RE *ONE SECOND* AND A *DOOR* AWAY FROM *FREEDOM?!*

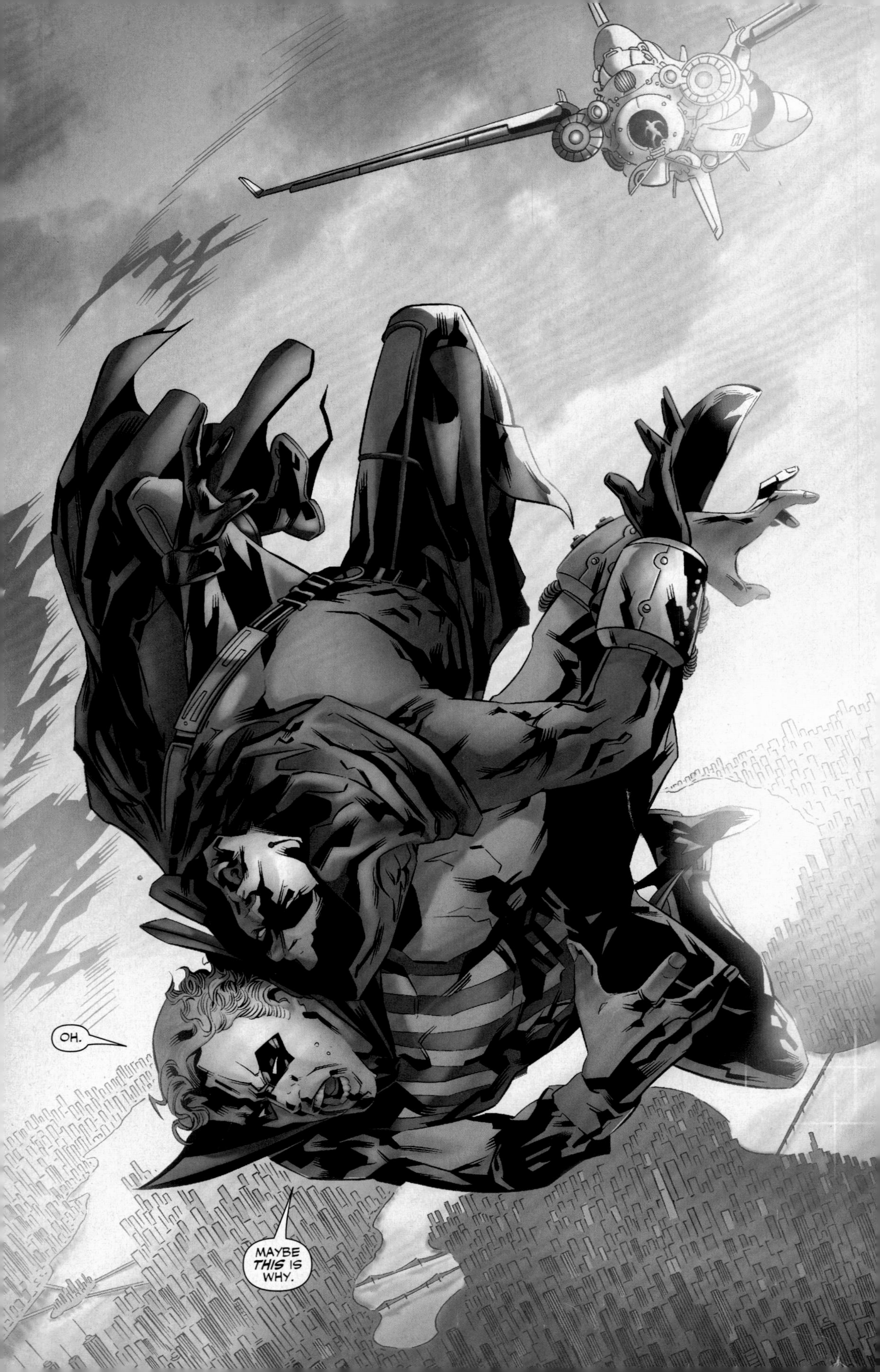
OH.
MAYBE THIS IS WHY.

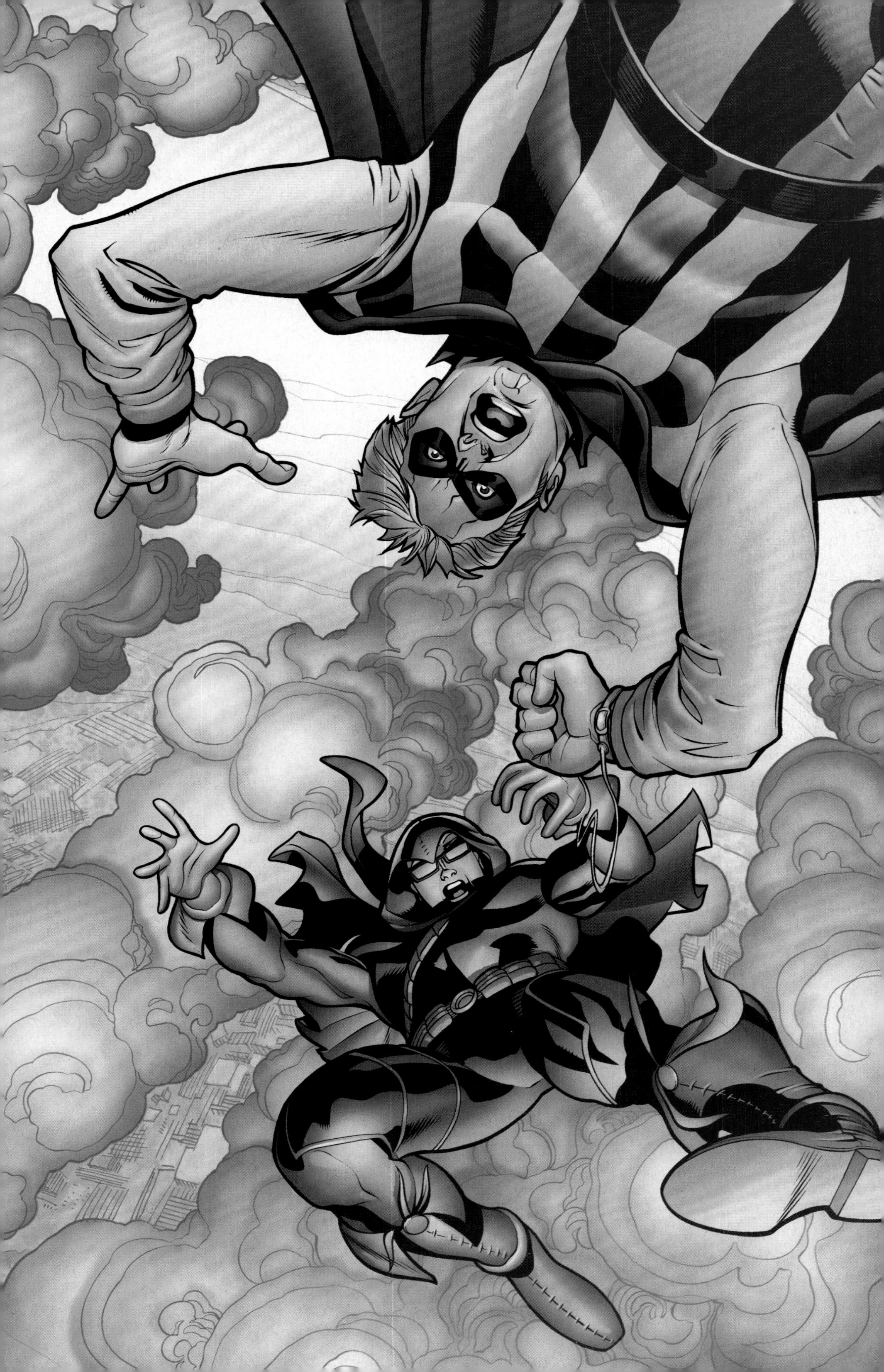

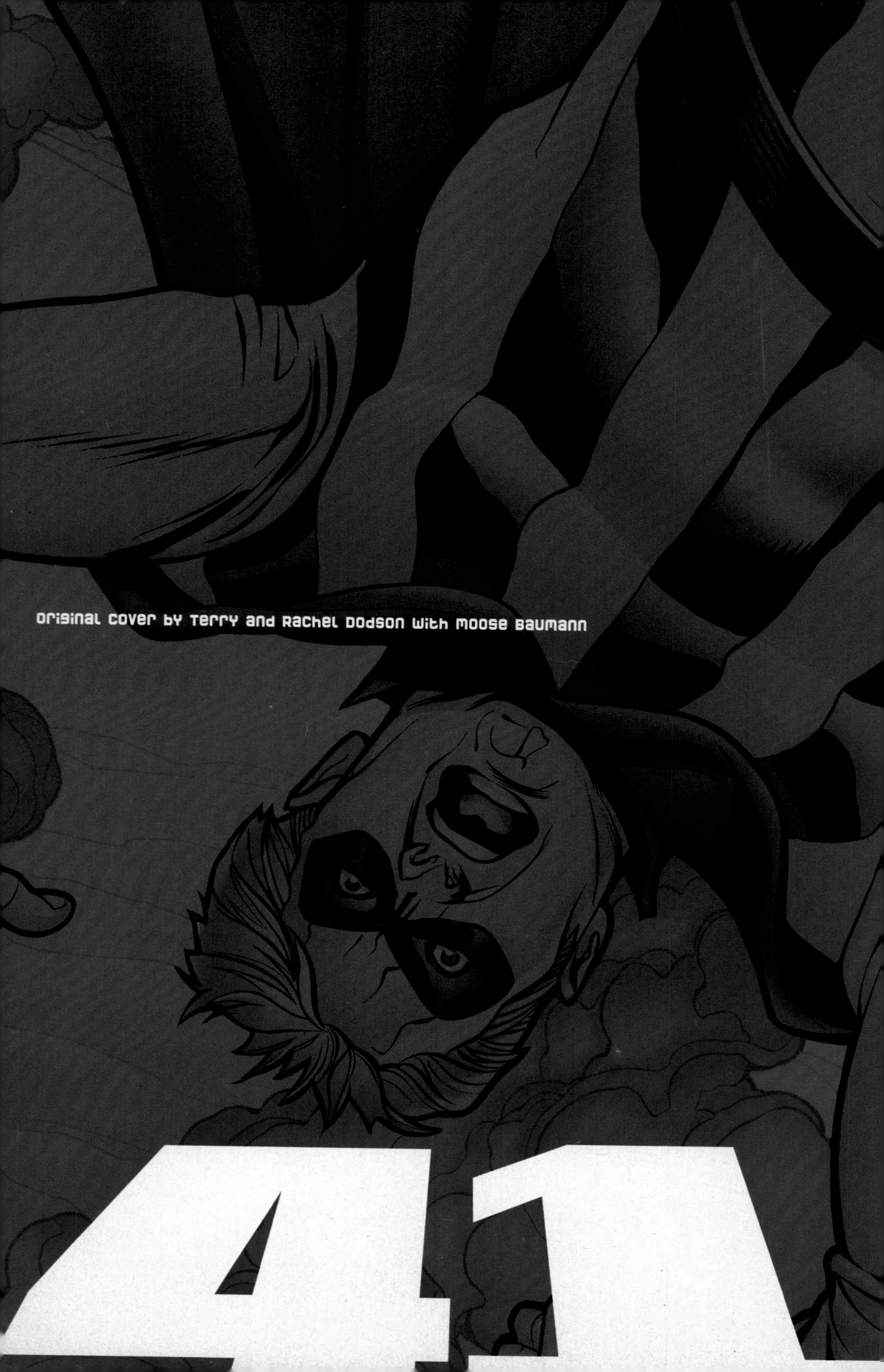
41

Original cover by Terry and Rachel Dodson with Moose Baumann

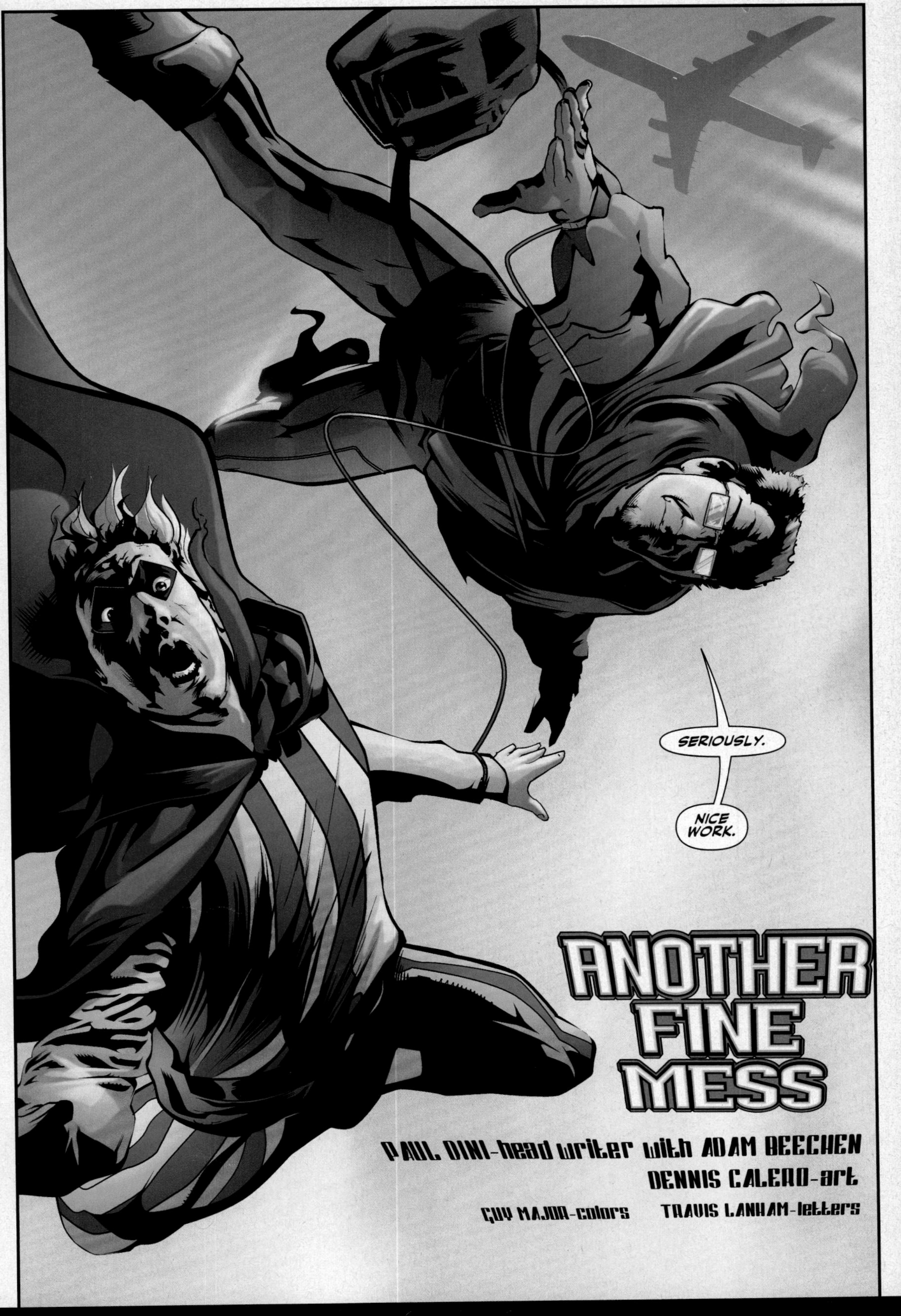
SERIOUSLY.
NICE WORK.
ANOTHER FINE MESS
PAUL DINI-head writer with ADAM BEECHEN
DENNIS CALERO-art
GUY MAJOR-colors
TRAVIS LANHAM-letters

FORTY-ONE AND COUNTING...

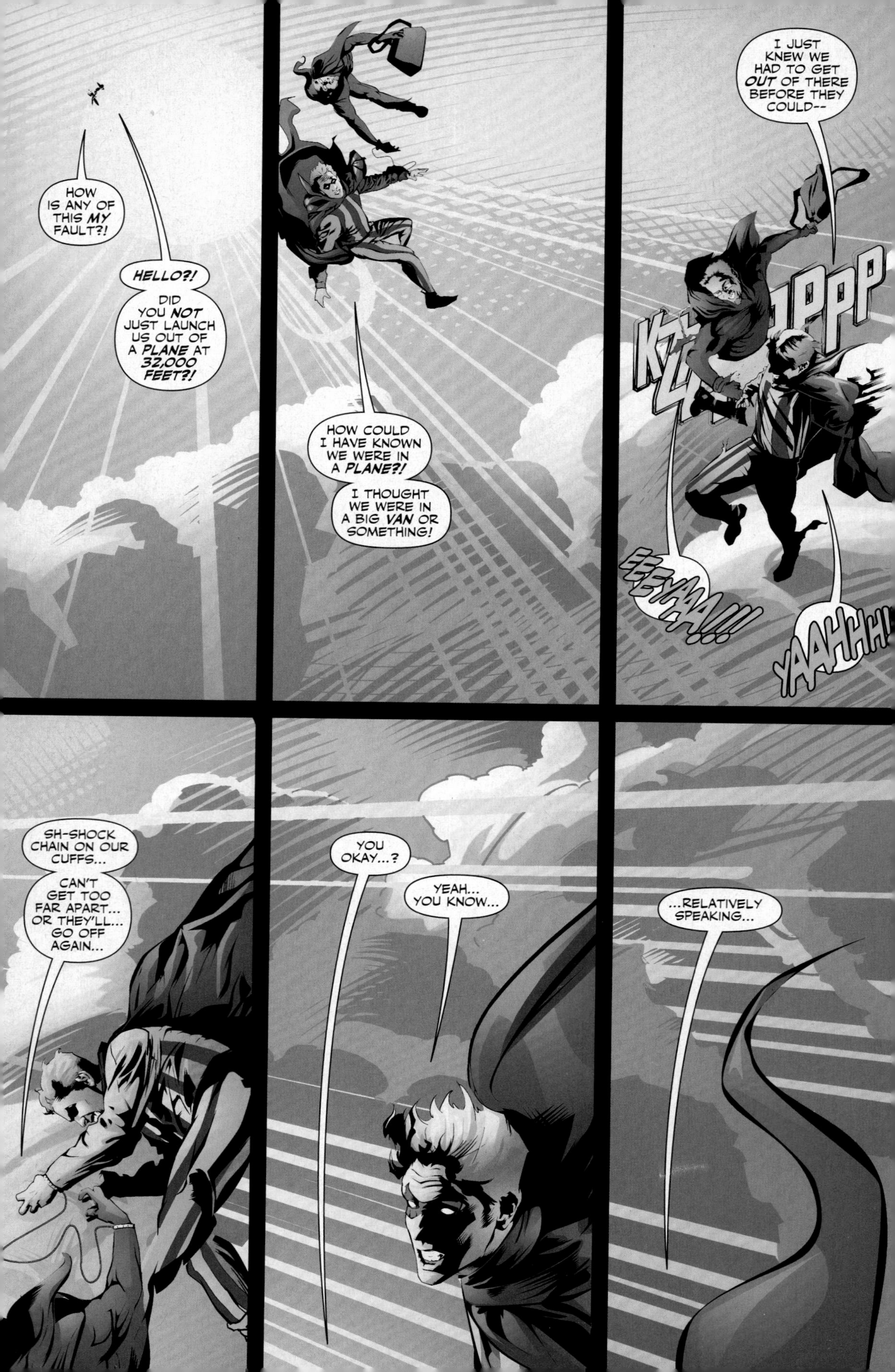
HOW IS ANY OF THIS *MY* FAULT?!
HELLO?!
DID YOU *NOT* JUST LAUNCH US OUT OF A *PLANE* AT *32,000 FEET?!*
HOW COULD I HAVE KNOWN WE WERE IN A *PLANE?!*
I THOUGHT WE WERE IN A BIG *VAN* OR SOMETHING!
I JUST KNEW WE HAD TO GET *OUT* OF THERE BEFORE THEY COULD--
PPP
EEEYAAA!!!
YAAHHH!
SH-SHOCK CHAIN ON OUR CUFFS...
CAN'T GET TOO FAR APART... OR THEY'LL... GO OFF AGAIN...
YOU OKAY...?
YEAH... YOU KNOW...
...RELATIVELY SPEAKING...

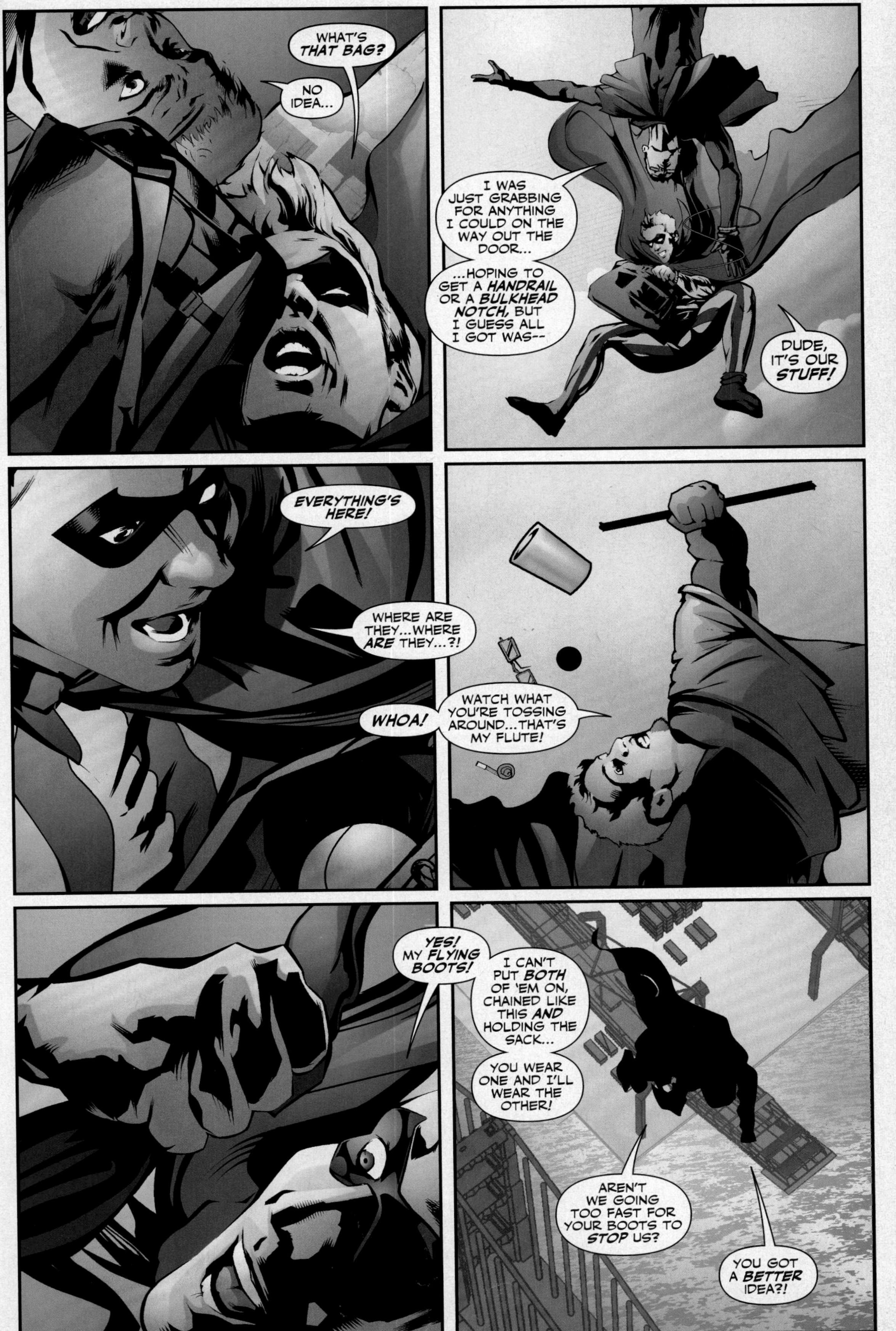
WHAT'S THAT BAG?
NO IDEA...
I WAS JUST GRABBING FOR ANYTHING I COULD ON THE WAY OUT THE DOOR...
...HOPING TO GET A HANDRAIL OR A BULKHEAD NOTCH, BUT I GUESS ALL I GOT WAS--
DUDE, IT'S OUR STUFF!
EVERYTHING'S HERE!
WHERE ARE THEY...WHERE ARE THEY...?!
WHOA!
WATCH WHAT YOU'RE TOSSING AROUND...THAT'S MY FLUTE!
YES! MY FLYING BOOTS!
I CAN'T PUT BOTH OF 'EM ON, CHAINED LIKE THIS AND HOLDING THE SACK...
YOU WEAR ONE AND I'LL WEAR THE OTHER!
AREN'T WE GOING TOO FAST FOR YOUR BOOTS TO STOP US?
YOU GOT A BETTER IDEA?!

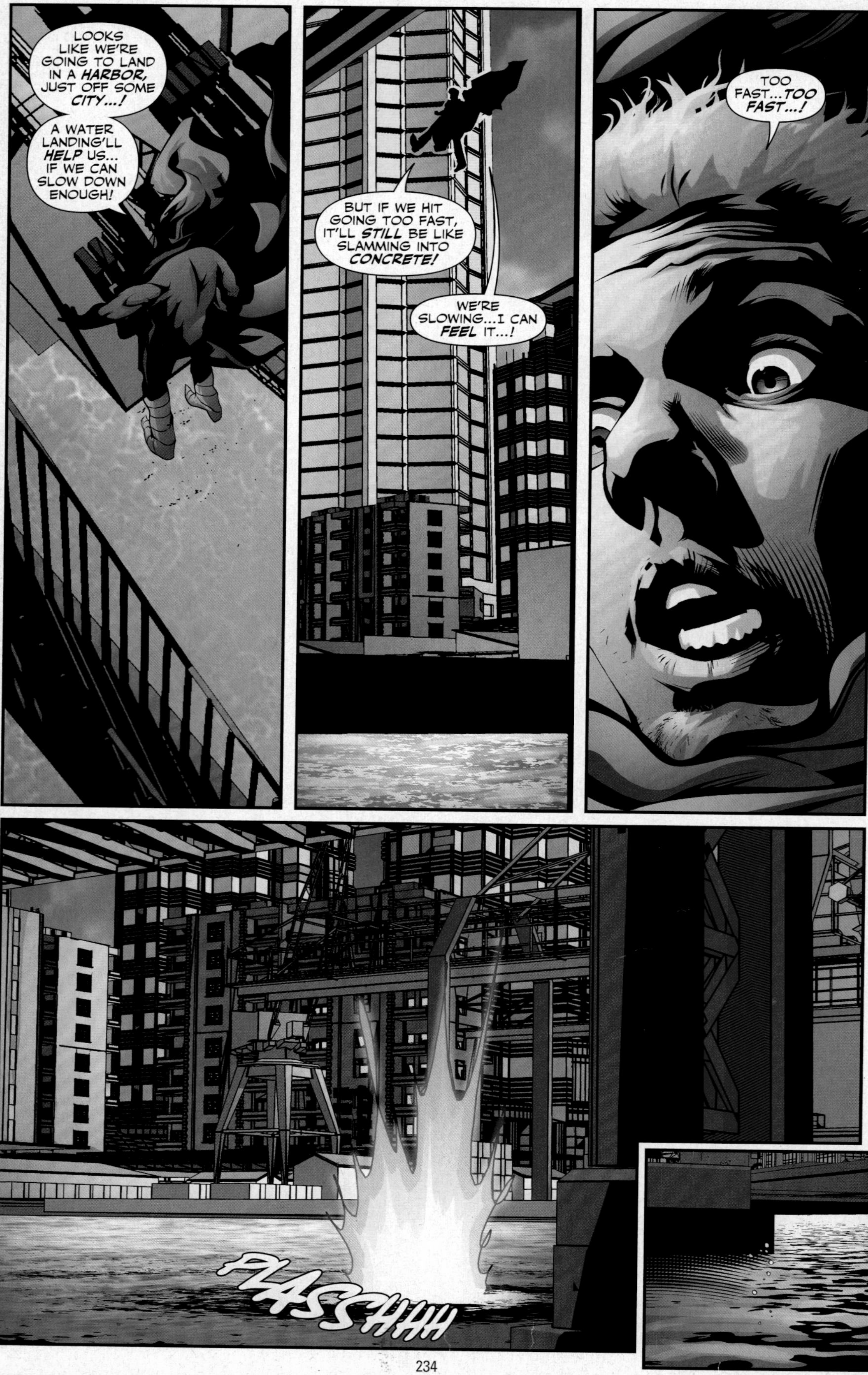
LOOKS LIKE WE'RE GOING TO LAND IN A *HARBOR,* JUST OFF SOME *CITY*...!
A WATER LANDING'LL *HELP* US... IF WE CAN SLOW DOWN ENOUGH!
BUT IF WE HIT GOING TOO FAST, IT'LL *STILL* BE LIKE SLAMMING INTO *CONCRETE!*
WE'RE SLOWING...I CAN *FEEL* IT...!
TOO FAST...*TOO FAST*...!
PLASSHHH

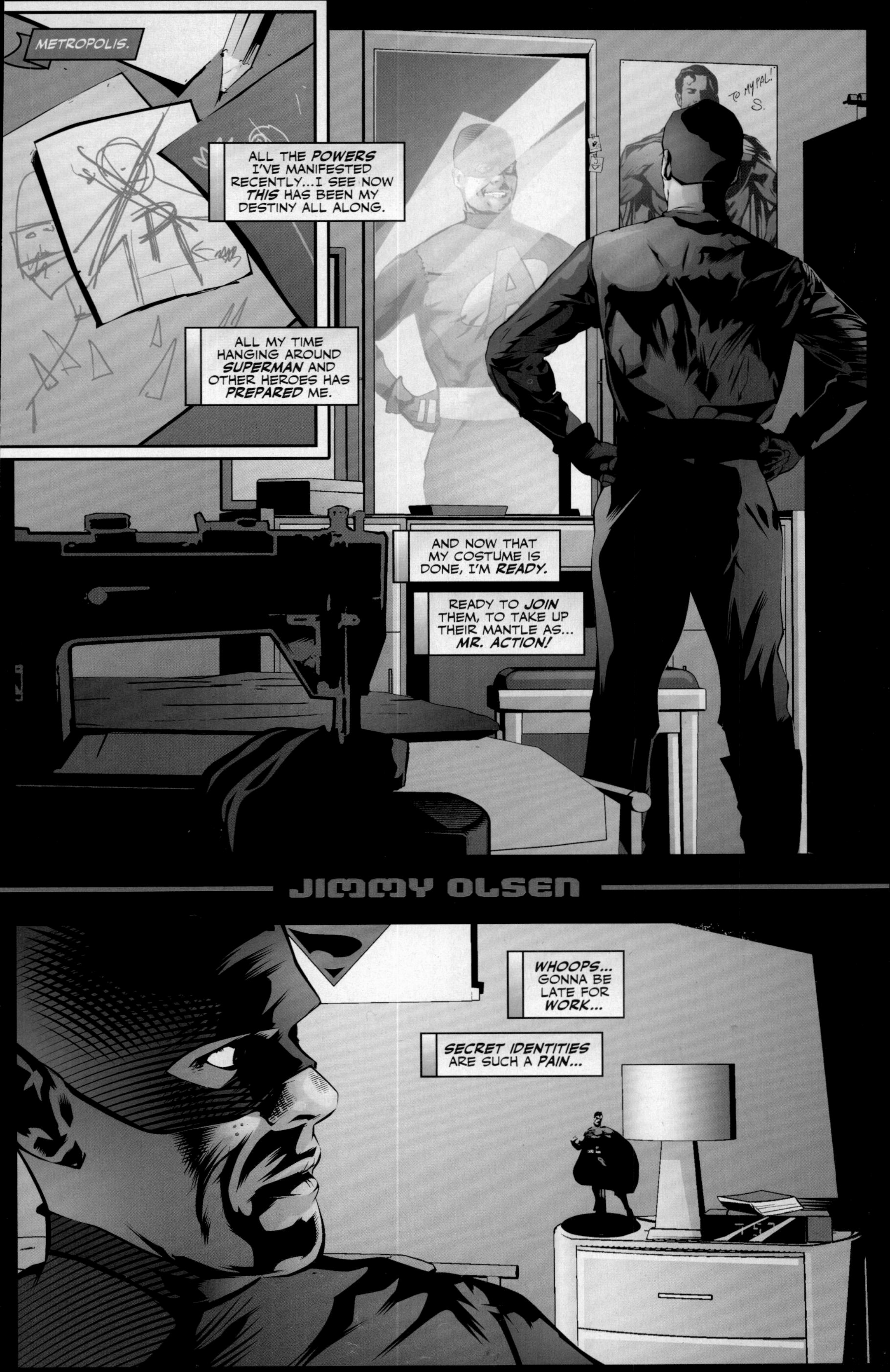
METROPOLIS.
ALL THE POWERS I'VE MANIFESTED RECENTLY...I SEE NOW THIS HAS BEEN MY DESTINY ALL ALONG.
ALL MY TIME HANGING AROUND SUPERMAN AND OTHER HEROES HAS PREPARED ME.
TO MY PAL! S.
AND NOW THAT MY COSTUME IS DONE, I'M READY.
READY TO JOIN THEM, TO TAKE UP THEIR MANTLE AS... MR. ACTION!
JIMMY OLSEN
WHOOPS... GONNA BE LATE FOR WORK...
SECRET IDENTITIES ARE SUCH A PAIN...

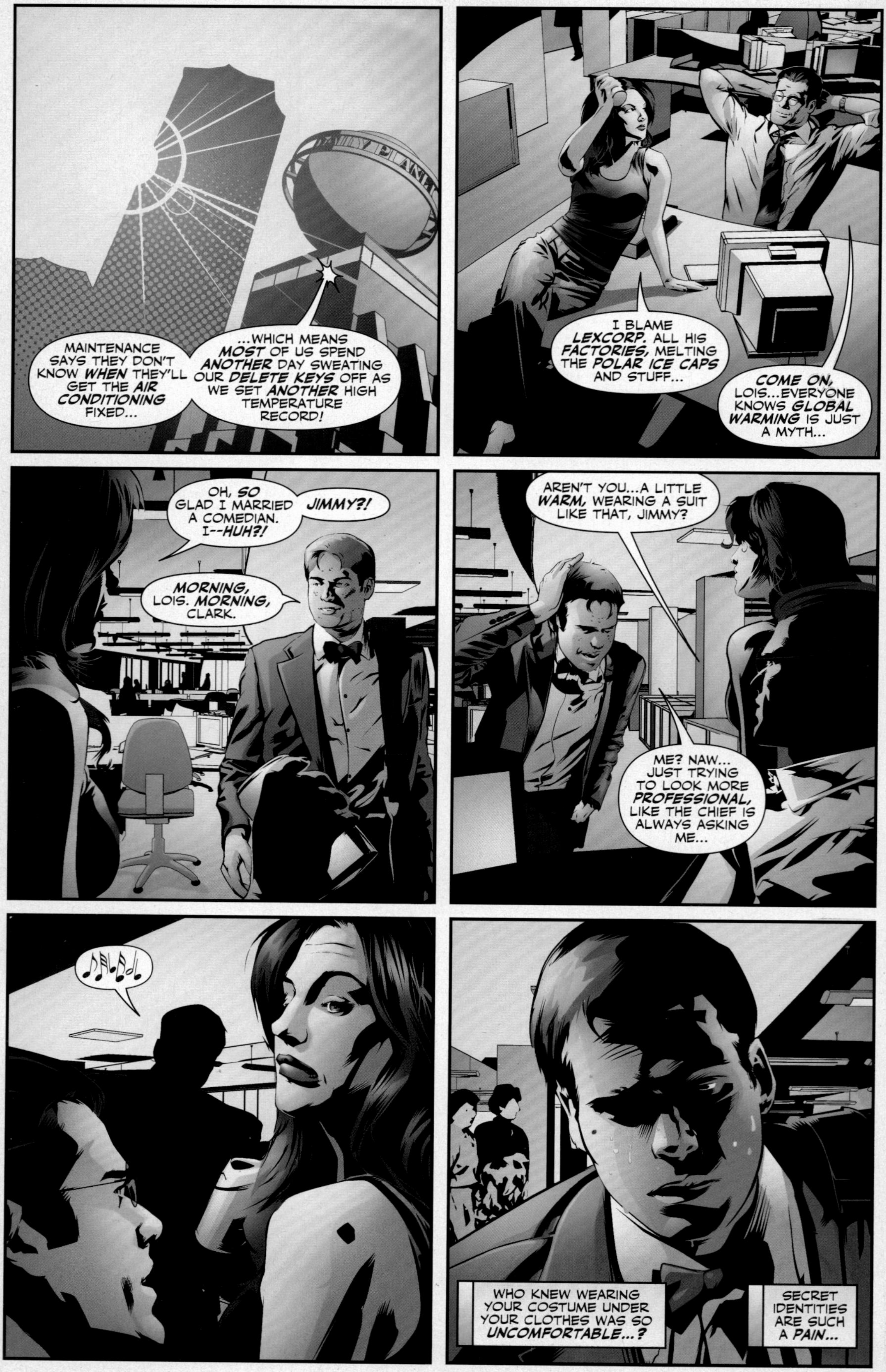
MAINTENANCE SAYS THEY DON'T KNOW WHEN THEY'LL GET THE AIR CONDITIONING FIXED...
...WHICH MEANS MOST OF US SPEND ANOTHER DAY SWEATING OUR DELETE KEYS OFF AS WE SET ANOTHER HIGH TEMPERATURE RECORD!
I BLAME LEXCORP. ALL HIS FACTORIES, MELTING THE POLAR ICE CAPS AND STUFF...
COME ON, LOIS...EVERYONE KNOWS GLOBAL WARMING IS JUST A MYTH...
OH, SO GLAD I MARRIED A COMEDIAN. I--HUH?!
JIMMY?!
MORNING, LOIS. MORNING, CLARK.
AREN'T YOU...A LITTLE WARM, WEARING A SUIT LIKE THAT, JIMMY?
ME? NAW... JUST TRYING TO LOOK MORE PROFESSIONAL, LIKE THE CHIEF IS ALWAYS ASKING ME...
WHO KNEW WEARING YOUR COSTUME UNDER YOUR CLOTHES WAS SO UNCOMFORTABLE...?
SECRET IDENTITIES ARE SUCH A PAIN...

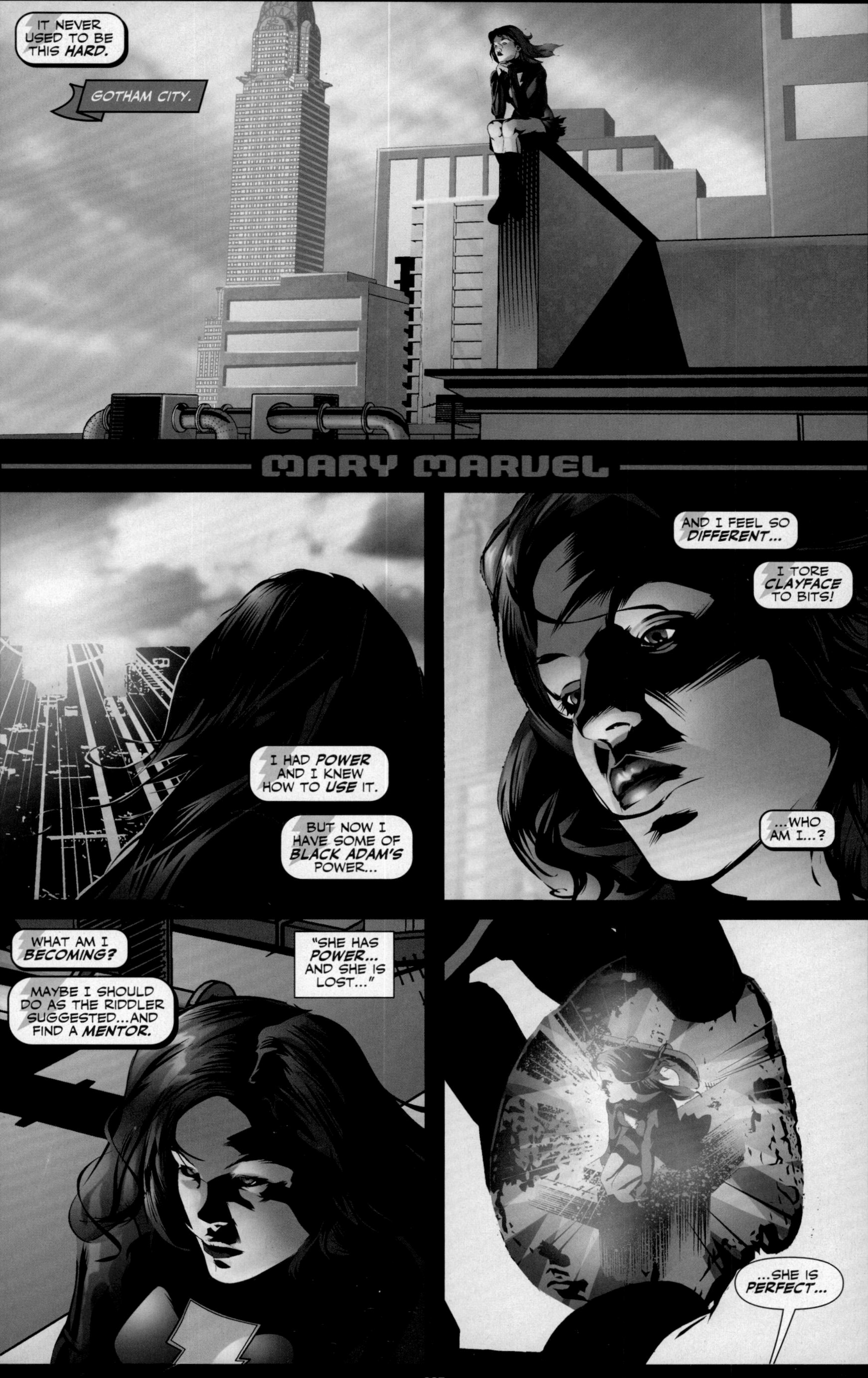
IT NEVER USED TO BE THIS HARD.
GOTHAM CITY.
MARY MARVEL
I HAD POWER AND I KNEW HOW TO USE IT.
BUT NOW I HAVE SOME OF BLACK ADAM'S POWER...
AND I FEEL SO DIFFERENT...
I TORE CLAYFACE TO BITS!
...WHO AM I...?
WHAT AM I BECOMING?
MAYBE I SHOULD DO AS THE RIDDLER SUGGESTED...AND FIND A MENTOR.
"SHE HAS POWER... AND SHE IS LOST..."
...SHE IS PERFECT...

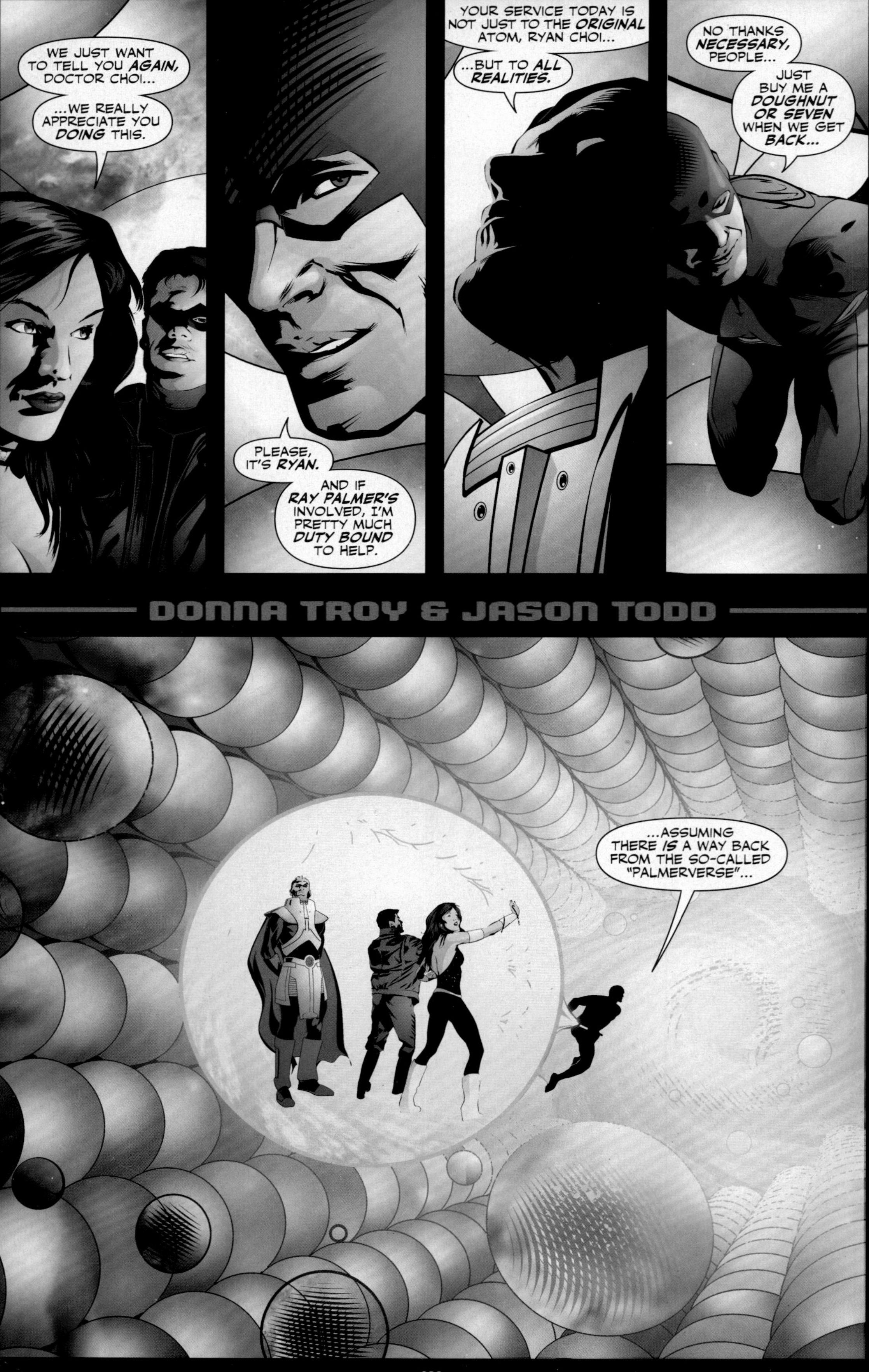
WE JUST WANT TO TELL YOU AGAIN, DOCTOR CHOI...
...WE REALLY APPRECIATE YOU DOING THIS.
PLEASE, IT'S RYAN.
AND IF RAY PALMER'S INVOLVED, I'M PRETTY MUCH DUTY BOUND TO HELP.
YOUR SERVICE TODAY IS NOT JUST TO THE ORIGINAL ATOM, RYAN CHOI...
...BUT TO ALL REALITIES.
NO THANKS NECESSARY, PEOPLE...
JUST BUY ME A DOUGHNUT OR SEVEN WHEN WE GET BACK...
DONNA TROY & JASON TODD
...ASSUMING THERE IS A WAY BACK FROM THE SO-CALLED "PALMERVERSE"...

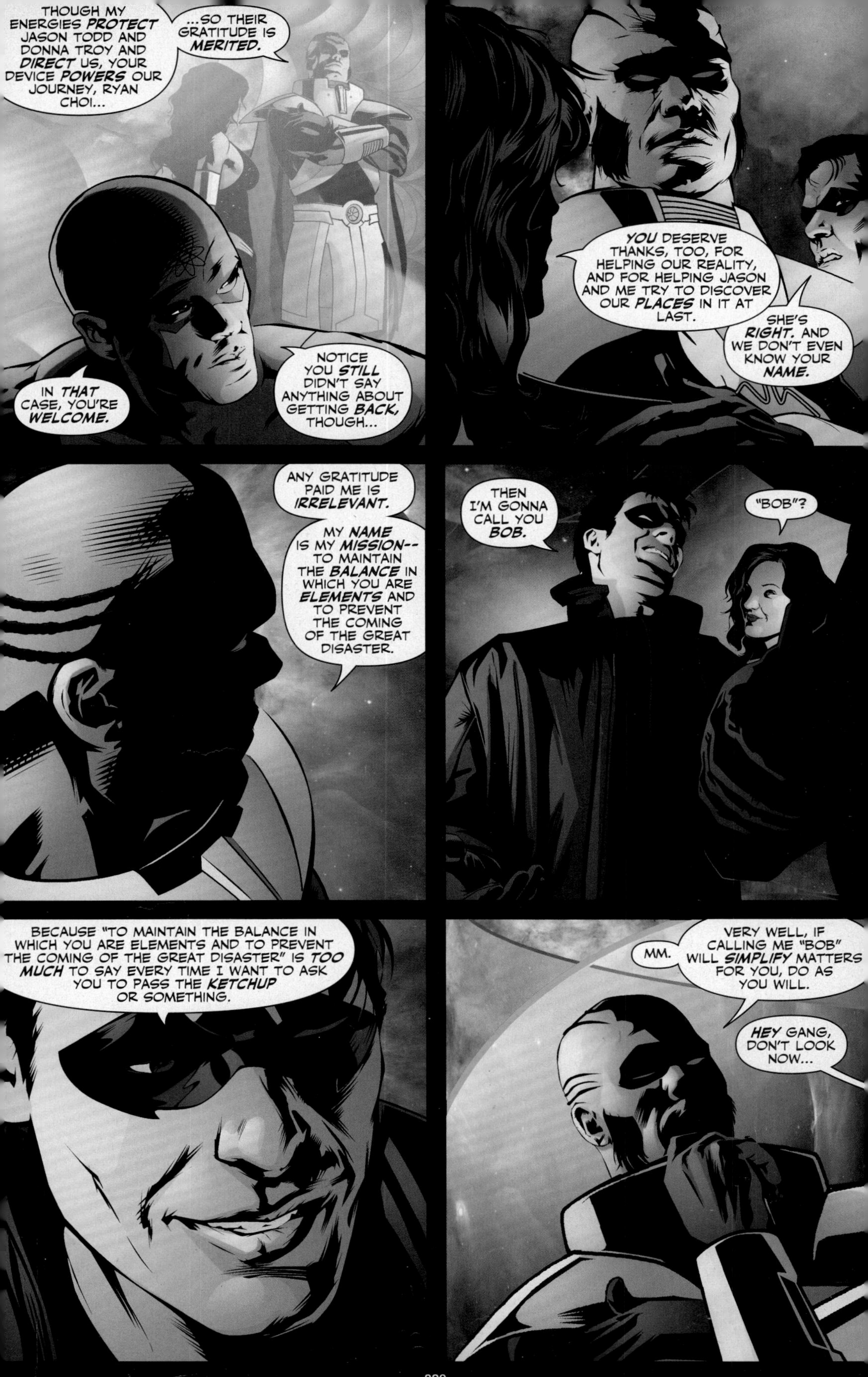
THOUGH MY ENERGIES PROTECT JASON TODD AND DONNA TROY AND DIRECT US, YOUR DEVICE POWERS OUR JOURNEY, RYAN CHOI...
...SO THEIR GRATITUDE IS MERITED.
IN THAT CASE, YOU'RE WELCOME.
NOTICE YOU STILL DIDN'T SAY ANYTHING ABOUT GETTING BACK, THOUGH...
YOU DESERVE THANKS, TOO, FOR HELPING OUR REALITY, AND FOR HELPING JASON AND ME TRY TO DISCOVER OUR PLACES IN IT AT LAST.
SHE'S RIGHT. AND WE DON'T EVEN KNOW YOUR NAME.
ANY GRATITUDE PAID ME IS IRRELEVANT.
MY NAME IS MY MISSION--TO MAINTAIN THE BALANCE IN WHICH YOU ARE ELEMENTS AND TO PREVENT THE COMING OF THE GREAT DISASTER.
THEN I'M GONNA CALL YOU BOB.
"BOB"?
BECAUSE "TO MAINTAIN THE BALANCE IN WHICH YOU ARE ELEMENTS AND TO PREVENT THE COMING OF THE GREAT DISASTER" IS TOO MUCH TO SAY EVERY TIME I WANT TO ASK YOU TO PASS THE KETCHUP OR SOMETHING.
MM.
VERY WELL, IF CALLING ME "BOB" WILL SIMPLIFY MATTERS FOR YOU, DO AS YOU WILL.
HEY GANG, DON'T LOOK NOW...

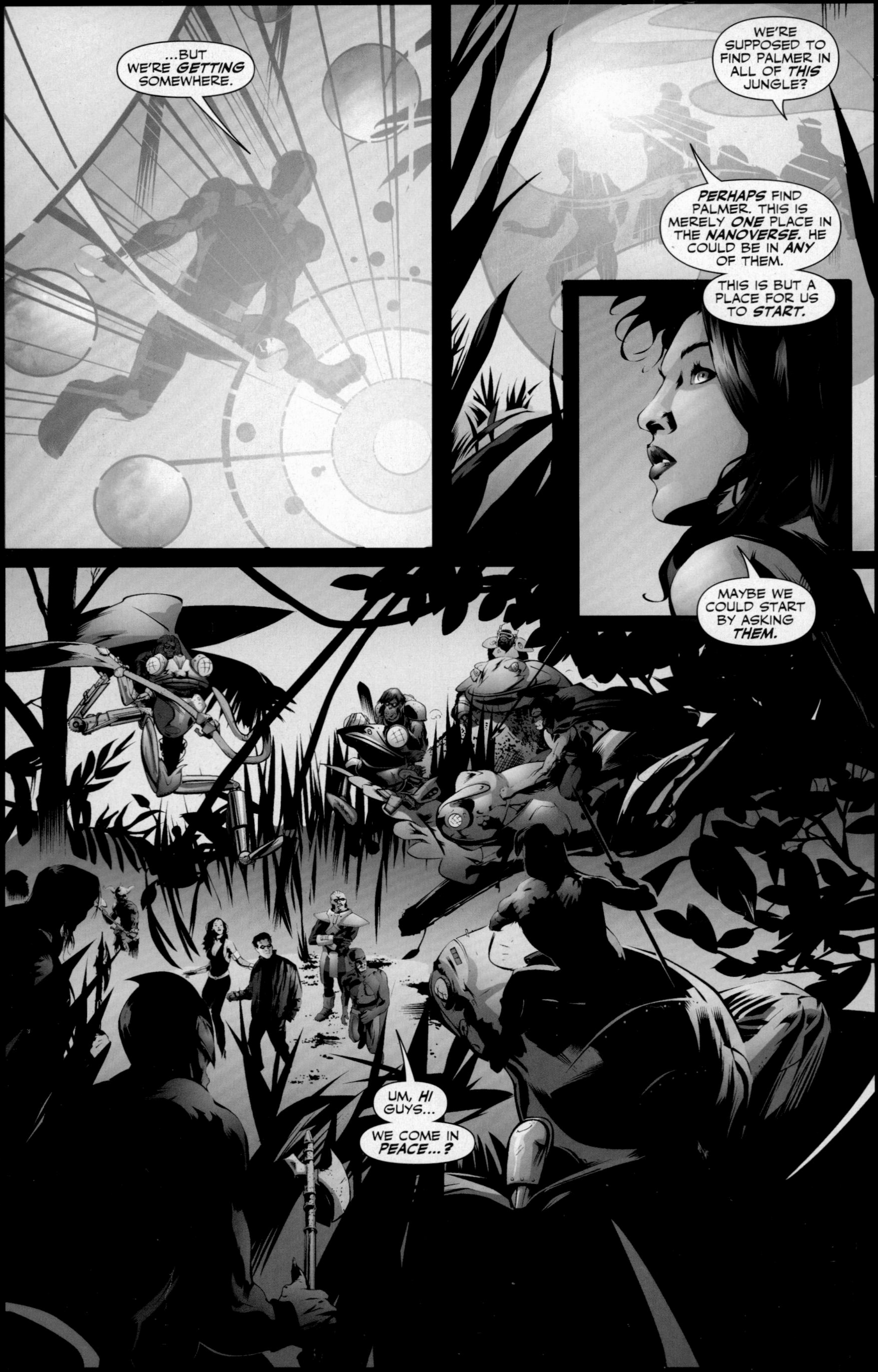
...BUT WE'RE *GETTING* SOMEWHERE.
WE'RE SUPPOSED TO FIND PALMER IN ALL OF *THIS* JUNGLE?
PERHAPS FIND PALMER. THIS IS MERELY *ONE* PLACE IN THE *NANOVERSE.* HE COULD BE IN *ANY* OF THEM.
THIS IS BUT A PLACE FOR US TO *START.*
MAYBE WE COULD START BY ASKING *THEM.*
UM, *HI* GUYS...
WE COME IN *PEACE...?*

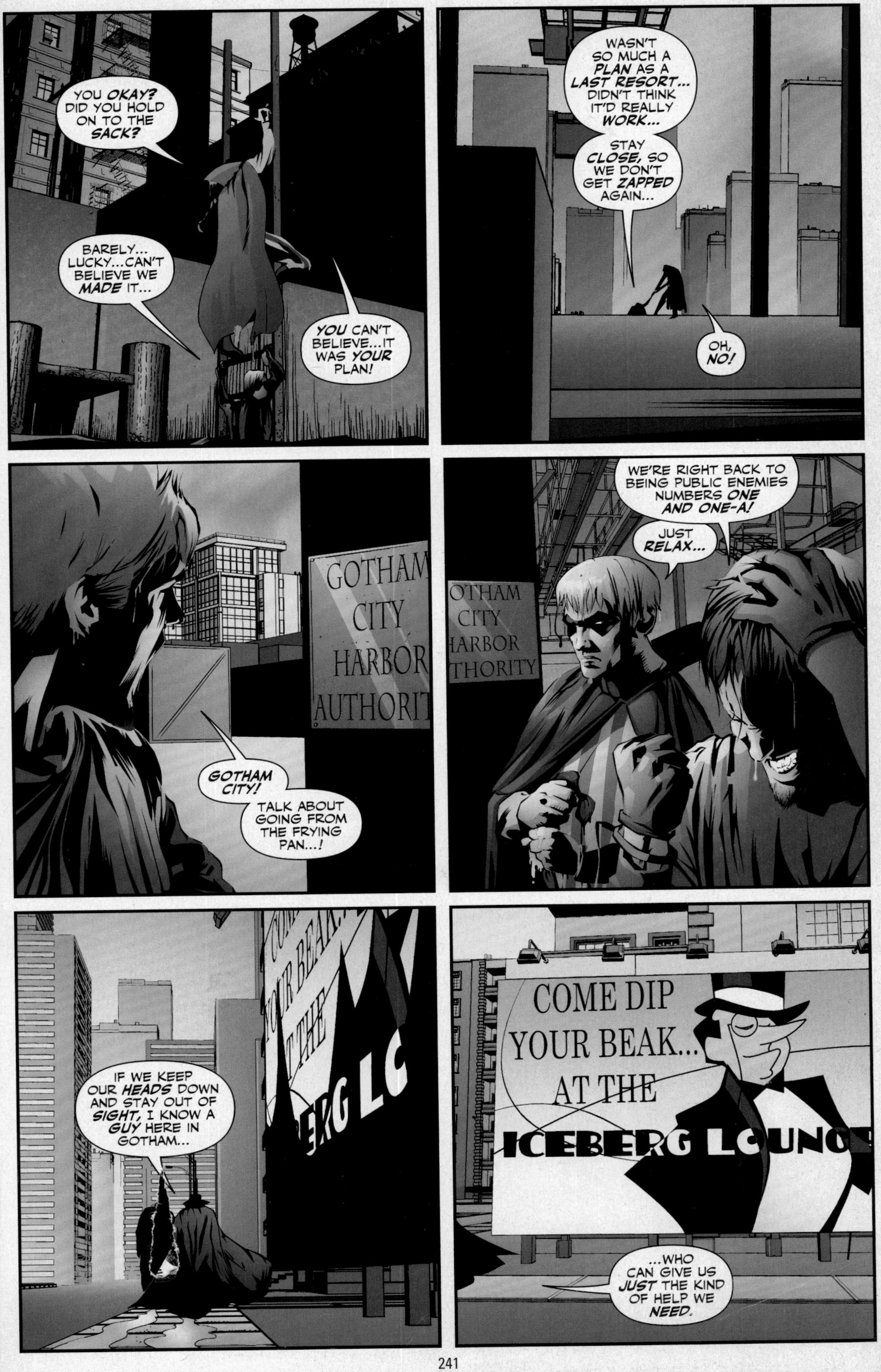
YOU OKAY? DID YOU HOLD ON TO THE SACK?
BARELY... LUCKY...CAN'T BELIEVE WE MADE IT...
YOU CAN'T BELIEVE...IT WAS YOUR PLAN!
WASN'T SO MUCH A PLAN AS A LAST RESORT... DIDN'T THINK IT'D REALLY WORK...
STAY CLOSE, SO WE DON'T GET ZAPPED AGAIN...
OH, NO!
GOTHAM CITY HARBOR AUTHORIT
GOTHAM CITY!
TALK ABOUT GOING FROM THE FRYING PAN...!
WE'RE RIGHT BACK TO BEING PUBLIC ENEMIES NUMBERS ONE AND ONE-A!
JUST RELAX...
OTHAM CITY HARBOR THORITY
IF WE KEEP OUR HEADS DOWN AND STAY OUT OF SIGHT, I KNOW A GUY HERE IN GOTHAM...
COME DIP YOUR BEAK... AT THE ICEBERG LOUNG
...WHO CAN GIVE US JUST THE KIND OF HELP WE NEED.

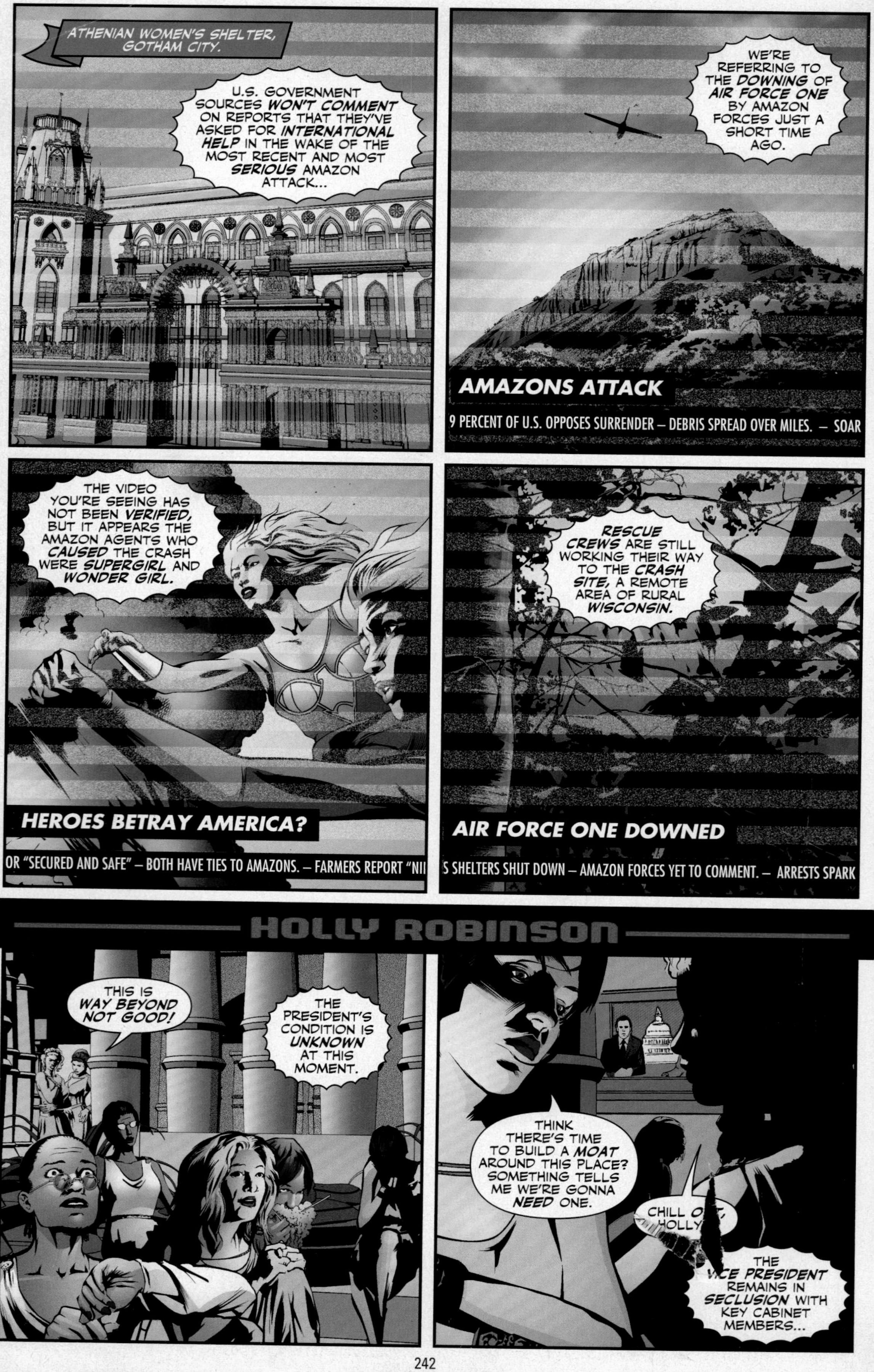

ATHENIAN WOMEN'S SHELTER, GOTHAM CITY.
U.S. GOVERNMENT SOURCES WON'T COMMENT ON REPORTS THAT THEY'VE ASKED FOR INTERNATIONAL HELP IN THE WAKE OF THE MOST RECENT AND MOST SERIOUS AMAZON ATTACK...
WE'RE REFERRING TO THE DOWNING OF AIR FORCE ONE BY AMAZON FORCES JUST A SHORT TIME AGO.
AMAZONS ATTACK
9 PERCENT OF U.S. OPPOSES SURRENDER – DEBRIS SPREAD OVER MILES. – SOAR
THE VIDEO YOU'RE SEEING HAS NOT BEEN VERIFIED, BUT IT APPEARS THE AMAZON AGENTS WHO CAUSED THE CRASH WERE SUPERGIRL AND WONDER GIRL.
HEROES BETRAY AMERICA?
OR "SECURED AND SAFE" – BOTH HAVE TIES TO AMAZONS. – FARMERS REPORT "NII
RESCUE CREWS ARE STILL WORKING THEIR WAY TO THE CRASH SITE, A REMOTE AREA OF RURAL WISCONSIN.
AIR FORCE ONE DOWNED
S SHELTERS SHUT DOWN – AMAZON FORCES YET TO COMMENT. – ARRESTS SPARK
HOLLY ROBINSON
THIS IS WAY BEYOND NOT GOOD!
THE PRESIDENT'S CONDITION IS UNKNOWN AT THIS MOMENT.
THINK THERE'S TIME TO BUILD A MOAT AROUND THIS PLACE? SOMETHING TELLS ME WE'RE GONNA NEED ONE.
CHILL OUT, HOLLY.
THE VICE PRESIDENT REMAINS IN SECLUSION WITH KEY CABINET MEMBERS...

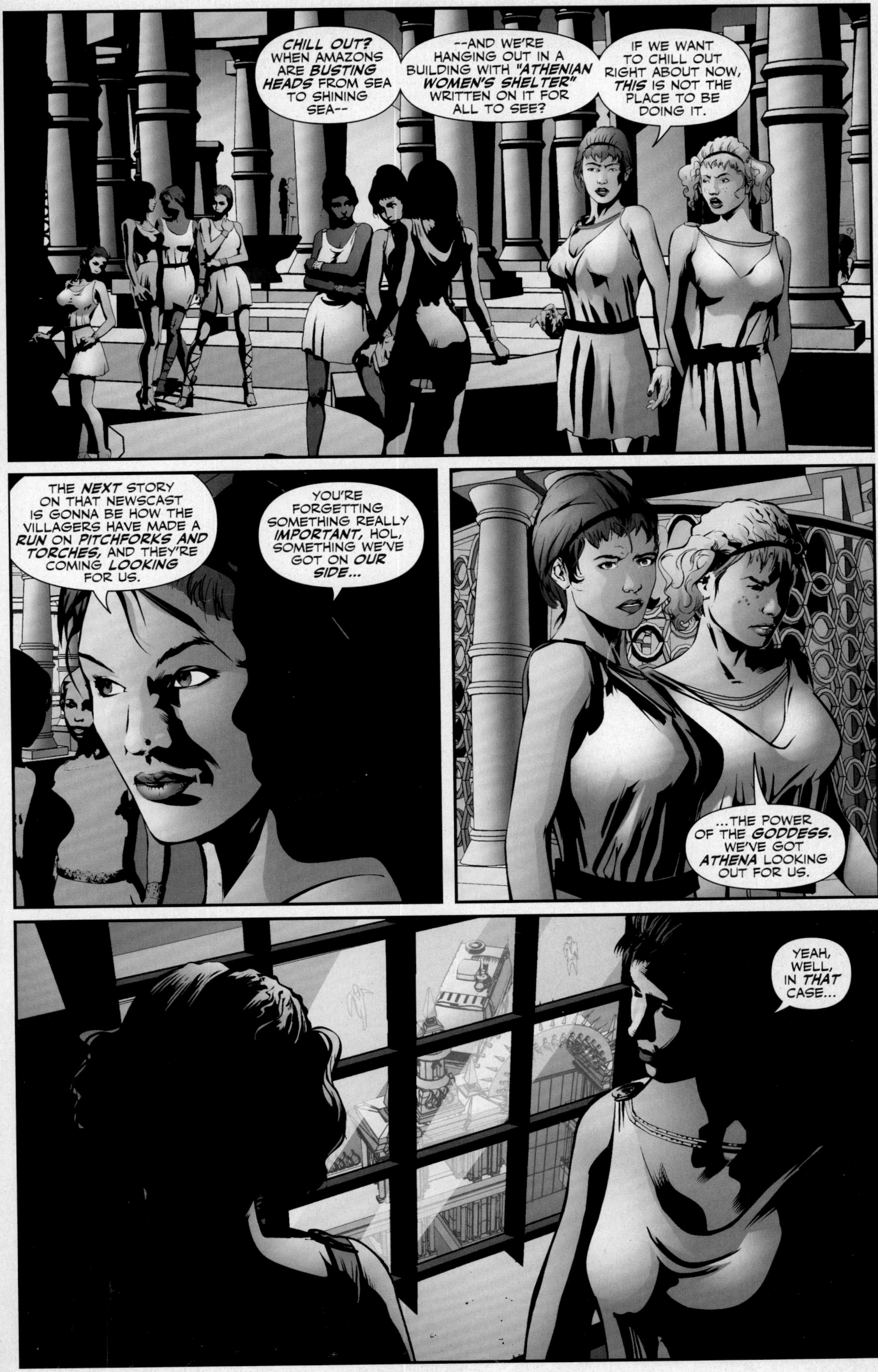

CHILL OUT? WHEN AMAZONS ARE BUSTING HEADS FROM SEA TO SHINING SEA--
--AND WE'RE HANGING OUT IN A BUILDING WITH "ATHENIAN WOMEN'S SHELTER" WRITTEN ON IT FOR ALL TO SEE?
IF WE WANT TO CHILL OUT RIGHT ABOUT NOW, THIS IS NOT THE PLACE TO BE DOING IT.
THE NEXT STORY ON THAT NEWSCAST IS GONNA BE HOW THE VILLAGERS HAVE MADE A RUN ON PITCHFORKS AND TORCHES, AND THEY'RE COMING LOOKING FOR US.
YOU'RE FORGETTING SOMETHING REALLY IMPORTANT, HOL, SOMETHING WE'VE GOT ON OUR SIDE...
...THE POWER OF THE GODDESS. WE'VE GOT ATHENA LOOKING OUT FOR US.
YEAH, WELL, IN THAT CASE...

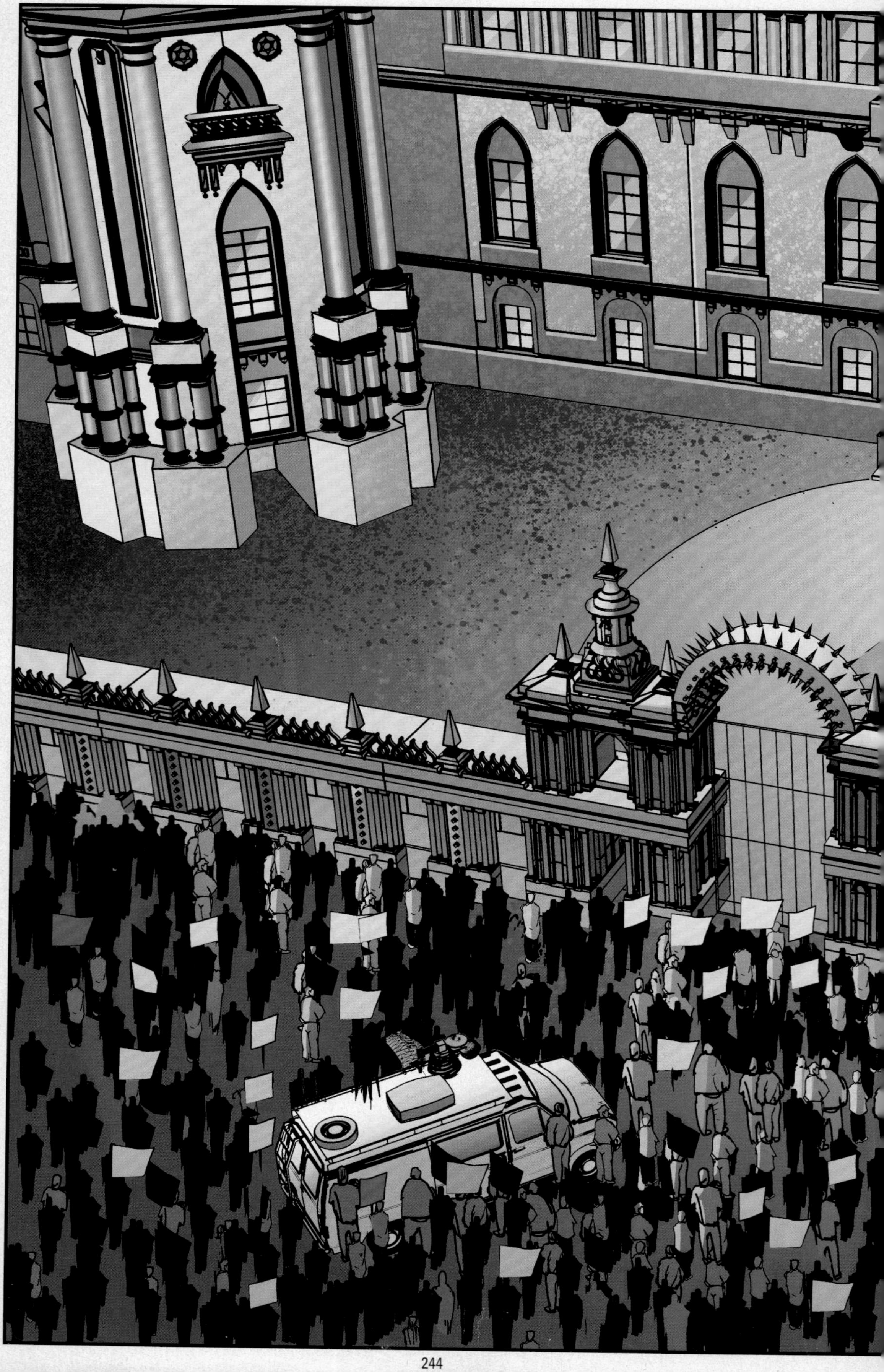

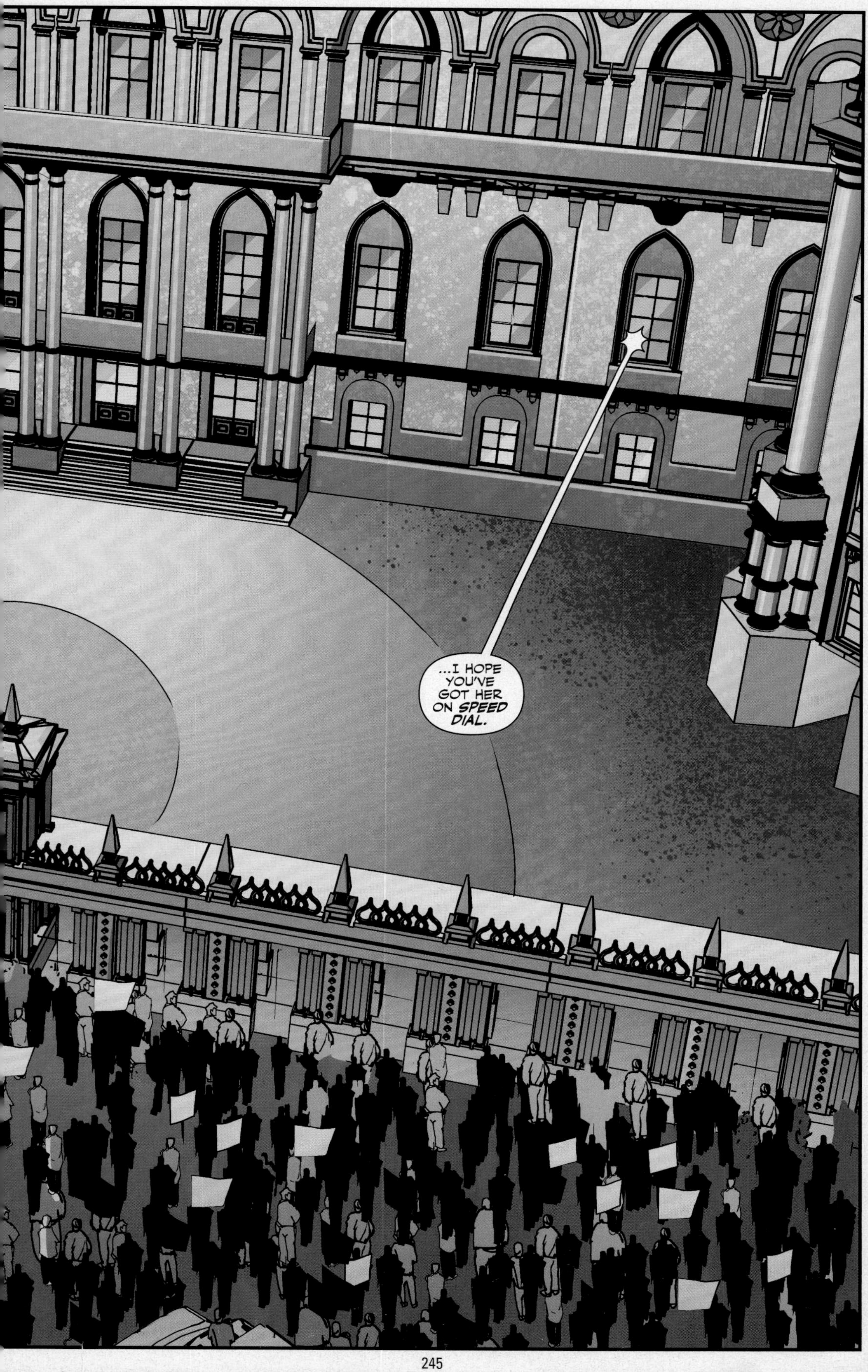
...I HOPE YOU'VE GOT HER ON SPEED DIAL.

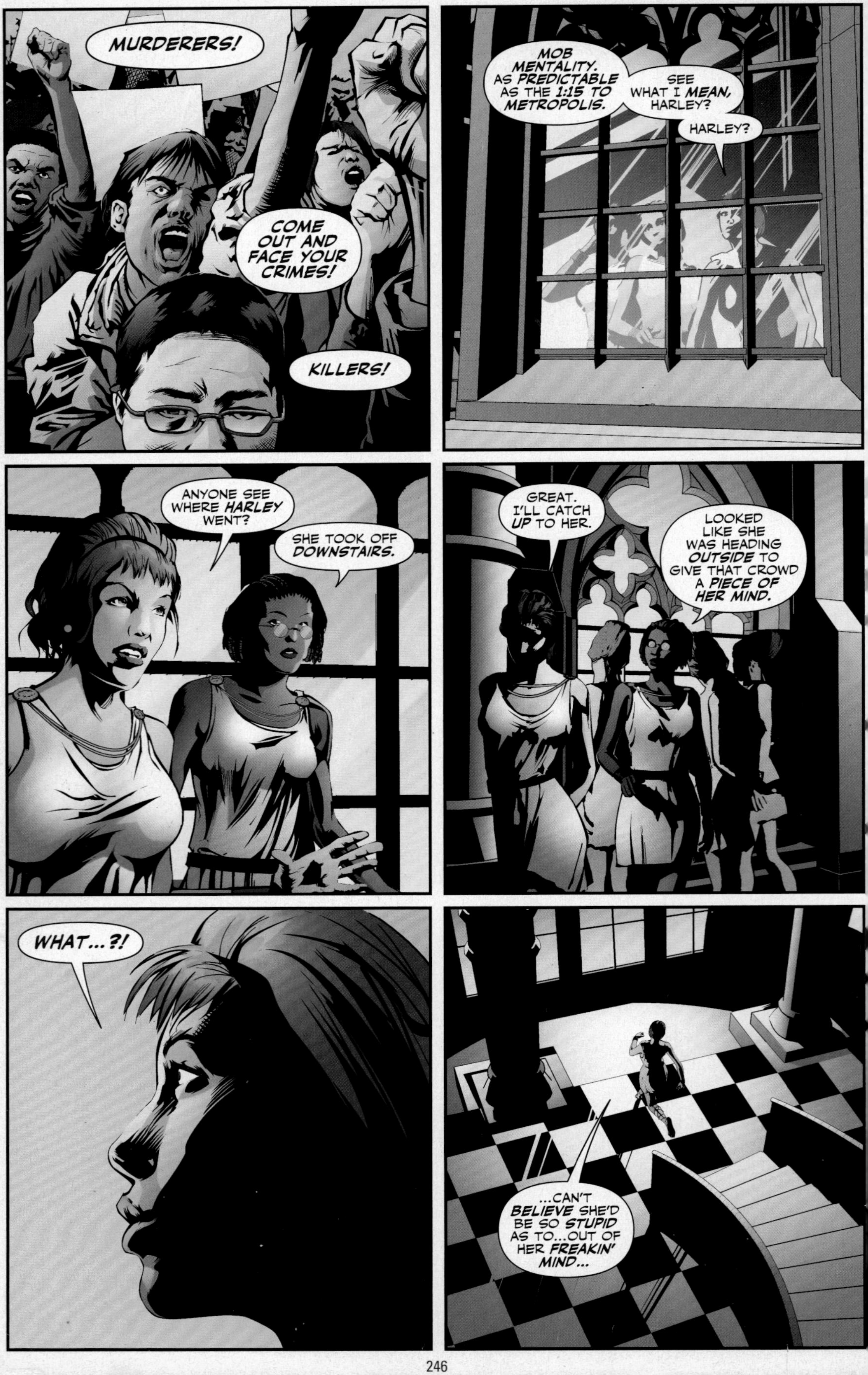
MURDERERS!
COME OUT AND FACE YOUR CRIMES!
KILLERS!
MOB MENTALITY. AS PREDICTABLE AS THE 1:15 TO METROPOLIS.
SEE WHAT I MEAN, HARLEY?
HARLEY?
ANYONE SEE WHERE HARLEY WENT?
SHE TOOK OFF DOWNSTAIRS.
GREAT. I'LL CATCH UP TO HER.
LOOKED LIKE SHE WAS HEADING OUTSIDE TO GIVE THAT CROWD A PIECE OF HER MIND.
WHAT...?!
...CAN'T BELIEVE SHE'D BE SO STUPID AS TO...OUT OF HER FREAKIN' MIND...

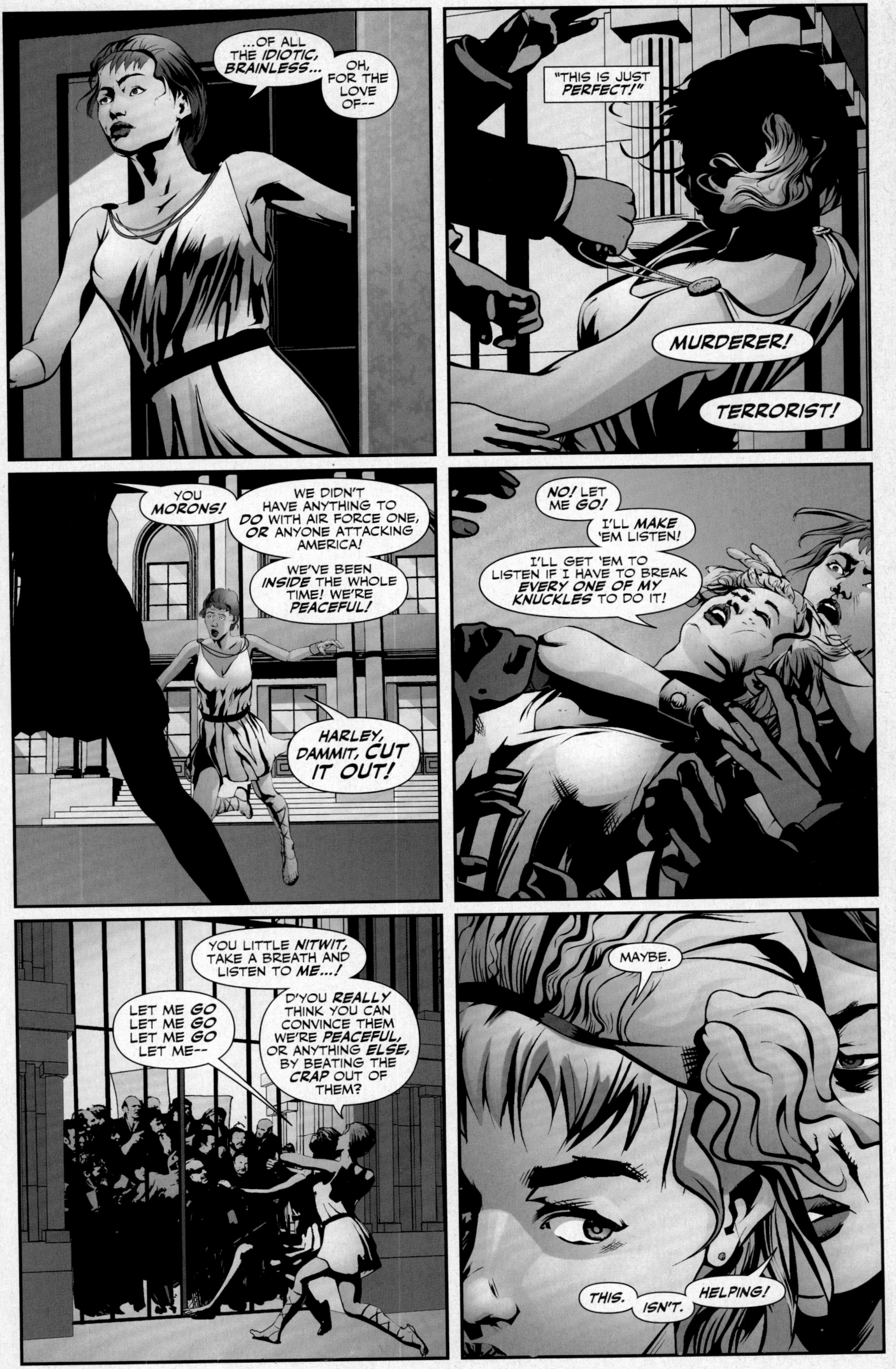
...OF ALL THE IDIOTIC, BRAINLESS...
OH, FOR THE LOVE OF--
"THIS IS JUST PERFECT!"
MURDERER!
TERRORIST!
YOU MORONS!
WE DIDN'T HAVE ANYTHING TO DO WITH AIR FORCE ONE, OR ANYONE ATTACKING AMERICA!
WE'VE BEEN INSIDE THE WHOLE TIME! WE'RE PEACEFUL!
HARLEY, DAMMIT, CUT IT OUT!
NO! LET ME GO!
I'LL MAKE 'EM LISTEN!
I'LL GET 'EM TO LISTEN IF I HAVE TO BREAK EVERY ONE OF MY KNUCKLES TO DO IT!
YOU LITTLE NITWIT, TAKE A BREATH AND LISTEN TO ME...!
LET ME GO LET ME GO LET ME GO LET ME--
D'YOU REALLY THINK YOU CAN CONVINCE THEM WE'RE PEACEFUL, OR ANYTHING ELSE, BY BEATING THE CRAP OUT OF THEM?
MAYBE.
THIS.
ISN'T.
HELPING!

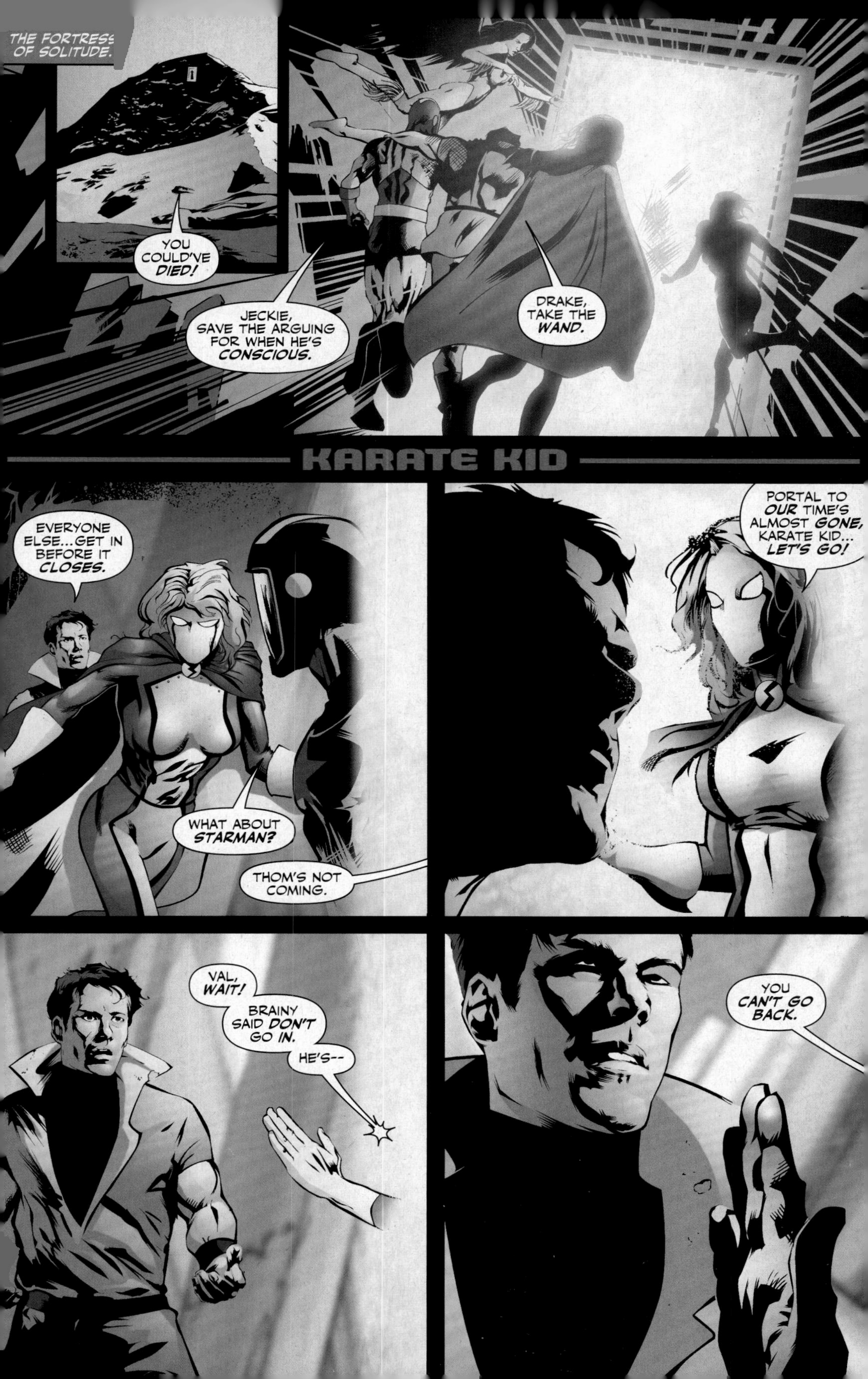
THE FORTRESS OF SOLITUDE.
YOU COULD'VE DIED!
JECKIE, SAVE THE ARGUING FOR WHEN HE'S CONSCIOUS.
DRAKE, TAKE THE WAND.
KARATE KID
EVERYONE ELSE...GET IN BEFORE IT CLOSES.
WHAT ABOUT STARMAN?
THOM'S NOT COMING.
PORTAL TO OUR TIME'S ALMOST GONE, KARATE KID... LET'S GO!
VAL, WAIT!
BRAINY SAID DON'T GO IN.
HE'S--
YOU CAN'T GO BACK.

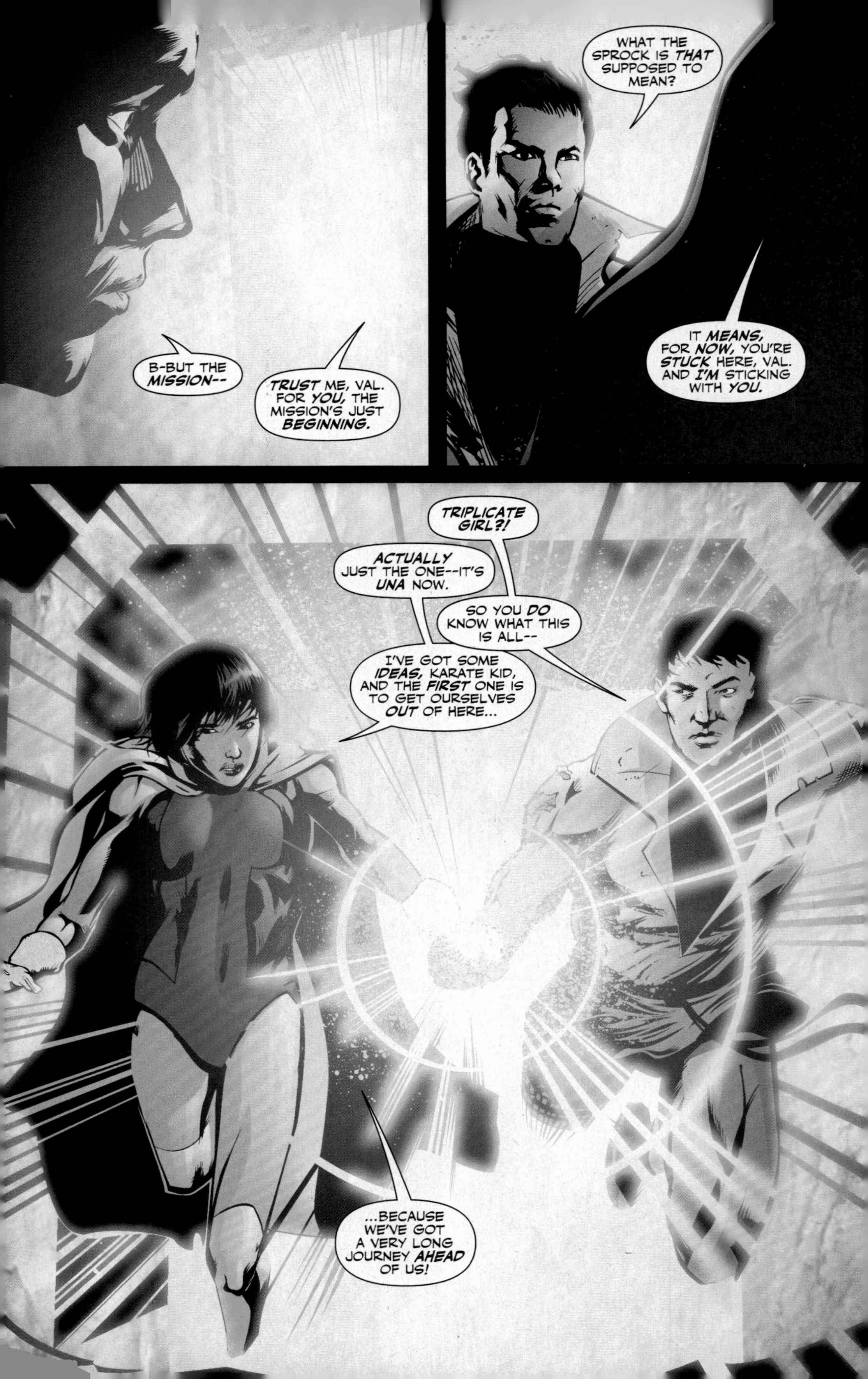
B-BUT THE MISSION--
TRUST ME, VAL. FOR YOU, THE MISSION'S JUST BEGINNING.
WHAT THE SPROCK IS THAT SUPPOSED TO MEAN?
IT MEANS, FOR NOW, YOU'RE STUCK HERE, VAL. AND I'M STICKING WITH YOU.
TRIPLICATE GIRL?!
ACTUALLY JUST THE ONE--IT'S UNA NOW.
SO YOU DO KNOW WHAT THIS IS ALL--
I'VE GOT SOME IDEAS, KARATE KID, AND THE FIRST ONE IS TO GET OURSELVES OUT OF HERE...
...BECAUSE WE'VE GOT A VERY LONG JOURNEY AHEAD OF US!

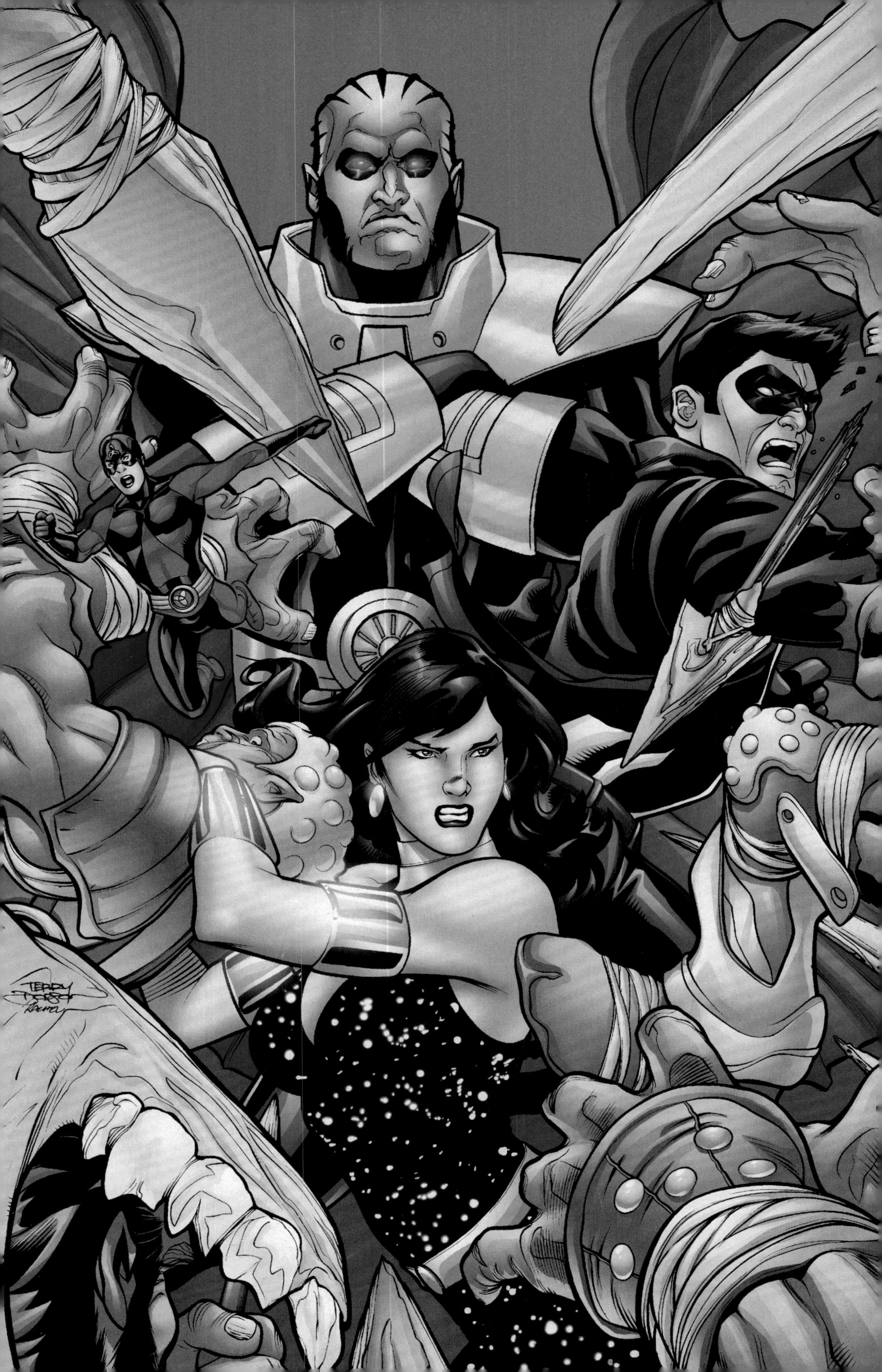

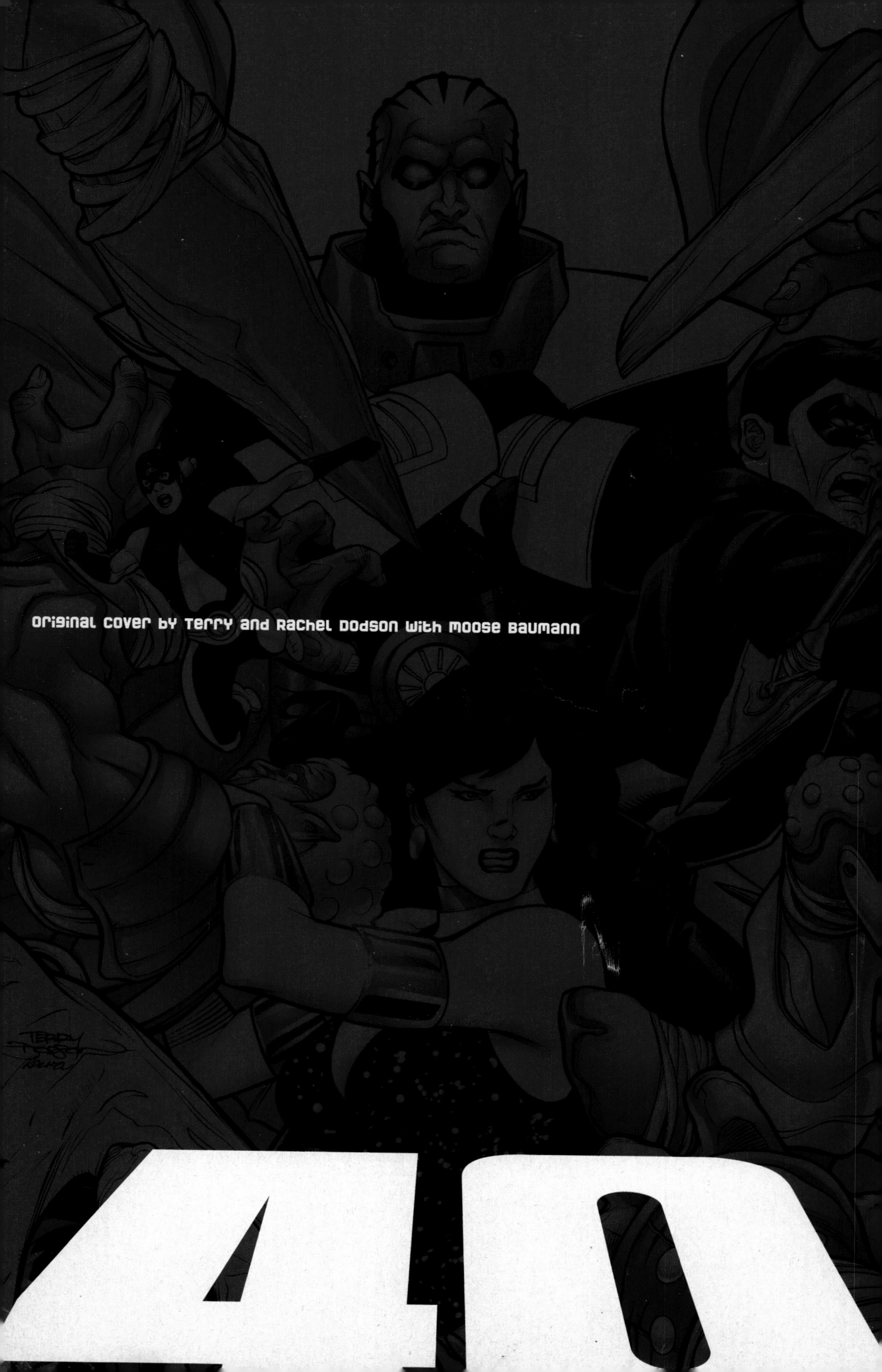
40

original cover by Terry and Rachel Dodson with Moose Baumann

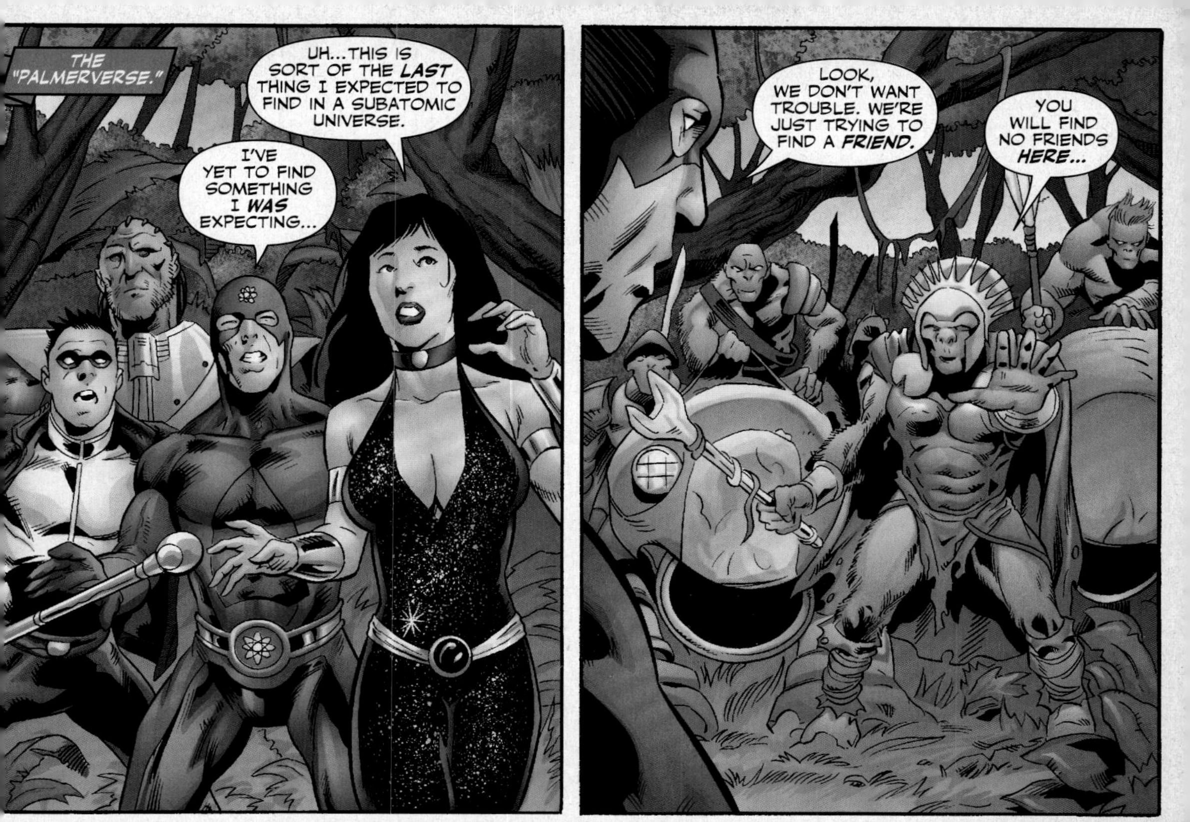
THE "PALMERVERSE."
UH...THIS IS SORT OF THE LAST THING I EXPECTED TO FIND IN A SUBATOMIC UNIVERSE.
I'VE YET TO FIND SOMETHING I WAS EXPECTING...
LOOK, WE DON'T WANT TROUBLE. WE'RE JUST TRYING TO FIND A FRIEND.
YOU WILL FIND NO FRIENDS HERE...

FORTY AND COUNTING...
DONNA TROY & JASON TODD

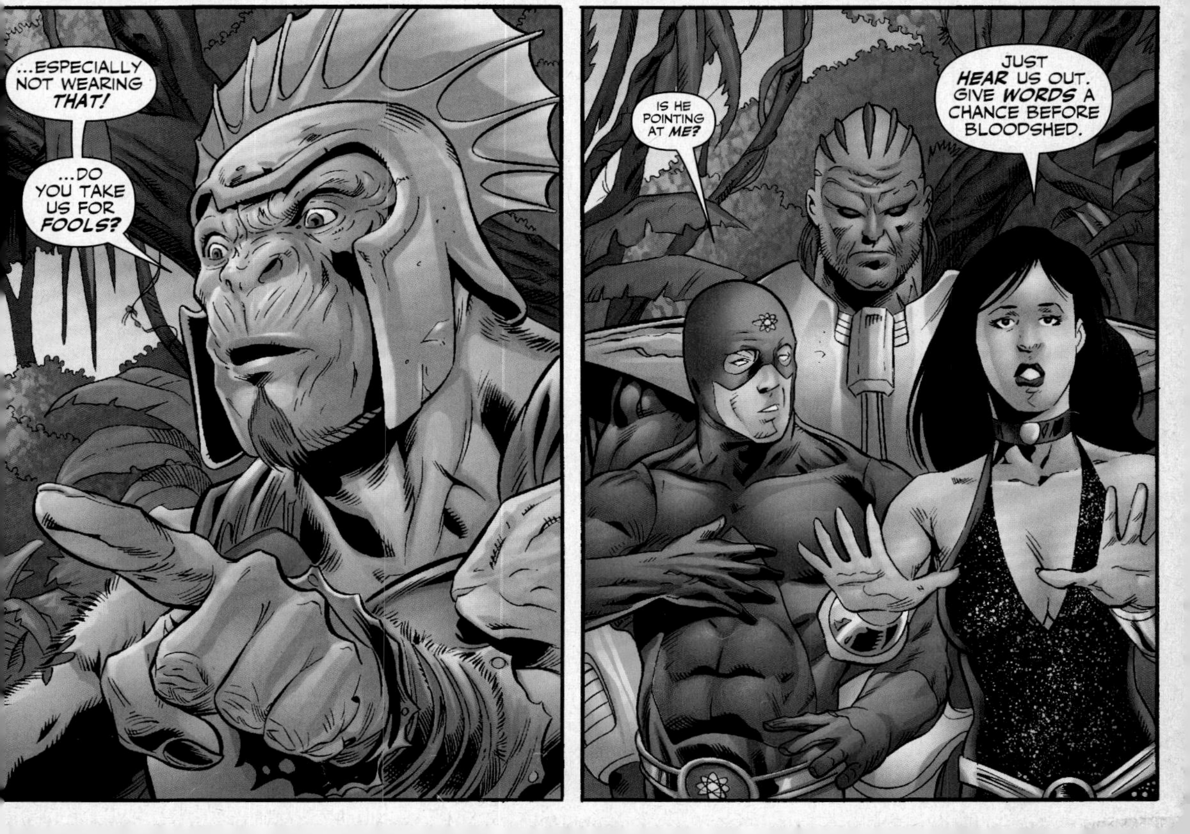
...ESPECIALLY NOT WEARING THAT!
...DO YOU TAKE US FOR FOOLS?
IS HE POINTING AT ME?
JUST HEAR US OUT. GIVE WORDS A CHANCE BEFORE BLOODSHED.

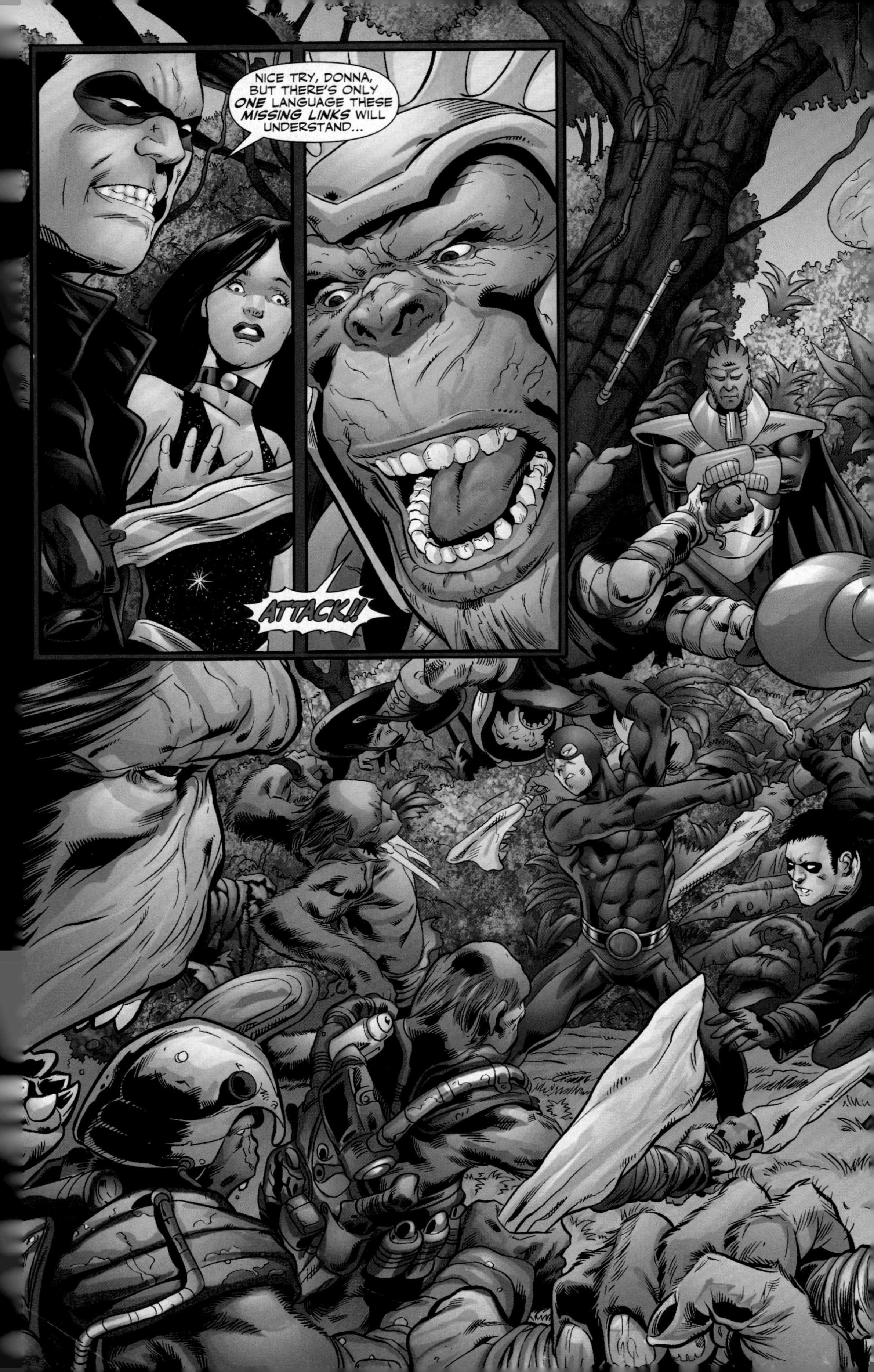
NICE TRY, DONNA, BUT THERE'S ONLY ONE LANGUAGE THESE MISSING LINKS WILL UNDERSTAND...
ATTACK!!

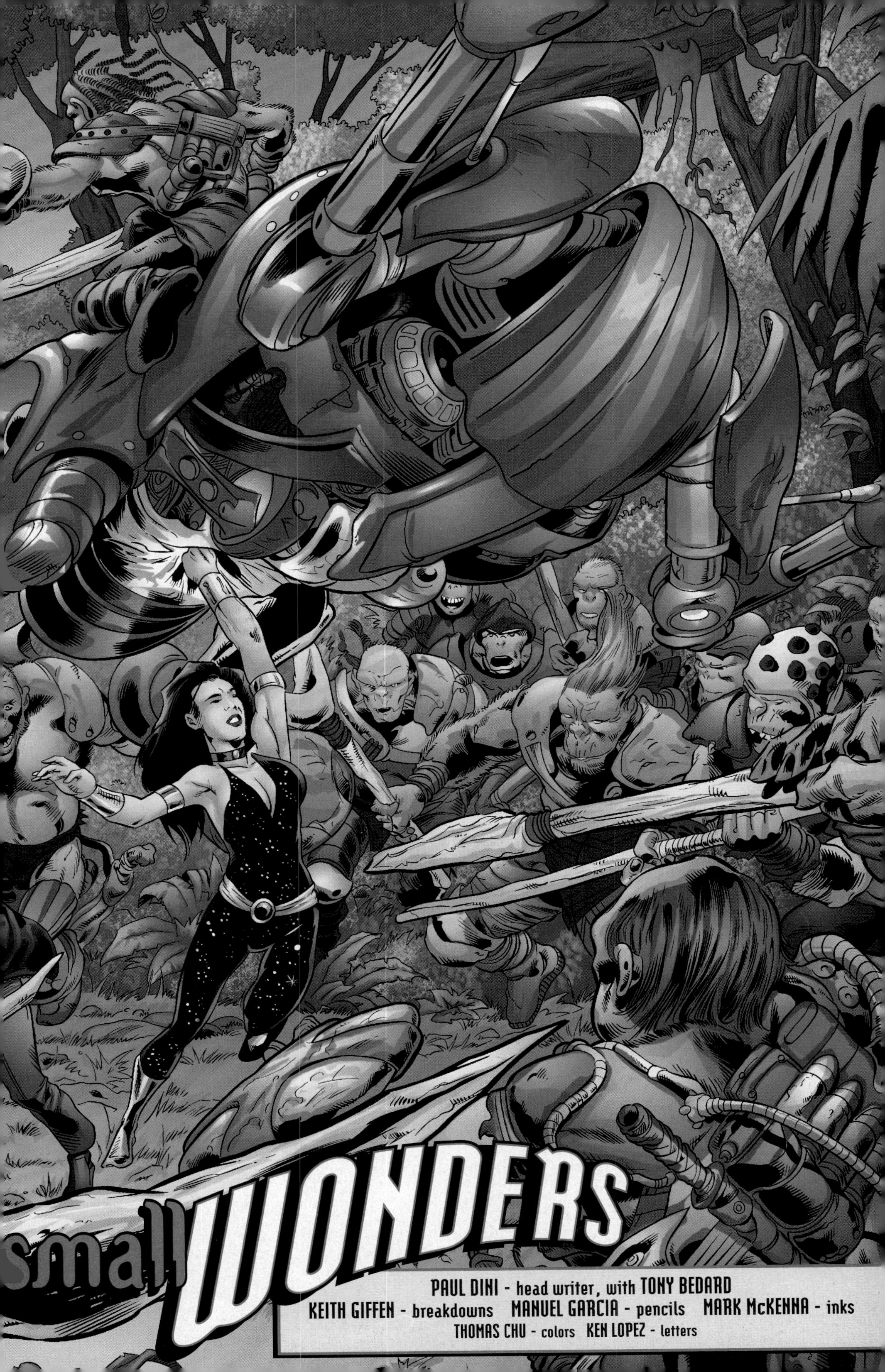
small WONDERS
PAUL DINI - head writer, with TONY BEDARD
KEITH GIFFEN - breakdowns MANUEL GARCIA - pencils MARK McKENNA - inks
THOMAS CHU - colors KEN LOPEZ - letters

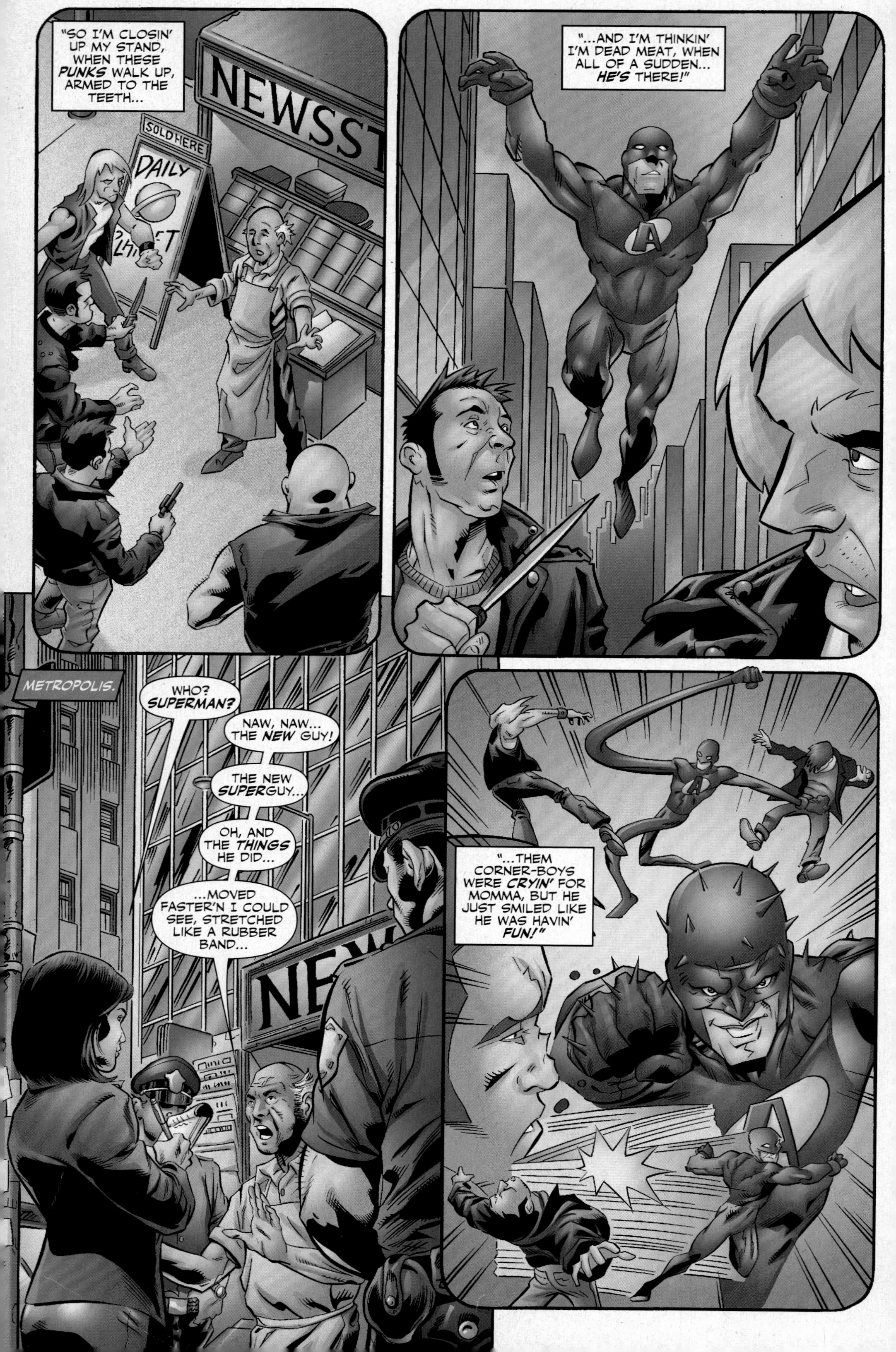
"SO I'M CLOSIN' UP MY STAND, WHEN THESE PUNKS WALK UP, ARMED TO THE TEETH...
NEWSST
SOLD HERE
DAILY
"...AND I'M THINKIN' I'M DEAD MEAT, WHEN ALL OF A SUDDEN... HE'S THERE!"
METROPOLIS.
WHO? SUPERMAN?
NAW, NAW... THE NEW GUY!
THE NEW SUPERGUY...
OH, AND THE THINGS HE DID...
...MOVED FASTER'N I COULD SEE, STRETCHED LIKE A RUBBER BAND...
"...THEM CORNER-BOYS WERE CRYIN' FOR MOMMA, BUT HE JUST SMILED LIKE HE WAS HAVIN' FUN!"

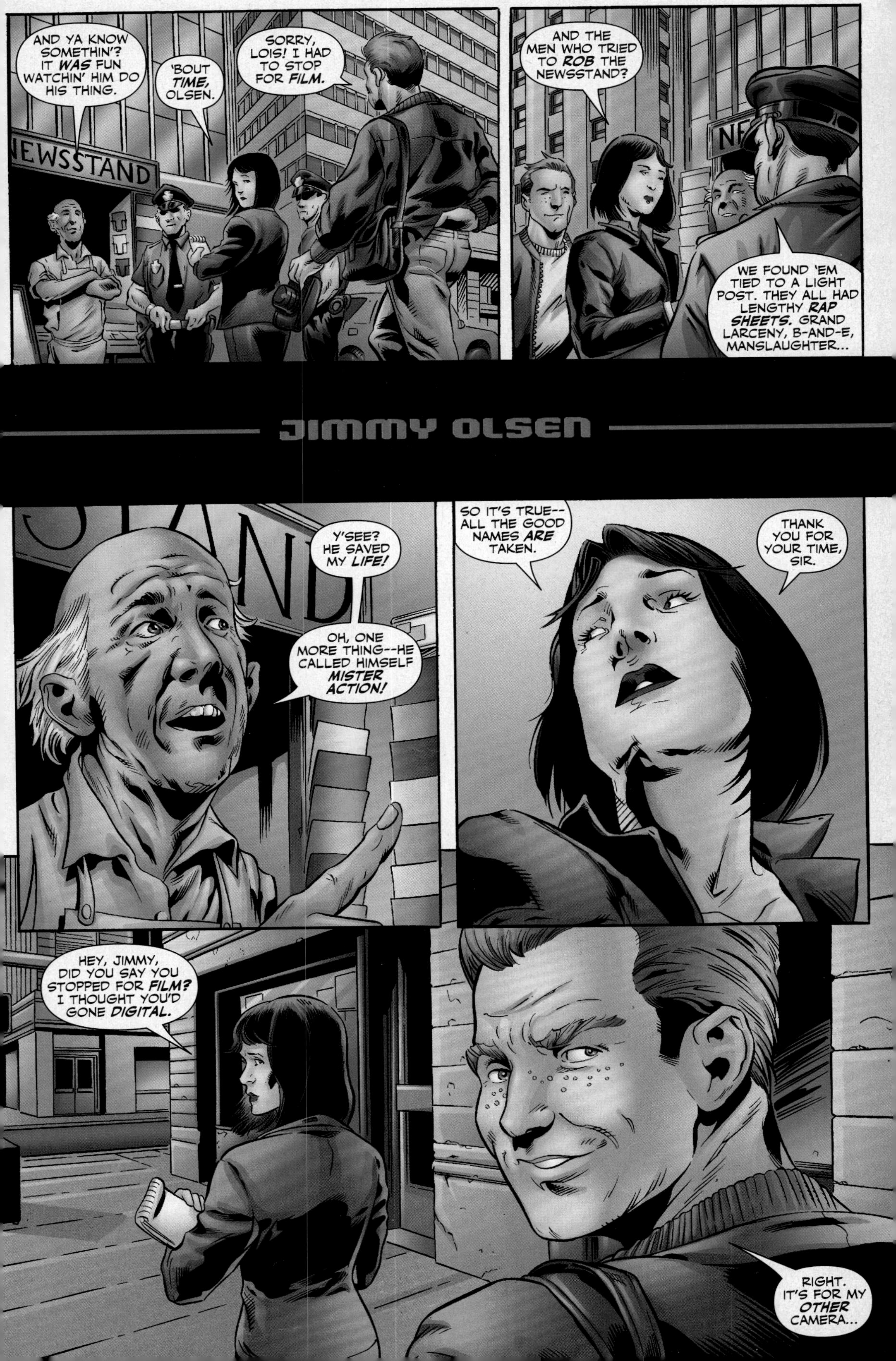
AND YA KNOW SOMETHIN'? IT WAS FUN WATCHIN' HIM DO HIS THING.
'BOUT TIME, OLSEN.
SORRY, LOIS! I HAD TO STOP FOR FILM.
NEWSSTAND
AND THE MEN WHO TRIED TO ROB THE NEWSSTAND?
WE FOUND 'EM TIED TO A LIGHT POST. THEY ALL HAD LENGTHY RAP SHEETS. GRAND LARCENY, B-AND-E, MANSLAUGHTER...
JIMMY OLSEN
Y'SEE? HE SAVED MY LIFE!
OH, ONE MORE THING--HE CALLED HIMSELF MISTER ACTION!
SO IT'S TRUE-- ALL THE GOOD NAMES ARE TAKEN.
THANK YOU FOR YOUR TIME, SIR.
HEY, JIMMY, DID YOU SAY YOU STOPPED FOR FILM? I THOUGHT YOU'D GONE DIGITAL.
RIGHT. IT'S FOR MY OTHER CAMERA...

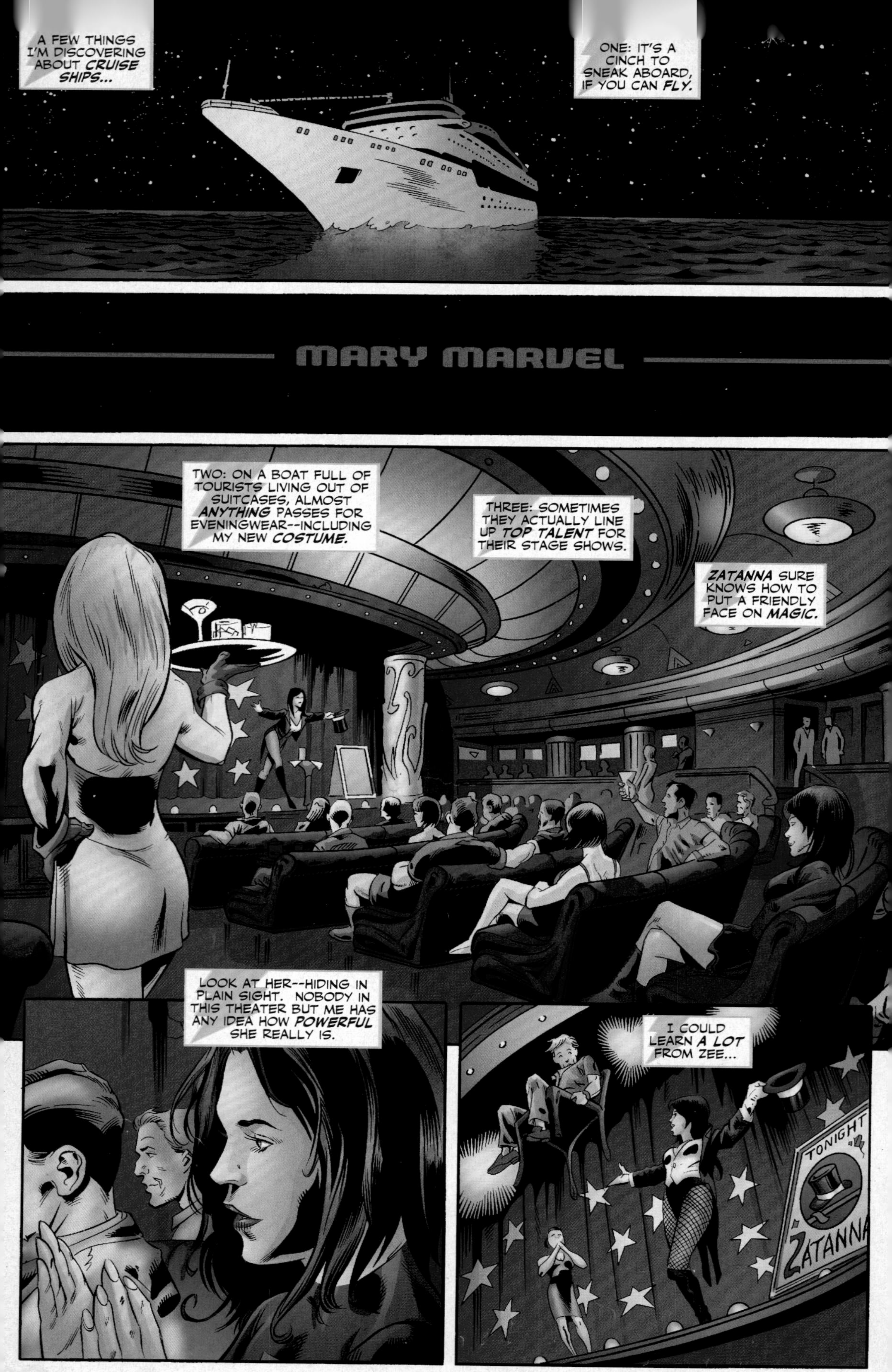
A FEW THINGS I'M DISCOVERING ABOUT CRUISE SHIPS...
ONE: IT'S A CINCH TO SNEAK ABOARD, IF YOU CAN FLY.
MARY MARVEL
TWO: ON A BOAT FULL OF TOURISTS LIVING OUT OF SUITCASES, ALMOST ANYTHING PASSES FOR EVENINGWEAR--INCLUDING MY NEW COSTUME.
THREE: SOMETIMES THEY ACTUALLY LINE UP TOP TALENT FOR THEIR STAGE SHOWS.
ZATANNA SURE KNOWS HOW TO PUT A FRIENDLY FACE ON MAGIC.
LOOK AT HER--HIDING IN PLAIN SIGHT. NOBODY IN THIS THEATER BUT ME HAS ANY IDEA HOW POWERFUL SHE REALLY IS.
I COULD LEARN A LOT FROM ZEE...
TONIGHT
ZATANNA

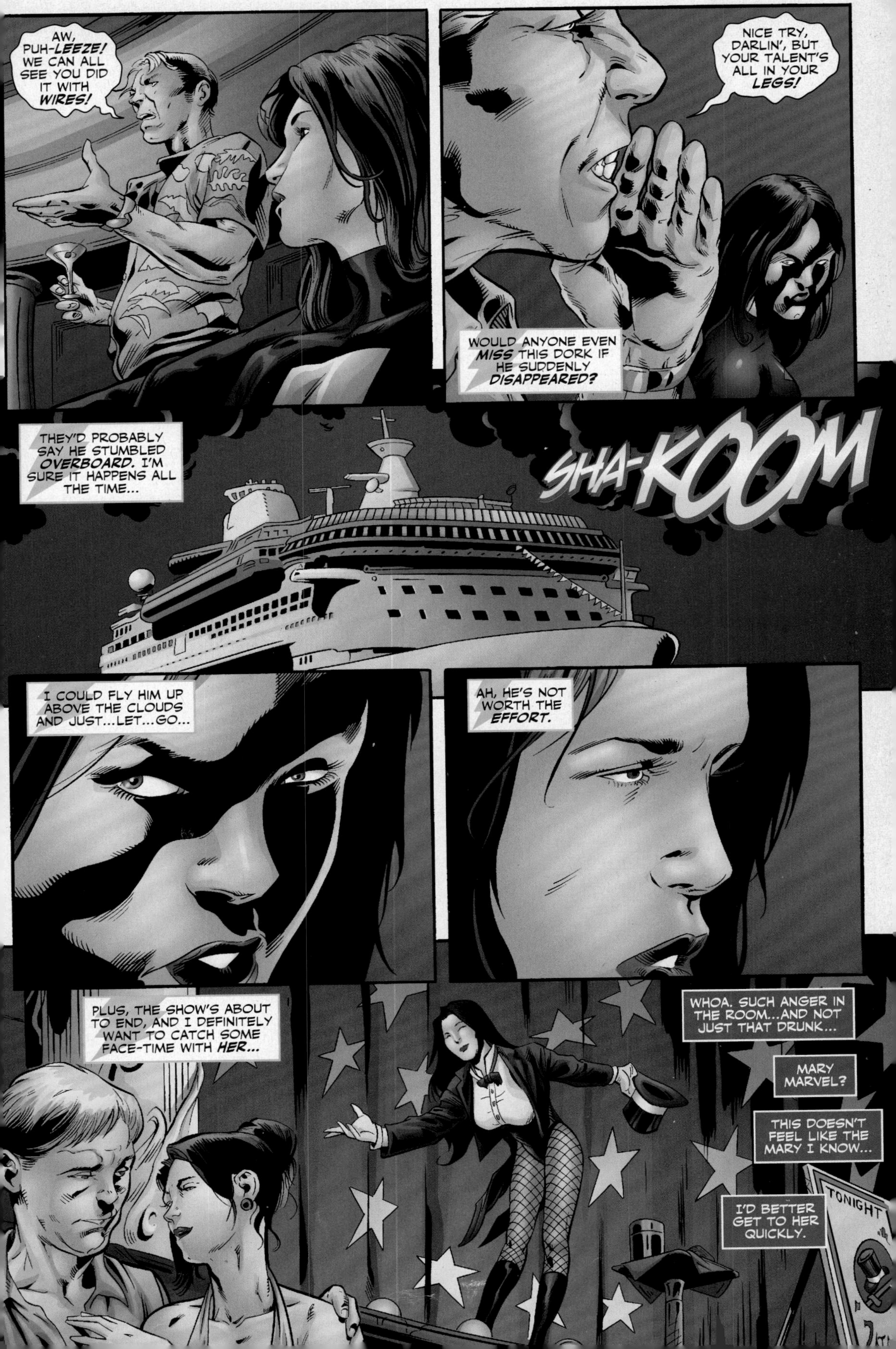
AW, PUH-LEEZE! WE CAN ALL SEE YOU DID IT WITH WIRES!
NICE TRY, DARLIN', BUT YOUR TALENT'S ALL IN YOUR LEGS!
WOULD ANYONE EVEN MISS THIS DORK IF HE SUDDENLY DISAPPEARED?
THEY'D PROBABLY SAY HE STUMBLED OVERBOARD. I'M SURE IT HAPPENS ALL THE TIME...
SHA-KOOM
I COULD FLY HIM UP ABOVE THE CLOUDS AND JUST...LET...GO...
AH, HE'S NOT WORTH THE EFFORT.
PLUS, THE SHOW'S ABOUT TO END, AND I DEFINITELY WANT TO CATCH SOME FACE-TIME WITH HER...
WHOA. SUCH ANGER IN THE ROOM...AND NOT JUST THAT DRUNK...
MARY MARVEL?
THIS DOESN'T FEEL LIKE THE MARY I KNOW...
I'D BETTER GET TO HER QUICKLY.
TONIGHT

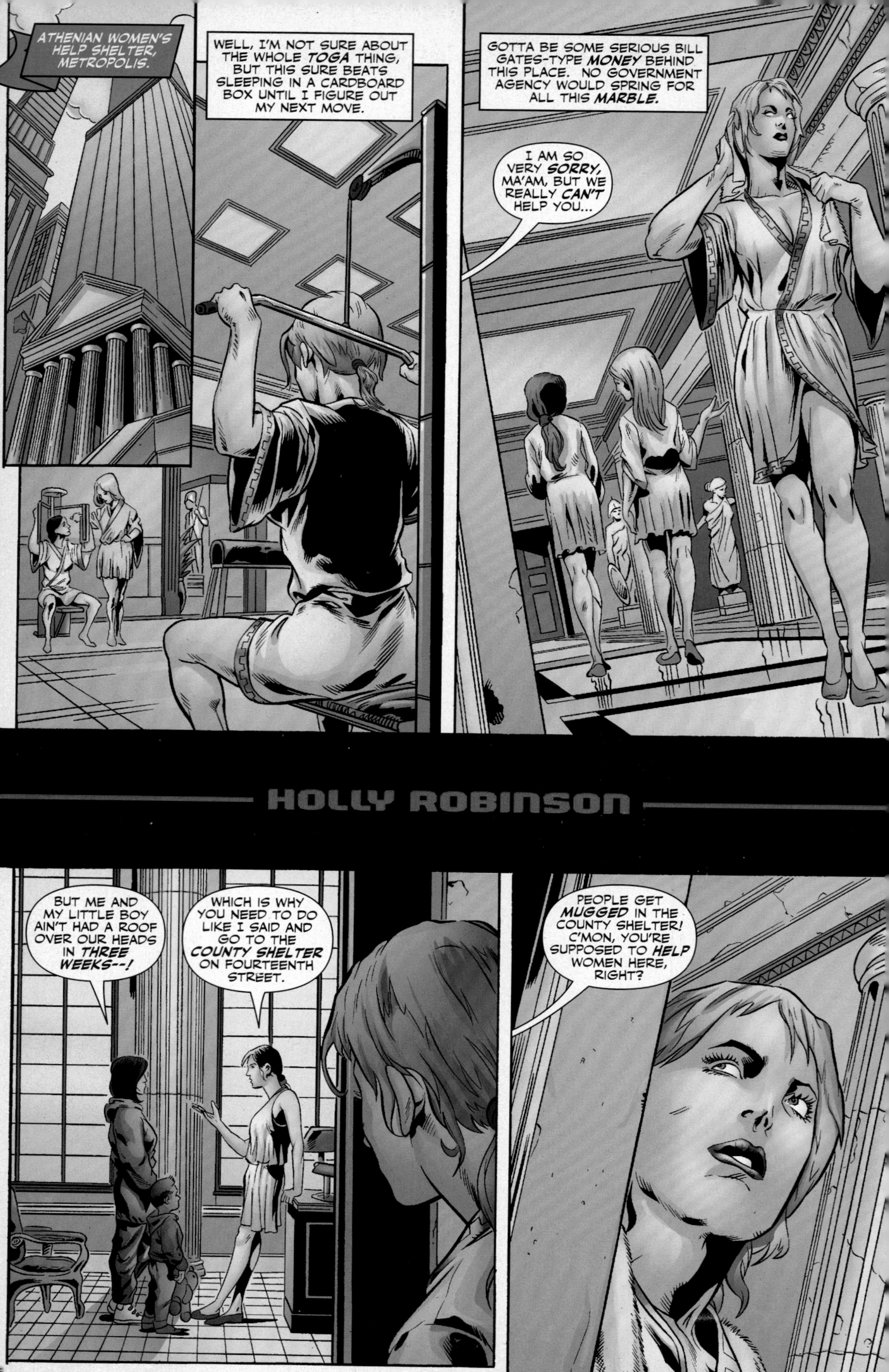
ATHENIAN WOMEN'S HELP SHELTER, METROPOLIS.
WELL, I'M NOT SURE ABOUT THE WHOLE TOGA THING, BUT THIS SURE BEATS SLEEPING IN A CARDBOARD BOX UNTIL I FIGURE OUT MY NEXT MOVE.
GOTTA BE SOME SERIOUS BILL GATES-TYPE MONEY BEHIND THIS PLACE. NO GOVERNMENT AGENCY WOULD SPRING FOR ALL THIS MARBLE.
I AM SO VERY SORRY, MA'AM, BUT WE REALLY CAN'T HELP YOU...
HOLLY ROBINSON
BUT ME AND MY LITTLE BOY AIN'T HAD A ROOF OVER OUR HEADS IN THREE WEEKS--!
WHICH IS WHY YOU NEED TO DO LIKE I SAID AND GO TO THE COUNTY SHELTER ON FOURTEENTH STREET.
PEOPLE GET MUGGED IN THE COUNTY SHELTER! C'MON, YOU'RE SUPPOSED TO HELP WOMEN HERE, RIGHT?

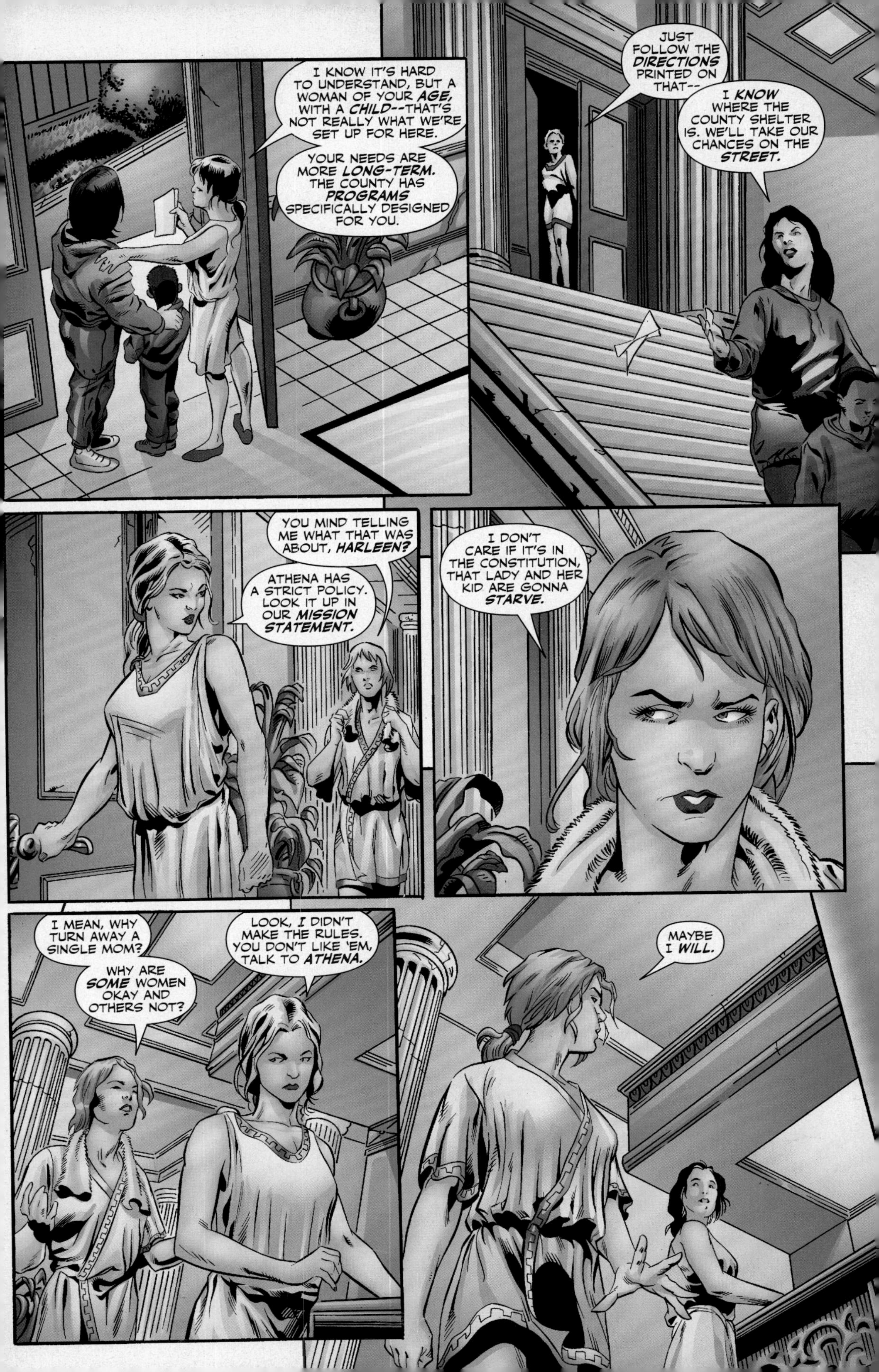
I KNOW IT'S HARD TO UNDERSTAND, BUT A WOMAN OF YOUR AGE, WITH A CHILD--THAT'S NOT REALLY WHAT WE'RE SET UP FOR HERE.
YOUR NEEDS ARE MORE LONG-TERM. THE COUNTY HAS PROGRAMS SPECIFICALLY DESIGNED FOR YOU.
JUST FOLLOW THE DIRECTIONS PRINTED ON THAT--
I KNOW WHERE THE COUNTY SHELTER IS. WE'LL TAKE OUR CHANCES ON THE STREET.
YOU MIND TELLING ME WHAT THAT WAS ABOUT, HARLEEN?
ATHENA HAS A STRICT POLICY. LOOK IT UP IN OUR MISSION STATEMENT.
I DON'T CARE IF IT'S IN THE CONSTITUTION, THAT LADY AND HER KID ARE GONNA STARVE.
I MEAN, WHY TURN AWAY A SINGLE MOM?
WHY ARE SOME WOMEN OKAY AND OTHERS NOT?
LOOK, I DIDN'T MAKE THE RULES. YOU DON'T LIKE 'EM, TALK TO ATHENA.
MAYBE I WILL.

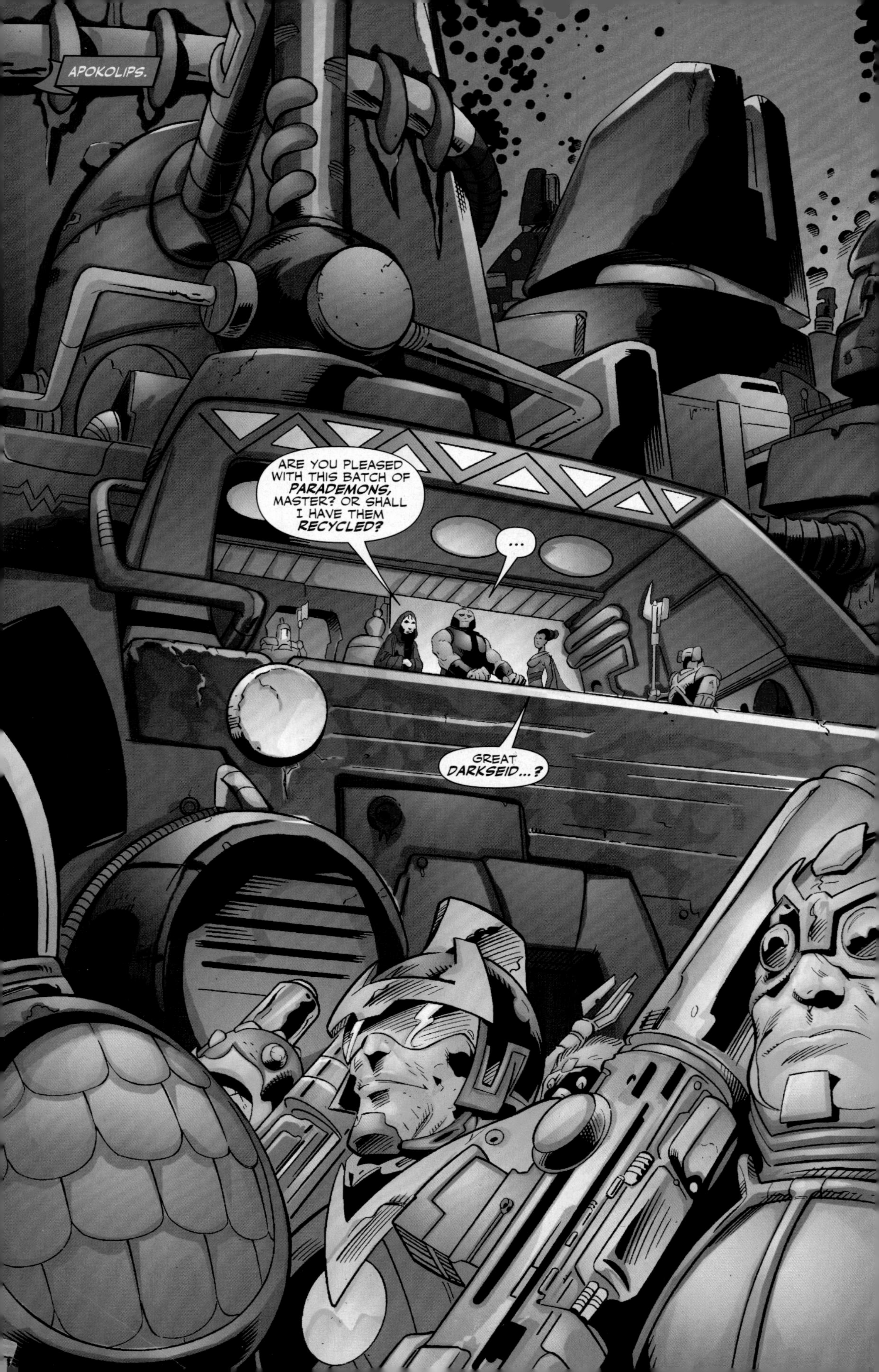
APOKOLIPS.
ARE YOU PLEASED WITH THIS BATCH OF PARADEMONS, MASTER? OR SHALL I HAVE THEM RECYCLED?
...
GREAT DARKSEID...?

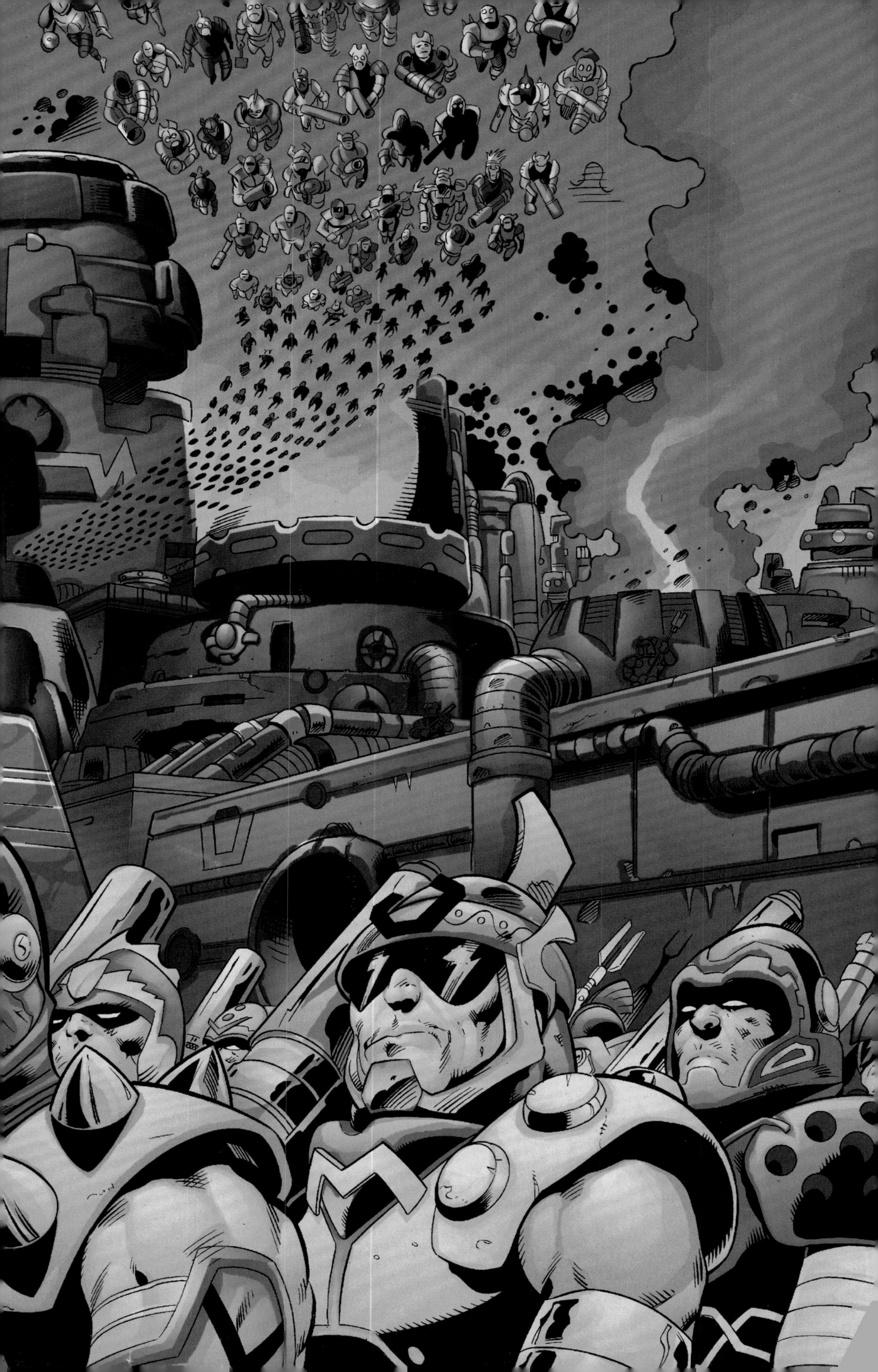

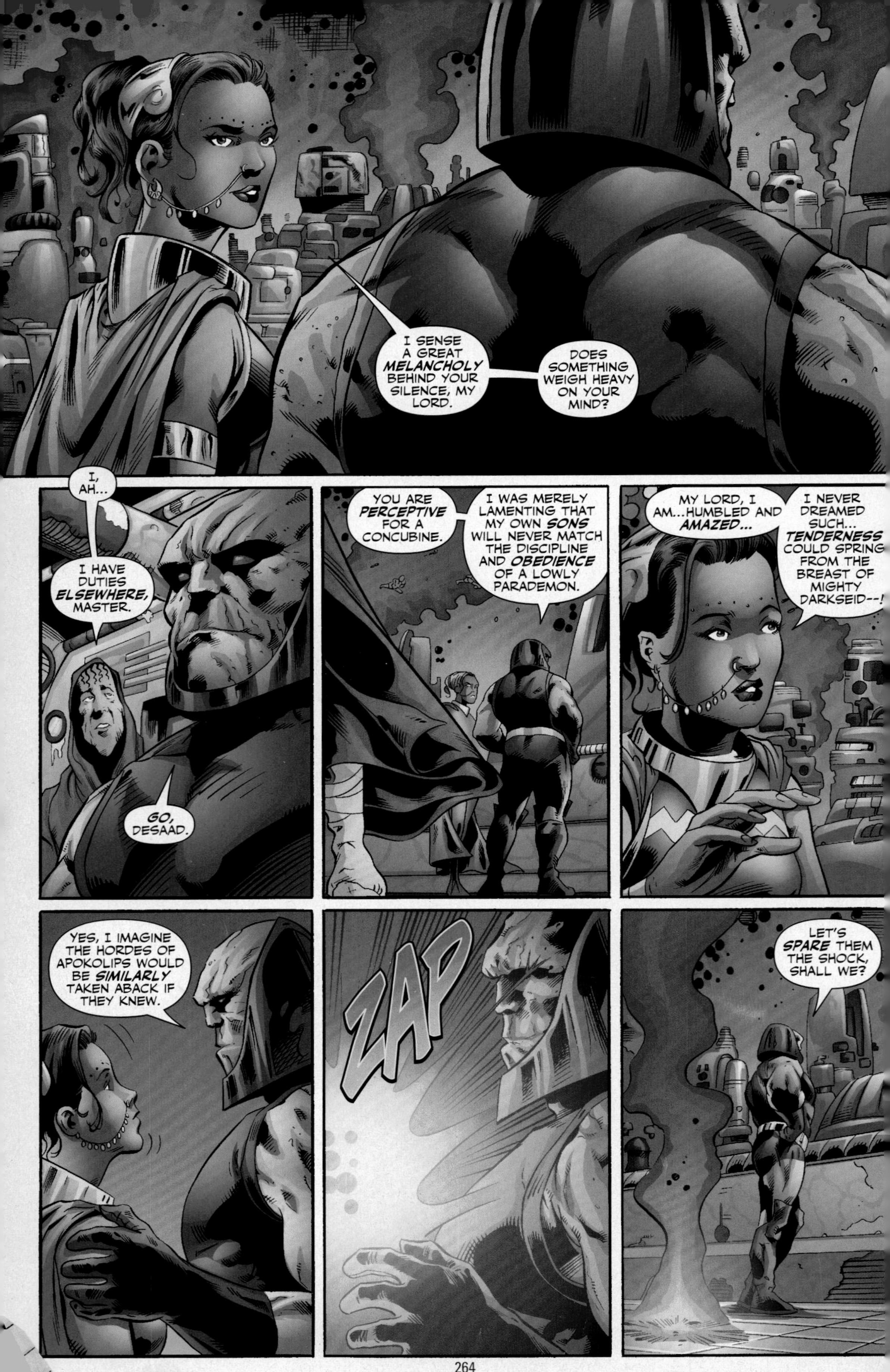
I SENSE A GREAT MELANCHOLY BEHIND YOUR SILENCE, MY LORD.
DOES SOMETHING WEIGH HEAVY ON YOUR MIND?
I, AH...
I HAVE DUTIES ELSEWHERE, MASTER.
GO, DESAAD.
YOU ARE PERCEPTIVE FOR A CONCUBINE.
I WAS MERELY LAMENTING THAT MY OWN SONS WILL NEVER MATCH THE DISCIPLINE AND OBEDIENCE OF A LOWLY PARADEMON.
MY LORD, I AM...HUMBLED AND AMAZED...
I NEVER DREAMED SUCH... TENDERNESS COULD SPRING FROM THE BREAST OF MIGHTY DARKSEID--!
YES, I IMAGINE THE HORDES OF APOKOLIPS WOULD BE SIMILARLY TAKEN ABACK IF THEY KNEW.
ZAP
LET'S SPARE THEM THE SHOCK, SHALL WE?

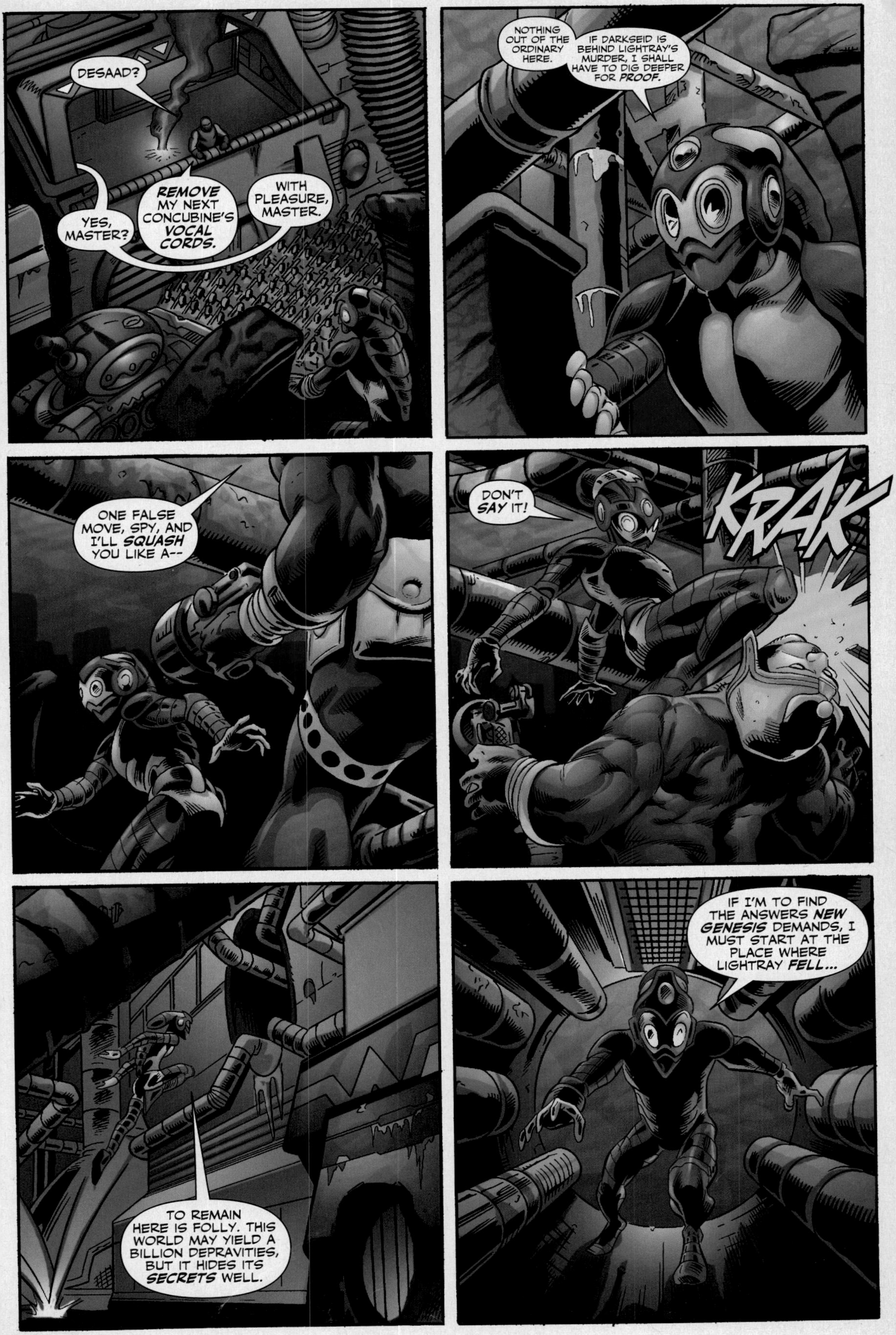
DESAAD?
YES, MASTER?
REMOVE MY NEXT CONCUBINE'S VOCAL CORDS.
WITH PLEASURE, MASTER.
NOTHING OUT OF THE ORDINARY HERE.
IF DARKSEID IS BEHIND LIGHTRAY'S MURDER, I SHALL HAVE TO DIG DEEPER FOR PROOF.
ONE FALSE MOVE, SPY, AND I'LL SQUASH YOU LIKE A--
DON'T SAY IT!
KRAK
TO REMAIN HERE IS FOLLY. THIS WORLD MAY YIELD A BILLION DEPRAVITIES, BUT IT HIDES ITS SECRETS WELL.
IF I'M TO FIND THE ANSWERS NEW GENESIS DEMANDS, I MUST START AT THE PLACE WHERE LIGHTRAY FELL...

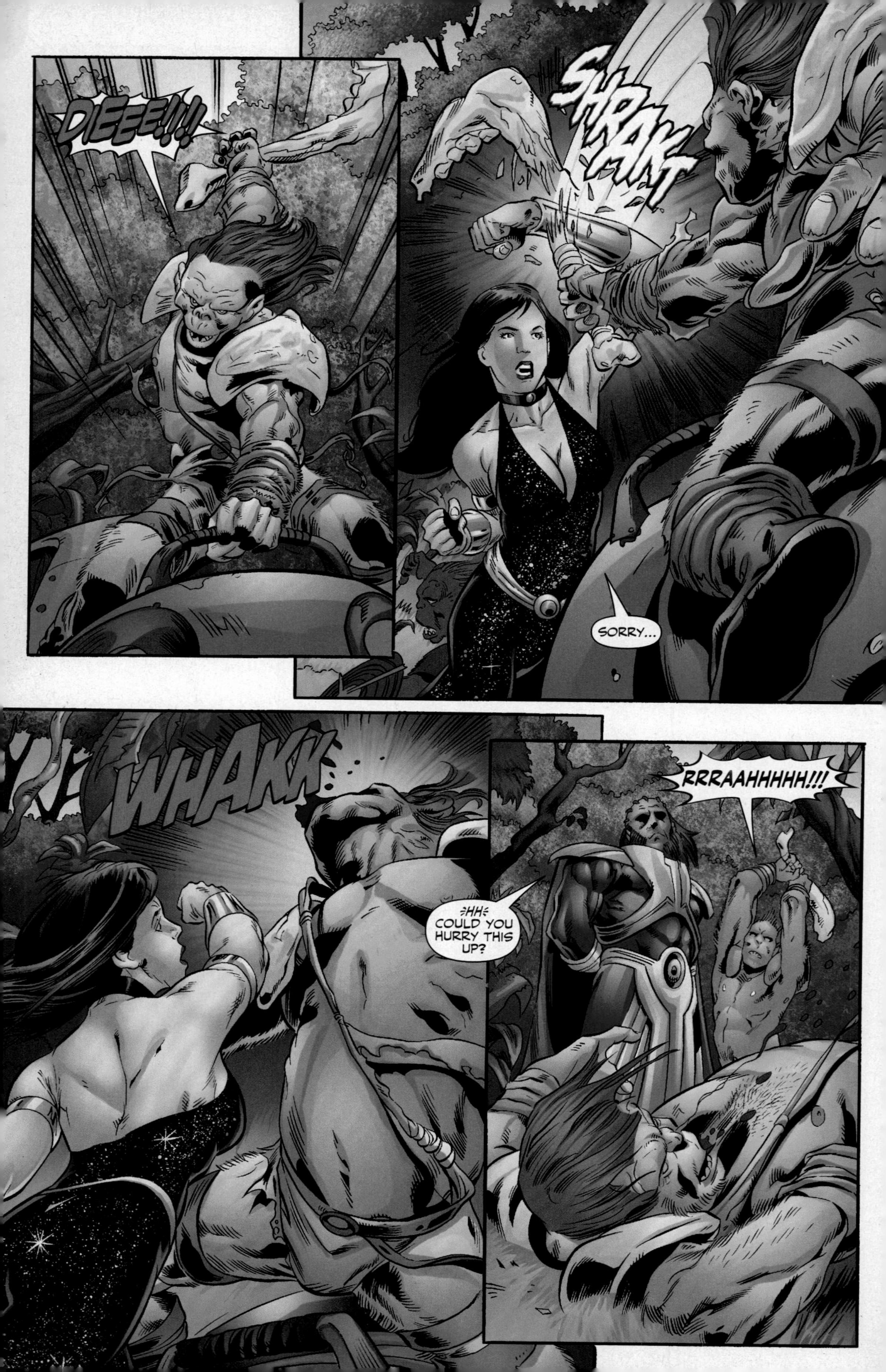
DIEEE!!!
SHRAKT
SORRY...
WHAKK
RRRAAHHHHH!!!
HH
COULD YOU HURRY THIS UP?

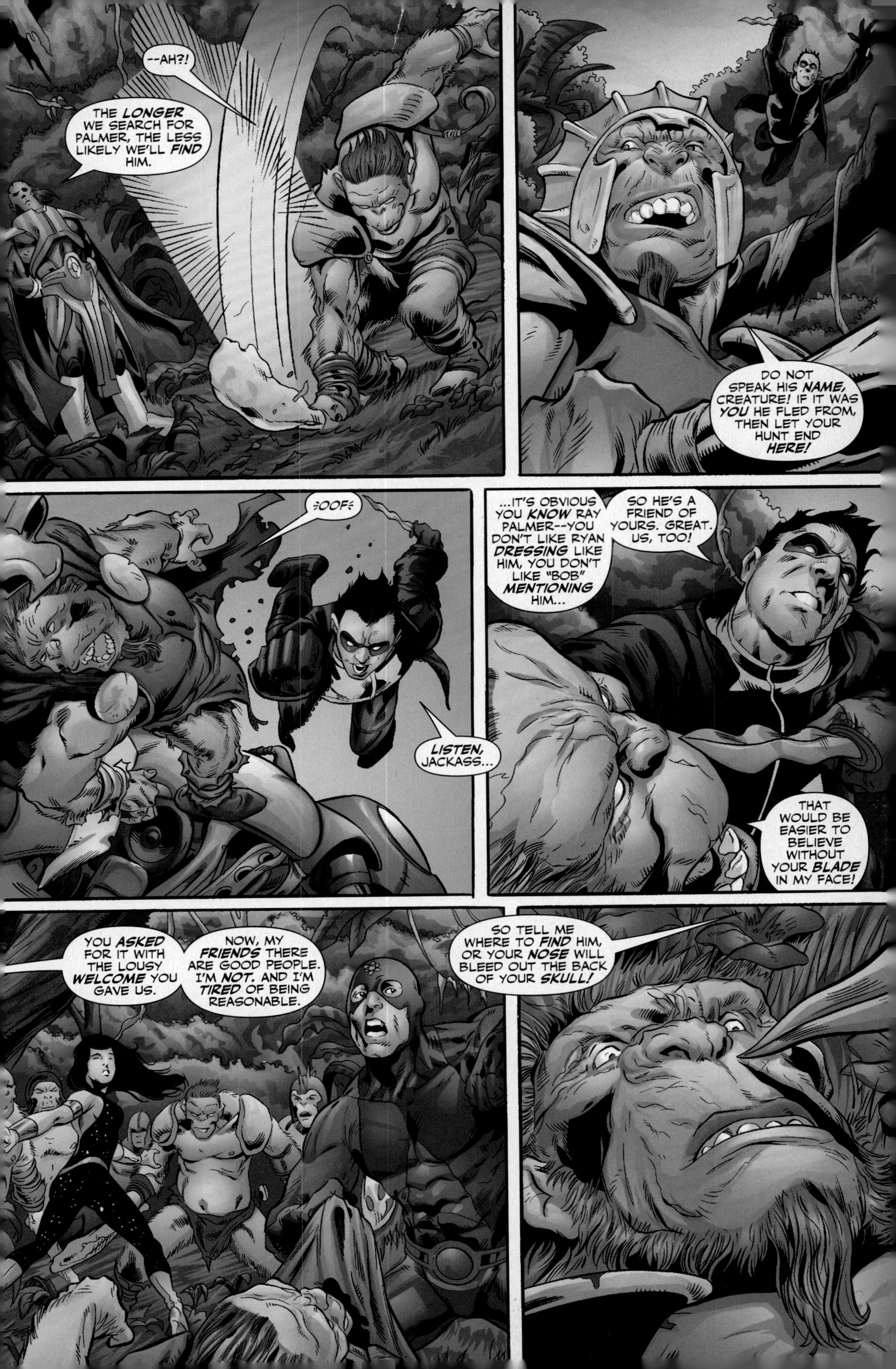
--AH?!
THE LONGER WE SEARCH FOR PALMER, THE LESS LIKELY WE'LL FIND HIM.
DO NOT SPEAK HIS NAME, CREATURE! IF IT WAS YOU HE FLED FROM, THEN LET YOUR HUNT END HERE!
OOF
LISTEN, JACKASS...
...IT'S OBVIOUS YOU KNOW RAY PALMER--YOU DON'T LIKE RYAN DRESSING LIKE HIM, YOU DON'T LIKE "BOB" MENTIONING HIM...
SO HE'S A FRIEND OF YOURS. GREAT. US, TOO!
THAT WOULD BE EASIER TO BELIEVE WITHOUT YOUR BLADE IN MY FACE!
YOU ASKED FOR IT WITH THE LOUSY WELCOME YOU GAVE US.
NOW, MY FRIENDS THERE ARE GOOD PEOPLE. I'M NOT. AND I'M TIRED OF BEING REASONABLE.
SO TELL ME WHERE TO FIND HIM, OR YOUR NOSE WILL BLEED OUT THE BACK OF YOUR SKULL!

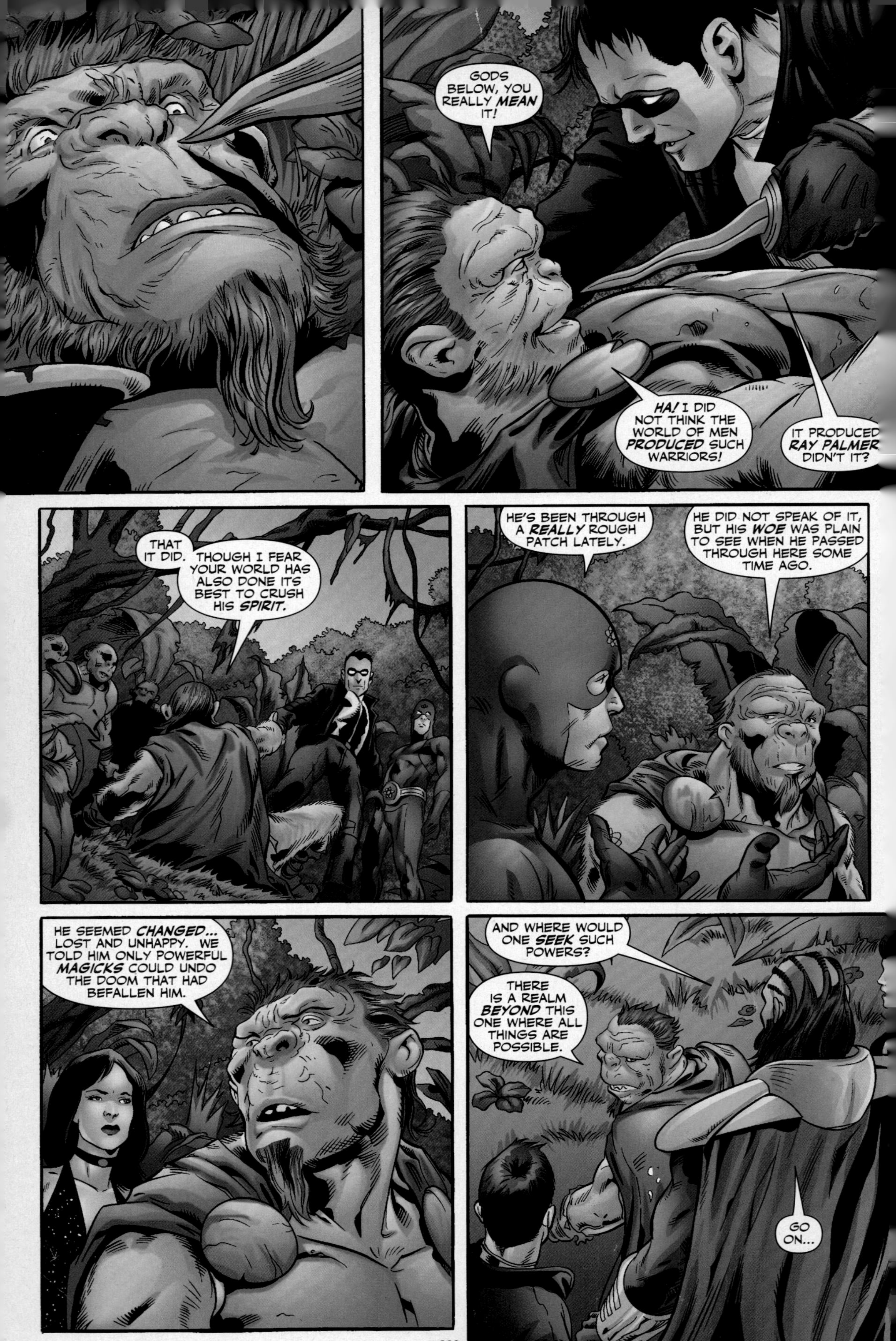
GODS BELOW, YOU REALLY MEAN IT!
HA! I DID NOT THINK THE WORLD OF MEN PRODUCED SUCH WARRIORS!
IT PRODUCED RAY PALMER DIDN'T IT?
THAT IT DID.
THOUGH I FEAR YOUR WORLD HAS ALSO DONE ITS BEST TO CRUSH HIS SPIRIT.
HE'S BEEN THROUGH A REALLY ROUGH PATCH LATELY.
HE DID NOT SPEAK OF IT, BUT HIS WOE WAS PLAIN TO SEE WHEN HE PASSED THROUGH HERE SOME TIME AGO.
HE SEEMED CHANGED... LOST AND UNHAPPY. WE TOLD HIM ONLY POWERFUL MAGICKS COULD UNDO THE DOOM THAT HAD BEFALLEN HIM.
AND WHERE WOULD ONE SEEK SUCH POWERS?
THERE IS A REALM BEYOND THIS ONE WHERE ALL THINGS ARE POSSIBLE.
GO ON...

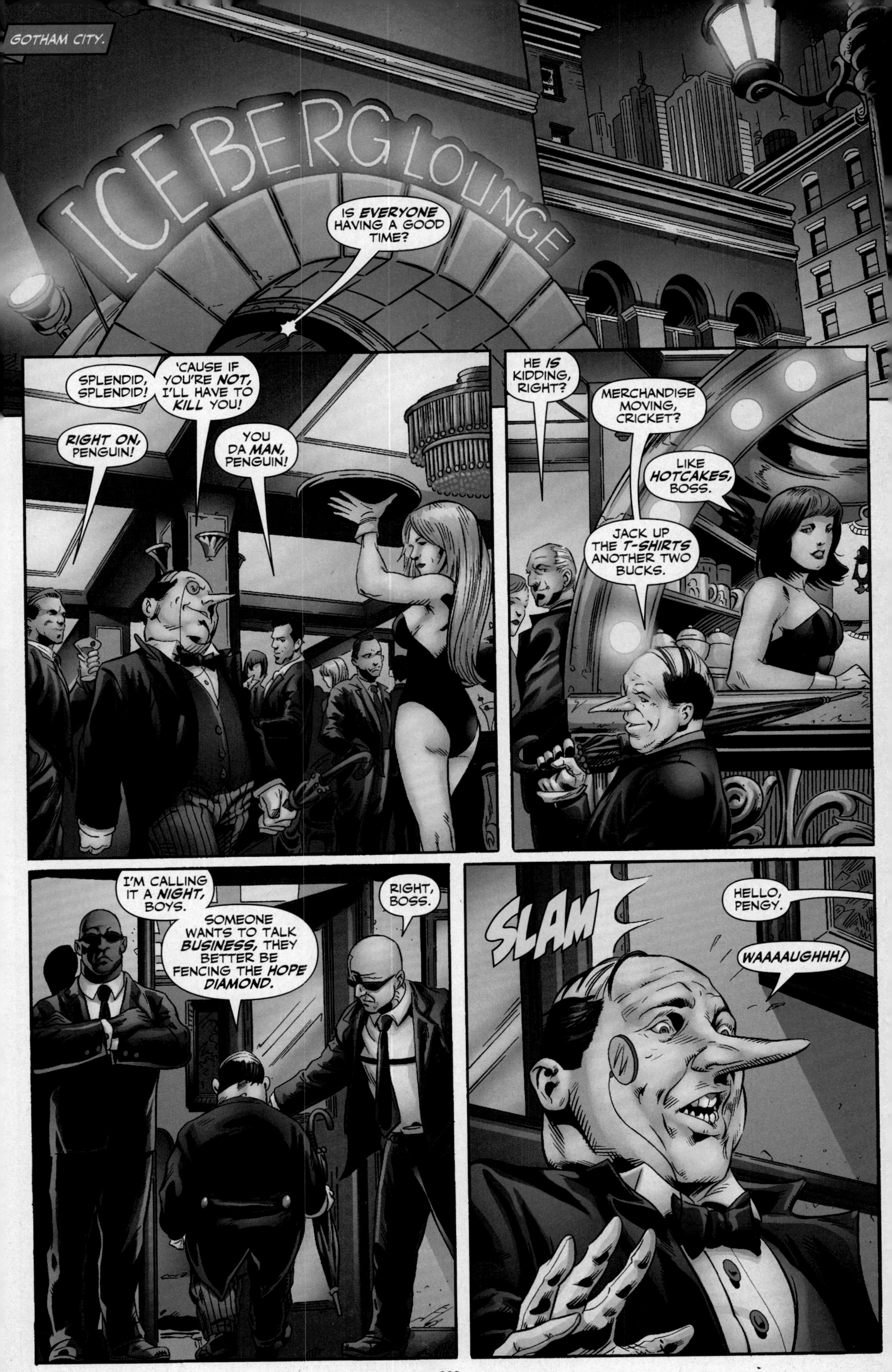
GOTHAM CITY.
ICEBERG LOUNGE
IS EVERYONE HAVING A GOOD TIME?
SPLENDID, SPLENDID!
'CAUSE IF YOU'RE NOT, I'LL HAVE TO KILL YOU!
RIGHT ON, PENGUIN!
YOU DA MAN, PENGUIN!
HE IS KIDDING, RIGHT?
MERCHANDISE MOVING, CRICKET?
LIKE HOTCAKES, BOSS.
JACK UP THE T-SHIRTS ANOTHER TWO BUCKS.
I'M CALLING IT A NIGHT, BOYS.
SOMEONE WANTS TO TALK BUSINESS, THEY BETTER BE FENCING THE HOPE DIAMOND.
RIGHT, BOSS.
SLAM
HELLO, PENGY.
WAAAAUGHHH!

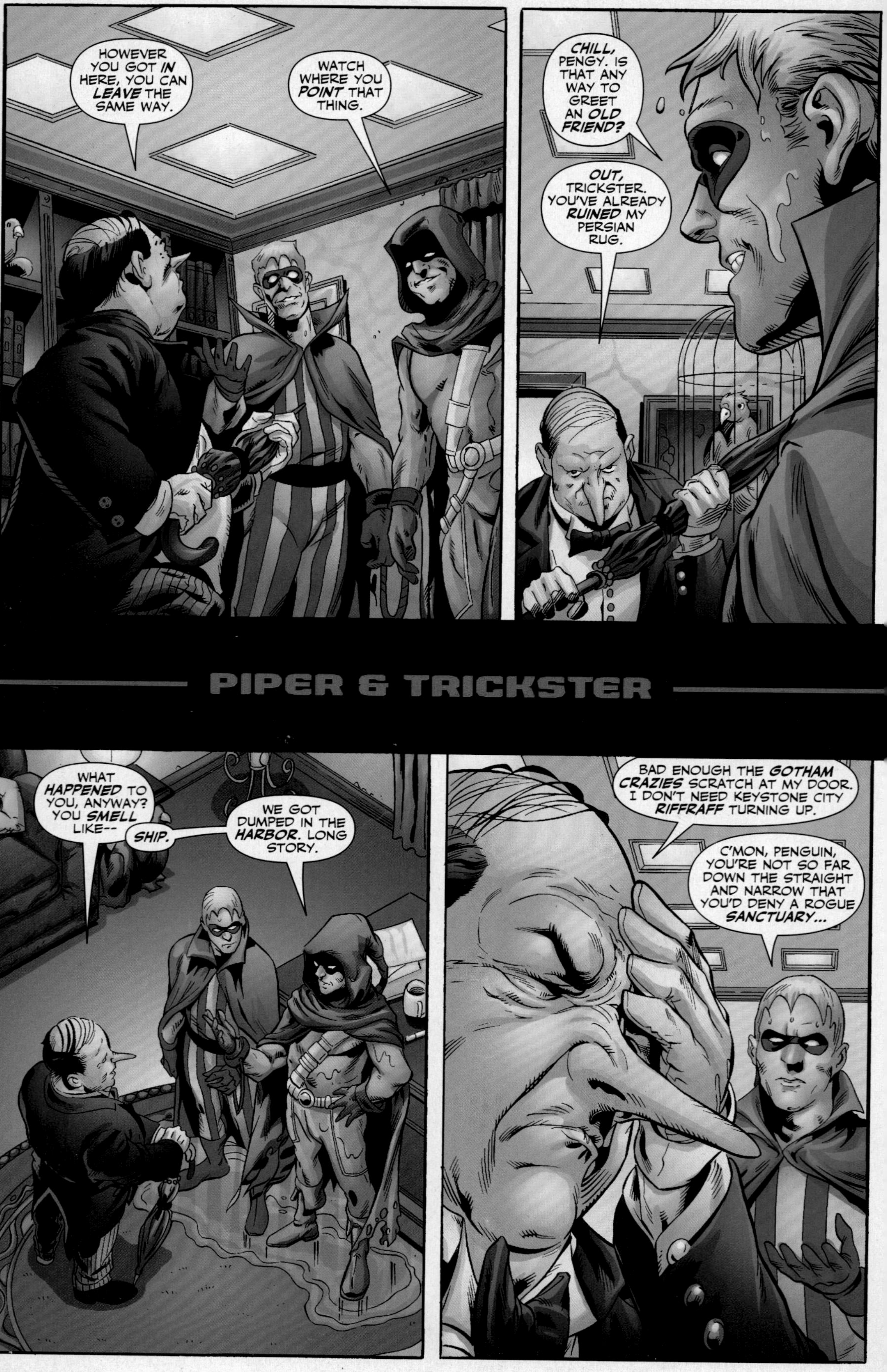
HOWEVER YOU GOT IN HERE, YOU CAN LEAVE THE SAME WAY.
WATCH WHERE YOU POINT THAT THING.
CHILL, PENGY. IS THAT ANY WAY TO GREET AN OLD FRIEND?
OUT, TRICKSTER. YOU'VE ALREADY RUINED MY PERSIAN RUG.
PIPER & TRICKSTER
WHAT HAPPENED TO YOU, ANYWAY? YOU SMELL LIKE--
SHIP.
WE GOT DUMPED IN THE HARBOR. LONG STORY.
BAD ENOUGH THE GOTHAM CRAZIES SCRATCH AT MY DOOR. I DON'T NEED KEYSTONE CITY RIFFRAFF TURNING UP.
C'MON, PENGUIN, YOU'RE NOT SO FAR DOWN THE STRAIGHT AND NARROW THAT YOU'D DENY A ROGUE SANCTUARY...

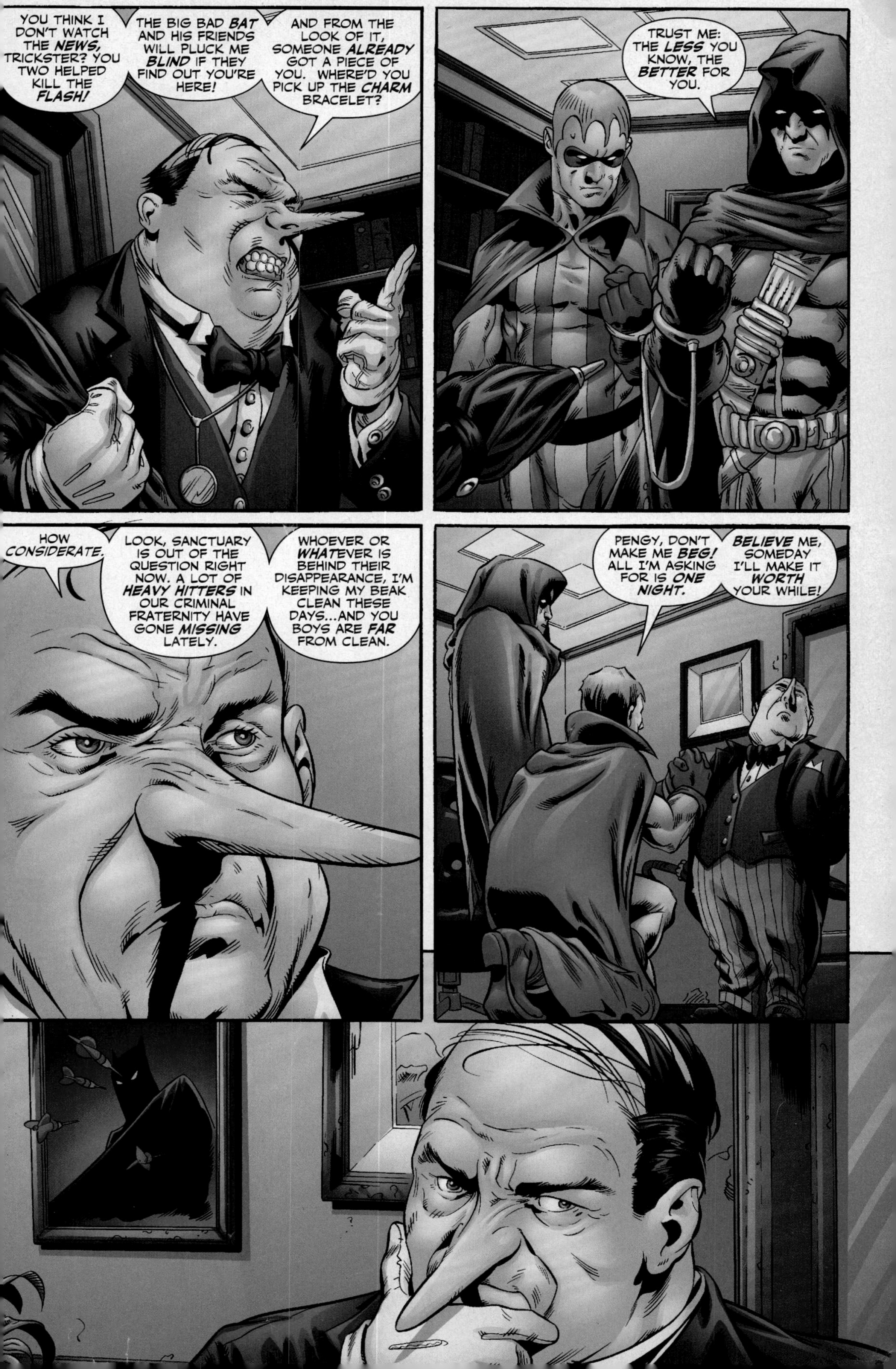
YOU THINK I DON'T WATCH THE NEWS, TRICKSTER? YOU TWO HELPED KILL THE FLASH!
THE BIG BAD BAT AND HIS FRIENDS WILL PLUCK ME BLIND IF THEY FIND OUT YOU'RE HERE!
AND FROM THE LOOK OF IT, SOMEONE ALREADY GOT A PIECE OF YOU. WHERE'D YOU PICK UP THE CHARM BRACELET?
TRUST ME: THE LESS YOU KNOW, THE BETTER FOR YOU.
HOW CONSIDERATE.
LOOK, SANCTUARY IS OUT OF THE QUESTION RIGHT NOW. A LOT OF HEAVY HITTERS IN OUR CRIMINAL FRATERNITY HAVE GONE MISSING LATELY.
WHOEVER OR WHATEVER IS BEHIND THEIR DISAPPEARANCE, I'M KEEPING MY BEAK CLEAN THESE DAYS...AND YOU BOYS ARE FAR FROM CLEAN.
PENGY, DON'T MAKE ME BEG! ALL I'M ASKING FOR IS ONE NIGHT.
BELIEVE ME, SOMEDAY I'LL MAKE IT WORTH YOUR WHILE!

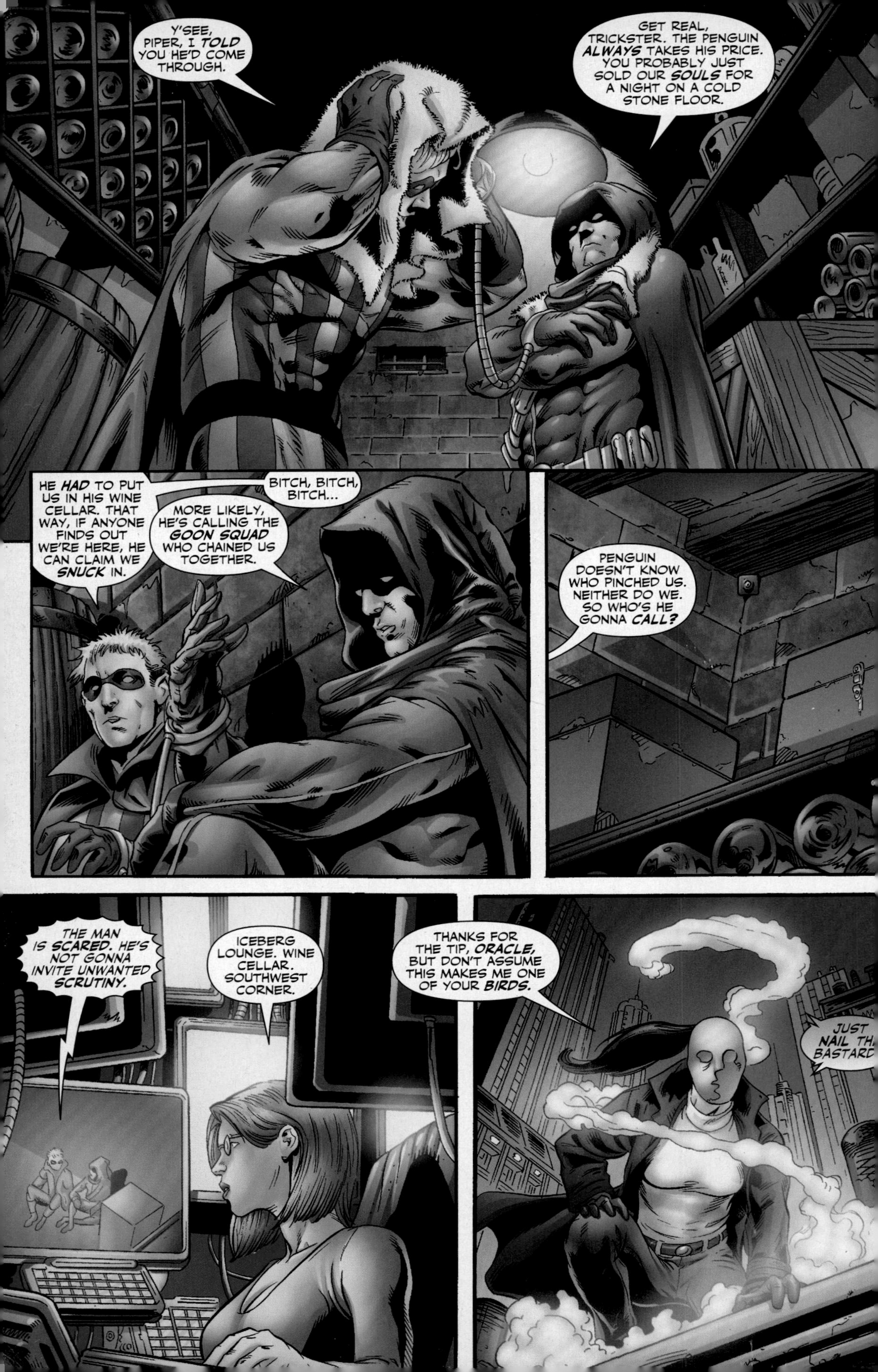
Y'SEE, PIPER, I *TOLD* YOU HE'D COME THROUGH.
GET REAL, TRICKSTER. THE PENGUIN *ALWAYS* TAKES HIS PRICE. YOU PROBABLY JUST SOLD OUR *SOULS* FOR A NIGHT ON A COLD STONE FLOOR.
HE *HAD* TO PUT US IN HIS WINE CELLAR. THAT WAY, IF ANYONE FINDS OUT WE'RE HERE, HE CAN CLAIM WE *SNUCK* IN.
BITCH, BITCH, BITCH...
MORE LIKELY, HE'S CALLING THE *GOON SQUAD* WHO CHAINED US TOGETHER.
PENGUIN DOESN'T KNOW WHO PINCHED US. NEITHER DO WE. SO WHO'S HE GONNA *CALL?*
THE MAN IS *SCARED*. HE'S NOT GONNA INVITE UNWANTED *SCRUTINY.*
ICEBERG LOUNGE. WINE CELLAR. SOUTHWEST CORNER.
THANKS FOR THE TIP, *ORACLE,* BUT DON'T ASSUME THIS MAKES ME ONE OF YOUR *BIRDS.*

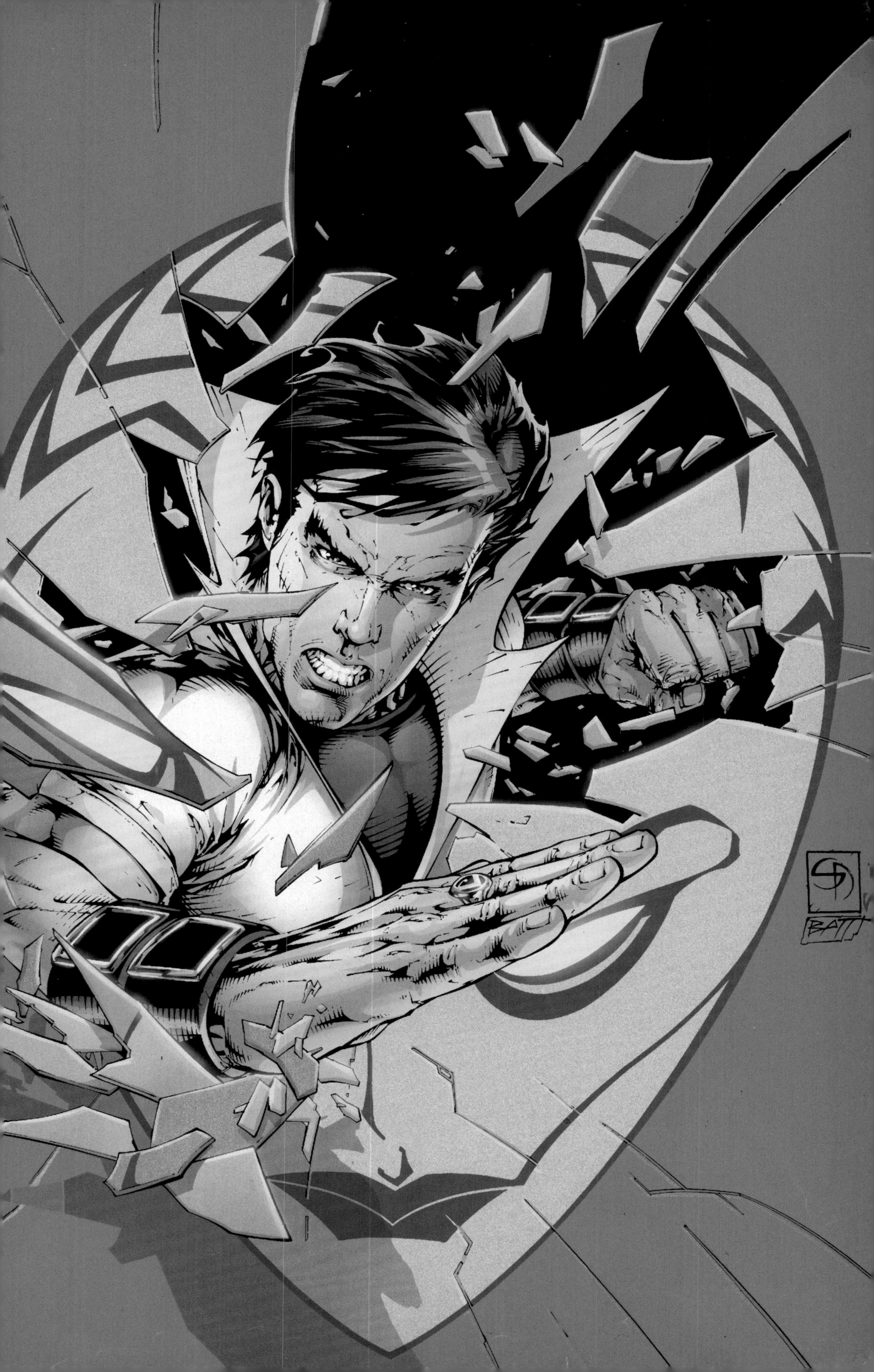
BATT

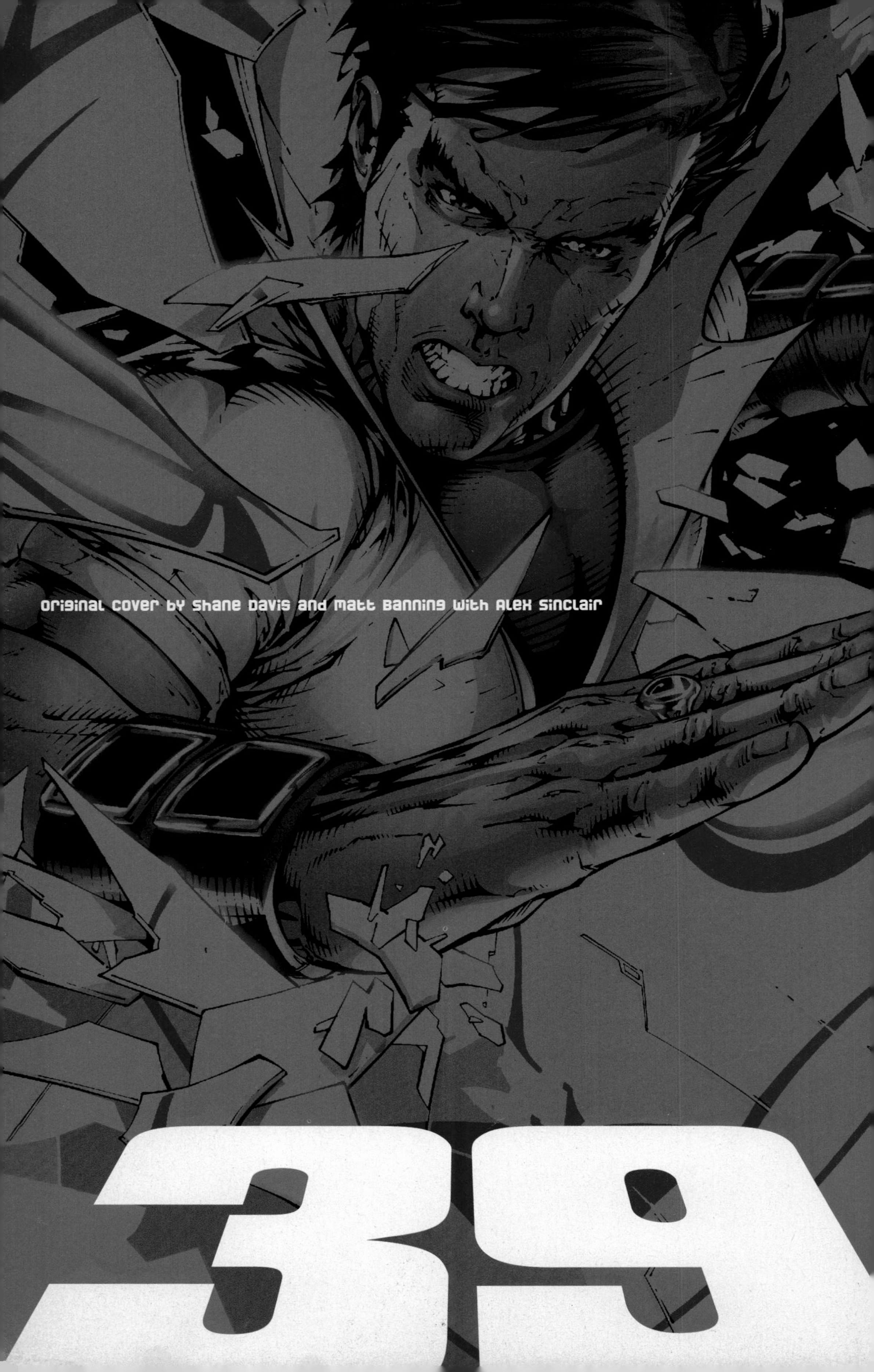
original cover by Shane Davis and Matt Banning with Alex Sinclair
39

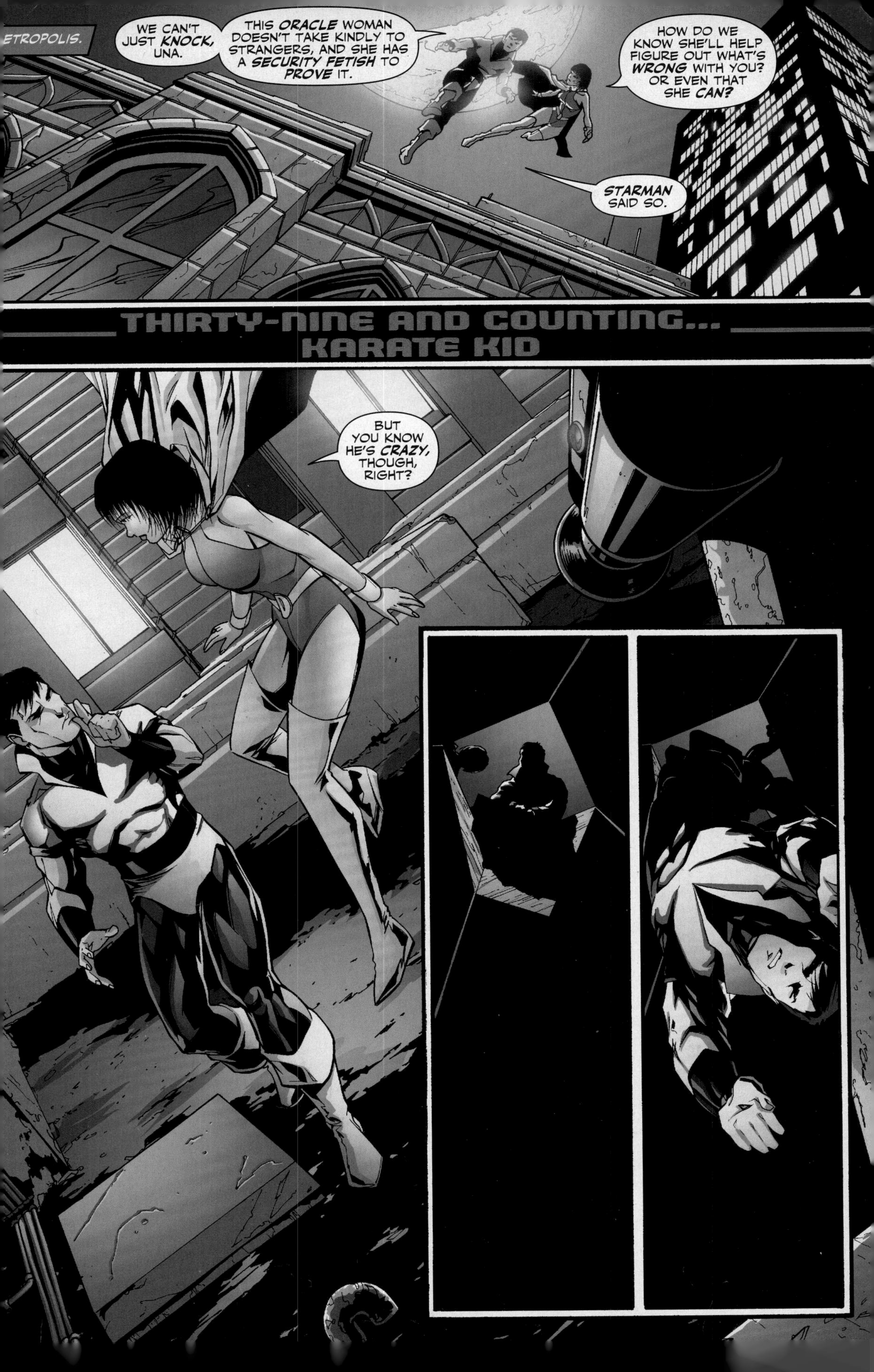
ETROPOLIS.
WE CAN'T JUST KNOCK, UNA.
THIS ORACLE WOMAN DOESN'T TAKE KINDLY TO STRANGERS, AND SHE HAS A SECURITY FETISH TO PROVE IT.
HOW DO WE KNOW SHE'LL HELP FIGURE OUT WHAT'S WRONG WITH YOU? OR EVEN THAT SHE CAN?
STARMAN SAID SO.
THIRTY-NINE AND COUNTING... KARATE KID
BUT YOU KNOW HE'S CRAZY, THOUGH, RIGHT?

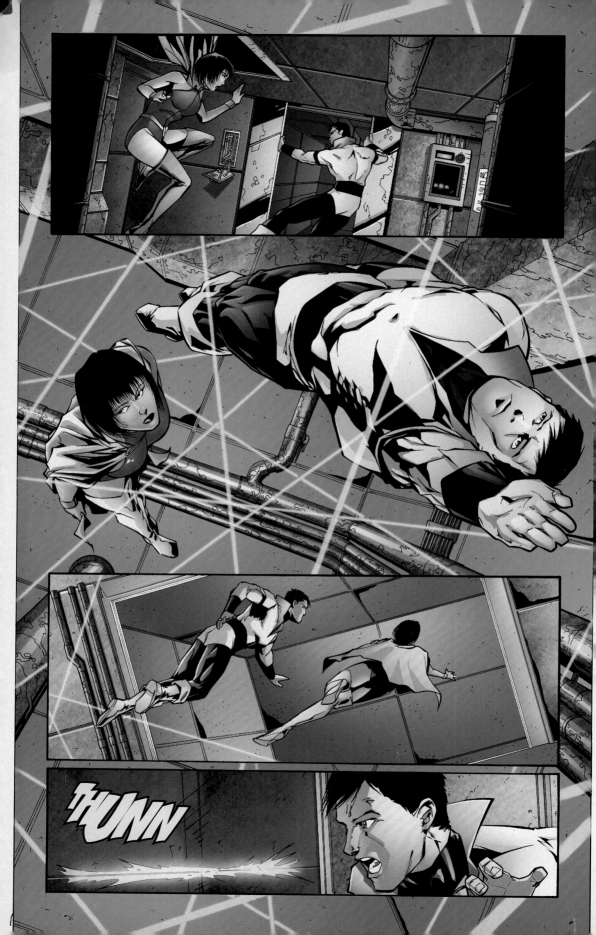

THUNN

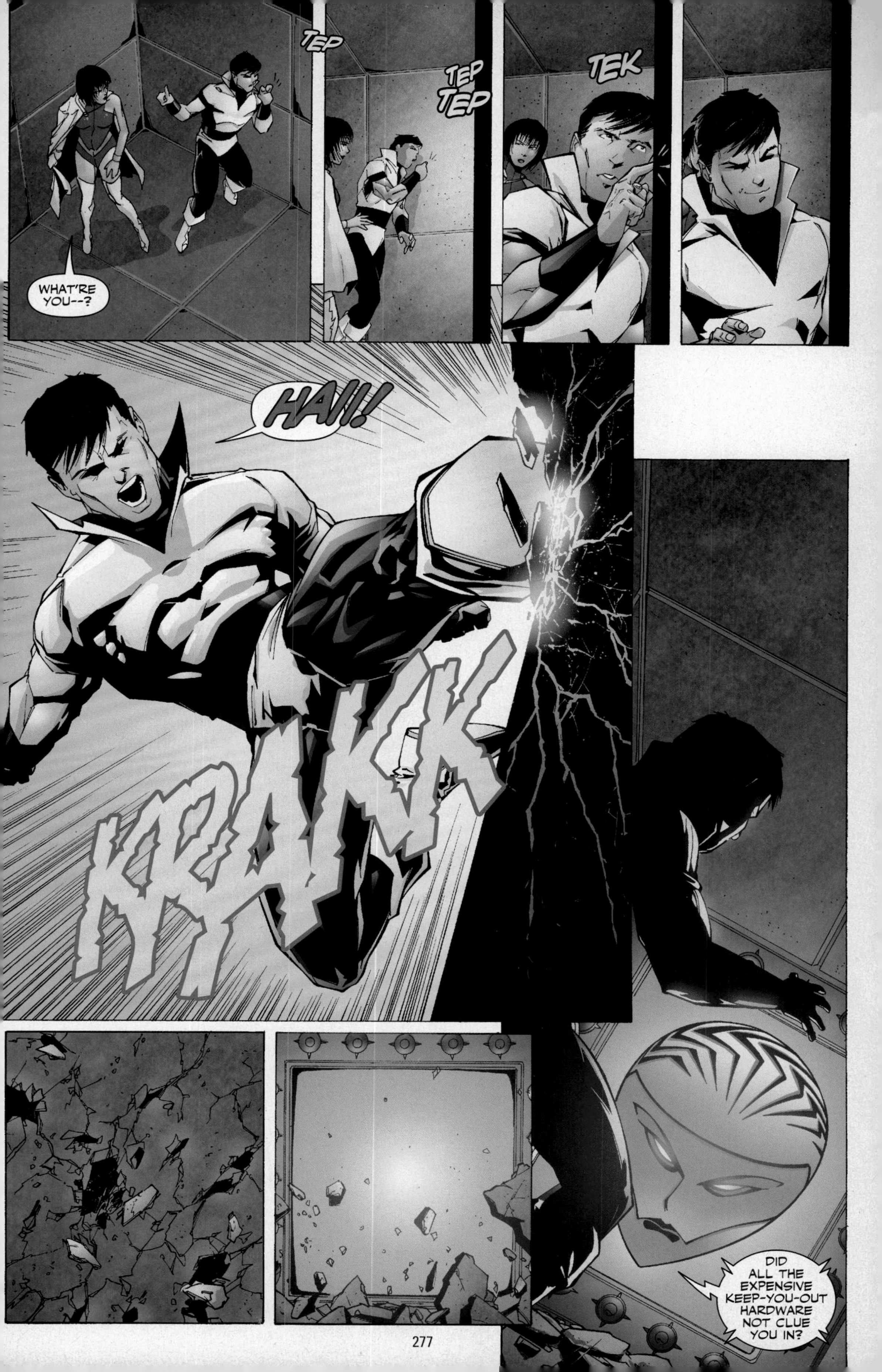
WHAT'RE YOU--?
TEP
TEP TEP
TEK
HAII!
KRAKK
DID ALL THE EXPENSIVE KEEP-YOU-OUT HARDWARE NOT CLUE YOU IN?

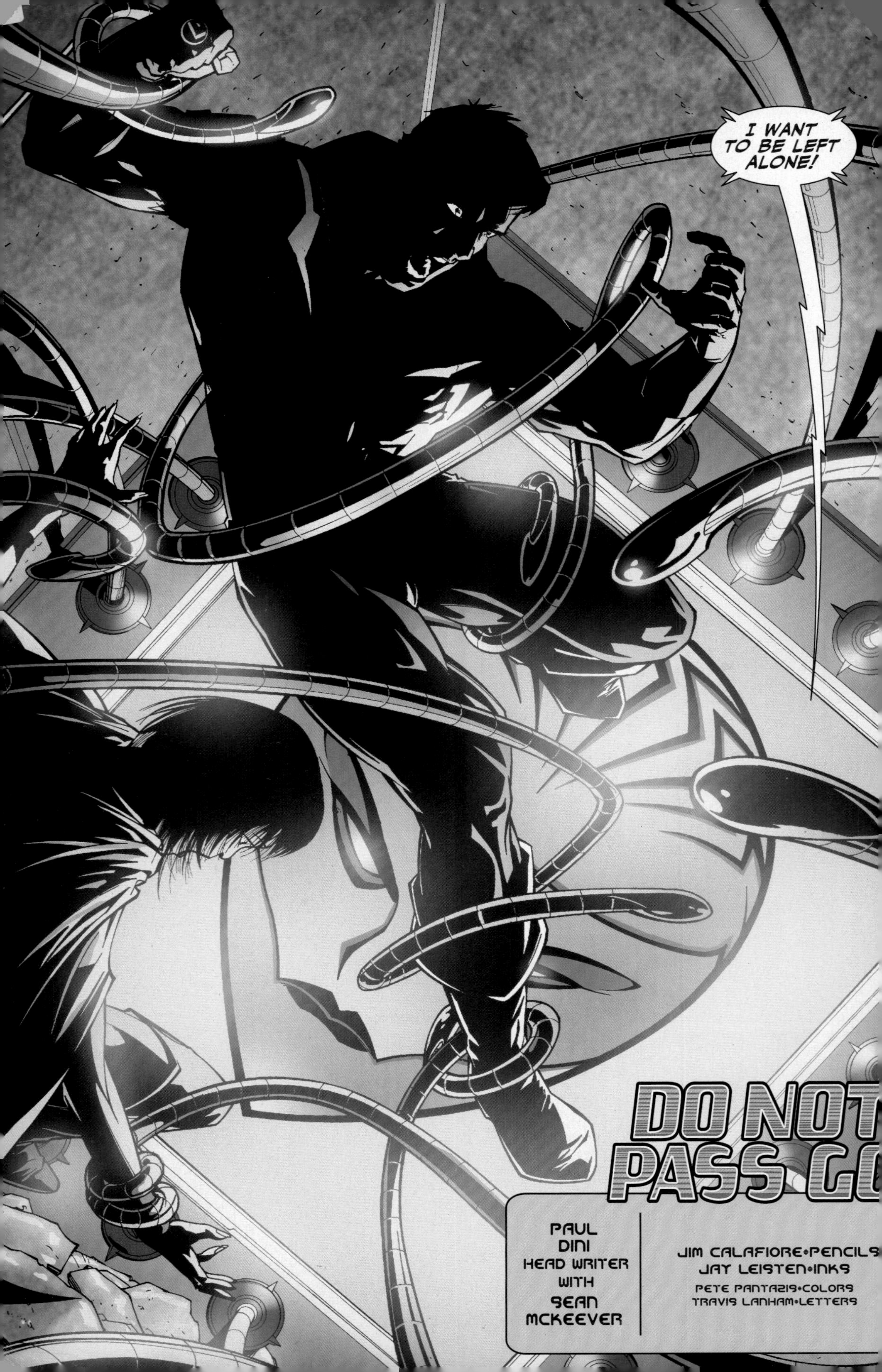
I WANT TO BE LEFT ALONE!
DO NOT PASS GO
PAUL DINI HEAD WRITER WITH SEAN MCKEEVER
JIM CALAFIORE•PENCILS
JAY LEISTEN•INKS
PETE PANTAZIS•COLORS
TRAVIS LANHAM•LETTERS

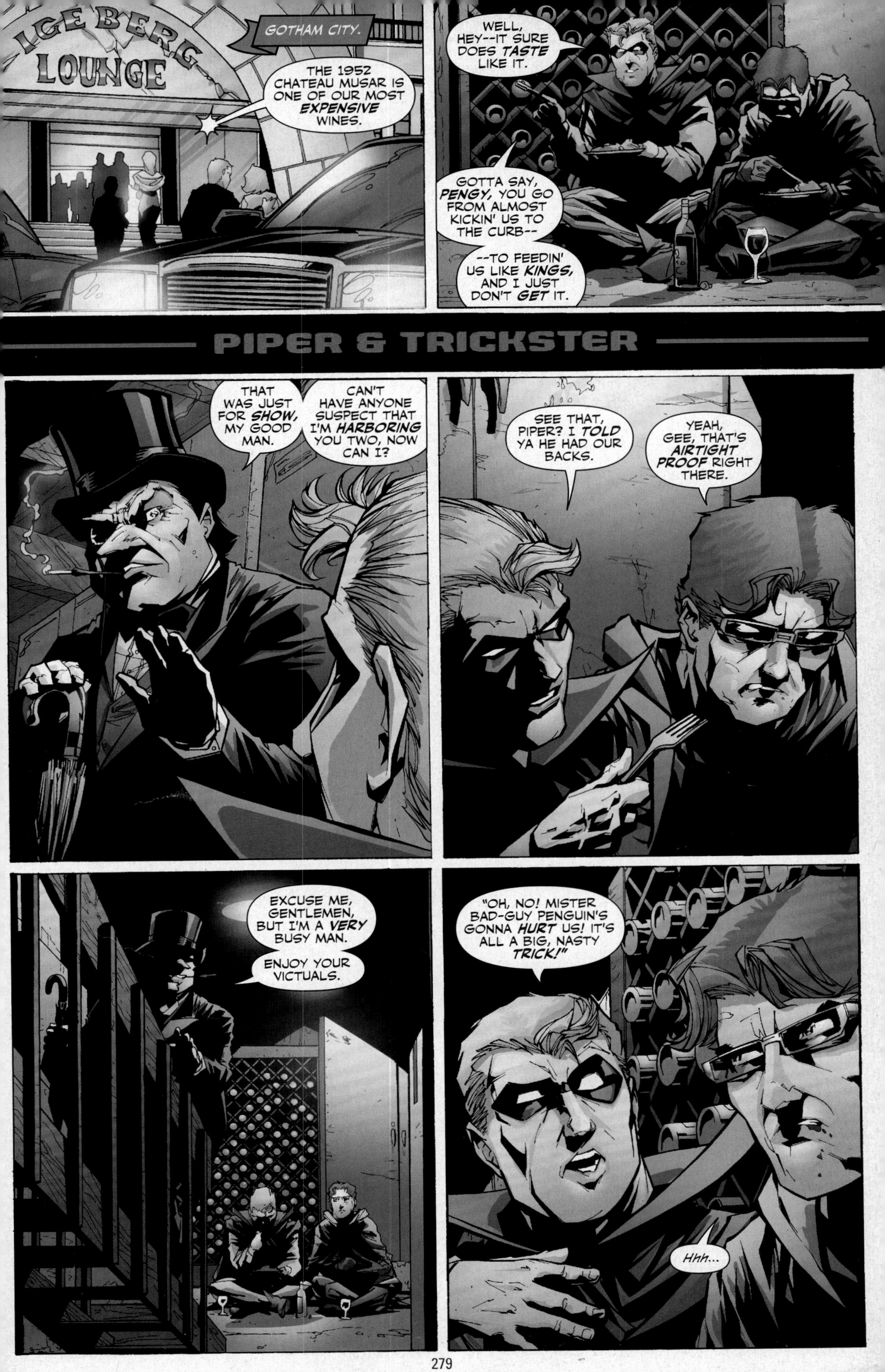
ICEBERG LOUNGE
GOTHAM CITY.
THE 1952 CHATEAU MUSAR IS ONE OF OUR MOST EXPENSIVE WINES.
WELL, HEY--IT SURE DOES TASTE LIKE IT.
GOTTA SAY, PENGY, YOU GO FROM ALMOST KICKIN' US TO THE CURB--
--TO FEEDIN' US LIKE KINGS, AND I JUST DON'T GET IT.
PIPER & TRICKSTER
THAT WAS JUST FOR SHOW, MY GOOD MAN.
CAN'T HAVE ANYONE SUSPECT THAT I'M HARBORING YOU TWO, NOW CAN I?
SEE THAT, PIPER? I TOLD YA HE HAD OUR BACKS.
YEAH, GEE, THAT'S AIRTIGHT PROOF RIGHT THERE.
EXCUSE ME, GENTLEMEN, BUT I'M A VERY BUSY MAN.
ENJOY YOUR VICTUALS.
"OH, NO! MISTER BAD-GUY PENGUIN'S GONNA HURT US! IT'S ALL A BIG, NASTY TRICK!"
Hhh...

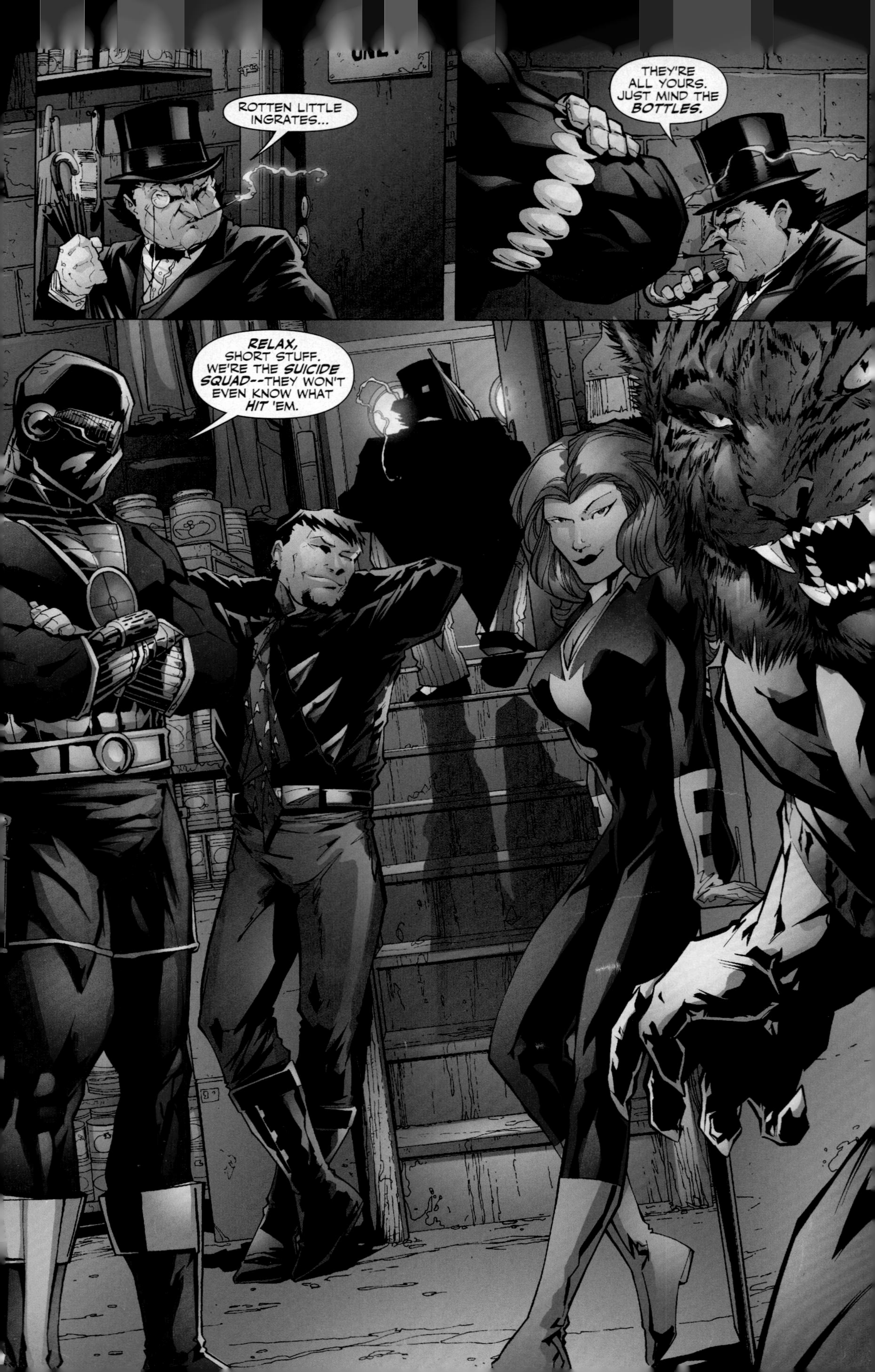
ROTTEN LITTLE INGRATES...
THEY'RE ALL YOURS. JUST MIND THE BOTTLES.
RELAX, SHORT STUFF. WE'RE THE SUICIDE SQUAD--THEY WON'T EVEN KNOW WHAT HIT 'EM.

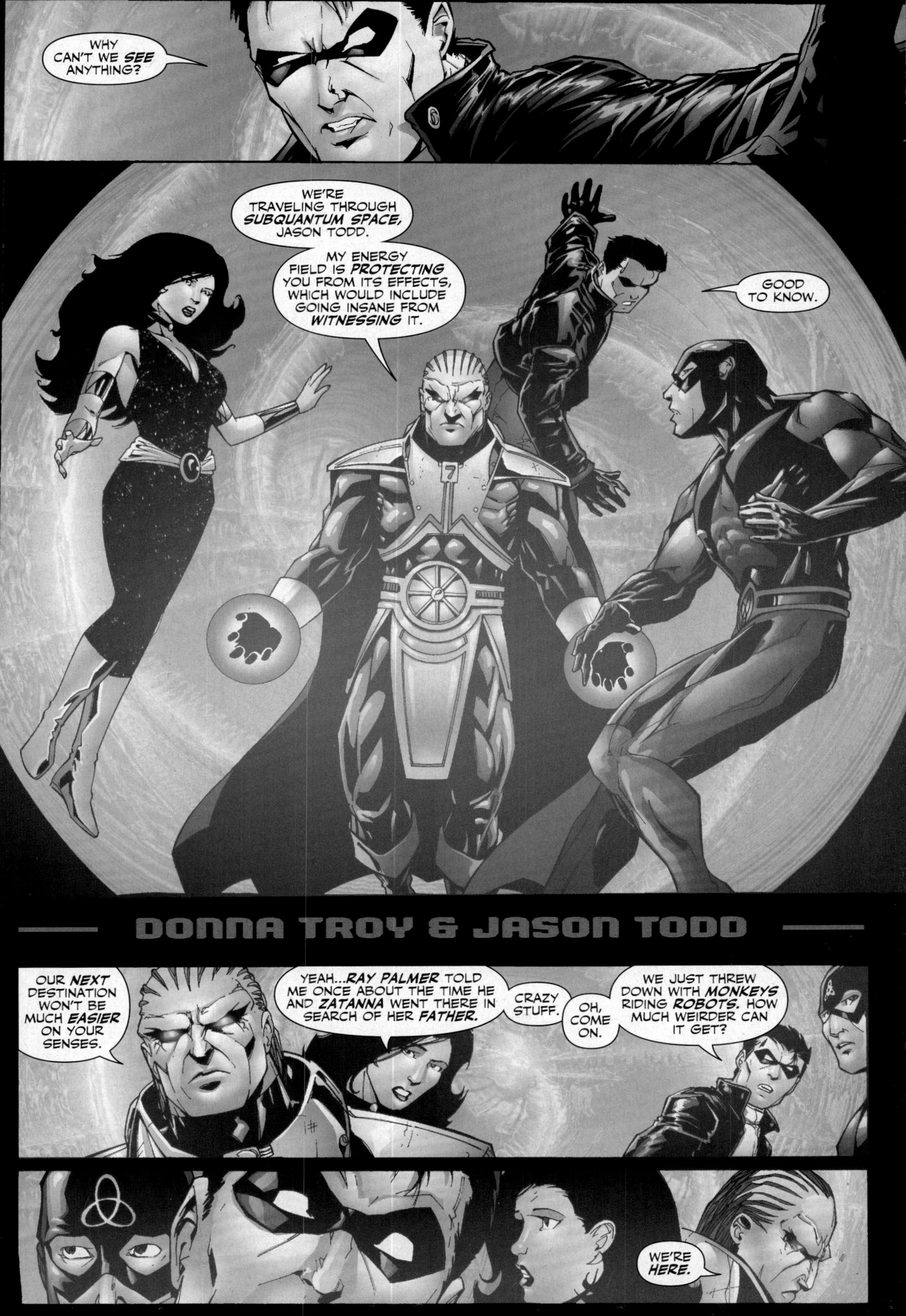

WHY CAN'T WE SEE ANYTHING?
WE'RE TRAVELING THROUGH SUBQUANTUM SPACE, JASON TODD.
MY ENERGY FIELD IS PROTECTING YOU FROM ITS EFFECTS, WHICH WOULD INCLUDE GOING INSANE FROM WITNESSING IT.
GOOD TO KNOW.
DONNA TROY & JASON TODD
OUR NEXT DESTINATION WON'T BE MUCH EASIER ON YOUR SENSES.
YEAH...RAY PALMER TOLD ME ONCE ABOUT THE TIME HE AND ZATANNA WENT THERE IN SEARCH OF HER FATHER.
CRAZY STUFF.
OH, COME ON.
WE JUST THREW DOWN WITH MONKEYS RIDING ROBOTS. HOW MUCH WEIRDER CAN IT GET?
WE'RE HERE.

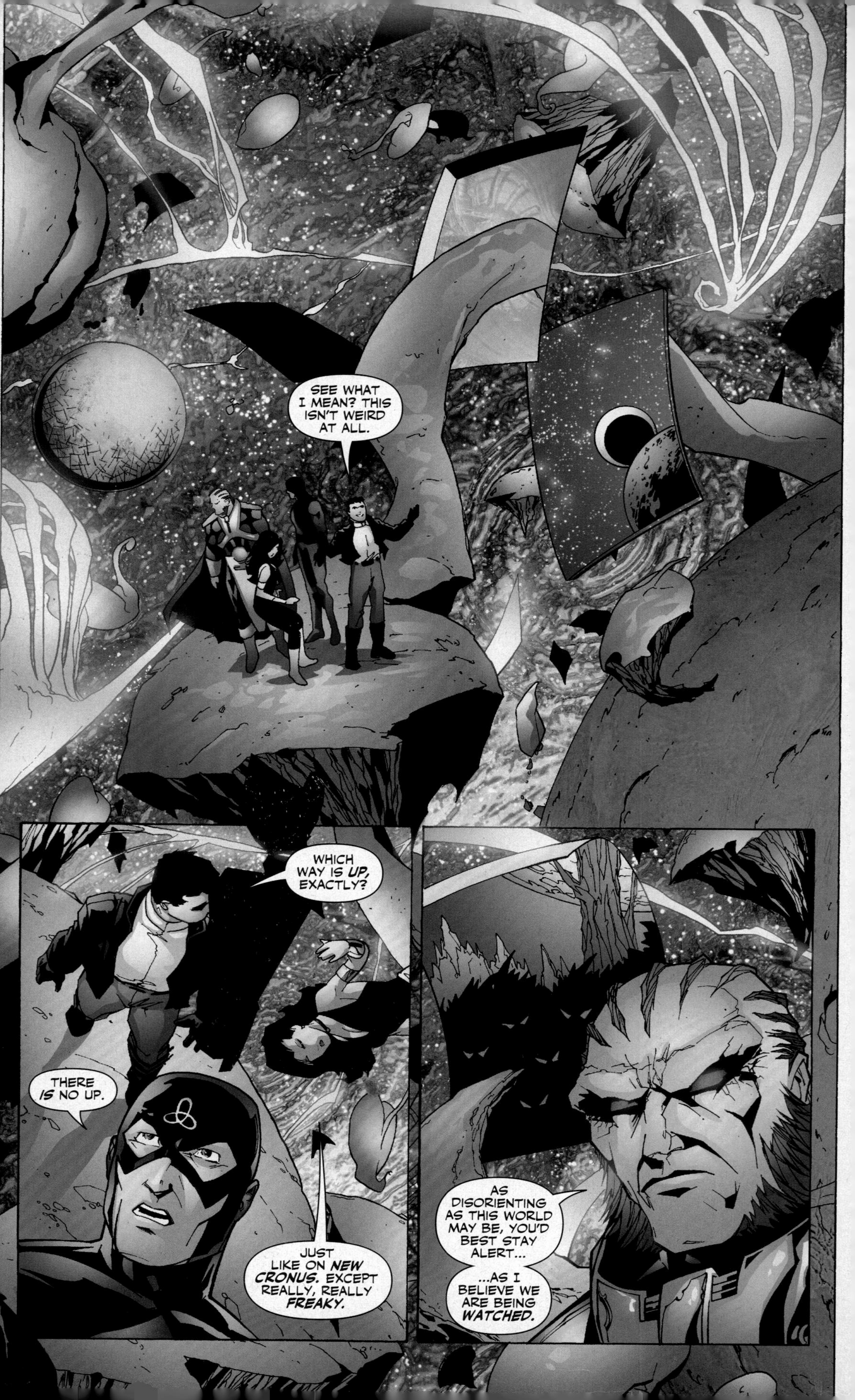
SEE WHAT I MEAN? THIS ISN'T WEIRD AT ALL.
WHICH WAY IS *UP*, EXACTLY?
THERE *IS* NO UP.
JUST LIKE ON *NEW CRONUS*. EXCEPT REALLY, REALLY *FREAKY*.
AS DISORIENTING AS THIS WORLD MAY BE, YOU'D BEST STAY ALERT...
...AS I BELIEVE WE ARE BEING *WATCHED*.

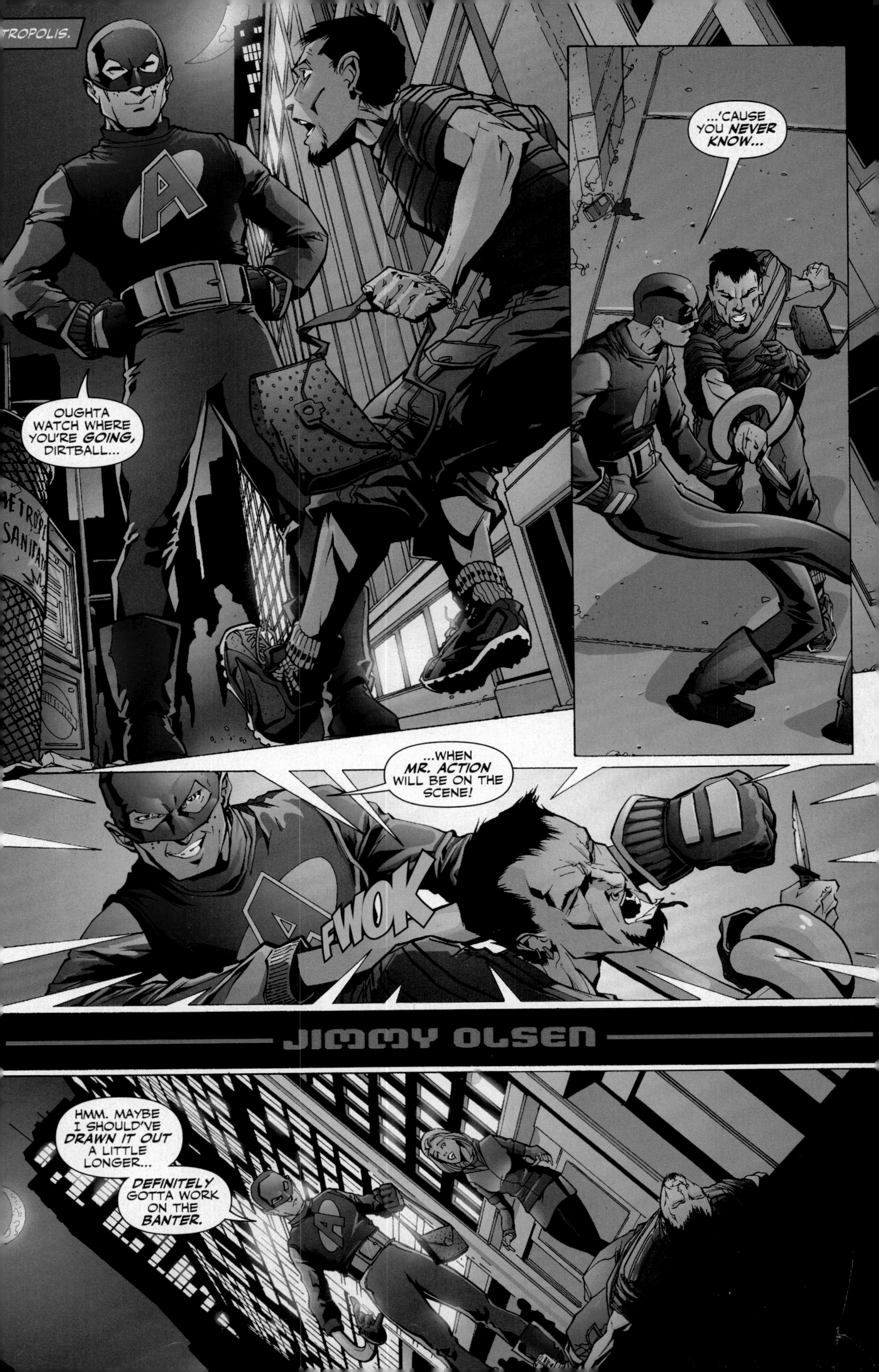
TROPOLIS.
OUGHTA WATCH WHERE YOU'RE GOING, DIRTBALL...
...'CAUSE YOU NEVER KNOW...
...WHEN MR. ACTION WILL BE ON THE SCENE!
FWOK
JIMMY OLSEN
HMM. MAYBE I SHOULD'VE DRAWN IT OUT A LITTLE LONGER...
DEFINITELY GOTTA WORK ON THE BANTER.

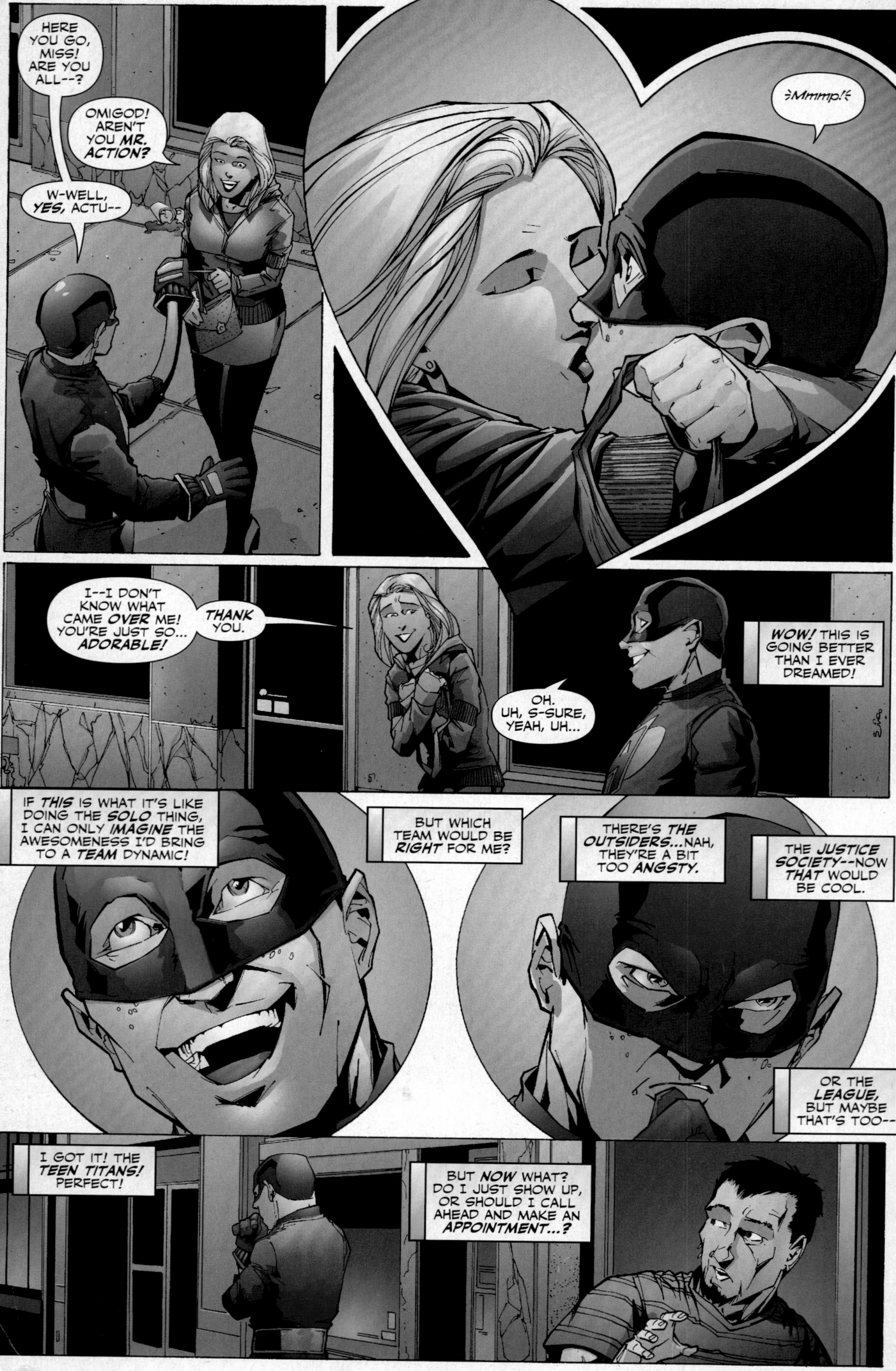
HERE YOU GO, MISS! ARE YOU ALL--?
OMIGOD! AREN'T YOU MR. ACTION?
W-WELL, YES, ACTU--
Mmmp!
I--I DON'T KNOW WHAT CAME OVER ME! YOU'RE JUST SO... ADORABLE!
THANK YOU.
OH. UH, S-SURE, YEAH, UH...
WOW! THIS IS GOING BETTER THAN I EVER DREAMED!
IF THIS IS WHAT IT'S LIKE DOING THE SOLO THING, I CAN ONLY IMAGINE THE AWESOMENESS I'D BRING TO A TEAM DYNAMIC!
BUT WHICH TEAM WOULD BE RIGHT FOR ME?
THERE'S THE OUTSIDERS...NAH, THEY'RE A BIT TOO ANGSTY.
THE JUSTICE SOCIETY--NOW THAT WOULD BE COOL.
OR THE LEAGUE, BUT MAYBE THAT'S TOO--
I GOT IT! THE TEEN TITANS! PERFECT!
BUT NOW WHAT? DO I JUST SHOW UP, OR SHOULD I CALL AHEAD AND MAKE AN APPOINTMENT...?

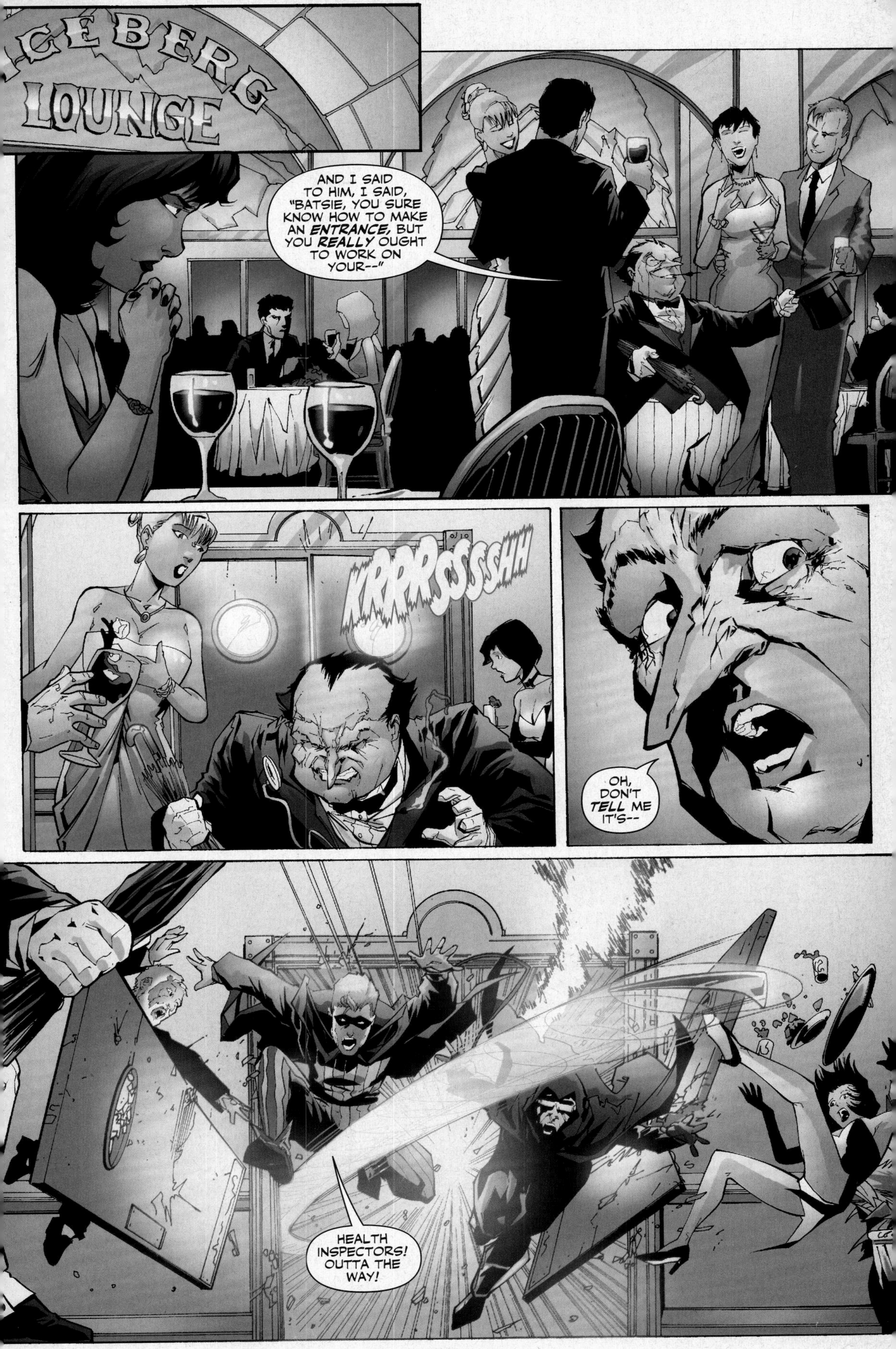
ICEBERG LOUNGE
AND I SAID TO HIM, I SAID, "BATSIE, YOU SURE KNOW HOW TO MAKE AN ENTRANCE, BUT YOU REALLY OUGHT TO WORK ON YOUR--"
KRPRSSSSHH
OH, DON'T TELL ME IT'S--
HEALTH INSPECTORS! OUTTA THE WAY!

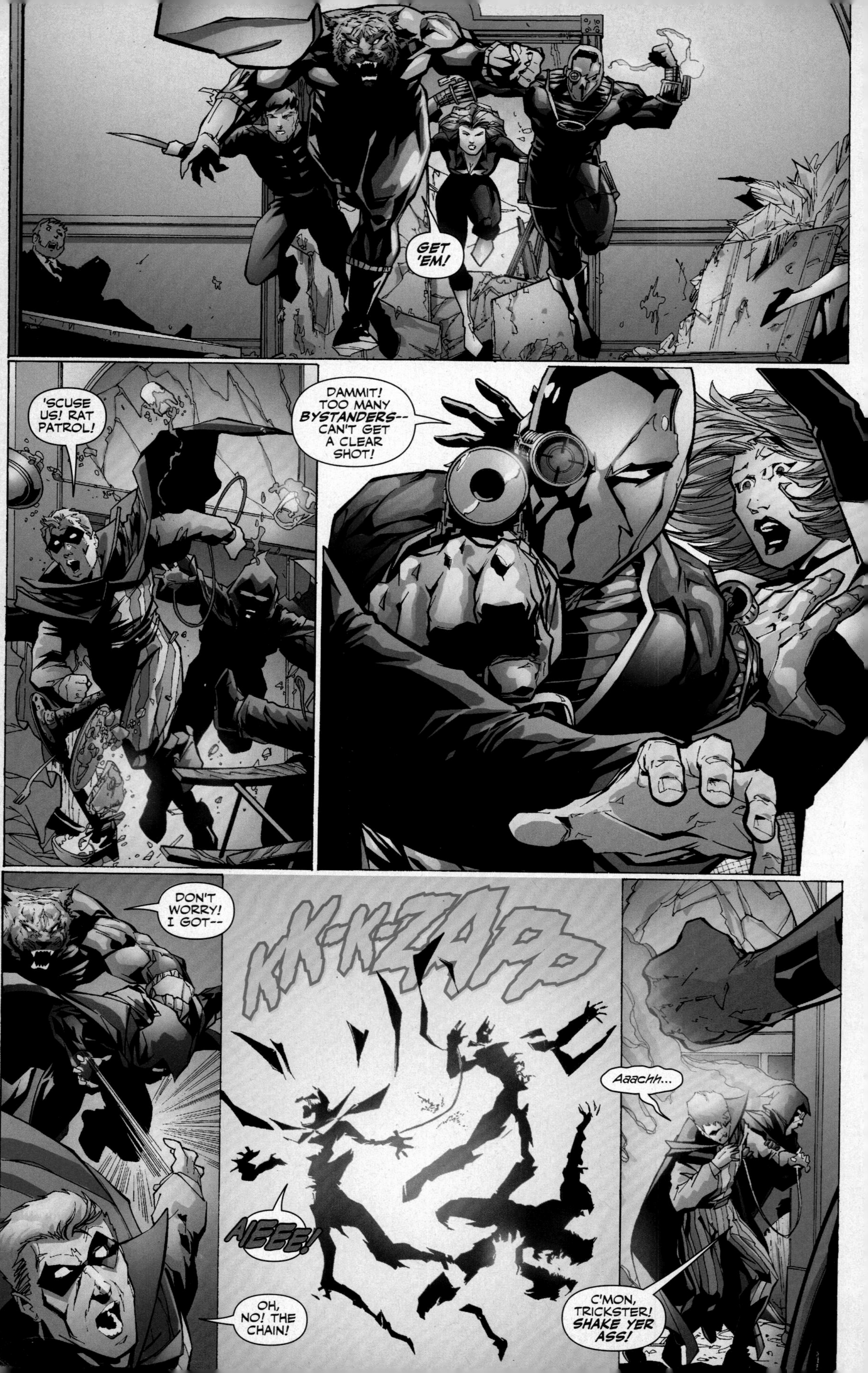
GET 'EM!
'SCUSE US! RAT PATROL!
DAMMIT! TOO MANY BYSTANDERS-- CAN'T GET A CLEAR SHOT!
DON'T WORRY! I GOT--
KK-K-ZAPP
AIEEE!
OH, NO! THE CHAIN!
Aaachh...
C'MON, TRICKSTER! SHAKE YER ASS!

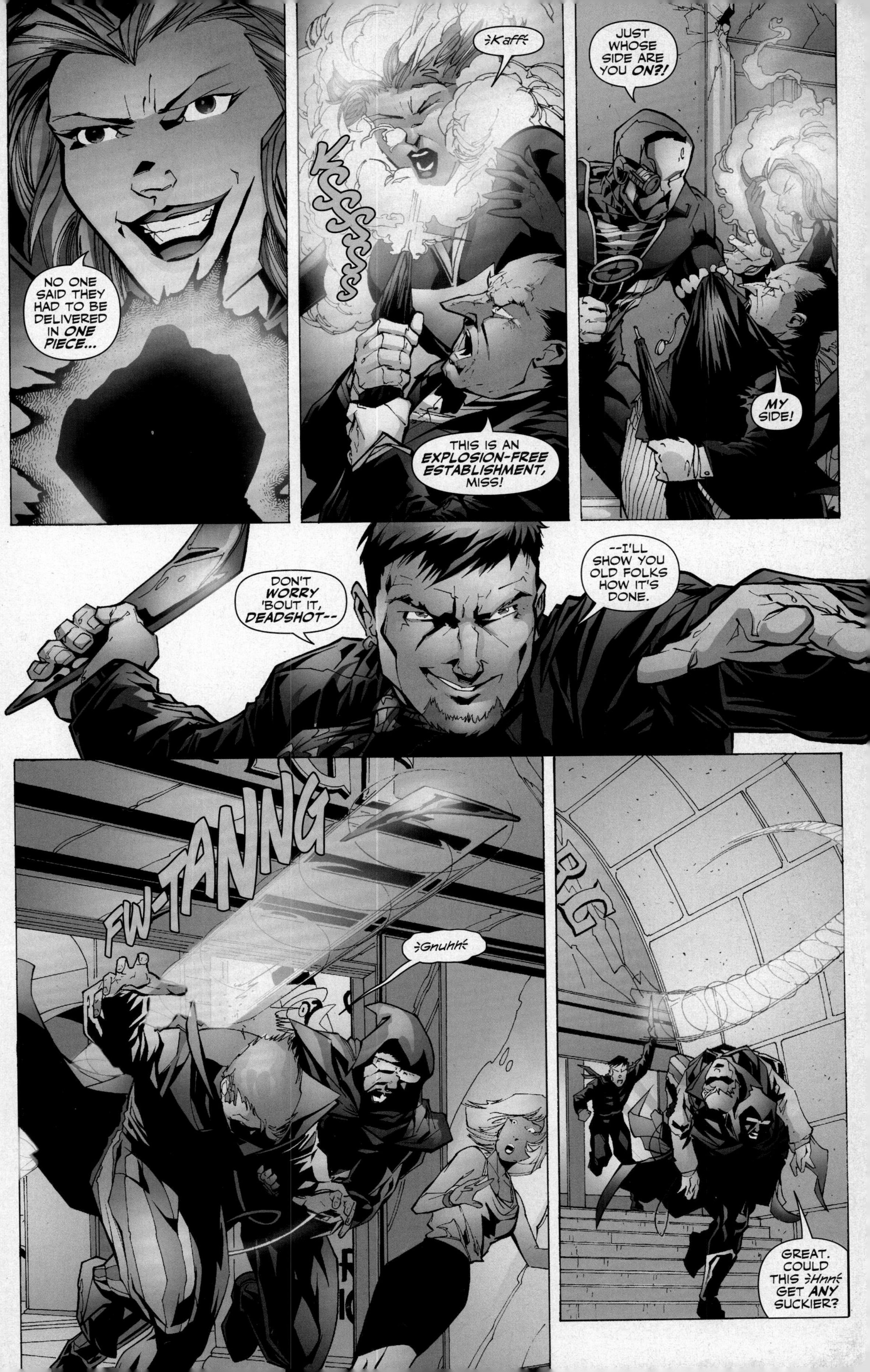
NO ONE SAID THEY HAD TO BE DELIVERED IN ONE PIECE...
KSSSSS
Kaff
THIS IS AN EXPLOSION-FREE ESTABLISHMENT, MISS!
JUST WHOSE SIDE ARE YOU ON?!
MY SIDE!
DON'T WORRY 'BOUT IT, DEADSHOT--
--I'LL SHOW YOU OLD FOLKS HOW IT'S DONE.
FW-TANNG
Gnuhh
GREAT. COULD THIS Hnn GET ANY SUCKIER?

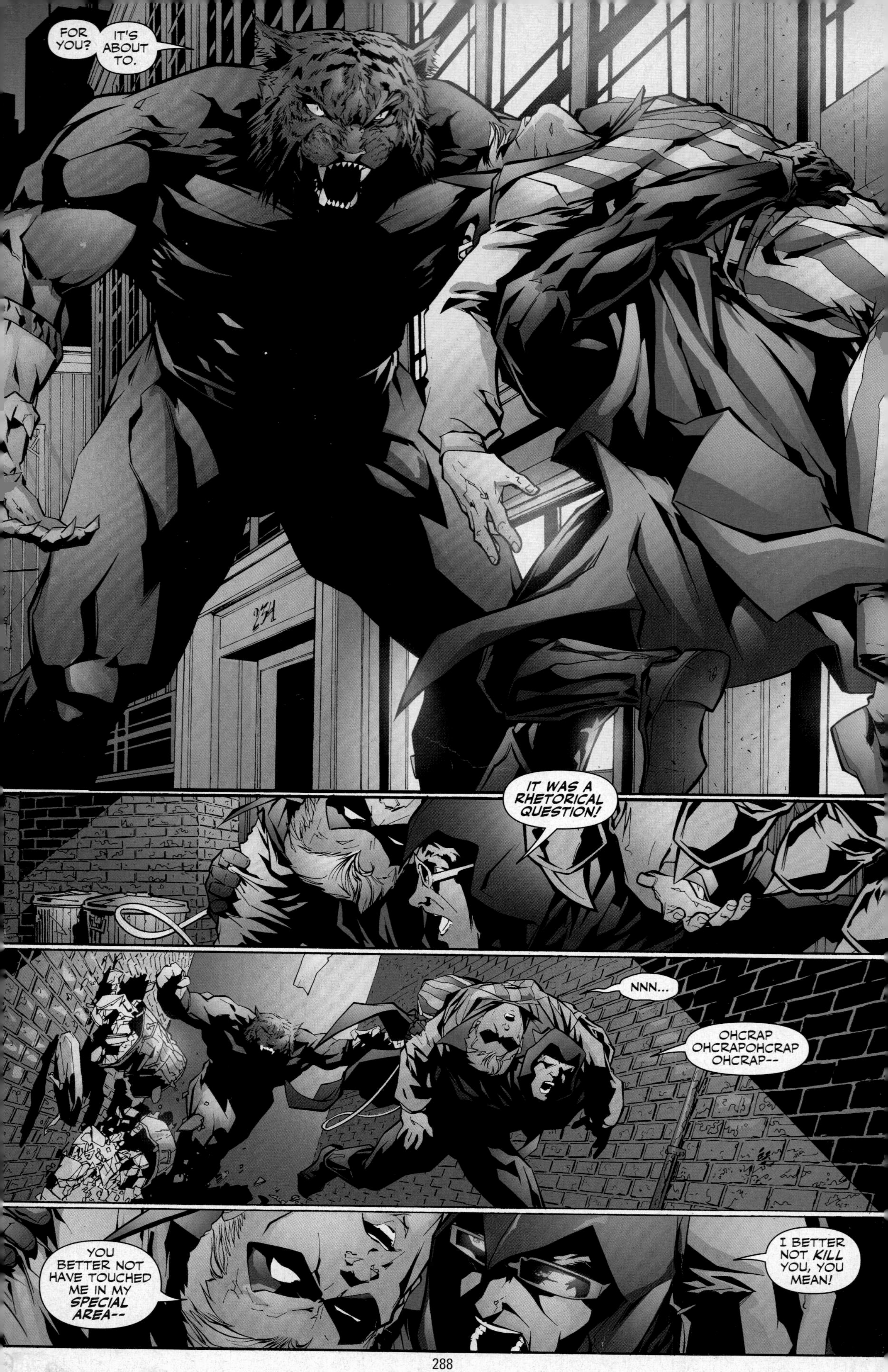
FOR YOU?
IT'S ABOUT TO.
IT WAS A RHETORICAL QUESTION!
NNN...
OHCRAP OHCRAPOHCRAP OHCRAP--
YOU BETTER NOT HAVE TOUCHED ME IN MY *SPECIAL AREA*--
I BETTER NOT *KILL* YOU, YOU MEAN!

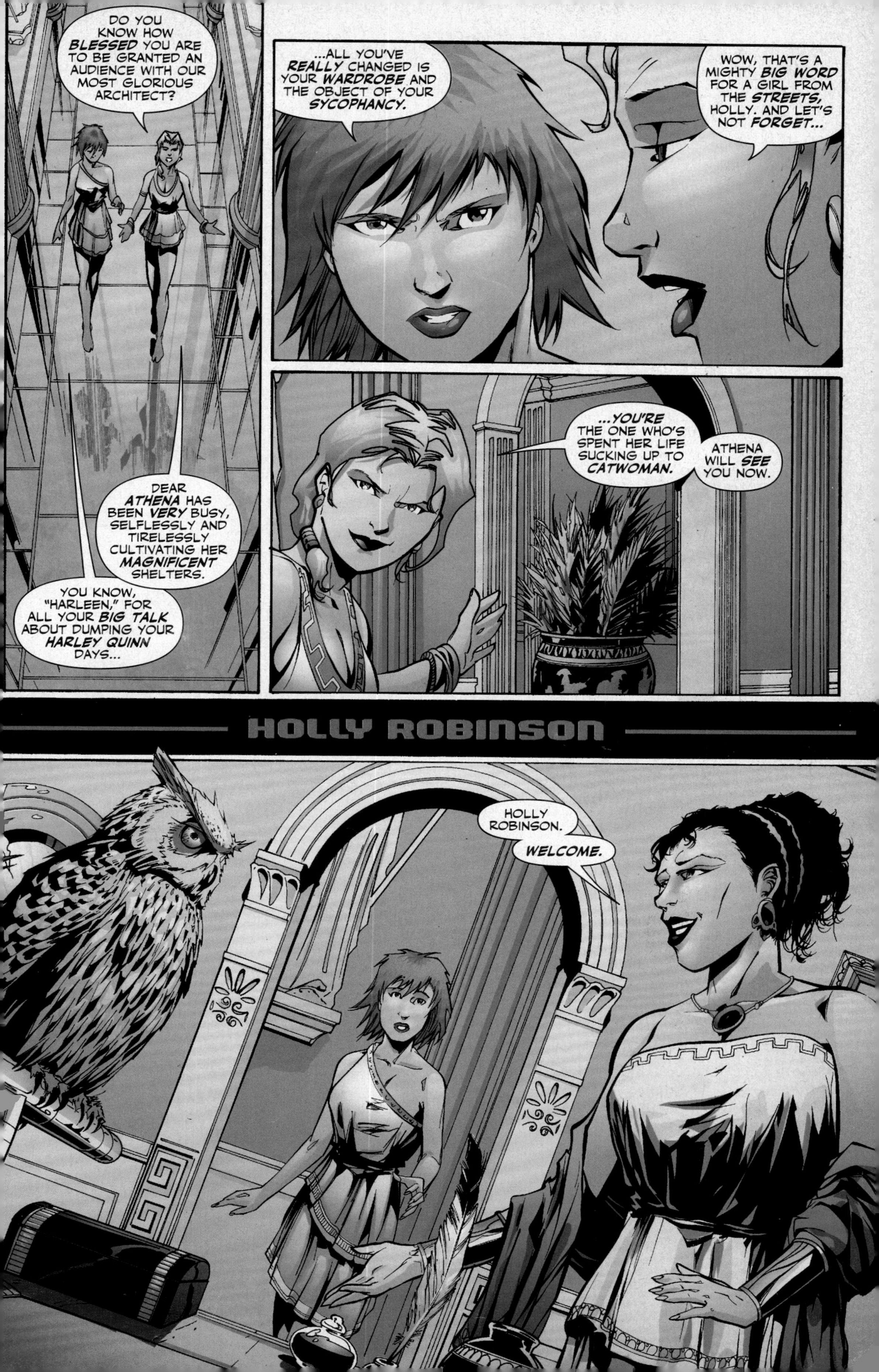
DO YOU KNOW HOW BLESSED YOU ARE TO BE GRANTED AN AUDIENCE WITH OUR MOST GLORIOUS ARCHITECT?
DEAR ATHENA HAS BEEN VERY BUSY, SELFLESSLY AND TIRELESSLY CULTIVATING HER MAGNIFICENT SHELTERS.
YOU KNOW, "HARLEEN," FOR ALL YOUR BIG TALK ABOUT DUMPING YOUR HARLEY QUINN DAYS...
...ALL YOU'VE REALLY CHANGED IS YOUR WARDROBE AND THE OBJECT OF YOUR SYCOPHANCY.
WOW, THAT'S A MIGHTY BIG WORD FOR A GIRL FROM THE STREETS, HOLLY. AND LET'S NOT FORGET...
...YOU'RE THE ONE WHO'S SPENT HER LIFE SUCKING UP TO CATWOMAN.
ATHENA WILL SEE YOU NOW.
HOLLY ROBINSON
HOLLY ROBINSON.
WELCOME.

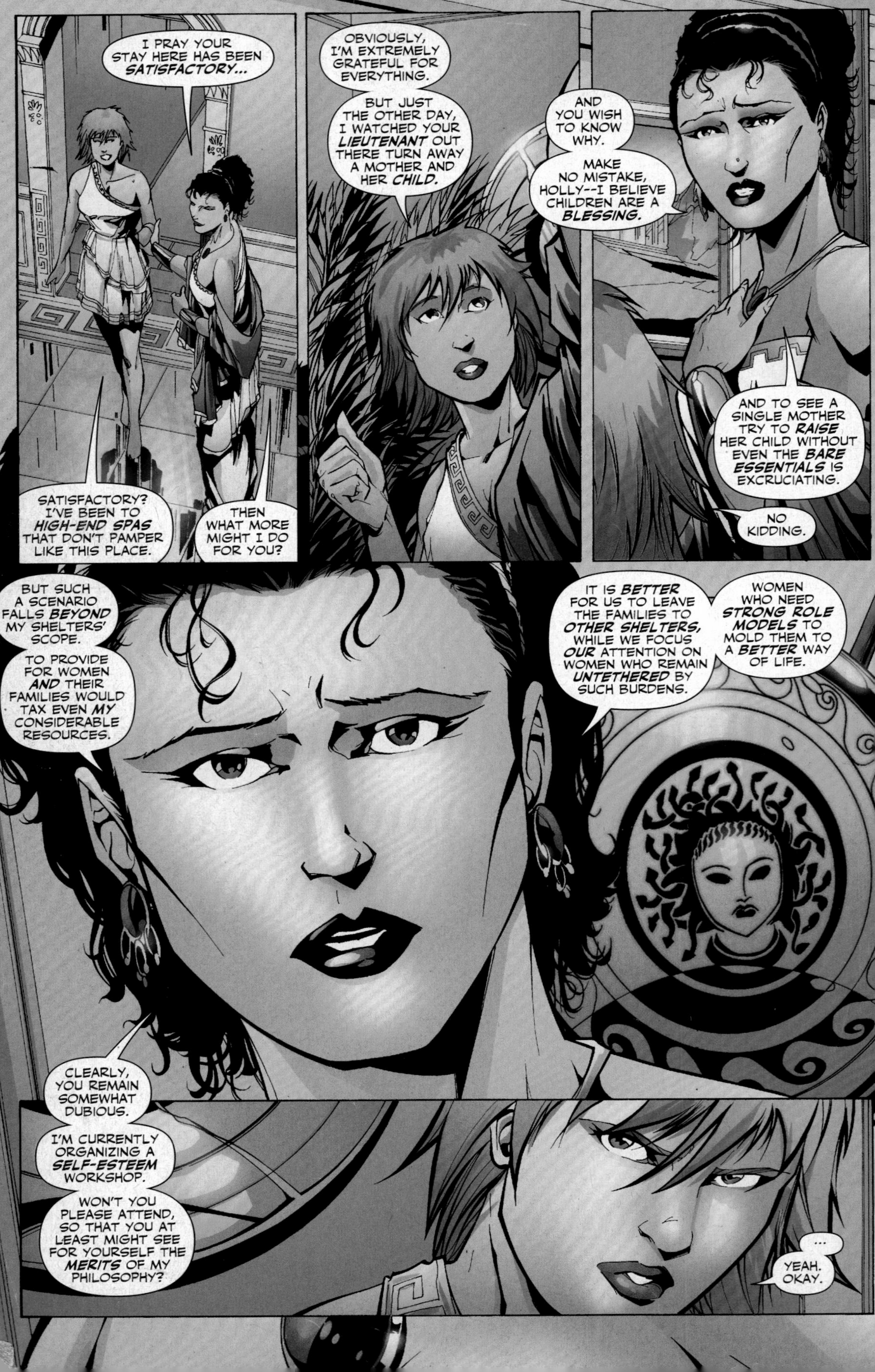
I PRAY YOUR STAY HERE HAS BEEN SATISFACTORY...
SATISFACTORY? I'VE BEEN TO HIGH-END SPAS THAT DON'T PAMPER LIKE THIS PLACE.
THEN WHAT MORE MIGHT I DO FOR YOU?
OBVIOUSLY, I'M EXTREMELY GRATEFUL FOR EVERYTHING.
BUT JUST THE OTHER DAY, I WATCHED YOUR LIEUTENANT OUT THERE TURN AWAY A MOTHER AND HER CHILD.
AND YOU WISH TO KNOW WHY.
MAKE NO MISTAKE, HOLLY--I BELIEVE CHILDREN ARE A BLESSING.
AND TO SEE A SINGLE MOTHER TRY TO RAISE HER CHILD WITHOUT EVEN THE BARE ESSENTIALS IS EXCRUCIATING.
NO KIDDING.
BUT SUCH A SCENARIO FALLS BEYOND MY SHELTERS' SCOPE.
TO PROVIDE FOR WOMEN AND THEIR FAMILIES WOULD TAX EVEN MY CONSIDERABLE RESOURCES.
IT IS BETTER FOR US TO LEAVE THE FAMILIES TO OTHER SHELTERS, WHILE WE FOCUS OUR ATTENTION ON WOMEN WHO REMAIN UNTETHERED BY SUCH BURDENS.
WOMEN WHO NEED STRONG ROLE MODELS TO MOLD THEM TO A BETTER WAY OF LIFE.
CLEARLY, YOU REMAIN SOMEWHAT DUBIOUS.
I'M CURRENTLY ORGANIZING A SELF-ESTEEM WORKSHOP.
WON'T YOU PLEASE ATTEND, SO THAT YOU AT LEAST MIGHT SEE FOR YOURSELF THE MERITS OF MY PHILOSOPHY?
...
YEAH. OKAY.

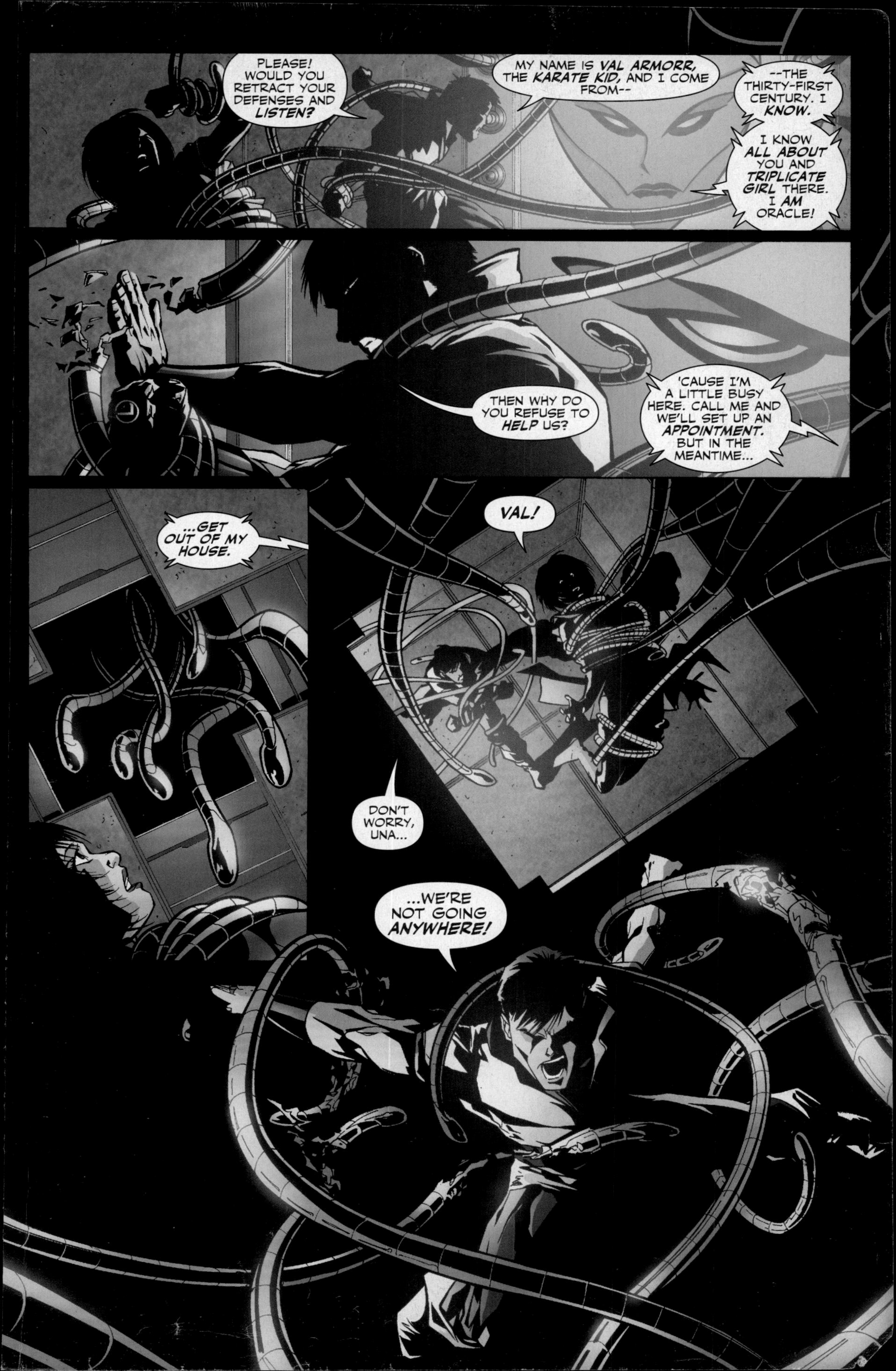
PLEASE! WOULD YOU RETRACT YOUR DEFENSES AND LISTEN?
MY NAME IS VAL ARMORR, THE KARATE KID, AND I COME FROM--
--THE THIRTY-FIRST CENTURY. I KNOW.
I KNOW ALL ABOUT YOU AND TRIPLICATE GIRL THERE. I AM ORACLE!
THEN WHY DO YOU REFUSE TO HELP US?
'CAUSE I'M A LITTLE BUSY HERE. CALL ME AND WE'LL SET UP AN APPOINTMENT. BUT IN THE MEANTIME...
...GET OUT OF MY HOUSE.
VAL!
DON'T WORRY, UNA...
...WE'RE NOT GOING ANYWHERE!

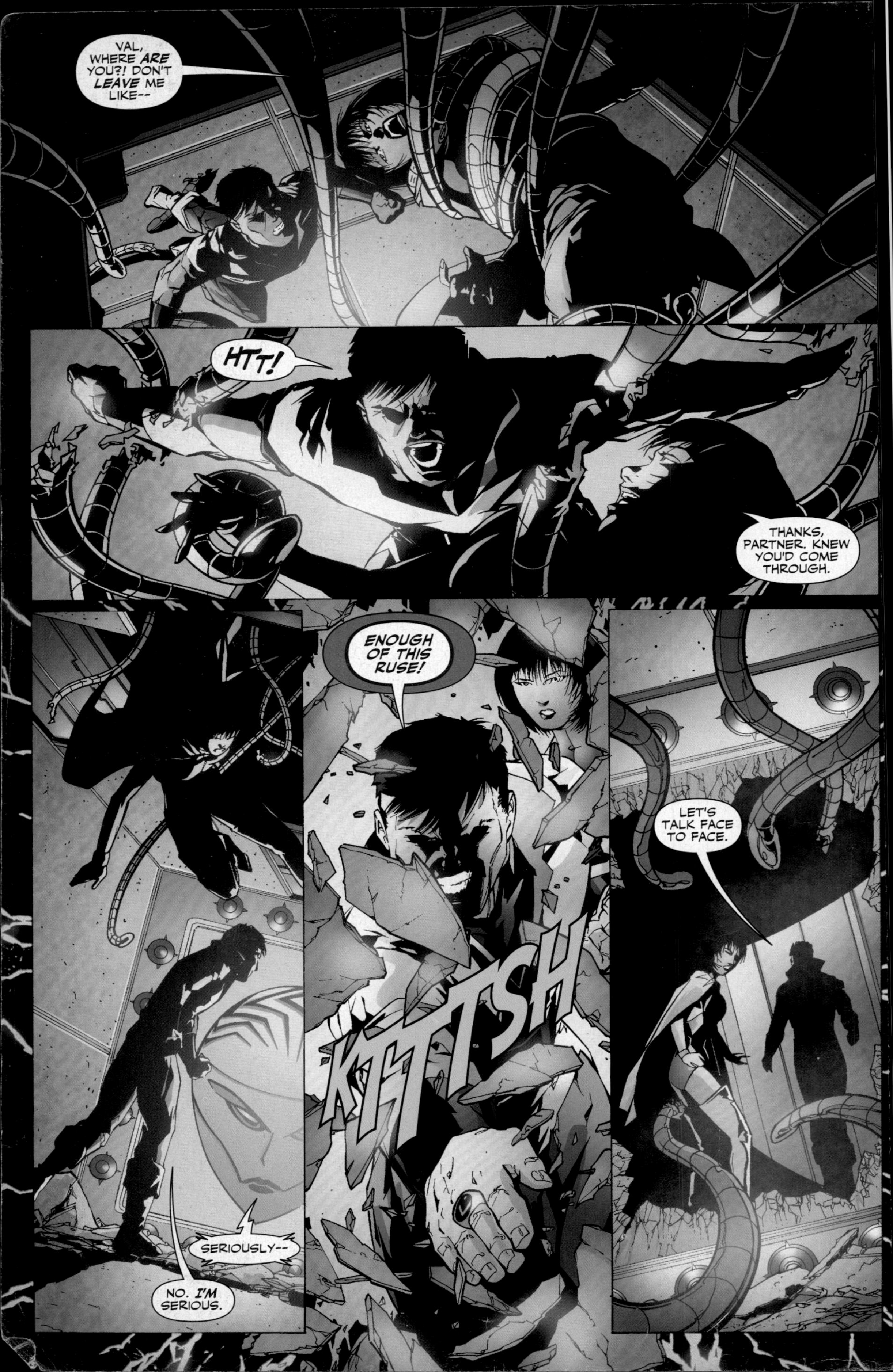
VAL, WHERE ARE YOU?! DON'T LEAVE ME LIKE--
HTT!
THANKS, PARTNER. KNEW YOU'D COME THROUGH.
SERIOUSLY--
NO. I'M SERIOUS.
ENOUGH OF THIS RUSE!
KTTTSH
LET'S TALK FACE TO FACE.

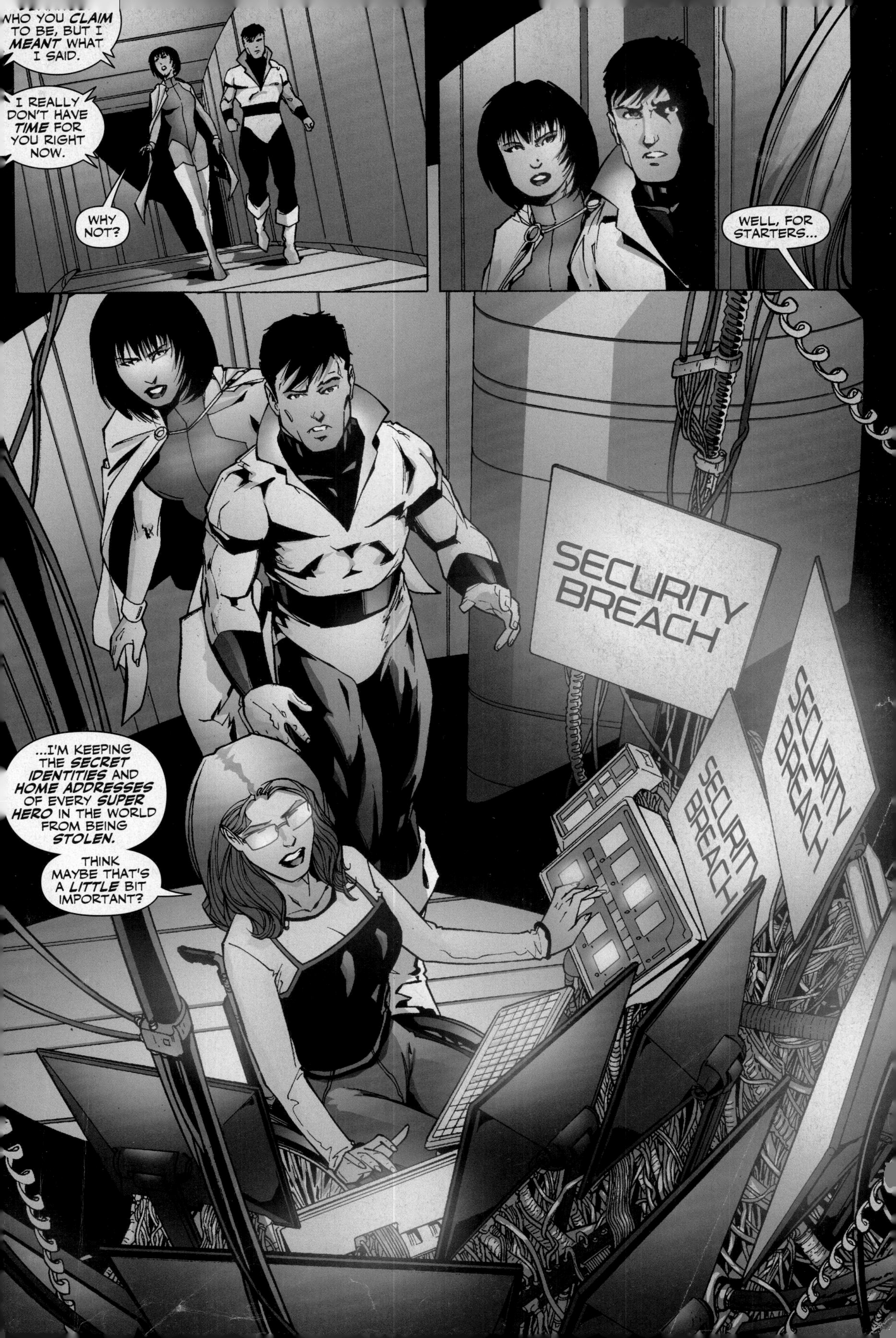

WHO YOU CLAIM TO BE, BUT I MEANT WHAT I SAID.
I REALLY DON'T HAVE TIME FOR YOU RIGHT NOW.
WHY NOT?
WELL, FOR STARTERS...
SECURITY BREACH
SECURITY BREACH
SECURITY BREACH
...I'M KEEPING THE SECRET IDENTITIES AND HOME ADDRESSES OF EVERY SUPER HERO IN THE WORLD FROM BEING STOLEN.
THINK MAYBE THAT'S A LITTLE BIT IMPORTANT?

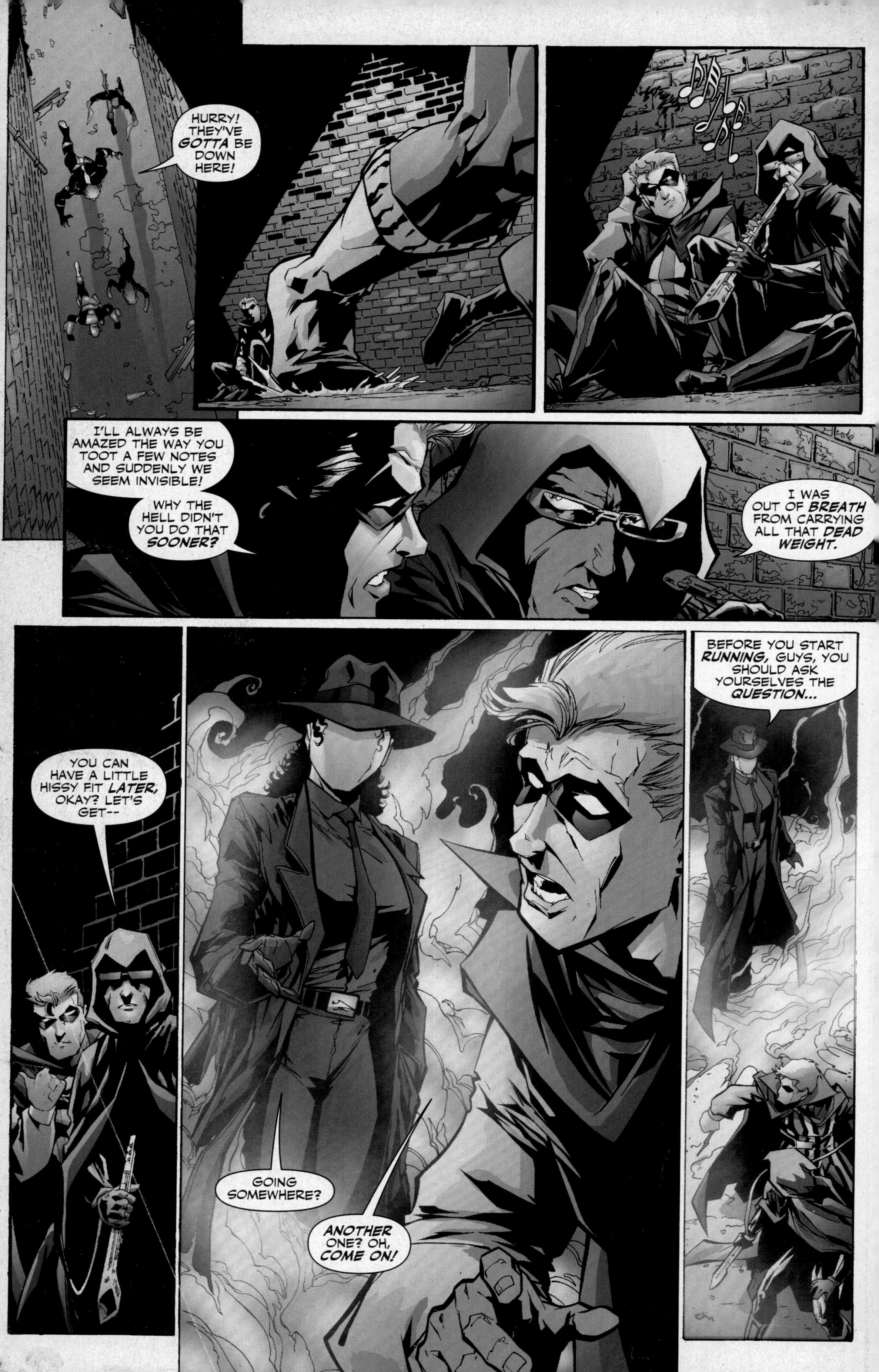
HURRY! THEY'VE *GOTTA* BE DOWN HERE!
I'LL ALWAYS BE AMAZED THE WAY YOU TOOT A FEW NOTES AND SUDDENLY WE SEEM INVISIBLE!
WHY THE HELL DIDN'T YOU DO THAT *SOONER?*
I WAS OUT OF *BREATH* FROM CARRYING ALL THAT *DEAD WEIGHT.*
YOU CAN HAVE A LITTLE HISSY FIT *LATER,* OKAY? LET'S GET--
GOING SOMEWHERE?
ANOTHER ONE? OH, *COME ON!*
BEFORE YOU START *RUNNING,* GUYS, YOU SHOULD ASK YOURSELVES THE *QUESTION...*

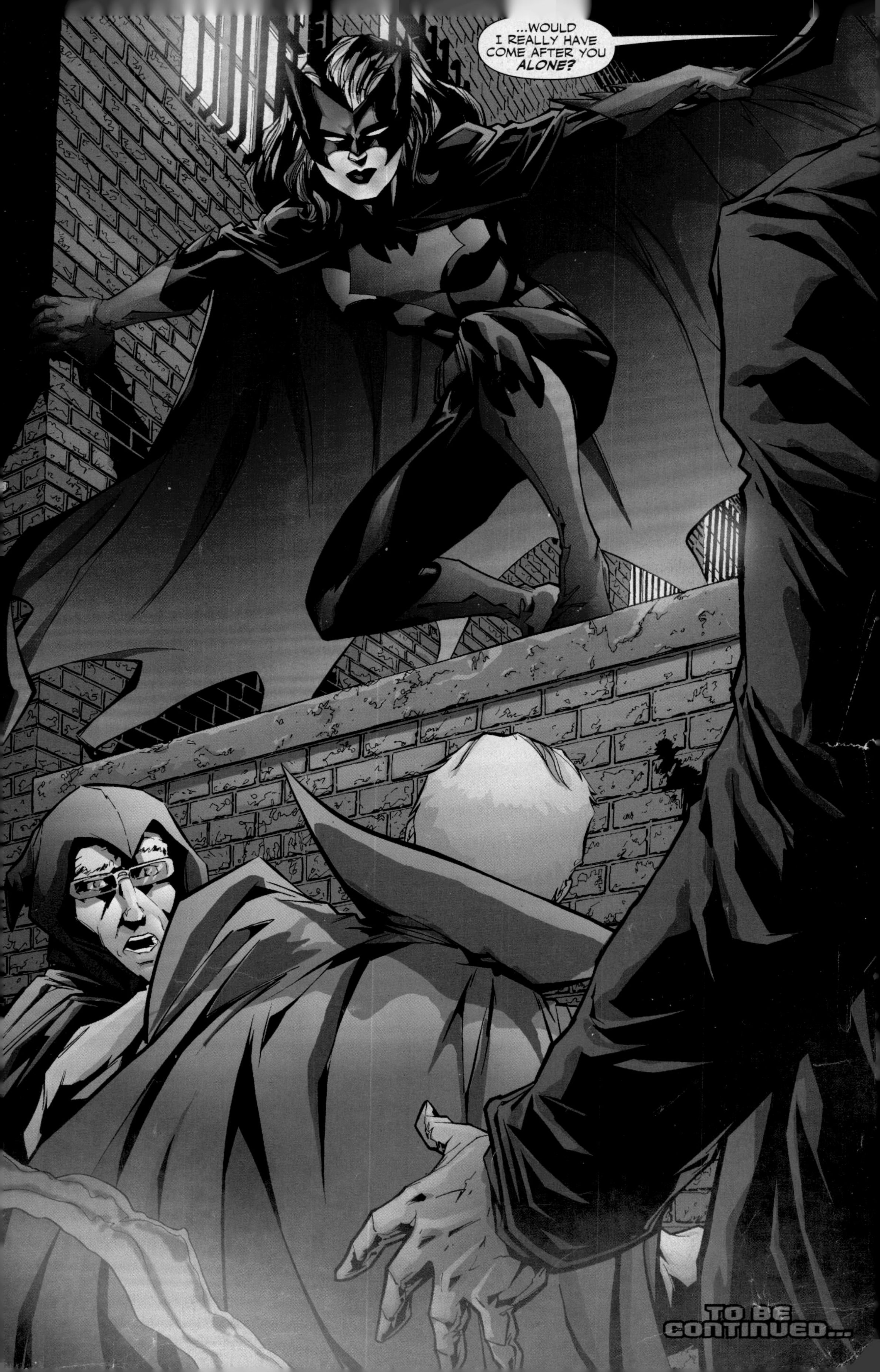
...WOULD I REALLY HAVE COME AFTER YOU *ALONE?*
TO BE CONTINUED...

READ MORE ADVENTURES OF YOUR FAVORITE HEROES IN THESE COLLECTIONS FROM DC COMICS:

KINGDOM COME

THE GREATEST SUPER HERO EPIC OF TOMORROW!
KINGDOM COME
Mark WAID Alex ROSS

Mark Waid and **Alex Ross** deliver a grim tale of youth versus experience, tradition versus change and what defines a hero. KINGDOM COME is a riveting story pitting the old guard — Superman, Batman, Wonder Woman and their peers — against a new uncompromising generation.

WINNER OF FIVE EISNER AND HARVEY AWARDS, INCLUDING BEST LIMITED SERIES AND BEST ARTIST

IDENTITY CRISIS

NEW YORK TIMES BEST-SELLING AUTHOR OF THE ZERO GAME
BRAD MELTZER
RAGS MORALES MICHAEL BAIR
IDENTITY CRISIS
Introduction by JOSS WHEDON, creator of BUFFY THE VAMPIRE SLAYER and FIREFLY

BRAD MELTZER
RAGS MORALES
MICHAEL BAIR

CRISIS ON INFINITE EARTHS

CRISIS ON INFINITE EARTHS
MARV WOLFMAN & GEORGE PÉREZ

MARV WOLFMAN
GEORGE PÉREZ

DC: THE NEW FRONTIER VOLUME 1

DC: The New Frontier

DARWYN COOKE
DAVE STEWART

SEARCH THE GRAPHIC NOVELS SECTION OF

www.DCCOMICS.com

FOR ART AND INFORMATION ON ALL OF OUR BOOKS.

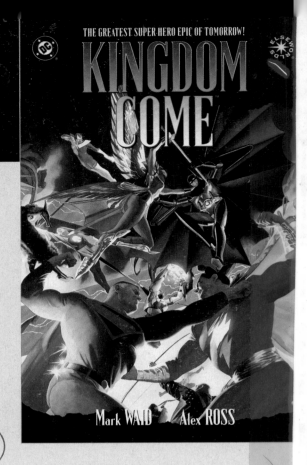

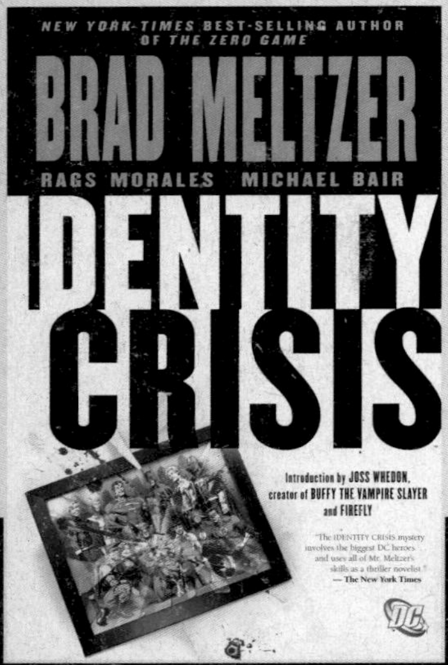